BLACK POETS OF THE UNITED STATES

BLACK POETS
OF THE UNITED STATES

From Paul Laurence Dunbar to Langston Hughes

BY JEAN WAGNER

Translated by Kenneth Douglas

UNIVERSITY OF ILLINOIS PRESS
Urbana   Chicago   London

The original French edition, published under the title *Les Poètes Nègres des Etats-Unis,* copyright 1962 by Librairie Istra, Paris.

Fifth printing, 1979

Grateful acknowledgment is made to the following for permission to quote from works under copyright. Rights in all cases are reserved by the owner.
Dodd, Mead & Co., for selections from *Oak and Ivy* by Paul Laurence Dunbar, *The Complete Poems of Paul Laurence Dunbar, The Life and Works of Paul Laurence Dunbar* by Lida Keck Wiggins, *Paul Laurence Dunbar and His Song* by Virginia Cunningham, and *The Negro Genius* by Benjamin Brawley; Carl Cowl, for selections from *Songs of Jamaica* by Claude McKay, *Constab Ballads* by Claude McKay, *Harlem Shadows* by Claude McKay, *A Long Way from Home* by Claude McKay, and miscellaneous articles and unpublished poems by Claude McKay; Twayne Publishers, Inc., for selections from *Selected Poems of Claude McKay;* Liveright Publishing Corporation, for selections from *Cane* by Jean Toomer; Mrs. Jean Toomer, for selections from *Essentials* by Jean Toomer and *Blue Meridian* by Jean Toomer; Harper and Row, for selections from *Color* by Countee Cullen, *Copper Sun* by Countee Cullen, *The Black Christ* by Countee Cullen, *The Medea and Some Poems* by Countee Cullen, *On These I Stand* by Countee Cullen, and *Caroling Dusk* by Countee Cullen; The Viking Press, for selections from the following books written or edited by James Weldon Johnson: *God's Trombones, Along This Way: The Autobiography of James Weldon Johnson, Negro Americans, What Now?,* and *The Books of American Negro Spirituals,* vol. 2; Alfred A. Knopf, for selections from *The Weary Blues, Fine Clothes to the Jew, The Dreamkeeper and Other Poems, Shakespeare in Harlem, Fields of Wonder, One-Way Ticket, Selected Poems, Montage of a Dream Deferred, Jim Crow's Last Stand,* and *Ask Your Mama,* all by Langston Hughes; Harold Ober Associates, for selections from *Fine Clothes to the Jew, Montage of a Dream Deferred, Scottsboro Limited, A New Song, Jim Crow's Last Stand,* and miscellaneous poems and articles, all by Langston Hughes; Hill and Wang, for selections from *The Big Sea* and *I Wonder As I Wander,* by Langston Hughes; and Sterling Brown, for selections from his *Southern Road, Negro Poetry and Drama,* and miscellaneous articles.

To Sterling and Daisy Brown
in lasting friendship and gratitude

CONTENTS

FOREWORD
by Robert Bone

Three or four years ago, during my tenure as a Fulbright lecturer in France, a social affair was arranged by my hosts at the University of Grenoble. Fulbright students and professors, and visiting Americans of whatever status at the University, were chatting over drinks with their French colleagues. As I conversed in English with an American undergraduate, we were joined for ten or fifteen minutes by Professor Jean Wagner. Toward the end of this conversation, my young countryman paid Wagner the magnificent (if unintended) compliment of asking, "And what part of the States are *you* from?"

To speak the American vernacular with a flawless accent is a point of pride with Jean Wagner. It is of course an indispensable skill for any critic who would cope with verse written in a foreign tongue. It is entirely characteristic of Wagner, and of his capacity for empathy, that he is able to surmount linguistic and cultural barriers, and by a supreme effort of imagination pass for a native. He is a living refutation of the argument, so widespread in this chauvinistic age, that no man can understand a woman, no Catholic a Protestant, no Frenchman an American, no white man a black.

Jean Wagner was born in 1919 in the province of Lorraine. He was educated at the lycée of Sarreguemines, a Catholic high school in Besançon, and the University of Strasbourg. Before receiving his Diplôme d'Etudes Supérieures in 1939, he made several trips abroad: two to England, two to Germany, and one to the United States, where he spent a year as an exchange student at Birmingham Southern College (B.A. 1938). This year at a white college in the Deep South was the source of a lifelong fascination with southern culture, and a particular concern with the literary expression of black Americans.

On his return to France, Wagner taught English at various lycées (1939-45) and at the National School of Engineering in Strasbourg (1945-59). In the meantime, he passed his qualifying examinations and chose American Negro poetry as the subject of his doctoral research. In 1958 he spent six months in the United States, doing research at Howard, Hampton, Atlanta, Fisk, and the Schomburg Collection in New York. He returned to France to complete his dissertation, and to obtain his Doctorat d'Etat from the Sorbonne in 1963. Currently professor of American Studies at the University of Grenoble, he is the author of *Black Poets of the United States* (1963), *Runyonese: The Mind and Craft of Damon Runyon* (1965), and a French translation of Jean Toomer's *Cane* (1971).

The book that you are reading is a product of the best traditions of European scholarship. Thorough and comprehensive, it reflects painstaking research, encyclopedic knowledge of its subject, and Olympian determination to view that subject in its largest possible perspective. The aim of such a work is to be definitive within its chosen field. From such a tradition we should expect neither timeliness nor "relevance," but rather a patient re-creation of the past. For the book is geared to a European sense of time. This is not your flimsy Hollywood modern, but stout Romanesque, vaulted and timbered to last for centuries.

The chronological focus of the book is a half-century of Afro-American poetry published from 1890 to 1940. In effect, two generations of black poets are treated in considerable depth: Paul Laurence Dunbar and his contemporaries, and the major poets of the Harlem Renaissance. Volume II is yet to come, in which Wagner will treat the middle generation of Gwendolyn Brooks, Robert Hayden, Margaret Walker, and Melvin Tolson, and the younger generation of LeRoi Jones, Don Lee, Nikki Giovanni, and the rest. Meanwhile, the present volume must be honored as the first and only full-length study of Afro-American poetry, and as a seminal work not likely soon to be replaced as the standard treatment of its field.[1]

Wagner's most enduring contribution is the religious frame of reference that he establishes. Such an approach may seem self-evident in the case of a tradition deriving from the spirituals, and owing its early forms, vocabulary, and evangelical fervor to Wesleyan hymnals. But before the publication of this book, the most substantial essays in the field were rather belligerently secular in outlook and sensibility. The first extensive criticism

[1] Sterling Brown's *Negro Poetry and Drama* (1937) is a short monograph, while Saunders Redding's *To Make a Poet Black* (1939) is a summary treatment both of poetry and of prose.

of black poetry appeared, after all, in the 1930's — a decade when social and political considerations were uppermost in the minds of literary men. Marxist-oriented critics like Richard Wright thus attempted to isolate the racial elements in Negro verse and to found a tradition based on protest and propaganda.[2]

It is Wagner's distinction to have demonstrated the essential fusion of racial and religious feeling in Afro-American poetry. In contrast to the critics of the 1930's, the author of this study is at bottom a religious man. Wagner is inclined to take the measure of a poet by his concern with ultimate reality — that is, by the transcendent values he succeeds in dramatizing in his verse. Such a frame of reference is far more appropriate to this group of poets than the sociological prepossessions of the 1930's.

Wagner's central thesis is the interdependence of racial and religious feeling in American Negro poetry. The two are joined in vital union — a symbiosis in which feelings of religious origin are often "racialized," while feelings arising out of racial conflict are often "spiritualized," or projected on a metaphysical plane. This symbiosis is most eloquently illustrated in the spirituals, where the slave's desire for freedom in this world and his hope for salvation in the next are closely intertwined. Curiously enough, the same interplay of racial and religious feeling may be found in the work of modern poets, most of whom have long since abandoned the forms if not the emotional ambience of their religious heritage.

What accounts for these interlocking planes of experience in the soul of the black poet, according to Wagner? A schizoid tendency in Western culture, which first appeared when the white man decided to evangelize those whom he enslaved. To reduce the black man to the status of a thing, and then to save his soul: such were the contradictory impulses of a culture hopelessly torn between greed and guilt, between its lust for empire and its commitment to Christ. This fundamental schism in the white man's soul was then transmitted, like some hereditary blight, to the Negro slave. For the black man perceived with a clarity born of suffering the contradictions of the system in which he was enmeshed. Once converted, his faith was placed in constant jeopardy by the odious spectacle of human slavery, as practiced by his Christian masters.

From the first, moreover, white Americans have tried to link the idea of God with that of white supremacy. With appropriate scriptural allusions, they have argued that slavery and segregation were ordained by God. They have thereby guaranteed that the black man's political rebellion, when it finally emerged, would be accompanied by an assault on Christian values.

---

[2] See Wright's essay, "The Literature of the Negro in the United States," *White Man, Listen!*, pp. 105-50.

How could it be otherwise? By a process of transference, feelings of hostility aroused by the white man's injustice came to be directed toward the white man's God. Among the black intelligentsia, in particular, Christianity became associated with the submissive attitudes of slavery times. Hence the dilemma of the Negro poet, who "felt constrained to choose between God and the race."

This fissure first appeared in the poetry of Paul Laurence Dunbar, for Dunbar was the first Negro poet to emancipate himself from Methodism. Casting off the cloak of piety which had muffled Negro verse, he turned inevitably to his folk tradition. That he managed to circumvent the stereotypes of Christian piety, only to fall victim to those of the plantation school, was the essential failure of his art. But Dunbar was the first Negro poet whose religious faith gave way to doubt and skepticism. In the next generation apostasy was commonplace, as the younger poets reflected bitterly on the impotence of God and of the Christian church in the face of growing racial violence.

According to their inclinations in this conflict of divided loyalties, the six major poets of the Harlem Renaissance may be classified as folklorists or spiritualists. James Weldon Johnson, Langston Hughes, and Sterling Brown regard their folk tradition as a primary source of inspiration. Their language and their forms are drawn from folk sermons, work and prison songs, blues and ballads, jazz and jive. In varying degrees, they view Christianity as the religion of slavery, the opiate of the people, and a major obstacle to black emancipation. Privately or publicly they reject religious faith as incompatible with their loyalty to the Negro masses, whom they wish above all to sustain and exalt.

The spiritualists, in contrast, affirm their loyalty to God. Claude McKay, Jean Toomer, and Countee Cullen are likewise victims of a splintered culture, but in their case the conflict deepens, even as it is internalized. For these poets discover in the end that the fundamental conflict is not between the white man and the black, nor between the black man and his God, but between each man and himself. It is through the transcendence of self, and a truly heroic conquest of spiritual values, that these poets surmount their dilemma and achieve a life-giving synthesis from which the soul of the black man can emerge transfigured and enlarged.

Such is the fault that fractures the terrain of the Harlem Renaissance. Whether the godly are more successful poets than their ungodly counterparts is something else again. Wagner tends to bestow his laurels on the spiritualists, rather than the folklorists. The oncoming generation of younger blacks will no doubt be disposed to reverse this judgment. Determined to disengage themselves from white cultural norms, they will conclude that the index to a poet's "whiteness" is precisely his allegiance to the white man's God. They will prefer the folklorists, on the grounds that they are more emancipated from European (i.e., Christian) standards.

However one apportions praise or blame between the folklorists and spiritualists, the categories themselves are likely to endure. For Wagner has demonstrated the fundamental importance of theology in formulating a history of Afro-American poetry. He has shown that a culture is stitched together in such a way that when it rips, it tears along the seams. Political disaffection, for example, is reflected at a deeper level of consciousness in the art forms and religious icons of an oppressed people. So it was, at any rate, among the poets of the Harlem Renaissance, and so it has remained among the poets of the Black Renaissance of the 1960's.

If we look beyond the boundaries of the present book to the contemporary scene, how does Wagner's central thesis fare? To the superficial eye, it would appear that religious subjects have yielded entirely to political concerns. But a closer inspection will reveal that beneath the surface of revolutionary rhetoric lies a desperate search for new gods. Whether these new icons take the form of a black Christ, of Allah, or of ancient voodoo gods, the religious motivation is unmistakable. Cultural nationalism, in short, opens a fissure extending to the throne of God.

Black nationalism, its incessant talk of power notwithstanding, is far more a religious than political phenomenon. It follows that the poets of the movement, who are responsible for creating its mythology, must be approached in religious terms. Secular in outlook as they may conceive themselves to be, they are in fact embarked on a religious quest. When a history of the Black Renaissance is written, it will follow the broad guidelines laid down in *Black Poets of the United States* by Jean Wagner.

ROBERT BONE

Teachers College
Columbia University

February, 1972

ACKNOWLEDGMENTS

This book is greatly indebted to many persons, some of them dead now, as well as to a number of institutions and organizations on both sides of the Atlantic.

In the United States, where our research was made possible through a Smith-Mundt-Fulbright grant of the State Department, Dr. Elizabeth P. Lam and Miss Mary Hoch, of the Conference Board of Associated Research Councils, Washington, D.C., were helpful in many ways.

To Howard University, our host institution for several months, our debt is exceptionally heavy. Precious assistance was received from Dean Charles H. Thompson, the staff and administration of the Founders Library, and especially from Mrs. Dorothy B. Porter, Curator of the Negro Collection, without whose competent and untiring devotion many a valuable document would have escaped our attention. Professor E. Franklin Frazier allowed us to share in some of his great learning. To Professor Sterling A. Brown our indebtedness is downright immeasurable. In hundreds of hours of conference, he taught us what cannot be learned in any library; he would have much more competently written this book.

It is impossible to say how much time, information, and aid of many kinds was generously contributed by Arna Bontemps, Langston Hughes, Richard Wright, Alfred Kreymborg, Carl Van Vechten, Melvin B. Tolson, Samuel W. Allen, Robert Hayden, Benjamin E. Mays, Saunders Redding, Harold Jackman, Warren M. Banner, Carl Cowl, N. P. Tillman, T. D. Jarrett, M. Carl Holman, Mrs. Countee Cullen, Mrs. Beulah Reimherr, Mrs. Naomi M. Garrett, and the librarians of the Schomburg Collection, Hampton Institute, Atlanta University, Fisk University, West Virginia State College, the College of William and Mary, and Vassar College.

In France, the Cultural Services of the United States Embassy in Paris, especially O. Rudolph Aggrey and Philip Di Tommaso, energetically supported this project from its very inception. Together with the Centre National de la Recherche Scientifique and the French Ministry of National Education, they made possible its completion and publication, while at the Sorbonne Professors Roger Asselineau, Maurice Le Breton, Louis Landré, and Jean Simon generously gave of their time and advice.

And yet, for close to ten years, in view of the qualms which its very dimensions induced in the editors of a number of publishing firms, this book has remained practically unknown to the American public. That it is now, at long last, available in an English-language edition is due to the courage of Richard L. Wentworth, editor of the University of Illinois Press, and to the no less courageous efforts of Kenneth Douglas, who did not shy away from the formidable task of preparing an excellent translation from the original French.

To each and all, we here express our sincere appreciation.

PREFACE

This book was originally published as a doctoral dissertation in Paris in the spring of 1963. It grew out of the need for a serious assessment of a group of writers who even then appeared as the classics of black American poetry. Neither in the United States nor outside had they at the time been the subject of an investigation in any way commensurate with their actual achievement, importance, and interest. In fact, black American writers as a whole were not discovered by literary critics until a comparatively recent date.[1] In 1931, Vernon Loggins published his thesis *The Negro Author: His Development in America.* This was mainly a historical survey, which attempted no evaluation of the personalities of the writers reviewed; moreover, its scope did not extend beyond 1900. Except for Sterling Brown's short *Negro Poetry and Drama* (1937), designed as a popular primer, and

---

[1] When the *Literary History of the United States* appeared some twenty-five years ago, the editors justified their initiative by invoking the necessity for each generation of Americans to redefine its literary past in its own terms (see the Preface, 4th printing, 1959, p. vii). In spite of such well-intentioned liminal declarations, however, this handbook, like most of its predecessors, gave short shrift to those American writers who happened not to be white, and one would have vainly searched its fifteen hundred pages for anything amounting to a redefinition, let alone a bona fide reevaluation of black American writing. For this omission the editors can hardly be held personally responsible. One should be aware, of course, that editors of general literary histories must rely for their estimates on previous research publications. As long as these are not forthcoming, the black American writer will not be adequately represented in handbooks of American literature. On the subject of discrimination against the black American writer, see our article "Littérature nègre et littérature américaine," *Rives* (Paris), December, 1960, pp. 16-20.

J. Saunders Redding's *To Make a Poet Black* (1939), also a brief survey, nothing appeared between the two world wars besides the uncritical and often tendentious works of Benjamin G. Brawley.[2] After World War II, black novelists were studied in Hugh M. Gloster's *Negro Voices in American Fiction* (1948), aptly supplemented ten years later by Robert Bone's *The Negro Novel in America*. But the poets remained as good as ignored. It is to them, therefore, that this book was intended to do justice.

The time span chosen is roughly the half-century extending from 1890 to 1940, though these dates should not be taken too strictly. Actually, we begin with Dunbar, whose first collection of poems did not appear until December, 1892, but who had been writing poetry more than seven years earlier. To evaluate Dunbar with any degree of fairness, however, one has to go farther back in the history of literary events, and farther back still in general history to provide the necessary background and perspective. At the far end, the boundary is set by such writers whose first publications in book form[3] appeared before 1940, though we did not cut short at that date the study of Langston Hughes, whose complete poetic production is included.

Another point of importance is the twin theme on which we have chosen to focus our attention. That the account of their life experience as black men in a white civilization was the capital point of interest in all of these poets is only too obvious. What needs a word of explanation is our choice not to isolate the study of their racial feeling, but rather to associate it with the study of their religious feeling. In so doing, we would, of course, have been amply justified by the mere historical fact that racial and religious themes have been traditionally associated in black lyrical expression from the days of the spirituals to present-day poetry. But, as we were soon to discover, racial and religious feeling do not simply coexist as independent themes; they are really interdependent, joined in a kind of symbiosis or vital union, so that variations in one result in variations in the other. This

---

[2] *The Negro Genius* (1937), a new edition of *The Negro in Literature and Art in the United States* (1930), in which Brawley undertook to draw up an inventory of the Negro's contribution to American culture, laid down the principle (Introduction, pp. 8-9) that "such distinction as the Negro has won in the arts is due primarily to the black rather than the mixed element in the race. People of mixed blood have given us the college presidents, the administrators, the government employees; but the blacks are the singers and seers. Black slaves gave us the spirituals; modern composers of a lighter hue transcribe them." Brawley's critical biography of Dunbar, *Paul Laurence Dunbar, Poet of His People* (1936), draws a portrait of the poet which is too carefully expurgated to be credible; this book fully deserves the severe censure to which Sterling Brown subjected it ("The Literary Scene: Biography," *Opportunity*, July, 1937, pp. 216-17). On the whole, Brawley's critical judgments, to which we will have occasion to return, cannot be accepted without great wariness.

[3] See the liminal note to our Bibliography.

will be shown both in our studies of individual authors and in our conclusion.

As the reader will readily realize, our concern lies somewhat beyond that of the conventional contributor to literary history, and our book was conceived more like a venture in the field of what has since come to be known as Black American Studies. Naturally, we make it a point not to abstract the writings from the life styles and declared intentions of the writers, their historical, social, and cultural environment, and the forces at play within or without. But we are also interested in discovering the psychological complexities of each writer's individual personality in order to arrive at a better understanding of the complexities of the black soul.

We hold no brief for any particular school of criticism, old or new, or for any particular aesthetic, black or white. The critic is naturally the product of his training and culture, and our own judgments must ultimately reflect a certain idea of man, in view of which the reader will easily understand that we reject as utterly childish and preposterous the contention that "black writers do not write for white people and refuse to be judged by them."[4]

Finally, we can only express the hope that, in the country with which it is mainly concerned, this book will be received with the same kind of intellectual honesty with which it was written.

J. W.

Université de Grenoble III

February, 1972

[4] Stephen E. Henderson, *The Militant Black Writer* (Madison, Wisc., 1969), p. 65.

It is a peculiar sensation, this double consciousness, this sense of always looking at one's self through the eyes of others, of measuring one's soul by the tape of a world that looks on in amused contempt and pity. One ever feels his two-ness, — an American, a Negro: two souls, two thoughts, two unreconciled strivings; two warring ideals in one dark body, whose dogged strength alone keeps it from being torn asunder.

— W. E. B. Du Bois
The Souls of Black Folk, 1903, p. 3

Lasst alle Völker unter gleichem Himmel
Sich gleicher Farbe wohlgemut erfreun.

— Goethe
Über Kunst und Altertum, 1827

Chapter One: INTRODUCTION

Black poetry's deserved place in the American literary domain does not depend solely on a heritage, now two centuries old, which abounds in works of unchallengeable beauty. An essential part of its interest is also to be found in the sum of human experience, individual and collective, from which this poetry springs and which it interprets, for it is the voice of several generations of human beings whose destiny, to the present day, has been strangely unlike that of the majority of their fellow citizens. Because of this destiny's extraordinary characteristics, black poetry is not an exclusively literary phenomenon and must be seen also as a body of psychological and social documents of exceptional value.

Consequently, no valid study of this material can be undertaken until one has first become aware of the highly complex problems confronting groups and individuals as a result of the presence, in a great country whose inhabitants are mainly white, of a black minority that today constitutes more than 10 percent of the population.

It is hard to evaluate even the work of a contemporary black poet like Langston Hughes if the whole history of the black race is to be set aside, from the deportations from Africa to the present moment. Yet history alone cannot explain everything. It is sociology that alerts us to the special nature of the links binding the Negro to his own racial community, as well as to that of the white majority. Sociology reveals the extent to which the life of the individual is determined by these communities, and also tells us of the conflicts between the communities and, on occasion, between the communities and the individual. Thus we find ourselves already in the realm of social psychology, whose function it is "to establish how each individual has adapted himself to the collective norms, how he fits into the milieux surrounding him, what role he plays therein, and what possible influence he exerts on them."[1] Incidentally, historians, sociologists, and psychologists still find it no easy matter to fix the boundaries of their respective disciplines.[2] It so happens that all of them have been concerned with the problems of the American Negro, and their countless studies differ not so much in the terrain they set out to explore as with respect to the aims they pursue and the methods they adopt.

We begin, therefore, with a rapid survey of the sort of insights that the sciences of man may be expected to offer an investigation such as ours.[3] Yet the reciprocal benefit is equally real, and we will deem the conclusions we may reach through a close study of that precious document concerning the black man, his poetry, to be not a whit less valid than the results attained by the social sciences. It has, in any case, long been recognized by such distinguished sociologists as E. Franklin Frazier and Robert E. Park that, by itself, black poetry can reveal to us many things about the multiple aspects of the black soul.[4]

While we will, therefore, not turn a deaf ear on history, sociology, or psychology, in the end our surest guide will prove to be the enlightened sympathy with which we approach our poets and their works.

1. THE NEGRO IN THE UNITED STATES

As early as the sixteenth century, the Spaniards had temporarily introduced

---

[1] Jean Maisonneuve, *Psychologie sociale,* p. 13.

[2] See, for example, the discussion that followed the account, by the historian Stanley M. Elkins, of the problem of the Negro's personality during the slave period. This discussion is reported in "The Question of 'Sambo': A Report of the Ninth Newberry Library Conference on American Studies," *The Newberry Library Bulletin,* December, 1958, pp. 14-40.

[3] It is clear that in this introduction we can do no more than outline the historical, sociological, and psychological problems that are at the base of any investigation concerning the Negro in the United States. Several of these problems will be examined more closely on various occasions in the course of this work. For more ample information, consult the selection of specialized studies listed in the bibliographical appendix.

[4] See E. Franklin Frazier, *The Negro in the United States,* pp. 492ff. Nevertheless, since Frazier utilizes secondary sources, not all of which are dependable, some of his remarks about such Negro poets as Dunbar are dubious at best. For Robert E. Park, see "Negro Race Consciousness as Reflected in Race Literature," *American Review,* September-October, 1923, pp. 505-16. This article is reprinted in the posthumous collection of his publications entitled *Race and Culture,* pp. 284-300.

some Negroes on the North American continent.[5] But the first Africans to take firm root within the boundaries of the present-day United States disembarked at Jamestown, Virginia, in August, 1619.[6] New England also imported its first Negroes less than twenty years later. They came from the West Indies, where they often went through an acclimatization period before being transferred to their ultimate destination. Little by little, each colony acquired its contingent of black labor.

Slaves and Free Men

For all that, slavery was put on a regular footing only by degrees, and in the earlier years, when the number of blacks was still rather low, their status differed little from that of indentured servants. The latter were often English laboring men, coming above all from the rural regions, whose poverty had induced them to emigrate. Unable to pay their passage, they indentured themselves for a certain period (usually five or seven years), after which they became free men once more. Among them were some, too, who had been taken to America against their will. These might have been rogues and vagabonds whom the British government had arranged to have deported and sold in America, or persons abducted on the streets of London by underworld gangs and then shipped overseas to be sold. Throughout the period of indenture, the civil rights of such individuals were largely held in abeyance — and it is in the laws formulated to clarify their place in society that we must seek the origin of all the black codes in the colonies.

The specific juridical status of Negroes was spelled out in case law and statutory law only as their numbers grew. It is believed that as late as 1682 Virginia Negroes could indeed claim their freedom, once their period of indenture had reached its end. But still extant rulings also reveal that, even before the mid-seventeenth century, Negroes were treated with greater severity in courts of law than were white indentured servants. Negroes are referred to as "slaves" for the first time in a Virginia law of 1662. Another law of that same year decided the fate of children born to parents of different race, proclaiming the child to be slave or free in keeping with the mother's own slave or free status. Beginning with the second half of the seventeenth century, the laws and regulations promulgated in most colonies

[5] Unless otherwise indicated, the information contained in this section is taken from Frazier, *The Negro in the United States;* Benjamin Griffith Brawley, *A Short History of the American Negro;* and John Hope Franklin, *From Slavery to Freedom.*

[6] On the doubts that still exist concerning this date, see the Federal Writers' Project volume, Roscoe E. Lewis, ed., *The Negro in Virginia*, pp. 1ff.

for the purpose of determining the Negro's place contented themselves, as a general rule, with consecrating already established usages.

Maryland, under a measure that became law in 1664, was the first colony to set up slavery as a separate institution from indenturing.[7] By its terms Negroes were bound to lifelong servitude. The same colony, seven years later, adopted another law that settled a hitherto controversial issue by decreeing that the fact of having received baptism would no longer liberate Negro slaves.

In any event, the distinction between indentured servants and slaves was to be automatically obliterated in the course of the eighteenth century. Since the purchase of a Negro slave, who was forced to render lifelong service, cost the planter little more than the acquisition of an indentured servant, whose period of service was strictly limited — and, furthermore, since it was easier to identify a runaway Negro, whose skin color betrayed him, than a white servant, who could melt into the crowd — the system of indenture disappeared almost completely during the eighteenth century, while at the same time slavery grew.

The expansion of slavery was inexorably linked with that of the plantation, which could be exploited only by the utilization of some form of forced labor. The plantation, moreover, was not merely an economic institution; since it operated under the supervision of the colonial administrators, it was a political institution also. Yet — for many plantations were situated in frontier regions and lacked contact with the outside world — it could form a tiny state within the state, where the planter exerted absolute power.

The principal products in the early days were tobacco, rice, and indigo, but in the pre-Revolutionary period planters from the West Indies introduced sugarcane into Louisiana. Besides, a series of inventions and technical developments within the English cotton industry created, in the course of the eighteenth century, an extraordinary demand for cotton; this could be met only by increasing the area of land under cultivation and by importing an ever greater number of slaves. The process received further impetus in 1793, when Eli Whitney invented the cotton gin. Thus, whereas there were only an estimated 700,000 slaves in the United States in 1790, ten years later there were about 900,000, more than 1.5 million in 1820, about 2.5 million in 1840, and some 4 million on the eve of the Civil War.

[7] The fact that slavery took root first of all in Maryland and Virginia explains why the earliest documents regulating it appeared in these colonies. For reasons it would take too much space to explain here, such regulations were introduced only much later into other colonies such as New Hampshire (1714), North Carolina (1715), and Georgia (1765).

Along with this increase in numbers went the progressive shifting of the Negro population to the South and Southwest — that is, into the regions which the cotton economy was taking over in its forward march.[8]

As the frontier receded and many plantations gradually emerged from their isolation, the power of the state and the force of public opinion imposed limits on the planter's absolute rule. In some regions the long-term consequences were to set up the planter as a kind of patriarch and to create between master and slave a system of social relations that favored, up to a certain point, the slave's acquisition of the master's culture. Thus there originated on the plantation the pattern of race relations that later would constitute the foundation of race relations in the South.

It is easy to imagine that social conditions varied enormously, depending on the region, the type of crop, and the dimensions of the enterprise. In 1850, 18 percent of the farms in the South were classified as plantations. Three-quarters of these specialized in the production of cotton and 15 percent in tobacco, while 8 percent grew hemp and roughly 2 percent, sugarcane. Many of them had only one or two slaves, as was the case with the tobacco-growers of Kentucky, whereas in the Deep South the average number of slaves on a plantation was much higher, rising to eighty-seven in certain Louisiana counties.

In the huge plantations of South Carolina, Georgia, Mississippi, and Louisiana, where the economy was at the level of industrial exploitation, the slaves sank to being mere beasts of burden. They had no contact with white men apart from their overseers, and these were recruited among the poor whites who looked on Negroes as animals. Wherever this state of isolation prevailed, the condition of the slaves was almost barbaric.

More humane relationships existed on the small and medium-sized plantations (in Virginia, for instance), where physical force as the decisive factor in social relations tended to be replaced by a complex of customs and traditions in which the master's feelings of superiority and responsibility were matched by the slave's feelings of fidelity and submissiveness. "All in all, the slave regime was a curious blend of force and concession, of arbitrary disposal by the master and self-direction by the slave, of tyranny and benevolence, of antipathy and affection."[9]

It still remains for us to distinguish the various categories of slaves making up the plantation's work force. At the very bottom of the ladder were the field hands, some of whom might nevertheless possess capacities that,

---

[8] This shift can be seen very clearly on the maps reproduced in Frazier, *The Negro in the United States,* pp. 31, 33, 35, 37.

[9] Ulrich B. Phillips, *Life and Labor in the Old South* (Boston, 1929), p. 195. Cited by Frazier, *The Negro in the United States,* p. 50.

attracting the attention of overseer or owner, could lead to some measure of authority being conferred on such a man over a group of his fellow slaves. Those with the requisite intelligence or manual dexterity sometimes became craftsmen (blacksmiths, shoemakers, cabinet-makers, and the like) who were highly regarded and were very proud of their skills. One can often note in them a marked spirit of independence, an evolution fostered by frequent permission to work on their own accounts outside the bounds of the plantation, against payment of a contractual indemnity to their owners. But those who were held in the very highest regard by their masters and by the other slaves were the servants in the master's house. They had a keen sense of their superior standing and derived from it no small measure of pride. There was ample cause for this prestige. Not only were the tasks they carried out much less arduous than the labors of the other slaves; these house Negroes were also treated with more consideration and were better clothed and lodged. They shared from near at hand in the daily life of the planter and his family, and had a natural tendency to identify with them rather than with the other slaves, whose existence so little resembled their own. Their intellect was generally more acute, they had better education and were more cultivated, and ultimately they assumed the manners and culture of the dominant class. Many of them were mulattoes, born of their masters' amours with mistresses chosen from among the most attractive slaves. In turn, the illegitimate offspring of such unions often profited from a status far above that available to others of their race, for it quite often happened that their masters, out of love for the mother, gave them their freedom and saw to it that they were educated.

As early as the seventeenth century there existed, in addition to the slaves, a class of free colored people. These were either onetime indentured servants who had earned their freedom, onetime slaves who had been set free under the terms of a will or for outstanding services rendered, or the children of free mothers. Yet others had been slaves who, having succeeded in earning some money, had purchased freedom from their masters. They numbered about 60,000 in 1790, more than 230,000 in 1820, and about 500,000 in 1860. Mulattoes made up the largest group among these free Negroes; in Louisiana, for example, they amounted to more than 80 percent of all such persons.

However, Negroes in this category were not truly free in every respect. Many states of the South and West regarded them as undesirables and barred them from residence under laws that, fortunately, were not always applied. It was the desire to get rid of these free Negroes that led to the 1822 creation of the colony of Liberia, which was declared independent

twenty-five years later. Though liable for taxes, the free Negroes could not
vote, and their frequently precarious financial position tended to be worse
in the North than in the South. But some still managed to assemble fortunes, among them the black owners of Louisiana cotton and sugarcane
plantations with their many slaves. It was traditional in such families to
send the children off to France for their education. But this wealth aroused
the envy of the white neighbors and, after a certain date, a Louisiana edict
forbade them to wear diamonds and elaborate coiffures.

Thus the lot of the free Negroes was utterly dissimilar from that of the
slaves, even though they were never treated, either *de jure* or *de facto,* as
full-fledged citizens. In the contexts of education and culture, above all,
they enjoyed opportunities beyond the reach of slaves, and so they found
themselves, after Emancipation, fully prepared to form the nucleus of the
future's black bourgeoisie.

The Negro "Inferior and Subservient"

The movement that resulted in the independence of the United States sent
a current of liberalism pulsing through the land. This also benefited the
cause of freedom for the slaves. In the North, most state constitutions contained clauses that provided for the rapid abolition of slavery. Under federal law it became illegal, as of January 1, 1808, to import slaves into the
United States.

But while the adoption of a liberal attitude called for no great sacrifice
in the North, where the demand for slaves had sunk to zero, the situation
was quite different in the South, where the booming cotton economy required ever more slaves. Thus the South, to protect its economic well-being,
was forced to defend and justify slavery against the attacks of northern
abolitionists. With the end of the War of 1812, the abolitionists found an
outlet in such specialized papers as Charles Osborn's *The Philanthropist,*[10]
and even in the South there were anti-slavery periodicals like *The Emancipator* of Tennessee, founded by Elihu Embree in 1820, and *The Patriot,*
a North Carolina Quaker journal. Efforts intensified after 1830 with the
founding, in rapid succession, of two anti-slavery organizations, the New
England Anti-Slavery Society (1831) and the American Anti-Slavery
Society (1833). In Boston, William Lloyd Garrison brought out *The Liberator* (1831), and a swarm of other journals disseminated their ideas,
while a veritable army of lecturers began to scour the country.

One of the first to draw up the South's response to the accusations made
by northern abolitionists was Thomas R. Dew, professor of history, meta-

[10] Founded in 1817.

physics, and political science at the College of William and Mary in Williamsburg, Virginia. The Virginia authorities had called on Dew to prepare a philosophical justification of slavery, and in 1832 he published the results of his investigation. After examining the history of slavery from ancient times and studying its economic and social impact on Virginia, Dew reached the conclusion that slavery was an undeniable good, that it contributed to Virginia's prosperity, and that it was the only possible form of coexistence between the races. While the Negro, according to Dew, had the appearance and strength of a man, his intelligence was that of a child. Thus it followed that he was not created to be free.

Dew, like his many emulators,[11] unhesitatingly turned to the Bible to find "proof" that slavery was the will of God: the Mosaic law recognized slavery; Jesus Christ never condemned it; Saint Paul had expressed his approval, since he had not only advised slaves to obey their masters, but had actually sent back the fugitive slave Onesimus to his master Philemon.

The 1857 decision of the southern-dominated U.S. Supreme Court in *Scott* v. *Sanford* (a case in which Dred Scott, a slave, confronted several of his successive masters, and which dealt with events going back to 1834) espoused completely the slaveholders' theses and interpreted the Constitution in accordance with them. The Supreme Court declared that Negroes "were at that time considered as a subordinate and inferior class of beings. . . . A Negro has no rights which a white man need respect."[12]

For the South's general acceptance of the theories of Negro inferiority and the legitimacy of slavery, a heavy portion of the blame must be attributed to the clumsiness and brutality that characterized the campaign waged by northern abolitionists.[13] The intransigence and lack of realism of a Garrison in the end submerged all southern slaveowners under the same moral opprobrium, although it has been shown that in the more northerly states of the South and in those fronting the Atlantic (with the possible exception of South Carolina) slavery produced such widespread feelings of guilt that a sense of kinship with the North might have resulted, rather than with the pro-slavery forces of Alabama and Mississippi. In Virginia, for example, where the economy had made considerable strides,

[11] Of these, we will name only Henry Hughes, *Treatise on Sociology, Theoretical and Practical* (1854); George Fitzhugh, *Sociology for the South, or the Failure of Free Society* (1854), and *Cannibals All, or Slaves without Masters* (1857); George D. Armstrong, *The Christian Doctrine of Slavery* (1857); Fred. A. Ross, *Slavery Ordained of God* (1857).

[12] For the text of this important decision, see Richard D. Heffner, ed., *A Documentary History of the United States* (Mentor ed.), pp. 125-33.

[13] See, on this question, Stanley M. Elkins, *Slavery: A Problem in American Institutional and Intellectual Life,* pp. 193ff.

slavery was no longer a vigorous institution and landowners desired nothing more, once a favorable occasion presented itself, than to get rid of their slaves — who were not only at the root of what was genuinely felt to be a sin, but who had, furthermore, first ceased to be profitable and later become a heavy financial burden. It so happened that an excellent opportunity did arise between 1832 and 1836, with an increase in the price of slaves. During these years Virginians sold an estimated 120,000 slaves to planters in the Deep South.[14]

Eventually, a stereotype of the Negro came to receive credence in every part of the South. He was depicted as "docile but irresponsible, loyal but lazy, humble but chronically given to lying and stealing; his behavior was full of infantile silliness and his talk inflated with childish exaggeration. His relationship with his master was one of utter dependence and childlike attachment: it was indeed this childlike quality that was the very key to his being."[15]

This customary southern view of the Negro was thus summarized by Stanley M. Elkins, who went on to raise the question of the portrait's accuracy.

We have already tried to demonstrate how dangerous generalizations can be in this area. Yet we are forced to admit at this juncture that Elkins's portrait of the Negro closely resembles the one painted in the South's militant literature through the nineteenth century and beyond.[16]

As for its accuracy, the numerous debates occasioned by this problem may be said to have given rise to three theories, none of which is really verifiable and which, in any case, are not mutually exclusive.

In Elkins's view (his explanatory hypothesis being the most recent and also, it must be admitted, a very tempting one), the portrait is essentially correct — not, however, because the Negro should be considered to be by nature an inferior, submissive creature, his evolution irremediably arrested at some infantile level, and not because he is destined by birth to be a slave, a conclusion that certain British colonizers expressed at a relatively recent date.[17] But Elkins, by comparing the closed world of the slave with the

[14] *Ibid.*, p. 211, n. 126.
[15] *Ibid.*, p. 82.
[16] Cf. below our Ch. 2.
[17] Frazier, *The Negro in the United States*, p. 82, cites a work by Harry H. Johnston, *A History of the Colonization of Africa by Alien Races* (Cambridge, 1913), in which the Negro is described as a born slave, strong, submissive, and cheerful, with no sympathy for his own racial brothers but inclined to recognize, follow, and imitate his master quite apart from any racial affinity. The British were not alone in seeing Africans in this light. See A. Memmi, *Portrait du colonisé, précédé du portrait du colonisateur.*

modern concentration camp, reached the insight that the slave who confronts his master and the prisoner who confronts his camp boss both find
themselves in the position of the child with respect to his father. The child
is dependent on him to the exclusion of everyone else and awaits reward or
punishment at his hands, in accordance with an identification with him (or
a failure to identify) and with the acceptance (or rejection) of the values
he incarnates. Thus, all by itself, the master's total, exclusive domination
has exerted an infantilizing effect on the slave, and this to the precise
degree that the universe of slavery is a more or less closed one.[18]

The second and much older response to this portrait of the Negro as
child is made by a great number of Negro critics. It consists of the categorical refusal to accept the facts as alleged: no Negro ever existed who corresponded to this portrait, which is simply the fabrication of white people
intent on finding some way to justify the legitimacy of slavery.[19]

The third explanation is often advanced in tandem with the second. It
does not deny that the Negro in fact often behaved like a child, but declares
this to be a mark of cunning on his part. The Negro puts on this show the
better to deceive his master, a theory that more than one aspect of black
folklore appears to confirm. Here, by way of example, is a stanza from "Me
and My Captain":

> Got one mind for white folks to see,
> 'Nother for what I know is me;
> He don't know, he don't know my mind,
> When he see me laughing,
> Just laughing to keep from crying.[20]

To this interpretation, however, the behaviorist psychologists and such
sociologists as Robert E. Park propose an emendation of considerable importance.[21] Agreed, they say; in our everyday existence we all more or less

---

[18] See Elkins, *Slavery*, Ch. 3. Of course, Elkins did not invent any of this, and
social psychologists had already noted the tendency of the persecuted to identify
with their persecutors. See, for example, Abram Kardiner and Lionel Ovesey, *The
Mark of Oppression: A Psychosocial Study of the American Negro*, p. 351. But
Elkins has lent much more substance to this observation by comparing the reactions noted in Nazi concentration camp detainees with those of some American
Negro slaves. Furthermore, this is only one facet of his thesis, which tends to explain the special character of slavery in America as due to the fact that, in the
United States, any forces that might have acted as a counterweight to the excesses
of the slave system found no organized institutional expression.

[19] This, more particularly, is the view held by critics of plantation literature.
On this, see below our Ch. 2.

[20] Quoted by Sterling A. Brown et al., eds., *The Negro Caravan*, p. 471.

[21] See Robert E. Park, "Die menschliche Natur und das Kollectiv-Verhalten"
("Human Nature and Collective Behavior"), *Kölner Vierteljahrshefte für Soziologie*, 6th yr. (1926-27), pp. 12-20.

consciously play one or more roles. In other words, we all wear masks. They find significance in the etymology of the word "person," derived from Latin *persona*, "a mask." But a price must be paid for wearing a mask, since in the long run the consequence of pretending to be what one is not is transformation, to some degree, into what one was only pretending to be.

Let it be declared right away that all these explanations are both true and false. They are assuredly false to the extent that any one of them is held up, to the exclusion of the others, as an explanation of the psychological behavior of all the blacks who have succeeded one another on American soil. Blacks have not always remained subservient as universally as some people have chosen to believe. We have in our hands accounts of slave revolts at every imaginable juncture: on the African continent before embarkation, on the slave ships before they had left the African ports, on the high seas, and on the American plantations. Among the most notable rebellions are Gabriel's in 1800, Denmark Vesey's in 1822, and Nat Turner's in 1831. We know that many Negroes, preferring death to slavery, jumped overboard during the Atlantic crossing. We know, too, that some slaves found so little to like in plantation life that sooner or later they ran away. Escapes became so frequent that in 1850 the slave-owning states induced Congress to pass a law requiring Northerners to return runaway slaves to their masters. That this law remained largely a dead letter is due to the Underground Railroad, a clandestine escape network whose agents helped the fugitive slaves to cross into Canada. Deservedly famous is the spirit of resistance that inspired a woman like Harriet Tubman, a fugitive slave who went back to the South twenty times and engineered the escape of three hundred slaves, among them her own parents. Famous, too, are the exploits of another escaped slave, Frederick Douglass, perhaps the most extraordinary leader the Negro race in the United States has ever produced.

Thus beyond a doubt there were rebellious slaves, and in their case it is only right to underline the spurious character of the Southerner's depiction of the Negro. But it is no less incontrovertible that rebellion remained ever the exception; on this point all historians and sociologists are in accord. An explanation must then be sought for the submissiveness and for the at times even infantile behavior, whether genuine or simulated, of the vast majority of the slaves. In this connection Elkins's hypothesis appears to offer an especially satisfactory solution for many cases to which the earlier theories could not readily be applied.

Taken as a whole, and providing the reasonable avowal is made that each one of them fits only a limited number of instances, the various explanations mentioned do finally furnish us, for the great mass of slaves, with a picture to which ordinary common sense must also lead: that of a vast throng of people profoundly human and diverging greatly in character, among whom can be discerned the resigned, docile individual as well as the sly and resourceful one, and in exceptional cases even the rebel.

The Mark of Oppression[22]

But it remains true that the experience of slavery has left a deep imprint on the personality of the Negro. Some one hundred years after Emancipation, the traumas that still afflict his psyche heal all the more slowly because his current status in American society does basically nothing more than psychologically prolong his status under slavery. Despite his freedom, despite the demolition of all the pseudo-scientific demonstrations of his inferiority and alleged congenital defects, he continues to be regarded very much as he was in the past. While he is no longer inferior essentially, the self-image thrown back at him by his human environment still mirrors his presumed inferiority.

This state of affairs leads to highly complex psychic repercussions that vary enormously with the individual and the precise circumstances in which they unfold. They may be grouped, in schematic fashion, into two basic types of reactions.

In the first place, the Negro gradually develops a poor opinion of himself. Ashamed of his appearance, self-despising and projecting his contempt on all who resemble him, he sometimes ends up by hating everyone of his own race. Thus the white man's outlook imperceptibly implants itself within him, since, for all practical purposes, no other outlook counts. As the old slogan has it, "White is right." One step further and the white man and his values are idealized, and the goal pursued is the closest possible resemblance to him in every respect. This tendency has brought wealth to cosmetics manufacturers, who sell Negro women products that straighten their hair and lighten their skin tone. Paul Laurence Dunbar called one of his musical comedies "Jes' Lak White Folks" (1900).

Yet, on the other hand, since he is constantly brought up short by the impossibility of becoming a white man, and since he knows how unfairly he is treated by white people, the Negro develops feelings of great hostility toward them. Rarely is an occasion found for venting this hostility in its raw state, whatever the degree of frustration experienced, because the Negro cannot at every instant launch an overt attack on those responsible. The requirements of life in society force him to repress his hatred and Ɡer, and this repression leads to a chronic fear of their consequences.

꜠le of the work by Kardiner and Ovesey already referred to, in which will detailed study of the psychological problems summarized here.

"The fear and the rage become almost interchangeable."[23] Ultimately this hostility is siphoned off in varied ways, depending on the individual and the precise situation. It may lead to abject submissiveness, or it may find an outlet in some intense physical activity, such as sports or dancing. It may also be sublimated and emerge as hedonism or, if no other safety valve is found, react adversely on the individual's health. Thus the poets Countee Cullen and Claude McKay died of high blood pressure.[24]

Here, as previously, we are forced to summarize and so to become excessively schematic: the living reality is infinitely more varied and complex. For example, in the lower classes the desire to be white may have a totally different origin. In this milieu the structure of the family is still severely affected by the destabilizing influences that slavery had imposed on it.[25] Since father, mother, and children could be sold separately and scattered far and wide, the family as an institution never had any *de jure* existence for the slave. Moreover, it existed infrequently *de facto*. The only link that for obvious reasons could not always be neglected was between mother and child. Thus the real head of the family was almost always the woman, whose role in the family therefore expanded to an excessive degree, while the man's role shrank proportionately. Even without considering the feeling of inferiority that came to haunt him, or the devices he employed in his search for psychological compensation, it is clear that the father finds himself less positively integrated in the family unit due to his inability to exert supreme authority within it, while he is also deprived of the respect and deference which would normally be his by right. Parents of the lower classes often fail to maintain a satisfactory living standard for the family; in any event, they belong to a racial group that the majority despises. But psychologists tell us that the ideal conceived by a child is derived from an idealization of his parents. In this particular instance the parents offer only an unimpressive ideal for the child to emulate, and this does much to motivate him in his search for a white ideal.

Finally, one should never lose sight of the basic factor which is at the root of all the problems we have touched upon. It is the American Negro's destiny to live simultaneously in two worlds, the black folks' and the white folks'. In his very depths he is the divided man so accurately portrayed in the quotation from W. E. B. Du Bois that serves as epigraph for our inves-

[23] Kardiner and Ovesey, *The Mark of Oppression*, p. 304.
[24] This is simply to record the fact. Negroes are not the only victims of this kind of psychosomatic repercussion. The example does no more than illustrate an observation made by Kardiner and Ovesey, *ibid.*, p. 305.
[25] See, on this topic, E. Franklin Frazier, *The Negro Family in the United States* (Chicago, 1939).

tigation. His entire life acquires its value as the struggle to rise above his conflicts and to achieve an inner unity. But this synthesis is always a heroic undertaking, and in it the best men may fail.

2. THE ORIGINS OF BLACK POETRY

Characteristically, black poetry in twentieth-century America is a venture to find an equilibrium between three movements in poetry which, until Paul Laurence Dunbar began to write at the beginning of the nineteenth century's last decade, had evolved side by side while remaining entirely, or almost entirely, oblivious to each other.

Though often unavowedly stated, two of these movements quite certainly had a thesis they wanted to prove. Broadly speaking, we may say that the poetry written by Negroes in the eighteenth and nineteenth centuries sought to convince the public that Negroes possessed essentially the same artistic and intellectual aptitudes as did whites, and that they too could write poetry in English. It cannot be said that the demonstration failed, for there is no lack of works to back it up.

As can well be imagined, the so-called Negro poetry written by white Southerners after the Civil War had a different goal. Its chief objective was to draw a portrait of the Negro conforming to the southern view of him and bearing witness also, in a bold, retrospective sweep, to the bliss of the Negro and the greatness of his master under the defunct institution of slavery. In the following chapter we will consider this poetry in more detail.

But it should be noted at once that the very preoccupations of these two poetic movements kept them isolated from the taproots of genuine black creativity. This certainly flourished with a greater authenticity in the anonymous outpourings of oral folk poetry, whose expression of human values and whose beauty would be acclaimed only much later. For this to occur, the aesthetic canons of poetry first had to proceed toward the rehabilitation of originality and sincerity, while ceasing to evaluate a work in accord with the formal perfection shown in its imitation of Pope, Scott, or Byron.

Written Poetry in the Eighteenth and Nineteenth Centuries

Written black poetry originated about the middle of the eighteenth century.[26] The earliest authors were a few highly favored slaves whose

---

[26] All we can do here is to survey very rapidly Negro poetry in the eighteenth and nineteenth centuries. Furthermore, we refer only to those aspects that have

masters allowed or even took an interest in their education. A fillip to the master's vanity sometimes resulted, for the bystanders regarded such slaves as prodigies, brilliant exceptions to the general rule which would have it that the Negro was incapable of intellectual progress.

The oldest extant poem by an American Negro is the work of Lucy Terry, who was owned by an Ebenezer Wells of Deerfield, Massachusetts. In her poem of twenty-eight lines, "Bars Fight," she relates how Indians attacked Deerfield on August 25, 1746, and describes the havoc wrought among the inhabitants. The poem tells us nothing of its author, unfortunately, and has nothing specifically Negro about it.[27]

Jupiter Hammon,[28] consequently, is still looked on as the first American Negro to have had a poem printed. If the quality of his verse were the only criterion we might consign him to oblivion forthwith, for his poems, inspired by the Methodist hymns of the period and taking over their phraseology, are crudely composed. Yet Hammon deserves mention above all for his first poem, "An Evening Thought: Salvation by Christ with Penitential Cries" (1760), which is very close in tone to folk poetry. It represents a halfway stage between the guileless art of the unknown composers of spirituals and the already much wordier manner of the black popular preacher. It is known that Jupiter Hammon was a convert and that his master allowed him, outside working hours, to preach to the blacks. He can readily be imagined using this poem to appeal to his fellows, until the sonorous repetition of the word "salvation" at regular intervals finally stirs the rhythm that has so often channeled the religious emotions of Negroes. Attention has also been paid to certain interesting aspects of Hammon's versification. A shifting of tonic accents and even bold syncopations characterize a poem destined to be heard rather than

relevance for the rest of our investigation. For remarks that are somewhat more detailed, see Vernon Loggins, *The Negro Author: His Development in America,* a survey of the entire literary production of Negroes from the beginnings to the end of the nineteenth century. But there exists no in-depth study of the poetry of this period. Sterling Brown's *Negro Poetry and Drama* is extremely brief, being intended as a popular introduction. J. Saunders Redding, in his *To Make a Poet Black,* examines the whole body of Negro literature. His views are extremely fragmented, and the conclusions he reaches often spring from bias rather than from an objective examination of the texts.

[27] Lucy Terry and her poem were brought to light fairly recently as a result of the publication of the Langston Hughes and Arna Bontemps anthology, *The Poetry of the Negro, 1746-1949.* See pp. 3, 406.

[28] Jupiter Hammon (1720?-1806?) was the slave of one Henry Lloyd of Queen's Village, Long Island. Almost nothing is known of his life and doings. His first poem, "An Evening Thought...," is dated December 25, 1760. Another poem, addressed to Phillis Wheatley, appeared eighteen years later. "A Dialogue, Entitled, the Kind Master and Dutiful Servant" bears no date.

seen and read. Employing a subtle, complex rhythm, the preacher's voice brings the verse to life, and so he can with impunity set aside the traditional rules of prosody. Hammon probably relied on the extraordinary precision of his auditory sensibility, while remaining unaware of the process. Yet his experiment should be borne in mind, for the black poets of the twentieth century will take it up again.

One can find much less to praise in Jupiter Hammon's religious fervor, which overlaid a strange torpor in his racial sensitivity. For here we are confronted with a neophyte who has been carefully indoctrinated by his entourage and whom kindly treatment has rendered docile. He ultimately ceases even to long for the future restoration of his freedom. More curious still are his endeavors to lull to sleep the same desire in his fellow slaves by turning their thoughts away from terrestrial realities and directing them toward the joys of eternity.[29] In "The Kind Master and Dutiful Servant,"[30] basically a dialogue on salvation and God's mercy, the great gap that separates master and slave is conscientiously insisted upon, on the lines of the "aristocratic contempt for the sodden mass of the people,"[31] a feature of the Calvinistic outlook that Hammon adopted with a somewhat naïve enthusiasm:

MASTER

Come, my servant, follow me,
According to thy place;
And surely God will be with thee
And send thee heavenly grace.[32]

. . . .

SERVANT

Dear master, *that's my whole delight,*
Thy pleasure for to do;[33]

. . . .

This passiveness and resignation obscure the genuineness of Hammon's religiosity, so that today we view his Christian faith as something alien to him. His morality also remains undeveloped, and seemingly restricted to Saint Paul's admonition: "Slaves, obey your masters!" He lets fall not a word that might be taken to criticize slavery, in which he sees only the

[29] *An Address to Negroes in the State of New York* (1787).

[30] The text of this poem is reproduced in Oscar Wegelin, *Jupiter Hammon, American Negro Poet,* Heartman's Historical Series no. 13 (New York, 1915), pp. 41-46.

[31] Vernon Louis Parrington, *Main Currents in American Thought* (New York, 1927), I, 14.

[32] First stanza (italics added).

[33] Fourth stanza (italics added).

manifestation of divine foresight and mercy. Thus the deportation of Africans to America becomes a kind of providential pilgrimage toward knowledge of the one true God.

A very different figure is cut by that "fascinating little poetess"[34] Phillis Wheatley,[35] whose culture and poetic talents can arouse in us even today a measure of astonishment. Displaying the influence of Pope, whom she studied closely, her poems are cast in a classical mold and find in that same source their images and turns of phrase. Beneath the reserve that is natural to her, there come to unambiguous expression the convictions of an already developed racial consciousness and the exigencies of a religious faith that was enlightened and well balanced. To appreciate the gulf separating her from the servile simplicities of a Hammon, one need but refer to her poem, "On Being Brought from Africa to America":

> 'Twas mercy brought me from my pagan land,
> Taught my benighted soul to understand
> That there's a God — that there's a Saviour too;
> Once I redemption neither sought nor knew.
> Some view our sable race with scornful eye —
> "Their color is a diabolic dye."
> Remember, Christians, Negroes black as Cain
> May be refined, and join th' angelic train.[36]

The first four lines were penned by the Christian, who subordinates everything to God. Though perhaps somewhat reminiscent of Hammon,

[34] Arthur P. Davis, "Personal Elements in the Poetry of Phillis Wheatley," *Phylon*, second quarter, 1953, p. 191.

[35] Phillis Wheatley (1753?-1784) was a young Senegalese(?), carried off as a slave and sold in 1761 in Boston, where she was bought by a rich tailor of the town, John Wheatley. The liveliness and intelligence of the little slave girl were soon noticed, and this encouraged the Wheatley family to further her education. In sixteen months' time she knew English so well that she could "read any, the most difficult parts of the sacred writings" (letter from John Wheatley to Phillis's London publisher, November 14, 1772). She was also taught Latin, and at the age of sixteen she could read Virgil and Horace. When seventeen years old she published her first poem. Her health aroused concern, and the doctors prescribed a sea voyage, so her masters set her free and sent her to England (1773), where she created a sensation and was received by the Countess of Huntingdon, the protectress of Whitefield. Her first volume of verses, *Poems on Various Subjects, Religious and Moral*, came out that same year in London. But the death of her masters and the marriages of their children broke up the home that had taken her in. In 1778 she entered into an unfortunate marriage, and she died on December 5, 1784. There were many editions and reprints of her works, the most readily available being the Julian D. Mason, Jr., edition (Chapel Hill, 1966).

[36] Phillis Wheatley, *Poems and Letters* (Heartman ed.), p. 92. This poem is also included in James Weldon Johnson, *The Book of American Negro Poetry* (1931 ed.), p. 29.

they are qualified forthwith by the African, who implicitly refutes all racial arguments on both human and spiritual planes. Negroes also have a capacity for culture — what better proof of that than she herself? As for God, she has the assurance that into his paradise he will welcome blacks and whites alike, and on a footing of equality. Her first poem already voices that conviction in a passage which exhorts Africans also to receive Christ, the "impartial Saviour," who by his sacrifice opened a path to the Kingdom's supreme rewards for all the disinherited of the earth.

> Take him, ye Africans, he longs for you;
> Impartial Saviour is his title due;
> Washed in the fountain of redeeming blood,
> You shall be sons, and kings, and priests to God.[37]

Elsewhere she boasts time and again of her African origin and proclaims her solidarity with the entire black race of Africa. Her sole passing regret is that the Muses looked with less favor on her than they had on Terence, that other African, whose renown she could not hope to rival with her verses.

At least she has the renown of being the first of her race to exalt the love of liberty and to protest to a high authority against the abominations of tyranny and slavery, as she did in the lines addressed to William, Earl of Dartmouth, on his appointment as secretary for North America:

> Should you, my lord, while you peruse my song,
> Wonder from whence my love of Freedom sprung,
> Whence flow these wishes for the common good,
> By feeling hearts alone best understood;
> I, young in life, by seeming cruel fate
> Was snatch'd from Afric's fancy'd happy seat;
> What pangs excruciating must molest,
> What sorrows labor in my parent's breast?
> Steel'd was that soul and by no misery mov'd
> That from a father seiz'd his babe belov'd;
> Such, such my case. And can I then but pray
> Others may never feel tyrannic sway?[38]

Phillis Wheatley has incurred the disapproval of black critic Saunders Redding for the expressions "seeming cruel" and "fancy'd happy." Without citing or even taking into account the lines immediately following, he

---

[37] "On the Death of the Reverend Mr. George Whitefield" (1770). This was her first published poem.

[38] "To the Right Honorable William, Earl of Dartmouth, His Majesty's Principal Secretary of State for North America," *Poems and Letters,* pp. 73-74. Also in Johnson, *The Book of American Negro Poetry,* p. 29.

uses these expressions as a pretext for the judgment that Phillis Wheatley did not really believe in the cruelty of slavery and the good fortune of free men in Africa.[39] This accusation is without merit, since it does violence to the text and also fails to recognize what extraordinary importance the discovery of the Christian message could have for Phillis Wheatley and many of her fellows. Moreover, a more careful examination of the texts has led another black critic to reach conclusions which, happily, exonerate the poetess.[40]

Just as the verses of Jupiter Hammon had done, those written by George Moses Horton,[41] the slave poet of Chapel Hill, frequently utilize the rhythms of Methodist hymns. But Horton is far removed from Hammon's submissiveness. There is strong reason to believe that, because of their excessive frankness, many of Horton's poems were omitted from his collections of poems published in the South. Yet the works that have come down to us reveal how heavily slavery's chains weighed on him. The tone he favors most is that of lamentation:

> Alas! and am I born for this,
>   To wear this slavish chain?
> Deprived of all created bliss,
>   Through hardship, toil and pain!
>
> How long have I in bondage lain,
>   And languished to be free!
> Alas! and must I still complain —
>   Deprived of liberty.

[39] Redding, *To Make a Poet Black,* pp. 10-11. Johnson, *The Book of American Negro Poetry,* p. 28, appears to be no more convinced than is Redding, for he writes: "one looks in vain for some outburst or even complaint against the bondage of her people."

[40] Davis, "Personal Elements . . . Phillis Wheatley."

[41] George Moses Horton (1797?-1883?) was born on a North Carolina plantation and spent the greater part of his life in the service of various members of the Horton family. Like Hammon and Phillis Wheatley, he seems to have profited from relatively lenient conditions of slavery. It is not known precisely when he was authorized to offer his services elsewhere, against payment to his master of a fifty-cent fee per day. He soon turned up at Chapel Hill, where he was in the service of the president of the University of North Carolina and also was somewhat the campus bohemian. He used to write love poems to order for the students, his charges ranging from twenty-five to fifty cents a poem, depending on the ardor desired. His first volume of poems, *Hope of Liberty,* was published at Raleigh in 1829. He had hoped that the financial returns would enable him to purchase his liberty, but in that he was disappointed. Several of his poems also appeared, perhaps without his knowledge, in a number of northern papers. His second collection, *Naked Genius,* was published in 1865. After Emancipation he went to live in Philadelphia and disappeared from public view. Nothing whatever is known of his last years.

> Oh, Heaven! and is there no relief
> This side the silent grave —
> To soothe the pain — to quell the grief
> And anguish of a slave?[42]

But there is already an embryonic protest in the following stanza of his poem, "The Slave," whose imagery has all the savor and ingrained realism of folklore:

> Because the brood-sow's left side pigs were black,
> Whose sable tincture was by nature struck,
> Were you by justice bound to pull them back
> And leave the sandy-colored pigs to suck?[43]

Finally, there are other poems, such as "Jefferson in a Tight Place," in which he ridicules Jefferson Davis, president of the Confederacy, for letting himself be taken like a hunted fox.[44] Horton thus establishes himself as one of the earliest Negro humorous poets.

However, the majority of nineteenth-century Negro poets lacked Horton's independent outlook. Many of them battled with their pens in the ranks of the northern abolitionists. While such activity on their part is certainly praiseworthy, one can only regret that it contributed to the depersonalization and, consequently, to the monotony of their poetry, which does not differ noticeably from its white models in either theme or language.

George B. Vashon (1820-78), a professor at Central College, McGraw-ville, New York, lauds the spirit of liberty in his poem "Vincent Ogé."[45] The hero bearing that name was a Haitian mulatto, educated in France, who was executed at Cap-Français on March 12, 1791, after making an unsuccessful attempt to stir up the mulattoes of Santo Domingo and persuade them to wrest the island's independence from the French. Vashon took Scott and Byron as his models. Though his style and his skill in versification are those of a talented poet, his hero remains Byronic rather than black.

Frances Ellen Watkins Harper (1825-1911)[46] was perhaps the best-

---

[42] "On Liberty and Slavery," first through third stanzas; appeared in *Hope of Liberty*. The poem is reprinted in Brown et al., eds., *The Negro Caravan*, pp. 288-89.

[43] "The Slave" appeared in *Naked Genius*. Cited by Brown, *Negro Poetry and Drama*, p. 7.

[44] *Naked Genius*.

[45] Appeared in the collective volume *Autographs for Freedom II* (1854), pp. 44-60.

[46] Frances Ellen Watkins Harper was born to free parents in Baltimore, where she also studied. After 1850 she taught for some time at the Union Seminary of

known black abolitionist writer of the period. She is said to have sold more than fifty thousand copies of her first two volumes of poetry during the tours she undertook to preach against slavery. Her first collection, *Poems on Miscellaneous Subjects* (1854), shows the influence of Longfellow. Almost always she wrote narrative verse, and her aim clearly is to move the reader, to tears if possible, over the slave's wretched lot. There is, for example, the child torn from his mother ("The Slave Mother," "The Slave Auction"), or the wife fearful for her husband on the eve of his taking flight ("The Fugitive's Wife"), or again the heroic slave who, for refusing to give away the companions with whom he had conspired, is flogged until he dies. Anxious that the lesson might not sink in deeply enough, the writer often intervenes at the end of her story to underline the moral and to appeal to the kindly feelings of her readers. Today this tearful sentimentality wearies us. In contrast, some pieces included in a later volume, *Sketches of Southern Life* (1872), can still arouse a certain interest because of the characters evoked. The author's Aunt Chloe and Uncle Jacob actually constitute one of the first attempts at a rapprochement between black poetry and black people. But her language and her humor are far from being authentically of the people, who will not find their first true poet before the arrival of Dunbar.

More deserving of preservation is the work of the barber poet of Buffalo, James M. Whitfield (1830-70),[47] whose verses should probably be placed among the most violent produced by the campaign for abolition. "America," which gives its title to the collection *America and Other Poems* (1853), opens with a bitter paraphrase of the identically named patriotic song:

> America, it is to thee,
> Thou boasted land of liberty —
> It is to thee I raise my song,
> Thou land of blood, and crime, and wrong.

Columbia, Ohio. In 1853 she began to work for the Underground Railroad in Little York, Pennsylvania. Her first volume served to make her known, and she was hired in September, 1854, as official lecturer for the Maine Anti-Slavery Society. After the Civil War, she was active as an agent for the Women's Christian Temperance Union and traveled a great deal in the South.

[47] James M. Whitfield was born in Boston and, as a young man, settled in Buffalo, where he worked as a barber. After his volume of poems came out, it seems that he gave up his trade and, like Mrs. Harper, became an abolitionist speaker. He was a fervent believer in Negro emigration, since he thought it could solve the racial question. In 1854 he attended the National Emigration Convention of Colored Men, which was called together by Martin R. Delany. This attitude brought him into conflict with Frederick Douglass, against whose attacks Whitfield nevertheless defended his convictions with vigor. But the emigration scheme collapsed, and no further attention was paid to Whitfield.

> It is to thee my native land,
> From which has issued many a band
> To tear the black man from his soil,
> And force him here to delve and toil;
> Chained on your blood-bemoistened sod,
> Cringing beneath a tyrant's rod,
> Stripped of those rights which Nature's God
> Bequeathed to all the human race.[48]

Throughout his long poems the invective tone is astonishingly well sustained and has qualities that foreshadow certain polemical works to which the Negro Renaissance will give birth almost three-quarters of a century later. Scorning the sentimentality of many abolitionists, Whitfield displays a vigor of thought that has a thoroughly modern flavor and is surprisingly open to the consideration of every world problem.

He maintains, in the first place, that slavery is a flaw within democracy, whose founding cost the lives of blacks as well as whites during the Revolutionary War. But democracy can only be one and indivisible, and in his view the lot of the American slave is closely linked with that of the citizens of European countries, where the fragile hopes that sprang up during the revolutions of 1848 were extinguished by the aggressive return of the tyrants with their absolutism. We cite one short passage concerned with the "Russian Bear":

> I see the "Rugged Russian Bear"
> Lead forth his slavish hordes, to war
> Upon the right of every State
> Its own affairs to regulate:
> To help each Despot bind the chain
> Upon the people's rights again,
> And crush beneath his ponderous paw
> All constitutions, rights and law.[49]

One after the other, each European tyrant receives his just deserts. Napoleon III is "the shadow of a great name," Haynau, "the Austrian butcher"; even Pius IX is "the Fisherman" who spreads out his nets over the world to catch souls as he blesses the sabers, still reeking with blood, thanks to which his throne stands more secure.[50]

This brings us to Whitfield's second main argument. Slavery, which represents the bankruptcy of democracy, represents also that of a Chris-

---

[48] "America," verses 1-12, *America and Other Poems*, p. 9. (Also cited in Brown et al., eds., *The Negro Caravan*, pp. 290-91.)

[49] "How Long?" *ibid.*, p. 31.

[50] *Ibid.*, pp. 31-32.

tianity unable to remain true to itself, whose grave has been dug by the faithful themselves as they tried to impose their faith by fire and sword. If Whitfield professes traditional Christian beliefs in such poems as "A Hymn"[51] and "Christian Hymn,"[52] also visible in him are the first signs of a religious doubt that may even verge on despair, when he surveys the afflicting spectacle of Christianity's practical inefficacy.[53] Thus his skepticism is a prefiguration of Dunbar's doubting and of the agnosticism expressed by certain black poets of the twentieth century.

A word must still be said concerning that strange figure Albery A. Whitman (1851-1902)[54] who, as an imitator, was a genius. His narrative poems are perhaps longer than those of any other American poet, white or black. In some five thousand lines, his *Not a Man and Yet a Man* (1877) relates the adventures of a mulatto slave, Rodney, who saves his master's daughter from being massacred by Indians and then falls in love with her. But the master, breaking his promise to give his daughter in marriage to any man who would save her, sells Rodney to a planter from the Deep South. There Rodney falls in love with the beautiful slave girl Leeona, is separated from her for a while, and is permanently united with her in Canada. *The Rape of Florida* (1884) is another narrative replete with adventures and romantic episodes, in the midst of which the reader may be excused for losing his way. The plot deals with the expulsion from Florida of a group of Seminole Indians who had always extended a brotherly welcome to fugitive slaves. It is difficult to decide which series of exploits is the more admirable, the fictional hero's or the author's own, for at every moment the latter must perform a new feat in order to reach the end of the 257 Spencerian stanzas that make up his poem. His last volume, *An Idyl of the South* (1901), consists of two parts, "The Octoroon" and "The Southland's Charm and Freedom's Magnitude." The idyl takes place between a ravishing octoroon girl and her white master, both of them considerably idealized to meet the needs of the situation,

[51] *Ibid.*, p. 55.
[52] *Ibid.*, p. 16.
[53] "The Misanthropist," *ibid.*, pp. 54-55.
[54] Born in Kentucky, Albery A. Whitman remained a slave until Emancipation in 1863. He was orphaned at an early age and had only irregular schooling. He taught, to begin with, and then became the pastor of the African Methodist Episcopal Church in Springfield, Ohio, while at the same time carrying out administrative duties at Wilberforce University. To judge by his verses, he must have been an avid reader of Goldsmith, Scott, and Byron, as well as of such American poets as Longfellow and Whittier. Loggins (*The Negro Author*, p. 337) declares that *Not a Man and Yet a Man* is a genuine tour de force of metrical imitativeness. In addition to his longer poems, Whitman wrote several shorter pieces, some of them in a superior dialect form (e.g., "Tobe's Dream," at the end of his last volume).

for the poem is highly conciliatory in tone, and even flattering, with regard to the South. This is very much at odds with Whitman's earlier declaration that "the time has come when all 'Uncle Toms' and 'Topsies' ought to die."[55]

Folk Poetry

Despite all the interest that some of the above poets can still arouse in us, and despite the affecting beauty of some of their poems, it cannot be denied that for us today most of these writers appear unrelievedly dull. Yet could not the same be said of many of their white compatriots of the same period, however illustrious the names they bear?

How much fresher, by comparison, how eternally youthful is the lyric poetry of nameless folk poets! How much more eloquently it pleads in its naïve spontaneity for the cause of black humanity out of whose sufferings it has arisen! Everything here has been truly lived; it is inborn and authentic. Song is an immediate upwelling; issuing directly from the heart, it blithely disregards all accepted metrical notions.

However, years had to elapse before the incomparable beauty of folk poetry could be recognized. The prestige of the singer determines the prestige of the song: this often is the aesthetic criterion. It was not until these millions of slaves had been declared free men under the law that anyone deigned to listen, although over the centuries they had, by their singing, abundantly demonstrated their membership in the human race.

The first and for a long time the only slave songs known to a wider public were the spirituals. This fact gives rise on occasion to the hastily drawn conclusion that the Negro was unusually religious. But the religion of the African, which was based on the ancestor cult, represented for him something quite unlike the role allotted to religion by Western man. It was inseparable from his daily life, affecting and giving meaning to its every gesture. Thus the spirituals are not exclusively religious songs but must be considered as a body of documents dealing with slave life,[56] just as the African chants often constituted historical narratives handed down by oral tradition.

In America also, Negro religion had from the outset a very special character. The religious service was in reality the only form of social activity available to Negroes. There alone — and this was especially true

[55] *Twasinta's Seminoles: or, Rape of Florida* (1885 ed.), p. 8.

[56] One should not, however, commit the mistake of overstressing this aspect of the spirituals, as is done by Miles Mark Fisher, with little persuasive power, in his *Negro Slave Songs in the United States.*

for the plantations in frontier regions — could they come together and without hesitation unburden themselves of all the emotions that had to be held in check on every other occasion. The preacher, who inevitably was one of the better-educated slaves, soon became a good deal more than a minister of religion. He began to function at the same time as a genuine racial leader, concerning himself with the temporal needs as well as the spiritual life of the group. As a consequence, together with the step-by-step development of what would long continue to be the "invisible institution"[57] of the Negro Church, its social and political significance also came more clearly to the fore.

Thus the frequent prohibitions of religious services attended solely by Negroes, especially after the rebellions that occurred early in the nineteenth century. The gatherings that took place in spite of everything had to be held in secret. The seventeenth century already had its clandestine assemblies, in which the African drum was used to summon the participants. Virginia, in 1676, was the first colony to forbid the use of the drum.[58] Thereupon the spiritual often took on the character of a secret language which enabled the slaves to communicate among themselves with no fear of being found out. Later, in Underground Railroad days, the spiritual served as a code between runaway slaves and the agents of the Underground, and we may assume that it was similarly used on ordinary occasions, when slaves wanted to talk to each other without giving themselves away to whites who might be nearby.[59]

Thus from the outset overall circumstances proved highly conducive to the growth, within slave life, of that strange symbiosis of racial and religious feeling which can be observed in the folk poetry as well. Moreover, the condition of the Negro within slavery's closed world gave the Christian message a special resonance which, in a latent state, included this same symbiosis. The slave could hardly expect that through men's deeds he would experience liberation here below, whereas the Christian religion

[57] George F. Bragg, *History of the Afro-American Group of the Episcopal Church* (Baltimore, 1922), p. 39. Cited by Frazier, *The Negro in the United States*, p. 343.

[58] Fisher, *Negro Slave Songs*, p. 29.

[59] The use of the spiritual as a secret code was already noted by Frederick Douglass, who explained that Canaan stood for Canada, Pharaoh represented the masters, the people of Israel were the Negroes, and so on (cited by Brown, *Negro Poetry and Drama*, pp. 18-19). Concerning the spiritual "We'll Soon Be Free," one of whose lines declares that "De Lord will call us home," Thomas Wentworth Higginson ("Negro Spirituals," *Atlantic Monthly*, June, 1867, p. 692) relates that a young Negro drummer explained to him that, by "the Lord," everyone singing the spiritual actually meant "the Yankees." Consult also Fisher's *Negro Slave Songs, passim.*

offered him at least the hope of a happier lot and greater justice in the world beyond. This expectation enabled him to support more readily the burden of each day.

> I am a poor pilgrim of sorrow.
> I'm in this wide world alone.
> No hope in this world for tomorrow.
> I'm tryin' to make heaven my home.
>
> .   .   .   .
>
> I've heard of a city called heaven.
> I've started to make it my home.[60]

"Free," "freedom" — the spirituals repeat these words time and again, and the slave, as he sang them, undoubtedly tended to think of his freedom here below rather than of his redemption from sin. It is true that certain insincere Southerners like Newman Ivy White have chosen to flout the evidence and argue that the sufferings referred to in the spirituals were not those of slavery.

> The haunting melody of these "spirituals," their notes of sorrow, aspiration and jubilance, have given rise to a common belief, demonstrably false, that in these songs we have the Negro's expression of suffering under slavery and of his joy at liberation. Without pausing to expose this fallacy in detail, one needs only to call attention to the fact that a strain of supposed melancholy is a common property of folk-songs everywhere and does not always reflect a really melancholy mood.[61]

The strongest rejoinder to such partisan arguments is provided by the texts of the spirituals themselves:

> No more auction block for me,
> No more, no more,
> No more auction block for me,
> Many thousand gone.[62]

What induced the Negro to pick out, from the Bible stories, those very episodes that paralleled his own captive condition and the hope of his own liberation?

---

[60] "City Called Heaven," in Arna Bontemps and Langston Hughes, *The Book of Negro Folklore*, pp. 290-91. For Christianity's value to the slave, see also the fine passage in James Weldon Johnson, *The Books of American Spirituals*, I, 20-21.

[61] N. I. White, "Racial Traits in the Negro Song," *Sewanee Review*, July-September, 1920, p. 397.

[62] "No More Auction Block," in Bontemps and Hughes, *The Book of Negro Folklore*, p. 291.

> Go down, Moses,
> Way down in Egyptland,
> Tell old Pharaoh
> To let my people go.[63]

or this:

> Joshua fit de battle of Jericho,
> Jericho, Jericho,
> Joshua fit de battle of Jericho,
> And de walls come tumbling down.[64]

The Christian religion appeared to him as a means of escape into a universe still far away, perhaps, but where the slave would at last exercise a sure retribution on the slaveowners:

> Oh Mary, don't you weep, don't you moan,
> Oh Mary, don't you weep, don't you moan,
> Pharaoh's army got drownded.
> Oh Mary, don't you weep.[65]

The story of Lazarus and the evil rich man enables him to reach a similar conclusion:

> Poor man Laz'rus, poor as I,
> Don't you see?
> Poor man Laz'rus, poor as I,
> When he died he found a home on high
>
> .   .   .   .
>
> Rich man Dives, he lived so well,
> Don't you see?
> Rich man Dives, he lived so well.
> When he died he found a home in hell.[66]

These ambivalent themes are so distinctive in character that only with signal disingenuousness could one confuse them with those others that express religious fervor, as in this instance:

> Lord, I want to be a Christian
> In-a my heart, in-a my heart,
> I don't want to be like Judas,
> In-a my heart, in-a my heart.

---

[63] "Go Down, Moses," *ibid.,* p. 292.
[64] "Joshua fit de Battle of Jericho," *ibid.,* p. 300.
[65] "Oh Mary, Don't You Weep," *ibid.,* p. 299.
[66] "I Got a Home in Dat Rock," *ibid.,* pp. 297-98.

> Lord, I want to be more holy,
> In-a my heart, in-a my heart,
> Lord, I want to be like Jesus,
> In-a my heart, in-a my heart.[67]

Over the last fifty years or so, the question of the origin of the spirituals has occasioned numerous debates. While they cannot be accorded a detailed examination here, it is advisable at least to give a summary indication of the conflicting theses. As some view it, the Negro borrowed a great deal from white hymns with which he had become acquainted, particularly after the Great Awakening that got under way shortly before the middle of the eighteenth century. He was allowed to attend its great open-air camp meetings, which were organized on a regular basis by the Methodists and Baptists.[68] Others have held that the spirituals are the transposition, into the new language and surroundings in which he found himself transplanted, of the songs and rhythms the Negro had already possessed in Africa.[69] The truth probably lies somewhere in between. While some spirituals indeed appear to be so close to certain Methodist hymns that one can speak of influence, the structures of others, on the contrary, bear sure signs of their African origin. Their genuinely Negro character always emerges clearly when they are sung, or even subjected to a phono-photographic analysis, as Metfessel's study indicates.[70]

[67] "Lord, I Want to Be a Christian," in Johnson, *The Books of American Negro Spirituals* (2 vols. in 1), II, 72-73.

[68] In essence, this is already the view put forward by Richard Wallaschek, *Primitive Music: An Inquiry into the Origin and Development of Music, Songs, Instruments, Dances and Pantomimes of Savage Races* (London, 1893), who looked on the songs of the American Negroes as being mere imitations of European compositions. More serious than Wallaschek's investigation are those by Guy B. Johnson, *Folk Culture on St. Helena Island, South Carolina* (Chapel Hill, 1930), and George Pullen Jackson, *White Spirituals in the Southern Uplands* (Chapel Hill, 1933). Newman Ivy White, *American Negro Folksongs* (Cambridge, 1928), demonstrated in particular that the Negro had indeed taken part in the camp meetings held in the South. White also drew a parallel between white and black religious primitivism.

[69] The African-origins thesis was first defended by Henry Edward Krehbiel, *Afro-American Folksongs: A Study in Racial and National Music.* Most black critics have again taken up this thesis, especially James Weldon Johnson, who discusses it at length in the prefaces to the work cited above, note 67.

[70] Milton Metfessel and Carl E. Seashore, *Phonophotography in Folk Music: American Negro Songs in New Notation.* The problem of the African origin of the spirituals is but one part of a much vaster problem, that of the African contribution to the culture of the Negro in the United States, a matter on which unanimity is far from achieved. For some, including E. Franklin Frazier, the deportation of the Negro to the United States and the conditions of slavery he had to endure were enough to extinguish almost totally his African culture. Others, on the contrary, among them Melville J. Herskovits, have sought to attribute

What must be borne in mind here are the two principles that predominate in the typical structure of many forms of expression in Negro folklore. These are antiphony and improvisation.

Several studies, especially those of Krehbiel, James Weldon Johnson, and Herskovits,[71] have shown that Negro antiphony is indisputably of African origin. In the spirituals, the correspondence is with a type of song in which one verse, always sung by a soloist, alternates with a response that is always identical and is sung by all the participants — as, for example, in "Oh, Wasn't Dat a Wide Ribber":

> Oh, de Ribber of Jordan is deep and wide,
>   One mo' ribber to cross.
> I don't know how to get on de other side,
>   One mo' ribber to cross.
> Oh, you got Jesus, hold him fast,
>   One mo' ribber to cross.[72]
>   [Etc.]

Anyone who has attended a Negro folk religious service, especially in the South, knows that in a Negro church there are no passive spectators; everyone is an actor. During the singing the men's voices, sounding in unison from one side of the church, alternate with the women's voices, which come from the other side. The sermon is far from a monologue, and the pastor has scarcely started on his path when the signs of an incipient dialogue between him and the worshipers can be noted. To begin with, a few approving cries ring out from the "Amen Corner."[73] The temperature quickly rises, and after a time the whole congregation is engaged in a dialogue with the pastor. The rhythm of speech becomes increasingly staccato until it prefigures the rhythm of the spiritual into which the dialogue is imperceptibly transformed. Then, after the singing has set all hearts aglow, hysterical cries will arise here and there in the

countless features of African origin to the American Negro. We hasten to say that Herskovits's demonstration fails to convince, and that his conclusions are pushed altogether too far. There are indeed sporadic, fragmentary survivals, which are not nearly as widespread as Herskovits would have one believe. As for the particular problem that concerns us here, we would indicate that even today one may still hear, in rural regions of the Deep South, folksongs whose African character is undeniable. For one example, see the record prepared by Frederic Ramsey, Jr., *Music from the South*, vol. 5, "Song, Play and Dance," Folkways FP 654, side one, track 7, which reproduces the song "Blind Child," sung by the children of Perry County, Alabama.

[71] Melville J. Herskovits, *The Myth of the Negro Past*.

[72] Johnson, *The Books of American Spirituals*, I, 25.

[73] The "Amen Corner" is occupied by those members of the congregation who most persistently enter into a dialogue with the pastor.

church, and at last the "shout" begins. Women and men spin around, ravished by the Holy Spirit, finally entering into a trance and rolling on the ground, until charitable neighbors raise them to their feet.[74]

Antiphony, again, underlies the characteristic Negro pastime known as "playing the dozens." One of the participants hurls at his opponent observations that grow ever more malicious and offensive. In the end, the other either gives in and goes away or, on the contrary, flies into a rage and repays insults with blows.[75]

Alongside this use of antiphony, improvisation also plays a major role;[76] provision is even made for it in the structure of the song. For example, in the antiphonal form the soloist has time to invent a new verse while the group is singing the response. In the blues form, whose structure is approximated by some spirituals, the solo singer's time for invention is increased by repeating the first line, as in this version of "The Ship of Zion," transcribed by Thomas Wentworth Higginson:

> Dis de good ole ship o' Zion,
> Dis de good ole ship o' Zion,
> Dis de good ole ship o' Zion,
> And she's makin' for de Promise Land.[77]

In conclusion, let us recall that antiphony, and above all the art of improvisation, play a major role in the creation of jazz.[78] This lies outside the scope of our investigation, but one of jazz's constituent elements, the blues, belongs to poetry's domain no less than to music's.

The precise origin of the blues is scarcely more easy to ascertain than

[74] See the following recordings: Ramsey, *Music from the South,* vol. 9, "Song and Worship," side one, particularly tracks 4 and 5 (Folkways FP 658); *Noël et Saint-Sylvestre à Harlem,* Ducrétet-Thomson 260 V. 069; *Spirituals et Folklore,* recorded by Harry Belafonte, side one, track 6: "Noah," RCA 430-213.

[75] On the dozens, see Ralph F. Berdie, "Playing the Dozens," *Journal of Abnormal and Social Psychology,* January, 1947, pp. 120-21; John Dollard, "The Dozens: Dialectic of Insult," *American Imago,* November, 1939, pp. 3-25; William Elton, "Playing the Dozens," *American Speech* XXV (1950), 148-49.

[76] For the description of an actual improvisation, see Higginson, "Negro Spirituals," pp. 692-93.

[77] *Ibid.,* p. 691.

[78] The same holds true for the work songs, which we do not discuss here. They are the most functional of the slave songs, providing a rhythm for fieldhands, longshoremen, convicts, etc., and helping to increase the workers' productivity. For examples, see Brown et al., eds., *The Negro Caravan;* Bontemps and Hughes, *The Book of Negro Folklore;* and two works by Howard W. Odum and Guy B. Johnson, *The Negro and His Songs* and *Negro Workaday Songs.* Several work songs are to be found on the Belafonte record mentioned above, note 74.

that of the spirituals. Though the blues reach the light of day only toward the end of the nineteenth century, their folk beginnings probably predate Emancipation.[79]

Unlike the spirituals, the blues poem has a fixed form. It consists in principle of several stanzas of three lines each,[80] with the second line either the exact replica of or a slight variant on the first line. Each line has four stresses, but the number of unstressed syllables sometimes conforms to a metrical system more complex than classical metrics, which recognizes only disyllabic and trisyllabic feet. This system, which permits a practically unlimited number of syllables between the tonic accents, is the specifically Negro or African rhythmic element. The blues line may, as a consequence, run to a considerable length that for printing purposes sometimes must be broken up, as is at times done with the ballad, into two lines (of equal or unequal length).

While the spirituals are community songs that express collective emotions, the blues are essentially an individual matter. Thus there are *choirs* that sing spirituals, but *singers* of blues. This individual character of the blues is probably due to their origins, which by general agreement are sought in the "field holler"[81] used by the plantation worker to communicate with his comrades dispersed some distance away in the fields. It is the characteristically Negro modulation of this shout, the "blue note,"[82] that provides both the name[83] and the usually melancholy theme.

The blues, it is sometimes thought, speak only of the pangs of love. Thousands of poems do indeed exist dealing with every aspect of love betrayed and love frustrated, but the themes evoked by the blues cover a much wider range. The singer can bemoan with equal readiness catastrophes to crops and damage wrought by flood and tornado, the ravages of sickness, the harmfulness of drink, cruel deeds of the police, and hardships brought on by an economic crisis. Ever since blacks started their mass migrations from the rural South to the cities of the North, they have

[79] Brown, *Negro Poetry and Drama*, p. 27; Ramsey, *Music from the South*, vol. 4, side one, track 2 (Folkways FP 653) reproduces the statements on this subject of an inhabitant of Perry County, Alabama, to the effect that the blues go back to the slave period.

[80] But two-line and four-line stanzas are also found.

[81] See Willis Lawrence James, "The Romance of the Negro Folk Cry in America," *Phylon*, first quarter, 1955, pp. 15-30. Contains a discography.

[82] The blue note is a "downward inflection of a semitone in the third and seventh notes of the major scale." André Hodeir, *Hommes et problèmes du jazz*, p. 393, under "blue note."

[83] But it appears that the blues were also called "cornfield song" and "reel." See Ramsey, *Music from the South*, vol. 4, side one, tracks 2 and 5 (Folkways FP 653).

often entrusted to the blues their expression of longing for the region they have left, or the recurrent desire to abandon the heartless city and let the train bear them off to sunnier skies. Langston Hughes, during World War II, even wrote a "Go Get the Enemy Blues"![84]

It follows from this that the inspiration behind the blues — the same holds true for spirituals also — is far from exhausted. But today the former often take on a commercial guise, while the latter prefer the garb of the "gospel song."

Another type of Negro poetry deserves brief mention. This is the ballad. The Negro attained familiarity with English ballads brought over by immigrants and proceeded to compose others of his own. The ballad rivals the blues in its thematic variety. It may relate the adventures of a "bad man" like the dangerous Stackalee, tell of lovers' quarrels that end with a shot ("Frankie and Johnnie"), or even describe the misdeeds and peregrinations of "Mr. Boll Weevil" ("De Ballit of de Boll Weevil"). But incontrovertibly the most famous ballad of them all is devoted to the story of the legendary John Henry. Using nothing but his hammer, he had sworn to outrace the steam drill that had been set up to pierce a tunnel. He wins indeed, only to collapse a moment later, dead of exhaustion.[85] The legend symbolizes man's last attempt to beat the machine, but in its multiple variants it also exemplifies the spirit of the "tall tale," which is as Negro as it is American.

We have seen above how the world of slavery brought together the factors favoring the development, within the black soul, of that fusion of racial and religious feeling whose most eloquent exemplar was and is the spiritual.

From the outset, however, slavery forced Christianity to contradict itself. The Negro was admitted to baptism, on the one hand, while on the other he was declared devoid of a soul.[86] Slavery, by simply existing, offered unceasing defiance to the teachings of Christ, and there was nothing in Christian institutions that could justify it. The sanctity of marriage was only a tragic irony for the Negro family, which at any moment could be wrenched apart by sale and dispersal, while Negro wives were practically

[84] The most exhaustive thematic study of the blues is that by Paul Oliver, *Blues Fell This Morning*.

[85] On the John Henry legend, see Guy B. Johnson, "John Henry: A Negro Legend," in Charles S. Johnson, ed., *Ebony and Topaz*, pp. 47-51; and the same author's *John Henry: Tracking Down a Negro Legend*.

[86] Some persons still clung to this conviction at the beginning of the twentieth century. See Charles Carroll, *The Negro, a Beast* (St. Louis: American Book and Bible House, 1900).

at the mercy of their masters' appetites. For the masters, the slave's religion was often nothing but a huge farce; witness the ribald comments made in literary works and on the stage.[87]

The Negro himself saw his faith continually shaken by the abominable spectacle of the reality in which the strange religion of the white man ultimately resulted. The values it held up for emulation were often robbed of meaning for the black, who was acutely sensitive to the contradictions of the system that hemmed him in. So there is no cause for astonishment if his religious ardor was less universal, perhaps, than some would have us believe. To some extent this is just a pious legend which, like the assertion of the Negro's inferiority, does not survive confrontation with the actual facts.

The legend found such ready credence because, beginning with the very earliest published versions, samples of Negro folklore were carefully expurgated, while whatever seemed altogether reprehensible in content was not published at all. Overly violent songs of protest might have undermined the slave system's fundamental thesis, and obscene or irreverent songs might have given the lie to those who insisted that Negroes did not use "coarse expressions."[88] Thus it is not certain that an accurate reflection of reality is presented by the disproportionate bulk, in the published literature of folklore, of spirituals and of relatively inoffensive secular songs.

Whatever the truth of the matter, some of the secular songs that do survive demonstrate sufficiently that, even though weighty factors militated in favor of a symbiosis between racial and religious feeling, others of equal significance tended to introduce a split between the two. Spirituals came from the faith of the people, but disillusion also sought an outlet in songs that hold faith up to mockery, as in this parody of the Lord's Prayer which harshly exposes the system's basic inconsistency:

> Our Fader, who art in heaven,
> White man owe me 'leven, pay me seven,
> Thy kingdom come, thy will be done,
> And ef I hadn't tuck that, I wouldn't git none.[89]

[87] Examples of this will be found in the following chapters. See also Elkins, *Slavery*, pp. 195ff., and n. 113.
[88] Lily Young Cohen, *Lost Spirituals* (New York, 1928), p. x. Cited by Fisher, *Negro Slave Songs in the United States*, p. 14. (Fisher relates various examples of bowdlerization, *ibid.*, pp. 14-15.) For his part, White declares that, out of a hundred and fifty songs he had collected on one of his trips, one-third simply could not be published ("Racial Traits in the Negro Song," *Sewanee Review*, July-September, 1920, pp. 399-400). See also Oliver, *Blues Fell This Morning*, pp. 127ff.
[89] Cited by Brown, *Negro Poetry and Drama*, p. 21.

Elsewhere, the Negro's protest against the cruelty and hypocrisy inflicted on him by this pseudo-Christian world found expression in obscenity. "Well, if what is happening to me is right, then, dammit, anything is right";[90] that, in effect, was his reaction. It explains why songs like the "dirty dozens" voice approval of every sort of irregularity, including incest and homosexuality. Some go so far as to doubt whether God ever had the ability to create a rational universe.

This popular poetry, considered as a whole, thus offers us a much more subtle and realistic picture of the world of oppression than one could possibly find in the written poetry of the same period. The latter took shape in part on the fringes of the people's existence, whereas folk poetry was the very emanation of this existence.

The cleavage between these two forms of expression, which was maintained throughout the nineteenth century, also reflects a divergence in their social origins, for by definition folk poetry expresses the feelings of the masses, while written poetry gives outer shape to the aspirations of the middle class or bourgeoisie.

The sensed need to reestablish contact between poetry and life led to attempts at a fusion of these two branches of poetry; this reached its culmination in the twentieth century with the writers of the Negro Renaissance. The aim of our investigation is, to a considerable extent, to study the problems, both aesthetic and psychological, to which this development gave rise.

[90] Richard Wright, *White Man, Listen!*, p. 131. Wright is probably the only person then to have published some examples of the dirty dozens (*ibid.*, pp. 131-32.)

PART ONE: PAUL LAURENCE DUNBAR AND HIS TIME

Chapter Two: THE NEGRO IN THE AMERICAN TRADITION IN DUNBAR'S TIME

The period of Reconstruction that followed the Civil War confronted the newly liberated blacks with political, social, economic, and psychological problems of unprecedented importance. Politically, they had to serve their apprenticeship as citizens while simultaneously being forced to defend their brand-new citizenship against attempts from every side to reduce it to zero. Socially, unless the circumstances were quite exceptional, the virtual equality that had just been accorded them remained a dead letter. Economically, they were almost human jetsam, unless they stayed as so-called free workers with the employers whose slaves they had been hitherto.

But their most severe problems were, then as now, in the psychological domain. Who are they? Or, rather, who can they hope to be, and who is it advisable for them to be, in order to engage in the struggle for life with some prospect of survival? For it is immediately obvious that no one, with a stroke of the pen, could raise them from their state of human non-entity and transform them into men like other men. The dead hand of the past rests heavily on their persons and on their personalities. Their inferior status had not been simply a legal edict but — far worse — it was and would long remain confirmed by the thousand-and-one usages of daily existence. Nor were the realms of literature and art exempted from these servitudes — very much to the contrary.

The black poets who strove to gain a hearing, toward the close of the nineteenth century, felt that they had a heavy burden to bear: it was made up of all the badges of inferiority pinned on the Negro as he was traditionally characterized in stage plays, poems, and novels. The poets

found their freedom of expression restricted to some degree by this traditional framed portrait of the Negro, which public opinion had readily
taken over from these literary forms. Acceptance was all the more total
since, reciprocally, literature had taken over this view of the Negro from
public opinion.

Thus, if it is to be valid, any assessment of Dunbar and his contemporaries presupposes familiarity with every feature of the heritage that the
poets had been obliged to assume. Of these features, only the two most
significant will receive consideration here. They are the minstrel tradition
and the plantation tradition, which had the most direct impact on the
black poetry written during the nineteenth century's closing years.

1. THE MINSTRELS

The minstrel show was a major factor in spreading the popularity of the
stock figure of the Negro throughout the land. Its influence was all the
more pervasive because, given the structure and versatile borderlines of
the genre, there crystallized around it a number of related artistic ventures, including popular drama, song, and poetry. Though not identical
with any of them, just as they did not turn to it alone for an outlet, it
nevertheless absorbed elements from them all, and they were all drawn
into its orbit.

If a single phrase could characterize the minstrels' activities, they might
be said to constitute an entertainment whose base is Negro folk art, either
comic or lachrymose, plagiarized, staged, and frequently falsified by low-
grade white actors who "play Negroes" by blackening their faces with
burnt cork.[1] It is immediately apparent how many potential contradictions
and psychological problems such an offshoot must contain, and to what
a degree it could generate complexes and conflicts.

By Dunbar's time, the minstrel show had already been long established
in popular favor. The beginnings can be traced to a time long before the
Civil War, and the tradition is at least as old, and the roots are as deep,
as the plantation tradition — possibly more so. To attribute a birth date
to it is a ticklish matter.[2] As for the originators: in contrast to the founders
of the plantation tradition, they are Northerners,[3] some even quite recent

[1] For this reason the minstrel show is often called "burnt cork comedy."
[2] Carl Wittke, *Tambo and Bones: A History of the American Minstrel Stage*,
p. 9.
[3] *Ibid.*, pp. 39-40. See also Jay Broadus Hubbell, *The South in American Literature 1607-1900*, p. 660. Constance Rourke seems to be alone in believing the opposite (*American Humor* [Anchor ed., 1955], pp. 74, 79) without, unfortunately,
supplying any references to back her allegations.

immigrants, whereas in the antebellum South humorous literature allotted only a very minor role to the Negro.[4] In the course of time, the frequent intermingling of the two traditions may be observed. They are indeed twin forms giving expression to the same public bias, for they share the same buffoon, "a simple, somewhat rustic character, instinctively humorous, irrationally credulous, gifted in song and dance, interesting in spontaneous frolic, endowed with artless philosophy."[5] Even before the Negro, viewed in this light, provided occasional entertainment for his plantation masters, he had often been obliged to amuse the slave-traders on the ship carrying him off into slavery.[6] There grew up quite early a widespread appreciation of his sometimes plaintive, sometimes humorous melodies, which he sang while accompanying himself on the banjo and displaying the innate virtuosity of his dance steps. Appreciated, too, were his religious fervor and the eccentricities of his behavior, dress, and speech.[7] But with equal certainty his black skin was enough to arouse levity, so that soon "to be black is to be funny."[8] This black buffoon with his performing skills was naturally regarded as treasure trove by the wandering entertainers who, early in the nineteenth century, needed something to freshen up their routines. For some time previously they had been exploiting to the hilt the figure of the stage Irishman with his unsteady gait, his shillelagh, and his red nose.[9]

---

[4] Hubbell, *The South in American Literature,* signals as sole exception Francis J. Robinson's *Kups of Kauphy* (1853).

[5] Francis Pendleton Gaines, *The Southern Plantation: A Study in the Development and the Accuracy of a Tradition,* p. 3.

[6] Wittke, *Tambo and Bones,* p. 6.

[7] Dailey Paskman and Sigmund Spaeth, *Gentlemen, Be Seated! A Parade of the Old-Time Minstrels,* p. 176. Cited by Wittke, *Tambo and Bones,* p. 7.

[8] Rourke, *American Humor,* p. 74.

[9] "The Irish were prominently displayed on the mid-nineteenth century stage. In the imported works of English dramatists that were put on in New York, practically all the Irish characters were blackguards or idiots..." (E. J. Kahn, Jr., *The Merry Partners: The Age and Stage of Harrigan and Hart,* p. 66). See also Wittke, *Tambo and Bones,* pp. 25, 200; Robert P. Nevin, "Stephen Foster and Negro Minstrelsy," *Atlantic Monthly,* November, 1867, p. 608. One could draw an extensive parallel between the figure of the Irishman and the Negro. See Sterling A. Brown, "A Literary Parallel," *Opportunity,* May, 1932, pp. 152-53. Very early, perhaps because of their joint existence on the stage, the Irish and Negroes were often associated in the public mind. *Uncle Tom's Cabin* has as its pastiche *Uncle Pat's Cabin.* On this, see Harry Birdoff, *The World's Greatest Hit, Uncle Tom's Cabin,* pp. 434-45. Other caricatures of ill-assimilated immigrants appear from time to time on the minstrel stage, to match current events, as long as the genre survives. The German (Wittke, *Tambo and Bones,* pp. 121, 191) is followed in his turn by the Jewish old-clothes dealer (*ibid.,* p. 156); both are provided with jokes and songs supposedly taken from the appropriate folklore material and delivered in the supposedly genuine accent. It may be said in conclusion that the

The first borrowings were no more than separate songs, sung in black-face during the intermissions. But as early as 1769, during a New York performance of Isaac Bickerstaff's *The Padlock,* an actor portraying a Negro slave entranced the audience by getting drunk on the stage.[10] In October, 1824, George Nichols, a circus clown who is looked on as one of the very first minstrels, sang a "Negro" song in New York's Chatham Garden Theater. His songs were adapted from tunes he had heard sung by blacks, who might be Mississippi firemen, Louisiana banjo-players, or such others as "Old Corn Meal," a combination of cornmeal peddler and singer who not only pushed his cart along the country roads but was also privileged to sing in one of the largest hotels in New Orleans.[11]

But it is the actor Thomas Dartmouth ("Daddy") Rice (1808-60) who, as the creator of "Jim Crow,"[12] has earned the right to be called the father of the minstrels. This song was written between 1828 and 1831.[13] There are several accounts of the circumstances that gave rise to the song,[14] but all concur on the sole point that interests us here: Rice obtained it from a black. He was sauntering through the streets of Cincinnati one day when he noticed a black man with a limp who was singing, as he associated word with deed:

> Turn about an' wheel about an' do jis so,
> An' ebery time I turn about I jump Jim Crow.

Rice must have grasped at once how he could utilize this personage and his refrain, trivial though it was. He was performing in Pittsburgh at the time, and there at the Hotel Griffith was a black called Cuff, who made a meager living by carrying bags between the hotel and the wharf or even

---

Negro is only one of the non-Anglo-Saxon personages at whose expense the American public can jest and laugh.

[10] Wittke, *Tambo and Bones,* p. 9. The stereotype of the Negro in the minstrel shows owes much to earlier models on the eighteenth-century English stage, especially in the utilization of dialect and of "plantation melodies." See Gilbert Chase, *America's Music from the Pilgrims to the Present,* p. 261; Richard Walser, "Negro Dialect in Eighteenth Century Drama," *American Speech,* December, 1955, pp. 268-76.

[11] Wittke, *Tambo and Bones,* pp. 16-18.

[12] However, some authors attribute the paternity of this famous song to G. Nichols (*ibid.*). As for the expression "Jim Crow," it is known that it was first used to designate the black man himself, and then the racial segregation and discrimination of which he has been the victim, especially in the South.

[13] *Ibid.,* p. 21. Yet Nevin, "Stephen Foster and Negro Minstrelsy," p. 608, asserts that the date is 1831.

[14] Wittke, *Tambo and Bones,* pp. 24-25. We give here Nevin's version, which he declares to be "authentic in every particular" ("Stephen Foster and Negro Minstrelsy," p. 610).

by offering his open mouth as a target for small boys who tried to toss in coins from three feet away. Rice had an inspiration. Taking Cuff by the hand and leading him backstage, Rice ordered Cuff to undress and in the meanwhile blackened his own face. He put on the clothes thus acquired; at the end of the regular performance he walked onto the stage in the ragged jacket, patched shoes, and no less dilapidated straw hat surmounting a bushy "Negro mop."[15] Then, to music provided by the orchestra, he began to sing:

> O, Jim Crow's come to town, as you all must know,
> An' he wheel about, he turn about, he do jis so,
> An' ebery time he wheel about he jump Jim Crow.[16]

It was an overwhelming success, and thunderous applause greeted each new stanza. But the laughter reached its crest when Cuff, who suddenly realized that it was time for the boat and feared that Rice would never leave the stage, himself appeared to ask for the return of his clothes. The next day the song was on everyone's lips, and it found its way into print without delay.

No more was needed to set the tone. Back up the singer with a partner for dialogue, a rudimentary chorus arranged in a semicircle, a banjo, a fiddle, and, most important, a tambourine and castanets.[17] There is your little minstrel troupe with all it requires to take off on its own with an evening's entertainment of sketches, gags, songs, and the great dance finale[18] which throws the performers into a frenzy.[19] It was with a troupe organized very much on these lines that in February, 1843, Daniel Decatur Emmett,[20] another king of the minstrels, gave New York its first complete minstrel show. He had no lack of emulators,[21] and up to the end of the

[15] A wig imitating the hair of blacks.

[16] Cited by Nevin, "Stephen Foster and Negro Minstrelsy," p. 609.

[17] "Tambo and Bones" are the minstrel's traditional attributes. They are played by the two endmen, one of whom sits at either end of the semicircle. So they are called Mr. Tambo and Mr. Bones.

[18] This is the "hoe-down" or "breakdown," which may have originated in the "shout" of the blacks. See Henry Edward Krehbiel, *Afro-American Folksongs: A Study in Racial and National Music*, p. 33.

[19] For the reproduction, in sound, of a minstrel show, see *A Complete and Authentic Minstrel Show*, Album P-1600, High Fidelity Somerset (Miller International Co., Media, Pa.).

[20] It is Emmett (1815-1904) who, within the framework of the minstrel show, will launch in 1859 the celebrated "Dixie," the future martial hymn of the Confederates. On the 1843 performance, see Chase, *America's Music*, p. 259.

[21] Let us cite the name of Edwin P. Christy (1815-1862), who was the first to sing a large number of Stephen Foster's songs.

century the genre enjoyed popularity.[22] Yet there were two peak periods in the minstrel show's long career, the first between 1850 and 1870 and the second in the century's last five years.[23] Troupes beyond number were then traversing the land, putting on their shows in theaters and circuses.[24] In these conditions, one can readily conceive the minstrel shows' success in establishing their mythical portrait of the Negro. This was etched even more deeply into people's minds by the countless songs the minstrels helped put into circulation.

The portrait is mythical indeed. Just as the traditional plantation Negro is always foolish, lazy, and careless of the morrow, the minstrel Negro loves watermelon which, as if it were a harmonica, he slides across his huge mouth. He wears clothes of startling colors,[25] drinks to excess, and cannot go by a henhouse without making off with one of the hens. As with the mythical plantation Negro, his handling of the English language is rendered all the more disastrous by a predilection for long words he does not understand. Boastfulness, ignorance, superstition, and cowardice make up one aspect of the caricature.[26]

The other aspect is represented by the sugary sentimentality attributed to the slave and expressed quite characteristically in the songs of Stephen Collins Foster (1826-64), the minstrel shows' illustrious supplier.

> 'Way down upon the Swanee river, Far, far away,
> There's where my heart is turning ever, there's where
>   the old folks stay!
> All up and down the old creation, Sadly I roam,
> Still looking for the old plantation, and for the old
>   folks at home!

So sings the black man of "Old Folks at Home" (1851), as interpreted by the minstrel Christy, the song's first singer. In "My Old Kentucky

[22] We still witnessed performances in the South on the eve of World War II. Although these shows are not quite extinct even today, in the twentieth century it is above all the cinema that has taken them over.

[23] Wittke, *Tambo and Bones,* pp. 64, 110-11.

[24] Because of the shared elements (clownlike characters, the music, the love of the spectacular and of din, etc.), minstrel show, theater, and circus continue to maintain close relations.

[25] With the minstrels, the hankering after gorgeous attire is looked on as typical of the northern black, while the other weaknesses are deemed, rather, to be those of the black slave in the South. See John Tasker Howard, *Our American Music, Three Hundred Years of It,* p. 176. In fact, the psychological significance of out-of-the-ordinary dress — essentially, a compensatory phenomenon — is a great deal more complex. See Abram Kardiner and Lionel Ovesey, *The Mark of Oppression: A Psychosocial Study of the American Negro,* pp. 92, 109, 313, 349.

[26] Wittke, *Tambo and Bones,* pp. 8-9, 39-40, 142, 157, 163, and *passim.*

Home" (1853), Foster tries the effect of contrast. The opening scene presents the black folks' cabin drenched in sunlight:

'Tis summer, the darkies are gay!

But "by'n bye hard times come a-knocking at the door" and, doubtless because the master is reduced to selling off his slaves, the atmosphere darkens:

The day goes by like a shadow o'er the heart,
With sorrow where all was delight;
The time has come when the darkies have to part . . .

but not until the affectionate slaves find time, before they go, to dry the tears of their mistress, who is very much upset by the parting:

Weep no more, my lady, O weep no more today!
We will sing one song for the old Kentucky home,
For the old Kentucky home far away!

This weepy sentimentality is Stephen Foster's chief contribution to the minstrel songs. If the mythical portrait of the Negro found such a long-lived acceptance in America and throughout the world that even today it still lingers in people's minds, the popularity of Foster's songs is in great measure responsible.

But the sentimentality is not to be attributed to Foster's individual temperament; rather, it must be viewed as a concrete exemplification of the taste of that period. Ambitious to succeed, Foster was all the more ready to conform since he had no personal conception of the Negro on the plantation, of which he had no immediate knowledge. He did, as it happens, spend the month of February, 1852, on the steamboat *James Milligan*, which took him to New Orleans,[27] but several of his hits predate this brief sojourn in the South. What he does know of the black man is derived from songs he heard sung by longshoremen and firemen on the wharves of Pittsburgh or Cincinnati. [28] He also knew the hymns and the atmosphere of the little black church where his parents' mulatto servant, Olivia Pise, sometimes took him when he was still a child.[29] As he would later tell his brother Morrison, several of his songs originated in his recollections of the black melodies heard in this church.[30] It would therefore be erroneous to credit him with the desire and, more especially, with the

[27] Chase, *America's Music,* p. 294.
[28] J. G. Burtnett, "National Elements in Stephen Foster's Art," *South Atlantic Quarterly,* October, 1922, p. 324.
[29] *Ibid.* See also Chase, *America's Music,* pp. 287-88.
[30] Chase, *America's Music,* pp. 287-88.

merit that are not his: that of having been the interpreter of the black soul.[31]

Coming as it does at the century's halfway mark, Foster's sentimentality clearly reveals that his main concern is conformity with the romantic perspective then beginning to exercise a decisive influence on public taste. Foster represents the merging of frontier vitality and primitivism with "the genteel tradition of the urban fringe, dominated by sentimentality, conventionalism, and propriety."[32] Those were the days when the covers of song books were adorned with pictures of loving couples frozen in stilted, romantic postures.[33] But it was at this time, too, that America and the world were shedding tears over *Uncle Tom's Cabin*. Mrs. Stowe's well-intentioned sentimentality reinforces Stephen Foster's; both feel obliged to make their original black models more refined. Otherwise, how could young ladies of good family sing Foster's ditties in the drawing room? The changes Foster made in the texts of some of his songs evince his eagerness to observe the proprieties of this American Victorianism. Thus, while "Poor Uncle Tom, Good Night!" (the first version of "My Old Kentucky Home") was in the Negro vernacular, the definitive version is painstakingly purged of this barbaric dialect.[34]

Even the minstrel show itself, previously rather crude on occasion, shows signs of increasing urbanization as it becomes progressively remote from its Negro sources and makes more lavish use of extraneous materials.[35] By 1855 things had gone so far that a Southern slaveowner could complain of finding, in an entire volume of "Negro" songs, "only ten with any trace of genuineness."[36]

But if the charge of mere falsification were to be the final word on the minstrel shows during the ten years before the Civil War, only one aspect of the total phenomenon would have been treated. For in the eyes of the public of that day and, to some extent, of our own day, the minstrel show's depiction of the Negro was more than a caricature. In their eyes it was

[31] Yet this is done by Burtnett, who describes him as the "true interpreter of the thoughts and the emotions of a race" ("National Elements in Stephen Foster's Art," p. 324).

[32] Chase, *America's Music*, p. 297.

[33] *Ibid.*

[34] *Ibid.*, p. 294.

[35] In particular, the British ballads. Current happenings also begin to find a place in the songs.

[36] Letter printed in *Putnam's Monthly*, January, 1855, pp. 72-79. Cited by Wittke, *Tambo and Bones*, p. 120. On the minstrel show's increasing infidelity to its origins, see *ibid.*, pp. 104-5, 122. Wittke regards this infidelity as being one of the principal reasons for the premature demise (if that is the fitting expression!) of the minstrel show.

not even that essentially, but a faithful representation of reality. Musicologists, too, have actually gone astray here. Among these scholars is Louis C. Elson, with his assertion that *"Old Folks at Home* is the chief American folk-song, and Stephen Collins Foster is as truly the folk-song genius of America as Weber or Silcher have been of Germany."[37] But one step further, and one is convinced that the Negro is really identical with the personage who cavorts on the minstrel stage. This step is taken with all the greater ease since everything conspires to endow the portrait with an authentic air. In the first place, there is the constant repetition, which in the end induces one to accept as true what is not true. Another factor is the utilization, in many minstrel songs, of the poetic and musical forms of the ballad. This facilitates the blending and final absorption of Negro elements into the Anglo-Saxon folklore with which the public was familiar.[38]

[37] Louis C. Elson, *History of American Music* (1904). Cited by C. Alphonso Smith, in W. P. Trent et al., eds., *Cambridge History of American Literature,* II, 353. See also Burtnett's remark, note 31 above. One thing that helped greatly in making Foster's songs sound like genuine folklore was, in addition to the use of the ballad meter, the adoption of the pentatonic scale, which is met with in the folklore of many continents. It is common especially to the Scottish songs and the Negro spirituals. Foster has no hesitation about using it, for example in "Old Folks at Home" (Chase, *America's Music,* p. 299). A wealth of information on folklore and the pentatonic scale will be found in Krehbiel's *Afro-American Folksongs.*

[38] One may reach the conclusion that in the process of assimilation — and that is to say, of Americanization — of the Negro type, which in the end is incorporated into the national heritage, it is to a great extent the popular Scottish contribution, and at times the Irish, which provided the materials for this amalgamation, while the minstrels functioned mainly as catalysts. Above, we have placed the first borrowings of the minstrels from the blacks at about 1828-31, and the last period during which the shows enjoyed great popularity in the final years of the nineteenth century. It might be enlightening to set beside these dates those which mark the diffusion of the Scottish ballads in America. "Comin' thro' the Rye" was introduced in 1828, the melody being an authentic strathspey to words by Burns (Sigmund Gottfried Spaeth, *A History of Popular Music in America,* p. 66). Ten years later, "Annie Laurie" appears in the third volume of Paterson and Roy's collection, *Vocal Melodies of Scotland.* And, finally, at the other limit of our period, the five volumes of Francis James Child's *English and Scottish Popular Ballads* were published between 1883 and 1898. At the very least, these dates form a strange series of coincidences. It should be borne in mind, too, that the black rubs shoulders on the stage with other "non-American" personages, a situation that both facilitates the merging of their characteristics and also, as it were, their reduction to a common denominator which is inevitably American. Finally, we will note below how, in their poems, poets like Irwin Russell and Paul Laurence Dunbar exploited the Scottish or Irish vein as well as the Negro one. Thus in every domain — in stage show, song, and popular poetry alike — the association of these elements became remarkably widespread, and it is hard to believe that this fact did not lead to a fusion of elements so often presented in association.

Thus the chief consequences brought about by the minstrel troupes through their portrayal of the black are the dissemination and the authentication of a mythical portrait which became deeply rooted in the American popular tradition.[39]

2. THE PLANTATION TRADITION IN POETRY

Though the South went down to military and economic defeat in the Civil War, its vital parts remained intact; its ideology was not crushed by force of arms. While hoping for a better day, the South bowed its head beneath the yoke of the military men and political adventurers who installed in the conquered territory a regime of occupation which used black men as a facade. Yet it was clear to everyone that this state of affairs could not last forever. So the South, after the storm had blown over, once again bore itself with a proud spirit. It did more — it set out to regain the ground lost and pushed ahead to seize positions which, before the war, would have been quite unattainable.

The postbellum era in the South, where 95 percent of the blacks in the nation then lived, is notable for the countless devices introduced to prevent the freedmen from enjoying their newly acquired civil rights. The Thirteenth Amendment (1865) had confirmed the abolition of slavery, the Fourteenth (1868) had granted citizenship to the freedmen, while the Fifteenth (1870) defended, against any restrictive legislation, their right to vote. But, as soon as martial law no longer reigned, the South saw to it that the blacks would not be able to exercise their rights effectively. There were acts of intimidation by the Ku Klux Klan, founded in 1865; the theft of ballot boxes; secret voting available for whites only — these and countless other chicaneries effectively circumvented the law.[40] The num-

[39] The stage stereotype created by the minstrels is so intimately associated with the black as a person that, in the public mind, each inevitably summons up the other. In response to public demand, the stage performances of *Uncle Tom's Cabin* began to feature music and dances of the kind the public had come to know in the minstrel shows. Sometimes even some stanzas of "Jim Crow" are sung. See Richard Moody, "Uncle Tom, the Theater and Mrs. Stowe," *American Heritage*, October, 1955, pp. 29, 31, 102; also Birdoff, *The World's Greatest Hit*. One can no longer deny the primordial role played by the minstrels in diffusing Negro stereotypes. Here is what James Weldon Johnson has to say on the subject: "Some of the most persistent of them were formed on the minstrel stage. . . . And it was from the minstrel show that millions of white Americans got their conceptions of Negro character. . . . To the minstrel stage can be traced the difficulty which white America finds in taking the Negro seriously" (*Negro Americans, What Now?*, pp. 91-92).

[40] Benjamin Griffith Brawley, *A Short History of the American Negro*, p. 152.

ber of lynchings, twelve in 1872, rose to 255 in 1892.[41] Not only were discrimination and segregation more and more widely applied in practice; gradually they were embodied also in the legislation of the states. In 1890, Mississippi passed the first measure aimed at suppressing the black vote by introducing the poll tax and an examination on the Constitution. In 1898, Louisiana invented the "grandfather clause," which virtually deprived blacks of the vote.[42] Nothing was overlooked that might help "put the Negro in his place."

Literature sped to the aid of politics in this endeavor. It worked out the themes and reflected the ideology, most signally by breathing back life into the plantation tradition.[43] Originating about 1830, this tradition is at bottom a romantic and thus idealized image of pre–Civil War southern plantation life. Apart from an occasional variant, the picture it presents closely resembles the one sketched below.

In the center of the plantation, where the slaves bustle about so joyously that they laugh and sing all day, rises a splendid colonial-style dwelling. There the aristocratic owner, who is always immensely rich and has a swarm of contented colored servants at his beck and call, leads in the midst of his family a semi-idyllic, almost entirely leisured existence, from which the slaves are usually not excluded. Happy clusters of pickaninnies frolic around the house. Rarely absent from the scene is the black mammy who lavishes her every care on the most recently born "Young Mahsr," to whom she will remain fondly attached as long as she lives. All else attests to the cordial relations the masters have established with their slaves, the latter being treated with unflagging generosity and subjected to an unending flood of encouragement and good advice. The slaves, for their part, know how much they have to thank their master for; thus their devotion to him knows no bounds. It must be said that they are content with little, for they are simple, credulous creatures, inherently comical yet endowed at times with a certain philosophy. But they excel above all in dancing, singing, and story-telling.

It is no longer possible merely to wonder whether this tableau might not be far removed from reality. One need but compare it to the circumstances

---

[41] *Ibid.*, p. 154.

[42] Rayford Logan, *The Negro in American Life and Thought*, p. 209.

[43] Still the main work on the plantation tradition is Gaines, *The Southern Plantation*. However, Gaines's views require emendation in certain areas, and should therefore be studied in conjunction with several works by Sterling Brown, *The Negro in American Fiction; Negro Poetry and Drama;* "Negro Character as Seen by White Authors," *Journal of Negro Education*, April, 1933, pp. 179-203; "The American Race Problem as Reflected in American Literature," *ibid.*, July, 1939, pp. 275-90.

as they emerge from the testimony of former slaves, which has been the object of much research in the last few years.[44] Perhaps the portrait had some validity early in the nineteenth century for the situation in Virginia — though not in the Deep South — as painted by John Pendleton Kennedy in *Swallow Barn* (1832), or by his contemporary William A. Caruthers, though with them the Negro remains very much in the background.

After 1830, however, conditions changed rapidly in the Deep South. With the extension of cotton-growing into Texas, the increased size of the plantations, and the greater number of slaves owned by one planter, that individual could no longer have any direct contact with most of his Negroes. On the big estates, relations were dehumanized by the introduction of the overseer or "nigger driver" who, as the Negroes saw him, was a devil incarnate.[45] Henceforward slavery would form the base of an inhuman economic system that aroused the wrath of northern abolitionists,[46] while Southerners reacted to their accusations by gradually assembling a coherent plan of defense. In its turn the plantation tradition, as one can well understand, became increasingly laden with political and social overtones that had been foreign to it, and with rare exceptions it evolved into an apologia for slavery. The outstanding figure here was, to the day of his death, the theoretician and leading orator John C. Calhoun. In this perspective too must be situated, as an early example, Beverley Tucker's novel *The Partisan Leader* (1836), along with the later poem, *The Hireling and the Slave,* which William J. Grayson brought out in 1854 as a rejoinder to *Uncle Tom's Cabin.* In it he contrasts the easy life of the South Carolina slave with the servitude suffered by the workers in New England.

[44] The picture of reality that Gaines tries to draw (*The Southern Plantation,* pp. 143ff.) requires a word of caution. As a Southerner, and even when he claims to be reestablishing the truth, Gaines is inclined to leave unmentioned the most offensive aspects of slavery. Besides, at the time his book was published (1924), the reality was still inadequately known because of lack of documentation. For a critical examination of the frequently highly relative objectivity of slavery's historians, see Stanley M. Elkins, *Slavery: A Problem in American Institutional and Intellectual Life,* Ch. 1, which is the best account of the matter that we possess. For the testimony of former slaves, see B. A. Botkin, ed., *Lay My Burden Down: A Folk History of Slavery,* particularly the section "The Slave's Chances," pp. 174-90. See also Charles H. Nichols, Jr., "Slave Narratives and the Plantation Legend," *Phylon,* third quarter, 1949, pp. 201-10; Frenise A. Logan, "Old South Legend," *Phylon,* third quarter, 1950, pp. 234-39. See also the bibliography provided by Elkins, *Slavery,* p. 17, n. 22.

[45] "Nigger driver second devil," declares one of their songs, "The Driver," cited by Thomas Wentworth Higginson in "Negro Spirituals," *Atlantic Monthly,* June, 1867, p. 693.

[46] Let us recall that William Lloyd Garrison founded *The Liberator* in 1831.

In the revival of the plantation tradition a scant ten years after the Civil War had ended, the outlook adopted is, naturally, less than ever the faithful replica of a reality now embellished by its remoteness in time. Besides, to add to the weight of bygone quarrels, there came the new southern resentment of the Negro, who was regarded as primarily responsible for the four years of bloodletting. Whether consciously or not, the writers of the New South chose to echo the pleas from beyond the grave in favor of the vanquished way of life. Their writings now place the Negro in the foreground, since they fully realize that their attitude must be defined in relation to him.

This rebirth of interest in the Negro on the part of postwar southern writers first manifests itself in poetry.[47] The inaugurator is Thomas Dunn English (1819-1902), who, in 1871, published four Negro dialect poems in various periodicals.[48] Next on the scene were brothers Sidney and Clifford Lanier, with a jointly written dialect poem entitled "The Power of Prayer, or: The First Steamboat up the Alabama," published in June, 1875, by *Scribner's Monthly*.[49] But the dialect poems of these writers are greatly surpassed in importance by those of another southern poet, Irwin Russell.

Irwin Russell

The work of Irwin Russell[50] proved exemplary in a highly stimulating

[47] See, on this topic, John Herbert Nelson, *The Negro Character in American Literature*, pp. 97ff.

[48] "Mahs' Lewis's Ride," *Appleton's*, May 6, 1871, pp. 519-20; "Caesar Rowan," *Scribner's*, July, 1871, p. 300; "Leonard Grimleigh's Shadow," *Lippincott's*, September, 1871, pp. 256-59; and "Momma Phoebe," *Scribner's*, November, 1871, pp. 62-63. These poems were reprinted in the *Select Poems of Dr. Thomas Dunn English*, ed. Alice English (Newark, 1894). We are indebted for this information on English to an article by Rayburn S. Moore, "Thomas Dunn English: A Forgotten Contributor to the Development of Negro Dialect Verse in the 1870's," *American Literature*, March, 1961, pp. 72-75. In addition to establishing English as the initiator of "Negro poetry" in dialect, a distinction that had been given the Lanier brothers, Moore notes that English made use of the poem in monologue form spoken by a Negro, and he points to striking analogies between "Caesar Rowan" and "Momma Phoebe" by English, and "Unc' Edinburg's Drowndin" and "Marse Chan," two stories in Page's collection *In Ole Virginia*. It would seem, then, that English was, alongside Russell, one of Page's models.

[49] Pp. 239-40. The following year, they publish in the same *Scribner's Monthly*, May, 1876, p. 142, "Uncle Jim's Baptist Revival Hymn." For the text of these poems see Sidney Lanier, *Centennial Edition*, 10 vols. (Baltimore, 1945), I, 215-17. See also, in the fifth volume of this edition, "Timeo Danaos! A Voice in the Night," pp. 200-203, and "The New South," p. 348, an interesting article in which Lanier reveals some of his personal views concerning the Negro. (This article had been published originally in *Scribner's Monthly*, October, 1880, pp. 840-51.)

[50] Irwin Russell (1853-1879) from the age of sixteen began to publish poems

way, especially for Joel Chandler Harris and Thomas Nelson Page,[51] who there learned how one could build up around the Negro a flattering panorama of the Old South.[52]

Russell was born in Mississippi and spent a great deal of time wandering along the river's banks and beyond. He had had frequent opportunities to observe the southern Negro from close at hand and, despite the slightly earlier publication date of Laniers' poems, he was the first writer to conceive of utilizing, in his poetry, this personage whose poetic temperament had taken his fancy. One day, in answer to a question, he responded:

> Many think the vein a limited one, but I tell you that it is inexhaustible. The Southern negro has only just so much civilization as his contact with the white man has given him. He has only been indirectly influenced by the discoveries of science, the inventions of human ingenuity, and the general progress of mankind. Without education or social intercourse with intelligent and cultivated people, his thought has necessarily been original . . . You may call it instinct, imitation, what you will; it has, nevertheless, a foundation . . . I have long felt that the negro, even in his submission and servitude, was conscious of a higher nature, and must some day assert it . . . I have felt that the soul could not be bound, and must find a way for itself to freedom. The negro race, too, in spite of oppression, has retained qualities found in few others under like circumstances. Gratitude it has always been distinguished for; hospitality and helpfulness are its natural creed . . . It does not lack courage, industry, self-denial or virtue . . . So the negro has done an immense amount of quiet thinking; and with only such forms of expression

---

in different newspapers and periodicals, often anonymously or under one of a variety of pseudonyms. It was his "Uncle Cap Interviewed" (*Scribner's Monthly*, January, 1876) that attracted attention to him. Only after his death were his poems assembled by Joel Chandler Harris, who also wrote a preface for their publication in book form (*Poems by Irwin Russell* [New York, 1888]). A new, slightly enlarged edition appeared in 1917 with the title *Christmas-Night in the Quarters*. All our references are to the 1888 edition.

[51] Concerning Russell's influence on Harris, see Hubbell, *The South in American Literature*, p. 788; for his influence on Page, *ibid.*, pp. 795-96. Page and Gordon dedicate their volume of poems, *Befo' de War* (1888), "To the Memory of Irwin Russell who awoke the first echo," and the book ends with a poem, "One Mourner," in which they represent a Negro as paying posthumous homage to Russell.

[52] The backward-turning character of all these writings is striking. Significant is the title, *Befo' de War*, of the Page-Gordon collection. Note also Harris's declarations about Russell who, he said, had succeeded in focusing attention on "the unique relations existing between the two races *before the war* . . . the old life *before the war* is reproduced with a fidelity that is marvelous" (*Poems by Irwin Russell*, Introduction, p. x; italics added). On this backward-turning, see also the remark made by William Stanley Braithwaite, "The Negro in American Literature," in Alain Locke, ed., *The New Negro*, p. 31: "It must be sharply called to attention that the tradition of the antebellum Negro is a post-bellum product, stranger in truth than in fiction."

as his circumstances furnished him he indulges in paradox, hyperbole, aphorism, sententious comparison. He treasures his tradition; he is enthusiastic, patient, long-suffering, religious, reverent. Is there not poetry in the character?[53]

What strikes him about the Negro then, are his spontaneity and originality, maintained intact on the fringes of that legally constituted society which scarcely knows whether to treat him as object, animal, or child. But we should also point out that Russell, like the rest of his southern compatriots, will not grant the Negro any culture or civilization of his own. These, in Russell's view, could only come to the Negro through eventual contact with whites. Nor does Russell seem to have the least notion that what he deems to be black originality and spontaneity — in short, whatever makes the black different — this religion, this poetry, and these traditions are actually the remnants of a civilization and culture from which the black was brutally torn to be transported into slavery and set down in a milieu and amid a culture to which he was refused access. Thus Russell's reaction to the personage he appears to have discovered consists principally of a wonderment that reveals, too, a slight tinge of condescension, as in these lines from "Christmas-Night in the Quarters":

> We form our minds by pedants' rules
> And all we know is from the schools;
> And when we work, or when we play,
> We do it in an ordered way —
> And Nature's self pronounce a ban on,
> Whene'er she dares transgress a canon.
> Untrammeled thus the simple race is
> That "wuks the craps" on cotton places.
> Original in act and thought,
> Because unlearned and untaught.
> Observe them at their Christmas party:
> How unrestrained their mirth — how hearty!
> How many things they say and do
> That never would occur to you![54]

Russell, it can be sensed, was aiming at a target well above mere farce of the Jim Crow type and endeavoring to portray the Negro sympathetically so as to stress all the basically human qualities. Nevertheless, though sympathetic, the presentation cannot shake off a certain paternalism. As a Southerner Russell despite himself maintains the prejudices of his up-

[53] Cited by William Malone Baskervill, *Southern Writers* (Nashville, 1896), pp. 117-19.
[54] *Poems by Irwin Russell*, p. 4.

bringing intact in his heart. When all is said and done, most of his poems fall within the plantation tradition and do not invariably echo the sympathy he had expressed elsewhere for his black literary model. The situations in which he places his characters do not go beyond those that the regional etiquette of race relations was prepared to tolerate, and when on some rare occasion he relates how the Negro slyly outwits the white man, there can be no doubts concerning Russell's interpretation of racial hierarchy.

The 1888 volume contains only one poem that presents the black as anything but a humorous character. "Going,"[55] perhaps the best and certainly among the best poems in the collection, conducts us to the bedside of a dying man who already glimpses the splendors of paradise. In this atmosphere, there is a most successful blending of the images found in the spirituals and the somewhat superstitious religious outlook of some blacks. Russell works the humorous vein in the other poems, as though the black man were not fit to be the subject of a serious poem.

The best-known poem by Russell, "Christmas-Night in the Quarters,"[56] has been described by Joel Chandler Harris as a "Negro operetta."[57] It deals with the Christmas festivities which the slaves were traditionally allowed to enjoy. There are several tableaux in Negro dialect, utilizing the heptasyllabic line of the ballad and kindred forms, and the whole is linked with connecting verse passages in standard English. The opening tableau shows us the guests arriving in an ox-drawn wagon, with the "coachman" railing against the laziness of the yoked oxen. At this moment the Negro pastor steps forward. He is a pronounced casuist, and he begs the Lord to bless the dancing that is about to start. Though well aware that this pleasure is sinful, he makes bold to hope that God in his infinite mercy will deign to look favorably on the humble rejoicings that bring together his servants, after their season of heavy labor.[58] Josey the fiddler is already tuning his fiddle, and until daybreak the gathering's high spirits will seek to vent themselves in the cotillion. The sole interruption is for supper, an occasion that Russell refuses to describe, for "the

[55] *Ibid.*, p. 110.
[56] *Ibid.*, pp. 1-15.
[57] *Ibid.*, Introduction, p. x.
[58] This biased presentation is certainly not in keeping with the spirit of the Negro popular tradition. Sterling Brown has told us how one day, while he was reading this poem to rural Negroes, they were so scandalized by the attitude of Russell's pastor they insisted the reading be stopped, fearing that the sacrilege might draw down a thunderbolt on the house. For a similar reaction to a pastor addicted to dancing, see Dunbar's "De Critters' Dance," stanza 10, lines 1-2, *Complete Poems*, p. 293.

most inventive modern poet ... could form no phrase to do it justice."[59] While all this is going on, the old gossips stand aside and listen to Aunt Cassy tell her tales of conjurors, ghosts, and devils who nightly hold their revels in the smoke-house.

> So wears the night, and wears so fast,
> All wonder when they find it past,
> And hear the signal sound to go
> From what few cocks are left to crow.[60]

The unvoiced suggestion is that so few roosters survive because the others have already found their way into the dancers' pockets. But before the dancers part, a last song is called for. Without waiting to be coaxed, Booker takes his banjo off the nail and sings a ballad whose story dates back to the Flood. Ham, the only Negro on Noah's Ark and the ship's barber — here, the Ark assumes the features of a Mississippi steamboat — was feeling bored, so one day he took a piece of wood and held it over steam, curving it to make a banjo. But what could he use for strings? The notion occurred to him of using hairs from the opossum's tail, and that is why today the opossum has no hair on his tail. And Russell adds: "... whar you finds de nigger — dar's de banjo an' de 'possum!"[61] Everyone is sorry the party has to end, and one of the young blacks voices his regret that Santa Claus did not have a twin brother, so that there could be two Christmases each year instead of one.

The tableau drawn is not an entirely friendly one, for we are discreetly reminded, between the roars of laughter, that the Negro is a thief, that he is lazy, and that he does nothing but eat opossum and play the banjo. In short — and in reaching this conclusion Russell joins hands, by and large, with the legislators of his native state — the Negro has remained very much a child. Furthermore, "Christmas-Night in the Quarters" contains in embryo nearly all the themes forming the base of Irwin Russell's work.

There is, to begin with, the theme of the Negro sermon, which Russell was the first to introduce into literature and which will be borrowed not only by the minstrels[62] but also by Negro poets.[63] Russell's Negro pastor,

[59] *Poems by Irwin Russell,* pp. 9-10.

[60] *Ibid.,* p. 10.

[61] *Ibid.,* p. 14.

[62] To the best of our knowledge, no one has stated that several minstrels appropriated Russell's poems for use as monologues on the stage. Wittke, *Tambo and Bones,* p. 171, cites a Negro sermon in verse, "Uncle Pete's Sermon," as an item in a collection of minstrel texts, *Dick's Ethiopian Scenes* (New York, 1879), p. 108. This sermon, which Wittke does not identify, is nothing other than the direct

pretty much on the lines of all pastors and priests in humorous literature, is always eager to receive. This holds true for the pastor in "Half-Way Doin's"[64] who, after having in his sermon exhorted his flock not to do anything halfway, repeats this advice when the hat is being passed around for the collection. In another respect, the fidelity with which Russell reproduces not only the portrait of the pastor — who for a long time would remain quite ignorant[65] — but also the often highly unexpected imagery of the metaphors and allegories that compose the sermon, lead us to infer that the poet found numerous opportunities to look at and listen to Negro pastors as they preached. Hence it is the poems on a religious topic, even when religion is allied with humor, that present Irwin Russell's conception of the Negro in its most attractive guise.[66]

More tendentious, as he is portrayed, is the theme of the crafty, thieving black who is into the bargain too clever by half, since in his naïve ignorance he dares to boast of his wiles, convinced that his white interlocutor will not be smart enough to see through him. At times such roguery succeeds, as it did for Uncle Pete, who made a dollar selling a wretched mongrel fit only to be done away with:

> Drownin' time wuz comin' fur him mighty precious fas'!
> Sol' him fur a dollar — well! An' goodness knows de pup
> Isn't wuf de powder it'd take to blow him up![67]

But in "Business in Mississippi"[68] the Negro meets with a setback. He tries, through the use of a misleading sample, to sell good old Master Johnny a

---

transcription of Russell's "Half-Way Doin's," with only the title changed. Wittke, *Tambo and Bones,* pp. 187-88, similarly reprints the actual text of the famous ballad on the origin of the banjo, which formed part of *Christmas-Night in the Quarters,* as having appeared under the title "Ham's Banjo" in the collection of the minstrel Al. G. Field, *History of the American Minstrelsy* in *The Kit Kat* VIII, n.d. This sort of plagiarism, common at the time, must have been rendered all the more easy and frequent by the fact that Russell's poems appeared in periodicals without the author's name or under a pseudonym. In any event, it serves to indicate that there was no great difference between Russell's outlook and that of the minstrels, and that the stereotyped portraits of the Negro were regarded as no less valid in poetry than on the stage.

[63] Especially Paul Laurence Dunbar and James Weldon Johnson.

[64] *Poems by Irwin Russell,* p. 54.

[65] The ignorance of the pastors, Negro or white, in certain sects is due in part to the fact that the vocation or "call" took the place of every other requirement. Some Negro pastors were entirely illiterate. See Carter G. Woodson, *The History of the Negro Church,* pp. 150-51 and *passim.*

[66] See, in addition to the poems already cited, "A Sermon for the Sisters," *Poems by Irwin Russell,* pp. 55-58; "The Old Hostler's Experience," *ibid.,* pp. 63-65; "Rev. Henry's War-Song," pp. 66-67.

[67] "Selling a Dog," *ibid.,* p. 24.

[68] *Ibid.,* pp. 19-22.

bale of cotton containing a heavy ballast of stones, and is utterly discoun-
tenanced when subsequently exposed as a cheat. Brazenly mendacious,
finally, is the hero of "Wherefore He Prays That a Warrant May Issue."[69]
He has the effrontery to ask the judge for a warrant of arrest against his
employer, whom he charges with attempted murder. But as the story
unfolds we learn that in reality this Negro, after stealing a chicken, had
gone on to steal the wood with which to cook it. To scare the thief, the
employer had hidden a pound of gunpowder in a hollow log, so that the
"attempted murder" occurred when the log was in the fireplace. Chicken,
wood, pot, and ashes went up with a bang and flew across the kitchen.

These humorous monologues are not just farce. Russell's little tableaux
are put together with remarkable skill, and the mere idea of choosing the
genre of the monologue, and having a Negro speak it, was a find in itself.
What better means could he have hit upon to persuade the reader of the
truth of any declaration or insinuation than to have the Negro himself
utter it? It rendered the association of ideas, in the minds of Russell's audience, all the more solid and lasting. Again, the psychology of the thief has
been admirably worked out. To attain his goal he presents himself as obsequious, amicably disposed, and loyal, and he feigns amazement, should the
need arise, when he is unmasked. This is the living image of the rogue
against whom one must be on guard but whom it would be pointless to
attack openly. He can be thwarted only if one remains vigilant, and reduced to harmlessness only through recourse to stratagems and extralegal
methods. Thus beneath the farce the thesis makes itself evident, and it is in
this fashion that Russell's themes join ranks with those from the plantation
tradition.

Two particular poems from this collection are written in this selfsame
spirit. They are "Mahsr John" and "Uncle Cap Interviewed"; they have
as their goal no longer the simple portrayal of the Negro, but the defense
and glorification of the antebellum South.

The main thing about Master John that the slave who speaks in the
first poem wishes to tell us is that he was immensely rich:

> He shorely wuz de greates' man de country ebber growed.
>
> .   .   .   .   .
>
> He alluz wore de berry bes' ob planters' linen suits,
> An' kep' a nigger busy jes a-blackin' ob his boots;
> De buckles on his galluses wuz made of solid gol',
> An' diamon's! — dey wuz in his shut as thick as it would hol'.[70]

---

[69] *Ibid.*, pp. 31-34.
[70] "Mahsr John," *ibid.*, pp. 43-46.

He owned five cotton plantations, as well as a sugarcane plantation in Louisiana, and one thousand slaves. Any of them whose occupations receive some closer mention do indeed appear to have lived in blissful idleness:

> I reckon dere wuz forty ob de niggers, young an' ol',
> Dat staid about de big house jes to do what dey wuz tol';
> Dey had a' easy time, wid skacely any work at all —
> But dey had to come a-runnin' when ol' Mahsr John' u'd call![71]

The masters sometimes held dances, having an orchestra come all the way from New Orleans for the purpose. But since the war everything has changed:

> Well, times is changed. De war it come an' sot de niggers free,
> An' now ol' Mahsr John ain't hardly wuf as much as me;
> He had to pay his debts, an' so his lan' is mos'ly gone —
> An' I declar I's sorry fur my pore ol' Mahsr John.[72]

As for the second poem's speaker, Uncle Cap, his greatest pride is to bask at second hand in the glory that surrounded the Virginia aristocrats:

> So you thought 'twas Souf Ca'lina, sah, whar I was born an' raised?
> No! I'm from ole Virginny, an' fur dat de Lord be praised!
> Virginny niggers always wuz de best dat you could buy;
> Poor white trash couldn't git 'em, 'ca'se de prices wuz so high.[73]

> .   .   .   .   .

> Whut do I t'ink of freedom? I dunno; it's true I's free,
> But now I's got so awful old, whut good is 'at to me?
> I nebber bodders 'bout it much . . .[74]

Was it really worth it, just for this, to have waged war against the South and treated its leaders, anachronistically, as "war criminals"? You can see for yourselves, Russell tells us; even the Negroes look back longingly to the good old antebellum days. And their freedom? Just see how little importance that has for them. So rely on the Southerners! They know the Negro better and have more genuine affection for him than you Northerners do. You went off to war in support of an idea but couldn't bear to live with blacks for even a day.

Once again, the case is shrewdly argued. Russell not only avoids speaking in his own right; he strengthens his overall plausibility by using Negro

[71] *Ibid.*, p. 45.
[72] *Ibid.*, pp. 45-46.
[73] "Uncle Cap Interviewed," *ibid.*, pp. 60-61.
[74] *Ibid.*, pp. 61-62.

dialect[75] and the stylistic devices favored by Negroes. The result is a greater naturalness, while the ballad meter situates the work more convincingly within the Anglo-Saxon popular tradition.[76]

There is, therefore, no cause for surprise that Joel Chandler Harris and Thomas Nelson Page, those two grand masters of the plantation tradition and illustrious advocates of postbellum southern ideology, should have claimed Irwin Russell as their own and, after his untimely death, have paid him solemn homage. Thus Russell's importance lay not merely in his having been the first writer to discover a rich vein of inspiration in the Negro and in his dialect, but also in having built an enduring foundation for the stereotypes of the black in the American literary tradition.

Joel Chandler Harris

Russell deserved credit, in the opinion of Harris,[77] above all for having introduced Negro folklore into literature. Ham's famous ballad on the origin of the banjo, which Russell utilized in his "Christmas-Night in the Quarters," was well known in the oral tradition of the Negro folktale. It was in this spirit that Harris wrote his "Negro" songs, the earliest group appearing in January, 1877, in the *Atlanta Constitution,* which had admitted Harris to its editorial staff the year before. Then, from 1878 on and in the same paper, there came the famous Uncle Remus stories, which had enormous success in every corner of the land.[78] Harris, who had a remarkable command of the Negro dialect of his own region, had heard Negroes tell these tales and had modified them, to some extent, in deference to the plantation tradition.

[75] While sufficiently accurate to be plausible, Russell's use of dialect is not always equally skilled and often tends to be a mere dislocation of spelling. This is the opinion of Joel Chandler Harris, an expert on the matter: "The dialect is not always the best, — it is often carelessly written..." (*Poems by Irwin Russell,* p. xi). Harris's judgment is presented in strange fashion by James D. Hart, *Oxford Companion to American Literature* (1948), p. 659: "His accuracy of language and understanding of character were recognized by Joel Chandler Harris...."

[76] Russell is another example of a poetic temperament made sensitive to black folk values through a close intimacy with those of Scotland. "Burns," he declared, "is my idol" (Smith, *Cambridge History of American Literature,* II, 353-54). Several of his poems are Scottish or Irish pastiches ("Larry's on the Force," "The Irish Eclipse," "Nine Graves in Edinbro," "Studies in Style — Burns"). We have already noted the same association in the case of the minstrels. Should this be looked on simply as a reflection of the geographical association that took place in the South, where farmers of Scottish or Irish ancestry live side by side with the blacks in their service? We raise the question here, without attempting to answer it.

[77] 1848-1908.

[78] The first collection in volume form, *Uncle Remus, His Songs and His Sayings,* appeared in 1880.

Yet his attitude is akin to Russell's, for there are times in his evocation of bygone days when he allows himself a genuine sympathy for his human subject. Indeed, some of Harris's contemporaries voiced (and in their wake some more recent critics have voiced) a suspicion that Harris, through the mouth of Uncle Remus, was insinuating that the black man was superior to the white.[79] Brer Rabbit was a disguise for the black man, while the white man appeared variously as wolf, bear, or other animal more noted for strength than cunning.

But this is not the occasion for even a rapid examination of Harris's writings. We would simply call attention to the influence he sought to exert on public opinion and actually did exert on some of the numerous writers, in the main second-raters and third-raters, who were then writing "Negro" poetry. At times Harris not only heaped upon them whole-hearted praises that their verses did little to justify; he also deliberately encouraged them to magnify the brilliance in which they bathed the Old South.

An interesting case history, in this connection, is that of Harriet Weeden.[80] We have no intention of trying to refurbish the almost forgotten name of this Alabama poetess. Though many of her poems still make agreeable reading, she is scarcely more distinguished for depth than for originality, and that is slight. She devoted her talent exclusively to writing humorous and sentimental "Negro" poetry, and her themes and attitudes were pretty much those of the whole plantation school. The very first page of her first volume alerts the reader to this fact, for as epigraph stands a line of Emerson's that was an excellent choice for this position:

"Oh, South winds have long memories."

This no doubt explains why Harris took an interest in her; by so doing, he appears to have established not only the worth of her poetry but also the lady's financial well-being. Her first collection, *Shadows on the Wall* (1899), was privately published by the author in Huntsville, Alabama. But probably because of Harris's support (in the form of a long preface to this new collection of poems) Miss Weeden's second volume, *Bandanna Ballads* (1900), bore the imprint of Doubleday, in New York. It proved a highly profitable genre, for the very next year witnessed the publication, by the same publisher, of Miss Weeden's third book of poems, *Songs of the Old South*.

As might be suspected, the interesting feature in the case of Miss Weeden is Joel Chandler Harris's famous preface. This document, in our

[79] For an interpretation of Harris from this point of view, see Bernard Wolfe, "Uncle Remus and the Malevolent Rabbit," *Commentary*, July, 1949, pp. 31-41.
[80] 1847-1905.

view, does so much to illuminate both its author's mentality and ambitions and the public resistance that the southern claims encountered at the end of the century that, despite its length, we reproduce the central passage here:

It is safe to say that never before has an artist caught with such vital and startling distinctness, such moving fidelity, the characters which gave to the old plantation, if not its chiefest charm, at least one of its most enchanting features. Moreover, these memorial portraits arrive upon the scene in the very nick and point of time. A new generation has arisen, and it has become incredulous and sceptical in regard to the traditions and legends of the old plantation in general, and of the old-time quality negro in particular. These newcomers find a touch of romance in the reports that come to them from their forbears; their curiosity receives a fillip; they would like to believe in the substance of what they hear; but they live in a commercial age, and have a hard grip on what is practical and concrete. They look about them for some confirmation of the stories that are told, and they find not a shred. If there were negroes in the old days so quaint and gentle, so tender-hearted and devoted, that novelists and writers of tales never tire of crowning them with the halos that are convenient to fiction, what has become of them? Why have they disappeared from the face of the earth, leaving no trace behind? Why have they left no successors? Such is the attitude of an incredulous generation, engaged in trying to snatch a few tufts of hair from the seventy-and-seven thousand prongs of the money-demon's tail.

Not long ago, a Northern gentleman, who has been in the South long enough to make his mark there, wrote to an author of his acquaintance protesting the wholesale method of making saints of the old-time negroes. "If you want to display genuine art," he said, "give it the relish of reality. Paint the negroes as they now are. When you do this, I'll take a thousand copies of your book, and send them broadcast among my friends in New York and Massachusetts."

Well, the art of Miss Weeden's book is not only an answer to the sceptical, but is a welcome and necessary explanation of the plantation legends that have been preserved. Whatever the negroes are now, whatever they may become in the cold-storage conditions of our commercial environment, these portraits present unimpeachable evidence of what they were.[81]

This document is its own best commentary. It leaves no doubt as to Harris's ambition, which was to impose the plantation-school thesis on a hesitant public opinion — whose skepticism, furthermore, was attributed to the materialism that had taken hold of northern industrialized society. Thus the South was seen by contrast as the protector of genuine human values; in this crusade the pious plantation legends became irrefutable proof of

[81] *Bandanna Ballads,* pp. x-xii.

antebellum southern society's idyllic character. Finally, the whole debate centered upon the Negro, since the southern case ultimately depended for its success on the art with which this retrospective portrait of the Negro was painted.

Thomas Nelson Page and Armistead C. Gordon

The only aspects which Thomas Nelson Page took from Russell's work were the manner and the basic lesson of "Mahsr John" and "Uncle Cap Interviewed." He was little concerned with depicting the Negro as he was in himself, for the role allotted to the black was, primarily, to glorify his masters and to keep alive the thesis of their former splendor. Page bases his defense of the Old South on the forthright conviction, which he never for a moment questions, that the Negro is inferior. In "The Negro Question," one of the essays that make up *The Old South* (1892), he heaps up the arguments that tend to demonstrate this mental and social inferiority: "These examples cited, if they establish anything, establish the fact that the Negro race does not possess, in any development which he has yet attained, the elements of character, the essential qualifications to conduct a government, even for himself, and that if the reins of government be intrusted to his unaided hands, he will fling reason to the winds and drive to ruin."[82]

These declarations must be borne in mind, when one comes to consider both the short stories of *In Ole Virginia* (1887) and the poems he published jointly with his friend Armistead C. Gordon in the volume entitled *Befo' de War* (1888). Page and Gordon are indebted to Irwin Russell for both the form and the technique of the poem: its ballad meter and the monologue, which is invariably placed in the mouth of a former slave and couched in Negro dialect. In quality, however, this dialect is more closely akin to Harris's than to Russell's. And the themes, while modeled on those of "Mahsr John" and "Uncle Cap Interviewed," are much more heavily underscored and are, at times, preposterously exaggerated.

Uncle Gabe, in his eagerness to convey the wealth of his former masters, tells us that their hogs were so numerous that the fields were black with them,[83] that the slaves were as plentiful as the grains of corn in the granary,[84] and that their mistress never went farther on foot than from the house to the carriage.[85]

---

[82] Cited by Hugh Morris Gloster, *Negro Voices in American Fiction*, pp. 9-10.
[83] "Uncle Gabe's White Folks," Page and Gordon, *Befo' de War*, p. 3.
[84] *Ibid.*, p. 1.
[85] *Ibid.*, p. 3.

The slaves' devotion to their masters is hymned in the same lofty tone. Irwin Russell, portraying his blind violinist Ned, had refrained from stating how he had become blind,[86] whereas Jucks, the crippled violinist of Gordon's poem, met with disaster as he saved his master's two little girls who, while playing, had blown up the sawmill steam engine. "An' he never shall want," adds Mars' Thomas, "while I'm livin', no way!"[87] Kree, a young black, drowned while saving the life of his young Mars' Charley, who is so upset at the loss of his playmate that he too dies. They are buried beside each other in the mansion lawn.[88] Ashcake, the illegitimate son of his Ole Marster, also drowns as he saves his father in a boating accident. In his grief, the master soon follows to the grave the son he had sired on one of his former slave women.[89] In "Little Jack," a former slave on the brink of death entrusts his son with the savings that had been destined to purchase his freedom. But the war, coming too soon, set him free without any payment. The son is instructed to hand over the money to Young Marster, who is in greater need of it than is the young freedman:

> "Now, chile, you teck dat money,
> Git on young Marster's track,
> An' pay it ter him, honey;
> An' tell him Little Jack
> Worked forty year, dis Chris'mus come,
> Ter save dat sum:
>
> "An' dat 'twas for ole Marster,
> Ter buy your time f'om him;
> But dat de war come farster,
> An' squandered stock an' lim' —
> Say you kin work an' don't need none,
> An' he carn't, son.
>
> "He ain' been use ter diggin'
> His livin' out de dirt;
> He carn't drink out a piggin,
> Like you; an' it 'ud hurt
> Ole Marster's pride, an' make him sw'ar,
> In glory dar!"[90]

The discreet hints dropped by Page and Gordon let us surmise that some of these Negro characters owe their existence to the dalliance of the

---

86 "Blind Ned," *Poems by Irwin Russell,* pp. 39-42.
87 "Jucks," Page and Gordon, *Befo' de War,* p. 88.
88 "Kree," *ibid.,* pp. 34-37.
89 "Ashcake," *ibid.,* pp. 89-93.
90 "Little Jack," *ibid.,* pp. 115-16.

master with a slave woman.[91] With this paternity, the former slave can in part adopt for himself those aristocratic qualities which he lauds in his masters,[92] and so can display the most unqualified contempt for his ethnic brothers in the service of poor whites.[93]

Viewed as a whole, the poems of *Befo' de War* repetitively stress the harm done by the changes that resulted from the Civil War and the ensuing emancipation of the slaves. The war did not merely destroy immense natural riches;[94] more regrettably, it wrecked a harmonious ordering of things and of social relations, together with the happiness and well-being of those presumed to have been set free. Out of the former slaves it made, not men, but rootless creatures unable to support themselves[95] and incapable, too, of benefiting from the education[96] and the voting rights[97] that had been granted them. Freedom too often means, as they see it, the freedom not to work.[98] Now their heads are filled with grandiose ambitions,[99] which seem all the more crass in contrast with the often unexpected mani-

[91] "Poke o' Moonshine," *ibid.*, p. 47; "Ashcake," p. 91.

[92] Southern writers used this convenient means of creating for themselves a glorious past which often existed nowhere outside their own imaginations. "I'm F. F. V.," declares the black speaker in "To You" (*ibid.*, p. 107), these letters standing for "First Families of Virginia." "We wuz de ve'y top de pot," says the speaker in "Marse Phil" (p. 119), who had "gone to college" with his young master, but as his servant!

[93] See, for example, "Uncle Gabe's White Folks" (*ibid.*, p. 2):
> "My folks war'n' none o' yo' po'-white trash;
> No, sah, dey was ob high degree — :
> Dis heah nigger am quality."

In the use of the expression "my folks," there is a play on the two meanings, "bosses" and "parents." Since he is the son (and though the natural son, nevertheless the son) of a white man, the whole white family becomes his family. Thus the title of the poem, "Uncle Gabe's White Folks," actually means "the family of Uncle Gabe's white ancestors."

[94] "The Lament of Orpheus," *ibid.*, p. 48; "Home Again," p. 123.

[95] Those in "Departed Luck," *ibid.*, pp. 30-33, having burned their last log and eaten their last bit of bread, simply wait for deliverance by death, as they dream of the good old days when, for Christmas, the daughter of the house brought them a tray laden with good things.

[96] "Ebo," *ibid.*, pp. 25-29; "Ichabod," pp. 94-97.

[97] "At Whitehall," *ibid.*, pp. 67-69.

[98] "Virginia Creepers," *ibid.*, pp. 60-62.

[99] The black in "De Ole 'Oman an' Me," *ibid.*, pp. 13-16, complains that his wife has been putting on airs since the war ended. She used to call him Ichabod, or Ich, or "Ole Fool," and he called her Anniky, but now it's always "Mister Brown" and "Mistis Brown." At home they eat only white bread now instead of the cornmeal cake the husband would much rather eat, and the buttermilk has yielded to tea and coffee. She doesn't walk any more but takes the mule when she goes to town, and comes back with clothes in which her husband doesn't feel comfortable.

festations of their ignorance and fixity of outlook.[100] Emancipation has overthrown even the Negroes' religious beliefs. True, a great deal of superstition was involved. But whatever the nature of the beliefs, discarding them has done nothing but upset an equilibrium which would have been a thousand times better left intact.[101]

Gordon and Page will not be the last to offer us, within the form of the popular ballad in Negro dialect, this cheery vision of the old relationship between masters and slaves. The plantation poem will, like the minstrel song, continue to tempt a horde of writers. But very few will depart noticeably from the models examined above.

Yet there is one miscellany, slightly prior to *Befo' de War*, that deserves brief mention. Published by J. A. Macon in 1883 and entitled *Uncle Gabe Tucker: or, Reflection, Song and Sentiment in the Quarters*, its varied contents were in part noted by the author on the base of direct observation, and in part consisted of stories and poems which he wrote utilizing these materials.

J. A. Macon does not adhere to the plantation tradition, his standpoint being that of a collector whose good faith is unquestionable. It is no exaggeration to see in him a forerunner of the folklore-hunters who will later descend upon the country's obscurest backwaters, noting and so preserving for posterity the treasures they discover. Macon, in short, is what Harris might have been if the latter had not set out to preach a holy crusade.

In addition to the humorous pieces, Macon most commendably records realistic comments on the less agreeable aspects of slave life. In "Harvest Song," for example, the exhausted harvesters wait in the oppressive heat for the return of the young boy who has gone off with his bucket to fetch water while the boss, mounted on horseback, watches them from the shade:

> De lead-cutter stan'in' right up to de wheat,
>   But his foot sort o' draggin' like dey lame,
> De boss settin' up on his horse in de shade,
>   An' he say, "Dat nigger mighty game!"
> Nigger so tired tell he's mos' drap down,
>   But he holler an' sing all de same.[102]

---

[100] The black in "Nigger Twist" (*ibid.*, pp. 6-9) will have nothing to do with matches; he uses a glowing log, as in the past. The speaker in "Ebo" (pp. 25-29) makes fun of the schoolteacher who has taught his son that the earth is round and turns on its axis. Anyone can see that the earth is flat; besides, if it did turn around, the water bucket that is always put on the shelf would have fallen off long ago!

[101] "Zekyl's Infidelity," *ibid.*, p. 17.

[102] J. A. Macon, *Uncle Gabe Tucker*, p. 125.

The slaves depicted by Macon, unlike those of Russell or Page, do not spend their time in idleness and their work day, while officially scheduled to begin at daybreak, in fact often begins earlier, for it is the slaves' overseer who decides when day dawns!

> Oberseer use to reggerlate de daybreak.[103]

The realism in more than one of these poems is sufficient to convince us that they are based on the account of a former slave who feels a cold chill running down his back as he recalls what he has gone through. "Patter-Roller," for instance, evokes the patrols that nightly combed the plantation lands for runaway slaves. No less anxious to avoid discovery were those other slaves who had a moonlit rendezvous with a sweetheart:

> Oh, patter-roller down in de new-cut road,
>   Wid long bull-whip in his han';
> He ridin' 'long slow, an' he lookin' on de groun'
>   For fresh nigger track in de san'.
>
> .   .   .   .   .
>
> But, take keer, ladies! — jes' no use talkin', —
>   Dis nigger got to hurry up an' go;
> He kin dodge 'long close to de new-cut road,
>   An' slip by de patter-roller, sho'![104]

But we repeat that Macon is a lone voice amid the concert of those who chant the delights of the old-time plantation and strive for a moral victory over the conquerors of yesterday.[105]

3. The South's Revenge

As one can readily imagine, the plantation writers did not elaborate their defense either exclusively or even primarily for the edification of southern

---

[103] *Ibid.*, p. 137.

[104] "Patter-Roller," *ibid.*, pp. 126-27.

[105] Let us mention, nevertheless, the Georgian poet Frank Lebby Stanton (1857-1927), who was also employed for a time on the *Atlanta Constitution. Songs of the Soil* (1894), with a preface by Joel Chandler Harris, was followed by *Comes One with a Song* (1899), *Songs from Dixie Land* (1900), *Up from Georgia* (1902), and *Little Folks Down South* (1904). Unlike Page and Gordon, Stanton does not make systematic use of the Negro in his poems and, although a Southerner, he cannot be looked on as a militant. Some of his poems even constitute an implicit protest against the Negro's victimization by poverty and harsh treatment. Here and there one may note rather pronounced similarities with the poems of Dunbar. However, because of the date of these poems, many of which had appeared in the press before being published in book form, it would be rather difficult to establish the influence of Stanton on Dunbar, or vice versa.

readers.[106] Northern readers were also envisaged with the intent, which was achieved beyond anyone's wildest hopes, of rehabilitating the lost cause.

Immediately following the Civil War, Northerners lent a singularly ready ear to the renascence of the vanquished ideology. Even before the outbreak of hostilities, the abolitionists were far from having reached agreement on their program;[107] by the time hostilities had ceased, their ardor was considerably diminished, and during the Gilded Age people's minds were being worked on by appeals that had no connection with the humanitarian ideal.

Speaking on the topic of the New South to a New York audience in December, 1886, Henry W. Grady,[108] a Georgian and editor-in-chief of the *Atlanta Constitution*, asked in effect that the South be given a free hand to solve its own problems. "To liberty and enfranchisement is as far as the law can carry the Negro. The rest must be left to conscience and common sense. It must be left to those among whom his lot is cast, with whom he is indissolubly connected, and whose prosperity depends upon their possessing his intelligent sympathy and confidence."[109]

The northern businessmen, who had Congress practically in their pockets,[110] were only too ready to accede to this request. If the prosperity of a region where they had invested heavily[111] could be assured by their handing over to the South the task of regulating its relations with the Negroes, then the Northerners' eagerness not to endanger their investments dictated that they should grant the requested carte blanche. Surely they had enough to do in keeping their heads above water, with the West opening up and the North itself becoming ever more heavily industrialized. And, after all, the war had ended long ago; it made no sense to keep on fighting. Appeasement was in the wind, and the North gave its assent.

---

[106] Yet the South looked on the works of its postbellum writers as documents that justified slavery. See Hubbell, *The South in American Literature*, p. 802.

[107] On the disputes that reduced the efficacy of the abolitionists, see Elkins, *Slavery*, pp. 175ff.

[108] Grady presided over a group that undertook to work out the terms on which the South could once more be fully accepted within the nation. From this group emerged the slogan "the New South." See Henry Nash Smith, "The Second Discovery of America," in Robert E. Spiller et al., eds., *Literary History of the United States*, p. 791.

[109] Henry W. Grady, *Complete Orations and Speeches*, pp. 17-18. Cited by Gloster, *Negro Voices in American Fiction*, p. 6. Concerning this important New South speech, as it was called, see Logan, *The Negro in American Life and Thought*, pp. 176-78. For the reaction of the northern press, *ibid.*, pp. 178-82, 258-61.

[110] Roi Ottley, *Black Odyssey: The Story of the Negro in America*, p. 207.

[111] Brawley, *A Short History of the American Negro*, p. 154; also Logan, *The Negro in American Life and Thought*, pp. 176ff.

This is not to say that the Negro was forgotten, or that people no longer took an interest in him. At this time he actually enjoyed a vogue he had never previously known in the North.[112] The interest aroused by the original publication of *Uncle Tom's Cabin* took on fresh life after 1870, when the stage version of the work was presented.[113] By 1879 one could count some fifty companies who were touring the land with the play. Their number, twenty years later, has been estimated at over five hundred, and it was not unusual for an actor to appear in this one play throughout his life. The success was so great that new words were coined for the performance ("Tomming") and the actors ("Tommers"). Endemic, too, in the precise meaning of the word, was the popularity of the minstrel show, in which the so-called Negro song or "coon song" flourished. The impact of these shows, as we have already said, can hardly be overstated.[114]

Finally, this was the period when for the first time the general public in the North actually heard Negro spirituals, previously known only by repute, in particular through the accounts written by travelers returning from the South.[115] Discharged soldiers played a considerable part in making these melodies known, for many men had learned by heart or even transcribed these "jubilee songs," as they were then called.[116] In 1867 Thomas Wentworth Higginson, who had commanded the first Negro regiment during the Civil War, published one of the first articles ever written on spirituals.[117] But above all else it was the extraordinarily successful tour undertaken in 1871 by the Jubilee Singers of Fisk University that drew the attention of the country and the world to these unappreciated or unknown treasures of black folklore. Sometimes an audience was moved to tears, and everywhere the singers went the enthusiasm was immense. It was a natural supposition that the country would be affected for a long time to come by this impressive revelation.[118]

[112] On this vogue, which flourished roughly between 1870 and 1880, see Wittke, *Tambo and Bones,* p. 91; also Smith, "The Second Discovery of America."

[113] For everything concerning *Uncle Tom's Cabin,* see Birdoff, *The World's Greatest Hit,* and Moody, "Uncle Tom, the Theater and Mrs. Stowe."

[114] From 1848 on there appeared in a steady stream a considerable number of collections of minstrel songs. The rate of publication accelerated immediately prior to 1870. These collections were soon so widely distributed that hardly any American household was without one (Wittke, *Tambo and Bones,* p. 188). For a selection of titles of such collections, *ibid.,* p. 189, n. 67.

[115] Sterling A. Brown et al., eds., *The Negro Caravan,* p. 412.

[116] Wittke, *Tambo and Bones,* p. 189.

[117] Higginson, "Negro Spirituals," pp. 685-94. Higginson was not the first to write of the spirituals, since a short time before Fanny Kemble had mentioned them in her *Journal of a Residence on a Georgia Plantation: 1838-39* (1863).

[118] Gaines, *The Southern Plantation,* pp. 138-39. Many collections of spirituals were published in this period. Wittke, *Tambo and Bones,* p. 91, refers to that of Biglow and Main (New York, 1872) as immensely successful.

However, people were also beginning to see the Negro in another light. It went hand in hand with the cooling of abolitionist ardor that the Negro was no longer seen as an oppressed human being for whose freedom one must battle. In the eyes of northern citizens, who every day felt the tentacles of the industrial octopus a little tighter around their throats, the Negro came to incarnate instead the natural man who, because of his essentially rural activities, was still privileged to live, like the primitive, in harmony with the seasons. Purer and fresher than civilized man, he was, so to speak, the last vestige of an age of innocence, in a world plagued with financial scandals, corruption, and the cult of Mammon.[119] On the morrow of a murderous war, when everyone before all else desired appeasement, the Negro assumed the quality of an escapist dream incarnate. He is, if you will, more or less our French eighteenth century's "noble savage." Nevertheless, the northern city-dwellers were especially prone to find him a trifle more savage than noble when they witnessed the arrival of the first hordes of black immigrants from the South. For these new arrivals were likely to present acute new problems in municipal administration and in the daily life of the citizens.[120]

In this combination of circumstances, the northern public was more than ever willing to pay close attention to the southern case, and on that side there was no hesitation to make it known.

The first men to do so were the southern exiles, onetime wealthy planters ruined by the war, who hoped to achieve for themselves a less disastrous material situation among their adversaries of yesteryear. Such men were Richard Malcolm Johnson and Charles Colcock Jones, Jr., that dyed-in-the-wool Southerner who started a law practice in New York but returned to die in his native Georgia where, in obedience to his orders, he was buried in uniform and draped in the Confederate flag.[121]

But it was more especially the southern writers who put into circulation the southern thesis that the Negro, inherently inferior, had been satisfied with his lot in the feudal society of prewar days. For a full ten years these writers dominated the scene in every American periodical.[122] *Scribner's*

---

119 One may compare this notion with the views that were expressed about the Negro by Irwin Russell, note 53 above, and by Joel Chandler Harris, note 81 above. We will see below how widely read were the works of these two writers in the northern states.

120 Elkins, *Slavery,* p. 13.

121 Smith, in Trent et al., eds., *Cambridge History of American Literature,* II, 316-17.

122 "The Southern writers of fiction ... for a decade all but dominated the American magazines" (Smith, "The Second Discovery of America"). See also Lo-

Monthly, as recorded above, published among other works the poems of the Lanier brothers and of Irwin Russell. *Century Magazine* presented Thomas Nelson Page's first story, "Marse Chan," in 1884. In 1888 it was Century of New York that brought out Irwin Russell's posthumous collection of poems, and the following year Scribner's published Page's stories in book form. When the southern writers do not come to town, the Northern publishers seek them out at home. Appleton sent a special representative to Joel Chandler Harris in Atlanta with an offer to publish his Uncle Remus stories.[123]

The northern reading public, during the last twenty years of the nineteenth century, reveled in the literary apologias for plantation life, "for which readers all over the country showed an apparently insatiable appetite."[124] As these writings were read, the ideas they contained were also eagerly swallowed and accepted; as a result there was, in the North, a gradual but nonetheless total reversal of opinion. "If the Southern writers conceded to the nation the fact of union, the nation conceded to the South its view of the race problem."[125] "Abolitionism was swept from the field; it was more than routed, it was tortured, scalped, 'mopped up.' "[126]

Thus the plantation tradition won its return engagement with *Uncle Tom's Cabin,* and the former abolitionist Thomas Wentworth Higginson could be observed shedding warm tears over the death of a slaveowner in Thomas Nelson Page's "Marse Chan."[127] *"Graecia capta ferum victorem cepit!"*[128]

Moreover, this outcome had nothing fleeting about it, and one must await the years following World War I before seeing any definitive imposition of limits on the southern ideology. To cite the conclusion recently reached by the historian Stanley M. Elkins, the whole course of development had signified "the triumph, North and South, of a view on slavery whose basic premise was racial inferiority. At no time in American history

gan, *The Negro in American Life and Thought,* pp. 258ff., where he refers to *The Century* as particularly ready to welcome the Southerners; Smith, *Cambridge History of American Literature,* II, 315; Hubbell, *The South in American Literature,* p. 800; Gaines, *The Southern Plantation,* p. 63; and the M.A. dissertations of Howard University, Washington, D.C., on the Negro in the press of the period (references in Logan, *The Negro in American Life and Thought,* pp. 363-64).

[123] Hubbell, *The South in American Literature,* p. 789.
[124] Smith, "The Second Discovery of America." See also Hubbell, *The South in American Literature,* p. 859.
[125] Smith, "The Second Discovery of America."
[126] Gaines, *The Southern Plantation,* p. 62.
[127] Smith, "The Second Discovery of America."
[128] Horace, *Epistles,* Book II, Epistle 1, line 166. ("Conquered Greece conquered its savage victor.")

were Southern race dogmas so widely accepted throughout the entire nation as in the early years of the twentieth century."[129]

Returning to the purely literary domain, one has every right to believe that the relative ease with which the North accepted the thesis propounded by southern writers may be explained largely by the plantation school's having offered itself to the public as the southern wing of the regionalist movement, which reached its crest late in the nineteenth century. The two have in common many essential components. In one as in the other, the gaze is resolutely fixed on the past, a past whose glorious effulgence and wealth of charms are made all the more certain by the careful elimination of every shady element. So there is nothing to weigh down the imaginative flights of the reader who, to his heart's content, can center on this past his regrets and longings. In one movement as in the other, it may be noted that the background is filled with huge, stereotyped landscapes in front of which pose personages who themselves are almost always equally stereo-typical. And all these literary works are filled to the brim with dialect, either Negro, Pike, or New England. None of these dialects is entirely faithful to the original, nor is it meant to be. Finally, connecting with the escapist urge previously noted, these writers have a tendency to direct our attention to rural characters, especially frontier types. Now the South, at least until the Civil War, was a frontier region — lock, stock, and barrel.[130]

There is, consequently, sound reason to maintain that the banner of regionalism played no small part in lending plausibility to the plantation writers' thesis. On its path, this thesis met with a form of support no less effective for being involuntary, since none other than the Negro himself, through the interest he aroused, helped to sustain the ideology of his former masters.

Thus at the nineteenth century's close, when black poet Paul Laurence

---

[129] Elkins, *Slavery*, p. 13. This "reconquest" of the North by southern ideology stretches over approximately one-half century of American history, since it began shortly after 1875 and went on until after 1920. Thomas Nelson Page (1853-1922) was, as we have said, one of its chief architects, and it is rather curious that the movement petered out just as Page was dying. We cannot refer here to every stage in this crusade, but mention should at least be made of Thomas Dixon (*The Leopard's Spots* [1902]; *The Clansman* [1905]) and of the plea for racial purity, *The Passing of the Great Race* (1916), by the amateur ethnologist Madison Grant. Concurrently with the advance of southern ideology, there also developed a hostility to the Negro in the North. On this (attitude of the man in the street; segregation in Boston, the onetime capital of abolitionism; discrimination at Harvard; etc.), see Ray Stannard Baker, *Following the Color Line: An Account of Negro Citizenship in the American Democracy*, pp. 109ff.

[130] See especially W. J. Cash, *The Mind of the South* (Anchor ed.), Ch. 1, esp. p. 24.

Dunbar was beginning to write, credence was given to the same conception of the Negro in popular literature, in literature proper, and in vast
areas of American public opinion. This view resulted from many influences, the most important of which we have tried to characterize above.
The minstrels established the Negro as the nation's buffoon, and the
literary legend of the plantation portrayed him as an inferior creature satisfied to be treated as such. Neither of these portraits permits him to be
taken seriously, since the only fitting tones in which he can be depicted
are humor and pathos — or, even more accurately, sentimentality alone.
It was utterly unthinkable at this time that he should be depicted in any
other way; no one would have regarded the resulting work as genuine.
The racial stereotypes so widely accepted, in North and South alike, were
not simply the artists' fantasies. They had sunk their roots deep in the
political order and in the life of society.

Chapter Three: PAUL LAURENCE DUNBAR

> ... my sad people's soul
> Hidden by a minstrel smile.
> — Gwendolyn B. Bennett[1]

Paul Laurence Dunbar is probably the black poet it is most difficult to evaluate fairly, and one has a strange but inevitable feeling of embarrassment in turning to him. Even after the lapse of half a century, his contradictions and his complexity have yet to lose their disconcerting quality.

"Ambiguous" is the word that spontaneously occurs to anyone who sets out to characterize him, and the adjective does sum up the man and his work. Ambiguous, to begin with, is his popularity with whites and blacks alike; ambiguous, too, is this southern-style poetry written by a black man from the North a quarter-century after Emancipation; ambiguous, finally, is the destiny which decreed that he should pass into posterity, in spite of all, as a poet of his people.

But to be born black, and a poet, in the United States in 1872 — was that not ambiguous at the outset?

1. BIOGRAPHY

Childhood Years (1872-91)

The son of parents who had been Kentucky slaves, Paul Laurence Dunbar was born on June 27, 1872, in Dayton, Ohio.[2] His father, Joshua Dunbar,

---

[1] "Heritage," *Opportunity*, December, 1923, p. 371.

[2] The best biography is Virginia Cunningham, *Paul Laurence Dunbar and His Song*. It also contains the most complete bibliography on Dunbar (pp. 267-83). Still useful are the works by Lida Keck Wiggins, *The Life and Works of P. L.*

73

had been a plasterer on a plantation. Abandoning all hope of ever purchasing his freedom, he used the Underground Railroad to escape to Canada, and then returned to fight in northern uniform during the Civil War. In 1871 he was already advanced in years when he married, in Dayton, a young widow, Matilda Murphy, not yet thirty years old. Unlike his father, who was barely literate and had become embittered under slavery, Dunbar's mother had a remarkable personality. Witty and prepossessing, and with a certain taste for beauty which she had acquired in the home of her former masters, she excelled in telling stories of the old days. Desirous of an education, she had taught herself to read and write, and took enough time away from her work as a laundrywoman to follow several evening courses. She wanted Paul to profit by the education that had been denied his parents.

Thus hedged about by his mother, Dunbar grew up in a kind of special universe she had created around him, protecting him both against his father and against those outside who might threaten him because of his color.

Joshua Dunbar was an authoritarian, domineering individual, totally incapable of understanding a son whose mind soared aloft on the wings of fancy. There was never any love or genuine intimacy between them. While Dunbar often alluded to his mother, rarely does he mention his father, and then only in connection with some quarrel they had, as in "In the Morning,"[3] where the father rages at his young son 'Lias, who rebels

---

Dunbar, with biography pp. 19-136; and Benjamin Griffith Brawley, *Paul Laurence Dunbar, Poet of His People.* One may also consult with profit the psychoanalytical interpretation by Walker M. Allen, "Paul Laurence Dunbar: A Study in Genius," *Psychoanalytic Review* XXV, no. 1 (January, 1938), 53-82. Our biographical sketch is based in the main on these four sources. For the poems we cite Dunbar's *Complete Poems* (New York, 1955), which is the most readily available edition today and which also, like the Wiggins edition mentioned above, reproduces William Dean Howells's introduction to *Lyrics of Lowly Life.* Nevertheless, nearly one hundred poems are missing from all the so-called complete editions. A list (also incomplete, unfortunately) of these poems will be found in Cunningham, *Dunbar and His Song,* pp. 270-72. For these poems we refer, of course, to the original printing.

[3] *Complete Poems,* p. 307. See also "At Night," *ibid.,* p. 418. The following comments by Abram Kardiner and Lionel Ovesey, *The Mark of Oppression: A Psychosocial Study of the American Negro,* pp. 346-47, cast some light on the relationship between Dunbar and his parents. "Let us consider the instance of the male who does not desert the family, but stays on and lets his wife take up the slack. She works to supply the main support of the family while his sporadic earnings help occasionally. He is now definitely subordinate to his wife. Some of the histories indicate that under these conditions the man is submissive and unassertive, or he is overassertive and domineering over his children. . . . The common imprecations are indolence, good-for-nothingness and moral lassitude."

against paternal authority and seems utterly unable to do anything that could win his father's approval. The death of Joshua Dunbar in 1884 was assuredly a decisive event for the young poet, then twelve years old. For one thing, it obliged him to do manual labor, and so helped to increase his feelings of inferiority; for another, it strengthened his close dependence on his mother, a tie that he would never be able to shake off entirely.

Dunbar's earliest works date from the time when he was still a schoolboy in Dayton, and often the only black in the class. "An Easter Ode" was written in 1885, a few weeks before he entered the Methodist Church, and in 1888 Dayton's Republican newspaper, *The Herald,* published two of his poems, "Our Martyred Soldiers" and "On the River." These first indications of his literary ability helped the timid boy to find some compensation for his sense of racial inferiority. When he showed his poems to his teachers and friends, sometimes with a persistence that bordered on exhibitionism, he was looking for recognition from those around him, eager to be esteemed and regarded as an equal. But he found the encouragement he needed above all in the love of his mother. He soon took over the role and the responsibilities of his dead father and looked forward to supporting her. His mother had thought he might enter the ministry;[4] he would have preferred a career as journalist or lawyer himself. But when his secondary education ended in 1891, these dreams of the future were suddenly dissipated. Higher education was out of the question, in view of the family's limited resources, and the office jobs that his actual education might have put in his way were at that time almost all barred to persons of his race. So he had to accept employment as an elevator boy at four dollars a week.

Early Successes (1891-96)

His new occupation at least had the advantage of allowing him time to read, and he soon turned his elevator into a study. What did he read? The classics, of course, Tennyson being one of his favorites.[5] But his biographers depict him as alert above all to the literary successes of the day. He found them in *The Century,* not missing a single issue, and in other magazines and papers to which the syndicates, formed during the Civil War, distributed their weekly pabulum of journalistic poetry. These light pieces, frequently in dialect, are sometimes the work of James Russell Lowell, but

---

[4] His first novel, *The Uncalled* (1898), relates this very story of a rebellion against the ministry (which he is being constrained to accept) on the part of a young white man, Freddie Brent, in whom Dunbar paints his own portrait.

[5] Alice Dunbar also speaks of his liking for Lowell (*Paul Laurence Dunbar, Poet Laureate of the Negro Race,* p. 6).

more often of Eugene Field or James Whitcomb Riley, or of the less-known Ella Wheeler Wilcox.

Riley[6] above all seems to have impressed Dunbar, as he had impressed the whole nation. But no doubt the financial rewards, rather than the quality of his poetry, awakened in young Dunbar the ambition to emulate the Indiana poet laureate. Coldly and industriously he began to dismantle Riley's devices, with an eye to appropriating them, just as Riley himself had done with those of the *Farm Ballads,* Will Carleton's gold mine. The everyday philosophy, the tearful sentimentality, the sighs for the good old days, the longing for the farm, all presented in ordinary colloquial speech — there was a good market for that in the last decade of the nineteenth century. So Dunbar too will write poems that appeal to the public. These are the years when he turns out "A Banjo Song," "A Drowsy Day," and other poems whose highly significant titles are "The Ol' Tunes," "The Old Apple Tree," "The Old Homestead," and "An Old Memory," some of which even borrowed Riley's Hoosier dialect.

In June, 1892, the Western Writers Association met in Dayton, and Dunbar was asked by one of his former teachers to come and read, outside the regular program, some of his poems to the gathering. His talent made a marked impression, and a delegation was instructed to get in touch with him. He was asked for several unpublished poems; these appeared soon afterward, together with favorable comments about their author, in papers as far away as New York and Denver. In Denver, Riley himself happened to see them and, on November 27, he wrote a very kind letter to Dunbar, congratulating and encouraging him.[7]

But the great event of the year was the December publication of his first volume of poems, which he called *Oak and Ivy.* He managed to recover the printing costs within two weeks by setting out to sell most of the copies himself. They slowly made their way through the region and were reviewed in a number of papers. As a result, the poet received invitations to give readings of his poems.

His material situation continued, nevertheless, to be worse than uncertain. So he decided to try his luck in Chicago, where, in 1893, the World's Fair was being held. Thanks to Frederick Douglass, he found work in the Haitian pavilion. There he got to know James David Corrothers and James Edwin Campbell, young Negro poets like himself, and also the composer Will Marion Cook, with whom he would later collaborate in the music halls. But in the meantime his trip to Chicago had done

---

[6] See Dunbar's poem of homage to J. W. Riley (*Complete Poems,* p. 475), whom he praises for his simplicity, sentimentality, and didactic tone.

[7] For the text of this letter, see Cunningham, *Dunbar and His Song,* p. 74.

nothing to mend his finances — helped by the generosity of a Toledo lawyer, he barely succeeded in preventing the seizure of the house where he lived with his mother. The end of 1894 found him plunged in despair. To a friend he wrote on November 7: "There is only one thing left to be done, and I am too big a coward to do that."[8]

But the following year the horizon began to clear. *The Century* at last accepted three of his poems, "A Negro Love Song," "Curtain," and "The Dilettante," which appeared respectively in April, May, and July, 1895. It also happened about this time that *Oak and Ivy* attracted the attention of an influential Toledo doctor. Learning of the poet's poverty, this Dr. Tobey sent him money and then saw to it that a second volume of his poems was published. It is thanks to him that *Majors and Minors* came out at the beginning of 1896 and thanks to him, too, that these new poems were received by Robert G. Ingersoll and the actor James A. Herne, who in his turn called them to the attention of William Dean Howells.

Fame and Its Drawbacks (1896-1902)

Howells published in *Harper's Weekly* on June 27, 1896, a lengthy review of *Majors and Minors*.[9] So favorable was its tenor that suddenly Dunbar found himself famous. The literary agent with whom Howells put him in touch had him travel to New York immediately, and the publishing house of Dodd, Mead agreed to bring out a new collection of poems. These were *Lyrics of Lowly Life,* for which Howells wrote an introduction. This new volume bore Dunbar's reputation as far as England; it was decided to send him there early in 1897, to give poetry readings.

On his return to the United States he settled in Washington, where, as he had promised, Robert Ingersoll obtained a position for him in the Library of Congress. There he finished a partly autobiographical novel, *The Uncalled,* and a series of stories, *Folks from Dixie.* He had obtained the living documentation for the series from former slaves living in Howard Town, the capital's Negro quarter. Finally, he wrote the book for a musical comedy by Will Marion Cook, *Clorindy, or the Origin of the Cakewalk,* which opened at the Casino Roof Garden in New York during the summer of 1898.

[8] Cited by Wiggins, *Life and Works of Dunbar*, p. 41.

[9] "Life and Letters," *Harper's Weekly,* June 27, 1896, pp. 630-31. This article is reprinted in Cunningham, *Dunbar and His Song*, pp. 144-48. Concerning the impact made by this review, Van Wyck Brooks remarks that "Howells was perhaps the only critic in the history of American literature who has been able to create reputations by a single review" and records that, as a result of Howells's article, Dunbar received two hundred letters of congratulation (Van Wyck Brooks, *The Confident Years* [New York, 1952], p. 142, note).

Now that material prosperity and success were his, why did he almost secretly marry his beloved Alice Ruth Moore? It was in rather curious fashion that he had become acquainted with this young New Orleans elementary school teacher who, like him, wrote verses. For he had fallen in love with her three years earlier, upon seeing her photograph and several of her poems in a magazine. They had exchanged letters and had even celebrated a hasty betrothal just before Dunbar left for England. Yet, on one side as on the other, a great deal of hesitation had not been overcome. The bride's parents looked askance at the somewhat offhand way in which their daughter had fallen for a laundrywoman's son who was "black as sin," whereas Alice had an almost white complexion. Then, again, was their daughter going to marry a buffoon who got involved in minstrel shows like *Clorindy*? As for Dunbar, he was not sorry to postpone the moment when, perhaps with marked reluctance, he would set up a rival against his hitherto exclusive love for his mother. He and Alice were married in New York on March 6, 1898.

Late that year, under Alice's influence, he resigned from the Library of Congress and devoted himself entirely to writing. At the beginning of 1899 there appeared a new collection of poems, *Lyrics of the Hearthside*. That spring, Booker T. Washington invited him to Tuskegee; there Dunbar made his first fleeting contact with the South. In April, during a stay in New York, he fell gravely ill. First it was pneumonia, and then tuberculosis became evident. He had to undergo a serious operation and seek convalescence, first in the Catskills and later in Colorado. But he was the victim of his fame and could never find the rest he needed. He continued to write, publishing another novel, *The Love of Landry*, and a second volume of stories, *The Strength of Gideon*, in 1900.

In January, 1900, he set off hastily for New York in order to settle his differences with the actor Ernest Hogan concerning a new musical comedy. *Uncle Eph's Christmas* was written, like *Clorindy*, in collaboration with Will Marion Cook. The show had been in performance since Christmas, 1899, at the Boston Music Hall when Dunbar, probably at Alice's instigation, decided to withdraw his name. Alice was furious that he should continue to involve himself in minstrel shows; reviewers consequently referred to him as the "prince of the coon song writers."[10] So in Hogan's presence she made a frightful scene which Dunbar probably held against her in secret, though he forgave her at the time. From then on their marriage slowly deteriorated, quarrels became more frequent, and the stretches of fair weather were only intermittent.

[10] Cited by Cunningham, *Dunbar and His Song*, p. 204.

When Dunbar first fell ill, the doctors recommended spirits by way of a stimulus. With the return of his cough, he now had ever more frequent recourse to whisky, and his best friends began to talk about it. The situation turned to disaster on October 19, 1900, in Evanston. He arrived late, and quite drunk, for a recital in a Methodist church; one after the other his hearers left the church, disgusted. The press reported the incident. Alice was embarrassed, humiliated, and furious, but once more things were patched up between them.

A new novel, *The Fanatics,* reached the bookstores in 1901. Its theme was the fate of two lovers separated by parental fanaticism during the Civil War. In May of that year *Lippincott's Monthly Magazine* published his last novel, *The Sport of the Gods,* which dealt with the misfortunes of a Negro family that had left a little southern town to go to New York.

Despite his illness and despite the more and more frequent coughing of blood, Dunbar kept on working furiously, giving frequent recitals and supplying the magazines with stories and articles. To induce him to take a little rest, James Weldon Johnson invited him to spend a few weeks at his Florida home in March. In May he went for a rest to the Chesapeake shore. But immediately after his return he plunged once more into an excessive variety of tasks. The domestic situation was not improved by this, and in October Alice wrote her mother-in-law: "We quarrel all the time."[11] In January, 1902, when Dunbar had barely returned from a reading in South Carolina, yet another quarrel broke out; this time Alice threw him out of the house. They never saw each other again.

The End (1902-6)

Upon leaving Washington, Dunbar first went to New York, where he finished writing a new musical comedy, *In Dahomey.* Then he took up residence in Chicago with his mother. "I am greatly discouraged," he wrote, "and if I could do anything else, I should give up writing. Something within me seems to be dead."[12] Nevertheless, he continued to give the requested readings at numerous places in that part of the country.

May, 1903, found him in Boston, where Alice had lived before their marriage. All of a sudden he felt he wanted to see her again. He wrote her, and begged old friends to intervene on his behalf. But it was all in vain — Alice remained deaf to his appeals.

A new volume of poems, *Lyrics of Love and Laughter,* appeared in 1903, and also a collection of stories, *In Old Plantation Days.*

[11] *Ibid.,* p. 226.
[12] In a letter dated July 27, 1902, cited by Wiggins, *Life and Works of Dunbar,* p. 96.

Finding Chicago too noisy, toward the end of the year he moved to Dayton, the familiar setting of his childhood. There, as long as he lived, many friends found their way to his house.

Poems referring to his unhappy love appeared in *Lippincott's* and other magazines. They have such titles as "Forever," "Parted," and "Heartbreak Hill." Then came yet another volume of stories, *The Heart of Happy Hollow* (1904), and, the following year, his final sheaf of poems, *Lyrics of Sunshine and Shadow.*

When disease gained its last victory, on February 9, 1906, friends gave him the burial he had wished:

> Lay me down beneaf de willers in de grass,
> Whah de branch'll go a-singin' as it pass.
>   An' w'en I's a-layin' low
>   I kin hyeah it as it go,
> Singin', "Sleep, my honey, tek yo' res' at las'."[13]

2. DUNBAR AND THE PLANTATION TRADITION

We have indicated above[14] the essential traits of that idealization of the past that has been baptized "the plantation tradition." It will be recalled that the southern writers who continued within this tradition after the Civil War were not alone in holding an optimistic vision of days gone by. Such a vision is shared by many writers in a period of waning romanticism; it is the reaction of the partisans of an old, agrarian civilization against the swelling tide of industrialism with all its evils. As such it is to be found, with a greater or lesser degree of prominence, in the regionalist writers, especially among popular poets like Eugene Field and James Whitcomb Riley — who had, as we have seen, a decisive influence on Dunbar. But for the southern writers this vision is the last tremor of the plantation system, and thus of slavery, in opposition to the settlement that Reconstruction tried to impose on the South. As such, it is of an undeniably retrograde nature.

Dunbar runs the gamut of this backward-looking optimism, from mere praise of the good old days to the actual hymning of the Old South. This latter aspect must necessarily occupy the center of our attention, for it is important that we know to what degree it may be inferred that Dunbar had adopted a certain philosophy of history — important since he is in fact no neutral or foreign observer who takes a stand before certain historical facts in which he had no direct involvement. To the contrary,

---

[13] "A Death Song," *Complete Poems*, p. 228.
[14] See Ch. 2 above.

Dunbar is the son of former slaves who had felt slavery's yoke; yet he is willing to use the same colors as did his former masters to depict conditions in the Old South.

Dunbar and the Plantation

Following in the footsteps of Stephen Foster and Thomas Nelson Page, Dunbar does indeed offer us, for the most part, pleasing views of the old plantation. The masters are kind, the slaves are happy and filled with devotion, and as they give expression to their reciprocally tender feelings, they both feel how the tears spring to their eyes.

"A Corn Song" is the very embodiment of such traditional stereotypes. The master is sitting on the big white veranda, which is bathed in the warm light of the setting sun; in the distance one can hear the song of the slaves as they return from the cornfields, physically weary but light of heart and holding their heads high. The inevitable tear falls in the final stanza:

> And a tear is in the eye
> Of the master sitting by,
> As he listens to the echoes low-replying
> To the music's fading calls . . .[15]

Only seldom does the master voice his displeasure, as in the dialect poem "Spring Fever."[16] At that, it is but a passing mood, for he knows that spring, the rascal, is responsible for the indolence that seizes men and beasts every year at this same time.

Much more often it is a smiling master, like that of "A Back-Log Song,"[17] who during the Christmas celebrations watches with patent satisfaction the happiness of his slaves, whose hearts overflow with joy.

A place is also reserved in the picture for the black mammy, who is devoted to the master's children and sings them lullabies,[18] and for the "uncle" who has the essential role, and enjoys the unvoiced delight, of telling them stories just like Uncle Remus's, in which the little animals use their cunning to defeat the stronger, bigger ones.[19]

When the masters are absent, the slaves idle away the sunlit hours courting the girls or, at night, dancing to the sound of the banjo while the moon

[15] *Complete Poems*, p. 94.

[16] *Ibid.*, p. 283.

[17] *Ibid.*, p. 229.

[18] "Lullaby" (*ibid.*, p. 230) is addressed to a white child. "Scamp" (p. 388) conveys the tenderness the black mammy feels for her own child.

[19] "A Cabin Tale: The Young Master Asks for a Story," *ibid.*, p. 247. See also "The Visitor" (p. 284). These two poems may be compared with Gordon's "God Knows," Thomas Nelson Page and Armistead C. Gordon, *Befo' de War*, p. 56.

bathes the cottonfields in its light.[20] In addition to dancing, the slaves' favorite sports (in which they receive the full encouragement of their masters) are fishing and hunting opossums and 'coons.[21]

Dunbar has a special liking for happy domestic scenes in which, after a day of strenuous labor, the slave who has no quarrel with his lot[22] idealizes men and their surroundings. Thus the couple in "Chrismus Is A-Comin" bend adoringly over their child and find him more handsome than any of the master's children:

> Ol' Mas' Bob an' Missis
> In dey house up daih
> Got no chile lak dis is,
> D' ain't none anywhaih.[23]

And when the slave in "Long To'ds Night" returns home at day's end with a song on his lips,

> De cabin's lak de big house, an' de fiah's lak de sun;
> His wife look moughty lakly, an' de chile de puttiest one.[24]

To do Dunbar justice, however, it must be noted that on occasion he does offer us brief glimpses of the miseries of slavery which the plantation

[20] "A Warm Day in Winter," *Complete Poems*, p. 269; and "A Frolic," *ibid.*, p. 325.

[21] See "Fishing," *ibid.*, p. 276; "Expectation," p. 209; "Hunting Song," p. 242; "Snowin'," p. 271. For rabbit hunting, see "Winter's Approach," p. 421. The Negro's liking for opossum is a theme shared by the plantation tradition and the minstrels, and Dunbar pays it ample homage; see "Possum," p. 226; "Christmas," p. 446; "A Preference," p. 347; "The Party," lines 73-74, 82, p. 137. In "A Coquette Conquered," p. 98, Dunbar plunges headlong into the ridiculous with his account of a youthful coquette, who had long spurned the advances of one of her suitors, but yields now that she is offered an opossum. Another related cliché is that of the gormandizing Negro, for which see "The Visitor," p. 284; "Reluctance," p. 330; "De Way T'ings Come," p. 367; also "Signs of the Times," p. 122; "Soliloquy of a Turkey," p. 275; "The Capture," p. 453. Also related is the theme of the Negro thief, especially the chicken thief, as in "Accountability," p. 6. From the same source comes the theme of the Negro ignoramus, which finds expression in the last two lines of "A Letter," p. 244, and in "A Love Letter," p. 440. We have written at some length about these not very interesting themes in our Ch. 2, and the references given above will serve to convey the extent to which Dunbar borrowed from his forerunners. Though he usually utilizes them in an inoffensive way, the fact that they are found in his poetry in itself bears witness to the influences that we have signaled elsewhere in these pages.

[22] "Song," stanza 2, lines 1-2, *ibid.*, p. 286; and "Twell de Night Is Pas'," stanza 3, lines 1-2, p. 415, are particularly concerned with the farmworker who is contented with his lot. For the modest pleasures of rural life, see "Time to Tinker Roun'," p. 215; "At Candle-Lightin' Time," p. 251; "Noddin' by de Fiah," p. 326.

[23] *Ibid.*, pp. 246-47.

[24] *Ibid.*, p. 303.

literature had totally ignored. But they are only glimpses, and their effect
is rapidly eliminated by the resurgence of optimism.

Typical in this respect is "Parted," the lament of a slave who has been
separated from his beloved because his master has just sold him and a boat
is taking him deeper into the South. To appreciate Dunbar's handling of
this theme, one must bear in mind the terror that the threat of being "sold
down the river" aroused in a slave, for this was the direst punishment that
could be inflicted on the insubordinate.[25] But the slave of "Parted" goes
off almost light-hearted, confident that God, who can read lovers' hearts,
will one day bring them together again:

> De breeze is blowin' 'cross de bay,
>   My lady, my lady;
> De ship hit teks me far away,
>   My lady, my lady;
> Ole Mas' done sol' me down de stream;
> Dey tell me 't ain't so bad's hit seem,
>
>   .   .   .   .
>
> I'll stan de ship, I'll stan de chain,
> But I'll come back, my darlin' Jane,
>
>   .   .   .   .
>
> God knows ouah hea'ts, my little dove;
> He'll he'p us f'om his th'one above.[26]

To see things in this way is, as Sterling Brown discerningly remarked in
his consideration of this poem, "a cruel misreading of history."[27]

Less grave is the separation suffered by Samuel in "When Sam'l Sings."[28]
His wife works on a plantation twenty miles away, and he returns gay as
a lark every time he has been able to visit her.

A few sad notes, along with tears of pity, are to be observed in "A Banjo
Song." But the weariness of the slave overwhelmed by distress and wor-
ries cannot long resist the consoling tones of the banjo. It is on this com-
forting note that Dunbar ends, as if the slave's tears must inevitably yield
to a happy smile:

>   .   .   .   .
>
> Oh, dere's lots o' keer an' trouble
> In dis world to swaller down;

---

[25] See, for example, Roi Ottley, *Black Odyssey: The Story of the Negro in America*, p. 133.

[26] *Complete Poems*, pp. 234-35. For a similar consoling reflection, see "A Plantation Melody," stanzas 3 and 4, *ibid.*, pp. 313-14.

[27] Sterling A. Brown, *Negro Poetry and Drama*, p. 33.

[28] *Complete Poems*, p. 339.

> An' ol' Sorrer's purty lively
>   In her way o' gittin' roun'.
>
> . . .
>
> Oh, de music o' de banjo,
>   Quick an' deblish, solemn, slow,
> Is de greates' joy an' solace
> Dat a weary slave kin know![29]
>
> . . .

The idealization of the plantation is even more obvious when Dunbar has a former slave speak, with a change in the viewpoint that makes the poem a panorama of the past. An excellent example of this process is provided by "The Old Cabin," in which a former slave, lying sleepless, recalls the days of slavery:

> In de dead of night I sometimes
>   Git to t'inkin' of de pas'
> An' de days w'en slavery helt me
>   In my mis'ry — ha'd an' fas'.
> Dough de time was mighty tryin',
>   In dese houahs somehow hit seem
> Dat a brightah light come slippin'
>   Thoo de kivahs of my dream.
>
> An' my min' fu'gits de whuppins,
>   Draps de feah o' block an' lash
> An' flies straight to somep'n joyful
>   In a secon's lightnin' flash.
> Den hit seems I see a vision
>   Of a dearah long ago
> Of de childern tumblin' roun' me
>   By my rough ol' cabin do'.[30]

And he goes on through another four stanzas to recollect the good aspects of the dead era: his old hut, which in his eyes was much more beautiful than the splendid house of his masters; his old friends, who in the evening came to his house to enjoy themselves and play the banjo; and above all else the laughter and jokes which constituted the essential beauty of those good old days. The poem is no different from many others in its evocation of these details, and in its use of the same clichés.

---

[29] *Ibid.*, pp. 30-32. For other examples of consolation through banjo and violin, see "Blue," p. 416; "Christmas," p. 446; and "My Sweet Brown Gal," p. 282. It should be noted that this is yet another theme often used by the minstrels and the plantation writers.

[30] *Ibid.*, p. 429.

But to the poet's credit is a certain integrity in his presentation of the subject. This sets him off markedly from the plantation school and is something that, to the best of our knowledge, has not hitherto been stressed. For, in the first two stanzas of the poem cited above,[31] Dunbar actually indicates in the clearest possible way just what the function of memory is: spontaneously suppressing the evil recollections, while hastening to dredge to the surface only the happiest images. In this way he appears to be saying, as though to defend himself in advance, that *he* cannot be accused of having kept silent about the horrors of slavery; that, on the contrary, his poems are extraordinarily faithful renderings of the psychology of the former slave, who has a natural tendency to forgive and forget. Nor does it seem to us that there is any bad faith in Dunbar's implicit defense. Yet it cannot be denied — and here, in spite of everything, the poet may deserve reproof — that the reader takes away with him a much stronger impression of the agreeable recollections, since the others occupy no more than one of the six stanzas in the poem.

In "The Voice of the Banjo," that instrument itself begins to sing the delights of the former era to the old man sitting alone in his cabin. There were the nighttime songs when the day's work was over, the joy of finding the wife at the hearthside and of dandling the little one on his knees, and also the softness of those southern nights when the moon spread its silvery gleams over the stretches of sand. The voice of the banjo ends on the suggestion that these memories of the past provision us for our journey into the future:

So the future cannot hurt us while we keep the past in mind.[32]

As for "Speakin' o' Christmas,"[33] a poem more in the manner of Riley than of Page, it looks back longingly on the old-time Christmas for the reasons that always lend glamour to times past, while "Long Ago,"[34] more or less in the same vein, has a certain relationship with the spirit of "Auld Lang Syne."

On the basis of this, it might seem that Dunbar had simply borrowed from the literature of his own day, especially from Riley, the general notion that the good old days were preferable to the present. He perhaps fused this nostalgia with an idealized picture of the plantation borrowed

---

[31] Stanza 1, lines 6-7; stanza 2, lines 1-4.
[32] *Ibid.*, p. 199.
[33] *Ibid.*, p. 125.
[34] *Ibid.*, p. 312.

from the Page school, which also expressed much the same nostalgia, though for reasons of its own.[35] In addition, we have noted that Dunbar tended to tone down the more outrageous features of the plantation school's portrait, particularly by inserting brief evocations of slavery's abominations.

Unfortunately, there are other poems whose topic is not the antebellum plantation but the post-Emancipation one. Here Dunbar, in a way that is astonishing for a man of his race, espouses the southern ideology[36] as we have seen it expressed in *Befo' de War* by Page and Gordon.

The most equivocal poem in this group is undoubtedly "When Dey 'Listed Colored Soldiers."[37] The blue uniform of the North and the grey uniform of the South are juxtaposed, without its being entirely clear that the poet's sympathies are not extended to both. The happenings evoked by the young Negro woman in the poem occurred during the Civil War, after the Emancipation Proclamation, on a plantation situated in territory already occupied by the northern armies. She recalls the grief she felt at the imminent separation when 'Lias, her beloved, came to tell her that he was leaving to fight on the northern side. At first she would have wished to stop him, but how could she not approve his decision to earn his newly granted liberty on the battlefield? And she felt proud of him, standing so strong and so handsome in his splendid blue uniform with its shiny buttons!

Her two masters, father and son, had already left for war, wearing grey uniforms, of course; seeing her mistresses cry at the news of their death, she had cried also. Then she was told that her 'Lias, too, had fallen somewhere in the South.

One cannot fail to see that Dunbar has chosen a highly delicate topic, since he lets his young freed girl shed the selfsame tears for her masters and her 'Lias, whose status in life and whose loyalties were in conflict, without making any mention of the personal affection she might have felt for any of them. Here Dunbar is dancing on a tightrope, and he sheds a revealing light on the art of compromise he had to practice to avoid angering either of his two publics, the black or the white. The reader can but lament his embarrassment.

"The News"[38] takes up once more, in the most literal fashion, the situations, technique, and southern-style ideology of *Befo' de War,* with

[35] See our Ch. 2.

[36] In addition to the poems that will be discussed below, see "To the South: On Its New Slavery," which will be considered at greater length later in the chapter.

[37] *Complete Poems,* p. 293.

[38] *Ibid.,* p. 218.

the goal of demonstrating the boundless loyalty of the blacks to their masters, and the kindness of the masters to them. Dunbar's poem, like those of Page and Gordon, adopts the procedure of having a black utter the monologue, to enhance the plausibility of identifying the character with the sentiments attributed to him.

The speaker is an old slave whose working days are over. The poem does not reveal whether or not he has been set free, for the question of his freedom never arises. The war had not yet ended, and in the first stanza the old servant anxiously interrogates those around him, for their strange behavior leads him to suppose that they are hiding bad news from him. These four lines suffice to delineate and characterize a whole social nexus, with greater force and persuasiveness than a whole treatise could have achieved. Yes, his master has died in battle. They finally break the news to him. Yet with what a sense of delicacy, and with what stratagems, the attempt was made to hide from the faithful old servant, as from the most venerable member of the family, the bad news that might have caused his death, in view of the love his kind master had inspired in him!

Then it is learned that one of the master's soldiers had returned with the news of his death. What, asks the old slave, how can the wretch bear to remain alive, now that his leader is no more? The old man himself would have gone off to fight with his master — wearing, of course, the grey uniform — but he had been made to see that he was too feeble, and he had promised to look after his young master. But now there is no more reason for him to remain alive. So, after two lines interrupted by death rattles, he goes to his reward in the last stanza!

"The Deserted Plantation" describes the distressing spectacle of a plantation ravaged by war. The tools lie rusting in a corner and the fields where once the golden corn swayed in the wind are now invaded by weeds. Swallows have taken over the buildings; silence reigns in the master's big house, once crowded with guests, and in the huts of the slaves where the happy sound of the banjo is no longer heard. Despite this picture of desolation, the former slave has returned out of a sense of loyalty, as one seeks out a home where one has known true happiness. He judges harshly the ingratitude of the other slaves who have not followed his example:

> Gone! not one o' dem is lef' to tell de story:
>> Dey have lef' de deah ole place to fall away.
> Couldn't one o' dem dat seed it in its glory
>> Stay to watch it in de hour of decay?
> Dey have lef' de ole plantation to de swallers,
>> But it hol's in me a lover till de las';

Fu' I fin' hyeah in de memory dat follers
All dat loved me an' dat I loved in de pas'.
So I'll stay an' watch de deah ole place an' tend it
Ez I used to in de happy days gone by.[39]

. . . .

Too evident to require the least stressing is the thesis that the self-pro-
claimed war of liberation destroyed the genuine happiness that Negroes
had enjoyed under the old dispensation, turning them into rootless creatures who instinctively make their way back to the home, even though it is
ruined, of those who had been their real friends. *Ubi bene, ibi patria!*

The scene evoked by "Chrismus on the Plantation" is a dreary Christmas
Eve. On that day the old master, impoverished by the war, calls together
the freedmen he has been paying since the Emancipation and informs
them that he is ruined. He is forced to sell the plantation, and it breaks
his heart that he must dismiss them. The former slaves shed tears, and in
the master's eye too a tear glistens.

At this moment Ben steps forward to speak in the name of them all.
Does their master, he asks, think they have no gratitude? Now that he
is poor, are they going to forget all his past kindness? If that is the effect
liberty has, well, let Mr. Lincoln take back "his" liberty! Come what may,
they will never abandon their master, and even if he cannot pay them, the
strength of their arms will still be able to obtain from the old plantation
everything they need to support everyone:

Er in othah wo'ds, you wants us to fu'git dat you's been kin',
An' ez soon ez you is he'pless, we's to leave you heah behin'.
Well, ef dat's de way dis freedom ac's on people, white er black,
You kin jes' tell Mistah Lincum fu' to tek his freedom back.
We gwine wo'k dis ol' plantation fu' whatevah we kin git,
Fu' I know hit did suppo't us, an' de place kin do it yit.[40]

Thus, as tears fill the master's eyes and a smile lights up his lips, the
day that had started out so badly ends with the innocent joys of an old-
time Christmas.

Dunbar and the South

This apologia for the plantation, the main features of which have just
been depicted, verges on a neighboring theme which may also serve to
throw some light upon it. We refer to a certain longing for the South that

[39] *Ibid.*, p. 108.
[40] *Ibid.*, pp. 219-20.

finds expression even in Dunbar's earliest poems. The two themes cannot always be readily distinguished and are sometimes presented together, as we have seen with the longing for the plantation and longing for the days gone by. Nevertheless, they are markedly different in character. In the case of the plantation, the basis is the comparison drawn between past and present, while longing for the South springs from the opposition, sometimes only implicit but always undeniable, of North and South and extends beyond that to contrast urban and rural existence. This last aspect, on which we will have more to say, allows the theme to emerge from the purely ideological character it had, when connected with the plantation, and to acquire a certain documentary value concerning the psychology of the freedman who heads for the North.

This is the very context of "Goin' Back,"[41] which takes the form of a monologue in which a freedman, who has gone to live in a northern town after the Emancipation, explains how his homesickness, after thirty years' absence, is now taking him back to his native Kentucky. His case is presented as typical:

> It's the same ol' tale that I have to tell, —
> An' thar's few o' my race but knows it well, —[42]

The poem is not altogether devoid of southern ideology. It is insinuated that freedom was a divine gift in appearance only:

> Freedom, it seemed, was a gift divine.[43]

But the old freedman's disappointment is based above all on the contrast between North and South; this is not to the advantage of the former, which lacks the warmth and cordiality in human relations and does not have that charm of existence which has traditionally characterized the South:

> Well, I caught the fever that ruled the day,
> An', finally, northward made my way.
> They said that things were better North,
> An' a man was held at his honest worth.
> Well, it may be so, but I have some doubt,
> An' thirty years ain't wiped it out.
> Thar was lots of things in the North to admire,
> Though they hadn't the warmth an' passion an' fire
> That all my life I'd been ust to seein'
> An' thought belonged to a human bein'.

[41] *Oak and Ivy*, pp. 58-59.
[42] *Ibid.*, p. 58.
[43] *Ibid.*

> An' a thing I couldn't help but miss
> Was the real ol' Southern heartiness.
>
> .   .   .
>
> Oh, praise the Lamb, that I shall see
> Once more the land so dear to me.[44]

"After a Visit" praises the friendliness and hospitality of Kentucky people, who

> Feed you tell you hear the buttons
> Crackin' on yore Sunday vest.[45]

We have already noted the longing expressed in "The Voice of the Banjo" for the balmy, moonlit southern nights. In another poem, "To Her," the same theme is developed, but with an oriental touch reminiscent of Bayard Taylor or Richard Henry Stoddard:

> To-night we sit where sweet the spice winds blow,
> A wind the northland lacks and ne'er shall know
>
> .   .   .
>
> As in Arabia in the long ago.[46]

More convincing, because genuinely experienced, is the treatment of the same theme in "A Florida Night," which ends with the exclamation:

> Florida, oh, Florida's de lan' fe me —[47]

But the ultimate is assuredly reached when Dunbar expresses his longing for the South, and in places defends the Old South, in a poem whose stated aim is to protest against the "new slavery" practiced there since the Civil War, in the form of peonage, disfranchisement, and the lynching of blacks. This poem, "To the South: On Its New Slavery," actually contains Dunbar's outcry, "Oh, Mother South."[48] Coming after several praise-filled stanzas of the kind we have already cited, the cry acquires the significance of a heartfelt allegiance. It is impossible to escape the conviction that for Dunbar, as for so many of his brothers, the South is the black's true homeland.

This longing for the South seems to have had a more down-to-earth validity in some other poems, where it occurs together with the expression

---

[44] *Ibid.*, pp. 58-59.
[45] *Complete Poems*, p. 64.
[46] *Ibid.*, p. 440. For another "oriental" poem by Dunbar, see "In the Tents of Akbar," p. 363.
[47] *Ibid.*, p. 310.
[48] *Ibid.*, p. 355.

of hostility for the city. The objection might be raised that this feeling, far from being a mark of realism, is on the contrary pulled right out of the romantics' stock in trade. Yet this is not entirely the case, for the loathing of the city felt by the mass of those freedmen who had settled in the North, like the hero of "Goin' Back," must be interpreted in the first place as the expression of their disillusionment in contact with city life, and as a symptom of their difficulty in adapting to urban conditions. As a corollary, their longing for the South indicates no desire for romantic escapism or for a return to nature; it is simply a commonsense reaction in favor of a live-lihood less painfully gained and better remunerated.

In Dunbar's own case, his dislike of the city is also, assuredly, the re-action of the tuberculosis victim against the city's noise and pollution.

Now that these aspects have been noted, it may be added that this anti-city bias borrows its forms of expression from the romantics. In "The Voice of the Banjo," for example, the isolated cabin is situated "out of noisy traffic's way,"[49] and the old plantation of "To the Eastern Shore" wins back the emigrant slave with an alluring

> ... my sandy roads is gleamin' w'ile de city ways is black.[50]

As for Possum Trot, the idyllic little village celebrated in the poem of that name,

> The circuses don't come that way, they ain't no railroad line.
> It ain't no great big city, where the schemers plan an' plot.[51]

The poet himself speaks in "Bein' Back Home," and the delight he ex-periences in being home once more, probably after his Chicago sojourn of 1903, is due mainly to his having left the city:

> D'want to be too nigh to town.[52]

"Ballade," finally, voices his disappointment at seeing industrialization spread even to West Medford, Massachusetts, so that the river no longer is what it used to be when he first fished in it:

> Oh, once loved, sluggish, darkling stream,
>   For me no more thy waters swell,
> Thy music now the engines' scream,
>   Thy fragrance now the factory's smell;
>   Too near for me the clanging bell;

49 *Ibid.*, p. 199.
50 *Ibid.*, p. 329.
51 *Ibid.*, p. 236.
52 *Ibid.*, p. 428.

> A false light in the water shines
> While Solitude lists to her knell —
> Arcadia has trolley lines.[53]

In conclusion, let us note that in Dunbar's works one finds probably the earliest portrayals of the city Negro who seeks in outrageous garb some compensation for his sense of inferiority.[54] He is simply mentioned in "Li'l' Gal,"[55] but "Jealous" offers a complete portrait, while both poems speak of him as an unattractive and even dangerous type.[56] Not until the arrival of the Negro Renaissance, and particularly of Langston Hughes, will he be presented in poetry in a more sympathetic light.

The Poet and His Theme

The themes examined above are not all, strictly speaking, a forthright defense of the plantation and its slave economy. But we believe it has been demonstrated that the same psychological substratum is common to them all, and that the drift of the argument basically points to the conclusions reached by the plantation school. Even such a topic as anti-city feeling allies itself, when all is said and done, with the arguments advanced by a Grayson.

One may legitimately wonder how much Dunbar's idealization of ante-bellum society corresponded to his personal convictions. In other words, had Dunbar himself come to accept in some respects the Southerners' theories? Or was he merely bowing to the taste of the day and utilizing these views with an eye toward achieving speedy popularity?

The first thing to bear in mind is that Dunbar, who was born seven years after the Civil War had ended, had no extensive, direct knowledge of the South.[57] His longest period of residence there was probably the six weeks he spent with the Johnsons in Jacksonville, Florida, in 1901. Several of his readings had also taken him to the South, especially to Tuskegee and to South Carolina. He was also acquainted with a few Negro communities in Kentucky, as well as on the eastern shore of Maryland, where he often went while living in Washington.

[53] *Ibid.,* p. 332.
[54] For the psychological aspect of this phenomenon, see the cases cited by Kardiner and Ovesey, *The Mark of Oppression,* pp. 92, 109, 313, 349.
[55] *Complete Poems,* p. 338, stanza 3, line 1.
[56] *Ibid.,* p. 232.
[57] Nor does he appear to have been acquainted with country life. See, for example, "A Summer Pastoral," *ibid.,* p. 460, in which plowing goes on (stanza 5, line 1, and stanza 8, line 3) while the children hide in the haystacks (stanza 1, line 6).

But all that is scanty, compared to the fund of knowledge he obtained, at one remove, from former slaves living in the Howard Town section of Washington and, more especially, from his mother. She had always striven mightily to veil the most horrendous aspects of slavery, though well acquainted with them, when she told her son stories of those prewar days.[58] If she could have stopped him, he would never have so much as set foot in the South. "I never permitted Paul to go South until he became a man and I couldn't help it."[59] While Dunbar was still a child, her stories about the plantation concerned amusements and joyous gatherings, and the less happy memories were relegated to the time when he had grown up. One might hazard the guess that these later revelations made less mark on the consciousness of the young man than had the earlier stories on the fresher, more receptive mind of the child.

Whether he had them from his mother or from the old men in Howard Town, the pictures of the Old South that Dunbar had garnered were in either case already partially winnowed, perhaps deliberately, perhaps through the normal functioning of the memory mechanism. Thus, in contrast, the biased exaggerations of the plantation school may have appeared less shocking to him than they do to the twentieth-century reader. Yet it cannot be denied that Dunbar might well have eliminated the ambiguity in which he was content to leave the real feelings of the freedmen, for the tenderness they expressed for the South of another era was that of an old man for the familiar scenes of childhood, or of a country-dweller transformed into townsman for his bygone rural life — and not in the least a longing for the state of slavery.

Allowance must also be made for the sense of inferiority and the self-contempt that prolonged oppression inevitably imposes on the oppressed class. As a consequence, this class espouses in some measure the mythical portrait of itself drawn by the oppressors. This well-known phenomenon has often been described, notably by Robert E. Park.[60] In a somewhat different context, that of the relations between the colonizer and the native, here is Albert Memmi's characterization:

> Desired and disseminated by the colonizer, this degrading mythical portrait is finally, in some degree, accepted and experienced by the native. In this

[58] Cunningham, *Dunbar and His Song,* pp. 15-16.

[59] This is a statement made by the mother of the poet to a journalist, according to an unidentifiable newspaper clipping preserved in the Dunbar file of the Moorland Collection, Howard University, Washington, D.C.

[60] See, for example, Robert E. Park, "Die menschliche Natur und das Kollectiv-Verhalten" ("Human Nature and Collective Behavior"), Kölner Vierteljahrshefte für Soziologie, 6th yr. (1926-27), pp. 12-20.

fashion it acquires a certain reality and comes to form part of the real portrait of the native . . . The ideology of a ruling class, as one knows, is taken over in large measure by the subordinate classes . . . By accepting this ideology, the subordinate classes ratify in a certain way the role that has been allotted them.[61]

This phenomenon was assuredly at play in the case of Dunbar and his informants, so he cannot be blamed entirely for presenting his fellows in an unfavorable light. He simply presented them, quite often, as they really were.[62]

For an entirely fair evaluation, it would still be necessary to put oneself in the shoes of a poor but ambitious young Negro boy, who was also extremely timid and reserved, in the last years of the nineteenth century. What thoughts occurred to him when he heard Booker T. Washington declare to the New South that it would have "at all times the patient, sympathetic help"[63] of his race? And how could he fail to line up with those wise men who "understand that the agitation of questions of social equality is the extremest folly"?[64] Life had already taught him that one had to get on with white people, and hadn't he to rely on them to buy what he wrote?

It is easy to understand that the supporters of the New Negro movement felt embarrassed or even annoyed, twenty-five years later, by the servitudes that had hampered the first great poet of their race. But probity obliges us to disagree with one of them, when he speaks of Dunbar's "rebellion"[65] against the traditional stereotype of the Negro. Dunbar did not set out to challenge his era; to a very considerable extent he headed in the same direction. And the current was running in favor of accommodation and

[61] Albert Memmi, *Portrait du colonisé, précédé du portrait du colonisateur,* p. 116.

[62] This appears to be confirmed by the view of psychiatrists, as is shown by this remark on the black: "The slaveholder was not only his persecutor; he was also his benefactor and protector. This is the strange fate of a persecuted people who become acclimated to the passive and dominated role; they tend to identify themselves with their persecutor. The self-hatred of the Negro is the best testimony we can offer in evidence; he hates himself as the white man hates him (or as he thinks the white man hates him)" (Kardiner and Ovesey, *The Mark of Oppression,* pp. 351-52).

[63] Booker T. Washington, in an address delivered during the opening ceremonies of the Cotton States Exposition, September 18, 1895. See Washington, *Up from Slavery* (World's Classics ed.), p. 166.

[64] *Ibid.* Dunbar's approval of Washington is also clearly indicated in his sonnet, "Booker T. Washington" (*Complete Poems,* p. 341), and in "On the Dedication of Dorothy Hall, Tuskegee, Ala., April 22, 1901" (*ibid.,* p. 348).

[65] "His rebellion against the minstrel tradition," J. Saunders Redding, *To Make a Poet Black,* p. 61.

useful compromises, not toward futile outbursts of nationalism and rebellion.

Thus the plantation tradition in Dunbar's work must be looked on as essentially "the mark of oppression."[66] This theme of maladjustment is, in the last analysis, the price he paid for his fame.

3. RACE CONSCIOUSNESS AND HISTORY

It may seem paradoxical, at first glance, to speak of race consciousness in connection with a poet who, as we have seen, so closely espoused the attitudes of white people toward his own race. His attempts to make his avowed feelings match the norms of the plantation tradition and of the minstrels would indeed be the negation of all race consciousness, had not the poet sensed with poignant sharpness the ambiguities and the total disarray of the situation in which he found himself.

Following the Emancipation Proclamation it had slowly dawned on the Negro that he was, in fact, being relegated to the fringes of history. Slavery had struck him with "cultural amnesia"[67] — that is to say, it had left him rootless, without a country, without institutions, and, above all, without a past. Worse than that, while reluctantly conceding him a nominal liberty, his onetime masters continued their oppression by inflicting on him a past they had conceived, and in which the personality of the oppressed existed only in its subordinate relationship to the personality of the masters.[68]

In these circumstances, is it surprising that Dunbar should have experienced unending bewilderment in his endeavors to place himself and his race in the historical context? Such an undertaking calls for a choice to be made at every step. This choice, which is tinged by reality's hues as much as it affects them, and is constantly being reoriented by the chooser's subjectivity, constitutes in itself a value judgment. The present cannot be evaluated without any reference to the past, and vice versa. Moreover, in the case that concerns us, to opt for one or the other inevitably forces one to take a specific cultural and racial attitude.

The strength of the emotional factors that tie Dunbar to the South and to everything it represents; the necessity of writing for a twofold public with differing requirements; the uncertainties of an era when the Negro's

---

[66] The title of the work by Kardiner and Ovesey.

[67] The expression is used by Memmi, *Portrait du colonisé*, p. 135.

[68] On the mentality of the freedman, viewed in this perspective, see W. T. Fontaine, "The Mind and Thought of the Negro of the United States as Revealed in Imaginative Literature, 1876-1940," *Bulletin of Southern University* (Scotland-ville, La.) XXVIII, no. 3 (March, 1942), 8ff.

political and social status was rapidly evolving and, sometimes, beating a retreat — all these things made it highly distressing, if not entirely impossible, for the poet to make such a choice. Through all the hesitations, ambiguities, and differences that mark his evaluation of both past and present, what chiefly becomes apparent is the consuming urge to equality and integration in the mainstream of American national history.

Past and Present

By taking over and adopting a considerable portion of the plantation tradition, Dunbar was already manifesting a certain attitude toward the problem of the past. But fundamentally he realized that this was a way of deceiving himself, and no more than an escape from the distressing features of the present. So this past seemed to him, at one time and another, to be a devil's gift that followed him like a specter and which not even the passage of time could exorcise:

> The past which held its share of bitter pain,
> Whose ghost we prayed that Time might exorcise,
> Comes up, is lived and suffered o'er again . . . [69]

In those all too rare moments when Dunbar is himself (that is, when he becomes conscious of his race), he sees the past in a very different light from the idealized plantation picture. His "Ode to Ethiopia," printed in his first volume, apostrophizes Ethiopia as the incarnation of the black race:

> I know the pangs which thou didst feel,
> When slavery crushed thee with its heel,
>   With thy dearest blood all gory.
>
> Sad days were those — — ah, sad indeed![70]

In a poem written five years before his death, he makes mention of

> . . . the midnight of the gloomy past . . .
> . . . the sorrows of departed years . . .[71]

and, by way of antithesis, regards the present with an exaggerated optimism:

> The plant of freedom upward sprung,
> And spread its leaves so fresh and young —
>   Its blossoms now are blowing.[72]

[69] "Ere Sleep Comes Down to Soothe the Weary Eyes," *Complete Poems*, p. 3.
[70] *Ibid.*, p. 23.
[71] "On the Dedication of Dorothy Hall," *ibid.*, p. 348.
[72] "Ode to Ethiopia," *ibid.*, p. 23.

Flowers of charity, peace and devotion
   Bloom in the hearts that are empty of strife;
Love that is boundless and broad as the ocean
   Leaps into beauty and fulness of life.[73]

He actually goes on to describe the present as the advent of the golden age.[74]

These contradictions cannot be explained as due entirely to an evolution in the poet himself. Yet we know that his view of the present grew gloomier in his last years, as shown by a number of poems in the 1903 collection.[75] In those difficult times he turned beyond the grave to invoke Frederick Douglass, whom he looked on as the great leader of the race, and to ask him for help:

Ah, Douglass, we have fall'n on evil days,
   Such days as thou, not even thou didst know,

    . . .

Oh, for thy voice high-sounding o'er the storm,
   For thy strong arm to guide the shivering bark,
The blast-defying power of thy form,
   To give us comfort through the lonely dark.[76]

"Slow through the Dark" envisages the progress of the black race as a slow ascent through the shadows, whose very density appears to the poet to herald the nearness of the summit:

Slow moves the pageant of a climbing race:
   Their footsteps drag far, far below the height,
   And, unprevailing by their utmost might,
Seem faltering downward from each hard won place.

    . . .

Heed not the darkness round you, dull and deep,
   The clouds grow thickest when the summit's nigh.[77]

In "By Rugged Ways," the black people go along rocky roads as they unseeingly march through the dark toward the light:

[73] "Ode for Memorial Day," *ibid.*, p. 36.
[74] "The golden present" ("On the Dedication of Dorothy Hall," *ibid.*, p. 348).
[75] "The darker side of the problems of the race life was being brought home more and more forcibly to him as he grew older," remarked the poet's wife, with reference to the poems "Slow through the Dark" and "By Rugged Ways" (Dunbar, "The Poet and His Song," in *Dunbar, Poet Laureate of the Negro Race*, p. 17).
[76] *Complete Poems*, p. 339.
[77] *Ibid.*, p. 344.

> By rugged ways and thro' the night
> We struggle blindly towards the light;
> And groping, stumbling, ever pray
> For sight and long delaying day.[78]

The same idea is expressed by "Joggin' Erlong"[79] in a lighter tone and with the familiarity of dialect.

These poems, so modest in presentation, are important in our eyes for the changed perspective they reveal in Dunbar and for the kind of awakening of a more precise historical sense that can be divined. Here the happy days are no longer placed in a past bathed in glory and borrowed from others, but in a future which the black race can attain solely through its own efforts.

The Search for Heroes

Dunbar's eyes, in spite of this, remain fixed on the past, and he sets out to people it with heroes of his race, whether real or legendary. Nevertheless, his way of choosing them is a proclamation of loyalty to America rather than to his race, and their example serves as a plea to the nation that the black be recognized as a full-fledged American.

Here, to begin with, is a ballad that celebrated the black Samson. This giant, according to the legend recorded by C. M. Skinner in his *Myths and Legends of Our Land*, traversed the battlefield at Brandywine, scythe in hand, mowing down before him Cornwallis's redcoats and, adds Dunbar, leaving no work for the gleaners wherever he had passed as harvester of death. Firm in tone and meter, the poem breathes an authentic racial pride, though for some tastes it lays rather too much stress on the loyalty of the black hero,

> ... the loyal black giant
> Who fought for his country that day.[80]

He could fight for the freedom of his country, while his black brothers were still enslaved.

These reserves also apply to the poems that praise the black soldiers who wore the northern uniform and died in the Civil War, though Dunbar does seize this occasion to condemn (incidentally and in terms that remain very timid) those who perpetuate the unequal treatment of the two races.

In "The Unsung Heroes,"[81] the poet asks the god of battles to endow

[78] *Ibid.*, p. 350.
[79] *Ibid.*, p. 265. The same conception is found in "After While, a Poem of Faith," *ibid.*, p. 81.
[80] *Ibid.*, p. 334.
[81] *Ibid.*, p. 319.

some bard with the strength needed to celebrate these obscure heroes, "who feared the master's whip, but did not fear the fight," until the day arrives when all hatred between the races shall have disappeared.

"The Colored Soldiers," while it sings of "those noble sons of Ham . . . the gallant colored soldiers/Who fought for Uncle Sam," is unusual in addressing white America directly. The poet begins by reminding whites that, at the outset of the war, the services of blacks had been contemptuously refused. Then he mentions several battles in which black troops took part, and sketches a savage portrait of the combatants:

> And like hounds unleashed and eager
> For the life blood of the prey,
> Sprung they forth . . .[82]

The final two stanzas broach the question of equality of the races:

> They were comrades then and brothers,
> Are they more or less today?
>
> .   .   .   .
>
> They were citizens and soldiers
>
> .   .   .   .
>
> And their blood with yours commingling
> Has enriched the Southern soil.[83]

But here too he persists in his timidity, expressing no open indignation at injustice and limiting himself to dropping hints.

He is more successful in the sonnet addressed to Robert Gould Shaw, the only son of a rich and famous New England family, who agreed to head the 54th Massachusetts Regiment, made up entirely of blacks. He and they were slaughtered while attacking Fort Wagner, near Charleston, on July 18, 1863. In this sonnet, Dunbar was able to disguise his emotion and restrain his bitterness and disillusionment, until in the last three words of the last line he gives them free rein. Why, he asks in a long apostrophe of the young hero, had he left family and studies to confront death,

> Since thou, and those who with thee died for right
> Have died, the Present teaches, but in vain![84]

"The Conquerors," finally, is a poem in memory of the black troops who fought in Cuba in 1898, during the Spanish-American War. This homage is only provisional, declares the poet, and he awaits the time when the

[82] *Ibid.*, p. 78.
[83] *Ibid.*, p. 79.
[84] *Ibid.*, p. 360.

nation itself, its voice for the moment "muffled and dumb, out of fear," can voice a gratitude "that the present yet knows not to ply."[85]

Again, all the soldiers in these poems are *American* heroes, not *racial* heroes — even if the black fighters in the Civil War happened to battle to free the slaves.[86]

What authentic heroes of the race can then be found in Dunbar's work? Alexander Crummell, the black missionary to Africans and builder of churches?[87] Frederick Douglass[88] and Booker T. Washington,[89] between whose achievements Dunbar scarcely seems to distinguish? This is truly a sparsely populated gallery of heroes, and one which does not go back very far in the history of the race since, actually, it coincides with the independence of the United States. Nor is there a genuine rebel among them, though Dunbar had sung the praises of men who refuse to compromise with injustice and stand alone as they brave the elements:

> Right arms and armors, too, that man
> Who will not compromise with wrong;
> Though single, he must front the throng,
> And wage the battle hard and long.
> Minorities, since time began,
> Have shown the better side of man;
> And often in the lists of Time
> One man has made a cause sublime![90]

But these exalted hopes come from a man easily swayed by conflicting impulses; they are a counterweight to his sense of inferiority and his frustrations. Dunbar's real heroes are those modest and conformist individuals who know and remain in the place to which the decisions of the majority entitle them:

> Not they who soar, but they who plod
> Their rugged way, unhelped, to God
> Are heroes . . .

·   ·   ·   ·

[85] *Ibid.,* p. 180.

[86] The same holds true for Lincoln, Whittier, and Harriet Beecher Stowe, to whom Dunbar also paid homage, in the poems "Lincoln," *ibid.,* p. 295; "Whittier," p. 28; "Harriet Beecher Stowe," p. 191. One could not expect that he would make Lincoln a champion of Emancipation, since this would falsify history. But it is to be regretted that the Whitter poem fails to allude to Whittier's anti-slavery struggle. Only Mrs. Stowe is presented as a true champion of liberty for blacks.

[87] "Alexander Crummell, Dead," *ibid.,* p. 181.

[88] "Frederick Douglass," *ibid.,* p. 7; "Douglass," p. 339.

[89] "Booker T. Washington," *ibid.,* p. 341; "On the Dedication of Dorothy Hall," p. 348.

[90] "Right's Security," *ibid.,* p. 120.

> 'Tis they whose backs have felt the rod,
> Whose feet have pressed the path unshod,
> May smile upon defeated care,
> Not they who soar.[91]

Between the intransigence of a Frederick Douglass and the modesty of a Booker T. Washington, he inclines toward the latter:

> God give to these within this temple here,
> Clear vision of the dignity of toil ...[92]

It would be no easy matter to interpret all this as the glorification of his race. All in all, Dunbar will not achieve the goals he proclaimed in the last stanza of his grandiloquent "Ode to Ethiopia":

> Our ears shall list thy story
> From bards who from thy root shall spring,
> And proudly tune their lyres to sing
> Of Ethiopia's glory.[93]

Dunbar and Racial Injustice

These aspects of Dunbar's personality also explain why he wrote so few poems protesting the injustice and violence that were victimizing ·his fellows. The poet was not unaware of the state of affairs, and had even suffered personally during a race riot in New York in July, 1900.[94] But if we overlook the kind of implicit protest to be found in the above poems that recall the deeds of Negro soldiers, there are only a few poems of outright protest.

The most lyrical of these is assuredly the poem inspired by the action of a young Negro woman, Mary Britton, a teacher in Lexington, Kentucky, who rose up in the state assembly and delivered a passionate speech against a bill providing for segregation in public transport. The rhetorical force of the first two stanzas echoes in some measure the indignation expressed by Milton in his sonnet on the slaughtered Piedmontese:

> God of the right, arise
>   And let thy pow'r prevail;
> Too long thy children mourn
>   In labor and travail.

[91] "Not They Who Soar," *ibid.*, pp. 27-28.
[92] "On the Dedication of Dorothy Hall," *ibid.*, p. 349. See also "Limitations," p. 410, in which Dunbar offers lavish counsels of modesty that are certainly addressed to his racial brothers.
[93] *Ibid.*, p. 24.
[94] Cunningham, *Dunbar and His Song*, pp. 209-10.

> Oh, speed the happy day
> When waiting ones may see
> The glory-bringing birth
> Of our real liberty!
>
> Grant thou, O gracious God,
> That not in word alone
> Shall freedom's boon be ours,
> While bondage-galled we moan!
> But condescend to us
> In our o'erwhelming need;
> Break down the hind'ring bars,
> And make us free indeed.[95]

Yet here too the protest remains indirect, for it is addressed to God and not to men, while the tone is that of prayer rather than denunciation.

Even less overt is the one poem that attacks lynching, "The Haunted Oak," in which the poet allows the oak to speak. The content is a story told to Dunbar by an old Negro of Howard Town whose nephew had been falsely accused of rape:

> They'd charged him with the old, old crime.[96]

The bloodthirsty Alabama mob had dragged him out of prison and hanged him from the branch of an oak tree. The branch had withered instantly, while the others continued to flourish. Dunbar's poem is well contrived, and, though the forcefulness of the protest is somewhat mitigated by the legendary trappings,[97] the poet in any event succeeded in imbuing the story with the mysterious atmosphere that envelops the punitive raids of the Ku Klux Klan. And he actually named, as the guilty parties, the local judge, doctor, and pastor:

> Oh, the judge, he wore a mask of black,
> And the doctor one of white,
> And the minister, with his oldest son,
> Was curiously bedight.[98]

At the time, this required a certain courage.[99] Indeed, at the very moment the poem appeared in *The Century* (December, 1900), the Negro was still

---

[95] *Oak and Ivy*, p. 30.
[96] *Complete Poems*, p. 356.
[97] Indeed, there appear to be reminiscences of Goethe's "Erlkönig" here. Dunbar may have known the poem in translation; *ibid.*, stanza 6.
[98] *Ibid.*, p. 357, stanza 11.
[99] For the limitations under which the Negro author labored during this period, see Charles Chesnutt, "Post-Bellum, Pre-Harlem," *The Crisis*, June, 1931, pp. 193-94.

widely regarded as an animal without a soul, and with less intelligence than a dog.[100] The few lines that Dunbar had sent to the *Chicago Record* the previous year, after the race riots in Wilmington, North Carolina, had made use of even more veiled expressions.[101]

Why didn't Dunbar protest more often and more boldly against racist excesses? Did he fear that too much frankness would lose him part of his readership, which was almost entirely white? There can be no doubt that financial considerations affected his attitude. But the pressure of public opinion cannot be held altogether responsible for the poet's failure to resolve the conflict of loyalties that was tearing him apart.[102]

In connection with this psychological entanglement, the outstanding work is certainly "To the South: On Its New Slavery." The title leads one to expect a protest directed against this new form of slavery, made up of disfranchisement, peonage, and the lynchings that became steadily more frequent as the South shook off its defeat. But a reading of the poem utterly disposes of such expectations. The first stanza, with its grammatical inadequacies, plunges us at once into total confusion.[103] Besides, the tone does

---

[100] Cunningham, *Dunbar and His Song*, pp. 207-8; and Charles Carroll, *The Negro, a Beast* (St. Louis: American Book and Bible House, 1900), p. 339.

[101] "Loud from the South, Damascan cries
Fall on our ears, unheeded still.
No helping powers stir and rise.
Hate's opiate numbs the nation's will.
Slumbers the North (while Honor dies!)
Soothed by the insidious breath of lies."
Cited by Cunningham, *Dunbar and His Song*, p. 185, from the *Toledo Journal*, December 11, 1898, which gave as its source the *Chicago Record*. These lines were never reprinted in any of Dunbar's collections of poems.

[102] Dunbar appears at times to have persuaded himself that discussions of the racial issue were pointless. "Trouble in de Kitchen" (*Complete Poems*, p. 445), which records such a debate, has partial recourse to the tale of the pot calling the kettle black: "Dey slurred each othah's colah and dey called each othah names" while the kerosene can pours "oil erpon the flames" and the canisters of seasonings on the shelf dig their elbows into each other's ribs. In the end, the fire reestablished harmony by going out, and so cooling the ebullition of the speakers. See also "Speakin' at de Cou'thouse," *ibid.*, p. 332.

[103] "Heart of the Southland, heed me pleading now,
Who bearest, unashamed, upon my brow
The long kiss of the loving tropic sun,
And yet, whose veins with thy red current run."
(*Complete Poems*, p. 352.)
It will be noted, first of all, that the relative pronouns "who" and "whose," though coordinated, have different antecedents. Nor is it easy to see, furthermore, why Dunbar marks off with commas the word "unashamed" in the second line. Should the South find it unbearable, and be ashamed, that the sun should implant a kiss on the poet's forehead, since he is a Negro? No more satisfactory meaning is arrived at by assuming that the South itself kisses the poet's forehead. The kindest thing one can say about this stanza is that it is not entirely clear.

not suggest protest but is, rather, that of a son speaking affectionately to his mother. The irresistible conclusion is that in his heart the poet had established a hidden equivalence between his mother in the flesh and this southern earth, uniting the two in the same excessive and almost unnatural love.

Any thought of reproach is soon abandoned, and the "new slavery" of the title yields to a mere "weakness"[104] in the body of the poem, with praise for the Old South far outweighing the blame. So we slip back imperceptibly into the plantation tradition. The two stanzas that contrast the happiness of the slave in the past and the despair of the freedman in the present treat the latter, and not the slave, as a pathetic prisoner:

> There was a time when, jocund as the day,
> The toiler hoed his row and sung his lay,
> Found something gleeful in the very air,
> And solace for his toiling everywhere.
>
> Now all is changed, within the rude stockade,
> A bondsman whom the greed of men has made
> Almost too brutish to deplore his plight,
> Toils hopeless on from joyless morn till night.[105]

In itself, this picture may not be entirely inaccurate; but, situated in this idealization of the old ways, its effect is annihilated. What is retained from the poem is the immense outpouring of tender feeling at the end, and the fictitious conflict between the poet and the South is thereby reduced to a harmless lovers' quarrel:

> Oh, Mother South, hast thou forgot thy ways,
> Forgot the glory of thine ancient days,
>
> . . . . .
>
> It cannot last, thou wilt come forth in might,
> A warrior queen full armored for the fight;
> And thou wilt take, e'en with thy spear in rest,
> Thy dusky children to thy saving breast.[106]

Nothing could more accurately depict the ambivalent nature and the real limits of Dunbar's racial consciousness.

4. THE POET OF THE PEOPLE

While ill at ease in its relationship with the major themes of race, Dun-

---

[104] Stanza 3, line 2, *ibid.*, p. 353.
[105] Stanzas 11 and 12, *ibid.*, p. 354.
[106] Stanza 18, lines 1-2, and stanza 19, *ibid.*, p. 355.

bar's personality was especially suited to harmonize with the more modest themes of the life of the people.[107] The *New York Times* called him "a true singer of the people — white or black."[108] This explains not only his precocious affinity with such poets as Riley, but also his more compromising kinship with the southern poets and the wordsmiths of the minstrel songs who had set out, earlier than Dunbar, to portray the Negro in their own fashion.

Not everything was false in those portraits. The minstrels had authentic Negro material as a foundation, and the poets of the South had utilized their personal acquaintanceship with blacks. Yet they all passed on and supported the presuppositions of a social system into which was built the black man's inferior status, the result too often being a biased or ill-intentioned caricature. From these ingredients, nevertheless, there had arisen the official portrait of the black, accepted without question and sanctioned by opinion throughout the country, since it recognized in this portrait its own notions and its own prejudices. It was so universally held that Dunbar could hardly have brushed it aside without losing at the outset any chance of attracting an audience.

Under what conditions did Dunbar come to terms with this mythical portrait? His debt to southern ideology has already been recounted. Still to be examined is his depiction of the people; this divides into the two aspects of speech and temperament.

The Problem of Dialect

To have the black farmworker talk "pidgin English" served not only to contribute an element of local color to the monologue he spoke on the stage;[109] it was also a subtle way of demonstrating that this person was poorly acquainted with the national language and even, perhaps, permanently incapable of speaking correctly. Furthermore — and this was no drawback — it was a ready source of sure-fire humor.

The Negro, for his part, conscious of his recently acquired status as a human being and a citizen, came to look on the situation differently. To begin with, he noticed that the "literary" language often diverged widely from his own habits of speech. Besides, the linking of this dialect to a certain number of myths concerning him quickly led him to the conviction

---

[107] In this connection, see "Common Things" (*Oak and Ivy*, p. 57) and "A Choice" (*Complete Poems*, p. 201).

[108] Kathryn M. Leigh, *The American Negro, 1877-1900, as Portrayed in the New York Times* (M.A. dissertation, Howard University), Ch. 4. Cited by Rayford Logan, *The Negro in American Life and Thought*, p. 318, p. 364, n. 3.

[109] See, on this topic, our Ch. 2.

that the dialect was itself a myth whose chief aim it was to ensure that the mark of oppression should attach itself to him indelibly.

There is no doubt that Dunbar himself shared this view, for more than once he defended his use of dialect on the grounds of necessity. "You know of course, that I didn't start as a dialect poet," he told James Weldon Johnson one day. "I simply came to the conclusion that I could write it as well, if not better, than anybody else I knew of, and that by doing so I should gain a hearing. I gained the hearing, and now they don't want me to write anything but dialect."[110] And Johnson thought there was a tone of self-reproach in what Dunbar said.

But Dunbar's declaration is in serious conflict with the actual facts. Let us see what these facts are.

His most successful biographer depicts him as very eager, from the age of nineteen, to detect from their ways of speaking the geographical origins of the people who used his elevator. He even noted their favorite exclamations, their slang expressions, and their character traits.[111]

This was when he read assiduously the poems of Field, Riley, and Lowell, and probably those of Russell and others as well, trying to grasp their techniques. So it is clear that he had a spontaneous interest in the phenomenon of dialect as such, and that when he comes to use it himself it will be out of choice,[112] and not from necessity.

His statements are also refuted by his first volume, *Oak and Ivy,* which makes heavy use of dialect.[113] The proportion is indeed less than in later collections,[114] and in such poems as "The Ol' Tunes"[115] it is the Hoosier dialect that predominates. But "Goin' Back"[116] is already an attempt to utilize Negro dialect, and in "The Chronic Kicker,"[117] most of which is in standard English, the spelling and the turns of phrase reveal a marked tendency in the direction of dialect.

[110] James Weldon Johnson, *Along This Way,* p. 160.

[111] Cunningham, *Dunbar and His Song,* p. 57.

[112] He had, no doubt, informed Alice of his liking for dialect, for in a letter dated May 7, 1895, she answers him as follows: "You ask my opinion about the Negro dialect in literature. Well, I frankly believe in everyone following his bent. If it be so that one has a special aptitude for dialect work, why it is only right that dialect work should be made a speciality." (Cited by Cunningham, *Dunbar and His Song,* p. 125.)

[113] See also note 118 below for "Lager Beer," a poem that precedes *Oak and Ivy* by two years.

[114] We have some five hundred poems by Dunbar, and about one-third of them are in dialect. A very considerable part of his fiction is also in dialect. On this subject, see Hugh Morris Gloster, *Negro Voices in American Fiction,* pp. 46-56 and *passim.*

[115] *Complete Poems,* p. 82.

[116] *Oak and Ivy,* p. 58.

[117] *Ibid.,* p. 36.

There appears to have been little awareness hitherto of Dunbar's interest in all dialect speech — or, to be more precise, the interest is mentioned but left unexplained.[118] Thus Sterling Brown finds it incomprehensible that he should have written in Irish dialect.[119] The poem he has in mind is, no doubt, "Circumstances Alter Cases."[120] Yet this offers no difficulty to anyone who has followed the succession of decisive influences experienced by Dunbar. We have already indicated that Irwin Russell let Scottish[121] and Irish[122] pastiches stand beside his Negro dialect poems. The same propinquity is firmly established on the minstrel stage.[123] Thus once again we are led to record the attraction that the southern poets and the minstrels had for Dunbar, and to recognize his indebtedness to them.

But it should also be mentioned that he endeavors, for the most part, to free his Negro dialect of the purely orthographical distortions and the gross mispronunciations that Russell, Page, Gordon, and above all the minstrels tended to pass off as the Negro's actual way of speaking. "His grasp upon folk-speech is generally sure," says Sterling Brown.[124] James Weldon Johnson also is convinced that Dunbar pushed the traditional Negro dialect to the outermost limits of what it could be made to do;[125] the study of those who preceded him,[126] as well as of his contemporaries,[127] inevitably leads us to make these conclusions our own, where his poetry is concerned.

[118] The only phonetic study of Dunbar's dialect is the dissertation by Ralph Glassgow Johnson, "The Poetry of Dunbar and McKay: A Study," Ch. 2, pp. 63-109, and Ch. 3, pp. 230ff. Johnson calls attention to the poem "Appreciation" (*Complete Poems*, p. 404) which is, he maintains, an attempt to imitate the Creole speech of New Orleans, while the mother in the poem is Dunbar's mother-in-law, seen through Alice's eyes. Allegedly, the reason why Dunbar did not continue to use this dialect was his hostility to his in-laws, and the existence of tensions between Alice and the poet. But Johnson's arguments are not persuasive, and some features might lead one to believe just as readily that what was aimed at was an imitation of German dialect on the lines of *Hans Breitmann's Ballads* (1869) by Charles G. Leland, with which Dunbar could have become acquainted. In any event, he had written a poem in German dialect, "Lager Beer," published in the *Dayton Tattler*, December 13, 1890, under the pseudonym Pffenberger Deutzelheim. On this, see Cunningham, *Dunbar and His Song*, pp. 50, 271.

[119] Brown, *Negro Poetry and Drama*, p. 35.

[120] *Complete Poems*, p. 431.

[121] For a "Scotch" poem by Dunbar, see "A Border Ballad," *ibid.*, p. 73.

[122] For two "Irish" poems by Russell, see "Larry's on the Force," *Poems by Irwin Russell*, p. 68, and "The Irish Eclipse," *ibid.*, p. 72. See also our Ch. 2 above.

[123] See our Ch. 2 above.

[124] Brown, *Negro Poetry and Drama*, p. 35.

[125] James Weldon Johnson's remarks on Dunbar will be found in *The Book of American Negro Poetry*, pp. 3-5, 34-37, 49-52; and in *Along This Way*, pp. 151-52, 159-62.

[126] See our Ch. 2 above.

[127] See our Ch. 4 below.

Yet truth compels us to acknowledge that Dunbar, whose addiction to wordplay is well known,[128] did not always shun an appeal to a low level of public taste by offering for its delectation (especially in stage performances) samples of Negro pseudo-dialect whose exaggerations no minstrel could have pushed further. Here, for example, is a conversation between father and son in the musical comedy *Uncle Eph's Christmas:*

— Pappy, where was de possum first perskivered?
— Don't you know der's no sich word in the dictionumgary as perskivered?[129]

and Aunt Chloe states:

— I's got de best edjumingation.[130]

These lapses are to be attributed not to Dunbar the poet, but to Dunbar the black minstrel, for he was that also.

So dialect, whether German, Scottish, Irish, Hoosier, or Negro, possessed an extraordinary fascination for Dunbar, and he did not await public demand before utilizing it in his poetry. The demand was aroused by W. D. Howells's review of *Majors and Minors,*[131] and by then Dunbar had been writing in dialect for six years. Howells did not dissimulate his preference for the dialect poems in which, he declared, Dunbar "has been able to bring us nearer to the heart of primitive human nature in his race than anyone else has yet done."[132]

While Howells, through this review, established Dunbar as a writer, he also caused him distress, for Dunbar esteemed his poems in standard English much more than he did the others, since he felt that only there could he truly be himself. As Alice Dunbar declared, concerning the view Howells had expressed: "It was in the pure English poems that the poet expressed *himself.* He may have expressed his race in the dialect poems; they were to him the side issues of his work, the overflowing of a life apart from his dearest dreams."[133]

[128] See "Deacon Jones' Grievance," *Complete Poems,* p. 60, stanza 8, lines 1-4; "Whip-Poor-Will and Katy-Did," *ibid.,* p. 301; and the facetious title of a story in *The Heart of Happy Hollow,* "The Race Question," which deals with horseracing, not with racial matters.
[129] Cited by Brawley, *Dunbar, Poet of His People,* p. 86.
[130] *Ibid.*
[131] The text of Howells's article is reproduced by Cunningham, *Dunbar and His Song,* pp. 144-48.
[132] *Ibid.,* p. 146. See also his introduction to *Lyrics of Lowly Life,* reprinted in *Complete Poems,* pp. vii-x.
[133] Dunbar, "The Poet and His Song," in *Dunbar, Poet Laureate of the Negro Race,* pp. 6-7.

When it became clear that the public shared Howells's preference, Dunbar was upset almost to the point of despair. As early as March 15, 1897, he wrote from London to a friend: "I see now very clearly that Mr. Howells has done me irrevocable harm in the dictum he laid down regarding my dialect verse."[134]

For the expression of all the bitterness this disappointment had aroused in him, one must turn to a poem that has become famous, "The Poet," published in the 1903 collection:

> He sang of life, serenely sweet,
> With, now and then, a deeper note.
> From some high peak, nigh, yet remote,
> He voiced the world's absorbing beat.
>
> He sang of love when earth was young,
> And Love itself was in his lays.
> But ah, the world, it turned to praise
> A jingle in a broken tongue.[135]

In part, this is admittedly the lament of an artist conscious of not being appreciated as he deserves, when he sees his most trivial pieces winning praise to the neglect of those he deems superior. But the comparative downgrading of the former, in the mind of Dunbar, cannot be explained as due solely to the literary merits of the two types of work.[136] To a much greater degree it is a manifestation of his race complex.[137]

[134] Cited by William Stanley Braithwaite, "The Negro in American Literature," in Alain Locke, ed., *The New Negro*, p. 38.

[135] *Complete Poems*, p. 309.

[136] The white public, Dunbar was convinced, could not help believing that the Negro poet inevitably oscillated between the two poles of humor and pathos. "Misapprehension" (*Complete Poems*, p. 187), resembling in this "The Poet," shows the extent to which Dunbar was wounded by the reaction of the white public to his poems in standard English:

> Out of my heart, one day, I wrote a song,
> With my heart's blood imbued,
> Instinct with passion, tremulously strong,
> With grief subdued;
> Breathing a fortitude
> Pain-bought.
> And one who claimed much love for what I wrought
> Read and considered it,
> And spoke:
> "Ay, brother, — 'tis well writ,
> But where's the joke?"

[137] Walker M. Allen, in his psychoanalysis of Dunbar, sees in this a manifestation of the Oedipus complex as well. Indeed, dialect is one of the elements affectively associated with his mother, since it is from her that he learned the major part of the Negro dialect he knew. Thus his rejection of dialect would also be the

With his dialect poems, Dunbar actually takes a stand on the side of his own race and proclaims to Negroes that he is a Negro. Presented to his white audience, however, this work in dialect appears to be an avowal that he is indeed inferior and a sign that he accepts the mythical portrait of the black man. Thus the poet interprets the public's refusal to recognize his standard English poems as superior to his dialect poems to be a rejection of the "white man" in him — since his poems in standard English must be regarded as a projection of his "will to whiteness" and as a compensation for his feeling of inferiority.[138] Dunbar's refusal to recognize his work in dialect is another way of rejecting his blackness, for at this level the problem of dialect is no longer purely linguistic; it becomes laden with a number of racial associations. Thus to speak of dialect is to speak of the plantation tradition, of the caricature of the black in minstrel style, and of black inferiority.

Again, we need not summarily dismiss the possibility that Dunbar, by rejecting his dialect works that identify him with the people, was also rejecting his lowly social origins. In a certain sense, he may be considered as belonging to the developing black bourgeoisie[139] which, in its urge to climb the social ladder, feels obliged to deny everything it might share with the lower class.

---

attempted resolution of the mother fixation — that is to say, it is an effort to transcend the infantile level at which his love for her has remained. (See Allen, "Dunbar: A Study in Genius," pp. 77ff.) It is interesting to compare with this point of view that of the poet's mother, which is similar to Dunbar's own in every respect and may have been its source. Here is a journalist's account of the interview he had with Matilda Dunbar, probably a short while before her death on February 23, 1934: "Mrs. Dunbar spoke perfect English. The dialect which her son used in many of his poems was learned in the streets, not at home, she said. Dunbar honored his mother in the poem dedicated to her, 'When Malindy Sings.' Mrs. Dunbar did not approve of dialect, and so he feared to use her name, Matilda. Instead he used 'Malindy.' " (See a newspaper clipping, which unfortunately it is impossible to identify, in the Dunbar file of the Moorland Collection, Howard University, Washington, D.C.) The negative attitude adopted by Mrs. Dunbar is clearly at odds with the truth (see Cunningham, *Dunbar and His Song*, pp. 15-16; and Brown, *Negro Poetry and Drama*, p. 33), but it is a typical manifestation of such an attitude associated with a feeling of inferiority. It can usefully be compared with her statements on the South, which are mentioned in note 59 above.

[138] Allen, "Dunbar: A Study in Genius," p. 80. For statements by Dunbar that lend support to this view, see Brawley, *Dunbar, Poet of His People*, pp. 76-77. Wiggins, *Life and Works of Dunbar*, p. 109, relates, on the other hand, how one day Dunbar told her that from then on he would publish dialect poems only under a pseudonym. This declaration throws a strong light on the dissociation Dunbar was seeking between the black man and the white man coexisting within him, and cast him in the role of a new Dr. Jekyll and Mr. Hyde. Note, too, the curious impression made on Howells: "Here . . . is white thinking and white feeling in a black man" (Cunningham, *Dunbar and His Song*, p. 147).

[139] See E. Franklin Frazier, *Black Bourgeoisie*, Ch. 5, pp. 112ff.

It does not seem possible, therefore, to follow Howells completely in his attempt to establish the similarity of Dunbar and Burns: "I do not think one can read his Negro pieces without feeling that they are of like impulse and inspiration with the work of Burns when he was most Burns, when he was most Scotch, when he was most peasant."[140] This parallel does not seem to be entirely correct. Whereas Burns identified himself completely with his people, Dunbar is torn between identification and rejection. Burns, too, wrote in the authentic speech of the people, while Dunbar's dialect is at best a secondhand instrument irredeemably blemished by the degrading themes imposed upon it by the enemies of the black people. Finally, Burns wrote for his people, while Dunbar's own people made up only an insignificant part of his audience.

All things considered, it is still a mistake to pose the problem as though the racial character of a poem could be found in its language alone. It is not in his use of dialect that Dunbar is, perhaps, more especially representative of his race, but in his way of sensitizing one to the popular temperament.

Dunbar and the Negro Popular Temperament

However outrageous their exaggerations may have been, the minstrels had not missed the target when they singled out, in the character of the black, his gifts as entertainer and showman. So it is not astonishing that, toward the end of the nineteenth century, ever greater numbers of Negroes felt drawn to the minstrel show.[141] There, in spite of the distortions, they discovered elements in accord with their own artistic temperament: their frenzied love of the dance, their extraordinary talents as actors and musicians, their love of color and costume, and their vivacity.

Up to this time this popular vein had remained almost entirely neglected by Negro poets; none had as yet affirmed what is, basically, the specific artistic genius of his race. Adhering to the accepted notion of poetry which, for the Western mind, is today quite separate from such other forms of artistic expression as music, dance, and theater, Dunbar's forerunners had artificially denied themselves those popular sources of inspiration in which the predominantly synthesizing character of their race's artistic genius affirms itself. Concerning this, some explanatory comments may be in order.

It is indeed difficult for us to conceive of unwritten poetry, since a poem almost always becomes known to us in the form of printed characters on

[140] Critical article on *Majors and Minors*, reproduced in Cunningham, *Dunbar and His Song*, p. 145.
[141] See, on Negro performers in show business about 1900, James Weldon Johnson, *Black Manhattan*, Ch. 8-11.

a page. To the extent that the writer is accustomed to enclosing his art within the material limits that determine the way his work is put into circulation, the work may succeed in arousing in the reader's mind the entire range of resonances the poet had intended. But we all know that, for the full development of the poetic line's sonorousness, it is sometimes necessary to read it aloud and so compensate for the inadequacies of a mere silent reading.

The problem becomes slightly more complex when the poem, if it is to unfold freely, needs a melodic underlay. In such a case it is usual to speak of a song, not a poem. But it goes without saying that this distinction is often tenuous and the boundary between the two hard to assign — especially when the music of a song far outstrips the words, which in many songs are too threadbare to merit the name of poetry.

The situation becomes a trifle more complex when the interpreter of the sung poem is so imbued with the rhythm of the lines that it runs into his feet, which tap out a rhythmical accompaniment to the poem, much as would the rhythm section in a jazz combo.

Finally, to the resources of speaker, singer, and dancer may be added simultaneously those of the mime or actor. Then the poem no longer leads its own autonomous existence. Attracting to itself a whole gamut of related artistic forms, it becomes a kind of global, spontaneously synthesized art. This sort of poetry is characteristically African. "The African has few poems that he can recite merely as poems. He loves poetry when it can be dramatized and sung and danced."[142] "The poet sings the verses with such vivacity as will create a dramatic scene in which he is the hero."[143] It is also inseparable from the actions of everyday life.

Before Dunbar's time this global conception of poetry had remained the possession of the people, and to Dunbar must go the credit for reestablishing a bond between poetry and the people. We were able to detect a few traces of such a connection in the work of Hammon and of Horton, but virtually none survived in the work of any other nineteenth-century black poet.[144]

Dunbar's reactivation of this bond was done spontaneously, for he was a showman as well as a poet. Toward the end of the nineteenth century there did actually come together a group of musicians, composers, and actors who sought to create Negro shows and songs that would be outside

[142] Mbonu Ojike, *My Africa* (New York, 1946), p. 225. (Cited by Johnson, *The Poetry of Dunbar and McKay*, p. 102.)
[143] Ojike, *My Africa*, p. 227 (cited by Johnson, *ibid.*).
[144] Except for the timid attempts by F. E. W. Harper and A. A. Whitman; see our Ch. 1 above.

the minstrel tradition, taking over its more valid features while avoiding its exaggerations and coarseness.[145] Dunbar was drawn into this world of song and musical shows by the composers Will Marion Cook[146] and John Rosamond Johnson, brother of the poet James Weldon Johnson, who set several of Dunbar's poems to music.[147]

If these relationships were to be overlooked, one would risk losing at the same time all that lies behind the specific worth and delightfulness of Dunbar's popular poetry. The reader will not be able to re-create for himself the rhythmic and dramatic integrity of these poems unless he uses his voice and his imagination to reawaken the underlying sound and rhythm and even the actual setting, which Dunbar never failed to provide in his recitals. Never far removed from song, stage show, and popular entertainment, these works are designed not for reading but for live performance.

We had a personal experience of this when one day in New York a young black actor[148] decided to re-create for us, in the very conditions Dunbar was said to have used for his reading, the poem entitled "A Negro Love Song."[149] It is in Negro dialect but otherwise not very obviously Negro when simply read from the printed page. This poem is known to have originated during the Columbia Exposition of 1893 in Chicago, while Dunbar and several other blacks were working as cooks in a restaurant. When they had nothing else to do they used to chat, and the previous day's erotic exploits were a frequent topic of conversation. But this crowding together did not make for efficiency, and when another waiter arrived with his laden tray he used to open a path for himself by calling out, "Jump

[145] See note 141 above, and also Johnson, *Along This Way*, pp. 152-53.
[146] For *Clorindy, or the Origin of the Cakewalk* (1898), *Uncle Eph's Christmas* (1899), *Jes' Lak White Folks* (1900), and *In Dahomey* (1902). See, on the collaboration between Dunbar and Cook for the first of these shows, W. M. Cook, "Clorindy, or the Origin of the Cakewalk," in Rosamond Gilder et al., eds., *Theatre Arts Anthology: A Record and a Prophecy* (New York, 1950), pp. 227-33.
[147] See, for a list of these poems, Cunningham, *Dunbar and His Song*, pp. 274-76. On the collaboration between Dunbar and John Rosamond Johnson, see Johnson, *Along This Way, passim*, but esp. pp. 161-62, for the circumstances in which the music for "Li'l Gal" and "The Colored Band" was composed. In fact, Dunbar's fondness for the stage can be traced back to the time when he was still a schoolboy. In 1888 he had become a member of the Dayton lodge of the Knights of Pythias, which arranged many dances and theatrical performances. One evening he had a long conversation with the actors of a minstrel troupe who, after giving their show in the Park Theater in Dayton, had been invited to a reception by the lodge. This had inspired in him the notion of founding a drama group in his school, and his fellow pupils elected him president. It was he who wrote the first play staged by the group, *The Stolen Calf*. On this, see Cunningham, *Dunbar and His Song*, pp. 34ff.
[148] Roscoe Brown.
[149] *Complete Poems*, p. 75.

back, honey, jump back." It occurred to Dunbar to incorporate their amorous confessions into a poem, each stanza of which is interrupted three times by the exclamation "Jump back, honey, jump back." This serves as a response that could be picked up by a choir, giving the poem an antiphonal structure reminiscent of certain African songs and of the spirituals. Dunbar's talent, and above all his auditive sense, enabled him to endow the lines of his poem with an extraordinary rhythm which to some extent anticipates ragtime rhythm. Yet "A Negro Love Song," like so many poems of its kind, does not really come to life unless it is accompanied by what our young actor called the "hambone shuffle." To carry this out, the speaker places his right foot on a chair and leans forward slightly so that the right shoulder comes close to the right knee. The palm and the back of the right hand go from shoulder to knee and back again with extraordinary dexterity, suggesting the jazz sticks of a jazz rhythm section. Against the rhythmic background so created, the simultaneous recitation of the poem achieves an effect one would never dream of, when simply reading the poem.

An experience of this kind provides a more concrete grasp of the special nature and circumstances of popular poetry as a genre. It also throws light on the importance of the physical contribution in explaining Dunbar's hold on his audiences. "Dunbar's success on the platform, and it was great, was due not only to his fame as a poet, but also to his skill as a reader. His voice was a perfect musical instrument, and he knew how to use it with extreme effect."[150] Whether or not his African ancestry is responsible, alongside the Western-style poet in Dunbar there was also an African-style poet, as defined above. If today he is still considered, despite his ideological failings, to be the poet of his people, this is largely because the histrionic aspect of his art corresponded to fundamental tendencies of his race and because the poem, through its themes and rhythms, communicates to the audience an emotion that sets off motor activity. In similar situations the same effect is produced between the black preacher and his flock, or between the jazz musician and his hearers.

Thus Dunbar won over his audience at the recital he gave on Narragansett Pier, on August 25, 1896, with his poem "The Cornstalk Fiddle."[151] The poem begins like a popular song in Riley's manner, and its tripping meter, in which anapest and iamb alternate, admirably evokes the old melodies of the country-dance or the quadrille with their contagious beat, while the shrill note of the village fiddle reigns over all. The second stanza tells us how to make this rustic instrument out of cornstalks. When Dunbar

[150] Johnson, *Along This Way*, pp. 159-60.
[151] *Complete Poems*, p. 25.

began to recite, to the muted accompaniment of a string orchestra, the heads of the listeners in the hall began to sway and their feet to beat time. By the time he had reached the sixth stanza, which deals with the village dancers, the poet's own feet could not stay still, and he began to dance the successive figures of the country-dance described in the poem.

> His lithe form, graceful as a gazelle's, glided about the stage, with a rhythm of movement which showed that his whole being responded to the music of the orchestra and to the beauty of his own conception. Every emotion depicted in the lines came out upon his face and found expression in his wonderful eyes. The audience went wild with excitement and the wine of their applause only served to stimulate his efforts. The recital was a great success, and the southern people who had been carried back to "old plantation days" by the vivid poem-pictures and skillful acting of the wonderful negro boy, were the most enthusiastic of the audience.[152]

No one previously had combined all the talents of the poet, musician, dancer, and actor to the same degree. This made Dunbar the first truly great interpreter of the popular Negro temperament.[153]

The Themes of Dunbar's Popular Poetry

Through its vigor, this authentically Negro vein saves a noteworthy proportion of his popular poetry from oblivion, and sets it off from those of his works which are uninspired copies of the plantation tradition or of the pastoral sentimentalities of Field and Riley. Nevertheless, these works are not distinctive so much on account of their themes, which often are simply those of Dunbar's models, as for the fresh way in which they are handled. Here Dunbar is truly in his element. His actor's temperament is clearly advantageous in enabling him to embody the personages staged in his poems, for he can live with them and through them, whereas his forerunners had treated the same subjects from the outside as observers who, though often lucid, preserved their detachment.

"An Ante-Bellum Sermon"[154] reveals the advance that has been made,

[152] Wiggins, *Life and Works of Dunbar*, p. 65.
[153] In the case of some poems, Dunbar proceeded as if he had actually been a composer. 'Whistling Sam" (*Complete Poems*, p. 252) is interspersed with musical notations of the tunes that Sam is whistling. Concerning the writing of this poem, Alice Dunbar recounts that "Whistling Sam" caused much expenditure of energy. "All had to whistle Sam's tunes, and then the music teacher must come and play them out on the piano, and transcribe the musical notation to be sure there were no mistakes" ("The Poet and His Song," in *Dunbar, Poet Laureate of the Negro Race*, p. 15). When engaged on this sort of poem, Dunbar acted it out as he wrote it (*ibid.*).
[154] *Complete Poems*, p. 20.

from Russell to Dunbar, in depicting the Negro pastor. The idea of treating a Negro sermon in a poem was, of course, initiated by Russell. But Dunbar's preacher is no ignoramus, as were the minstrels' preachers. Chosen as theme of the sermon is the episode of Moses and his mission to the Pharaoh; it is treated much as in the spiritual "Go Down, Moses," with its implied parallel between the freeing of the Hebrew children from the Egyptian yoke and of the blacks from the southern planters. This preacher also has a sense of humor. Even after the parallel he has been drawing is quite obvious, he denies several times that he is referring to the present:

> But fu' feah some one mistakes me,
> I will pause right hyeah to say,
> Dat I'm still a-preachin' ancient,
> I ain't talkin' 'bout to-day.[155]

Actually, however, he is so closely concerned with the present that in his oratorical fervor he forgets about Moses, and at the end of the poem he all but commits the unpardonable error of speaking openly:

> But when Moses wif his powah
> Comes an' sets us chillun free,
> We will praise de gracious Mastah
> Dat has gin us liberty;
> An' we'll shout ouah halleluyahs,
> On dat mighty reck'nin' day,
> When we'se reco'nised ez citiz' . . .
> Huh uh! Chillun, let us pray![156]

This takes us far beyond the grotesque Negro preacher that the minstrels put on the stage. It is clear that on this occasion Dunbar was writing for a Negro audience. The situation is reversed, the laughter being directed against the oppressor, not against the oppressed.

A new way of presenting the pastor is also found in "The Party"[157] and "De Critters' Dance,"[158] two poems for which Dunbar's immediate source of inspiration was "Christmas-Night in the Quarters." But whereas Russell's parson committed the sacrilege of asking a divine blessing for the sinful frolics of the dancers, in "The Party" the preacher does no more than say grace hastily at the beginning of the meal, since he is impatient to get to the dish of opossum. The question is seen in a different light in "De Critters' Dance," for which Dunbar devised a very ingenious use of

[155] *Ibid.*, p. 21.
[156] *Ibid.*, pp. 22-23.
[157] *Ibid.*, p. 134.
[158] *Ibid.*, p. 291.

Negro folklore, transporting Russell's entertainment from the human to the animal world.[159] This allows Dunbar full liberty, with no risk of disapproval, to make of Parson Hedgehog a frenzied dancer — though this is enough nevertheless to scandalize the parishioners. For that matter, is Parson Hedgehog actually a Negro? Evidence is lacking, except perhaps for the dialect in which the poem is written.

In a number of other poems, religious scruples play their part in modifying the dance theme. The speaker in "Temptation"[160] barely has the necessary strength to resist, while those in "Itching Heels"[161] and "How Lucy Backslid"[162] give in, despite their struggles. "Angelina"[163] is not entirely convinced that dancing is a sin; her view probably reflects Dunbar's own skepticism concerning the religious externals within which such popular sects as the Baptists and Methodists had allowed themselves to fossilize. Losing sight of the essential, they put out excessively severe edicts against dancing, gambling, and drinking.

But Dunbar's superiority incontestably asserts itself in the wild rhythm he imparts to all his characters.[164] They strut, swagger, jig around, and arouse everyone present to frenzy when they begin to sing, as did pretty Lindy in "The Party."[165] If we could see how Dunbar himself breathed life into this poem, we would note how the repetition of its motifs has some of the obsessive and bewitching qualities of jazz rhythm, and like the poem's Uncle Jim we would find ourselves swept up in the contagion.

All these works successfully attempt to multiply relations between poetry and popular music, and in the process Dunbar reveals himself as a genuine forerunner of the Negro Renaissance. A similar tendency is apparent in two other poems that try to express in words the unique value of the musical interpretations characteristic of Negroes. In "The Colored Band" — which could serve as a document in the history of jazz, since in this poem the Negro band parading through the streets of the town is already playing a Sousa march in ragtime — Dunbar essays a comparison between white

---

[159] See, for a similar recourse to the animal world, "A Cabin Tale," *ibid.,* p. 247.

[160] *Ibid.,* p. 235.

[161] *Ibid.,* p. 362. See also "The Dance," p. 274.

[162] *Ibid.,* p. 255.

[163] *Ibid.,* p. 220.

[164] See also "The Spellin'-Bee" (*ibid.,* p. 65), which, though written in Hoosier dialect, exhibits the same temperament.

[165] *Ibid.,* p. 135. The poem is remarkable also as being the first, to our knowledge, to record that the Negro women present on this occasion had slicked down their hair: ". . . haih breshed back ez slick ez grease" (line 8). See, on the meaning of this desire to attain the white ideal, Kardiner and Ovesey, *The Mark of Oppression,* pp. 309ff. See also p. 334 in the same work, on the dance as an expression of dissatisfaction and of feelings of frustration.

and black musicians.[166] The celebrated "When Malindy Sings,"[167] in which
Dunbar recalls how his mother used to sing spirituals,[168] also has this
intention.

Several of Dunbar's love poems also make him a forerunner of the
Negro Renaissance, for in scattered places they already sing the praises of
black beauty in and for itself. "Song"[169] relates the passion of a black
suitor for his beautiful African girl, and "Dinah Kneading Dough"[170]
lauds the charms of a pretty girl as she works. She has jet-black eyes, hair
that all the same is too frizzled for some people's tastes, and beautiful arms,
whose ebony tones stand out in contrast against the whiteness of the dough
she is kneading. Frizzled hair is also part of the charm of Mandy Lou
("A Plantation Portrait"[171]), who is "browner den de frush's wing."
"Dely," finally, delivers an almost racist panegyric of ethnic purity, and
in places one can sense a touch of contempt for the "compromise" that
those of mixed descent represent:

> Dely brown ez brown kin be
> An' huh haih is curly;
>
> .   .   .   .
>
> She ain' no mulatter;
> She pure cullud, — don' you see
> Dat's jes' whut's de mattah?
> Dat's de why I love huh so,
> D' ain't no mix about huh....[172]

5. The Lyricism of Heartbreak

We have yet to speak of what is, it must be confessed, the most engaging
aspect of Dunbar's poetic work — that in which, as a genuine lyric poet,
he gives vent to the cry of pain torn from him by the tragic destiny of his
brief existence. For over his entire life there hovers the dramatic feeling
of a double falling short and a double failure: one his work, the other
his love:

[166] *Complete Poems,* p. 286, stanzas 3 and 6.
[167] *Ibid.,* p. 131, stanza 2, lines 1-4; stanza 3, lines 5-6; stanza 8, lines 1-2.
[168] Faint echoes of the spirituals can also be found in "Deacon Jones' Grievance," *ibid.,* p. 58; "The Ol' Tunes," p. 82; "A Spiritual," p. 314; and "W'en I
Gits Home," p. 316.
[169] *Ibid.,* p. 19.
[170] *Ibid.,* p. 305.
[171] *Ibid.,* p. 278. Mandy Lou's complexion is also praised in "Dreamin' Town,"
p. 417.
[172] *Ibid.,* p. 239.

> To have come near to sing the perfect song
> And only by a half-tone lost the key,
>
> . . . .
>
> To have just missed the perfect love,
>
> . . . .
>
> This, this it is to be accursed indeed;
> For if we mortals love, or if we sing,
> We count our joys not by the things we have,
> But by what kept us from the perfect thing.[173]

This curse that the poet felt weighing him down has been interpreted in various ways, by the poet himself and by the critics.

Black critics have been unanimous in wishing to present Dunbar as a writer who was victimized by the prejudices, and even by the indifference, of his public.[174] We have ourselves repeatedly noted the power possessed by the mythical portrait of the Negro, that creation of majority opinion and of its writers, and we have stressed to what degree Dunbar was hemmed in by it. Striving first of all for popularity, he had risked playing the buffoon before his public, hoping that, once the audience had been won over, he could turn about and gain a hearing for the more serious things he believed he must say to them. Not until too late did he realize that he had entered into a pact with the devil — for the public, once they had come to know him as a buffoon, would refuse to see him as anything else.

This is one facet of Dunbar's tragic situation which it would be futile to deny, and which has inspired several of his most moving poems. "Sympathy" is the heartfelt cry of a poet who finds himself imprisoned amid traditions and prejudices he feels powerless to destroy:

> I know what the caged bird feels, alas!
> When the sun is bright on the upland slopes;
>
> . . . .
>
> I know why the caged bird beats his wing
> Till its blood is red on the cruel bars;
>
> . . . .
>
> I know why the caged bird sings, ah me,
> When his wing is bruised and his bosom sore, —
> When he beats his bars and he would be free;

[173] "Life's Tragedy," *ibid.*, p. 367.

[174] See Johnson references cited above, note 125; Redding, *To Make a Poet Black*, pp. 56-57, and J. Saunders Redding, "American Negro Literature," *The American Scholar* XVIII, no. 2 (Spring, 1949), 137-38.

> It is not a carol of joy or glee,
>> But a prayer that he sends from his heart's deep core,
>> But a plea, that upward to Heaven he flings —
> I know why the caged bird sings![175]

But the tragedy of Dunbar cannot be restricted to the dimensions of what was imposed upon him from outside, and it is going too far to accuse his readers of systematically underestimating his poems in standard English and of accepting only his works in dialect.[176] Most of his poems in English share several basic defects with many other works of the same period, not the least of which are banality and a lack of sincerity. Dunbar was not blind to them. Indeed, it is at those moments, when he perceives his own inadequacies and measures the distance separating his goals and his abilities, that his situation appears to him in its true light and lets him glimpse his tragedy as one of failure. He had taken Shelley as his model, but his lyric flights had neither the momentum nor the ardor of Shelley's:

> We have no singers like the ones whose note
>> Gave challenge to the noblest warbler's song.
> We have no voice so mellow, sweet, and strong
> As that which broke from Shelley's golden throat.
>
> The measure of our songs is our desires;
>> We tinkle where old poets used to storm.
> We lack their substance tho' we keep their form:
> We strum our banjo-strings and call them lyres.[177]

This conviction of failure was not due entirely, perhaps, to the faltering powers of his lyricism; it may have originated in equal measure in his awareness that he had not been the poet his race deserved, and had not truly sung its virtues. He had spoken to James Weldon Johnson of his plan one day to write works in which he would be his real self. It is not known what these works would have been, but they probably would have represented a glorification, as he envisioned it, of the black race.[178] Yet we are entitled to doubt whether these unwritten works would have greatly differed from those we know. The main thing is that they were never written, for Dunbar was a creature of whim, unable to seize the flying moment.[179] Perhaps he was all the more inclined to postpone what grieved

[175] *Complete Poems*, p. 162.
[176] Redding, "American Negro Literature," pp. 137-38.
[177] "Prometheus," stanzas 4 and 5, *Complete Poems*, pp. 188-89.
[178] Johnson, *Along This Way*, pp. 160-61.
[179] He was aware of this. See his poem "Till the Wind Gets Right" (*Complete Poems*, p. 433).

him most, and for him this was assuredly his race, since a feeling of inferiority was inseparable from it: "My position is most unfortunate. I am a black white man."[180] The poet's self-estimate, in its poignant lucidity, sums up what must be regarded as the heart of his problem, for he is venting his distress at not having bridged the contradictions that afflicted him with a synthesis that could have led to an internal equilibrium. Thus, all things considered, Dunbar was much less the victim of public indifference than a man whose basic contradictions remained unresolved.

Pessimism and Religious Doubts

One of the many derelictions laid at the door of Dunbar's public is that of having caused the poet's pessimistic attitude toward existence.[181] The charge is groundless. Dunbar's pessimism, though it may have been deepened by public indifference to certain portions of his work, is essentially the manifestation of his feeling of inferiority. In any event, it precedes the publication of his first volume, where a number of poems give it expression.

"A Career" may be said to prefigure the failure that Dunbar would later view as his. This poem, with its two unequal parts, contrasts the poet's aspirations and the reception given by the world:

> "Break me my bounds, and let me fly
> To regions vast of boundless sky;
>
> . . . .
>
> Oh, circumscribe me not by rules
> That serve to lead the minds of fools!
> But give me pow'r to work my will,
> And at my deeds the world shall thrill.
> . . . . "
>
> He lived a silent life alone
> And laid him down when it was done;
> And at his head was placed a stone
> On which was carved a name unknown![182]

"Promise" and "Fulfillment"[183] are a diptych similar in tone. The poet had devoted all his love to growing a splendid rose, but when one fine

---

180 Cited by Wiggins, *Life and Works of Dunbar*, p. 81.

181 Speaking of public indifference to him, Redding declared: "Dunbar felt it, and the purest stream of his lyricism was made bitter and all but choked by it" ("American Negro Literature," p. 137).

182 *Complete Poems*, p. 471.

183 *Ibid.*, pp. 18-19.

morning he went to pluck it, a child had already snatched and run off with it. Refusing to be discouraged, the poet renewed his efforts, and stood guard over the flower night and day:

> At last, oh joy! the central petals burst apart.
> It blossomed — but, alas! a worm was at its heart![184]

No less bitter are his definitions of life:

> A crust of bread and a corner to sleep in,
> A minute to smile and an hour to weep in,
> A pint of joy to a peck of trouble,
> And never a laugh but the moans come double;
>   And that is life![185]

and elsewhere:

> . . . this low, long, lethargic night,
> Worn out with strife
> Which men call life.[186]

Even in the last of his poems, written at a time when he had achieved a degree of resignation,[187] the same pessimistic outlook persists. Thus his pessimism is an absolutely central attitude; it is not always very convincingly patched over by the facade of beautiful, exhibitionistic optimism which he and his ethnic brothers prefer to present to the world.[188]

This tragic perspective must be borne in mind if one would understand the real meaning of his humor, the grinning mask donned by the black buffoon to hide the tears that rise from his grieving heart:

> We wear the mask that grins and lies,
> It hides our cheeks and shades our eyes, —
> This debt we pay to human guile;
> With torn and bleeding hearts we smile,
> And mouth with myriad subtleties.
>
> Why should the world be overwise,
> In counting all our tears and sighs?
> Nay, let them only see us, while
>   We wear the mask.

[184] *Ibid.*
[185] "Life," *ibid.*, p. 9.
[186] "The Change Has Come," *ibid.*, p. 92. See also "One Life," p. 114; "Compensation," p. 420; "Worn Out," p. 474.
[187] "Resignation," *ibid.*, p. 169; "At Sunset Time," pp. 435-36, stanza 3, lines 7-8.
[188] See the protest song "Me and My Captain," cited in our Ch. 1, note 20.

We smile, but, O great Christ, our cries
To thee from tortured souls arise.
We sing, but oh the clay is vile
Beneath our feet, and long the mile;
But let the world dream otherwise,
We wear the mask.[189]

Together with the poet there weeps, beneath the smile of the black minstrel, the soul of his whole people.

One can hardly refrain from drawing a parallel between the deceptive
role of humor and the seemingly orthodox religiosity that finds expression
in most of Dunbar's poems. Both might simply be different forms of the
same conformist facade.[190]

Dunbar was received at the age of thirteen into the Methodist Church
of his native town. There is no evidence of devotional enthusiasm on his
part, however, and when his mother sought to steer him toward a career
in the ministry, his response was a flat refusal. His novel, *The Uncalled*
(1898), contains a slashing attack on the hypocrisy of official religion.[191]
Nor should one overlook the influence that may have been exerted on him
by the agnosticism of Robert G. Ingersoll, whose patronage won him a
post at the Library of Congress in 1897. Revealing in this respect is the
verse dedication he wrote on the endpaper of the copy of *The Uncalled*
which he sent to Ingersoll:

To R. G. I.
A wit that pricks th' inflated Gods,
Gives life, love's nobler leaven —
Laughs hell to scorn and takes the rods
Out of the hands of Heaven.
                    Paul Laurence Dunbar[192]

[189] "We Wear the Mask," *ibid.,* pp. 112-13.

[190] It is strange, to say the least, that Benjamin E. Mays, who at the time was
Dean of the School of Religion at Howard University, Washington, D.C., should
have chosen to say nothing whatever about these poems of doubt and unbelief in
the chapter he devoted to Dunbar in his work *The Negro's God as Reflected in His
Literature* (1938), pp. 130-39. Since Dunbar was the "poet of his people," nothing
must be done to diminish his great stature. Such an attitude closely resembles that
of black critics who insist that the pressure exercised by a white public is itself
sufficient to account for the poet's ideological deficiencies.

[191] See, on the same theme, "Religion" (*Complete Poems,* p. 58) and "A Little
Christmas Basket" (*ibid.,* p. 280).

[192] This copy, with Ingersoll's bookplate, is now in the Spingarn Collection of
the Howard University library in Washington, D.C., where Mrs. Dorothy Porter
was kind enough to point it out to us.

But here, too, it is clear that Ingersoll's influence could do no more than strengthen previous attitudes, for even in the 1892 collection of poems a religious skepticism is felt at times amid the more numerous orthodox works. Thus alongside "A Prayer,"[193] in which Dunbar asks God's aid on the thorny path which poverty and the poet's color have made his, other lines reveal a man in whom doubt has sunk deep, as when he speaks of

> The summer sounds, and summer nights,
> That set a restless mind to rights
> When grief and pain and raging doubt
> Of men and creeds have worn it out;[194]

"The Mystery" is centered upon the same problem, but by now the poet's attitude is that of a potential agnostic. Stress is placed on the question of the conclusion to be drawn from the silence of the heavens by which one is confronted:

> I grope without direction and by chance.
> Some feign to hear a voice and feel a hand
> That draws them ever upward thro' the gloom.
> But I — I hear no voice and touch no hand
> Tho' oft thro' silence infinite I list,
> And strain my hearing to supernal sounds;
>
> .   .   .   .
>
> I question of th' eternal bending skies
> That seem to neighbor with the novice earth;
> But they roll on, and daily shut their eyes
> On me, as I one day shall do on them,
> And tell me not the secret that I ask.[195]

If there were still any need to demonstrate the fact, "Mare Rubrum" makes plain that Dunbar's religious doubts are motivated by the powerlessness of God and the church in the face of racial injustice:

> In Life's Red Sea with faith I plant my feet,
>   And wait the sound of that sustaining word
>   Which long ago the men of Israel heard,
> When Pharaoh's host behind them, fierce and fleet,
> Raged on, consuming with revengeful heat.
>   Why are the barrier waters still unstirred? —
>   That struggling faith may die of hope deferred?
> Is God not sitting in his ancient seat?

[193] *Complete Poems*, p. 16.
[194] "In Summer Time," *ibid.*, p. 463, lines 25-28.
[195] *Ibid.*, p. 27.

> The billows swirl above my trembling limbs,
> And almost chill my anxious heart to doubt
> And disbelief, long conquered and defied.
> But tho' the music of my hopeful hymns
> Is drowned by curses of the raging rout,
> No voice yet bids th' opposing waves divide![196]

Finally, in "Behind the Arras," the poet's faith collapses under the pressure of a doubt he can no longer bear. The poem is a bitter denial of the existence of another life, perhaps even of God himself:

> ... the soul ... marks with eye intent
> That mystic curtain o'er the portal death;
> Still deeming that behind the arras lies
> The lambent way that leads to lasting light.
> Poor fooled and foolish soul! Know now that death
> Is but a blind, false door that nowhere leads,
> And gives no hope of exit final, free.[197]

Did Dunbar persist in his unbelief to the end? No one can say, for over his last moments hovered the same ambiguity that had hovered over his entire life. A minister was present at his deathbed; he read the twenty-third Psalm. The dying man listened peacefully. When the minister had finished, Dunbar began to repeat the psalm in a voice that grew ever weaker. He reached the line, "Yea, though I walk through the valley of the shadow of death," and breathed his last.[198]

However that may be, Dunbar is the first great Negro poet whose personal religious feelings were so clearly at odds with religious orthodoxy, which until then it had been traditional to associate with the expression of racial feeling.[199] The cleft between the two will widen; from now on it will become one of the distinguishing marks of the inner disarray experienced by black poets.

[196] *Ibid.*, pp. 177-78. "Vagrants," p. 191, is another poem expressing doubt, while "A Hymn," p. 156, is a prayer to be freed from doubt.
[197] *Ibid.*, p. 150.
[198] Wiggins, *Life and Works of Dunbar*, p. 131.
[199] Yet there is already a note of doubt and despair in Whitfield's poem, "The Misanthropist," for which see our Ch. 1 above.

Chapter Four: DUNBAR'S CONTEMPORARIES

During the years between the Civil War and World War I, Negro poetry produced no personality that can be set beside Dunbar's. His inadequacies may be deplored, yet one must admit that none of his contemporaries had the same delicate sensibility, the variety of inspiration, or the extraordinary feeling for rhythm and musicality that served him equally well in his English verses and in his dialect poetry. Nor did anyone else suffer as he did from the sense of his own weaknesses. In short, throughout this long period he remained the only genuine lyric poet.

Must the works of his contemporaries be consigned, then, to oblivion? We have not felt inclined to adopt this course, and those whom we consider will introduce more than one desirable nuance into this picture of a period transitional and uncertain of itself. Yet two writers whose place in this chapter would have been chronologically justified are omitted nevertheless.

James Weldon Johnson, who was one year older than Dunbar, actually wrote, as early as 1900, what came to be known as the Negro National Anthem, but his first collected volume of poems did not appear until 1917. Moreover, the poems he wrote in the style of Dunbar were totally eclipsed by his later work. This played its part in the Negro Renaissance, and it is in that setting that Johnson will be considered.[1]

Very different is the situation of William Stanley Braithwaite,[2] whose

[1] For James Weldon Johnson, see our Ch. 9 below.

[2] Born in Boston in 1878, he was literary critic on the *Boston Transcript* and lived in the "Sugar Hill" section of Harlem.

127

work constitutes a kind of disavowal of the race which, according to the ethnic norms of the United States, was undeniably his. Born in Boston to parents who had come from the West Indies, Braithwaite was so light-skinned that his African origins could go unnoticed. In his three volumes of verses, *Lyrics of Life and Love* (1904), *The House of Falling Leaves* (1908), and *Selected Poems* (1948), one would seek in vain for the shadow of any avowal, or disavowal, of his race. Braithwaite's persistent silence certainly amounts to the rejection of his blackness, for it is extremely difficult to accept the polite but specious explanation offered by James Weldon Johnson, who himself had a West Indian background: "He has written no poetry motivated or colored by race. This has not been a matter of intention on his part; it is simply that race has not impinged upon him as it has upon other Negro poets."[3]

Even if Johnson's supposition could be considered valid for Braithwaite's own poetry, it would fail to account for the biased tendency that also marks his activity as an anthologist. Setting aside the anthologies of magazine poetry that he published almost every year from 1913 on, we find it strange that he could bring out in succession *The Book of Elizabethan Verse* (1906), *The Book of Georgian Verse* (1909), *The Book of Restoration Verse* (1910), *The Book of Modern British Verse* (1919), an *Anthology of Massachusetts Poets* (1922), and even *A Contemporary Anthology of Verse by Catholic Sisters* (1931), but not a single anthology of Negro poetry. We cannot be convinced that it just so happened that he felt a greater kinship with poetry written by Catholic nuns than with that of Negro writers! The facts impose on us the conclusion that Braithwaite had not the least desire to be identified with the black world and what it stands for. There is, consequently, no need to examine him here.

The three poets, the core of whose work is studied here, have been selected not so much on account of their literary qualities as for their representative and explanatory value. Dunbar was not the first Negro poet to write in dialect; the attempts made by Mrs. Harper and A. A. Whitman have already been mentioned. Almost simultaneously with Dunbar there appeared a number of other dialect poets who have been named "the Dunbar school"[4] — rather inappropriately, for if it is undeniable that J. Mord

---

[3] James Weldon Johnson, *Book of American Negro Poetry*, p. 99.
[4] Campbell, Davis, and Allen are the outstanding members of this group. But they will be followed by many practitioners of dialect, whose popularity fully equaled that of the minstrel shows. Among the disciples of Dunbar whom we have not chosen to consider are J. S. Cotter, Sr. (1861-?), the author of many quite mediocre poetic pamphlets; J. W. Holloway (1865-1935), *Bandannas* (n.d.) and *From the Desert* (1919); J. D. Corrothers (1869-1919), *Selected Poems* (1907) and *The Dream and the Song* (1914). These writers are lacking in personality;

Allen borrowed from Dunbar, James Edwin Campbell had his own highly original talent and was in no sense a borrower. As for Daniel Webster Davis, he worked directly from the models provided by the minstrels and the southern poets, pushing their clichés to the outermost limits of the possible. His writings convey the true dimensions of the effort to filter out the dross that, comparatively speaking, Dunbar's work represents.

Campbell, Davis, and Allen are, above all else, witnesses to their own times. In contrast to Dunbar, Campbell reveals the upsurge, among blacks, of a racial consciousness that chafes under every yoke. His poetry already contains budding qualities that the climate of the Negro Renaissance will bring to full flower. Like Allen, he introduces into poetry a satirical spirit almost entirely lacking in Dunbar, one which is the direct descendant of that inexhaustible treasure house of good sense and practical shrewdness, the wisdom of the people. Their work also foreshadows the intellectuals' break with the forms of traditional Negro religiosity, still paralyzed by its crushing burden of subservience and unable to offer genuine spiritual sustenance to the elite of a people in search of its soul.

1. James Edwin Campbell

Little is certain concerning relations between Dunbar and James Edwin Campbell,[5] a fellow Ohioan five years Dunbar's senior. The two men be-

it would have required a great deal of indulgence to welcome their writings into what is called the literary domain, and this study would have gained nothing essential by paying attention to them.

[5] James Edwin Campbell was born September 28, 1867, in Pomeroy, Ohio, and received his elementary and secondary education there. After graduating from Pomeroy Academy in 1884, he taught for two years at Buck Ridge near Gallipolis, Ohio, and then joined the staff of the *Pioneer* in Charleston, West Virginia. He soon left the paper to head the Langston School in Point Pleasant, West Virginia, and then, in 1892, the West Virginia Colored Institute, which is now the West Virginia State College. But there was much opposition to his administration, and this induced him to leave for Chicago where, up to the time of his death in December, 1895, he was on the staff of the *Chicago Times Herald*. His early poems in Negro dialect were published in various newspapers. *Driftings and Gleanings* (1887) is a volume of poems in standard English, followed by two essays. The poems are mediocre and often have an artificial character. The choice of subjects makes most of them appear to be academic exercises ("Mucius Scaevola," "Defeat of Boadicea by the Romans," "Death of Dentatus," "To the River Tiber," are some examples). Whenever racial topics are taken up, they are nearly always clumsily handled. Campbell's second collection, of poems exclusively, is entitled *Echoes from the Cabin and Elsewhere* (1895), and it contains those of his poems that deserve to survive. On Campbell, see Carter G. Woodson, "J. E. Campbell: A Forgotten Man of Letters," *Negro History Bulletin*, November, 1938, p. 11, and the brief remarks devoted to him by Johnson, *Book of American Negro Poetry*, pp. 64-65; Sterling A. Brown, *Negro Poetry and Drama*, pp. 36-37; J. Saunders

came acquainted in Chicago in 1893, and one may suppose that on this occasion they told each other how they felt about the merits of the Negro dialect which they had both tried to use in their poems. But nothing entitles one to speak of influence in this connection since, despite obvious resemblances in their work, there are also signs that point to basically different personalities in the two authors. The most striking thing about Campbell is, indeed, the openness with which he takes a stand, the firmness of his personality, and his independence.

The Theme of Interracial Love

Unlike Dunbar, Campbell owes almost nothing to the plantation poets. A poem such as "Linkum,"[6] the only one that clearly reveals any influence from Page and Gordon, gives the impression of following their ideology in order to reject it all the more firmly in the end. The poem recounts the tragic circumstances which led to the death of a ten-year-old black, Lincoln, as he was trying to save a little white girl. Lincoln's father tells us that he was a nice boy with a great love for music. Little Ellen was very fond of him and followed him wherever he went. One day the mother left her sleeping child in Lincoln's care. But, as he is watching over her, he hears a band of musicians approaching. As they pass the house, he can resist no longer; he runs out of the house to follow them. A short while later the alarm bell sounds, and the little boy realizes at once that the Bradley house is on fire. He slips through the crowd that has been attracted by the fire, and he dashes through the flames and smoke until he gets to little Ellen. But no sooner has he carried her out, safe and sound, in his arms and put her down on the ground than he collapses and dies from his wounds.

> "De one dat sabed all udders, hisse'f he couldn't sabe."[7]

These are the words that a grateful Miss Ellen, a big girl now, has had cut into the tombstone of her young rescuer.

One might feel tempted to interpret this poem as intended to demonstrate how devoted the blacks were to their white superiors, but to do so would be to miss an essential point. At this date a southern writer would have found it unthinkable to present a young Negro, perhaps already at

---

Redding, *To Make a Poet Black*, pp. 51-53. On the meeting between Dunbar and Campbell at the time of the Columbia Exposition (Chicago, 1893), see Virginia Cunningham, *Paul Laurence Dunbar and His Song*, p. 99, where mention is also made of J. D. Corrothers (also *ibid.*, pp. 93-94).

[6] *Echoes*, p. 24.
[7] *Ibid.*

the age of puberty, holding a young white girl in his arms. And Campbell does not merely dare to create this tableau, a really audacious action in 1895[8] — he actually imagines bonds of affection between Lincoln and Ellen. These are only lightly sketched in, for the protagonists in "Linkum" are still children. But the theme is developed more fully in other poems.

"A Love Dream"[9] is the impassioned dream of a night of ardent love between the poet and a white mistress who has given herself to him on a beach against which the waves beat, and beneath a tropical sky that is spangled with stars. The mistress personifies the South; the poem leaves no doubt at all on that score. Nevertheless, the meaning of the poem does not emerge very clearly. It does not express that longing for the South which we have observed in Dunbar, and of which no symptom is anywhere to be discovered in Campbell. Thus it seems, rather, that the poet utilized this theme to show that the might of love can triumph over racial inequality. Through the tone of the poem, whose phrasing is not always beyond reproach, one can also sense the satisfaction experienced by the seducer at having this one time subjugated the woman who proclaims him to be inferior, especially since desire has not wiped out every trace of hatred from the woman's eyes. Let us bear in mind, however, that the poem is only a dream, as Campbell himself assures us, and that at the same time it expresses primarily the poet's desires and aspirations.

In "Compensazione,"[10] it is not inequality of race but of rank and fortune that must yield in secret to the love of a young commoner whose family background and poverty prevent him from marrying the woman he loves and who loves him. While he watches her ride by, on horseback, with the young lord to whom she has become engaged, he secretly savors his revenge for the contempt that this social superior feels for him, the only man she truly loves:

> O, rich young lord, thou ridest by
> With looks of high disdain;
> It chafes me not thy title high,
> Thy blood of oldest strain.
> The lady riding at thy side

---

[8] The first time that an American Negro novelist (and perhaps any American novelist) mentions a love relationship between a Negro and a white woman seems to have been in the novel *Hearts of Gold* (1896) by J. McHenry Jones. On this topic, see Hugh Morris Gloster, *Negro Voices in American Fiction*, pp. 31-32. Thus, if nothing has been overlooked, Campbell is the first writer to utilize the theme.

[9] *Echoes*, p. 78.

[10] *Ibid.*, p. 69.

Is but in name thy promised bride,
  Ride on, young lord, ride on!

Her father wills and she obeys,
The custom of her class;
'Tis Land not Love the trothing sways —
Her fair white hand, young lord, is thine,
Her *soul*, proud fool, her *soul* is mine,
  Ride on, young lord, ride on![11]

But the theme of love as victor over inequality is nowhere so explicitly developed as in "The Pariah,"[12] the longest and most prosaic of Campbell's poems. It relates the vicissitudes of a love between the daughter of a white industrial tycoon (probably in the Chicago area, where Campbell lived for a long time) and a mulatto who is practically white. The first section insists at length upon the absurdity of the obstacles that social prejudices set up against this love. Not only is the mulatto as white as the industrialist himself; his family has been longer on American soil than the industrialist's.

When the story opens, the girl, who has always been very friendly toward the mulatto, now changes her attitude because she has learned that he has Negro blood in his veins. Bitterness and rebelliousness take up their abode in the heart of the "pariah," so he does not hesitate to accept the invitation of the factory employees, who have gone on strike against the industrialist, to harangue them. He is just about to inspire his own hatred in them when the thought of the girl he loves gives him pause. The words he utters, in addressing the strikers, will speak of reconciliation, with the result that the men make no use of the weapons they are carrying. Filled with gratitude, the tycoon's daughter flings herself into the mulatto's arms, avowing her love.

The literary quality of this poem is slight, and the story is clumsily constructed and told. There is no doubt that here Campbell has tackled something beyond his powers. But this failure does not in the least subtract from the interest of the theme, which probably makes use of a number of autobiographical features.

Is it permissible to conclude that Campbell had a secret relationship with a white woman? The supposition is not entirely gratuitous, if one considers the attention, unusual for this time, lavished in his poetry upon the theme of interracial love, and the conquering air he adopts in treating it. It might have been relatively easy for him to establish such a liaison, for

[11] *Ibid.*
[12] *Ibid.*, p. 82. The poem runs to about 150 lines.

Campbell, to judge from a photograph, appears to have been a rather light-skinned mulatto with features sufficiently Caucasian to enable him to pass as white, just like the hero of "The Pariah," the following lines of which perhaps describe the poet himself:

> Fair was I as her complexion,
> Honest came my fairness, too,
> For my father and my mother
> Were in wedlock banded true.[13]

If it was indeed thus, his fairness of skin, no less than the legitimacy of his birth, could account for Campbell's extraordinary self-assurance and for his utter lack of any feeling of inferiority.

He possessed, too, the qualities of a genuine agitator, a role for which both his oratorical skill and his serious concern with people's problems well fitted him. The episode of the speech made to the strikers in "The Pariah" is quite certainly a recollection of a similar address made by Campbell to a crowd of Negro miners in West Virginia, when he tried to persuade them to use their leisure and their money more wisely than in drinking and gambling. The success of this speech has been attested to by Carter G. Woodson, who relates that many miners, influenced by Campbell's words, changed their way of life and flocked to the West Virginia Colored Institute which Campbell was directing.[14]

The People in Campbell's Poetry

Campbell displays greater talent in his popular poetry in dialect than in his English poems. But even if he rarely attains the formal mastery of verse that was at Dunbar's command, one can sense that he adhered more closely to folk reality and was prouder of belonging to his people. Unlike Dunbar, Campbell did not have to gain a livelihood by means of his poetry; he could consequently afford to exhibit a greater independence regarding accepted stereotypes. This he showed both in his use of dialect and in his choice and handling of subjects.

In Dunbar's poems, the dialect is often Negro in name only. One need but examine Lowell's *Bigelow Papers* or Riley's Hoosier poems to discover parallels that throw a clear light on Dunbar's procedures. His aim seems to have been to create a universally applicable American dialect that would be accepted and understood without further ado by the wider public, to whose requirements he was always far too ready to accede.

---

13 *Ibid.,* lines 21-24.
14 Woodson, "J. E. Campbell."

Campbell's dialect, on the contrary, usually conveys the genuine Gullah tone of the black islanders of the Carolinas and Georgia. This is related to the Jamaican speech found in the first two volumes of poetry by Claude McKay (1912).[15]

The plantation and slavery themes are altogether absent; there can be no more convincing proof that the poet maintained his independence vis-à-vis his white readers. On the positive side, Campbell shows himself to be the people's careful observer in social realities, religious formalism, and folk values.

"Uncle Eph's Horse Trade"[16] contains probably the first reference made in all literature to the matriarchy that characterizes the Negro family. The family to which the poem introduces us is ruled over by Aunt Susan, and it is a good thing that this is so. She has a firm grip both on her family responsibilities and on economic reality, while her husband, Uncle Eph, whom she had sent to sell the heifer, has the effrontery to return from town with the smell of booze on his breath and in charge of a one-eyed, broken-winded, rheumatic old mule he had accepted in return for the heifer. Susan has all the needed authority to see to it that, before five in the morning, the mule is taken back to town and the heifer returned to the barn. Uncle Eph listens without a murmur to the blame he so richly deserves:

> Dat blood *do* tell in muleses; it tells in niggahs mo' —
> De Browns was allus triflin', an' Efum, youse *mo'* so.
> I wucked ha'd all lars' summah, w'en you wuz loafin' roun'
> Spen'in' yo lars' nickel in de dram shops in de town,
> Ur sweatin' and ur gruntin' in dat ol' washin' tub
> Ter buy dat Jussey heffah an' keep you all in grub.[17]

Susan, who stands guard over the financial security of her home, also tries to maintain the moral edicts of the church. On her return from a camp meeting where she had gone to worship, she routs a boon companion

---

[15] Characteristic, indeed, of Campbell's language is the use of the subject personal pronoun (less often, of the object pronoun) as a possessive adjective. Also, as in certain Germanic dialects, the adverb of place *where* sometimes serves as a relative pronoun. The verbal copula *to be* is usually left unexpressed, but is sometimes replaced by the repetition of the subject in the form of the pronoun. Finally, one may note the unusual closeness of the vowel *i* and its concomitant lengthening. For instance: *"He* yurs *dee* so long an' *he* eyes so *beeg,* / An' *he* laigs so spry dat he dawnce ur *jeeg"* ("Ol' Doc' Hyar," *Echoes,* p. 13) ; "Dar's Tempie wid dat niggah *whar* waits at de St. Cla'r" ("Church Rally," *Echoes,* p. 37) ; "de one *whar* raise mos' moneh gwi' git ur silbah cup" (*ibid.*). On McKay, see our Ch. 6 below.

[16] *Echoes,* p. 17.

[17] *Ibid.*

who had profited by her absence to indulge, along with Uncle Eph, in the forbidden pleasures of drink and gambling.

But these rough-hewn moral precepts, far from obtaining Campbell's backing, appear to have estranged him from the church. In "De S'prise Party,"[18] which closely resembles Dunbar's "The Party," he lets virtuous Aunt Susan succumb to the sin of dancing. Responsible is the wily Uncle Eph who, while playing hymns on his banjo, imperceptibly moves on from "Neah-row my Gawd ter Dee" to an irresistible country-dance tune. In " 'Sciplinin' Sister Brown,"[19] Campbell vividly shows how little the very censors of morals are convinced that their prohibitions have any validity. The members of the board of deacons, apprised of Susan's downfall, have sought in vain to bring the sinner to repentance. They do not stir from the house until they, too, under the influence of Uncle Eph's invincible rhythm, yield to the impulse to dance. In these circumstances it would be boorish of them not to declare that Susan is innocent. They fall back on the old though specious excuse that no dancing has occurred as long as the feet have not been crossed:

> Sistah Brown wa'n't guilty, caze she nebber crossed her feet![20]

Campbell has a no less cavalier attitude toward the precepts than toward the preachers of this external moralizing. His contempt for it is underlined both by the humorous tone he employs in treating such scenes and by the fact that Aunt Susan's virtuousness and Uncle Eph's indifference are one. It cannot even be asserted that Campbell bothers to condemn the churches and churchly morality, for the gap between them and real life has grown so great that comedy and indulgence are all they deserve. While taking a different route to reach Dunbar's religious skepticism, Campbell's indulgent smile is another sure sign of the black elite's incipient estrangement from the churches.[21]

Yet Campbell's satire does not take for its target either the people or religious feelings per se.[22] On the contrary, he shows a deep sympathy for the people in their direct communication with God, and in the poem

---

[18] *Ibid.*, p. 19.

[19] *Ibid.*, p. 22.

[20] *Ibid.*, p. 23.

[21] On this estrangement, see Carter G. Woodson, *The History of the Negro Church*, Ch. 12, pp. 224ff.

[22] See, with regard to this distinction, the poem "To G. H. G." (*Driftings and Gleanings*, pp. 39-43), stanzas 7 and 8, in which Campbell refuses to criticize religion as such. What he despises, he declares, is the Pharisee who clings to the outer form, but "who letting go the genuine substance of all things, of his religion boasteth so."

"When Ol' Sis' Judy Pray" he depicts with a particularly fortunate touch the precise quality of religious exaltation that marks a divine service in a Negro popular church:

> When ol' Sis' Judy pray,
> De teahs come stealin' down my cheek,
> De voice ur God widin me speak';
> I see myse'f so po' an' weak,
> Down on my knees de cross I seek,
> When ol' Sis' Judy pray.
>
> When ol' Sis' Judy pray,
> De thun'ers ur Mount Sin-a-i
> Comes rushin' down f'um up on high —
> De Debbil tu'n his back an' fly
> While sinnahs loud fur pa'don cry,
> When ol' Sis' Judy pray.
>
> When ol' Sis' Judy pray,
> Ha'd sinnahs trimble in dey seat
> Ter hyuh huh voice in sorro' 'peat:
> (While all de chu'ch des sob an' weep)
> "O Shepa'd, dese, dy po' los' sheep!"
> When ol' Sis' Judy pray.
>
> When ol' Sis' Judy pray,
> De whole house hit des rock an' moan
> Ter see huh teahs an' hyuh huh groan;
> Dar's somepin' in Sis' Judy's tone
> Dat melt all ha'ts dough med ur stone
> When ol' Sis' Judy pray.[23]

But here we are already close to the frontiers of folklore for which, as for everything that concerns the people, Campbell shows an interest filled with respect. In "De Cunjah Man"[24] he enables us to sense the power of the village sorcerer and of the superstitions that lie behind it, and he arouses in us some of the terror that the magician's rites inspire in young and old. If "Negro Lullaby"[25] and "Negro Serenade"[26] show no great departure from Dunbar's songs, "Song of the Corn"[27] is an early attempt to rediscover the functional simplicity of the work song.

Campbell's most notable achievement in this area is perhaps his "Mobile

[23] *Echoes,* p. 44.
[24] *Ibid.,* p. 41.
[25] *Ibid.,* p. 33.
[26] *Ibid.,* p. 40.
[27] *Ibid.,* p. 27.

Buck,"[28] which captures the abrupt rhythm of the Negro dance that bears this name. In a preliminary note, the author explains the circumstances in which he had been able to watch at close range the performance of the dance by the Negro longshoremen on the Ohio or the Mississippi. This sheds light on the difference between the attitudes of Campbell, the respectful and almost anthropological observer of folklore, and of Dunbar, who had primarily the concerns and talents of a showman.

Nevertheless, Campbell does not disdain to utilize the framework of the folktale, with its animal personages, to paint a satirical social portrait. Among such works, "Ol' Doc' Hyar" is a remarkably lively and keenly observed study of a Negro doctor confraternally related to Jules Romains's celebrated Dr. Knock:

> He doctah fur all de beas'es an' bu'ds —
> He put on he specs an' he use beeg wu'ds,
> He feel dee pu's den he look mighty wise,
> He pull out he watch an' he shet bofe eyes;
> He grab up he hat an' he grab up he cane,
> Den — "blam!" go de do' — he gone lak de train,
> > Dis ol' Doc' Hyar
> > Whar lib up dar
> Een ur mighty fine house on ur mighty high hill.[29]

By means of this "Dr. Hare," Campbell is condemning the activities of the new black bourgeoisie, greedy for social standing and lured by wealth (as was the whole American middle class of this Gilded Age), but which remained indifferent to the welfare of the black masses, with whom it had no wish to be identified. Dr. Hare is totally unmoved by the condition of his patients. When he learns of the death of Master Bear, who was in his "care," all he does is scratch his head and remind the family that his fees have to be paid all the same:

> "Ef pahsons git well ur pahsons git wu's,
> Money got ter come een de Ol' Hyar's pu's;

[28] *Ibid.*, p. 36. He states that what he had tried to recapture was "the shuffling, jerky rhythm of the famous negro dance. The author has watched by the hour the negro roustabouts of Ohio and Mississippi river steamboats 'buck' against each other. . . . One roustabout called on by the crew steps out and begins to shuffle. Suddenly he makes a tremendous slide forward on one foot, like the swift stroke of a skater, while with the other foot he beats a perfact tattoo. Each dancer in succession tries to outdo his predecessor, while all are cheered on by the comments and laughter of their rude but picturesque audience."

[29] *Ibid.*, p. 13. "The Courting of Miss Lady Bug" (*ibid.*, p. 34) similarly utilizes animal folklore.

> Not wut folkses does, but fur wut dey know,
> Does de folkses git paid" —[30]

All this bears witness to Campbell's sincere concern for the people and to his feeling that they should be defended against any and all exploiters. Elsewhere, in this shifting and uncertain period, one would seek in vain for equal uprightness and boldness in self-affirmation. Campbell therefore remains the most attractive and the most interesting of Dunbar's contemporaries. In any event, he deserves something better than the neglect he has suffered at the hands of anthologists for the last forty years.[31]

2. DANIEL WEBSTER DAVIS

The name of the Reverend Daniel Webster Davis[32] is remembered, not for the literary excellence of his works, but because of the considerable success enjoyed by his broad comedy in moving popular audiences to gales of laughter. His two collections of poems, mainly in dialect, are *Idle Moments* (1895) and *'Weh Down Souf* (1897). Only a few of these poems fail to employ minstrel-style buffoonery or to take over the servility of the characters inhabiting the plantation tradition. It is, furthermore, far from clear whether Davis was completely sincere or whether he instead set out to win easy popularity from an audience whose demands were slight.

No one was less concerned than Davis with attaining authenticity in the use of dialect, and his pointlessly fantastic orthography[33] had, seemingly, no more important goal than to arouse laughter. The same might be said of his characters. Poems with evocative titles such as "Bakin an' Greens,"[34] "De Biggis' Piece ub Pie,"[35] or "Hog Meat"[36] are obviously and smugly happy to keep alive the reputation for gluttony that the minstrels had foisted on the Negro, whose liking for watermelon had never been held up

[30] *Ibid.*

[31] Only in the anthologies compiled by Johnson, *Book of American Negro Poetry*, pp. 64-71, and Sterling A. Brown et al., eds., *The Negro Caravan*, pp. 316-18, is Campbell represented.

[32] Daniel Webster Davis was born in North Carolina in 1862. Shortly after the Civil War his parents settled in Richmond, Virginia, where Davis completed his secondary schooling in 1878. He began to teach in 1880 and, in 1885, he became a minister. On Davis, see Redding, *To Make a Poet Black*, pp. 53-56; Johnson, *Book of American Negro Poetry*, p. 81; Brown, *Negro Poetry and Drama*, pp. 37-38.

[33] Such as *kows, vizhuns* (*'Weh Down Souf*, p. 19); *politishuns, sum* (for *some*) (*ibid.*, p. 20).

[34] *Ibid.*, p. 10.

[35] *Ibid.*, p. 14.

[36] *Ibid.*, p. 16.

to crasser ridicule than in "Why He Saved the Engine"[37] or "Is Dar Wadermilluns on High?"[38] While almost displaying the indulgence of an accomplice toward thieves — who are blamed for getting nabbed, not for having stolen[39] — Davis finds a sly pleasure in extending suspicion even to his fellow preachers and in heaping them with ridicule, as the minstrels had done. To the preacher of "Fell frum Grace,"[40] who begs indulgence for a chicken thief, he allots this declaration:

> Should Gabul such dis congregashun
> Fur de chickins dat don' gone,
> I'm mighty feard we'd all be lackin',
> So don' let us cast a stone.[41]

His remaining preachers are skinflints[42] or ignoramuses endowed with a certain picturesqueness who entertain their congregations by interpreting Holy Writ in a highly personal fashion,[43] and with all the imaginative virtuosity for which the Negro preachers of that time were celebrated.[44]

As for the chances of progress on the part of his ethnic brothers, Davis appears to have shared the doubts of their white detractors. "Signs"[45] and "When You Gits a Rabbit Foot"[46] seem to demonstrate that Negroes cannot be educated out of their superstitions. But the author finds this consoling, for in his view no good can come from book learning, which is

[37] *Ibid.*, p. 25.

[38] *Ibid.*, p. 116.

[39] "Pomp's Case Argued," *ibid.*, p. 81.

[40] *Ibid.*, p. 37.

[41] *Ibid.* Nevertheless, "Mat" (*ibid.*, p. 85) breaks a lance in favor of unfortunate children, and if Mat, the eleventh child of an impoverished family, is a thief, blame falls in the first place on society, which lets human beings live in such wretched conditions. Note, too, Davis's irony in a poem on a related subject, "My Childhood's Happy Days" (*ibid.*, p. 60).

[42] "Payin' fur de Hydin'," *ibid.*, p. 110.

[43] "Skeetin' on de Ice" (*ibid.*, p. 72), in which the preacher explains that the people of Israel crossed the Red Sea with so little trouble because God had frozen it over. Thus the crossing of the Red Sea becomes a skating party.

[44] The most renowned of these Negro preachers exercised his sacred office in Virginia, as did Davis. This was John Jasper (1812-1893) who, after preaching for some time on Brown's Island, in the James River, established his church in Richmond, where Davis was able to hear him. His most famous sermon was and continues to be "The Sun Do Move, and the Earth Am Square," in which he proved — in a highly imaginative fashion, it goes without saying — that the earth is square, and that the sun revolves around it. See, on this odd character, Roscoe E. Lewis, ed., *The Negro in Virginia*, pp. 250-51. The text of the famous sermon will be found in Langston Hughes and Arna Bontemps, *The Book of Negro Folklore*, pp. 225-33.

[45] *'Weh Down Souf*, p. 43.

[46] *Ibid.*, p. 83.

more or less condemned in "Stickin to de Hoe."[47] Let the Negro stick to manual tasks, which offer him the greatest likelihood of making his way in the world!

> I s'pose dat I'm ol' fashun',
> But God made man to plow,
> An' git his libbin' by de sweat
> Dat trickles down his brow.
>
> While larnin' an' all dem things
> Am mighty good fur sho',
> De bes' way we kin make our pints
> Is stickin' to de hoe.[48]

One can readily distinguish here echoes of Booker T. Washington's theories; Davis quite clearly is his ardent follower. The Tuskegee celebrity also conferred on Davis the privilege of composing an ode, which Davis read at the opening ceremony in the Negro pavilion of the Atlanta Cotton States Exposition on October 21, 1895.[49] Where the master race is concerned, Davis's tone is more than conciliatory.[50] Though he does venture on the way a few timid allusions to the injustices that still victimize the black man,[51] he carefully stresses the pleasantness of life on the plantation of former days,[52] the kindness of the old mistress toward her slaves,[53] and the counterpart of their faithfulness to her. There are long passages that amount to a dithyrambic exaltation of the sweetness of existence to be found only in the South. Davis recognizes Dixie as the homeland of the Negro and declares it to be "the fairest spot on earth."[54]

Davis was more a conformist than any of his contemporaries, and he had

[47] *Ibid.,* p. 57.
[48] *Ibid.*
[49] "Exposition Ode," *ibid.,* p. 65.
[50] When dealing with the heroes who fell during the Civil War, Davis takes good care not to offend either side:
> 'Tis the blessing that we celebrate, and not the cause now lost,
> For that was dear to other hearts as this can be to us.
> And who were right or who were wrong, we are not here to say,
> For, still in death, they're heroes all — the blue, likewise the gray.
>   ("Emancipation," stanza 14, *ibid.,* p. 32)
[51] "Exposition Ode," stanza 16, line 1: "God is not dead, though justice sleeps..." and stanza 17, line 3: "Disfranchisement, injustice and prejudice gone, / We'll both rejoice..." (*ibid.,* p. 71).
[52] "Night on de Ol' Plantashun," *ibid.,* p. 122 and *passim.*
[53] "Ol' Mistis," *ibid.,* p. 112.
[54] See "Exposition Ode," stanzas 13-15, *ibid.,* p. 70, where Davis specifically declares: "The South's our home..." (stanza 13, line 1). The poem ends with this line: "For Dixie Land is still to us the fairest spot on earth." Similar statements are made in, for example, "Ol' Virginny Reel," p. 75, stanza 1; "'Weh Down Souf," p. 7, stanza 1; "Cookin' by de Ol' Time Fireplace," p. 118.

scarcely any other concern than to flatter the white majority. It was to provide them with amusement that he presented his own people as a race of obedient buffoons. Thus Sterling Brown is not far from the truth when he calls Davis the Negro Thomas Nelson Page.[55]

3. J. Mord Allen

Allen,[56] whose modest volume of tales and poems was published in the year of Dunbar's death, was already in certain respects a transitional figure. It is for this reason we believe him to deserve attention, despite the undeniable weaknesses in versification and literary inventiveness.

Most of his subjects exhibit few signs of originality in either conception or treatment, and more than one of his poems might well be presented under a title taken from the corresponding poem by Dunbar. Like his predecessor, Allen celebrates humble folk, and he does not always shun platitude and excessive length in his loving evocation of their reflections on the alternating months and seasons.[57] He hits upon a pleasantly humorous touch in portraying a number of attractive idlers who savor the delight of postponing the chores that await them, either because they cannot resist the allures of a siesta[58] or the joys of fishing,[59] or perhaps because they can place the blame for their laziness on the ravages of a microbe.[60]

Admittedly, Allen distinguishes himself from Dunbar by not becoming the explicit defender of the Old South. He may, nevertheless, have had some inclination in that direction. In "Holding Hands," a black Philemon and Baucis adopt a pathetic tone to express the longing they feel for the Alabama of their youth.[61] The Negro protagonist of "November" recalls the countryside where he used to live and deplores the harshness of his city existence, with a flour bin less often full than empty.[62] Finally, the speaker in "Kivver" is also bitterly disappointed by the northern urban setting, where the struggle to keep alive so absorbs him that he cares

[55] Brown, *Negro Poetry and Drama,* p. 37.

[56] Little is known of J. Mord Allen. Born in Montgomery, Alabama, on March 26, 1875, he left high school without finishing his studies. In 1892 he became a boiler-maker in St. Louis. His miscellany, *Rhymes, Tales and Rhymed Tales,* was published in 1906 in Topeka, Kansas.

[57] "Shine On, Mr. Sun," *Rhymes,* p. 59; "The March Rain," *ibid.,* p. 87; "Ground-Hog Day," p. 102.

[58] "The Coming of the Nap," *ibid.,* p. 123.

[59] "When the Fish Begin to Bite," *ibid.,* p. 23.

[60] "A Victim of Microbes," *ibid.,* p. 7.

[61] *Ibid.,* p. 89.

[62] *Ibid.,* p. 43.

nothing for the lot of his black brothers who are being lynched in the South.[63]

More clearly than by subject matter, Allen is marked off from Dunbar by the mocking, sometimes even violently satirical tone that begins to peep out from beneath the humor. This establishes a certain kinship between his manner and that of Campbell.

With respect to the Negro preachers and their formalized religion, the satire remains within pretty harmless limits. The pastor in "Christmas Coming"[64] satisfies his gluttony at the expense of his parishioners, rendered so sluggish by their digestive processes that they seize on this as an excuse for not attending the Christmas service. In "The Devil and Sis' Viney,"[65] another pastor finally succumbs (within the bonds of wedlock be it said, and after lengthy qualms of conscience that confront the Devil's arguments and those of Saint Paul) to the charms and culinary skills of a pretty widow who has set her cap at him. "The Test,"[66] which is lamentably weakened as a piece of humorous writing by clumsiness and verbosity, pokes fun at the casuistry of a pastor who has to decide a case of con-science involving a checkers player. Paralleling Campbell's poem " 'Scip-linin' Sister Brown," Allen's preacher becomes fascinated by the game, and his morality has to adjust itself to the circumstances. So he will declare the game of checkers to be not a game, but a science. It follows that no sin has been committed.[67]

The theme of the dancer at odds with religious morality, so frequently met with in the Negro poetry of this time, is barely touched upon by Allen in "The Squeak of the Fiddle."[68] But the poem is noteworthy for other rea-sons. Its rhythm and liveliness do not fall far short of the best of Dun-bar's poems. Allen also shows that he has genuine powers of observation, and his asides, which are both subtle and penetrating and carom off satirically in the direction of white people, throw a great deal of light on what the dance means for Negroes. Because of the pleasure they take in it, with the awareness that only they can exploit all its possibilities, dancing becomes, as psychologists have shown,[69] a safety valve releasing their hostility against whites; at the same time, it provides a sense of superiority as an intense enjoyment that whites cannot know.

[63] *Ibid.*, p. 133: "He don' kyer nothin' bout de lynchin's in de South," stanza 3, line 1.
[64] *Ibid.*, p. 99.
[65] *Ibid.*, p. 10.
[66] *Ibid.*, p. 47.
[67] "Yer playin' is er science, en I votes 'It ain't no sin' " (*ibid.*, p. 58).
[68] *Ibid.*, p. 25.
[69] Abram Kardiner and Lionel Ovesey, *The Mark of Oppression: A Psycho-social Study of the American Negro*, pp. 333-34.

(White folks dances jes' fer style;
  Darkies lets dey ankle smile,
  When de fiddle's laffin' at em,
  En dey hyeah de prompter call)[70]

. . . .

(White folks dey got all de money;
  Po' ole darky ain't got none;
  But he's havin all de fun —
  'Deed he is. En kinder tickled,
  Too, ter leave it dat er way)[71]

Letting his sense of inferiority speak, as Dunbar had done, Allen too appears to be arguing in favor of the thesis that the Negro, delighted with his lot and averse to any change, readily resigns himself. This attitude is developed with greater explicitness in what must indeed be looked on as the two most astonishing poems by Allen, "Eureka"[72] and "His Race's Benefactor."[73]

The former is a satire skillfully directed against the ambitions of the new black bourgeoisie, which longs to escape the social boundaries that color imposes on it. Allen imagines that an inexpensive medical preparation has been discovered which, upon ingestion, immediately endows all Negroes with a white skin and straight hair. In the poem's most revealing passage, the Negro speaker, addressing his wife, speculates on what their social relationships will be like once they have changed color. His panorama of the future constitutes an actual inventory of the black man's subconscious, in which lies slumbering his longing for social equality with whites, together with contempt for his own coloring:

En den we'll j'ine er white church
  Ter match our white-folks clo'es.
En I b'lieve I'll run fer office
  Lak de other white men does.
En dese hyeah common darkies —
  We'll quit speakin' ter 'em all;
We'll git 'quainted wid some white folks,
  En ax dem in ter call.
Now, Mandy — Mandy, honey,
  Don't it kind o' make yer smile,
Ter think o' dem white ladies
  Drappin' in ter set er while,

[70] "The Squeak of the Fiddle," *Rhymes*, p. 26.
[71] *Ibid.*, p. 27.
[72] *Ibid.*, p. 61.
[73] *Ibid.*, p. 126.

En us er talkin' ter 'em
'Bout serciety en books,
En "Love, yer cheeks is rosy,"
En "Dear, how pale yer looks"?

Long time I been er figgerin'
How I could pass fer white:

    .   .   .   .

En now it's figgered fer me

    .   .   .   .

We gwine ter change de census
O' de white folks out dis way.[74]

"Eureka" probably contains the first utilization of this theme, which embodied a persistent aspiration of many blacks.[75] So it is not surprising to find it taken up again twenty-five years later in George Schuyler's novel, *Black No More* (1931), which has not been forgotten.

"His Race's Benefactor" is a sometimes blatant diatribe directed against black intellectuals who are committed to the struggle for the advancement of their race. Allen denounces them as parasites living at the people's expense, as dreamers too proud of their own learning to bother themselves with the problems of everyday life, and as Don Quixotes tilting against phantom enemies of the black race. These intellectuals are represented in the poem by Peter; his activities are related to us by his brother who, for his part, is clearly a partisan of Booker T. Washington. The following lines will convey some idea of how Peter is portrayed:

... fer *him*, he knows he's called
Ter help his people out o' whar de white folks got' em stalled.
So, day in, day out, any time er place,
Pete he's in de battle front, fightin' fer de race.

But what makes Pete so sorry is, dat he kain't hol' er job
En fight de race's battles, too, erginst de white-skin mob.
He 'lows it looks so selfish, ter be fingerin' yer gains,
When dar's nine million darkies groanin' under yokes en chains.
En so, he's workin' on dem chains; he leaves de res' ter me —
Ter buy de meal en meat en clo'es, ter dress his famerly.[76]

Peter's attacks on the white oppressors remain purely verbal, and his grandiose plans for saving his whole race have yet to save a single man.

---

[74] *Ibid.*, pp. 62-63.
[75] Yet we should note that, in "The Brown-Skin Girl," Allen celebrates, as Dunbar had done, the ethnically unalloyed black beauty: "Ain't nary lily, nary rose / Mixed up wid her complexion" (*ibid.*, p. 45, lines 3-4).
[76] *Ibid.*, p. 127.

The solution of the race question by means of emigration or intermarriage has remained a dead letter, for the Negroes refuse to emigrate, while the whites refuse to marry blacks.

Allen is especially cynical in his account of the failure of Peter's plan to end lynching:

> Den Pete he got ter figgerin' on mobs en lynchin'-bees.
> He 'lowed de sho' en proper way ter stop sich things wid ease
> Wuz ter tax dese Southern gennermen fer ev'y man dey hung —
> Say — 'bout ten thousan' dollars. But I reck'n dat's too strong;
> 'Kaze I notuss in de lynchin's dat takes place f'um time ter time,
> Dat de darky in de middle would be high-priced at er dime.[77]

No black poet pushed self-contempt so far as to endorse the lynching of his fellows. One may wonder, consequently, whether the hostility expressed by Allen, a boiler-maker by trade, against the intellectuals among the new black bourgeoisie was not, all things considered, the resentment of a jealous, envious inferior.

Today, a major portion of Allen's work has lost all validity. But his social satire, markedly different from Campbell's since it arises from a sense of inferiority, still presents a testimony that helps one in understanding the basic psychological reasons for the resistance, coming from the very depths of the people, that an initiator like W. E. B. Du Bois had to confront in the early years of the twentieth century.

[77] *Ibid.*, p. 130.

PART TWO: THE NEGRO RENAISSANCE

Chapter Five: THE NEGRO RENAISSANCE

Dunbar's death marked the end of an era. Although he survived by a few years the century of his birth, the attitude he embodied to the very end was that of a bygone age. It was the ambivalent attitude of the Negro during Reconstruction — uncertain of himself, subservient, and still a quasi-prisoner within the mentality that two hundred and fifty years of slavery had transformed into second nature. In addition to that, the flaccid, falsely distinguished poetry of the late nineteenth century, which constitutes so large a part of Dunbar's work, was also headed for extinction as a result of the renewal which, beginning in 1912, would so significantly alter the appearance of American poetry. Thus the first prominent poet of the black race was at the same time the last representative of a world doomed to disappear.

Any doubt on this score dwindled to nothing when the years immediately following World War I witnessed an unprecedented literary and artistic flowering among Negroes in the United States. The black race produced one after the other such remarkable poetic personalities as Claude McKay, Jean Toomer, Countee Cullen, Langston Hughes, and Sterling Brown, without counting a number of lesser poets. Even James Weldon Johnson, who was one year older than Dunbar, seemed poetically rejuvenated in this springtime of letters, which the Depression of 1929 slowed but could not stifle.

The dimensions of the phenomenon were equaled only by its suddenness — at least, that is the impression gained by contemporaries. James Weldon Johnson speaks of it as a "sudden awakening" and an "instantaneous change,"[1] excellent characterizations of the astonishment that befell those who were themselves responsible for the development. The movement soon acquired a name: it was called the Negro Renaissance.[2] Alain Locke, the coiner of the term, also provided it with a kind of collective manifesto, *The New Negro*,[3] published in 1925.

This "New Negro" who made his appearance in the world of arts and letters was not simply the creature of some fluke of fate. He came into the world only after a long period of gestation, during which he slowly reached an awareness of his person and his destiny, once the bewilderment following the shock of Emancipation had been overcome. Again, this renewal did not occur solely in literature, which simply reflected the profound social and psychological transformations taking place in the black masses. The writer felt close to these masses, for he had emerged from them. He could thus affect, and provide a stimulus for, their way of seeing things, by contributing a meaning and a value for the changes under way within them.

This Negro renewal would not have been possible but for the particularly favorable combination of circumstances that existed after the armistice of 1918. On the one hand, the period witnessed the materialization of efforts that had been made since the turn of the century to gradually mobilize the black populace and provide it with leadership. For its part, the war brought about or accelerated certain decisive population trends, with repercussions that had an effect on people's minds. Finally, the rebirth of nationalistic feeling throughout Europe was a contributing factor in the birth of Negro nationalism.

[1] James Weldon Johnson, *Black Manhattan*, p. 260.

[2] The value of this appellation will be discussed later. For the moment let us say merely that hitherto the term has been limited to the period that stretches from the end of World War I to the stock market crash of 1929. This terminal date, in our view, does not mark such a decisive rupture that the limitation should be accepted. So we shall utilize the expression "Negro Renaissance" for the entire period lying between the two World Wars, and 1929, a crucial date nevertheless, will be regarded as the boundary line between two phases.

[3] The term "New Negro Movement" is often understood as a synonym for the "Negro Renaissance." According to J. Saunders Redding, *To Make a Poet Black*, p. 98, the originator of the term "New Negro" is Rollin Hartt, who wrote an article entitled "The New Negro" that appeared in *The Independent*, January 15, 1921, pp. 59-60, 76. It is quite certain, however, that the expression is much older. Prior to this date, William Pickens had already published a work called *The New Negro: His Political, Civil and Mental Status* (New York, 1916). But Pickens also is not the originator of the term, and the first to use it appears to have been, by an irony of fate, none other than Booker T. Washington, in his book entitled *A New Negro for a New Century: An Accurate and Up-to-Date Record of the Upward Struggle of the Negro Race* (Chicago, [1900]). Should no even earlier document be brought to light, the earliest use of the term must be situated in the first days of this century.

In the artistic and literary domain, the world was engaged in discovering the Negro at the very moment he was busy rediscovering himself. American poetry, after the appearance of Lindsay, Frost, Masters, and Sandburg, set out on an even more far-reaching revolution with such poets as Eliot, Pound, and Hart Crane. This onward drive also spread to the Negro poetic renewal, which was thus able to benefit, in widely divergent areas, from many helpful factors. Our immediate task will be to examine these, before going on to say what the Negro Renaissance was and what, in particular, were its poets.

1. NEW FORCES

The Role of W. E. B. Du Bois

Booker T. Washington's policy of compromise was on the decline even before the death of its author in 1915. For a dozen years before that, it had been thoroughly battered by one of his most distinguished disciples, W. E. B. Du Bois,[4] who had long been in agreement with the Tuskegee program but finally came to oppose it. He openly took issue with Washington's attitude in the essay "Of Mr. Booker T. Washington and Others," which appeared in 1903 as part of the exceptionally influential book, *The Souls of Black Folk*.[5]

Washington, who was a most accomplished diplomat, had assured himself of the good will and financial support of both North and South, had spoken soothingly into the president's ear and won the favor of a large majority of the black population by envisaging nothing beyond manual and professional training for his people. In return, he was willing to accept for a time a certain limitation in political rights, a status of *de facto* inferiority, and the abandonment of higher education. When addressing his ethnic brothers he tended to speak less of rights than of duties, with regard to both the black and the white racial communities.

At the outset, the two men were brought close to each other by the

---

[4] This account of the Washington-Du Bois controversy is compiled, in the main, from these sources: Johnson, *Black Manhattan,* pp. 131-44; John Hope Franklin, *From Slavery to Freedom,* pp. 384-90; Gunnar Myrdal, *An American Dilemma, passim;* E. Franklin Frazier, *The Negro in the United States,* pp. 523-27, and *Black Bourgeoisie,* pp. 18-19, 66-70; August Meier, "From 'Conservative' to 'Radical': The Ideological Development of W. E. B. Du Bois, 1885-1905," *The Crisis,* November, 1959, pp. 527-36; "How the N.A.A.C.P. Began," *The Crisis,* February, 1959, pp. 71-78; Charles S. Johnson, "The Social Philosophy of Booker T. Washington," *Opportunity,* April, 1928, pp. 102-5, 115.

[5] Pp. 41-59.

shared desire to work for the progress of their race. Washington could only profit by obtaining the sympathy and collaboration of this young Negro scholar, whose thesis *The Suppression of the African Slave-Trade in the United States, 1638-1870* had been brilliantly defended at the oral examination in 1895 and was published as the first volume in the series of Harvard Historical Studies, when its author was still only twenty-seven years old.

When the break occurred, it involved not so much the program to be followed as the urgency that should be attributed to each of its aims. It would be incorrect to state that Washington was opposed to higher education for Negroes, or that Du Bois did not believe they should be given manual and technical training. But the former held that the cultivation of the mind was a luxury that could wait, and that what was needed first of all was the centering of every effort on the economic advancement of the race. Du Bois noted, on the other hand, that benefiting by Washington's conciliatory attitude the South had simply proceeded to disfranchise the Negro, had given legal sanction to his lesser civil status, and had by degrees reduced the aid granted the institutions of higher education open to Negroes. Nor had the number of lynchings decreased.

Faced with this situation Washington maintained his conciliatory tone, whereas Du Bois, on the contrary, decided to raise his voice in protest, both in word and deed, against what he rightly considered to be a return to *de facto* slavery.

To put an end to it, it was clear that the black masses would need leaders, and that Booker T. Washington's program of professional training would never provide any. It would be necessary to pick out a black intellectual elite and educate them at the highest level. This is the program called the "Talented Tenth."[6]

In the interim, it was at once necessary to initiate action. So Du Bois called together a group of black leaders at Niagara Falls in 1905, and they decided to organize a movement in defense of Negro rights. The first congress of this "Niagara Movement" was held the following year at Harpers Ferry, West Virginia, the very scene of John Brown's celebrated raid. The congress demanded for all Negroes the full range of civil and social rights to which every citizen of the United States is entitled, the end of racial discrimination, the right to maintain relations with any other person who is not unwilling to participate, the application of the law to all persons without distinction of financial standing or race, and the right of all chil-

[6] See Du Bois's essay, "The Talented Tenth," pp. 31ff., in his collective volume *The Negro Problem: A Series of Articles by Representative American Negroes of To-day* (New York, 1903).

dren to an education. This impulse led to the formation, in 1909, of the National Association for the Advancement of Colored People, which appointed Du Bois head of the propaganda section and editor of its monthly organ, *The Crisis*, which began publication in 1910. The circulation of this periodical amounted to about 16,000 copies in January, 1912,[7] and by 1918[8] the printing was well above 100,000.

While the N.A.A.C.P. thus became, in the struggle for unrestricted citizenship, a militant organization with hitherto unknown power, other efforts were being made in the cities of the North, especially in New York, to ease the adjustment to the new working environment of the many thousands of Negroes who had left the southern rural regions to look for better-paying work and more humane treatment in the North's urban centers. In 1911 the National Urban League was born, as a result of the fusion of several older committees.

Black Migrations

Since the abolition of slavery, Negroes had become an essentially mobile group in the population. On the one hand, the rural exodus tended to enlarge the urban communities in both North and South.[9] On the other hand, a pattern of migration from the South to the great northern cities was also coming into existence.[10]

As early as 1879, the mistreatment suffered in the South, on top of the setbacks experienced as the result of a poor cotton crop, had led a group of black rural folk from the states bordering the Mississippi to answer the summons of Benjamin "Pap" Singleton, who urged them to emigrate to what appeared to be the new Promised Land, Kansas.[11]

But a much greater shift in population began in 1915 and is still continuing today. It is referred to as the Great Migration. A series of poor

[7] Frazier, *The Negro in the United States*, p. 526.

[8] Hugh Morris Gloster, *Negro Voices in American Fiction*, p. 21.

[9] By 1910, 79.3 percent of all northern Negroes were living in cities, against 64.3 percent in 1860. During the same period, the proportion of the urban Negro population rose from 6.7 percent to 22 percent of the entire Negro population in the South. Between 1910 and 1940, the proportion of the southern Negro population living in cities rose from 22 percent to 37.3 percent (Myrdal, *An American Dilemma*, pp. 183-85). Concerning this whole question of migration, see *ibid.*, pp. 182ff.; also Frazier, *The Negro in the United States*, pp. 527ff. and *passim*. For the personal aspect of these migrations, see Charles S. Johnson, "The New Frontage on American Life," in Alain Locke, ed., *The New Negro*, pp. 278-98.

[10] Between 1910 and 1940, this trend involved about 1,750,000 Negroes (Myrdal, *An American Dilemma*, p. 183).

[11] For Singleton and the 1879 exodus, see Frazier, *The Negro in the United States*, pp. 154-55. More than 40,000 Negroes took part in this exodus (Myrdal, *An American Dilemma*, p. 1230, n. 5).

harvests, floods, and the ravages of the boll weevil produced a serious crisis in the South's rural economy. At the same time, the war that had broken out in Europe caused an acute shortage of labor in the industrial centers of the North. Not only had the flood of immigrants suddenly dried up; many European immigrants had gone back to fight in Europe. Agents were dispatched to the South to recruit workers for northern industry.[12] The Negro press,[13] and in particular the *Chicago Defender,* also helped attract thousands of blacks to the North by dazzling them with tales of the high wages they could earn and the more humane treatment they could hope to receive. In the North, it was said, "a man was a man." Within a few years, half a million Negroes emigrated to the big northern cities.[14]

After the war was over, the movement that had been so thoroughly launched went on at a stepped-up pace. In the twelve months prior to August 21, 1923, almost another half million Negroes left the South.[15] In big cities like New York, Chicago, and Detroit, residential concentrations of blacks grew up in previously unknown proportions.[16]

If Harlem came to be called "The Mecca of the New Negro,"[17] it was not only because this Manhattan neighborhood had become the largest black metropolis the world had ever seen, but also because it could be looked on as the crucible from which a new spirit would emerge.[18] There

[12] See Willis D. Weatherford and Charles S. Johnson, *Race Relations: Adjustment of Whites and Negroes in the United States,* pp. 331-48, on the concrete details of this migration.

[13] On the development of the Negro press throughout this period, see Frazier, *The Negro in the United States,* Ch. 19; and Roi Ottley, "The Negro Press Today," in Sylvestre C. Watkins, ed., *Anthology of American Negro Literature,* pp. 89-100. It should be borne in mind that this expansion of the press could not have occurred without a parallel expansion in education. At the outbreak of the Civil War, more than 90 percent of southern Negroes (who made up about 95 percent of the total Negro population of the United States) were illiterate. After Emancipation, illiteracy shrank regularly year after year, declining from 80 percent in 1870 to 70 percent in 1880, 57.1 percent in 1890, 44.5 percent in 1900, 30.4 percent in 1910, 22.9 percent in 1920 and 10 percent in 1930. Figures taken from W. E. B. Du Bois's "Negro in America," *Encyclopedia Americana* (New York, 1937), XX, 51, col. B.

[14] Franklin, *From Slavery to Freedom,* p. 464.

[15] Frazier, *The Negro in the United States,* p. 193.

[16] Between 1920 and 1930, the Negro populations of New York, Chicago, and Cleveland doubled, while those of Detroit, Gary, and Buffalo tripled (*ibid.,* pp. 193-94).

[17] "Harlem, Mecca of the New Negro" is the title of the special number of the *Survey-Graphic* of March, 1925, prepared under the direction of Alain Locke.

[18] See the article by Locke, "Harlem," *ibid.,* pp. 629-30; and the article by James Weldon Johnson, "The Making of Harlem," *ibid.,* pp. 635-39. This article of Johnson's was, no doubt, the starting point for his book, *Black Manhattan,* which may be consulted. On Harlem, see also Claude McKay, *Harlem, Negro Metropolis.*

the black race acquired consciousness of its unity; there Negroes from North and South, from the United States, the West Indies, and Africa learned in close proximity that the selfsame destiny ruled over them all.

Radicalism and the New Spirit

The new spirit expressed itself basically through the renewed assertion of the dignity of the individual, and by adopting a more manly and resistant attitude toward oppression in all its forms.

Since the United States had taken up arms to defend democracy abroad, democratic principles were more outrageously slighted at home than ever before. In the army camps, Negro recruits were subjected to all kinds of humiliation and unworthy treatment. In the cities of the North, the flood of migrants from the South gave rise to riots. White mobs in East St. Louis, Illinois, were guilty of a massacre in the black quarter on July 2, 1917. They set fire to the houses after nailing up windows and doors so that the black victims could not escape the flames. Screaming children, looking for their already murdered parents, were cold-bloodedly struck down in the streets and tossed half-dead into the bonfires. The balance sheet of this ghastly atrocity amounted to six thousand shelterless Negroes, several hundred dead, and property damage of some half a million dollars.[19]

On their return from France, where the population had treated them like human beings despite the orders of the American High Command,[20] black veterans had decided that they would no longer passively accept injustice and violence. During the race riots that saw bloodshed even in the federal capital as the "Red Summer" of 1919 ran its course, Negroes were not the only ones to pay the ultimate price. Whites learned that from now on blacks were resolved to meet violence with violence.[21] Once again it was W. E. B. Du Bois who voiced the feelings of all blacks as they returned home from fighting for democracy: "Under similar circumstances, we would fight again. But by the God of Heaven, we are cowards and jackasses if now that that war is over, we do not marshal every ounce of our brain and brawn to fight a sterner, longer, more unbending battle against the forces of hell in our land."[22]

In official circles such statements, which Du Bois was not alone in uttering and circulating, were held to be radical and seditious. A witch

[19] See Johnson, *Black Manhattan*, pp. 238-44.
[20] *Ibid.*, pp. 244-45; and Franklin, *From Slavery to Freedom*, pp. 460-61. See also the text of a circular by Albert Sarraut on this matter in Nancy Cunard, ed., *Negro Anthology*, p. 559.
[21] *Ibid.*, p. 246.
[22] W. E. B. Du Bois, "Returning Soldiers," *The Crisis* XVIII (1919), 14.

hunt was organized, with results that may be read in a Senate document entitled *Radicalism and Sedition among the Negroes as Reflected in Their Publications.* We cannot better characterize the spirit of the "New Negro" and, at the same time, the regressive and reactionary mentality of the Department of Justice of the period, than by allowing this document to speak briefly for itself: "There can no longer be any question of a well-concerted movement among a certain class of Negro leaders of thought and action to constitute themselves a determined and persistent source of a radical opposition to the Government, and to the established rule of law and order."[23]

To refuse to be slaughtered or burned alive was, consequently, to threaten public order! But we reproduce below the principal seditious attitudes with which black leaders were charged:

1. The ill-governed reaction toward race rioting;
2. The threat of retaliatory measures in connection with lynching;
3. The more openly expressed demand for social equality, in which demand the sex problem is not infrequently included;
4. The identification of the Negro with such radical organizations as the I.W.W.[24] and an outspoken advocacy of the Bolsheviki and Soviet doctrines;
5. The political stand assumed toward the present Federal administration, the South in general, and incidentally, toward the peace treaty and the League of Nations.

Underlying these more salient viewpoints is the increasingly emphasized feeling of a race consciousness, in many of these publications always antagonistic to the white race and openly, defiantly assertive of its own equality and even superiority ... The boast is not to be dismissed lightly ... The sense of oppression finds increasingly bitter expression ... Defiance and insolently race-centered condemnation of the white race is to be met with in every issue of the more radical publications ... The Negro is "seeing red." ...[25]

[23] *Radicalism and Sedition among the Negroes as Reflected in Their Publications,* Exhibit no. 10, pp. 161-87 in 66th Cong., 1st sess., *Senate Documents,* vol. 12, Document no. 153, "Investigation Activities of the Department of Justice." Letter from the Attorney General transmitting in response to a Senate resolution of October 17, 1919, a report on the activities of the Bureau of Investigation of the Department of Justice against persons advising anarchy, sedition and the forcible overthrow of the Government. Serial no. 7607, p. 162.

[24] These letters stand for Industrial Workers of the World, a workers' organization of the far left, founded in Chicago in 1905, which demanded the abolition of the system of wages and the establishment of international socialism. They were popularly known as the "Wobblies."

[25] *Radicalism and Sedition,* p. 162. It was, doubtless, an oversimplification to

In these terms the sleuths of Attorney General A. Mitchell Palmer have recorded for posterity the spirit of an age, "the dangerous spirit of defiance and vengeance at work among the Negro leaders."[26]

The Rehabilitation of the Negro Past

A famous name from the exhibits[27] cited in the above document is that of Marcus Garvey,[28] the extraordinary black prophet who, through his speeches no less than his person, galvanized the black masses of the United States for more than four years.

Born in Jamaica in 1887,[29] there Garvey had tried in vain to establish his "Universal Negro Improvement Association." But fortune smiled on him in the United States, where he transferred his activities in 1916. His project was absolutely fantastic. He envisaged the creation of an independent Negro nation in Africa, establishing the Black Star Line Steam-

look on Negro radicalism as nothing more than a phase of the "Red Scare" which struck terror into the hearts of solid citizens at this time. But there is no denying that from this time on some blacks, Claude McKay among them, had close connections with the "Reds." The Communist party of the United States subsequently made ever greater efforts to gain sympathy among blacks. Thus, in the fall of 1928, the proposal was made that Negroes in the southern states — in the so-called "Black Belt," where they then made up more than half of the population — should be granted the right of "national self-determination." On this, see Frank A. Scott, *An Inquiry into the Communist Program for the National Self-determination of Negroes in the Black Belt* (M.A. dissertation, Howard University, 1951). The Communist party of the United States did not drop this point from its program until its seventeenth congress met in Harlem in December, 1959. In the meantime, many prominent Negroes, including W. E. B. Du Bois and Langston Hughes, became at the very least strong sympathizers with the Party.

26 *Ibid.*, p. 187.

27 The Senate document surveys the whole "radical" press: *The Negro World, The Crusader, The Challenge, The Messenger, The Chicago Whip,* etc. Cited as "seditious" is an article entitled "The Glory of Death" that appeared in the last-named periodical on July 13, 1919. The writer of the article rejoiced in the death of Booker T. Washington because, he declared, this spared the Negro race "at least five years under ether" (*Radicalism and Sedition,* p. 186). Also see, on this radical press, Johnson, *Black Manhattan,* pp. 246-51.

28 Among the countless books and articles devoted to Garvey, one may consult, in addition to Garvey's own writings, E. David Cronon, *Black Moses: The Story of Marcus Garvey and the Universal Negro Improvement Association* (Madison, 1955); McKay, *Harlem, Negro Metropolis,* pp. 143-80; Johnson, *Black Manhattan,* pp. 251-59; Charles S. Johnson, "After Garvey — What?" *Opportunity,* August, 1923, pp. 231-33; A. F. Elmes, "Garvey and Garveyism: An Estimate," *Opportunity,* May, 1925, pp. 139-41; E. Franklin Frazier, "The Garvey Movement," *Opportunity,* November, 1926, pp. 346-48; Birgit Aron, "The Garvey Movement: Shadow and Substance," *Phylon,* fourth quarter, 1947, pp. 337-43.

29 This is the date given by, among others, McKay and Johnson, in the works cited in the previous footnote. Other writers give Garvey's birthdate as 1885.

ship Company to transport there all the blacks of America, and founding a weekly, *The Negro World,* to disseminate his ideas. Arrested for fraud, he was imprisoned in the Atlanta penitentiary and then expelled from the United States.

In material terms, Garvey's projects suffered a resounding defeat. His shipping line never owned more than a few vessels too badly in need of repair to take to sea. Those who had been naïve enough to purchase shares in his corporations lost their money, and the Republic of Africa, whose provisional president he had at once proclaimed himself to be, was never born. Yet all this matters very little, for Garvey's real importance lies elsewhere. It lies in his having brought into being the greatest mass movement Negroes had had to that time. For the millions of Negroes who spent several years under the thrall of his person and his central idea, Garvey was the living incarnation of their deepest dreams. While peoples' right to self-determination was being proclaimed, with cries of Poland for the Poles and Ireland for the Irish, Garvey arrived at the critical juncture to go them one better with Africa for the Africans! No American Negro was ever actually taken to Africa in a ship of the Black Star Line; not one might even have wanted to go back to live in the land of his ancestors. But this sea route, though amounting to no more than a line drawn on a map, at least symbolically reestablished a vital artery between the descendants of slaves and their true motherland. "Mother Africa!" Langston Hughes will call out, as though to hurl defiance at America and make it jealous, since it had never been more than a cruel stepmother for its dark-skinned children.

For the first time, Garvey aroused in all these children of Africa the consciousness of their unity, their nobility, and their greatness. Though still only provisionally the president of the great Africa of the future, Garvey had already taken care to surround himself with a black nobility of dukes and duchesses, of Knights Commanders of the Distinguished Order of Ethiopia or of the Sublime Order of the Nile. The man who labored all day as dishwasher in a Lenox Avenue eatery or as shoeshine boy near a subway entrance donned, that same evening, the resplendent uniform of his grade in the Household of the Provisional President, and he set off to file through Liberty Hall together with the sick nurses of the Black Cross and the officers of the African Legion in gala uniform, to the cheers of the frenzied black crowds. To the frustration and disillusionment that embittered the masses, Garvey applied the balm of a vision, but this vision seemed to have begun already to find its embodiment. To those whom slavery had stamped with the shame of their color, Garveyism, a veritable black racism, restored the pride in their color. Beyond this, Garvey added a spiritual sanction to the solemnly proclaimed beauty and nobility of blackness, for in the Orthodox African Church that he had founded God and the angels were black, while Satan was white.

Today Garvey's body, like John Brown's, lies mouldering in the grave, but his soul goes marching on.

The rehabilitation of Africa was not the work of Garvey alone, however. Though others may have contributed in less spectacular fashion to this goal, they were no less efficient.

The years following World War I witnessed in succession the first four Pan-African Congresses. They met in Paris (1919), London (1921, 1923), and New York (1927), with W. E. B. Du Bois the driving force behind them. Though what they achieved in the short run was quite modest, they nevertheless contributed, on other lines than Garvey's, to propagating the Pan-African idea in the black world and keeping it alive in people's minds.[30]

A much more direct and lasting influence on the cultural life of blacks in the United States was exerted by another initiative. In 1915, the son of onetime slaves, Carter G. Woodson, who had obtained his doctorate at Harvard University, founded the Association for the Study of Negro Life and History. When the first issue of the Association's journal, *The Journal of Negro History*, appeared in January, 1916, half of the articles dealt with Africa. Woodson's step would lead to many historical and sociological studies, which made it possible to bring to light a mass of documents concerning the history of the black race.[31] In their endeavor to reach a scientific assessment of historical happenings, the publications of the Association and its sympathizers were in fact going to refute the conclusions of a biased historical school which, as one of its chief aims, sought to establish by pseudo-scientific means the inferiority of the black and so provide a better justification for slavery or segregation.[32] Africa today is still at the center of the Association's preoccupations, and it is thanks in part to Woodson that one can no longer think of teaching young Americans that "Africa is

[30] On the Pan-African movement, see Philippe Decraene, *Le Panafricanisme,* and W. E. B. Du Bois, "Pan-Africa and New Racial Philosophy," *The Crisis,* November, 1933, pp. 247, 262.

[31] References to the principal works by Carter G. Woodson will be found in our bibliography. On Woodson and Africa, see Ulysses Lee, "The ASNLH: The Journal of Negro History and American Scholarly Interest in Africa," John A. Davis, ed., *Africa Seen by American Negroes* (Paris, 1958), pp. 401-18.

[32] On the highly relative objectivity of some white American historians in their writings dealing with the Negro, see Stanley M. Elkins, *Slavery: A Problem in American Institutional and Intellectual Life,* pp. 1-26.

noted for its burning climate, its vast deserts, and for the dark color and degraded character of its inhabitants."[33]

Not the least among Woodson's qualities is the fact that, looking beyond his intellectual equals, he also envisaged the cultural needs of the great mass of black people. It is for them that he founded, alongside the *Journal of Negro History,* the *Negro History Bulletin,* to diffuse more widely the results gained in research. He also organized Negro History Week, which even today makes a special effort, often with the collaboration of the civil authorities, to remind Americans of both races of the part played by Negroes in the material and cultural building of America.

In the anthology-manifesto *The New Negro* (1925), Arthur A. Schomburg proclaims the enormous importance of the Negro's rediscovering his own history:

> The American Negro must remake his past in order to make his future. Though it is orthodox to think of America as the one country where it is unnecessary to have a past, what is a luxury for the nation as a whole becomes a prime social necessity for the Negro. For him, a group tradition must supply compensation for persecution, and pride of race the antidote for prejudice. History must restore what slavery took away, for it is the social damage of slavery that the present generations must repair and offset.[34]

2. THE PROBLEM OF SELF-DEFINITION

The lexicographer Littré declares that "Renaissance" is a word "sometimes used to denote a lively movement in people's minds, after a period of oppression."[35] Thus the Negro Renaissance is fittingly named, for it was basically the artistic expression of a lively movement in people's minds. Its birth was made possible by the events we have summarily evoked, and it had its prime importance as a reaction that would succeed in liquidating the aftermath of the period of oppression and slavery, and in barring any return of such practices.

When Alain Locke gave the movement the name "Renaissance," he was thinking primarily of an analogy with the Irish Renaissance,[36] whose earliest stirrings became manifest shortly before the turn of the century. "Harlem," he said," has the same role to play for the New Negro as Dublin

[33] Sidney E. Morse, *A System of Geography for the Use of Schools* (New York, 1855). Cited by Lee, "The ASNLH," p. 402, n. 2.

[34] Arthur A. Schomburg, "The Negro Digs up His Past," in Locke, ed., *The New Negro,* p. 231.

[35] Emile Littré, "Renaissance," *Dictionnaire de la langue française* (Paris, 1958).

[36] Alain Locke, *Le Rôle du nègre dans la culture des Amériques,* p. 62.

has had for the New Ireland."[37] In both instances the literary revival had a political and social aspect, and it drew its strength from the concentrated urge to freedom on the part of a people long oppressed. In each case, too, the projected emancipation had to confront the problem of cultural dualism. Would the literature of the New Ireland discard everything British? And, in the Negro Renaissance, what would be the proportion of Negro and American ingredients?

To answer this question amounted to venturing a self-definition. But how could a man say who he was, or who he wanted to be, except by referring to what he had previously been forced to be? There could be no question of self-definition without a new evaluation of the past.

Like the great European Renaissance, the Negro's "Little Renaissance"[38] had, in addition to an Antiquity to excavate and extoll, a Middle Ages to repudiate. Africa, whose artistic treasures were only currently being discovered, was its Antiquity, and slavery its Middle Ages, whose shadows were at last being dispersed in the dawn of a new age:

> We have tomorrow
> Bright before us
> Like a flame.
>
> Yesterday
> A night-gone thing
> A sun-down name.
>
> And dawn-today
> Broad arch above the road we came.[39]

It was with reference to this dual past that the New Negro tried to define his real personality.

The Negro Renaissance emerges in its entirety out of a new vision of the race's common past. Its history had been distorted by pro-slavery ideology; now the Negro labors to restore the true image of that history. Long ashamed of it, he now finds in it a legitimate cause for pride: "There has come to us a realization of that past of which for long years we have been ashamed, for which we have apologized. We thought nothing could come out of that past which we wanted to remember, which we wanted to hand down to our children. Suddenly, this same past is taking on form, color and reality, and in a half shame-faced way we are beginning to be

[37] Alain Locke, "The New Negro," in Locke, ed., *The New Negro*, p. 7.
[38] Derived from the title of an article by Alain Locke, "Our Little Renaissance," in Charles S. Johnson, ed., *Ebony and Topaz*, pp. 117-18.
[39] Langston Hughes, "Poem," *The Weary Blues*, p. 108.

proud of it."[40] While engaged in rehabilitating his past, he also redeems his black color and all that it stands for. For this is the visible sign that testifies to the common destiny uniting him with all other Negroes in the world, especially with those of the African mother country.

The Discovery of the Negro and of Negro Art

This proved a singularly favorable moment for a fresh evaluation of the black cultural heritage since, in the years that followed World War I, the wider public of the Western world was itself occupied in discovering Negro art in all its manifestations.

The British punitive expedition which had taken the town of Benin in January, 1897, had carried off between two and three thousand master-pieces in bronze and ivory; these were placed on exhibition in the museums of London and Berlin.[41] In Brussels, visitors to the 1897 exposition saw assembled a magnificent collection of African sculptures and masks. In Paris, African sculpture was first proclaimed art by a group of painters[42] who had learned to appreciate it in the galleries of the old Trocadéro or on the premises of the dealer Paul Guillaume, whose collection attracted a whole crowd of artists, including painters, sculptors, decorators, musicians, and writers. In Merion, Pennsylvania, the collector Albert C. Barnes had just founded the museum of Negro art that bears his name. The Negro cultural periodical *Opportunity*, founded by the National Urban League in 1923, had enlisted the collaboration of Guillaume and Barnes to spread knowledge of African art among Negroes in the United States. Special numbers on Negro art[43] were published in May, 1924, and May,

[40] W. E. B. Du Bois, "Criteria of Negro Art," *The Crisis*, October, 1926, p. 292. On history as a source of race pride, see James Weldon Johnson, *Negro Americans, What Now?* pp. 45-48.

[41] On the artistic discovery of Benin, see Denise Paulme, *Les Sculptures de l'Afrique noire*, p. 23. For some of the information contained in this paragraph, we are indebted to the opening chapter of this work.

[42] Especially Vlaminck, Matisse, and Derain. The last-named spent long hours in the ethnographic section of the British Museum. "In 1908, there were some twenty African statues in Henri Matisse's collection; Derain, Braque and Picasso own a number of African masks" (*ibid.*, pp. 1-2).

[43] In particular, the issue of May, 1924, contained articles by Alain Locke, Albert C. Barnes, and Paul Guillaume. In the issue of May, 1926, see above all the article by Paul Guillaume, "The Triumph of Ancient Negro Art," pp. 146-47, which provides interesting details concerning "the discovery of Negro art" in Paris at the beginning of the twentieth century. The article summarizes a lecture he had given at the Barnes Foundation on April 4, 1926. See also Albert C. Barnes, "Primitive Negro Sculpture and Its Influence on Modern Civilization," *Opportunity*, May, 1928, pp. 139-40, 147. The influence of African art on the spirit of the Negro Renaissance is also attested in the collective volume, Locke, ed., *The*

1926; interspersed among the articles were poems of African inspiration by Langston Hughes, Claude McKay, and Lewis Alexander.

In literature, too, the Negro was in vogue on both sides of the Atlantic. The year 1920 saw Blaise Cendrars's Paris publication of his *Anthologie nègre*, which brought together tales, legends, fables, poetry, and songs by black Africans. The following year, the West Indian writer René Maran won the Goncourt Prize for his *Batouala*, subtitled "An Authentic Negro Novel." It was translated into English without delay and had considerable influence on Negroes in the United States. When André Gide's *Voyage to the Congo* appeared in 1927, with a sequel published in 1928, black America saw its impression confirmed that France was "turning to vital, genuine sources."[44] The writers of postwar America, in their revulsion both against the machine and against the Victorian prudery that still dominated small-town life, often came to look on the Negro as a kind of noble savage whose primitive spontaneity had been left untouched by the horrors of the civilization they were condemning.[45] This is partially true for Waldo Frank (*Holiday*, 1923) and for Sherwood Anderson (*Dark Laughter*, 1925). The theme is employed more extensively than ever in the southern novel: T. S. Stribling (*Birthright*, 1922), Julia Peterkin (*Green Thursday*, 1924; *Black April*, 1927), Du Bose Heyward (*Porgy*, 1925;[46] *Mamba's Daughters*, 1929), E. C. L. Adams (*Congaree Sketches*, 1927; *Nigger to Nigger*, 1928), Roark Bradford (*Ol' Man Adam and His Chil-*

New Negro. See Albert C. Barnes, "Negro Art and America," *ibid.*, pp. 19-25; Alain Locke, "The Legacy of the Ancestral Arts," *ibid.*, pp. 254-67, and illustrations. The same holds true for Cunard's *Negro Anthology*, which devotes an entire section, with numerous illustrations, to African sculpture (pp. 656-733) and has lavish documentation concerning the ethnic surroundings in which it originated. See too the second part of Davis, ed., *Africa Seen by American Negroes*, esp. James A. Porter, "The Trans-Cultural Affinities of African Art," pp. 119-30; and J. Newton Hill, "African Sculpture: An Aesthetic Evaluation," pp. 131-41; and the illustrations.

[44] Sterling A. Brown, "The New Negro in Literature," *The New Negro Thirty Years Afterward*, p. 58. Brown regrets, however, that Paul Morand in *Magie Noire* (1929) could hit on nothing better than to include "absurd fantasies of American Negroes reverting at slightest provocation to ancestral savagery" (*ibid.*).

[45] It is clearly impossible for us to do more than touch on this subject. For a broader investigation, see Sterling A. Brown, *The Negro in American Fiction*, Ch. 8-12, pp. 115ff., and the same author's *Negro Poetry and Drama*, Ch. 7, pp. 93-102, and Ch. 9-10, pp. 115ff. See also his two articles, "Negro Character as Seen by White Authors," *Journal of Negro Education*, April, 1933, pp. 179-203; and "The American Race Problem as Reflected in American Literature," *Journal of Negro Education*, July, 1939, pp. 275-90. In Gloster, *Negro Voices in American Fiction*, and Robert A. Bone, *The Negro Novel in America*, will be found studies of novels written by Negroes.

[46] Staged in 1927 in a version by Du Bose and Dorothy Heyward. Gershwin based on it his opera *Porgy and Bess* (1935).

dren, 1928),[47] etc. The Negro is placed at the center of popular theater fare by Ridgely Torrence and Paul Green, and Eugene O'Neill, in two of his plays, fully develops the dramatic impact of black destiny. While *The Emperor Jones* (1920) is still much concerned with tom-toms, superstitions, and black atavism, Brutus Jones is nevertheless a tragic character who, in certain respects, might well have been inspired by Marcus Garvey. *All God's Chillun Got Wings* (1924) treats with unusual honesty and realism the psychological problems that arise from association between the two races. For various reasons the personage of the Negro matched, for all these writers, the preoccupations expressed in these words by Carl Van Doren in 1924: "What American literature decidedly needs at the moment is color, music, gusto, the free expression of gay or desperate moods. If the Negroes are not in a position to contribute these items, I do not know what Americans are."[48]

In this mass of literature, a place of special importance must be attributed to the novel *Nigger Heaven* (1926) by Carl Van Vechten, who was one of the principal promoters of a cultural rapprochement between blacks and whites during the Negro Renaissance.[49] Some idea of the influence he exerted is conveyed by the fact that this novel, in the seventeen months following publication, went into thirteen reprintings. Like its author, *Nigger Heaven* was a kind of symbolic hyphen between the two races, not only because the blues that speckle it throughout had been specially written for Van Vechten by Langston Hughes, but also because it epitomizes the shared taste for eroticism and primitivism which drew both blacks and whites to Harlem[50] as long as the jazz age lasted.

Jazz contributed more than any other art form to making the Negro known in the postwar world.[51] Crowds in the cities of America and Europe

[47] This is the source for Marc Connelly's famous play *The Green Pastures* (1930).

[48] Carl Van Doren, "The Younger Generation of Negro Writers," *Opportunity,* May, 1924, p. 145.

[49] On the role Carl Van Vechten played in the Negro Renaissance, see George S. Schuyler, "Carl Van Vechten," *Phylon,* fourth quarter, 1950, pp. 362-68, and also Van Vechten's own article in *The Crisis* of July, 1942, on the Negro collection he founded at Yale University. On the influence of *Nigger Heaven* and the controversies touched off by the book, see Hugh Morris Gloster, "The Van Vechten Vogue," *Phylon,* fourth quarter, 1945, pp. 310-14.

[50] On the Harlem atmosphere during the Negro Renaissance one may consult, in addition to the works cited in note 18 above, the series of articles by Wallace Thurman, "Negro Life in New York's Harlem: A Lively Picture of a Popular and Interesting Section," *The Light,* November 5, 1927 (the poor condition of the copy at our disposition makes it impossible to give pagination); November 12, 1927, pp. 10-12, 46; November 19, 1927, pp. 7-9; November 26, 1927, pp. 8-10. See also Nancy Cunard, "Harlem Reviewed," *Negro Anthology,* pp. 67-75.

[51] A selection of works on jazz can be found in our bibliography. See also J. A.

were avid for this music and its accompanying dances; soon, too, composers, music critics, and intellectuals of every stripe began to examine it closely.[52] They would have erred had they not taken it seriously, for it was a sign of something more meaningful than a mere revolution in the aesthetics of musical rhythm. Jazz summed up a whole life-style. It was a rebellion against the norms and servitudes of the past; it flaunted one's adhesion to a new scale of values. In the success it met with among the most varied races in every country in the world, the American Negro saw the assurance that his art, far from bearing the blemish of inferiority, had on the contrary a universal and deeply human value. Thus the addiction to jazz was in itself a rehabilitation of the Negro past.

Cultural Dualism and Its Problems

Slavery was undoubtedly the blot on the escutcheon, the most haunting shadow in the panorama of this past. Despite the legal measures by which emancipation was brought about, the mark of oppression had been pitilessly passed on from slaves to free men, as though it were some sort of original sin. As a consequence, the children of the generation which had suddenly stepped out of bondage into liberty on January 1, 1863, had peremptorily and totally renounced slavery and everything that could possibly call it to mind.

But around 1920 a third generation took over. Its attitudes obeyed the same psychological laws noted in the case of the descendants of immigrants. Immigrants' sons desire nothing more than to shake off every reminder of the culture from which they sprang; they are impatient to merge totally, if possible, with the already assimilated American masses. But when the third generation puts in an appearance, the problem is no longer how

Rogers, "Jazz at Home," in Locke, ed., *The New Negro*, pp. 216-24; and Cunard, ed., *Negro Anthology*, pp. 346-95. Linked with the fashionableness of jazz is that of black music-hall artists, actors, singers, and sports champions. See, on this, Cunard, ed., *Negro Anthology*, pp. 290-344; Johnson, *Black Manhattan*, pp. 104-25, 160-230; and Sterling A. Brown, "Athletics and the Arts," *The Integration of the Negro into American Society*, Papers Contributed to the Fourteenth Annual Conference of the Division of the Social Sciences, Howard University (1951), pp. 117-47.

[52] Frederick J. Hoffman, *The Twenties*, p. 270, n. 7, cites the following articles and books, a list that will convey some idea of the importance attached to jazz at that time: Jean Cocteau, *Le Coq et l'arlequin* (1918); Ernest Ansermet, "On a Negro Orchestra," *Revue Romande*, October, 1919; W. J. Turner, "Jazz Music," *New Statesman*, February 5, 1921; Marion Bauer, "L'Influence du 'Jazz-Band'," *La Revue Musicale*, April, 1924; Darius Milhaud, "Jazz-Band and Negro Music," *Der Querschnitt*, Summer, 1924; M. Ladoche, "Musique américaine," *Revue Politique et Littéraire*, June 5, 1926; Constant Lambert, "Jazz," *Life and Letters* (1928); Clive Bell, *Since Cézanne* (1929).

to become lost in the crowd but how to identify closely with one of the groups that make it up. The third generation feels the need to disinter what the preceding generation had spurned, for these grandchildren want to take root, and not drift like flotsam on the limitless wastes of human anonymity. This reassessment of the past is a phenomenon that characterizes the third generation. In the felicitous phrase of Marcus Hansen, "What the son wishes to forget, the grandson wishes to remember."[53]

For blacks of the postwar period this need was all the more urgent, since internal migration had given rise to a whole mass of rootless people in the northern cities. Torn from the southern rural habitat that had been the setting for the lives of many generations, they suddenly found themselves hundreds or thousands of miles removed from the familiar scenes, lost amid the crowd in an inhuman world where no one either knew or cared for them. Transplanted to this urban environment, Negroes needed more than ever to recall the past.

Nevertheless, the problem of the generations was not the only factor determining the new view of the past. It would be a mistake to underestimate the influence exercised, at the nascent stage, by an ever more pronounced social stratification within the Negro population.

The Renaissance was, indeed, closely linked to the masses of black people, just as were several of the ideological factors that had collaborated to produce it. It was a popular movement, not at all bourgeois or aristocratic. Garvey owed his rise and his successes to the support of the masses, not of the middle class. Writers like Claude McKay and Langston Hughes had not merely sprung from the people; they fought on its behalf in political or trade-union organizations of the left or far left. So it is not surprising that the reevaluation of the past undertaken by the Negro Renaissance should have tended to rehabilitate the people above all else. In truth, the phenomenon of black culture came from the people.

When one states that the Negro Renaissance was a negation of slavery, it is highly necessary to reach agreement on the precise content of the

[53] Marcus L. Hansen, *The Problem of the Third-Generation Immigrant* (1938), pp. 9-10. Cited by Will Herberg, *Protestant, Catholic, Jew: An Essay in American Religious Sociology*, p. 43. Yet we hasten to add that there is nothing absolute about this phenomenon, especially in the case of the Negro. The tendency to identify with the tradition of the racial group is constantly opposed and clouded over by the tendency to assimilate with the larger majority community, on which to a very great extent one must depend in order to achieve the economic goals of existence. Thus Langston Hughes, discussing "the younger colored people," remarked in 1927: "I found that their ideals seemed most Nordic and un-Negro, and that they appeared to be moving away from the masses of the race rather than holding an identity with them" ("Our Wonderful Society: Washington," *Opportunity*, August, 1927, p. 226).

term. Slavery is everything, whether *de facto* or *de jure,* which had aimed at robbing the Negro of his essential humanity. For the Negro himself, it included everything which, on his part, might contribute to the notion that he accepted the situation that had been forced on him. In short, slavery was a mask that had been affixed to the Negro and that had inevitably left deep stigmata on his personality. But now the time had come for him to snatch off the mask so that he might show his real face.

By some miracle, all the forces of oppression that had been unleashed against him had proved unable to smother his creative genius entirely. In these circumstances a half-century elapsed before the gathering and appreciation of his folklore treasures began. Thanks largely to the efforts of such men as James Weldon Johnson, America and the world became aware not only of the Negro spirituals but of a whole band of black poets, several of whom were born in slavery.

Everything considered, and to the extent that it had the good sense not to confuse slavery itself with those who had been its victims, the Negro Renaissance was as much a resurrection as it was a criticism of the past.

This attitude sometimes led to harsh confrontations with spokesmen for the black middle class, whose influence was growing along with its numerical importance as schooling became more general and the economic advances of the race were more firmly established. This black bourgeoisie, which had emerged from the class of those who had been free before Emancipation, was traditionally ill-disposed toward the tattered, unschooled black masses with which it had no desire to be lumped together. Its aim was to achieve a status modeled on that of the white middle class; the rowdy flamboyance of some forms of popular culture, whether jazz or the religious demonstrativeness of the popular sects, was basically antipathetic. Yet the white majority, by overlooking such all too subtle social distinctions and by subjecting the black masses and the black bourgeoisie to the same discrimination, forced the latter to seek a compromise with the former. If the black middle class sought identification with something different from the culture of the majority which offered only rebuffs, there was nothing for it but to make common cause, in some measure, with the black masses.[54]

Much the same pulling and hauling took place among the black intellectual elite, as it slowly took shape following the earlier efforts of W. E. B. Du Bois. Since their discomfiture was also to some extent that of the Lost Generation, black intellectuals were naturally up in arms against middle-

[54] See E. Franklin Frazier, *Black Bourgeoisie,* in particular Ch. 5, pp. 112ff.; and W. E. B. Du Bois, "On Being Ashamed of Oneself," *The Crisis,* September, 1933, pp. 199-200.

class hypocrisy and puritanism, both white and black. But if, almost to a man, they scorned to identify themselves with American industrial materialism, and if as Negroes they had an especially acute awareness of the chasm separating the democratic ideal from social reality, that nevertheless did not ensure universal agreement concerning the aspects of the Negro past that should be preserved and set up as values in the cultural heritage, reconstituted after the event, which the New Negro planned to bestow on himself.

In their choice of values, they were swayed at times by considerations other than those which dictated the attitude of the black middle class. While the latter looked forward to the disappearance of any feature that might mark it off from the white middle class, the black intellectuals had no objection in principle to adopting a dual culture. At a time when Western civilization was subjected to so much criticism by white writers, it appeared more opportune than ever to provide a certain number of improvements derived from the black cultural past currently in the process of reevaluation. Moreover, the Negro had no choice but to live in two worlds, showing himself "white" with whites and "black" with blacks. Cultural dualism, consequently, seemed far better fitted to the actual situation than did any exclusive option.

Also militating in favor of this solution were the conditions in which the writer could hope to be published and read. In spite of the extension of schooling among his own people, he could scarcely count on any audience but whites to buy and read his books. James Weldon Johnson relates that a New York publisher said to him one day: "I would publish any good book touching on the Negro that came to me, if I felt that I could count on three thousand colored people buying it." And Johnson gives us his response:

> I had to tell him that he could not count on three thousand; no, not on two thousand; not even on one thousand — not on one thousand out of twelve million!
>
> We are not book buyers. We are not book readers...We show small interest even in books that vitally affect us, either for good or for ill...If we had only twelve thousand Negro American book buyers...regularly... the publishers in the United States would take notice, and as a consequence there would come into being a corps of Negro writers to set themselves to the task of changing and forming public opinion.[55]

The necessity of writing for two different audiences imposed serious

[55] Johnson, *Negro Americans, What Now?* pp. 93-94. This book considers the principal aspects of the cultural problem of the Negro Renaissance.

constraints on the writer.[56] If he wrote for whites but failed to use the approved racial clichés, he was disbelieved. Certain aspects of Negro life — the moneyed classes, for instance, or facts derived from the past of the race — were unknown to whites and so could not be grasped by them. With the black audience, the difficulties were no less formidable. Each small social group had its own prejudices and claimed the right to decide who the real Negroes were. Sterling Brown cites typical reproaches, voiced after a perusal of some contemporary works: "But we're not all like that." "Why does he show such a level of society? We have better Negroes than that to write about." "What effect will this have on the opinions of white people?" "Negroes of my class don't use dialect anyway." And Brown mischievously adds this comment:

Which *mought* be so, and then again, which *moughtn't.*[57]

On all these problems which the necessity of a dual culture created, the divergence of opinion from one social class to another made it impossible to elaborate a collective point of view. Some artisans of the Renaissance would have liked to establish agreement on a kind of typical portrait of the New Negro,[58] but this was a utopian notion and no agreement was ever reached. In practice, each individual was left to define his own attitude, in keeping with his own personality, with regard both to the culture of the majority and to the cultural past of his own race. It was up to him to decide the extent and the manner of his identification with his racial group, and to skirt the dangers of a separatism that would have cut off the Negro from the American community, reduced the efficacy of indi-

[56] On this topic, see the following articles by James Weldon Johnson: "The Dilemma of the Negro Author," *American Mercury*, December, 1928, pp. 477-81; "Race Prejudice and the Negro Artist," *Harper's Monthly*, November, 1928, pp. 769-76; "Negro Authors and White Publishers," *The Crisis*, July, 1929, pp. 228-29. See also Langston Hughes, "The Negro Artist and the Racial Mountain," *Nation*, June 23, 1926, pp. 692-94.

[57] Sterling A. Brown, "Our Literary Audience," *Opportunity*, February, 1930, p. 42. See also his "The Negro Author and His Publisher," *Quarterly Review of Higher Education among Negroes*, July, 1941, pp. 140-46.

[58] The longing for a collective definition can be read out of many statements published at this time. But the most meaningful manifestation is, perhaps, the query circulated on this subject by *The Crisis* among people of both races prominent in the world of arts and letters. See "The Negro in Art — How Shall He Be Portrayed? A Symposium," *The Crisis*, February, 1926, p. 165; March, 1926, pp. 219-20; April, 1926, pp. 278-80; May, 1926, pp. 35-36; June, 1926, pp. 71-73; August, 1926, pp. 193-94; September, 1926, pp. 238-39; November, 1926, pp. 28-29. This longing still exists, as one can realize by reading the articles contained in the collective pamphet *The American Negro Writer and His Roots*, Selected Papers from the First Conference of Negro Writers, March, 1959 (New York, 1960).

vidual and group in this community, and, finally, resulted in an intellectual, cultural, and material impoverishment for all blacks, in much the same way as some white southern mountain folk were suffering because of their isolation.[59]

Art or Propaganda?

The very special relationship of the black writer to his dual audience led him, in the long run, to ask himself what his art was for. Could his art maintain a disinterested posture, or should it aid in the advancement of his people? As he reflected on this question, the writer may have cherished the illusion that he had a free choice, whereas psychological and social realities lying beyond his control still confined him within harsh limits.

Claude McKay was probably among the first to define his attitude in these matters. He tells how one of his teachers had previously convinced him that art and propaganda were incompatible. But later, he declared, he came to see that one of Milton's greatest sonnets was "pure propaganda," and that the work of some of the greatest minds in modern literature "had carried the taint of propaganda." He reached the conclusion that propaganda had "come into its respectable rights" in the literary domain, and he proclaimed himself proud to be a propagandist.[60]

The militant thinking of W. E. B. Du Bois led him to the same conclusions. "All art is propaganda," he bluntly declared, "and ever must be . . . I stand in utter shamelessness and say that whatever art I have for writing has been used always for propaganda. . . ."[61]

The outlook of Alain Locke, the spiritual father of the Negro Renaissance, is less rough-hewn. In an article that set out to examine the problem of "Art or Propaganda?" he clearly indicates that he is opposed to the latter: "Art in the best sense is rooted in self-expression and whether naive or sophisticated is self-contained. In our spiritual growth genius and talent must more and more choose the role of group expression, or even at times the role of free individualistic expression, — in a word must choose art and put aside propaganda."[62] But it is already noteworthy that this ex-

[59] This aspect of the problem is discussed by E. Franklin Frazier, "Racial Self-Expression," in Johnson, ed., *Ebony and Topaz,* pp. 119-21, and the same author's "A Folk Culture in the Making," *Southern Workman,* June, 1928, pp. 195-99. See also Charles I. Glicksberg, "The Alienation of Negro Literature," *Phylon,* first quarter, 1950, pp. 49-58.

[60] Claude McKay, "Soviet Russia and the Negro," *The Crisis,* December, 1923, p. 61.

[61] W. E. B. Du Bois, "Criteria of Negro Art," *The Crisis,* October, 1926, p. 296.

[62] Alain Locke, "Art or Propaganda?" *Harlem,* November, 1928, p. 12.

pression of his views puts more stress on the group than on the individual. A little further on he implicitly recognizes the special functions that Negro art must carry out: "The sense of inferiority must be innerly compensated, self-conviction must supplant self-justification and in the dignity of this attitude a convinced minority must confront a condescending majority."[63] Also, "Negro things may reasonably be a fad for others; for us they must be a religion. Beauty, however, is its best priest and psalms will be more effective than sermons."[64] Thus, though he does not care to put it as brutally as others would, Locke too sees the need for Negro art to possess a certain efficacy. While art and propaganda might be separated by an infinity of gradations, a total rupture was out of the question.

There is nothing astonishing in this, for what these writers called propaganda was nothing other than a particular form of social criticism. And why should this be incompatible with art, in the case of black writers, when this did not hold true for white American writers? The critical mentality of the muckrakers in the century's early years, though compelled to fall silent by the impassioned patriotism of the war, speedily reawakened with the coming of peace. Writers like Lewis and Dreiser had no qualms about censuring America and American society.

Moreover, in fact almost all Negro writers were "committed." During the decade that followed the war, their commitment was racial above all. They protested against every form of social injustice inflicted on the Negro because of his race, and, by celebrating the greatness of the race and of its African past, they challenged the racist views that made the Negro out to be inferior. Those Negro writers who had political ties with the left or far left,[65] like Du Bois and McKay, continued to be the exception. Their political sympathies left few traces in their writings, for race consciousness was far stronger than class consciousness.

No evolution occurred in this state of affairs until after the crash of 1929. Then new, closer bonds were established between black and white intellectual workers. On one side and the other they looked on themselves as identical victims of the capitalist machine, and, though race consciousness did not disappear on this account, it tended to take a place subordinate to class consciousness and direct social criticism. This tendency would only grow more pronounced after the Roosevelt administration created,

[63] *Ibid.*
[64] *Ibid.*
[65] At the time *The Crisis* was founded, Du Bois was already a member of the Socialist party (see his autobiography *Dusk of Dawn,* p. 235), and he seeks in his novel, *The Quest of the Silver Fleece* (1911), influenced by the example of Frank Norris, to expose the economic origins of racial oppression. For Claude McKay, see our Ch. 6 below.

within the framework of the Works Progress Administration, the Federal Writers' Project (1935), which provided work for unemployed intellectuals.[66] These years of crisis constituted a turning point in the production of some of the older writers like Fenton Johnson and Langston Hughes, and they left a characteristic mark on the writings of such newcomers as the poets Sterling Brown and Frank Marshall Davis, and the novelist Richard Wright.

Thus, throughout the whole period covered by this investigation, art and propaganda will remain, for one reason or another, inextricably combined.

3. The Poetry of the Renaissance

The most noteworthy personalities of the Negro Renaissance were undoubtedly its poets. It is in poetry, as Alain Locke already knew and said, that "we can see more clearly than anywhere else the ideals and objectives of the 'New Negro'."[67] Since poetry was one of the most ancient traditions of the black race, it was as a consequence best fitted to express the psychic states of a whole people on the point of acquiring self-awareness and beginning to articulate its demands for social and cultural emancipation.

Besides, is it not preeminently the poet's role to speak for his people, when any great national renaissance is under way? One has but to recall the part played, in stimulating the European uprisings of 1848, by a Vörösmarty and a Petöfi in Hungary, by John Kollar in Slovakia and George Asaki in Romania. When Langston Hughes sings, "I, too, am America," does he not echo the lines of Michael Vörösmarty, "The fatherland is not the exclusive property of the rulers. The poor peasant also contributes to its prosperity"?[68]

It is precisely insofar as the new poetry expresses this racial coming to consciousness that it is entitled to call itself Negro.

What, we may now ask, is Negro Poetry? Certainly not merely poetry by Negro writers.... Neither is Negro poetry the older dialect poetry of a peasant patois and a Ghetto world of restricted and genre types and sentiment. Negro poetry today represents many strains, having only one common factor — the fact of reflecting some expression of the emotional sense of race or some angle of the peculiar group tradition and experience. In the

---

[66] Sterling Brown was "Editor on Negro Affairs" in the Project.

[67] "The Negro in American Culture," in Watkins, ed., *Anthology of American Negro Literature*, p. 158.

[68] Cited by J. Ancel, *Histoire contemporaine*, new ed., by H. Calvet (Paris, 1942), p. 12.

case of the American Negro the sense of race is stronger than that of nationality; and in some form or other is a primary factor in the consciousness of the Negro poet.[69]

It is our intention to make a thorough study of the new Negro poetry, as defined above, by examining the works of Claude McKay, Jean Toomer, Countee Cullen, James Weldon Johnson, Langston Hughes, and Sterling Brown, who are the most remarkable poets of the period between the two wars, and with whom the six following chapters will deal.

But these poets were not alone in incarnating the new spirit, and they were not always the first to do so. It is, consequently, advisable to begin by considering them in relation to a number of minor poets who, though less gifted (or perhaps simply less productive), nevertheless contributed in some measure to shaping the character of the Negro Renaissance.

Again, before we proceed to treat either group, it may be useful to sketch briefly the material conditions in accordance with which these writers could establish contact with their public.

The Poets and Their Public

Communication between black poets and people was never closer than during the decade after World War I. Their poems made their way among the masses, chiefly through the numerous black periodicals that provided them with an outlet. Under the intelligent editorship of W. E. B. Du Bois, *The Crisis* had acquired a specifically cultural character and had risen to considerable prominence.[70] Beginning in 1923, its influence was seconded by *Opportunity*, under the direction of Charles S. Johnson. Every year each of these periodicals awarded poetry and short story prizes. Each month their columns printed the works of young black poets, and these poems were often reprinted by daily and weekly publications. If they attracted the attention of a Negro minister, they could be at the very least recited from the pulpit the next Sunday, and the whole sermon might be

---

[69] Alain Locke, "The Negro in American Culture," in Locke, ed., *The New Negro,* p. 159. See also his declarations on this subject in the article that preceded the previously mentioned essay, "The Message of the Negro Poets," *Carolina Magazine,* May, 1928, pp. 5-6; and his comment on the second edition of James Weldon Johnson's anthology, which he criticized because, in his view, it did not allot sufficient space to racial themes: "For after all, the justification of Negro expression, considered separately, lies in the content significance and its representativeness of group thought and feeling" ("We Turn to Prose: A Retrospective Review of the Literature of the Negro for 1931," *Opportunity,* February, 1932, p. 42).

[70] On this topic, see Du Bois, *Dusk of Dawn.* The passage dealing with the development of *The Crisis* is reproduced in Watkins, ed., *Anthology of American Negro Literature,* pp. 317ff.

taken up by a commentary on them. At large-scale gatherings, black orators utilized poems to enliven their speeches. In restaurant kitchens and barber shops, dishwashers and shoeshine boys passed poems from hand to hand and repeated them aloud.

Black and white intellectuals were beginning to fraternize during these years. From time to time *Opportunity* published the work of white poets and critics. Major publishing houses opened their doors to the black poets. Claude McKay and Sterling Brown were published by Harcourt, Brace, Jean Toomer by Boni and Liveright, Countee Cullen by Harper, Langston Hughes by Knopf, and James Weldon Johnson by Viking. The leading magazines showed themselves much more willing than in the past to accept their poems and articles. McKay was even invited to share in the editing of *The Liberator.* James Weldon Johnson, Carl Van Vechten, and Alfred Knopf, Jr., celebrated all their birthdays together. Finally, blacks and whites came together in the night spots of Harlem, which was then at its apogee as a nocturnal center.[71]

In no area was this cultural collaboration more noticeable, and more fruitful, than in the research on Negro folk poetry that was then carried out. The spirituals had already aroused interest in the years following the Civil War, but then interest had waned. In 1914 Henry Edward Krehbiel's *Afro-American Folksongs* signaled the starting point of renewed attentiveness. The following year there appeared *Folk Songs of the American Negro,* by John Wesley Work; in 1919, *Negro Folk-Songs,* by N. Curtis-Burlin; in 1922, *Negro Folk Rhymes,* by Thomas W. Talley, the first collection of secular songs. It is impossible to name everything published from this point on, the works are so numerous. The peak was reached in 1925, when half a dozen titles were published, including the works by James Weldon Johnson, Howard W. Odum and Guy B. Johnson, Elizabeth Scarborough, R. E. Kennedy, R. N. Dett, and others. Only after 1930 did the output diminish noticeably. It is significant that it is no longer the spirituals alone that attract attention, for more and more frequently the secular songs are rescued from oblivion. In this connection we will cite merely the blues anthology published by W. C. Handy and A. Niles in 1926.

Alongside these publications devoted to folk poetry, anthologies of written Negro poetry also appeared for the first time. E. C. Stedman, in his massive *Library of American Literature* (11 volumes, 1888-91), had found a place for Phillis Wheatley; the handful of poems he reprinted were actually accompanied by a portrait of the young African girl. His ninth volume contained several pages of "Negro Hymns and Songs." In another collec-

---

[71] For details, see the autobiography of Langston Hughes, *The Big Sea,* pp. 243ff.

tion, *An American Anthology* (1900), Stedman included half a dozen poems by Dunbar. But the wider public, and even the intellectuals, continued to be unaware of the existence of American Negro poets even after the end of World War I.

The first anthology to appear was James Weldon Johnson's *The Book of American Negro Poetry* (1922). It also had the good fortune to be published by a firm that specialized in poetry, so that it was widely distributed and became well known. In a forty-page preface Johnson was not satisfied to present merely a short survey of Negro poetry prior to Dunbar, the first poet included in the anthology; he also tried to estimate the Negro's contributions to American culture in the field of music. He went on to plead for the incorporation of Negro literature within American literature, expressing regret that the factor determining the choice made by anthologists was not always merit alone.

Robert T. Kerlin's anthology, *Negro Poets and Their Poems,* which came out the following year, fell far short of Johnson's. The principal blemishes which might be noted are a confused manner of presentation and a deficiency of critical sense.

An Anthology of Verse by American Negroes, which Newman I. White and Walter C. Clinton brought out in 1924, originated in the South but reveals only slight traces of its geographical origin. Nevertheless, a few remarks should be noted which would have sounded strange from any other source. For instance, the feeling of resentment toward the white race is presented as a distinguishing feature of the "small fry" among the Negro poets — who would, therefore, include men of the stature of Claude McKay! — while Dunbar, Allen, and Braithwaite receive an implicit commendation for having avoided this "weakness." But the most typical observation concerns the expression of racial consciousness which, the compilers assert, plays an important role especially among the less accomplished writers and which, in their view, is utterly devoid of literary value.

Alain Locke's *The New Negro,* published in 1925, was more than an anthology; it was a manifesto. In an introductory essay, "The New Negro," Locke defined and analyzed the new spirit. The first part of the book, under a heading that for the first time utilized the expression "Negro Renaissance," offered extracts from the works of Negro writers of the new generation — poems, short stories, or one-act plays. An article by William Stanley Braithwaite considered these first fruits of the Renaissance in the setting of American literature. Music and folklore were not neglected. Economists, sociologists, and leaders of the race shared the second part, whose aim it was to determine the social situation of the

Negro in 1925. This twofold division also placed emphasis on the fact that this new literature could not be severed from the movement in society that bore it up and whose spirit it endeavored to express. The entire work, owing to the significance of the documents it brought together, marked a memorable stage in the evolution of the American Negro.

Two years later, Locke sponsored a selection of poems by McKay, Toomer, Cullen, and Hughes, published in the form of a small brochure aimed at attracting a very wide public and entitled *Four Negro Poets*. That same year Countee Cullen's important anthology *Caroling Dusk* was published; it will be discussed later in connection with that poet.

These works, however, almost without exception began with Dunbar. So Benjamin Griffith Brawley filled a gap with his *Early Negro American Writers* (1935), in which prose and poetry were jointly represented.

In the meantime Negro literature also found its way to the schools, and in *Readings from Negro Authors for Schools and Colleges* (1931) by O. Cromwell, L. D. Turner, and E. B. Dykes, poems filled about one-seventh of the volume.[72]

With the crash of 1929, the left and far left entered the lists. Victor Francis Calverton's *Anthology of American Negro Literature*, published that year by Modern Library, was highly representative of Negro literature from its beginnings. No kind of writing was omitted,[73] but the sociological essay was accorded a very important place, as one would expect from a man with Calverton's outlook — though the compiler did not deviate, even in his introduction, from the most scrupulous objectivity.

The same cannot be said of the *Negro Anthology* (1934) of Nancy Cunard, for alongside its monumental, highly valuable documentation on every aspect of Negro life in America and Africa — on history, culture, sociology, and so on — there are also entire pages of blatant Communist propaganda. Poetry, in any case, was only sparsely represented, and it is obvious that some of the poems included were picked for their proletarian inspiration rather than for their aesthetic value.

Finally, still in 1934, there was published in New York, by the Maxim Gorki editions of the Union of Russian Revolutionary Art Workers domiciled in the United States, R. Magidov's anthology *Negry Poiut: Antol-*

---

[72] The same scholastic aim marks the following works: Elizabeth Lay Green, *The Negro in Contemporary American Literature* (1928); Sterling A. Brown, *Outline for the Study of the Poetry of American Negroes*, prepared to be used with *The Book of American Negro Poetry*, ed. James Weldon Johnson (1931); as well as the educational series of "Bronze Booklets," which contained several works of popularization concerning the Negro and his culture.

[73] In the more recent Modern Library ed. of 1944, bearing the same title and compiled by Watkins, poetry is no longer included.

ogija Negritjanskoi Poezii, which offered translations into Russian of a selection of American Negro poems notable in particular for their protest and demands.[74]

Whatever their ideological tendencies, the very existence of these anthologies, published at the rate of about one per year, was a phenomenon that had no precedent and revealed the interest taken by a public that had grown larger and more varied than ever before, in the works of Negro writers, and in particular of the poets.

The Poets and Their Themes

One might maintain that the new Negro poetry was first manifested by W. E. B. Du Bois (born 1868) in "A Litany at Atlanta." It was written in 1906, the year of Dunbar's death,[75] after four days of horrible slaughter involving whites and blacks in Atlanta that marked the campaign for election of a new governor. This caustic, violent poem is a modern forty-fourth Psalm addressed to God, whom the poet reproaches for his seeming slumber while his people are being butchered. Du Bois also finds room to attack Booker T. Washington and his ideal of racial progress through manual labor. In conclusion, he voices the uncertainty in which the Negro stands with regard to the color and, consequently, the trustworthiness of God:

> Sit no longer blind, Lord God, deaf to our prayer and dumb to our dumb suffering. Surely, Thou art not white, O Lord, a pale, bloodless, heartless thing?
> *Ah! Christ of all the Pities!*
> Forgive the thought! Forgive these wild, blasphemous words. Thou art still the God of our black fathers. . . .[76]

This God who the poet hopes is black foreshadows Garvey's God, just as the following hate-filled and unpoetic imprecations herald the nobler anger of a Claude McKay:

> I hate them, Oh!
> I hate them well,
> I hate them, Christ!
> As I hate hell!

[74] For anthologies of more recent date, see our bibliographical appendix.
[75] After appearing in various magazines, his poems were assembled in 1920 in *Darkwater,* where they were interspersed among the essays that make up the bulk of the volume. For "A Litany at Atlanta," see this same work, pp. 25-28, in the Jenkins ed. (Washington, D.C.) which we utilized.
[76] *Ibid.,* p. 27. See also the passage in "The Riddle of the Sphinx," *ibid.,* p. 54: "Bid the black Christ be born!"

> If I were God,
> I'd sound their knell
> This day![77]

Nevertheless, Du Bois is never led by his indignation at racial injustice into actual conflict with God, and his faith is never imperiled. In "The Prayers of God,"[78] he actually reveals very deep religious feeling. The poem, which is a dialogue between the white man and God, basically serves to demonstrate that any injustice inflicted on man is injustice toward God, and that God "needs men" in order to accomplish the task of redemption. *Darkwater* (1920), the volume in which these few poems were printed, ends with a hymn of hope in a great fraternity of all mankind. The poet's socialist faith and Christian faith are here blended into one:

> O Truce of God!
> And primal meeting of the Sons of Man,
> Foreshadowing the union of the World![79]

Du Bois, whose decisive influence on the actualization of the New Negro we have stressed above, is only occasionally a poet. Externally, his poems are sometimes reminiscent of the poetic prose of the biblical line, but his too numerous alliterations and his addiction to grandiloquence often lead him far from the sober style of Holy Writ. If he nevertheless deserves mention as a poet, it is because his fervent, militant tone, his racial pride, and the violence of his hatred and protest are already those of certain poets of the Negro Renaissance, more than one of whom would have subscribed to this "Credo":

> I believe in God, who made of one blood all nations that on earth do dwell . . .
> Especially do I believe in the Negro Race: in the beauty of its genius, the sweetness of its soul, and its strength in that meekness which shall yet inherit this turbulent earth.
> I believe in Pride of race and lineage and self . . .[80]

In marked contrast with the fiery, intensely racial lyricism of W. E. B. Du Bois stands the timorous, sentimental traditionalism of most Negro poets during the first twenty years of the twentieth century. The persis-

[77] "The Riddle of the Sphinx," *ibid.* It need scarcely be explained that "them" means whites.
[78] *Ibid.*, pp. 249-52.
[79] "A Hymn to the Peoples," *ibid.*, p. 275.
[80] "Credo," *ibid.*, p. 3. Other poems by Du Bois still remain scattered in magazines. See, for example, "The Song of America" and "Poem," *Palms* IV, no. 1 (1926), 18-19. But the poems of *Darkwater* which have been mentioned here are the most significant and reveal Du Bois as a forerunner of the Negro Renaissance.

tence of pseudo-dialect proves that Dunbar's example was still alive in everyone's memory, and that the recollection of his success brought him emulators more numerous than they were talented. Their very names would be forgotten today, were it not for the excessive generosity of some anthologists.[81]

The earliest poems by James Weldon Johnson, *Fifty Years and Other Poems* (1917), are among the best of this period. For all that, they are the work of a late arrival, who will require the stimulus of the young post-war generation before he will be moved to write those little masterpieces, the free-verse Negro sermons of *God's Trombones*.[82]

Among the minor poets, his namesake Fenton Johnson[83] is assuredly

[81] Of these writers, let us name Raymond Garfield Dandridge (1882-1930), whose *Penciled Poems* (1917), repeated in large part in his later collections *The Poet and Other Poems* (1920) and *Zalka Peetruza and Other Poems* (1928), are devoid of any real poetic inspiration. Even more mediocre is the collection of poems by Waverley Turner Carmichael, *From the Heart of a Folk* (1918). Much more talent is shown by Mrs. Georgia Douglas Johnson (1886-?), the author of three volumes of poems: *The Heart of a Woman* (1918), *Bronze* (1922), and *An Autumn Love Cycle* (1928). Only *Bronze* is explicitly racial, but there is no originality of theme, and the familiar simplicity of style makes her work appear to be a carry-over from the previous century. For writers even less interesting, one may see Johnson, ed., *The Book of American Negro Poetry*, and Robert T. Kerlin, *Contemporary Poetry of the Negro*.

[82] For James Weldon Johnson, see our Ch. 9 below.

[83] Fenton Johnson was born in Chicago on May 7, 1888, to a family that seems to have been fairly well situated. He obtained his higher education at the University of Chicago, taught for a year in the South, and at the age of nineteen had several of his plays performed in Chicago's Pekin Theatre. He published at his own expense three volumes of poetry, the first in Chicago in 1913, the other two in 1915 and 1916 in New York, where he lived for a short time and where, beginning in 1912, *The Crisis* published several of his short stories. He returned to Chicago where, together with Binga Dismond, from 1916 on he edited *The Champion Magazine*, and then *The Favorite Magazine*, modestly subtitled "The World's Greatest Monthly," and in which some of his poems and articles appeared. In the meantime, he established connections in his native town with the Harriet Monroe group, and several of his poems were accepted for *Poetry*. (Harriet Monroe will also retain several of them for her anthology, *The New Poetry*, published jointly with Alice Corbin Henderson.) Alfred Kreymborg published other poems by Fenton Johnson in *Others*. In 1920, Johnson himself brought out, under the imprint of his magazine, a volume of seven mediocre short stories, *Tales of Darkest America*, but he did not succeed in publishing, or finding anyone else to publish, his fourth collection of poems, *African Nights*. That, at least, is an unavoidable hypothesis, for Alfred Kreymborg, who speaks of it in *Our Singing Strength* as though it had been published, as later will be done also by Sterling Brown in *Negro Poetry and Drama*, has confessed to us that he had never seen a copy of *African Nights* in print. It must be assumed that Fenton Johnson had simply left the manuscript with him for a while, so that he might pick out a few poems for his anthology *Lyric America*. Furthermore, all our attempts to find a copy of *African Nights* in the great American libraries, even those with the appropriate specialization, remained fruitless. Apparently, then, this work never saw the light. Finally,

the most interesting. He, too, had begun to write familiar, sentimental pieces in Dunbar's manner, with no lack of backward glances, expressed in dialect, at the wonderful old-time plantation. His first book, *A Little Dreaming* (1913), contains the customary Scottish poem and Irish poem, even a Yiddish poem,[84] thus making abundantly clear the sources of his inspiration. But in *Visions of the Dusk* (1915) and *Songs of the Soil* (1916), certain attempts, such as his spirituals,[85] show that he has already reached an awareness of the cultural past of his race. "The Negro has a history," he declares, "and is something more than a peasant."[86] This feeling for history manifests itself most distinctly in "Ethiopia,"[87] which celebrates the past grandeur of African civilizations and gives vent to his impatient longing that the time of their resurrection may come:

> Thy hour! Thy hour! Oh when shall come thy hour?[88]

His reputation today depends not on his first three volumes, however, but on the fragments of his later work that have been published. These place Fenton Johnson among the poets who, toward the middle of the twentieth century's second decade, participated in the making of America's New Poetry.[89] The poems that made known Fenton Johnson's new manner appeared in *Poetry* and subsequently in the anthologies *Others* (1916, 1917, 1920), compiled by Alfred Kreymborg, with whom Johnson was friendly, and later in *The Liberator*.[90] Instantly we pass from the most commonplace traditionalism to the most revolutionary naturalism, from the rhymed, carefully scanned line to free verse, from conventionalized

---

there is a bulky collection of poems that has not been published, the product of a third period when Fenton Johnson was being supported by the Federal Writers' Project. A copy is in the library of Fisk University and there, thanks to the kindness of Arna Bontemps, we were able to examine it. A sampling of poems from this last collection, "The WPA Worker," will be found in our appendix of "Unpublished Poems" in the original French edition. Johnson died in Chicago on September 17, 1958.

[84] See "When I Speak of Jamie," *A Little Dreaming,* p. 62; "Kathleen," *ibid.,* p. 48; and "Mine Rachel," p. 58.

[85] See, for example, "Singing Hallelujah," *Visions of the Dusk,* p. 14; and "Jubal's Free," *ibid.,* p. 29.

[86] *Songs of the Soil,* p. iv.

[87] *Visions of the Dusk,* pp. 42-48.

[88] *Ibid.,* p. 42.

[89] Johnson refers to his friendship with Harriet Monroe, Carl Sandburg, Alfred Kreymborg, and other Chicago poets in an unpublished poem of the "WPA period." It is entitled "Rosemary for Chicago Poets."

[90] We have not ourselves gone through the files of *The Liberator,* but the library of Atlanta University, in the Fenton Johnson file, preserves two poems, "The Cotton Picker" and "The Sunset," with the annotation: "From *The Liberator,* no date; collected by WPA, Illinois."

Negro dialect to the brawny language of Sandburg's *Chicago Poems,* and from the confident optimism of Booker T. Washington to disillusionment, bitterness, and cynicism — even to unmitigated despair. "The Scarlet Woman" pillories society and its injustices, which it holds to be responsible for the degradation of a girl who had been "good like the Virgin Mary and the Minister's wife":

> My father worked for Mr. Pullman and white people's tips;
>   but he died two days after his insurance expired.
> I had nothing, so I had to go to work.
> All the stock I had was a white girl's education and a
>   face that enchanted the men of both races.[91]

She ends up as a prostitute, seeking forgetfulness in gin. Obliquely, this poem reaches out beyond the protests of a Du Bois. It tends to show how barren the hope is that education might one day contribute to the advancement of the race. The truth, as Fenton Johnson sees it, is that America has no place for a young black girl who has finished her schooling. Her education does not enable her to escape the fate of her less privileged sisters; she must choose between two forms of slavery, the lot of the proletarian or that of the prostitute. No less doomed are the hopes placed in the education of Negro ministers, for the churches are aiming not at the spiritual elevation of the masses but at monetary returns. This is the message of "The Minister," a poem in which Johnson voices the same criticism as his compatriot Sandburg who, in "To a Contemporary Bunkshooter," was denouncing at almost the same time religion's profiteers:

> I mastered pastoral theology, the Greek of the Apostles, and all the difficult subjects in a minister's curriculum.
> I was as learned as any in this country when the Bishop ordained me.
> And I went to preside over Mount Moriah, largest flock in the Conference.
> I preached the Word as I felt it, I visited the sick and dying and comforted the afflicted in spirit.
> I loved my work because I loved my God.
> But I have lost my charge to Sam Jenkins, who has not been to school four years in his life.
> I lost my charge because I could not make my congregation shout. And my dollar money was small, very small.
> Sam Jenkins can tear a Bible to tatters and the congregation destroys the pews with their shouting and stamping.

[91] "The Scarlet Woman." This poem has been reprinted in several anthologies. See, for instance, Johnson, ed., *The Book of American Negro Poetry,* p. 145.

Sam Jenkins leads in the gift of raising dollar money.
Such is religion.[92]

It seems possible to detect, in these poems on the pointlessness of education, an echo of Fenton Johnson's own disappointment, for his financial well-being was never so uncertain as after his period of study at the University of Chicago. He had paid for the publication of his first three volumes of poems but was unable to bring out the next, which was to have been called *African Nights*. It would have included those poems which establish him as a notable figure in the Negro literary movement of the time. This judgment is confirmed by the unpublished poem "Others," written at a later date, when he was enjoying the support of the Federal Writers' Project:

> We are Others, the great Forgotten, the scoffed at, the scum of the publishing houses;
>
> . . . .
>
> We have never known royalties and we will never know royalties; but empty pockets
> Will haunt us as the raven and tobacco cheer us as wine does a Wall Street royalist.
> We are not respectable. . . .[93]

Fenton Johnson must remain, ultimately, the poet of utter despair, the despair that engulfs one when every value has crumbled and all struggle has become useless. It is expressed to perfection in "Tired," his most frequently cited poem:

> I am tired of work; I am tired of building up somebody else's civilization.
> Let us take a rest, M'lissy Jane.
> I will go down to the Last Chance Saloon, drink a gallon or two of gin, shoot a game or two of dice and sleep the rest of the night on one of Mike's barrels.
> You will let the old shanty go to rot, the white people's clothes turn to dust, and the Calvary Baptist Church sink to the bottomless pit.
> You will spend your days forgetting you married me and your nights

---

[92] "The Minister," in Kreymborg, ed., *An Anthology of American Poetry, Lyric America: 1630-1930*, p. 538. The "shout" is that kind of well-known unleashed hysteria that makes up religious services in some popular Negro churches. The effect of this frenzy on the church fittings might be compared to the similar consequences of some jazz recitals, and the behavior of the pastor, as Johnson describes it, with that of some jazz singers whose emotion is deemed to be all the more sincere if they succeed, during their number, in tearing some of their garments and accessories.

[93] "Others," from which this passage has been taken, is part of the unpublished collection in the library of Fisk University.

hunting the warm gin Mike serves the ladies in the rear of the Last Chance Saloon.

Throw the children into the river; civilization has given us too many. It is better to die than it is to grow up and find out that you are colored.

Pluck the stars out of the heavens. The stars mark our destiny. The stars marked my destiny.

I am tired of civilization.[94]

This cry of despair, uttered by Fenton Johnson at a time when the Negro Renaissance had not yet begun, is unique in the whole body of black poetry. Its depths will not be plumbed again, even in the most dreadful days of the 1929 Depression.

If Fenton Johnson could find no one who would publish his despairing poems, the reason may be that, in the first ten postwar years and with the return of prosperity, the poets of the Negro Renaissance were above all seeking justification for hope in what was to come. White America, which had turned toward them in order that their primitivism might cure the ills of Western civilization, depicted by T. S. Eliot as a "Waste Land" (1922), was in no way reluctant to encourage this tendency in them. The optimism of Negro leaders, who were reassured by the growing power of the protective organizations they had patiently assembled, appeared to work in the same direction.

Among the poets of this renewal there were, admittedly, some who spoke of their souls' lacerations and clamored against the place allotted them in a white civilization, which still treated the black as half a man and still deprived him of the fruits of his labor:

> ... what I sowed and what the orchard yields
> My brother's sons are gathering stalk and root,
> Small wonder then my children glean in fields
> They have not sown, and feed on bitter fruit.[95]

[94] "Tired." This poem has been reprinted in many anthologies. See, for instance, Johnson, ed., *The Book of American Negro Poetry,* p. 144.

[95] Arna Bontemps, "A Black Man Talks of Reaping," in Langston Hughes and Arna Bontemps, *The Poetry of the Negro,* p. 111. Arna Bontemps, born in 1902, is one of the most brilliant minor poets of the Negro Renaissance. In 1926, his "Golgotha Is a Mountain" was awarded *Opportunity's* poetry prize, and the following year *The Crisis* awarded him its first prize in poetry for "Nocturne at Bethesda." His poems have been included in various anthologies, and were collected in *Personals* (London, 1963). Later, Bontemps was interested above all in writing novels. He is now curator of the James Weldon Johnson Memorial Collection, Yale University Library. In his poetry, protest and the African theme are expressed discreetly and are often tempered by the intensity of his religious feeling. Comparable in manner to his work is that of Joseph Seamon Cotter, Jr. (1895-

But even a Claude McKay does not always utter cries of revolt, as in *Spring in New Hampshire* (1920) and *Harlem Shadows* (1922), for there is also the sensual exoticism of his Jamaican poems. When Jean Toomer (*Cane*, 1923) evokes his pilgrimage to Georgia, his book opens with a series of portraits of black women, whose sensual beauty he stresses. The anguished laments of Countee Cullen (*Color*, 1925; *Copper Sun*, 1927) are accompanied by the obsessive rhythm of the African tom-tom, which he feels beating in his veins as we sense it in his verses. The frenzied rhythm of the jazz band is the living pulse both of the swarming city of Harlem and of the verses of its poet Langston Hughes (*The Weary Blues*, 1926; *Fine Clothes to the Jew*, 1927); it conveys in its essence the erotic atmosphere of the black metropolis' night spots.

The exaltation of instinct goes hand in hand with that of the primitive African homeland,[96] the memory of which Garvey had just brought back to life in the consciousness of the black masses. If the body's rights are asserted, they are those of a black body whose vigor, grace, and beauty are a polar antithesis to the insipid, frigid Caucasian aesthetic ideal. On parallel lines, the precolonial civilization of Africa, where once the Negro lived free and blissful, is contrasted with America's Western civilization, its anti-natural standards constituting shackles which oblige the Negro to vegetate behind glass, so to speak, as Helene Johnson picturesquely expresses it in her poem "Bottled":

> Say! That man that took that sand from the Sahara desert
> And put it in a little bottle on a shelf in the library,
> That's what they done to this shine, ain't it? Bottled him.
> Trick shoes, trick coat, trick cane, trick everything — all glass.
> But inside —
> Gee, that poor shine![97]

Thus, when all is said and done, all hope for a better future is based on the rediscovery and the celebration of the race's past. It is there too that racial pride finds fresh nourishment. The heroes of Africa are summoned back from the tomb and, if need be, new heroes will be created

---

1919) who published, shortly before his premature death, a far from voluminous poetic sheaf in *The Band of Gideon* (1918).

[96] These are also the most frequent themes of the minor poets whose verses appear in the magazines: Lewis Alexander, born in 1900; Gwendolyn Bennett, born in 1902; Edward Silvera, born in 1906; Waring Cuney, born in 1906; Helene Johnson, born in 1907.

[97] "Bottled," in Countee Cullen, ed., *Caroling Dusk*, p. 223. This poem also expressed the idea that the black is too beautiful to be able to flourish amid the ugliness of Western urban civilization. The same notion can be found in the work of many poets, including McKay and Hughes. See, too, the poem "No Images" by Waring Cuney, in Cullen, ed., *Caroling Dusk*, p. 212.

by making Negroes out of those who may not have been black. Garvey had announced that God was black, and the poets saw no reason why they should not do the same.

NIGGER

A Chant for Children

Little Black boy
Chased down the street —
"Nigger, nigger never die
Black face an' shiney eye,
Nigger . . . nigger . . . nigger . . ."

Hannibal . . . Hannibal
Bangin' thru the Alps
Licked the proud Romans,
Ran home with their scalps —
"Nigger . . . nigger . . . nigger . . ."

Othello . . . black man
Mighty in war
Listened to Iago
Called his wife a whore —
"Nigger . . . nigger . . . nigger . . ."

Crispus . . . Attucks
Bullets in his chest
Red blood of freedom
Runnin' down his vest
"Nigger . . . nigger . . . nigger . . ."

Toussaint . . . Toussaint
Made the French flee
Fought like a demon
Set his people free —
"Nigger . . . nigger . . . nigger . . ."

Jesus . . . Jesus
Son of the Lord
— Spit in his face
— Nail him on a board
"Nigger . . . nigger . . . nigger . . ."

Little Black boy
Runs down the street —
"Nigger, nigger never die
Black face an' shiney eye,
Nigger . . . nigger . . . nigger"[98]

[98] Frank Horne, "Nigger," *ibid.*, p. 120. Crispus Attucks, a Negro with Indian blood, is regarded as the first American to fall in the cause of national inde-

The things left unsaid are the most eloquent part of this poem by Frank Horne, which only ironically is a chant for children. In it one can glimpse the hope that tomorrow will see the realization of W. E. B. Du Bois's prophecy, made as early as 1903, to the effect that the problem of the twentieth century would be that of the color line.[99]

Accompanying the rediscovery of the past is the rediscovery of the folk, which falls into two distinct stages.

During the first postwar decade, the poets' interest is turned toward popular culture as much as and more than it is toward the people itself. Langston Hughes restores to a place of honor such ancient forms of popular poetry as the ballad and the blues. He tries to incorporate the popular jazz rhythms into his poems and to model other poems on the old pattern of the spirituals, while James Weldon Johnson, in the Negro sermons of *God's Trombones* (1927), seeks to immortalize the picturesque oratorical art of the old-time preacher and to create, as J. M. Synge had done for the Irish peasant, the literary equivalent of popular Negro speech while avoiding the ideological blemishes of the traditional Negro dialect popularized by the southern poets.

Admittedly, apart from this cultural interest there exists a militant poetry that pleads the cause of the black people, denounces the injustice and cruelty of which it is the target, heaps abuse on the lynch mobs, and demands in its name the protection of the democratic laws and institutions on which America hypocritically prides itself. But, for more than one-tenth of its loyal subjects, they remain a dead letter.

However, after the financial collapse of 1929, the people acquire a new dimension in poetry.[100] In the light of the Marxist critique, to which they had been exposed through participation in trade-union movements or the WPA, a number of poets began to regard the Negro not so much as a victim of racial prejudice, but rather as a proletarian victimized by economic exploitation and, as such, linked with all other proletarians through-

---

pendence. He was, indeed, the first man to be killed by an English bullet in the Boston Massacre, on the night of March 5, 1770, as he was leading a troop of some fifty citizens who were about to attack the English sentinels.

Note, also, the negrification of the Virgin in the poem by Albert Rice (born in 1903), "Black Madonna," in Cullen, ed., *Caroling Dusk*, p. 177. Cullen's own use of this theme is much more extensively developed. As for the black man's ability to conquer the white man or even, with the help of time, to overthrow and annihilate his civilization, the theme will be found in McKay, Brown, and others. See, for instance, Waring Cuney, "Dust," *ibid.*, p. 210.

[99] Du Bois, *The Souls of Black Folk*, p. 13.

[100] It goes without saying that tendencies of the previous period will be found to persist (in Sterling Brown, for instance), but interest is no longer centered exclusively on popular culture.

out the world, no matter what their race. Among these poets are Sterling Brown (*Southern Road,* 1932), Langston Hughes (*A New Song,* 1938), and also Richard Wright, who at the outset of his literary career tried his hand at poetry.

> I am black and I have seen black hands, millions and millions of them —
> They were tired and awkward and calloused and grimy and covered with hangnails,
> And they were caught in the fast-moving belts of machines and snagged and smashed and crushed,
> And they jerked up and down at the throbbing machines massing taller and taller the heaps of gold in the banks of bosses,
> And they piled higher and higher the steel, iron, the lumber, wheat, rye, the oats, corn, the cotton, the wool, the oil, the coal, the meat, the fruit, the glass, and the stone until there was too much to be used,
> And they grabbed guns and slung them on their shoulders and marched and groped in trenches and fought and killed and conquered nations who were customers for the goods black hands had made.
> And again black hands stacked goods higher and higher until there was too much to be used,
> And then the black hands held trembling at the factory gates the dreaded lay-off slip,
> And the black hands hung idle and swung empty and grew soft and got weak and bony from unemployment and starvation,
> And they grew nervous and sweaty, and opened and shut in anguish and doubt and hesitation and irresolution . . .[101]

More and more, on top of racial consciousness a layer of class consciousness tended to impose itself, and out of it was born at the same time an internal social critique directed on occasion against the Negro masses, to pillory their naïveté, their illusions, and their failings, and on other occasions against the black bourgeoisie, a milieu made up of social climbers and snobs, ever eager to stress their superiority to common folk (with whom they hated to be lumped together) and aping the ways of the white middle class.

Among the minor poets who gained some prominence during these years, the name of Frank Marshall Davis,[102] the author of *Black Man's*

---

[101] Richard Wright (1908-1960), "I Have Seen Black Hands," stanza 2, in Hughes and Bontemps, eds., *The Poetry of the Negro,* p. 155.

[102] Frank Marshall Davis, who was born in 1905 in Arkansas City, Kansas, studied journalism at Kansas State College and spent his summers on farms and on the road. He went to Georgia in 1931, where he helped to found the *Atlanta Daily World,* remaining on the staff until 1934. The following year he joined the Associated Negro Press in Chicago, and interrupted this work only to accept a Rosenwald Foundation grant in 1937. Since 1948 he has been running a paper mill in Honolulu.

Verse (1935), *I Am the American Negro* (1937), and *47th Street* (1948), is worthy of mention. Though Davis exhibits a certain talent in his better poems, it remains undisciplined and is too often wasted by recourse to facility. An untiring polemicist, he could not resist prosiness and verbosity, and his longer poems suffer from their patent lack of structure. But his principal defect is a sort of bad taste which his journalistic activities did nothing to mitigate. It is revealed in his search for forced or incongruous images, and in his flashy display of borrowed devices used in inappropriate contexts. All too frequently one notices the clumsily transposed influences of Vachel Lindsay, Carl Sandburg, and Langston Hughes. He is overly fond of orchestrations and indications of setting in the manner of Lindsay; these marginal scenic notations become irritating in the long run, since they so obviously are gratuitous additions. It is hard to see how a poem like "Lynched"[103] gains from being subtitled "symphonic interlude for twenty-one selected instruments," or why "Hands of a Brown Woman"[104] needs the accompaniment of a "quartet of two guitars, a banjo and a tom-tom." In some places he becomes positively grotesque, as at the beginning of "Modern Man — The Superman,"[105] with its subtitle, "A Song of Praise for Hearst, Hitler, Mussolini and the Munitions Makers," and accompanied by the marginal note, "Eight airplane motors, each keyed to a different pitch, are turned on and off to furnish musical accompaniment within the range of an octave." Sandburg, too, may not have been a suitable model for a mind already so devoid of discipline as was Davis's. For it is from Sandburg, rather than directly from Walt Whitman, that Davis seems to have derived the notion of his enumerative poems, or even poem-inventories, the graveyard of genuine poetry, as is demonstrated by such poems as "What Do You Want America?"[106] and "For All Common People."[107]

Yet his borrowings are, at times, thoroughly judicious. In his first two volumes, the sections entitled "Ebony under Granite"[108] amount to a

[103] *Black Man's Verse*, p. 25.
[104] *Ibid.*, p. 44. See also, in the same volume, "Chicago's Congo" (Sonata for an Orchestra), p. 17; "The Slave" (For a Bass Viol), p. 41; "Lullaby" (Melody for a 'Cello), p. 48; "Death" (Overture for an Organ), p. 49; "Tryst" (Melody for the Tenor Strings of a Harp), p. 67; "To You" (Aria for a Violin), p. 68; "Love Notes at Night" (Melody for a Zither), p. 69; and, in *I Am the American Negro*, the inflated, tasteless setting for the title poem. The same holds true for "Peace Quiz for America" (To Be Read Aloud by Eight Voices), *47th Street*, pp. 54ff.
[105] *I Am the American Negro*, pp. 51ff.
[106] *Black Man's Verse*, pp. 21ff.
[107] *47th Street*, pp. 65ff. Davis often takes the even more devious route via Langston Hughes, whose own work was in some respects indebted to Sandburg's.
[108] *Black Man's Verse*, pp. 77ff.; *I Am the American Negro*, pp. 59ff.

highly successful Negro prolongation of *Spoon River Anthology*. Here he takes Negro society as his main target, scoring a number of bull's eyes with his daring naturalism. Like Masters, Davis reveals to us, behind the facade of happiness and success, the meannesses and the nauseating appetites that provide the mainspring of the social climber and, on occasion, also put an end to his climbing. From the depths of the grave, the Reverend Joseph Williams informs us that he had scattered bastards liberally throughout his parish.[109] Benjamin Blakey, great contractor and swinger of deals,

> Would have died more content
> Had he ever learned
> From which of his mistresses
> He contracted
> That fatal social disease . . .[110]

Robert Whitmore, the successful businessman who three times was the ruler of the local Elks

> died of apoplexy
> when a stranger from Georgia
> mistook him
> for a former Macon waiter.[111]

Mrs. Clifton Townsend, who could count among her ancestors many prominent white Southerners, came of a family in which the marriages were always planned to preserve the light skin color of which she was so proud:

> It was not childbirth
> In her forty-second year
> That took the life
> Of Mrs. Clifton Townsend
> But shame at bearing
> Through inconsiderate Nature
> A penny-brown son . . .[112]

Ralph Williamson, editor of the weekly *News-Protest*, built his fortune and his nationwide reputation on his readiness to denounce racial injustice and discrimination. So it is easy to understand how he suddenly expires as the consequence of a frightful nightmare in which he dreams that America has become a land without blemish, where all ill feeling between the races has vanished in a trice.[113]

---

[109] "Rev. Joseph Williams," *Black Man's Verse*, p. 77.
[110] "Benjamin Blakey," *I Am the American Negro*, p. 63.
[111] "Robert Whitmore," *Black Man's Verse*, p. 79.
[112] "Mrs. Clifton Townsend," *I Am the American Negro*, p. 65.
[113] "Editor Ralph Williamson," *ibid.*, p. 66.

It would be minimizing Frank M. Davis's excellent qualities, were one to consider only the poems of "Ebony under Granite." His skill as a portraitist, his intimate understanding of racial psychology's subtle mechanisms, and his mordant irony create memorable frescoes such as that of "47th Street,"[114] which admirably brings to life the humble folk of this black district in Chicago. But one is entitled to believe that poetry as a means of expression was not well suited to Davis's special talents, and that the sketch or the short story would have been a more appropriate form.

Poets in Conflict

Starting from an examination of the interrelationship of racial and religious feeling in the poets of the Negro Renaissance, we have been led to conclude that two major tendencies can be distinguished, and we have arranged on parallel lines the two sections that embrace the six following chapters.

Both tendencies already existed in a latent state in the folk poetry of the slave period. They correspond to the contradictory elements existing embryonically in the Christianity that was offered the African upon his entrance into the American slave world.

On the one hand, the Christian religion proclaimed a message of liberty to the slave. The God of whom the whites spoke was, it seemed, a just, kind God, who had sent his own Son on earth to teach men to love one another and had even demanded of him the supreme sacrifice of Calvary, so that all men might be redeemed, without distinction of color or race.

Yet for the enslaved African this gospel of love stood in strange contrast to the attitude adopted toward him by the white slaveowners who had brought him the good tidings. In his daily life the Negro had some difficulty detecting any influence exerted by the ideals of Christian liberty, justice, and brotherhood. Not only this, but while the Christian message of the Bible was proclaimed, the Bible was also made to provide all the arguments needed to justify the institution of slavery. This was the will of God, as attested by the sacred book; to make sure that no one could overlook the fact, the Creator had inflicted a contemptible color and nonhuman features on the creatures he had destined to lead an eternally inferior form of existence.

The examples cited in our rapid examination of folk poetry during the slave period have demonstrated how the slave's own consciousness was divided against itself, at a very early date, by this contradiction. It had originated in the soul of his oppressors, and they had projected it into the

[114] *47th Street*, pp. 15ff.

soul of the oppressed as they concurrently imposed on him their own religion and their own civilization. The slave was fully aware of this latent cleavage at the center of the religion he was taught; this is proved by his singing, alongside the spirituals, sacrilegious songs that voiced his refusal to accept this conflict as his own and expressed his desire to expel it from himself. It should be remembered, too, that only infrequent echoes of this protest have reached us, the bulk of it having been lost or deliberately suppressed.

Not until after Emancipation could the Negro survey the entire extent of the irreparable damage wrought in his soul by this basic contradiction. He found himself confronted by it more often and more painfully than ever, as he tried to gain a footing in ever wider sectors of American social, cultural, and intellectual life. He found it more and more difficult not to take the blatant duplicity of the white man as a reason for inferring that God, too, was deceitful. Thus the black man found himself involved in an internal struggle, his own racial values clashing with those of Western culture and, more especially, with the spiritual values of Christianity.

This conflict remained obscured, for the most part, in the men of Dunbar's generation. Cautiously aiming at respectability and conformity, they went on writing as if they still believed in the national motto, "In God we trust," though in fact they were at the very least agnostics, as was James Weldon Johnson. But the issue burst into broad daylight with the poets of the younger generation, who no longer shared their elders' feeling that Emancipation represented the genuine liberation of the black people by the God of its fathers. Very much to the contrary, they were convinced that liberation still lay ahead and that, in the unceasing struggle that would have to be waged to attain it, the Negro would have to look on God as an adversary rather than as an ally. What had been in its origins a social conflict between two races thus became, by successive stages and through a process of association of ideas that was inherently irrational, a cultural and then a religious conflict. In this, God and the black people were set up as antithetical values that seemingly could never be reconciled, and between which the individual was cruelly torn.

With certain intellectuals of the new generation marked by the emergence of the New Negro, one can observe the disintegration of the simple faith to which the people had formerly clung.[115] This same faith was still

[115] There exists a contemporary document of high quality dealing with this disintegration. See Mordecai Wyatt Johnson, "The Faith of the American Negro," *The Crisis*, August, 1922, pp. 156-58. This article was originally a commencement address delivered at Harvard University in 1922 by the president-to-be of Howard University.

preached in countless Negro churches that had the adherence of the popular circles into which many Renaissance writers had been born. There
was an agonizing division between the intellectual level these individuals
had reached and that of the circles from which they came. They could
not be satisfied by this emotional religion, which had only in part shaken
off the shackles of superstition. This anthropomorphic theology, purely
external morality, and picturesque ritual could still minister to the frustrations of simple, credulous people, but it could have no purchase on
the realities of the new, richer life that would be led by those Du Bois
had baptized the "Talented Tenth." Such a religion could give no satis-
fying answer to the anguished questions these men were raising, particularly with regard to the problem of evil. In their autobiographies, James
Weldon Johnson and Langston Hughes tell us how, while they were still
children, they went through the motions of religious devoutness in order
not to shock their families;[116] but it is clear that at this early stage they
had already rejected the faith as absurd, ineffective, and possibly even
harmful. Though an avowed agnostic, Johnson went on writing traditional
religious poetry until the end of his life, without a word that might reveal
his own disbelief. Religion, in his view, was not merely an integral part
of the American creed; it was also an essential ingredient in Negro folklore, and only as such did it have a place in his writings. His poetry is
actually religious poetry with no belief behind it and whose aim it is to
express the attitude of the credulous masses, not the poet's own outlook.
Langston Hughes's stance is not very different from Johnson's, but he belonged to another generation and thus (at least for some years of his life)
could openly express his rebelliousness against God, in the guise of defending his own people more effectively. As for Sterling Brown, he looks on
religion as merely an aftermath of slavery which postpones the moment
when black people will at last be able to acquire self-consciousness.

Whether openly or in secret, all the poets of this group are united in
rejecting religion of any kind as irreconcilable with loyalty to their people,
for their primary aim is to rehabilitate, praise, and defend the people. To
be precise, this tendency was not fully manifest before the 1929 crash,
when the growing influence of Marxist materialism provided new backing
for religious skepticism. But skepticism could not have developed except
in a soil already prepared to receive it.

[116] See Langston Hughes, "Salvation," *The Big Sea,* pp. 18ff.; and James
Weldon Johnson, *Along This Way,* pp. 25ff. And Sterling Brown has informed us
that his father reproved him, not for his lack of faith, but for his refusal to stop
drinking and smoking, even in moderation. It would appear that smoking and
drinking were graver sins than utter disbelief in the existence of God.

Yet there were other poets, facing the same conflict of loyalties, who felt a greater need for an inner life and for spiritual sustenance than for material advancement. They were also better apprised of the complexity of Christian thinking and more keenly aware of its demands on the individual. They reached an entirely different vision of the racial problem and of the position of the black man within Western civilization. Not that they suffered less than others at being torn between their belief in God and their attachment to their own people — but with them the conflict took on an inner dimension and acquired greater profundity. These men, the great lyric poets of the Negro Renaissance, thus gained the insight that the basic conflict is not between the black man and the white man, or between the black man and God, but between man and himself. "Whatever stands between you and that person," Jean Toomer will write, "stands between you and yourself";[117] and Countee Cullen, in a mystical dialogue with the Most High, will learn from him that "The key to all strange things is in thy heart."[118] It is by transcending self and through a heroic appropriation of spiritual values that Claude McKay, Countee Cullen, and Jean Toomer will at last prove able to vanquish the dilemma in which they refuse with all the force of their being to become imprisoned, and to achieve an extraordinarily life-giving synthesis of elements that others had judged to be beyond any possible reconciliation. From this synthesis the black man will rise transfigured and ennobled.

[117] Jean Toomer, *Essentials*, 29.
[118] "The Shroud of Color," line 94 in Countee Cullen, *Color*, p. 30.

SECTION A: In Search of the Spiritual

Chapter Six: CLAUDE McKAY

Many Negro Renaissance intellectuals never looked on Claude McKay as being one of themselves,[1] in the first place because he belonged to an older generation and was already thirty at the end of World War I. They also had a slight tendency to regard as an interloper this Jamaican immigrant who arrived in Harlem one fine day after having earned his living in countless ways. Moreover, he preferred the company of the far left to the elegant surroundings of the drawing room. While the Renaissance was in full swing in America, Claude McKay was traveling in Europe and North Africa, and thus was rather cut off from Harlem, which in the meantime had become the center of the black world. Finally, his self-willed character with its violence and intransigence, and his passionate denunciations of his friends as well as of his enemies in the two races, often gained for him the reputation of being an unsociable person and a rebel.

With all his faults, however — and sometimes because of the virtues inherent in these very faults, but above all because of his outstanding gifts as a poet — he remains beyond a doubt the immediate forerunner and one of the leading forces of the Renaissance, the man without whom it could never have achieved what it did. His contribution served as a corrective and lent added stature. To the frivolities of the chaotic existence that was all the rage, and to the Harlem primitivism of which he soon had had enough, McKay opposed the solid qualities of his Jamaican heri-

[1] Claude McKay, *A Long Way from Home*, p. 321.

197

tage, the sureness and perspicacity of his judgment, and his desire for inner progress and ennoblement. Showing no self-indulgence, he instinctively sought the discipline of the sonnet. Exigent also vis-à-vis his ethnic brothers, he invited them to abandon the various forms of dead-end particularism in which they were wasting their racial pride, and he urged them to set out along with him on the high road that alone leads to the discovery of authentic values.

1. BIOGRAPHY[2]

The Jamaican Years (1889-1912)

Claude McKay was born on September 15, 1889, in the village of Sunny Ville, a dependency of the parish of Clarendon, in the Jamaican mountains. He was the youngest of the eleven children born to a family of peasant proprietors. His father, Thomas Francis McKay, was descended from the Ashanti of West Africa and seems to have been of pure black stock, whereas his mother, Ann Elizabeth Edwards, probably had a slight admixture of white blood. The poet, as it happens, describes her as "very brown,"[3] not as black. It follows that Claude was not a pure-blooded African, as has been asserted by Max Eastman[4] and Walter Jekyll.[5] But from both sides the poet inherited not only a sturdy independence of outlook, but also the racial pride that was traditional in the family. His father was an admirable narrator of African tales, which were no doubt handed down from generation to generation in an oral tradition. He succeeded in awakening very early in his children both an interest in the customs of their ancestral land and a distrust of the white man. "Your

[2] There is no biography, as such, of McKay. Ralph Glassgow Johnson, "The Poetry of Dunbar and McKay," pp. 19-29, does little more than reproduce the notices contained in various anthologies. Our own biographical note makes no claim to novelty. To supplement the information contained in the various anthologies and in McKay's volume of memoirs, *A Long Way from Home,* we have turned above all to his own declarations, made in "Right Turn to Catholicism"; "On Becoming a Roman Catholic," *The Epistle,* Spring, 1945, pp. 43-45; "Boyhood in Jamaica," *Phylon,* second quarter, 1953, pp. 134-45; "Why I Became a Catholic," *Ebony,* March, 1946, p. 32; and also Ellen Tarry, *The Third Door,* pp. 127ff. We insisted, however, on ascertaining the year of the poet's birth, which has been variously given as 1889, 1890, and 1891. In a letter dated November 8, 1957, the poet's daughter, Hope McKay Virtue, has kindly informed us that, in the family Bible, Claude McKay's birth is entered as having taken place on September 15, 1889. We are also indebted for numerous details to Carl Cowl, the friend and literary agent of Claude McKay.

[3] "Boyhood in Jamaica," p. 141.

[4] Biographical note, *Selected Poems,* p. 110.

[5] Preface to *Songs of Jamaica,* p. 9.

grandfather was a slave," he sometimes told them, "and knew how cruel the white man could be."[6] The poet's ancestors on the mother's side had also found a means to withstand the slave-dealers.

[Claude] learned in childhood how a family of his ancestors, brought over in chains from Madagascar, had kept together by declaring a death strike on the auction block. Each would kill himself, they vowed solemnly, if they were sold to separate owners. With the blood of such rebels in his veins ...Claude McKay grew up proud of his race and with no disposition to apologize for his color.[7]

Two individuals exercised a considerable influence on the poet during his formative years. These were his brother, an elementary school teacher, and an Englishman domiciled on the island, Walter Jekyll, whom McKay will present in his Jamaican novel, *Banana Bottom,* in the guise of Squire Gensir. Through them he had the run of two libraries, where he read the great writers and especially the poets. He read the Elizabethans, Milton, Pope, Keats and Shelley, and the Victorians, as well as Dante, Leopardi, Goethe, Villon, and Baudelaire.

The parents sent their six-year-old to the classes taught by his brother in a "denominational school." This brother was also a lay reader in an Anglican church and a self-confessed militant agnostic. "By the time I was ten," McKay relates, "my brother was pushing free-thinking books my way. I devoured Huxley and Lecky, Haeckel and Gibbon and others.... My sister-in-law was very religious. When she saw me reading Haeckel's *The Riddle of the Universe,* she said it was a bad book, and tried to stop me. My brother said: 'Let the boy read anything he likes.' "[8]

At sixteen he became friendly with another agnostic, the collector of Jamaican folklore Walter Jekyll, who at the time was translating Schopenhauer. He had the boy read the German philosopher and enrolled him with the Rationalist Press Association in London. Most significantly, he encouraged him to write poems in the speech of the island's country folk and to give up writing poems in English, which Jekyll found too imitative. Jekyll also saw to it that the first collection of poems, *Songs of Jamaica* (1912), was published. He himself wrote the preface and persuaded the governor of Jamaica, Sir Sydney Olivier, a founding member of the Fabian Society, to let the book be dedicated to him. "Thus I grew up," McKay tells us, "without religious instruction at home.... Also, I was not free-thinking alone. In one high mountain village there were ten of us boys

6 "Boyhood in Jamaica," p. 141.
7 Max Eastman, Biographical note, *Selected Poems,* p. 110. Carl Cowl states that he too heard this anecdote related by the poet himself.
8 "On Becoming a Roman Catholic," p. 43.

in a free-thinking band, and most of them were heathen from their own primitive thinking, without benefit of books."[9]

At seventeen, having received an apprentice's scholarship from the Jamaican government, he was apprenticed to a mulatto who was both cartwright and cabinet-maker in Brown's Town, in the parish of Saint Ann. But he did not like the trade and soon left to sign up, at the age of nineteen, with the island police at Kingston, the capital. There he remained only ten months.

> I had not in me the stuff that goes to the making of a good constable; for I am so constituted that imagination outruns discretion, and it is my misfortune to have a most improper sympathy with wrong-doers. . . . Moreover, I am, by temperament, unadaptive; by which I mean that it is not in me to conform cheerfully to uncongenial usages. We blacks are all somewhat impatient of discipline, and to the natural impatience of my race there was added, in my particular case, a peculiar sensitiveness which made certain forms of discipline irksome, and a fierce hatred of injustice. Not that I ever openly rebelled; but the rebellion was in my heart, and it was fomented by the inevitable rubs of daily life — trifles to most of my comrades, but to me calamities and tragedies.[10]

This stay in Kingston not only exposed McKay to the humiliations and the hazing of the barracks; it was also instrumental in revealing to him the brutality of race prejudice and in bringing him up for the first time against the realities of a caste hierarchy based on color. In his home in the Clarendon Mountains, where blacks made up almost the total population and where their activities set the rhythm for rural daily life, he had always seen blacks occupy the chief positions. But now, for the first time, in the city he saw them relegated to the bottom rungs, as much because they were the picture of the unsophisticated country bumpkin as on account of their black skin. In the city, they were looked on as vastly inferior not only to whites, but to mulattoes also. These latter found in the city possibilities of social advancement that were permanently barred to blacks, and the sense that they belonged to a privileged class induced in them a feeling of superiority over the blacks, whom they utterly despised.

So McKay, grieved by the interracial hatreds of the city, returned to his mountain retreat and published in rapid succession his first two collections of verse, *Songs of Jamaica* (1912) and *Constab Ballads* (1912). They aroused the interest of the public, with the result that he received

[9] *A Long Way from Home*, p. 12.
[10] Preface to *Constab Ballads*, p. 7.

at the same time the medal of the Jamaica Institute of Arts and Sciences, the first time it had been awarded to a Negro, and a substantial stipend that enabled him to study in the United States. He embarked that same year at Port Antonio.

The Years in the United States (1912-19)

Upon landing in Charleston, South Carolina, he set off for Tuskegee but stayed there for only a few months, preferring to pursue his study of agriculture at Kansas State College. But here, too, he realized at the end of two years that agriculture was not for him, and 1914 found him owner of a restaurant on West 53rd Street, New York, at that time still a Negro neighborhood. Several months later the enterprise expired and McKay began to live from hand to mouth, working in the kitchens of various New England hotels or as a pullman-car waiter.

Throughout this period he was, in fact, much more concerned with poetry than with commercial undertakings, and in December, 1917, *The Seven Arts,* an ephemeral publication started by James Oppenheim, Waldo Frank, and Van Wyck Brooks, published two of his sonnets, "The Harlem Dancer" and "Invocation," under the pseudonym Eli Edwards.[11] The following year Frank Harris became enthusiastic about him and published a number of his poems in *Pearson's Magazine.* Almost at the same instant McKay attracted the attention of Max Eastman, who made available to him the pages of *The Liberator,* the outlet for several of his poems from 1919 on.

It was through Max Eastman that he made the acquaintance of the far left at about this time, in particular the staff of *The Masses* with Floyd Dell and John Reed, who in 1922 would affiliate *The Liberator* with the Communist party. Though he never joined the party, McKay took over and defended its ideas, even in the columns of Marcus Garvey's *Negro World.* In consequence, he had the honor of mention in the *Congressional Record,* where he was assailed by the attorney general of the United States.

Years of Vagabondage (1919-34)

In 1919 McKay set out for Holland and Belgium, and then lived for over a year in London. There he collaborated with Sylvia Pankhurst on *The Workers' Dreadnought,* and he also became known and appreciated as a poet. In the summer, 1920, issue of *Cambridge Magazine,*[12] C. K. Ogden

[11] The pseudonym was based on his mother's name, Elizabeth Edwards.
[12] Pp. 55-59.

published twenty-three of his poems. That same year saw the publication in London of his third volume, *Spring in New Hampshire,* with a laudatory preface written by the famous Cambridge critic I. A. Richards.

He returned for a very brief stay in the United States the following year. Max Eastman made him associate editor of *The Liberator* and wrote the introduction to McKay's new collection of poems, *Harlem Shadows,* which appeared in New York in 1922. Once again it was Max Eastman who, that same year, took McKay to Russia, where they attended the Fourth Congress of the Communist party. In Moscow, Petrograd, Kronstadt, and elsewhere McKay was welcomed by the leaders of the new regime and feted as a comrade and as a black poet. He read his poems in public, and *Pravda* published a translation of the poem he wrote in Petrograd for May Day, 1923. He himself was somewhat staggered by the elaborate welcome extended him; it appeared to him as "an *Arabian Nights* fantasy transformed into reality."[13] But when he left Russia in June, 1923, his pro-Communist leanings had grown a little more hesitant, for he was disturbed by more than one aspect of Soviet society.

After a brief stop in Berlin he reached Paris at the end of the year, and there he made a living by modeling. But his lungs were infected, and he had to spend three months in a hospital. Nevertheless, his sturdy constitution soon pulled him round, and he went off to convalesce in the Midi in the spring of 1924, a stay made possible by the kindness of several friends.

First he settled near Marseilles, then in La Ciotat, and then in Toulon, where he learned that the Garland Fund had granted him a monthly stipend of fifty dollars. At the end of the summer he went back for a while to Paris. There he met Edna St. Vincent Millay and Sinclair Lewis, who gave him advice and helped him financially.

The following year found him once again in Marseilles with Max Eastman, preparing to set out for Bordeaux and Brittany. In Nice, in the late fall, he worked in Rex Ingram's film studios and mixed with the Eastmans, Frank Harris, and Paul Robeson. After once more spending some time in Marseilles, he moved in 1927 to Antibes, at the prompting of Max Eastman. There he finished his novel on the frivolous life in Harlem, *Home to Harlem.* The novel came out in New York in 1928 and proved to be an instant best-seller, reprinted five times in the next two months. A new edition was brought out three years after its author's death.[14] Finally, in late 1927 McKay went back to Marseilles and began his second novel,

[13] *A Long Way from Home,* p. 170.
[14] (New York, 1951).

Banjo. Except for a brief stay in Paris in 1929, the rest of the time away from America was to be spent in either Spain or Morocco.

Spain was a revelation for him. "It was particularly in Spain, as I came to know and understand the people and visited the marvellous cathedrals, that I fell in love with Catholicism. Spain uncovered to me the fact that not only is there a Catholic way of salvation, but also a Catholic way of life."[15] Thus he attributes the earliest stirrings of his conversion to Catholicism to his first trip to Spain, in 1928.[16]

Banjo came out in 1929 and was followed in 1932 by a collection of stories, most with a Jamaican setting, *Gingertown*, and in 1933 by a third novel, *Banana Bottom*, which offers a picture in depth of rural life and culture in Jamaica.

Home to Harlem (1934-48)

Returning to Harlem after a twelve-year absence, McKay found a certain pleasure in seeing once again the familiar places and faces, through eyes that had been enriched by the experiences garnered on the world's highways and byways. His first thought was to assemble his recollections. They were published in 1937 as *A Long Way from Home*, and they marked their author's definitive rupture with Communism.

While still the object of attacks from the Communist quarter, motivated by the autobiography, in 1938 McKay met a mulatto girl named Ellen Tarry, a Catholic, who wrote books for children. She invited him to Friendship House, the Catholic welfare and activities center founded in Harlem by Baroness de Hueck. "But, Tarry, I am an unbeliever!" McKay rejoined. In reply, Ellen Tarry uttered this challenge: "It is easier for an intellectual not to believe than to believe."[17] The impact of these words was decisive, leading him to reflect and starting him once more on the spiritual itinerary he had abandoned when he left Spain.

In 1940 he was still able to publish a series of essays on Harlem and its spiritual and political leaders. This was *Harlem, Negro Metropolis*. But during the winter of 1941-42 he fell gravely ill. Ellen Tarry discovered his whereabouts and, with a team from Friendship House, set about caring for him. Yet he was never to recover his health. During the summer of 1943 his high blood pressure grew worse, and he went to recuperate in a Connecticut cottage lent by friends. The following spring, he was invited to Chicago by Monsignor Sheil, and there, on October 11, 1944, he re-

15 "Right Turn to Catholicism," p. 1.
16 *Ibid.,* p. 4.
17 "On Becoming a Roman Catholic," p. 45.

ceived baptism. Although ill, he still found the strength to teach in the Catholic schools of Chicago. At the time of his death (in a Chicago clinic on May 22, 1948), he had been preparing an anthology of his poems. It was not published until 1953.

2. The Jamaican Sources (The 1912 Poems)

The year 1912, when Claude McKay left Jamaica for good, marks a turning point in his experience. It may therefore serve to conveniently divide into two groups the approximately two hundred poems that constitute his published poetic opus. Not that there is any cleavage between the 1912 poems and the later ones, for the principal lines along which the themes are organized are much more than simply sketched out in the earlier collections, and they will maintain themselves throughout the poet's multiple wanderings. At twenty-three, the personality of the poet was firmly enough molded to meet the challenge of widened horizons without allowing itself to be distorted by them. But it will grow richer and more extensive; it will gain in subtlety, too. Thus the two groups of poems are differentiated less by any renewal in the actual poetic substance than by their measure of quality and universality, and by a broadening of the human perspectives.

The two collections published in Jamaica in 1912 constitute a diptych of McKay's experience in his native island. The first, *Songs of Jamaica,* is a sort of highly colored epitome of the years of childhood and young manhood spent in the mountains, where he listened to Nature's great voice and shared the life of the black peasantry. Often in direct opposition to these first poems are those of *Constab Ballads,* which reveal the disillusionment and pessimism the poet felt when plunged into the life of the capital. These first two volumes are already marked by a sharpness of vision, an inborn realism, and a freshness which provide a pleasing contrast with the conventionality which, at this same time, prevails among the black poets of the United States.

Authenticity of Form

Not the least original aspect of these seventy-eight poems is the rough but picturesque Jamaican dialect in which most of them are written, and of which they constitute the earliest poetic use.[18] Thus we are far removed

---

[18] "Boyhood in Jamaica," p. 142. Walter Jekyll, in his preface to *Songs of Jamaica,* provides some interesting details on this dialect, which in many respects

from the dialect of the Dunbar school, which was taken over from the whites who had concocted it in order to maintain the stereotype of black inferiority and to limit blacks more surely to the role of buffoons under orders to entertain the master race. An instrument of oppression when handled by white writers, the dialect became an avowal of subservience in its use by Dunbar, most of whose readers were whites. Furthermore, the themes treated in it had also been exploited by the former oppressors before Dunbar's arrival on the scene. None of these afterthoughts need be entertained in the case of McKay's dialect. Here everything is entirely and authentically Negro. It all comes directly from the people and is rooted in the soil, alike the phonology, often flavored with a delightful exoticism, and the rather summary morphology; the typically fantastic placing of the tonic accent and the somewhat rudimentary syntax, seldom in accord with the Queen's English; and, finally, the often unexpectedly roughhewn words and images, which originate in the hard-working folk's immediate contact with a soil reluctant to part with its riches.

As long as he lived, McKay's own speech kept the stamp of this rustic accent, as the recordings that have been preserved bear witness.[19] As for the whimsicalities of the Jamaican tonic accent, they often preclude any certain solution to the problem of scanning many of his lines, whether in dialect or standard English.[20]

Every bit as much as their language, it is the poetic quality of these works that links them genuinely to the people for whom they were written. It was no mere rhetorical flourish when McKay entitled his first collection *Songs of Jamaica*. For six poems, he adds in an appendix melodies which he composed.[21] The songs and ballads he did not set to music are so rhythmical that a musical accompaniment could easily be provided.

Song is the natural and spontaneous expression of the Negro in Jamaica as in the United States. It embraces individual songs, strung together as the situation required, and collective work songs, destined to provide a rhythm for labor in the fields ("jamma songs").[22] Just as great composers

is close to the Gullah spoken by American Negroes in the coastal regions of the Carolinas and Georgia. For the vocabulary, see the glossary in *Constab Ballads*, pp. 81-94.

[19] See Arna Bontemps, ed., *Anthology of Negro Poets*, Folkways Records, FP 91, side one, for a recording of McKay reading three of his poems.

[20] See Walter Jekyll in *Songs of Jamaica*, and Max Eastman's introduction to *Harlem Shadows*, p. xvii. Both also had difficulty in adapting themselves to the scansion of Jamaican verse.

[21] *Songs of Jamaica*, pp. 135-40. The poems are "Taken Aback," "Pleading," "Ione," "My Pretty Dan," "My Soldier Lad," and "Jubba."

[22] On this topic, see "Boyhood in Jamaica," p. 138. For examples of the songs, see his *Banana Bottom*, pp. 112, 188, and *passim*.

have derived from the folksongs of their native land the sureness of their melodic gift, there can be no doubt that McKay's poetic genius was awakened and took on form in contact with the folksongs of his island, as much as it did from his reading the great poets. Thus it was not the poet in isolation who created these first Jamaican poems but, with him and through him, the folk. All the poet did, when he offered these poems to the people, was "to give back to others a little of what he had got from them."[23]

Realism of the Peasant Portraits

How close the bond of sympathy was between McKay and the people is manifested also by the realism with which he characterizes the black Jamaican peasant. Here, too, the contrast with Dunbar is embarrassingly evident. McKay's portraits at once transcend the limits which, in James Weldon Johnson's view, inevitably weighed on American Negro dialect and forced it to sound only the registers of humor and pathos. In any case, there is no humor to be found here, nor will it play any part in the later work. These peasants are not the ignorant, lazy, thieving clowns all too often held up for ridicule by Dunbar's school, stereotypes designed to amuse the members of a superior race. "Our Negroes were proud though poor," McKay will later declare. "They would not sing clowning songs for white men and allow themselves to be kicked around by them."[24] Unlike the character portraits usually associated with American Negro dialect, these portraits are the actual incarnation of a whole people's racial pride.

All in all, McKay's characterization of the Jamaican peasant is substantially that of the peasant anywhere in the world: deeply attached to his plot of land, over which he labors with an atavistic skill; and unsparing of himself, yet seemingly condemned to unalleviated poverty, since there is always someone to snatch the fruits of his labor. He owes his pride to the sense of work well done, and has no feeling of inferiority vis-à-vis the whites whom, when the occasion arises, he will address in the bluntest terms.

In "Quashie to Buccra,"[25] a Negro has this to say to a white who is looking at the field from beyond the hedge:

> You tas'e petater an' you say it sweet,
> But you no know how hard we wuk fe it;

[23] "Boyhood in Jamaica," p. 145.
[24] *Ibid.*
[25] In the Jamaican Negro dialect, "Quashie" is the Negro, and "Buccra" the white man.

You want a basketful fe quattiewut,
'Cause you no know how 'tiff de bush fe cut.

．　．　．　．

De fiel' pretty? It couldn't less 'an dat,
We wuk de bes', an' den de lan' is fat;
We dig de row dem eben in a line,
An' keep it clean — den so it *mus'* look fine.[26]

These lines clearly establish the relationship of the black peasant to the white man, as McKay sees it: based on economics, not on race. The white man is always trying to deny the black peasant his due and is all the meaner, the richer he is. The white in the poem above wants to buy a basket of sweet potatoes, which he judges to be excellent, for the ridiculous price of a quarter (that is, one quarter of sixpence, or a penny and a half). If he dares to offer such a pitiful sum, it is because he has no idea of the work the Negro has to do to clear the field, especially when

De sun hot like when fire ketch a town.[27]

In the end, however, the tidiness and beauty of the field win the admiration of the white speaker. For the Negro has gone to a lot of trouble, and is justifiably proud of his handiwork. Besides, when harvest time arrives, he will forget all the labor he has expended:

Yet still de hardship always melt away
Wheneber it come roun' to reapin' day.[28]

The same pride in his abilities and achievements motivates the Negro in "King Banana," a poem that celebrates the glory of the banana and of the agricultural techniques used by blacks. The beauty of his patch of soil and the high quality of his crop strike a spark of irony from the peasant in this poem, when he turns to the whites who are always ready to recommend their own techniques, deemed superior to those the blacks use:

Wha' lef' fe buccra teach again
Dis time about plantation?
Dere's not'in' dat can beat de plain
Good ole-time cultibation.[29]

The critique of society becomes more urgent in other poems by McKay, where the responsibilities of the whites are categorically stated. They have

---

26 "Quashie to Buccra," stanzas 1 and 6, *Songs of Jamaica*, pp. 13-14.
27 *Ibid.*, stanza 3, line 1.
28 *Ibid.*, stanza 7, lines 3-4.
29 "King Banana," stanza 5, *ibid.*, p. 31.

organized the economic life of the island so as to profit from the resources that nature had destined for the blacks. That is the force of the following lines, in which the poet apostrophizes his native island:

> You hab all t'ings fe mek life bles',
> But buccra 'poil de whole
> Wid gove'mint an' all de res'
> Fe worry naygur soul.[30]

"Two-an'-Six," a poem that runs to 136 lines, speaks out against the catastrophic effect of such an economy on the life of the peasants, who are plunged into bitter poverty by a drop in sugar prices. One Saturday morning at cockcrow, while the stars are still in the sky, everybody is already astir to make ready the products that Cous' Sun is going to take to the fair in the neighboring town — in a borrowed cart, McKay notes — and while on his way

> . . . he's thinkin' in him min'
> Of de dear ones lef' behin'
> Of de loved though ailin' wife,
> Darlin' treasure of his life,
> An' de picknies, six in all,
> Whose 'nuff burdens 'pon him fall:
> Seben lovin' ones in need,
> Seben hungry mouths fe feed;
> On deir wants he thinks alone,
> Neber dreamin' of his own,
> But gwin' on wid joyful face
> Till him re'ch de market-place.
> Sugar bears no price te-day,
> Though it is de mont' o' May.[31]

Even with these wretched prices, the buyers expect him to tamp down the measure!

> Cousin Sun is lookin' sad,
> As de market is so bad'
> 'Pon him han' him res' him chin,
> Quietly sit do'n thinkin'
> Of de loved wife sick in bed,
> An' de children to be fed —
> What de labourers would say
> When dem know him couldn' pay;
> Also what about de mill

---

[30] "My Native Land, My Home," stanza 9, *ibid.*, p. 85.
[31] "Two-an'-Six," lines 41-54, *ibid.*, pp. 87-88.

Whe' him hire from ole Bill;
So him think, an' think on so,
Till him t'oughts no more could go.

. . . .

In his ears rang t'rough de din
"Only two-an'-six a tin!"

. . . .

Ah, it gnawed him like de ticks,
Sugar sell fe two-an-six!

So he journeys on de way,
Feelin' sad dis market day;
No e'en buy a little cake
To gi'e baby when she wake, —
Passin' 'long de candy-shop
'Douten eben mek a stop
To buy drops fe las'y son,
For de lilly cash nea' done.
So him re'ch him own a groun',
An' de children scamper roun',
Each one stretchin' out him han',
Lookin' to de poor sad man.
Oh, how much he felt de blow,
As he watched dem face fall low,
When dem wait an' nuttin' came
An' drew back deir han's wid shame![32]

Here, with penetrating realism, McKay disdains to make a racial issue of his critique. Not once is the white man named. The poet lets the facts speak for themselves and, though it is clear that he is attacking white avariciousness, the reproach is situated nevertheless in the economic and social domain. Sun does not waste words lamenting the injustice of the white owners; he reacts as the genuine head of his family and his business enterprise, with an awareness of his responsibilities. How is he going to feed his sick wife and his six children? What will his workmen say when he tells them he cannot pay them, and what will happen to the sugar mill when he fails to pay the rent? McKay might have tried to utilize this case of social injustice by transferring it to the sphere of race. That, indeed, is the way a James Weldon Johnson would probably have developed it. Remember that this is only 1912! The black peasant might have set up, over against the injustice done him, all the service rendered by his race; he might have summoned Africa itself to aid him. But nothing of this sort

[32] *Ibid.*, lines 67-78, pp. 88-89; lines 81-82, p. 89; lines 88-106, pp. 89-90.

is permitted to weaken the pertinence and perceptiveness of McKay's social critique. Already apparent is the outline of that objectivity, with its disdain of dream and lamentation, which will distinguish him among his peers in the United States and lend depth to his vision of things.

While "Two-an'-Six" says nothing of the whites, "Hard Times," on the contrary, strikingly portrays the moneyed idleness of the white men and the harsh life led by the black peasant, with not the least prospect of shaking off his poverty. Taxes are a heavy burden; he is besieged by the bailiff, afflicted by his wife's illness and, despite his labors, forced to see his ragged children suffer the pangs of hunger.

> De mo' me wuk, de mo' time hard,
>   I don't know what fe do;
> I ben' me knee an' pray to Gahd
>   Yet t'ings same as befo'.
>
> De taxes knockin' at me door,
>   I hear de bailiff's v'ice;
> Me wife is sick, can't get no cure,
>   But gnawin' me like mice.
>
> De picknies hab to go to school
>   Widout a bite fe taste;
> And I am working like a mule,
> While buccra, sittin' in de cool,
>   Hab 'nuff nenyam fe waste.
>
> De clodes is tearin' off dem back
>   When money seems noa mek;
> A man can't eben ketch a mac,
>   Care how him 'train him neck.[33]

All these poems, nevertheless, end on a note of faith in the future. In "Two-an'-Six," Sun's discouragement is dispelled by the loving, consoling words uttered by his wife:

> An' de shadow lef' him face,
> An' him felt an inward peace
> As he blessed his better part
> For her sweet an' gentle heart.[34]

In "Hard Times," it is faith in Providence that resounds in the last stanza:

> I won't gib up, I won't say die,
>   For all de time is hard;

[33] "Hard Times," stanzas 1-4, *ibid.*, p. 53.
[34] "Two-an'-Six," lines 117-20, *ibid.*, p. 90.

Aldough de wul' soon en', I'll try
My wutless best as time goes by,
An' trust on in me Gahd.[35]

All in all, health, vigor, and self-assurance make up the impression left by this portrait of the black Jamaican peasant, whose age-old practical virtues and wisdom have not been sapped by his material poverty. Thus the optimism that McKay discovers in this rural milieu is derived, in the first place, from extant moral values. But there are racial reasons also. For it is highly significant that all these country folks are blacks, excluding the mulattoes whom McKay implicitly rejects as all too eager to see in their white ancestry a justification for disdaining the blacks. Finally, the real values that constitute the superiority of the black peasant reside in his closeness to the soil of Jamaica. One can scarcely overstress the importance of this element in McKay's trinitarian symbolism, which associates the good with the black race and the soil.

Primacy of the Earth

Thanks to the circumstances prevailing in his birthplace, McKay to a certain extent is spared the battle of loyalties that weighs on the black poet in the United States, in his ceaseless to-and-fro between acceptance and rejection of his surroundings. The Jamaican countryside, peopled almost entirely by blacks,[36] offered an admirably supportive, kindly milieu for the unfolding and stabilization of McKay's personality. Since no racial prejudice affected persons who were all of one color, he was able to grow up without having a sense of inferiority forced on him. In his eyes, consequently, rural Jamaica is the real Jamaica. Only with his homeland thus understood is his identification a total one.

His roots in the soil of his native island are amazingly deep and lasting. These roots make him one with the soil. Through them he draws in his nourishment; the island's enchanting scenes call forth his earliest verses, and no one will ever rival him in praise for the mildness of its climate, the vividness of its colors, the luxuriance of its vegetation, or the coolness of its streams.

Do people say that Negroes are a race without a fatherland, landless exiles? Nonsense, ripostes McKay, for it cannot be denied that Nature has

[35] "Hard Times, " stanza 6, *ibid.*, p. 54.
[36] In 1891, or two years after Claude McKay's birth, in a total Jamaican population of 635,868 there were 488,624 blacks, 121,955 mulattoes, 14,692 whites, 10,116 Hindus, and 481 Chinese ("Jamaika," *Brockhaus Konversations-Lexicon,* 1908 ed., vol. 9). On economic and social conditions on the island, see Fernando Henriques, *Jamaica, Land of Wood and Water;* see also our note 70 below.

installed them in the loveliest of homelands, on this blessed isle. In Jamaica, the Negro feels truly at home. His gratitude to this land is total, his loyalty without reserve, and there is not one Negro who, to defend it, would not shed his last drop of blood. One could not find in any American black poet so entire a sense of belonging and such unalloyed patriotism:

> There is no land dat can compare
>   Wid you where'er I roam;
> In all de wul' none like you fair,
>   My native land, my home.
>
> Jamaica is de nigger's place,
>   No mind whe' some declare:
> Although dem call we "no-land race,"
>   I know we home is here.
>
> You give me life an' nourishment,
>   No udder land I know;
> My lub I never can repent,
>   For all to you I owe.
>
> E'en ef you mek me beggar die,
>   I'll trust you all de same,
> An' none de less on you rely,
>   Nor saddle you wid blame.
>
>   .   .   .
>
> An' I hope none o' your sons would
>   Refuse deir strengt' to lend,
> An' drain de last drop o' deir blood
>   Their country to defend.
>
>   .   .   .
>
> Your fertile soil grow all o' t'ings
>   To full de naygur's wants,
> 'Tis seamed wid neber-failing springs
>   To give dew to the plants.[37]

But uniting the black man and the earth is a more intimate, subtle relationship, a secret harmony as it were, and simply to name the familiar scenes is enough to arouse in the poet's sensibilities a physical resonance, to send a tremor through his frame:

> Loved Clarendon hills,
> Dear Clarendon hills,
> Oh! I feel de chills,
> Yes, I feel de chills

[37] "My Native Land, My Home," stanzas 1-4, 6, 8, *Songs of Jamaica*, pp. 84-85.

Coursin' t'rough me frame
When I call your name.[38]

Thus the union of the poet and his land is consummated in a romantic ecstasy. This correspondence between Nature and the poet is indeed "the organic exaltation produced by physical agents"[39] or the recollection of them, "the joy of all the senses in contact with the world"[40] which Cazamian analyzed, many years ago, in the English Romantics. Like them, McKay felt constantly drawn to nature and sensed the need to become totally merged in it. The emotion it aroused in him transcended by far the exclusively aesthetic plane. For Nature is an ever renewed source of strength, and instinctively he returned to commune with it. To summon back his energies, he plunged once again into the waters of his beloved stream:

I shall love you ever,
Dearest Sukee River:
Dash against my broken heart,
Nevermore from you I'll part,
But will stay forever,
Crystal Sukee River.

Cool my fevered brow:
Ah! 'tis better now,
As I serpent-like lance t'rough
Your broad pool o' deepest blue!
Dis once burnin' brow
Is more better now.

.   .   .   .

Kiss my naked breast
In its black skin drest:
Let your dainty silver bubbles
Ease it of its lifelong troubles,
Dis my naked breast
In its black skin drest.

Floatin', floatin' down
On my back alone,
Kiss me on my upturned face,
Clasp me in your fond embrace,
As I'm floatin' down
Happy, yet alone.[41]

[38] "To Clarendon Hills and H.A.H.," lines 1-6, *ibid.*, p. 106.
[39] Louis Cazamian, "L'Intuition panthéiste chez les romantiques anglais," *Etudes de psychologie littéraire* (Paris, 1913), p. 44.
[40] *Ibid.*, p. 49.
[41] "Sukee River," stanzas 1, 2, 5, 6, *Constab Ballads*, pp. 78-79.

McKay, for whom the earth was at the origin of everything, would certainly have signed his name to the exclamation of Shelley's Prometheus: "O, Mother Earth!"[42] The earth is the whole man. He had already proclaimed this before he had turned twenty,[43] and he realized it all the more clearly after he had left it and experienced enormous disillusionment in contact with the city, whose inhabitants he looked on as rootless, in the most concrete sense of the word:

> Fool! I hated my precious birthright,
> Scorning what had made my father a man.[44]

He attributed to his native soil, the nurturer, all the strength of his character and his poetic vigor:

> There is an exaltation of man's life,
> His hidden life, that he alone can feel.
> The blended fires that heat his veins within,
> Shaping his metals into finest steel,
> Are elements from his own native earth,
> That the wise gods bestowed on him at birth.[45]

It should also be specified that, in his mind, this land is the habitat of black men, for it would seem that a veritable racial pact existed between the black man and the Jamaican earth. He will avow this later, when he comes to write of the green hills of his childhood: "I have sought to recapture their charm and influence, which in a wider sense is the shaping influence that makes the difference between the white and colored worlds."[46]

Between the black man and the earth there is a total identification. When, vexed by the city, he returns to his mountains, he will see in this return not only a reunion with the earth, but with his people also:

> But I'll leave it, my people, an' come back to you,
> I'll flee from de grief an' turmoil;
> I'll leave it, though flow'rs should line my path yet,
> An' come back to you an' de soil.[47]

Thus the racial values he associates with the soil also help to tinge his

---

[42] *Prometheus Unbound,* Act III, scene 3, line 84.

[43] McKay was eighteen years old when he first showed his poems to Walter Jekyll ("Boyhood in Jamaica," p. 142).

[44] "A Labourer's Life Give Me," stanza 4, lines 1-2, *Constab Ballads,* p. 71.

[45] "My House," stanza 3, *Opportunity,* November, 1926, p. 342. This poem is reprinted in Countee Cullen, ed., *Caroling Dusk,* p. 92.

[46] "Boyhood in Jamaica," p. 145.

[47] "The Heart of a Constab," stanza 7, *Constab Ballads,* p. 63.

feeling for nature, and in his mind he conceives nature and the city as mutually exclusive forces.

We propose to study, immediately below, the sources of the racial symbolism of the city as these can be read out of the two 1912 volumes, and will briefly treat McKay's feeling for nature when we come to examine his exoticism.

Rejection of the City

Hatred of the city is one of the principal motifs in McKay's Jamaican poems, and the American poems will offer variations on the same theme. In Dunbar's work one could already note some aversion toward urban civilization, but this was only sporadic, and the motivation behind it was entirely different. Dunbar was sensitive, above all, to the ravages wrought by industrialization which, as it spread ever wider, made men's lives ugly and polluted the air they breathed. His reaction might even be interpreted, in part, as the tuberculosis victim's struggle for the pure air he knew he needed.

But with McKay the theme is not merely more amply treated; it acquires in the racial context a symbolic importance not found in Dunbar. The city, presented as the antithesis of the land, is consequently the enemy of the black man also.

The origin of McKay's antipathy for the city must be sought in his own experiences in Kingston. Having known hitherto only the understanding that prevailed among people of the same region, he now saw for the first time the repercussions that an inequality of caste, based on color, inflicted on daily life.[48] Though blacks formed a majority of the Kingston population, they were nevertheless inferior. One gains the impression that McKay, without approving it, could accept the fact that blacks had to make way for white people, since this was a custom whose demise might reasonably be foreseen. But it roused him to indignation that blacks were treated as inferiors even by mulattoes — by persons, that is, who at least in part shared a common ancestry with blacks. What heightened his indignation at the arrogance of the mulattoes, who stood socially higher because of their descent from whites, was the fact that neither their individual worth nor even their dress justified, in his view, their privileged situation. In "Papine Corner," whose title is borrowed from a Kingston intersection where streetwalkers and underworld figures congregated, and where rum

[48] On this, see Henriques, *Jamaica*, pp. 92-109, 127-41. See also Everett V. Stonequist, "The Mulatto as Marginal Man," in Alain Locke and Bernhard J. Stern, eds., *When Peoples Meet: A Study in Race and Culture Contacts*, pp. 402-5.

flowed freely, McKay directs his barbs against the members of this caste
who plunged themselves into drink and debauchery:

> When you want meet a surprise,
>   Tek de Papine track;
> Dere some things will meet you' eyes
>   Mek you tu'n you' back:
> When you want to see mankind
>   Of "class" family
> In a way degra' them mind
>   Go 'p deh, you will see.[49]

There is no doubt in McKay's mind that the moral degradation of the
mulattoes is the price they have to pay for denying their black ancestry.
This lack of racial pride places them, as he sees things, irredeemably beyond the pale. Ellen Tarry relates[50] — and the fact has independent backing[51] — that "yellow Negroes" always aroused his ire. Rejecting them
along with the whites in a blanket condemnation, he looked on them as
strangers and even worse, for their presence in the city, where they preferred to live, made of it a kind of foreign enclave on the island. Here are
his impressions on arriving in Kingston, after spending his youth in the
country:

> De early days pass quickly 'long,
>   Soon I became a man,
> An' one day found myself among
>   Strange folks in a strange lan'.[52]

Debilitated by their rejection of their black blood, and deprived of all
contact with the soil, they have simultaneously lost all sense of genuine
values and turned the city into a slave camp that McKay cannot escape
from fast enough:

> My little joys, my wholesome min',
>   Dey bullied out o' me,
> And made me daily mourn an' pine
>   An' wish dat I was free.
>
> Dey taught me to distrust my life.[53]
>
> .   .   .   .

In conclusion, he judges them to be a seed of discord planted by the
white man in the land of the blacks, where their presence in the guise of

---

[49] "Papine Corner," stanza 9, *Constab Ballads,* p. 42.
[50] Tarry, *The Third Door,* p. 129.
[51] In particular by Carl Cowl, and in general by all those who knew McKay.
[52] "My Mountain Home," stanza 7, *Songs of Jamaica,* p. 125.
[53] *Ibid.,* stanza 8 and stanza 9, line 1.

a privileged caste introduced, if it is permissible to say so, evil into this earthly paradise. McKay, in order to become acquainted with evil, had to go to the city:

> Te-day I am back in me lan',
> Forgotten by all de gay throng,
> A poorer but far wiser man,
> An' knowin' de right from de wrong.[54]

To be noted, in addition to the end of the stanza, is McKay's characterization, in the first line, of his return from city to country. It is actually a return from exile abroad!

The city symbolizes an evil that is multiple. In part it finds expression in the traditional ways but also, and especially, it adopts other forms that are significant in the racial context.

We will not linger long over the former, which for the most part illustrate the corrupting power of the city, on which McKay superimposes his keen awareness of the corruption rampant among the police. "Disillusioned"[55] voices the complaint of a young country girl who has been seduced by the policeman who enticed her to the city. When he learns that he has made her pregnant, he abandons her in favor of a city girl. Even more total is the degradation of Lelia, in "A Country Girl,"[56] who leaves her country home and ends up as a city prostitute, too ashamed ever to return home. The corporal of "A Recruit to the Corpy"[57] steadily raises his elbow at the expense of the young recruits, who must spend their last pennies to maintain him in drunkenness. "Pay Day"[58] condemns the readiness of the policeman to go into debt. The poem presents a series of remarkably successful pen portraits of the crowd of creditors, and of the prostitutes, who throng before the barracks gate on pay day.

The police are also reputed to be a tool in the hands of the whites for oppressing the blacks. This is the lament of the apple woman in "The Apple Woman's Complaint," when the police forbid her to sell her wares in the street. If she is not allowed to ply her modest trade honestly, she will have to live by stealing, and in either case she will be at odds with the police, who in any event live at her expense. From this poem we cite only those passages that present the attitude of the police as having originated in hatred of the blacks:

[54] "Rise and Fall," last stanza, *ibid.*, p. 101.
[55] *Constab Ballads*, p. 43. The poem is linked with another poem in *Songs of Jamaica* ("My Pretty Dan," p. 114), in which, on the contrary, the girl celebrated the faithfulness of the man she loved.
[56] *Songs of Jamaica*, p. 119.
[57] *Constab Ballads*, p. 50.
[58] *Ibid.*, p. 52.

> Black nigger wukin' laka cow
> An' wipin' sweat-drops from his brow,
> Dough him is dyin' sake o' need,
> P'lice an' dem headman boun' fe feed.
>
> .   .   .   .
>
> De headman fe de town police
> Mind neber know a little peace,
> 'Cep' when him an' him heartless ban'
> Hab sufferin' nigger in dem han'.
>
> .   .   .   .
>
> We hab fe barter out we soul
> To lib' t'rough dis ungodly wul'; —
> O massa Jesus! don't you see
> How police is oppressin' we?[59]

The vehemence of this protest against oppression, here placed in the mouth of the apple woman, and the boundless despair of the last stanza, are in violent contrast with the cold objectivity of the social critique voiced in the rural poems of *Songs of Jamaica*. It heralds what will be McKay's stance in his American poems. Of all the Jamaican poems, "The Apple Woman's Complaint" is the most bitter, violent, and militant. Thus it serves to make entirely plain the changes that city residence brought about in McKay.

The changes were caused, to some degree, by the humiliations to which the poet's dark skin exposed him. The city dweller's contempt for the rustic black man was inescapable. "Flat-Foot Drill" is, no doubt, based on McKay's own recollections of the instructor who taught him "Right turn, left turn!" in the barracks, and it would not be surprising if the insults heaped on the "mountain man" of the poem were in reality addressed to the poet:

> But seems unno all do'n-ca',
>   Won't mek up you' min' fe larn;
> Drill-instructor boun' fe swea',
> Dealin' wid you' class all day,
>   Neber see such from A barn.
>
>   Right tu'n, you damn' bungo brut'!
>   Do it *so*, you mountain man;[60]

The poem has nothing to say concerning the instructor's skin color. However, if we may judge on the basis of his accent, and also by consid-

[59] *Ibid.*, pp. 57-58, stanzas 3, 5, 8.
[60] "Flat-Foot Drill," stanza 2 and stanza 3, lines 1-2, *Constab Ballads*, p. 13.

ering his attitude toward blacks, he must certainly have been a mulatto.[61] "Bungo" is an abusive term reserved for the black, and is never applied to mulattoes. It should be noted, too, that the insult links black color with rural origin.

It is this kind of humiliation that gives rise, between blacks, mulattoes, and whites, to the hatred which, for McKay, is symbolized by the city. Hatred exists everywhere in the city, on the outside, but also and above all in people's hearts.

> 'Tis hatred without an' 'tis hatred within.[62]

Racial discord turns the city into an inferno, and McKay's only wish is to flee to the peace of the mountains, where blacks are sheltered from evil:

> Do you not hear de battle's roar,
> De tumult ragin' on de shore?
> Do you not see de poisonous bait
> Man sets for man t'rough deadly hate?
>
> Come, flee de envy an' de strife,
> Before dey ruin our life:
> Come to de hills; dey may be drear,
> But we can shun de evil here.[63]

To flee the city is, assuredly, to flee from evil; but basically this is a means of saving one's own personality from alienation and of keeping intact the loyalty to one's own race. By remaining in the city McKay would have risked transformation, morally speaking, into a mulatto. That is to say, he might have been led to deny his black extraction and to espouse the hatred felt by the whites for men of his own color. There are at least two poems to justify the surmise that this is the precise problem of conscience that confronted McKay at every turn in Kingston. "The Bobby to the Sneering Lady" illustrates this conflict of loyalties that the

---

[61] Tarry, *The Third Door,* p. 131, declares — her source of information being a friend who had known the poet in Jamaica, at the time he was in the island police force — that his immediate superior, a mulatto, was "a stern, uncompromising, sometimes unreasonable taskmaster." It is highly probable that McKay was thinking of this man when he wrote "Flat-Foot Drill." However, it is possible to take issue with Tarry when she conveys the impression that this circumstance alone accounts for McKay's hatred of mulattoes. It is quite obvious that his hatred springs from far more numerous and varied causes. This is made manifest not only by the other poems but also by the way in which, for instance, McKay treats the arrival of Bita in the city, in the Jamaican novel *Banana Bottom,* pp. 295ff. Bita is victimized by the mulattoes' prejudices against blacks.

[62] "The Heart of a Constab," line 1, *Constab Ballads,* p. 62.

[63] "To W.G.G.," stanzas 2 and 3, *ibid.,* p. 76.

black policeman has to confront. A society woman — white or mulatto, the poem does not say — has asked the policeman to arrest her servant girl, who, like him, is black, for some offense that is left unspecified. But the policeman refuses to make the arrest:

> Our soul's jes' like fe you,
> If our work does make us rough;
> Me won't 'res' you servant-gal
> When you've beaten her enough.[64]

Even the lady's threat to report him to his superior, and the certain prospect of punishment to follow, cannot shake the policeman's resolve. At stake here is not only his sense of justice, but also racial solidarity:

> Ef our lot, then, is so hard,
> I mus' ever bear in mind
> Dat to fe me own black 'kin
> I mus' not be too unkind.[65]

If this policeman was Claude McKay himself, he must have been haunted by the possibility that he might yield to the temptation of failing in loyalty to someone of his own color and so betraying his race. This fear is expressed in "The Heart of a Constab." He knows full well that his identity is not simply a matter of his own wish to belong. He must also receive the recognition of the members of his own group, the blacks, and the fear that one day he might be the object of their merited disapproval motivates his departure from the city. It is a decision that commits him wholly, for by leaving he repudiates the city and the mulatto and, as a consequence, all compromise with the white man, in order to affirm his identity with the land and with the blacks. Simultaneously he chooses personal cohesion rather than an entity he could not have adopted without alienating himself from his true personality.

> Oh! where are de faces I loved in de past,
> De frien's dat I used to hold dear?
> Oh, say, have dey all turned away from me now
> Becausen de red seam I wear?
>
> I foolishly wandered away from dem all
> To dis life of anguish an' woe,
> Where I mus' be hard on me own kith an' kin,
> An' even to frien' mus' prove foe.
>
> · · · ·

[64] "The Bobby to the Sneering Lady," stanza 2, *ibid.*, p. 66.
[65] *Ibid.*, stanza 8, p. 67.

'Tis grievous to think dat, while toilin' on here,
  My people won't love me again,
My people, my people, me owna black skin, —
  De wretched t'ought gives me such pain.

But I'll leave it, my people, an' come back to you,
  I'll flee from de grief an' turmoil;
I'll leave it, though flow'rs here should line my path yet,
  An' come back to you an' de soil.

For 'tis hatred without an' 'tis hatred within,
  An' how can I live 'douten heart?
Then, oh for de country, de love o' me soul,
  From which I shall nevermore part![66]

The foregoing should not leave the erroneous impression that these poems, published in 1912, reveal McKay to be a racial nationalist, even a xenophobe.

Alongside this hymning of the blacks' earthy merits, there is to be noted from time to time a critical reference to their deficiencies. In "Hard Times," for example, the responsibility for the situation is not laid entirely at the white man's door:

> Dat Gahd would cuss de lan' I'd know.
> For black naygur too bad.[67]

In other places, he records the superstitions current among the rural population. A stanza of "Whe' Fe Do?" condemns magic and sorcery, which still flourish in the West Indies. Together with other factors they contribute, no whit less than does racial oppression, to braking black progress:

> We nigger hab a tas' fe do,
> To conquer prejudice dat due
> To obeah, an' t'ings not a few
> Dat keep we progress back fe true —
> But whe' fe do?[68]

Again, his rejection of the city should not be interpreted as a rejection of Western civilization. One need but set beside each other his reserved attitude toward Africa, from which he expects nothing, and his enthusiasm for the greatness of England's past, to illuminate adequately his eclecticism, or his actual cultural dualism. If Jamaica is referred to as "my native land,

---

[66] "The Heart of a Constab," stanzas 2, 3, 6, 7, 8, *ibid.*, pp. 62-63.
[67] "Hard Times," stanza 5, lines 3-4, *Songs of Jamaica*, p. 54.
[68] "Whe' Fe Do?" stanza 4, *ibid.*, p. 28.

222 Black Poets of the United States

my home,"[69] England is "de homeland England" in the poem entitled
"Old England,"[70] which expresses McKay's burning desire to go there, on
a genuine pilgrimage to the wellsprings.

It must be avowed, however, that in the 1912 poems the references to
Western culture are too fragmentary to provide scope for discussion here.
They will not take on form and substance until the poet has lived through
his period of residence in the United States.

3. THE LYRICISM OF MILITANCY

The poet's transplantation from his narrow island to the huge American
continent, and his transfer from a social setting within which racial fric-
tions were kept within bounds, relatively speaking, to an arena made foul
by the periodic eruption of hatred and acts of violence between the races,

[69] See notes 30 and 37 above.
[70] "Old England," stanza 2, line 1, *Songs of Jamaica*, p. 63. There may be some
value in indicating here how McKay's attitude toward England differed from that
of American black poets toward the United States. Let us recall, first of all, that
in the United States all persons having any black blood whatever in their veins
are classed as Negro, whereas in the West Indies those of mixed descent, called
"colored people" to distinguish them from "blacks" or "Negroes," form a separate
caste and occupy a position in society intermediary between blacks and whites.
Besides, these definitions are not applied with an American rigidity, and the
greater suppleness in racial stratification also explains in part the absence, in
Jamaica, of the stern barrier that marks off what behavior is and what is not
allowed Negroes in the United States. For the same reason, relations between the
races are less tense. Yet, though racial discrimination is no less real in Jamaica
than in the United States, it takes a different form. In the United States, the inequality of the races was a matter of law in a number of states and, historically,
had the foundation of an ideology, with pseudo-scientific pretensions, that declared
the Negro to be congenitally inferior. In Jamaica, on the other hand, inferiority
was a mere *de facto* condition, a custom whose legal base was eliminated by the
Act of Emancipation of 1833. Of even greater psychological importance was the
fact that all the island's inhabitants believed in the fairness and independence of
the judicial arm of government (in McKay's time, the Colonial Office), whose
remoteness made it even more imposing. The awareness of his rights, and of the
ever open possibility of defending himself by claiming his rights as a British citizen,
are the constitutive elements of the Jamaican Negro's sense of superiority. His
racial pride is often simply his pride in being British, combined with the spirit of
independence derived from the Maroons, slaves who had rebelled and gone off to
the mountains, forcing the English to recognize their special status. In conclusion,
it should be pointed out that the Jamaican peasant often owns his land, as did
McKay's father, and thus could have a much stronger sense of mastering his destiny
than did the Negro in the United States. All this enables one to see in the proper
light McKay's statement: "The direction of our schooling was, of course, English.
And it was so successful that we really believed we were little black Britons"
("Boyhood in Jamaica," p. 137). McKay consequently can be seen to have had a
kind of double loyalty, to Jamaica and to England, with none of the reservations
that hedge in the loyalty of the American Negro to his country.

first took effect by increasing and raising to the bursting point the ill-clari-
fied passions which, already in Jamaica, secretly smoldered within his
heart. His reason for moving to the United States was not so much to
study as to find a larger public, to escape from his isolation, and to benefit
from the great vital streams in circulation there.[71] But before he could
gain a hearing he had to ensure his survival. Confronted by the hostility
the society's white majority directed against his race, with a virulent
intensity he had previously never imagined, he sharpened his claws and
set out to develop his defense mechanisms.

Racial Pride

His American poems give vent to his racial pride with a forcefulness he
had never exhibited before. This outburst is so authentic, and so much in
keeping with his own fiery, passionate temperament, that little influence
need be attributed to the stimulus he could have found elsewhere in the
paeans to race that were being sounded by his compatriot Garvey. Furthermore, as he faced the onslaught of white insolence, his pride grew in mili-
tancy without losing any of its nobility:

> Your door is shut against my tightened face,
> And I am sharp as steel with discontent;
> But I possess the courage and the grace
> To bear my anger *proudly* and unbent.[72]

His pride is like that of a tree deeply rooted and prepared to withstand
the hostile elements:

> Like a strong tree that in the virgin earth
> Sends far its roots through rock and loam and clay
> And *proudly* thrives in rain or time of dearth ...[73]

As this pride is strengthened and tested by adversity, he raises racial consciousness to the aesthetic plane. One would almost be tempted to affirm
that the poet is inaugurating a hedonism of color, when one beholds how
with a supremely refined sensuality he savors the heady joy of his blackness,
gaining awareness of it amidst a community that tortures him, but to
which he feels superior in every fiber of his being:

[71] *A Long Way from Home,* p. 20.
[72] "The White House," lines 1-4, *Selected Poems,* p. 78 (italics added). The
poem was published in Alain Locke, ed., *The New Negro,* p. 134. Over McKay's
objections, Locke changed the title to "White Houses," fearing that an allusion
might be found to the presidential residence. On this, see *A Long Way from Home,*
p. 313-14.
[73] "Like a Strong Tree," lines 1-3, *Selected Poems,* p. 45 (italics added).

For this peculiar tint that paints my house,
Peculiar in an alien atmosphere
Where other houses wear a kindred hue,
I have a stirring always very rare
And romance-making in my ardent blood,
That channels through my body like a flood.

I know the dark delight of being strange,
The penalty of difference in the crowd,
The loneliness of wisdom among fools,
Yet never have I felt but *very proud,*
Though I have suffered agonies of hell,
Of living in my own peculiar cell.[74]

No one ever expressed with such a wealth of nuances the opposing eddies that swirl in a mind in search of equilibrium amid stupidly hostile surroundings. This attempt at introspective insight clearly demonstrates how racial pride can act as a redemptive force.

Yet it must meet a rude challenge when, gloriously garbed, the poet's sworn enemy, the White City, displays the whole spectrum of her seductive wiles in order to win him over and ruin him:

For one brief moment rare like wine
The gracious city swept across the line;
Oblivious of the colour of my skin,
Forgetting that I was an alien guest,
She bent to me, my hostile heart to win,
Caught me in passion to her pillowy breast;
The great, proud city, seized with a strange love,
Bowed down for one flame hour my pride to prove.[75]

Assailed by these totally feminine cajolings to which he knows he is about to succumb, to which all his senses urge him to succumb, eyeing this modern Trojan horse that the White City pushes toward him across the barrier which none other than she had clairvoyantly and cynically erected to separate the races — confronting these diabolical machinations, there is but one recourse for the poet. He must fan the flame and grant full liberty to the hatred which, until that moment, he had labored to constrain within his heart. To no lesser degree than the intoxication of being black, Claude McKay learned in America how intoxicating it is to hate. He vents his joy in "The White City":

I will not toy with it nor bend an inch.
Deep in the secret chambers of my heart

[74] "My House," stanzas 1 and 2, *Opportunity,* November, 1926, p. 342.
[75] "The City's Love," *Harlem Shadows,* p. 16.

I muse my life-long hate, and without flinch
I bear it nobly as I live my part.
My being would be a skeleton, a shell,
If this dark passion that fills my every mood,
And makes my heaven in the white world's hell,
Did not forever feed me vital blood.
I see the mighty city through a mist —
The strident trains that speed the goaded mass,
The poles and spires and towers vapor-kissed,
The fortressed port through which the great ships pass,
The tides, the wharves, the dens I contemplate,
Are sweet like wanton loves because I hate.[76]

Hatred

Hatred has acquired quite a power of transfiguration. It becomes the favored theme of the poet's song, for it alone can make his surroundings bearable. At times, his paroxysms even crest so high that no catchment of words can suffice:

O word I love to sing! thou art too tender
   For all the passions agitating me;
For all the bitterness thou art too tender,
   I cannot pour my red soul into thee.

O haunting melody! thou art too slender,
   Too fragile like a globe of crystal glass;
For all my stormy thoughts thou art too slender,
   The burden from my bosom will not pass.

O tender word! O melody so slender!
   O tears of passion saturate with brine,
O words, unwilling words, ye cannot render
   My hatred for the foe of me and mine.[77]

It was once declared that hatred is not a poetic emotion.[78] If this act of exclusion were to be acquiesced in, it would oblige us to find no poetic merit whatever in Claude McKay's most striking poems since he, among all black poets, is *par excellence* the poet of hate. This, when situated in its racial context, has a very special characteristic. As "The White City" so clearly shows, it is the actual prerequisite for his survival, since it transmutes into a paradise the base inferno of the white world. It is a sort of

[76] "The White City," *ibid.*, p. 23.
[77] "O Word I Love to Sing," *ibid.*, p. 63.
[78] Louis Cazamian, in his university course (1943-44) comparing Byron and Shelley as lyric poets.

antidote secreted throughout his being and which prevents the White City from emptying him of his substance — were it not for this fostering flood of hatred, which constantly provides him with fresh energies, he would be reduced by the city to the level of a skeleton, of a sea creature's abandoned shell. Hatred is the compensatory factor that assures the equilibrium of his personality, allowing him to adapt himself adequately to his environment.

The psychologists who have studied the effects of racial oppression on the psyche and personality of the American Negro give their backing to this estimate, looking on hatred as a stabilizing factor in his personality. The circumstances imposed on him by his environment arouse in him a certain quantum of hostility. Whether, fearing the repercussions, he manages to bottle up this hostility or, for the same reason, abandons any notion of questioning the status allotted him, in either case we have to do with a neurotic temperament, unless the personality itself is affected by psychoses of reaction.[79] Thus a hypertrophic hostility (especially when, as in McKay's case, it is kept under close surveillance by the will) is an unchallengeable symptom of psychic health. Without it, "the individual is overwhelmed by the hostile world in which he is forced to live."[80]

A proper appreciation has not always been extended to this aspect (which, after all, is valuable and healthy) of hatred in blacks, and for McKay this is especially true. The Department of Justice, through the mouth of Attorney General A. Mitchell Palmer, chose to see in it nothing but "radicalism and sedition."[81] Many Americans still speak of arrogance or "uppitiness." This shows a total unawareness of the psychological realities behind the phenomenon and, consequently, of its value in terms of human experience.

McKay's hatred, as John Dewey has so well put it, "is clean; never mean nor spiteful."[82] This is no suppurating, latent affliction that forms an ulcer. It might more accurately be compared to the red-hot iron that cauterizes and disinfects. In the following lines, which certainly have nothing morbid about them, the poet expresses the same thought:

> There is a searing hate within my soul,
> A hate that only kin can feel for kin,

[79] Abram Kardiner and Lionel Ovesey, *The Mark of Oppression: A Psychosocial Study of the American Negro,* pp. 113, 145-46.

[80] *Ibid.,* p. 263.

[81] McKay's sonnet, "If We Must Die," was actually cited in the Senate document entitled *Radicalism and Sedition among the Negroes as Reflected in Their Publications* (1919), p. 167. On this document see our Ch. 5, "The Negro Renaissance."

[82] Introduction to *Selected Poems,* p. 9.

> A hate that makes me vigorous and whole,
> And spurs me on inceasingly to win.[83]

McKay is fond of employing, as he does with great precision, this image of an inner flame to convey the ardor of the lyric inspiration that urges all his being onward to liberation. The purifying effect of this flame must be stressed: note the adjective "searing," with its host of surgical implications. On the other hand, this inner flame raises to the melting point all the alloyed metals that make up his steel-hard temperament:

> And I am fire, swift to flame and burn,
> Melting with elements high overhead.[84]

It would be easy, too, to detail all the connotations awakened in the passage reproduced below by the homonymous "metal" and "mettle."

> The blended fires that heat his veins within,
> Shaping his metals into finest steel . . .[85]

His experience of America was made up of

> . . . the years that burn,
> White forge-like fires within my haunted brain.[86]

The fire symbolism is complicated by the origin that McKay attributes to hatred. We have stated that this served him as a defense mechanism. Already the Jamaican poems indicate that it originated in the city, which he spurns because of this. In "The White House" he also treats hatred as a poison concocted by the whites, and of which he must beware:

> Oh, I must keep my heart inviolate
> Against the potent poison of your hate.[87]

His own hatred is thus an antidote that enables him to fight, on an equal footing, against the hatred that burns in the oppressor; the racial struggle becomes a fiery furnace in which flame confronts hostile flame. This is the meaning of the sonnet entitled "Baptism":

> Into the furnace let me go alone;
> Stay you without in terror of the heat.

[83] "Mulatto," unpublished sonnet, lines 5-8. We are indebted to Carl Cowl, thanks to whom we became acquainted with this and other unpublished poems.

[84] "Polarity," stanza 2, lines 1-2, *Harlem Shadows*, p. 83.

[85] "My House," stanza 3, lines 3-4.

[86] "America in Retrospect," lines 13-14, *Opportunity*, November, 1926, p. 342. See also "One Year After" (*Harlem Shadows*, p. 85), line 10 of the second sonnet: ". . . molten elements run through my blood."

[87] "The White House," lines 13-14.

I will go naked in — for thus 'tis sweet —
Into the weird depths of the hottest zone,
I will not quiver in the frailest bone,
You will not note a flicker of defeat;
My heart shall tremble not its fate to meet,
My mouth give utterance to any moan.
The yawning oven spits forth fiery spears;
Red aspish tongues shout wordlessly my name.
Desire destroys, consumes my mortal fears,
Transforming me into a shape of flame.
I will come out, back to your world of tears,
A stronger soul within a finer frame.[88]

The last two lines once again stress the transforming power of the fire of hatred, and the sonnet expresses the poet's ultimate goal, which is to take on his shoulders, when he emerges from this baptism of fire, the burden of all his race.

Once all his fears have been reduced to nothing through this ordeal by fire, the poet's embrace of his ordeal extends beyond the living to all those who died in slavery, now that the moment has come to avenge them:

... I am bound with you in your mean graves,
O black men, simple slaves of ruthless slaves.[89]

Impassive, as he stands over against mighty America to defy it, the poet instinctively places himself at the front of the rebellion:

... as a rebel fronts a king in state
I stand within her walls with not a shred
Of terror ...[90]

This was at a time when racial violence, during the "Red Summer" of 1919, was causing fire and bloodshed throughout America. At this time, when a new order was in its birth throes and the hope of victory was quickened by the promise of the October Revolution, McKay sounds a reveille for dead and living in "Exhortation: Summer 1919":

Through the pregnant universe rumbles life's terrific thunder,
And Earth's bowels quake with terror; strange and terrible storms break,
Lightning-torches flame the heavens, kindling souls of men, thereunder:
Africa! long ages sleeping, O my motherland awake!

In the East the clouds grow crimson with the new dawn that is breaking,
And its golden glory fills the western skies.

[88] *Harlem Shadows*, p. 52.
[89] "In Bondage," lines 13-14, *ibid.*, p. 28.
[90] "America," lines 8-10, *ibid.*, p. 6.

O my brothers and sisters, wake! arise!
For the new birth rends the old earth and the very dead are waking,
Ghosts are turned flesh, throwing off the grave's disguise,
And the foolish, even children, are made wise;
For the big earth groans in travail for the strong, new world in making —
O my brothers, dreaming for dim centuries,
Wake from sleeping; to the East turn, turn your eyes![91]

That same year he became, with the publication of "If We Must Die," the incarnation of the new spirit and the spokesman for a whole people at last resolved to witness no longer, in resignation and submissiveness, the massacre of its own brothers at the hands of the enraged white mob, but to return blow for blow and, if necessary, to die. With the possible exception of James Weldon Johnson's "Negro National Hymn," no poem by any black poet has been so frequently cited and extolled.

First published in Max Eastman's magazine *The Liberator,* the poem was reprinted in every Negro publication of any consequence. It forced its way into the Negro pulpit (a most interesting phenomenon for this black heretic). Ministers ended their sermons with it, and the congregations responded, Amen. It was repeated in Negro clubs and Negro schools and at Negro mass meetings. To thousands of Negroes who are not trained to appreciate poetry, "If We Must Die" makes me a poet. I myself was amazed at the general sentiment for the poem. For I am so intensely subjective as a poet, that I was not aware, at the moment of writing, that I was transformed into a medium to express a mass sentiment.[92]

That is what Claude McKay himself said of his poem, and his declarations are borne out in every respect by Sterling Brown, who writes of the poem's author:

When his poems first appeared in this country he became, that which is most difficult, something of a poet of the people. The chronicler has run across enthusiasts for his poems in as unexpected places as a hotel kitchen in Jefferson City and a barber shop in Nashville. The intelligentsia welcomed him as a harbinger.[93]

Here is the text of this famous poem:

If we must die, let it not be like hogs
Hunted and penned in an inglorious spot,

[91] Stanzas 1 and 2, *ibid.,* pp. 49-50.
[92] *A Long Way from Home,* pp. 227-28. And see *ibid.,* pp. 31-33, where McKay recalls not only the strained atmosphere that gave rise to the poem, but also the incident, involving McKay and Harris, which it triggered. The latter insisted that "If We Must Die" should appear in *Pearson's Magazine,* then under his editorship. But McKay had already given the poem to Max Eastman for *The Liberator.*
[93] "A Poet and His Prose," *Opportunity,* August, 1932, p. 256.

While round us bark the mad and hungry dogs,
Making their mock at our accursèd lot.
If we must die, O let us nobly die,
So that our precious blood may not be shed
In vain; then even the monsters we defy
Shall be constrained to honor us though dead!
O kinsmen! we must meet the common foe!
Though far outnumbered let us show us brave,
And for their thousand blows deal one death-blow!
What though before us lies the open grave?
Like men we'll face the murderous, cowardly pack,
Pressed to the wall, dying, but fighting back![94]

The welcome accorded this sonnet is also due, in part, to its being one of those poems in which McKay's poetic gift reaches beyond the circumstances of the day to attain the universal. Along with the will to resistance of black Americans that it expresses, it voices also the will of oppressed peoples of every age who, whatever their race and wherever their region, are fighting with their backs against the wall to win their freedom. Some twenty-five years after its initial publication, "If We Must Die" was reprinted in an English anthology at a time when England, alone and with its back to the wall, was withstanding the onslaught of the Luftwaffe. And the text of the poem was discovered in 1944 on the body of a young white American soldier who had been killed in action.[95]

Target of Hatred: Evil

It is important, at this juncture in our examination of McKay's hatred, to try to determine against what, exactly, his hatred was directed. One might, indeed, choose to regard him as a last-ditch defender of Negro culture, filled with a global detestation of America and the Western culture for which, in his eyes, it stood. This interpretation of his cultural attitude has actually found supporters.

A study of McKay's novels which had signaled his cultural dualism nevertheless found it possible to advance the view that he rejected Western civilization and entrenched himself in a prior primitivism that exalted instinct to the detriment of reason.[96] While a reading of McKay's novels

[94] *Harlem Shadows*, p. 53.
[95] McKay's declarations recorded on Folkways FP 91, side one (see note 19 above), where the poet reads "St. Isaac's Church," "The Tropics in New York," and "If We Must Die." It also seems true that one day, during the Battle of Britain, Sir Winston Churchill read "If We Must Die" in the House of Commons, but we have no confirmation of this.
[96] Robert A. Bone, *The Negro Novel in America,* ends his study of McKay (pp.

does to some extent lend backing to this conclusion, any attempt to extend it to the totality of his writings would be quite wrong. To place things in the proper perspective, one must bear in mind that the writing of these novels occupied no more than six years of Claude McKay's life — and one should note also that this period, which stretched from 1928 to 1933, remained strongly affected by the wave of primitivism that had inundated Harlem after 1920. Finally, and most especially, it is arbitrary to record 1933 as marking McKay's "end" and thus deliberately to set aside the last fifteen years of the author's life.

McKay appears to have expressed all the complexity of his real feelings about America in the sonnet entitled "America":

> Although she feeds me bread of bitterness,
> And sinks into my throat her tiger's tooth,
> Stealing my breath of life, I will confess
> I love this cultured hell that tests my youth!
> Her vigor flows like tides into my blood,
> Giving me strength erect against her hate,
> Her bigness sweeps my being like a flood.[97]

What is predominant here, and basic also, is his love for America, whose strength acts on the poet like a stimulant. The other half of the picture, the hatred that America has for blacks, does not obliterate the poet's love for it. McKay's hatred does not mean a rejection of America; it is a reproach directed against the country's inability to reconcile discriminatory practices with egalitarian democratic doctrines. In the last analysis, what he hates is not America, but evil. An unpublished sonnet makes this explicit:

> I stripped down harshly to the naked core
> Of hatred based on the essential wrong.[98]

We know that the essential evil is the division between man and man, the white man's hatred and contempt for his fellow man, and the exploitation of black by white. In the "civilized hell" of America, evil adopts the most varied guises. But a natural defense reaction leads McKay to note those in particular which deny the black man's humanity. The metaphors often depict America as a kind of vampire seeking to deprive the victim of his substance and to leave him a mere shell or skeleton. America

67-75) with this sentence: "If McKay's spiritual journey carried him 'a long way from home,' in the end he returned to his native island." Neither literally nor figuratively does this statement convey the truth.

[97] "America," lines 1-7, *Harlem Shadows*, p. 6.

[98] This poem, of which lines 7-8 are reproduced above, inaugurates a cycle of some fifty unpublished sonnets, the degree of final polish varying from poem to poem. See also note 107 below.

becomes, for instance, a tiger, his striped coat representing the stripes of the American flag, who seizes his prey by the throat and nourishes himself on the blood:

> The white man is a tiger at my throat,
> Drinking my blood as my life ebbs away,
> And muttering that his terrible striped coat
> Is Freedom's and portends the light of Day.
>
> . . . .
>
> Oh Lord! My body, and my heart too, break —
> The tiger in his strength his thirst must slake![99]

One may note, incidentally, that the image of the stripes here identifies the white man with America, whereas in the 1912 poems McKay had always distinguished between England and the whites he was criticizing.

In another poem, "Birds of Prey," whites are depicted as birds darkening the sky with their wings, then swooping down on their victims to gorge themselves on the hearts:

> Their shadows dim the sunshine of our day,
> As they go lumbering across the sky,
> Squawking in joy of feeling safe on high,
> Beating their heavy wings of owlish gray.
> They scare the singing birds of earth away
> As, greed-impelled, they circle threateningly,
> Watching the toilers with malignant eye
> From their exclusive haven — birds of prey.
> They swoop down for the spoil in certain might,
> And fasten in our bleeding flesh their claws.
> They beat us to surrender weak with fright,
> And tugging and tearing without let or pause,
> They flap their hideous wings in grim delight,
> And stuff their gory hearts into their maws.[100]

Blood and heart quite assuredly have a symbolic value in these poems, which denounce the depersonalization of the black man and his exploitation by society's rulers, who glut themselves on his financial and artistic substance. But this carnage also requires a more literal interpretation, so that the poems may be understood as a condemnation of lynching, like the sonnet "The Lynching,"[101] where McKay speaks more openly.

At times, too, McKay succeeds in utilizing a less violent mode to chant the horrors of racial discrimination. "The Barrier" is a delightful poem

[99] Lines 1-4 and 13-14 of the sonnet "Tiger," *Selected Poems*, p. 47.
[100] "Birds of Prey," *Harlem Shadows*, p. 47.
[101] *Ibid.*, p. 51.

which, in a manner that is partly light and partly serious, considers the interdict prohibiting any love between a black man and a white woman. It is reminiscent of those trials that judged a man's intentions when, in the Deep South, blacks used to be convicted of the "visual rape" of a southern white beauty:

> I must not gaze at them although
>   Your eyes are dawning day;
> I must not watch you as you go
>   Your sun-illumined way;
>
> I hear but I must never heed
>   The fascinating note,
> Which, fluting like a river reed,
>   Comes from your trembling throat;
>
> I must not see upon your face
>   Love's softly glowing spark;
> For there's the barrier of race,
>   You're fair and I am dark.[102]

In contrast, "One Year After" is a meditation, after the fact, on an overstepping of the sexual taboos. The poet confesses to his white mistress, one year later, that inhibitions have hampered their union by blocking him, in spite of himself, from giving himself to her entirely. This poem, even more clearly than the preceding one, conveys some idea of the psychic repercussions that result from the evil of racial discrimination. Though condemning it the poet still cannot shake himself free, and in retrospect this love that is forbidden by an inhuman law appears to him as something monstrous, since it is both a crime, in the view of white people, and an act of disloyalty toward his own race. He is left with a sense of guilt that leads him to believe he has been rejected by both blacks and whites:

> Not once in all our days of poignant love
> Did I a single instant give to thee
> My undivided being wholly free.
> Not all thy potent passion could remove
> The barrier that loomed between to prove
> The full supreme surrendering of me.
> Oh, I was beaten, helpless utterly
> Against the shadow-fact with which I strove.
> For when a cruel power forced me to face
> The truth which poisoned our illicit wine,
> That even I was faithless to my race

---

102 "The Barrier," *ibid.,* p. 13.

> Bleeding beneath the iron hand of thine,
> Our union seemed a monstrous thing and base!
> I was an outcast from thy world and mine.[103]

These are a few aspects of the evil that gnaws at America's side like a cancer. The awareness of this fault is ever before McKay's eyes. But America, on the contrary, most frequently remains blind to it. Dazzled by its own might, it cannot glimpse, soaring over its destiny, the shadow that one day, the poet believes, will avenge this wrong:

> I see your great all-sweeping lights that blind
> Your vision to the Shadow over you.[104]

McKay has a prophetic vision of atonement through the collapse of American power, its miracles of granite one day to be swallowed up by the sand:

> Darkly I gaze into the days ahead,
> And see her might and granite wonders there,
> Beneath the touch of Time's unerring hand,
> Like priceless treasures sinking in the sand.[105]

Fearing lest Destiny fail in her task, the poet calls for aid on the angel of Vengeance, that the day of retribution may be speeded:

> ... from the dark depths of my soul I cry
> To the avenging angel to consume
> The white man's world of wonders utterly:
> Let it be swallowed up in earth's vast womb,
> Or upward roll as sacrificial smoke
> To liberate my people from its yoke![106]

Since McKay's hatred pushes him to the extreme of calling for the destruction of America, one may well wonder how it is possible to speak of the love he feels. Yet there is a passage in the autobiography that provides us with assurance on that score. He is dealing with the time when he worked for *The Liberator:* "It was at this time that I wrote a series of sonnets expressing my bitterness, hate and love. Some of them were quoted out of their context to prove that I hate America."[107]

One can sense the force of the purely internal logic, tied to conflicting allegiances, that leads him to associate hatred and love. The latter can

---

[103] We cite the first of the two sonnets that make up "One Year After," *ibid.,* p. 84.

[104] "America in Retrospect," lines 3-4, *Opportunity,* November, 1926, p. 342.

[105] From the sonnet "America," lines 11-14, *Harlem Shadows,* p. 6.

[106] From the sonnet "Enslaved," lines 9-14, *ibid.,* p. 32.

[107] *A Long Way from Home,* p. 135.

survive only to the degree that the former succeeds in isolating, destroying, and rejecting everything in the beloved object that raises up obstacles to this love.

The Limits of Hatred

Though McKay may justifiably be called the poet of hatred and rebellion, his real personality would be seriously misrepresented if one were to treat him as an out-and-out rebel. Without meaning to do so, Richard Wright undoubtedly slights McKay in his nobility by asserting of him: "To state that Claude McKay is a rebel is to understate it; his rebellion is a way of life."[108] To adopt this point of view is to overlook the remarkable self-mastery that McKay could summon up, and to neglect the personal purification and, when all is considered, the moral elevation that McKay believed he could derive from his hate.

It is, indeed, admirable that in his case hatred and rebellion did not become, as they might have, a vehicle lurching onward without reins or brakes. Even when he revels in his hate, he does not wallow in it, and in the midst of the hurricane he retains his control:

Peace, O my rebel heart! . . .[109]

However passionate his rebellious flights of rhetoric, they are always lucid and dominated by an unflagging will to self-transcendence:

Oh, I must search for wisdom every hour
Deep in my wrathful bosom sore and raw.[110]

He simply does not look on hatred as an end in itself. It is but a stage on the path that ends in the divine charity, for which its purifying action prepares the way. Understood thus, McKay's hatred is a holy anger the manifestation of which occurs only in entire clarity of mind, as did the divine anger directed against the deleterious hypocrisy of the Pharisees, or against the merchants who had made of the temple a "den of thieves." Ultimately, what sets a limit to hatred is the spiritual. Such is the message of the sonnet "To the White Fiends," in which God compels hatred to stop on the brink of murder, directing it to a higher goal:

108 Richard Wright, *White Man, Listen!* p. 139. This remark characterizes Wright better than it does McKay. Rebellion was, indeed, Wright's only life style, and he never discovered the values on which he could rebuild everything that his negative criticism had destroyed. For McKay, on the contrary, rebellion and hate are but a first stage, after which the way is clear for authentic values.
109 "The Tired Worker," line 3, *Harlem Shadows*, p. 44.
110 "The White House," lines 9-10, *Selected Poems*, p. 78.

Think you I am not fiend and savage too?
Think you I could not arm me with a gun
And shoot down ten of you for every one
Of my black brothers murdered, burnt by you?
Be not deceived, for every deed you do
I could match — out-match: am I not Afric's son,
Black of that black land where black deeds are done?
But the Almighty from the darkness drew
My soul and said: Even thou shalt be a light
Awhile to burn on the benighted earth,
Thy dusky face I set among the white
For thee to prove thyself of higher worth;
Before the world is swallowed up in night,
To show thy little lamp: go forth, go forth![111]

Thus, far from being a "way of life," McKay's hatred undergoes a sublimation that induces it to consume itself. In its place comes a tranquillity that is not indifference, but a deepening and internalization of racial feeling. In this frame of mind the poet can address America in these serene words, which are not uttered by an ingrate:

Wistful, I feel no hatred deep and wild,
For you made me a stoic introvert.[112]

4. Exoticism and the Theme of Africa

In McKay's work, the feeling for nature occupies almost as important a place as racial feeling. One could, indeed, compose a Jamaican flora by citing not only his poems, but also the novel *Banana Bottom* and some of the short stories included in *Gingertown*. His nature poems are all the more admirable for sounding a truer note. Unlike Countee Cullen or Langston Hughes, who never vibrated in unison with nature (which usually remains a mere concept for them), McKay brings to it the understanding and sympathy of a person who grew up in it and whose rare sensitivity brought him to an authentic integration with it. In *Harlem Shadows*, the nature poems make up nearly one-third of the volume. The languorous sweetness of their lyricism is like a cool breeze from the Isles, introducing a note of most welcome tranquillity into the militant fierceness of the poems of rebellion.

It is only too evident that these poems must be regarded primarily as an expression of the poet's longing for his distant Jamaica. By way of example,

[111] "To the White Fiends," *ibid.*, p. 38.
[112] "America in Retrospect," lines 7-8.

here is an unpublished poem of the same period. It is called "Home
Song":

> Oh breezes blowing on the red hill-top
>   By tall fox-tails,
> Where through dry twigs and leaves and grasses hop
>   The dull-brown quails,
>
> Is there no magic floating in the air
>   To bring to me
> A breath of you, when I am homesick here
>   Across the sea?
>
> Oh black boys holding on the cricket ground
>   A penny race,
> What other black boy frisking round and round
>   Plays in my place?
>
> When picnic days come with their yearly thrill
>   In warm December,
> The boy in me romps with you in the hills —
>   Remember!

But along with this subjective, personal meaning, the evocation of
tropical languor also helped to strengthen the exotic trend that developed
on both sides of the Atlantic in the particularly favorable conditions of the
1920's. The trend is to be noted in both white and black writers.[113] The
easygoing quality of tropical life, whose primitive rhythm of existence
permits long reveries, is implicitly opposed, in the title "North and South,"
to the frenzied pace of industrial America:

> O sweet are tropic lands for waking dreams!
>   There time and life move lazily along.
> There by the banks of blue and silver streams
>   Grass-sheltered crickets chirp incessant song;
> Gay-colored lizards loll all through the day,
>   Their tongues outstretched for careless little flies,
> And swarthy children in the fields at play,
>   Look upward, laughing at the smiling skies.
> A breath of idleness is in the air
>   That casts a subtle spell upon all things,
> And love and mating-time are everywhere,
>   And wonder to life's commonplaces clings.
> The fluttering humming-bird darts through the trees,
>   And dips his long beak in the big bell-flowers.
> The leisured buzzard floats upon the breeze,

[113] See our Ch. 5, "The Negro Renaissance."

Riding a crescent cloud for endless hours.
The sea beats softly on the emerald strands —
O sweet for quiet dreams are tropic lands![114]

In the freshness of this panorama of idyllic life in the tropics, we find all that is antithetical to the ugliness and gloom of Western civilization, which is symbolized by the city, "The harsh, the ugly city."[115] Around this polarity more than one poem in *Harlem Shadows* is constructed. We reproduce a passage from "When Dawn Comes to the City." One notes on the way the depressing connotations of the epithets applied to men and things, and to the very stars, in the urban setting:

The *tired* cars go *grumbling* by,
   The *moaning, groaning* cars,
And the *old* milk carts go *rumbling* by
   Under the same *dull* stars.
Out of the tenements, *cold* as stone,
   Dark figures start for work;
I watch them *sadly* shuffle on,
   'Tis dawn, dawn in New York.

But I would be on the island of the sea,
In the heart of the island of the sea,
Where the cocks are crowing, crowing, crowing,
And the hens are cackling in the rose-apple tree,
Where the old draft-horse is neighing, neighing, neighing.[116]

In New York, that great, inhuman city, even the wind in the subway would flee to the freedom of the great open spaces:

. . . the deafening roar
Of captive wind that moans for fields and seas,[117]

It can be seen that McKay's feeling for nature has no autonomous existence. Since it is linked with the racial symbolism of the earth and remains closely subordinated to it, seen from this point of view it most often amounts to the enunciation of a sense of belonging.

Its expressive value, because of this role, falls together with that of the African theme as treated by many poets of the Negro Renaissance. For them, Africa is the land still unpolluted by the inhuman machine outlook of the white man, hungry to enslave his fellow men. But for them — those who are unable to identify with America, the land that treats them in-

[114] *Harlem Shadows*, p. 17.
[115] "The Tired Worker," line 14, *ibid.,* p. 44.
[116] "When Dawn Comes to the City," lines 1-13, *ibid.,* p. 60.
[117] "Subway Wind," lines 7-8, *ibid.,* p. 54.

humanely — Africa is the substitute land where they can seek their roots; Africa is the mother with whom, in the place of stepmotherly America which has rejected them, they try to form an *a posteriori* bond of relationship.

McKay is totally unconcerned with these substitute values. For he comes from a land where blacks are in the majority, where he struck roots both tenacious and extraordinarily deep, a land with which his identification was perfect, if one allows for the extraterritorial status he imposed on the city of Kingston. He has no need to go all the way to Africa to find the palm trees to which he can compare the black girls. Jamaica is his Africa, and its exoticism is a genuine exoticism, not a dream escape to some substitute fatherland the need for which springs from a feeling of frustration.

It is not surprising, therefore, that he keeps the African theme within much more modest limits than the other Renaissance poets, whose feeling of unqualified admiration for Africa he does not share. The whole body of his work contains scarcely more than half a dozen poems devoted to Africa, and not one of them can be considered an apologia.

In the 1912 poems, Africa is the subject of only eight lines. At that, they do not even make up the poem's major theme, since they occur only incidentally in "Cudjoe Fresh from de Lecture," when Cudjoe tells Cous' Jarge about the lecture on evolution he has just heard:

> Seems our lan' must ha' been a bery low-do'n place,
> Mek it tek such long time in tu'ning out a race.
>
> . . . .
>
> But I t'ink it do good, tek we from Africa
> An' lan' us in a blessed place as dis a ya.
>
> Talk 'bouten Africa, we would be deh till now,
> Maybe same half-naked — all day dribe buccra cow,
> An' tearin' t'rough de bush wid all de monkey dem,
> Wile an' uncibilise', an' neber comin' tame.[118]

In this passage, a vague consciousness of belonging to Africa may be noted, since it is referred to as "our land," that is to say, the land from which our ancestors came. The poet's "we" certainly includes all the blacks in Jamaica, and perhaps all those in America North and South, with whom he would thus be uniting himself, at least with respect to his origins. Here, too, is an echo of the McKay family's lively awareness of its African heritage. But the poet pushes identification no further, and the remaining lines reveal a curiously realistic McKay who coldly weighs all

[118] "Cudjoe Fresh from de Lecture," stanza 7, lines 1-2; stanza 10, lines 3-4; stanza 11, *Songs of Jamaica,* pp. 56-57.

the advantages he has derived from his ancestors' departure from the shadowy African continent. What a contrast between the impoverished land of Africa and the blessed soil of Jamaica! What would all the Jamaican blacks be doing today in Africa? Doubtless they would be forced to watch the cows of some white settler, and in their savage frolics would be cheek by jowl with the monkeys in the jungle. Their greatest misfortune — it is worthwhile to insist on this feature — would have been to remain "wild and uncivilized," and so without benefit of the white man's culture. This outlook, on McKay's part, brings him astonishingly close to Phillis Wheatley, the Africa-born poetess, more than a century after her time.

His attitude toward Africa is even less clearly defined in "On a Primitive Canoe," one of the poems in which he calls Africa "a dim unknown land":

> Here, passing lonely down this quiet lane,
> Before a mud-splashed window long I pause
> To gaze and gaze, while through my active brain
> Still thoughts are stirred to wakefulness; because
> Long, long ago in a dim unknown land,
> A massive forest-tree, axe-felled, adze-hewn,
> Was deftly done by cunning mortal hand
> Into a symbol of the tender moon.
> Why does it thrill more than the handsome boat
> That bore me o'er the wild Atlantic ways,
> And fill me with a rare sense of things remote
> From this harsh life of fretful nights and days?
> I cannot answer but, whate'er it be,
> An old wine has intoxicated me.[119]

One can, no doubt, credit to Africa the admiration the poet feels for the skill of the artisan who shaped the canoe. But what are the "thoughts stirred to wakefulness" at the sight of this object? He does not say. However, the last two lines of the third quatrain give him away and it becomes evident, on this occasion also, that the primitivism evoked by the canoe represents the opposite pole from the inhuman frenzy of city civilization. Thus Africa does not represent a positive value here.

Elsewhere, it is called "that black land where black deeds are done,"[120] a judgment based on ignorance, which delights in peopling *terra incognita* with mysterious crimes, rather than on any desire to glorify Africa.

But in "Africa" an unconcealed despair concerning the fate of Africa finds expression, as McKay establishes a harsh contrast between Africa's

[119] *Harlem Shadows*, p. 36.
[120] "To the White Fiends"; see note 111 above.

past grandeur and its present lamentable state. So, in the end, the whole
force of this fine sonnet serves only to present Africa as an object of pity:

> The sun sought thy dim bed and brought forth light,
> The sciences were sucklings at thy breast;
> When all the world was young in pregnant night
> Thy slaves toiled at thy monumental best.
> Thou ancient treasure-land, thou modern prize,
> New people marvel at thy pyramids!
> The years roll on, thy sphinx of riddle eyes
> Watches the mad world with immobile lids.
> The Hebrews humbled them at Pharaoh's name.
> Cradle of power! Yet all things were in vain!
> Honor and Glory, Arrogance and Fame!
> They went. The darkness swallowed thee again.
> Thou art the harlot, now thy time is done,
> Of all the mighty nations of the sun.[121]

"The Wise Men of the East" is a sonnet written by McKay a short while
before he died, when he had reached the end of his spiritual pilgrimage
and had made his peace with God. A close examination of the reasoning
implicit in the poem reveals that he looked on the debasement of the black
peoples, and especially those of Africa, as a spiritual bankruptcy, and on
their current servitude as the punishment for their disloyalty to the destiny
that God originally had assigned them.

He sees, in the presence of Balthasar the Negro among the Magi who
were led by the star to the manger in Bethlehem, a first sign of the equality
that had originally been promised to Negroes under God's plan. The
second quatrain alludes to an episode in Acts,[122] the account of God's
sending an angel to wake the apostle Philip so that he may go and meet
the minister of Queen Candace of Ethiopia. Philip is told to explain to
him a passage in Isaiah relative to the coming of Christ, and to bestow
baptism on him. This incident, together with the conversion of the black
empire of Ethiopia to worship of the true God — which had been pre-
figured by the visit to King Solomon of the Queen of Sheba, "long before
Rome its pagan fetters burst," and would be completed in the fourth century by the preaching of Saint Frumentius — in McKay's view are testimony to the love lavished by God on the black race in order to single it
out. Yet, though called to occupy the first rank, blacks failed to show
themselves worthy of the call God had addressed to them as his chosen
people. Hence their present lamentable state:

121 "Africa," *Harlem Shadows*, p. 35.
122 Acts 8:26-39.

From the high place where erstwhile they grew drunk
With power, oh God, how gutter-low have black men sunk.[123]

One cannot be sure that the defense of Africa is the main aim of "En-slaved," where the poet once again raises his voice in protest against the oppression inflicted on his race. This poem may be, rather, an expression of the solidarity felt by the oppressed blacks of America with their African brothers. This would make it anti-white, not pro-African:

Oh when I think of my long-suffering race,
For weary centuries despised, oppressed,
Enslaved and lynched, denied a human place
In the great life line of the Christian West;
And in the Black Land disinherited,
Robbed in the ancient country of its birth,
My heart grows sick with hate, becomes as lead,
For this my race that has no home on earth.[124]

In "Outcast,"[125] it is again the sense of being captive in the white man's empire that occupies the poet's mind, rather than any feeling of solidarity with Africa. Nevertheless, this second factor emerges with greater clarity here than in any other poem by McKay. But he is less in-tent on affirming his link with Africa than in regretting that the elements forming this link have been lost or forgotten. These forgotten jungle chants, this so vital substance torn out of his heart and beyond recall — is it not the very element of African culture which the poet has never known because the white man severed his ancestors from it, after they had been seized and borne off to slavery in a strange land? And is it not somewhat surprising to hear him declare, all of a sudden, that he has been born "far from my native clime," when we are thoroughly acquainted with his vigorous assertions of identity with his Jamaican isle? He must be taken to express his kinship with the blacks of the United States, whose spokes-man he has become, and to state the truth, as suggested by the poem's title, that he himself has been rejected by the white American majority. These two ingredients are more obvious than any putative avowal of genuine solidarity with Africa.

But another possibility to be considered is that this sonnet confronts us with one of the rare instances when McKay's lucid realism gave way before Marcus Garvey's African nationalist dream. This is undoubtedly the case with the following lines from "Exhortation: Summer 1919," where the poet sounds the reveille for Africa:

[123] "The Wise Men of the East," lines 13-14, *Selected Poems*, p. 48.
[124] "Enslaved," lines 1-8, *Harlem Shadows*, p. 32.
[125] *Ibid.*, p. 45.

Africa! long ages sleeping, O my motherland, awake!

. . . .

Sons of the seductive night, for your children's children's sake
From the deep primeval forests where the crouching leopard's lurking,
Lift your heavy-lidded eyes, Ethiopia! awake![126]

In no single instance does McKay play the part of an apologist for
Africa. He might even be blamed, if not for failing to foresee, at least
for not having hoped for and more boldly desired an African renewal.
Thus McKay's handling of the theme of Africa does not warrant the view
of W. T. Fontaine, who chose to see in him an "enflamed singer of African
glory."[127] Very much to the contrary, the firmness of his attachment to
Jamaica, as much as his intellectual probity and his clearsightedness, pre-
cluded his seeking an unrealistic solution for his own problems by evading
them in favor of participation in solving others' problems, even if these
others should be Africans.

Thus if McKay is a forerunner of the Negro Renaissance, this is not
due to his vision of Africa. The genuine quality of his Jamaican exoticism
had immunized him against the heady African mirage, and his ability to
stand resolute against its seductions attests, in the last resort, the cohesiveness and equilibrium of his personality.

5. HARLEM AND NEGRO ART

McKay has left us only a few poems dealing with Harlem, the "Mecca
of the Negro Renaissance." His 1922 volume, though entitled *Harlem
Shadows*, has but two poems on the theme, the title poem and "The Harlem Dancer." Three years later, a sequence of three sonnets appeared: "Negro Dancers." There are also three unpublished poems, "Note of Harlem,"
"Lenox Avenue," and "Black Belt Slummers." All this amounts to little,
compared to the extensive treatment of the theme in his prose works. Centering around it are one of his novels, *Home to Harlem*, half the stories in
Gingertown, and all the essays making up *Harlem, Negro Metropolis*, not
to mention various sections of the autobiography, *A Long Way from
Home*. It would be idle to speculate on the reasons for this imbalance.
Suffice it to say that the prose works are all of a later date than the poems,
and that Harlem did not acquire its full importance until after McKay's
second departure for Europe.

[126] Lines 4, 15-17, *ibid.*, pp. 49-50.
[127] "The Mind and Thought of the Negro of the United States as Revealed in
Imaginative Literature, 1876-1940," *Bulletin of Southern University and A. & M.
College*, March, 1942, p. 30.

Yet, though for these reasons he can scarely be called the poet of Harlem, at least he has the merit of being the first to introduce Harlem into Negro poetry. For in December, 1917, "The Harlem Dancer" appeared in *The Seven Arts,* and "Harlem Shadows" was included in *Spring in New Hampshire* (1920). Earlier than Langston Hughes, it is Claude McKay who provided the first annotations on the frivolous night life that, until the 1929 crash, would enable Harlem to prosper. These poems might also be said to constitute the first poetic documents on the reactions of the black man borne to the urban centers by the tide of the Great Migration. There is nothing astonishing in the fact that McKay, as a shrewd observer of every aspect of city life, paid particularly close attention to this phenomenon.

"Harlem Shadows" is a poem in a minor key on the prostitutes that urban civilization, with its lack of humanity, had thrown onto the Harlem sidewalks. The poem is reminiscent of those that McKay, in the 1912 volumes, had devoted to the moral debacle of two country girls as a result of their going to live in Kingston. But "Harlem Shadows" is an innovation in the sense that McKay attributes a primordial importance to the prostitutes' color (blackening them further by referring to them as shadows) and makes their downfall symbolic of the whole race's. In each case, the blame is implicitly allotted to racial oppression. This biased suggestion deviates significantly from McKay's usually realistic, objective manner, and one would have expected him to treat these prostitutes as victims of the city rather than as slaves of the master race. This deference to racial propaganda spoils the end of the poem, which otherwise would have been very much to the point:

> Ah, stern harsh world, that in the wretched way
> Of poverty, dishonor and disgrace,
> Has pushed the timid little feet of clay,
> The sacred brown feet of my fallen race!
> Ah, heart of me, the weary, weary feet
> In Harlem wandering from street to street.[128]

The fourth line of this last stanza is, patently, in deplorable taste.

"The Harlem Dancer"[129] plunges us into the atmosphere of one of the countless night spots that sprang up in Harlem after World War I. This sonnet raises the problem of another sort of prostitution, that of Negro art to popular (mainly white) demands. White people appear in the sonnet as drunken spectators who gobble up with their eyes the form of a naked

[128] Stanza 3, *Harlem Shadows*, p. 22.
[129] *Ibid.*, p. 42.

black dancer. Between the young whites, in search of venal pleasures, and the nobility of the black beauty, the comparison is to the advantage of the latter. She appears before us in all the pride of a tall palm tree swaying majestically in the wind, yet she is an uprooted palm tree, torn from a kindlier country where she has left her soul. Her natural grace and beauty contrast with the artificial setting into which she has been transplanted, and her forced smile cannot hide her longing for her native land. Underneath the exoticism of detail, we once again come upon a thesis greatly favored by McKay and the Negro Renaissance, maintaining that the white world, more often than was generally believed, was a setting unfit to receive all that blacks have to offer it. This is the equivalent, on the aesthetic plane, of the awareness that is expressed elsewhere of "the loneliness of wisdom among fools."[130]

One may establish a parallel between "The Harlem Dancer" and another sonnet, "Negro Spiritual,"[131] which, though leaving Harlem unmentioned, considers this same problem of the exploitation of Negro art by whites. In this magnificent sonnet, McKay gives particularly fortunate expression to all the glorious, grievous overtones awakened in the black soul when hearing spirituals sung. But the primitive natural beauty of these songs of the slaves' cruelly tested existence is doubly betrayed with an orchestration that falsifies the songs and in the setting of a too artificially beautiful auditorium. There they strike a false note, as did the almost feline grace of the black dancer in the decadent atmosphere of the Harlem joint. Between Negro art and the blundering receptivity of the white art-lover lies the abyss of "an alien spirit." McKay condemns this attitude adopted by whites, since they approach Negro art with the mentality of slaveowners. All they have in mind is to find diversion in this art, just as they used to make buffoons out of the slaves they owned.

The unpublished "Black Belt Slummers,"[132] left in a state that reflects its author's untimely death, also satirizes white people's clumsy fascination with Harlem in the years after 1920, and their inability to understand the Negro and to accept him as he is.

These fans of primitive sensations at any cost are totally blinded by their own preconceptions, so that the Negro soul inevitably will remain a closed book for them. To understand Harlem one must do as the poet did, and let himself be swept away by its living rhythm:

[130] See note 74 above.
[131] This poem, which McKay had given to Eugène Jolas for his *Anthologie de la nouvelle poésie américaine* (Paris, 1928), appears never to have been reproduced elsewhere.
[132] For the text of this poem, see our Appendix of unpublished poems in the original French edition.

> Rich is the flavor of this Harlem street;
> The dusk over the dark-warm scene is tender,
> The murmuring of fruit-ripe throats is sweet
> And gladly to the tumult I surrender.[133]

Once that is done, Harlem will be seen as the great stage of Negro life. McKay evokes this in "Lenox Avenue," pouring into the poem all the vivacity and abandon, all the music and the casual life-style that can be sensed even today on a stroll through its streets:

> The cabarets and dancing halls so loud
> Entrancingly with laughter and with song,
> Intoxicate my senses with the street,
> To take the rhythm of Harlem's moving feet.[134]

This is indeed Harlem's contagious beat.

McKay also tries to find his way to this same black popular temperament in "Negro Dancers,"[135] but going beyond appearances he seeks, on this occasion, to penetrate to the very soul of the dancers and to discover their philosophy of life.

Poets have often been attracted by the theme of black dancers. Dunbar, it will be recalled, has left us entertaining portrayals of evenings spent dancing the quadrille with, in his day, the added savor of forbidden fruit. Jazz, in its turn, will soon find its true poet in Langston Hughes. Thus it need not surprise us that McKay also should have chosen to see in the liberation of the dance, as in the spontaneity and the subtle rhythms of the dancers, an especially revealing manifestation of the "immortal spirit" of his race, since here one could note the urge to expand, to express oneself, to free oneself, instincts that in daily life had to be kept in check at every instant.

But whereas Dunbar and Hughes let themselves be swept away by the vortex of the dance, McKay remained the detached observer, though sensing the emotion that radiated from the dancers to him. His view is an external one; a space remains between him and the crowd of dancers and allows him no identification with them. He, unlike Dunbar and Hughes, is not one of the dancers he describes. The third sonnet of this sequence is laden with pity for this crowd without faith or hope, dizzy from the music and shouts of the dancing hall, as at other times the "shouts" of the

---

[133] "Note of Harlem," stanza 1. The poem may be read in our Appendix of unpublished poems in the original French edition.
[134] These lines are from "Lenox Avenue." For the complete text, see our Appendix of unpublished poems in the original French edition.
[135] This poem, a sequence of three sonnets originally published in *The Liberator*, is reprinted in Locke, ed., *The New Negro*, pp. 214-15.

churches in Harlem and elsewhere daze them. It can be sensed that McKay experiences a measure of despair vis-à-vis the tragedy of this superficial response of a whole race to the oppression and contempt by which it is victimized.

This is, we believe, another manifestation of McKay's reserved attitude when confronted by the folk temperament, with which he never felt entirely at ease. Other elements that lead us to the same conclusion are the total absence of humor throughout his poetry and his preference for such classical poetic forms as the sonnet. Spirituals, blues, and jazz, whose popular forms were taken over by Langston Hughes, Sterling Brown, and many other poets, have no place in McKay's poetic work. In this connection, it is necessary to correct the mistaken view propounded by Henry Lüdeke (no doubt on the basis of uncertain information) that in *Harlem Shadows* the rhythms were "strongly influenced by popular poetry, above all the spirituals."[136] Quite the contrary, McKay must have had a background awareness that the popular forms and outlook could become, as has in reality often occurred, an excuse for avoiding personal reflection, and so would have been only another sort of escapism for the poet. Thus, while he defends Negro art against the deformations that whites inflicted on it, he defended it no less vigorously against those Negroes who were tempted to ask of it something that it could not provide: a soul. Through the mouth of one of his characters in *Banjo,* he had declared: "Getting down to our native roots and building up from our own people is not savagery. It is culture."[137] But in Harlem he could now see to what a degree this culture was emptied of substance the moment it lost contact with the soil, which alone could give it life, and was transported to the city, which in McKay's eyes had ever been a corrupting influence. In a word, he judged Negro popular culture, as he had encountered it in America, to be incapable of fulfilling his need for an authentic spiritual life.

6. The Spiritual Journey

From the time of the anonymous creators of the spirituals to the poets of today, the expression of religious feeling has always been motivated, among blacks, by their social situation and conditioned by the racial context. Though McKay does not escape this yoke, there is nevertheless a vast

---

[136] Henry Lüdeke, *Geschichte der amerikanischen Literatur,* p. 506. Yet it is praiseworthy of Lüdeke to have discussed Negro writers in his book, since most authors of literary histories of the United States still let them go practically unmentioned.

[137] *Banjo,* p. 200.

distance separating the religious traditionalism of the people from his individual religious feeling.

The traditionalist poets took over *en bloc* a set of accepted beliefs when, in their view, these formed part of their racial heritage; or, on the contrary, they rejected them all when they held them to be narcotics that could only lull their racial consciousness to sleep, or outworn superstitions that had been handed down from the now extinct period of slavery. Dangerous superstitions, at that, insofar as they tended to turn the race away from its immediate goals and removed to the other world any hope of achieving the longed-for liberty, equality, and justice. Almost always the religious feeling of such writers culminates at the outset, for it is the casual acceptance of a fully worked-out tradition to which the individual can hardly feel totally committed. In a word, it is often purely decorative, as it was with J. W. Johnson — part of the local color the reader is looking for, and in the absence of which the portrayal of the traditional Negro would appear incomplete.

McKay, on the contrary, with his nonconformist temperament, was repelled by the idea of adhering to traditions that took the place of individual reflection. His religious poetry is the expression of an inner growth, and his discovery of God the result of his individual search for truth. From a more general vantage-point, his poetic opus may be considered as the account of a vast attempt at a synthesis between the antagonistic elements of the black world and the Western world warring within him. There can be no denying that McKay, like every black exiled in a white milieu, was for a long time a divided man, so that it is possible to speak of his cultural dualism. But he never acquiesced in being torn apart by this dichotomy. His whole being urged him to find unity. The critique to which he subjected the antinomies deprived them, little by little, of their contingencies and laid bare their authentic values. In Jamaica, he affirmed the primacy of the soil and contrasted it with the inanity of the dream, cherished by the mulattoes, of a heightened social status. He rejected the mirage of Africa as a source of racial pride, looking on it as merely pathetic. He shunned the nationalism of a Garvey, whom he regarded as a charlatan,[138] and while he defended Negro folklore against whites, who would have denatured it, he nevertheless could not find spiritual sustenance in it. On the other hand, it was his natural instinct to evaluate the possibilities of spiritual advancement offered by Western, Christian culture, but there too he perceived the corroding evil that sowed hatred between men. In his dialogue

---

[138] "A West Indian Charlatan," *A Long Way from Home*, p. 354. Nevertheless, he does not underestimate the importance of the mass movement unleashed by Garvey's crusade.

with the West, conducted through the medium of his hatred, this emotion was slowly filtered of its dross as he came to grasp the necessity of raising himself above it. Unless the individual is engaged in a ceaseless effort to transcend himself, no victory over hatred will ever be possible. Neither rationalism nor Communism could provide the higher principle capable of reconciling the conflicting theses of his cultural eclecticism. At long last he discovered this principle within himself, and at the same time he discovered God. Thus his spiritual itinerary is an account of the internalization of his racial feeling.

"I was always religious-minded as some of my pagan poems attest. But I never had any faith in revealed religion."[139] Thus McKay retrospectively characterized the period that preceded his conversion to Catholicism. He may have overestimated the depth and strength of his onetime paganism, which seems to have been merely a skeptical attitude toward the Christian revelation, devoid of any positive content.

The many rationalist works that his brother and Walter Jekyll gave him to read have left few traces in his writings.[140] There is a passage in "Old England" that platonically praises Reason, and in the same stanza his hope that science will light up "de real truths" contrasts with his statement to the effect that "de old fait' is a wreck":

> I'd go to de City Temple, where de old fait' is a wreck,
> An' de parson is a-preachin' views dat most folks will not tek;
> I'd go where de men of science meet togeder in deir hall,
> To give light unto de real truths, to obey king Reason's call.[141]

The City Temple referred to is doubtless Saint Paul's, and the "parson" Dean Inge, who had just come to the post in 1911, and whose views had touched off numerous controversies. Of greater significance is the poem "Cudjoe Fresh from de Lecture," already cited in connection with the African theme. It discusses the relative merits of the fundamentalist view of man's origins and the theory of evolution, with particular reference to the black man. For Cudjoe, who tells Cous' Jarge what he has heard at the lecture, the evolutionary theory was a revelation, a truly new creation of man. It also gave him a fresh sense of his own worth, for the lecturer had stressed the equality of all men in the evolutionary process. But is this thesis not basically in accord with what the pastor teaches in church?

---

139 "On Becoming a Roman Catholic," p. 43.
140 Apart, of course, from what he has to say about them in his own autobiographical writings.
141 "Old England," stanza 4, *Songs of Jamaica*, p. 64. The poem expresses the wish that possessed McKay, "from since I could form a t'o't," to pay a visit to England and the monuments of its culture.

> ... Yes, in a diff'ren' way,
> For parson tell us how de whole o' we are clay;
> An' lookin' close at t'ings, we hab to pray quite hard
> Fe swaller wha' him say an' don't t'ink bad o' Gahd.[142]

The evolutionist, on the other hand, asserts that we are descended from the ape, and this seems a little more plausible. In particular, he insists that God had no responsibility whatever for the creative process, and this leads to the immensely important consequence that the black's skin color is due to a fortuitous accident of birth, and not to God's having cursed Ham.[143] To what degree did McKay himself give his adherence to these theories? That question cannot easily be answered, since no document exists that could throw further light on the poem. But this much is certain, that the problem of the origin of a multiplicity of races must have beset the adolescent's mind, and that from this moment on he saw the question as revolving around God.

If, then, there ever was a McKayan paganism, it had always coexisted with a vague deism taken over from his family and his school surroundings.[144] The 1912 poems do, actually, reveal a strange religious faith, compounded of uncertainty and contradictions, and sometimes steeped in a resigned pessimism intensified by McKay's first exposure to the inferior position accorded blacks in the city.

God is everywhere present, but the contours of his personality remain vague, just as the directions taken by his sympathies remain unclarified. Though the poet never directly says so, on occasion one has the feeling that God is a personage whose bouts of ill humor blacks have reason to fear.

> De harmless tabby o' de house
> Plays kindly wid de frightened mouse,
> Till, when it nearly loses dread,
> Good Lard! de little thing is dead.
> So wid de man, *toy of a Will,*
> E'er playin' with him to its fill,
> To-day alive, to-morrow slain,
> Thus all our pleasure ends in pain.[145]

[142] "Cudjoe Fresh from de Lecture," stanza 4, *ibid.,* p. 56.

[143] Genesis 9:25.

[144] It seems fairly certain that McKay went to church in his native village, perhaps not regularly, but at least quite frequently. In "Boyhood in Jamaica," p. 134, he writes: "What used to tickle us children was the quietness of the church and the squeaking of the shoes of our elders, as they walked down the aisle to the front benches."

[145] "Consolation," stanza 5, *Constab Ballads,* pp. 24-25. See also the line in "To W. G. G.," *ibid.,* p. 77, in which the poet looks on himself as "de helpless playt'ing of a Will."

He is invisible, yet to him one prays every evening on one's knees.[146] He created the world, for blacks as well as for whites,[147] but if need be he punishes the wickedness of the blacks by cursing their country.[148] Despite this the black, in the midst of his wretchedness, puts his trust in him.[149]

This Divine Being remains far away and external to the poet, and it scarcely seems that belief in him implies any commitment. More than that, the most generous inclinations of the poet's soul — the turning away from vengeance and the sense of forgiveness, for instance — appear to him to be at odds with this belief, which he sees as antiquated and threadbare:

> Den let me not t'ink hard of those who use
> Deir power tyrannously an' abuse:
> Let me remember always while I live,
> De noblest of all deeds is to forgive.
>
> This, not revenge, is sweet: this lif's de soul
> An' meks it wort' while in a empty wul':
> Far better than an old an' outworn creed
> 'Tis each day to do one such noble deed.[150]

If this attitude is set beside that adopted with respect to the pastor in "Cudjoe Fresh from de Lecture," it seems almost justified to conclude that McKay's skepticism, which was aroused by rationalist influences, signifies an estrangement from the church rather than from God. It would seem equally likely that this estrangement was motivated by certain practices or pastoral attitudes on the part of the Anglican clergy. This interpretation could also find confirmation in the handling of the Anglican clergyman on the island in *Banana Bottom,* since Bita, the black heroine of the novel, drifts away from the Church because of the tyranny that the Anglican clergyman and his wife, whose protégée she was, tried to exert over her.

Be that as it may, the poet's critique of what we shall call the official faith soon led him to become his own spiritual advisor. This imbues him with a taste for that upward movement of the soul that a victory over his passions represents, and it accustoms him to view progress as a continual upgrading of the individual through self-transcendence, which alone makes existence worthwhile "in an empty world." These are the qualities of soul that McKay brings to the spiritual enrichment of black poetry, as his voice blends in with those of the American black poets.[151]

---

[146] "A Dream," stanza 2, *Songs of Jamaica,* p. 95.
[147] "Whe' Fe Do?" stanza 9, line 1, *ibid.,* p. 29.
[148] See note 67 above.
[149] See note 35 above.
[150] "Compensation," stanzas 3 and 4, *Songs of Jamaica,* p. 92.
[151] It is rather strange that, a few years earlier, we could observe how American

As was true for his rationalism, McKay's provisional sympathy for Communism does not become a striking feature in his poetry. We have already referred to the two lines of "Exhortation: Summer 1919" that heralded the Russian Revolution as a new dawn whose glory filled the Western skies. It is quite certain that McKay had had a fleeting belief in the possibility of a great brotherhood of all the races in a Bolshevist communion, whereupon "the artificial hate that breeds lynchings and race riots might suddenly die."[152] But this was before his trip to the USSR, "the Magic Pilgrimage,"[153] as he would meaningfully call it and which, as though by enchantment, dispelled the beautiful mirage. However, among the poems inspired by the Russian journey there is one, "Petrograd: May Day, 1923," which still voices with assurance the Communist hope. Its last stanza hails Petrograd as the New Jerusalem whose worker-soldiers have dethroned the bosses, kings, and priests, and have given as a holy day to all the pagan festival of the First of May:

> Jerusalem is fading from men's mind,
> And sacred cities holding men in thrall
> Are crumbling in the new thought of mankind —
> The pagan day, the holy day for all!
> Oh, Petrograd, oh proud triumphant city,
> The gateway to the strange, awakening East,
> Where warrior-workers wrestled without pity
> Against the power of magnate, monarch, priest —
> World Fort of Struggle, hold from day to day
> The flaming standards of the First of May![154]

It can be seen how, in the enthusiasm of the moment, the Communist

---

Negro poets, in a way rather like McKay's, had drifted away from the organized churches. To some extent, no doubt, this represented the phenomenon of de-Christianization that is not limited to blacks. Besides this, in the case of McKay (and, for instance, Dunbar also), it is undeniable that racial arguments provided additional motives for this alienation. Yet McKay never went as far as did Dunbar who, in a moment of utter despair, actually denied the existence of God. Again, while Dunbar's incredulity led to passivity and the adoption of a purely negative attitude, McKay's doubts already contained the seed of a spiritual rebirth, just as his hatred had prepared the way for a fresh upwelling of love.

[152] From a letter of McKay's to W. H. Ferris, the literary critic of the *Negro World*, as reproduced in this magazine on September 20, 1919. It is cited in *Radicalism and Sedition*, p. 164. The letter extolls the racial tolerance that, rightly or wrongly, McKay attributes to the Soviet regime, demands that Bolshevism be explained to the black masses, and — this should be borne in mind — ventures the hope that the black agricultural proletariat will seize the land on which they labor, thus despoiling the owners who have been exploiting them.

[153] *A Long Way from Home*, p. 151.

[154] "Petrograd: May Day, 1923," stanza 5, *ibid.*, p. 225.

faith actually functioned as one stage in McKay's spiritual journey. Petrograd, in this stanza, is bathed in a religious atmosphere. Yet, almost simultaneously with this obeisance to the false gods, the marble effigy of the Man of Woe at Saint Isaac's Church in Petrograd wrung from him a religious emotion of a quite different quality. A beautiful sonnet, "Russian Cathedral," preserves it for us:

> Bow down my soul in worship very low
> And in the holy silences be lost.
> Bow down before the marble man of woe,
> Bow down before the singing angel host.
>
> What jewelled glory fills my spirit's eye!
> What golden grandeur moves the depths of me!
> The soaring arches lift me up on high
> Taking my breath with their rare symmetry.
>
> Bow down my soul and let the wondrous light
> Of Beauty bathe thee from her lofty throne,
> Bow down before the wonder of man's might.
> Bow down in worship, humble and alone;
> Bow lowly down before the sacred sight
> Of man's divinity alive in stone.[155]

The above follows the typography of the 1925 text. We find it significant that, when the sonnet was reprinted in the *Selected Poems*, which the author was able to oversee before his death, the words "man" and "woe" in the third line, as well as "divinity" in the last line, were provided with initial capital letters, whereas the "Beauty" of the tenth line was demoted to lower case. It seems to us that the 1925 arrangement reveals, on the poet's part, a measure of resistance to the Divine, the determination to reduce it at any cost to the human or even to the material level, despite the holy tremor that chilled his whole being and prostrated him, as though against his will, in adoration before the majesty of the Eternal. This resistance to the Divine is all the more noteworthy, since at the same moment he was deifying beauty.

This was the period when McKay did battle with God and with America also, and perhaps in his heart of hearts these two antagonists were but one. Clearly, his attitude toward both remains fluctuating and ambivalent. The vastness and the power of each attracts him but, for this very reason, each represents the threat of tyranny and is equally formidable in his

---

[155] "Russian Cathedral," in Locke, ed., *The New Negro*, p. 135. In the *Selected Poems*, p. 84, this sonnet is entitled "St. Isaac's Church, Petrograd."

eyes.[156] Friend or foe, they are the unknown, that mysterious infinity which, once it has breached an individual, pursues him night and day and gives him no rest. The following lines from the sonnet, "I Know My Soul," in which the poet speaks of his soul, have this meaning:

> And I explored it *to determine why*
> *This awful key to my infinity*
> *Conspires to rob me of sweet joy and grace.*
> And if the sign may not be fully read,
> If I can comprehend but not control,
> *I need not gloom my days with futile dread,*[157]

and they are the words not of a pagan, but of a man who has already found God but still schemes and flees from a force which, he fears, may prove domineering and cruel — capable in a momentary mood of abandoning him to fate, as the star which had always guided the black man may betray him to his lynchers:

> All night a bright and solitary star
> (Perchance the one that ever guided him,
> Yet gave him up at last to Fate's wild whim)
> Hung pitifully o'er the swinging char.[158]

What finally overcomes the poet's apprehensions and sets him on the path that leads to surrender to God is, primarily, his longing to live his life more fully, to rise above a vegetative existence, to plumb deep into the mysteries of men and things so that he may discover, beyond their material substance, the surrounding spiritual regions which he will embrace in their totality:

> Like a strong tree that reaches down, deep, deep,
>
> . . . . .
>
> So would I live in rich imperial growth,
> Touching the surface and the depth of things,
> Instinctively responsive unto both,
> Tasting the sweets of being and the stings,
> Sensing the subtle spell of changing forms,
> Like a strong tree against a thousand storms.[159]

[156] The association of the Western world and its "alien gods" is particularly significant in the sonnet "Outcast," which presents their conjunction as the ultimate state of slavery that cannot be evaded.

[157] *Harlem Shadows*, p. 46 (italics added).

[158] Second quatrain of the sonnet, "The Lynching," *Harlem Shadows*, p. 51.

[159] Text of this sonnet, "Like a Strong Tree," in Locke, ed., *The New Negro*, p. 134. Reprinted in *Selected Poems*, p. 45, where it is incorrectly stated to have

This spiritual enrichment transforms reality, endowing it with a meaning all the more precious since only the poet, together with God, can
sense the overtones. Not only does this enable him to savor the rare delight of "the loneliness of wisdom among fools"; it also nourishes and
assures the continuation of his dialogue and intimate union with God,
who will thus become his confidant, his ally, perhaps even his accomplice
in confronting the stupid enmity of the surrounding world:

> ... each man's mind contains an unknown realm
> Walled in from other men however near,
> And unimagined in their highest flights
> Of comprehension or of vision clear;
> A realm where he withdraws to contemplate
> Infinity and his own finite state.
>
> Thence he may sometimes catch a god-like glimpse
> Of mysteries that seem beyond life's bar;
> Thence he may hurl his little shaft at heaven
> And bring down accidentally a star,
> And drink its foamy dust like sparkling wine
> And echo accents of the laugh divine.
>
> Then he may fall into a drunken sleep
> And wake up in his same house painted blue
> Or white or green or red or brown or black —
> His house, his own, whatever be the hue.
> But things for him will not be what they seem
> To average men since he has dreamt his dream![160]

Thus the spiritualization of reality nullifies the distinctions between houses,
that is to say, between races of different color. This is not the least victory that would have remained beyond his reach, but for his faith in God.

It would be legitimate to inquire to what degree the dream referred to
in the last line of "My House" might justify our treating McKay's reli-
giousness as an escape from reality, the artificial sublimation of his racial
experiences, or the attempt to apply a balm to his battered soul. But, if
that were so, his turning to God would be abdication in the face of conflict, downright desertion at the height of the battle. However, it is manifest that McKay never asked God to replace him in the battles that were
McKay's own responsibility. On the contrary; "To the White Fiends"
allows us to estimate the self-mastery, the whole self-imposed moderate-
ness, that the resolve to act in conformity with the divine plan demands of

been previously unpublished. The same mistake is made in connection with "Enslaved" (*ibid.*, p. 42), which had already appeared in *Harlem Shadows*, p. 32.
    [160] "My House," stanzas 3-6, *Opportunity*, November, 1926, p. 342.

the poet.[161] His fundamental expectation in turning to God, and the object of the prayers he addresses to Him, is the light of truth:

> 'Mid the discordant noises of the day I hear thee calling;
> I stumble as I fare along earth's way; keep me from falling.
>
> Mine eyes are open but they cannot see for gloom of night;
> I can no more than lift my heart to thee for inward light.
>
> The wild and fiery passion of my youth consumes my soul;
> In agony I turn to thee for truth and self-control.
>
> For Passion and all the pleasures it can give will die the death;
> But this of me eternally must live, thy borrowed breath.[162]

That this is the ultimate objective of his spiritual quest is confirmed by the sonnet "Truth," written shortly before he died:

> Lord, shall I find it in Thy Holy Church,
> Or must I give it up as something dead,
> Forever lost, no matter where I search,
> Like dinosaurs within their ancient bed?
> I found it not in years of Unbelief,
> In science stirring life like budding trees,
> In Revolution like a dazzling thief —
> Oh, shall I find it on my bended knees?
> But what is Truth? So Pilate asked Thee, Lord,
> So long ago when Thou wert manifest,
> As the Eternal and Incarnate Word,
> Chosen of God and by Him singly blest;
> In this vast world of lies and hate and greed,
> Upon my knees, Oh Lord, for Truth I plead.[163]

His prayer will be granted, and divine illumination will bring him to recognize at last that the "essential evil" he had spent his life hunting down and fighting is not outside, but within him. To track down injustice and oppression by hating America is to fight against shadows. The basic evil is hate itself, and that is what he must hate. It is hate that wrecks unity, setting men one against the other, and the individual against himself. But it is the farthest point to which the pagan doctrines can lead one. God alone can lead a man further on and conquer hate itself:

> Around me roar and crash the pagan isms
> To which most of my life was consecrate,
> Betrayed by evil men and torn by schisms

[161] See note 111 above.
[162] "A Prayer," *Harlem Shadows*, p. 58.
[163] "Truth," *Selected Poems*, p. 46.

> For they were built on nothing more than hate!
> I cannot live my life without the faith
> Where new sensations like a fawn will leap,
> But old enthusiasms like a wraith
> Haunt me awake and haunt me when I sleep.
> And so to God I go to make my peace.[164]

As he wrote these last lines, the poet was almost on the verge of death. Thus his personal conclusions take on the value of a message not for his own race alone but for all men, when he calls out:

> Oh, Segregation is not the whole sin,
> The Negroes need salvation from within.[165]

These conclusions come as no surprise from a man who had already written, more than ten years before his death: "The whites have done the blacks some great wrongs, but also they have done some good. They have brought to them the benefits of modern civilization. They can still do a lot more, but one thing they cannot do: they cannot give Negroes the gift of a soul — a group soul."[166] Having at last found serenity in God, as he passed away Claude McKay could take for his own the words that Milton penned, after another mighty warrior had breathed his last:

> His servants He, with new acquist
> Of true experience from this great event,
> With peace and consolation hath dismissed
> And calm of mind, all passion spent.[167]

[164] "The Pagan Isms," lines 1-9, *ibid.*, p. 49.
[165] "The Negro's Friend," lines 13-14, *ibid.*, p. 51.
[166] *A Long Way from Home*, p. 349.
[167] John Milton, *Samson Agonistes*, lines 1755 to end.

Chapter Seven: JEAN TOOMER

It is no easy matter to determine the specific share of the poet in the work of Jean Toomer, for the whole process of his thinking, and his art as a narrator, obey the behests of his poetry. His poetic inspiration spreads far beyond his verse writings,[1] and Jean Toomer could neither think, nor tell a tale, nor describe except as a poet. So any attempt to cling to the traditional distinctions between the literary genres would be vain in the case of a writer who, like many other creative artists of his generation, subjects form to ceaseless experimentation in his endeavors to forge a truly fitting instrument of expression for himself.

There is nothing in the least arbitrary in this search for a personal literary form, and if the barriers partitioning off the expression of self tend to be lowered or even discarded, the primary reason is that Toomer regarded all such boundaries as outdated: the new generation required a new form. But beyond this — and herein resides its profound significance — form does nothing but reflect the ultimate concern, which is to break through the internal partitionings that obstruct the unification of the personality. The search for form, then, is simply another aspect of the search for self. "I am," he said, "what I am and what I may become I am trying to find out."[2]

[1] These amount to less than one thousand lines.
[2] Cited by Gorham B. Munson, "The Significance of Jean Toomer," *Opportunity*, September, 1925, p. 263, col. B. This article is reprinted, with two paragraphs added, in the author's *Destinations: A Canvass of American Literature since 1900*.

1. THE DESTINY OF JEAN TOOMER

Who was this man, actually? Was he a Negro or a white? He entered the world in Washington, D.C., on December 26, 1894, having inherited from his parents a complexion so light that he could "pass."[3] His marriage, which took place on October 30, 1931, united him with a white woman, the novelist Margery Latimer.[4] The following year she died in childbed, and in September, 1934, Toomer married another white woman, Marjorie Content, who was the daughter of a prominent Wall Street broker.[5] When asked about his race at the time his second marriage took place, according to one report he answered: "I really do not know whether I have Negro blood in me or not."[6]

Yet the facts are entirely clear. Toomer was the son of a Georgian farmer, Nathan Toomer, and a descendant, through his mother Nina E. Pinchback, of a lieutenant governor of Louisiana during the period of Reconstruction. This was Pickney Benton Stewart Pinchback, who, if we are to believe Toomer, at that time claimed to have black blood in his veins for the sole purpose of winning the support of black voters.[7] But it is incontrovertible that during the Civil War P. B. S. Pinchback donned a Northern uniform and fought as captain in one of the regiments making up the "Corps d'Afrique" under the command of General Butler.[8] And,

[3] There are few reliable sources for Toomer's biography. In addition to those cited in the notes that follow, see also "Toomer," *Who's Who in America* XVII (1932-33).

[4] Margery Latimer (1899-1932), born in Portage, Wisconsin, studied at Wooster College, the University of Wisconsin, and Columbia. She published short stories, articles, and reviews in various literary periodicals including *The Reviewer, Echo, The Century, The New Masses, Transition,* and *Bookman;* two collections of short stories, *Nellie Bloom and Other Stories, Guardian Angel and Other Stories;* two novels, *We Are Incredible* and *This Is My Body.* See Alfred Kreymborg et al., eds., *The Second American Caravan* (1928), p. 869; also *The New Caravan* (1936), pp. 659-60.

[5] Marjorie Content had been previously married to Leon Fleischmann, described by the papers of the day as a former counsellor in the French Ministry of Foreign Affairs (*Afro-American,* November 17, 1934). Toomer's second marriage took place at Taos, New Mexico, where he had been the guest of Mabel Dodge Luhan.

[6] *Kansas City American,* November 22, 1934.

[7] *New York Herald Tribune,* November 10, 1934. See also the reference given in note 5 above, and the *Afro-American,* early December, 1934 (the exact date is not included on the clipping we have seen in the Toomer file in the Moorland Collection, Howard University).

[8] John Hope Franklin, *From Slavery to Freedom,* p. 287. All the officers of this "Corps d'Afrique" (in French in the original) were Negroes. P. B. S. Pinchback was acting governor for six months during the winter of 1873 (*ibid.,* p. 314).

into the bargain, he protested against the discrimination to which he was subjected within his regiment on account of his race.[9]

Moreover, Toomer went for his schooling to Negro schools in Washington, Dunbar High School among them. He began his college work in 1914 at the University of Wisconsin, transferring to the College of the City of New York for the 1917-18 academic year. This was followed by four years given over entirely to writing; the earliest specimens of his work were accepted by *The Double Dealer* of New Orleans.[10]

Soon a number of his sketches, poems, short stories, and pieces of criticism began to appear in such periodicals as *Broom, The Crisis, The Liberator, The Little Review, The Modern Review, Nomad, Prairie, S 4 N,* and later in *Pagany, Bifur* (Paris), and *Adelphi* (London). Through these publications he came into contact with a literary and artistic group embracing personalities of the stature of Waldo Frank, Kenneth Burke, Alfred Stieglitz, Paul Rosenfeld, Gorham P. Munson, and Hart Crane, among others.[11]

In 1921 he went away to teach grade school in Sparta, in Hancock County, Georgia, but he left after four months.[12] This short stay in Georgia had been a veritable pilgrimage to the origins, as became undeniably clear in 1923 with the publication of Toomer's first volume, *Cane,* where the experience is quintessentially contained. The audacity of the technique — "fully two decades in advance of the period"[13] — and, even more decisively, the formal beauty of this work make it one of the most remarkable in all postwar American literature. Yet *Cane* went almost unnoticed, with Negro publications almost alone in calling attention to its merits. Though the book had been brought out by a well-known New York publisher, sales barely totaled five hundred.[14] This undeserved setback is, no doubt, partly responsible for Toomer's subsequent relative silence. Apart from a collection of "definitions and aphorisms" that came out in 1931

[9] For this piece of information we are indebted to Arna Bontemps, who researched the matter in the *New Orleans Picayune* of the period.

[10] See the biographical sketch he prepared for the Cullen anthology, *Caroling Dusk,* pp. 93-94.

[11] *Ibid.* See, for the group associated with the avant-garde periodicals *Broom* and *Secession,* Malcolm Cowley, *Exile's Return,* pp. 179-81 and *passim.* Several members of the group, especially Crane, Frank, Munson, Burke, and Toomer himself, for some time took an interest in the mystical thought of the Russian P. D. Ouspensky (1878-1947), who for a while was himself associated with Gurdjieff, and who brought out his *Tertium Organum* in 1922.

[12] Alain Locke, ed., *The New Negro,* p. 415; also Eugene Holmes, "Jean Toomer, Apostle of Beauty," *Opportunity,* August, 1932, p. 252, col. A.

[13] Robert A. Bone, *The Negro Novel in America,* p. 81.

[14] *Ibid.,* p. 88.

as *Essentials, Cane* was the last volume entirely from his hand ever published.

He continued, nevertheless, to trace that person he did not know: himself. In this enterprise, he was to receive providential aid from another. For it so happened that on January 4, 1924, George Ivanovich Gurdjieff embarked with forty of his pupils in order to give two series of performances of his "movements," one in New York's Neighborhood Playhouse and the other at Carnegie Hall.[15] Gurdjieff was a Russian who, after spending several years in Central Asia in order to acquaint himself with Oriental thought and disciplines, had founded his Institute for the Harmonious Development of Man in 1922, at the Prieuré d'Avon, near Fontainebleau. His doctrine, Unitism, with a wide base of inspiration in yoga, envisaged the reconstruction of man by teaching him to unify, transcend, and dominate himself.[16] Was this not precisely Toomer's own preoccupation?

Freud had already caught on in Greenwich Village, and soon Gurdjieff did also. After feeling maladjusted and suffering from repressions, now people went about unifying themselves. Besides, almost at the moment the master reached New York, his chief disciple also arrived. This was A. E. Orage, editor of the *New English Weekly;* his preaching made many converts in the Village. Also in New York was Margaret Anderson, who had already published Toomer, and who had followed Gurdjieff across the ocean, transferring to Paris the publishing of *The Little Review,* founded in Chicago ten years before.[17]

Who was the intermediary responsible for Toomer's being touched by Unitist grace? Perhaps the credit should go to Orage, for it appears that he bore Toomer off to Chicago to establish a branch of the Gurdjieff Institute.[18] But it was to the Prieuré d'Avon that Toomer went, during the summer of 1924,[19] to receive his initiation into Unitism.

[15] G. Gurdjieff, *Rencontres avec des hommes remarquables* (Paris, 1960), p. 16.
[16] On Gurdjieff and his teachings one may consult, among other works, Louis Pauwels, *Monsieur Gurdjieff* (Paris, 1954).
[17] On Margaret Anderson and Gurdjieff, *ibid.,* pp. 208-16; also Cowley, *Exile's Return,* pp. 60-61.
[18] Holmes, "Jean Toomer," p. 254, col. A.
[19] Bone, *The Negro Novel,* p. 81, proposes 1926 as the date of Toomer's stay in Fontainebleau. Yet this is clearly wrong, for Munson already refers to this stay in his article on Toomer published by *Opportunity* in the issue for September, 1925 (see our note 2 above). If one takes into account the lapse of time between the writing and the publication of an article, the summer of 1925 can scarcely be meant. We adopt 1924 as the most likely date. Gurdjieff had come to New York in February of that year, and Orage had followed him "in the spring" (Cowley, *Exile's Return,* p. 61, note). In that event, Toomer must have made up his mind rather rapidly.

Upon his return to the United States he proceeded, with the zeal be-
fitting a neophyte, to preach Gurdjieff in Harlem.[20] Among the most distinguished of his Negro disciples were Dorothy Peterson, the painter Aaron
Douglas, and the novelists Wallace Thurman and Nella Larsen. But the
laboring masses did not have the necessary time for these Unitist retreats.
So Toomer went downtown to convey the good word to white people and
departed, one day, to convert Chicago. "And the Negroes," declared Langston Hughes, "lost one of the most talented of all their writers."[21]
For the black community, with which Toomer had implicitly identified
himself until then, this departure from Harlem did indeed amount to a
denial of his race and a passing over to the whites. Added to his two marriages with white women, an incident that occurred in 1931 seemed to
confirm this notion of a repudiation. When James Weldon Johnson was
preparing the new edition of his anthology, *The Book of American Negro
Poetry,* he asked Toomer for authorization to include in it a number of
poems, but Toomer refused.[22] Langston Hughes perhaps judges this refusal
rather too severely, since something other than a repudiation of blackness
might serve to explain it — for instance, personal ill-feeling between
Toomer and Johnson.[23] In any event we are obliged to record that, ten
years later, Toomer allowed his work to appear in *The Negro Caravan,*
the anthology compiled by Sterling Brown, Arthur P. Davis, and Ulysses
Lee. And once again, with the permission of his publisher if not with his
own direct acquiescence, he is represented in the anthology that Langston
Hughes himself, together with Arna Bontemps, brought out in 1949 under
the title *The Poetry of the Negro.*[24]
To accuse Toomer of having denied his race would, consequently, be a
rash judgment. It would be more accurate to say that his aspirations to a
lofty spirituality, to which the masses are not necessarily sensitive, led him
to transcend the very notion of race. Some time after he had retired to
live in a Quaker community in Pennsylvania,[25] Toomer made this affirma-
tion: "A true individual belongs, on the one hand, to no less than himself;

[20] See Langston Hughes, *The Big Sea,* pp. 241-43 ("Gurdjieff in Harlem").
[21] *Ibid.,* p. 242.
[22] *Ibid.* Hughes is simply passing on a fact that was widely known. It should
also be borne in mind that Toomer could not have been represented in the first
edition (1922) of Johnson's anthology, which predated *Cane* by a year.
[23] This is the view of the matter held by Sterling Brown, as he was good enough
to inform us.
[24] Long after the rebuff administered to James Weldon Johnson, Toomer published in *The Crisis* (see his poem, "As the Eagle Soars," in the April, 1932 edition, p. 116). Would he have done this if he had been intent on "passing"?
[25] An echo of Toomer's Quaker experience will be found in his *The Flavor of
Man,* William Penn Lecture, 1949.

and, on the other, to no less than mankind and the entire human world."[26] "I am of no particular race. I am of the human race, a man at large in this human world, preparing a new race. I am of no specific region, I am of earth."[27]

Walt Whitman himself would have subscribed to this declaration of identity,[28] which bears witness to the transcendence and sublimation of race, not to its repudiation. We will see the new race emerge in that great poetic upsurge, "Blue Meridian," which still, more than a quarter-century after publication, unfortunately remains almost unknown. In this long poem,[29] Toomer reaches the last stage of a spiritual experiment whose point of departure was *Cane,* and which aims at the reconstruction of man. Like Claude McKay and Countee Cullen, and perhaps earlier than they, Jean Toomer recognized that, when all things are considered, the racial problem is but one aspect of an immensely larger problem. On the one hand, man is eternally divided against himself: "Whatever stands between you and that person stands between you and yourself."[30] Yet in the postwar world of the "Lost Generation" this problem acquires a special resonance for a thinking being who looks for renewal, is torn between today and tomorrow, and beyond that is condemned, as was Toomer, to the torture of living within two races at the same time, or of opting for one and so betraying the other.

Toomer rejected neither horn of the dilemma; it was the choice itself that he rejected. From the outset he placed himself above the mediocre plane on which this choice would have to be made. Not that in these higher regions the problems simply disappear — they change their nature. The antinomy loses none of its fearsome dimensions, and he who would overcome it must enter the "strait gate" of self-transcendence, for this alone leads to synthesis and peace in an inner harmony.

2. The Poetry of *Cane,* or, the Pilgrimage to the Origins

It would be easy enough to paint the portrait of Jean Toomer as a child of the "Lost Generation." But in so doing one must take care not to overdraw certain features. "The postwar writers, in their feeling that their experiences were unique, revealed their ignorance of the American

---

[26] *Essentials,* 22.
[27] *Ibid.,* 24.
[28] See, for example, Whitman's "Salut au Monde," in particular stanza 9.
[29] In Kreymborg et al., eds., *The New Caravan,* pp. 633-53. There are 741 lines in the poem.
[30] *Essentials,* 29.

past."[31] While Toomer to some extent shared their sense of unease, he in no way shared their misappreciation of the past.[32] On the contrary, his ceaseless introspection and his clairvoyance in recognizing the sources of his anxiety helped him to reach an awareness, not only of his own uprootedness, but also of the values embodied in the past, and more particularly in the earth that is inseparable from it. Admittedly the time had arrived to shake off all subjection to the past, to put off the old man and enter fully into the light of a new age. But would it not be an adventurer's blind folly to commit oneself to the future without finding out, first of all, from where one came? Very early Toomer came to see such a pilgrimage to the origins as a necessity, and from it he brought back the magnificent sheaf of *Cane*. Contact with the land of his fathers, of which he knew only what family gossip had related, revealed him to himself: "Georgia opened me. And it may well be said that I received my initial impulse to an individual art from my experience there. For no other section of the country has so stirred me. There one finds soil, soil in the sense the Russians know it, — the soil every art and literature that is to live must be imbedded in."[33]

Cane is an impressionist symphony[34] in which Toomer brings together into a vast choir all Georgia's earth and people. His purpose is not to describe them to us, but to allow himself to be fused with the soul of the South which they epitomize and breathe out, and to relive an obliterated past through the echoes they awaken within his own consciousness. For Waldo Frank, *Cane* is the South.[35] Yet there looms all the more mightily within it Jean Toomer himself, soliciting us to participate in his new creation of these impressions.

In its external form, the book is almost entirely in prose;[36] this may be

[31] Cowley, *Exile's Return*, p. 8.
[32] In that, he simply takes his place behind Walt Whitman in the preface (1855) to the first edition of *Leaves of Grass*, par. 1 and *passim*. This influence becomes especially apparent with the publication of *Essentials* in 1931.
[33] Cited by Locke, ed., *The New Negro*, p. 51.
[34] "It is interesting to know that Toomer, before he began to write, thought of becoming a composer." The assertion is made by Munson, "The Significance," p. 262, col. A. One should also stress the influence that may have been exerted on Toomer by his friend Alfred Stieglitz (1864-1946), not only as an experimentalist with color photography even before the turn of the century, but above all as owner of a New York art gallery. As early as 1908, Stieglitz introduced contemporary French painters to the United States.
[35] Preface to *Cane*, p. vii.
[36] There can be no question of submitting Toomer's work in prose to a close examination here, since that falls outside the limits of our study. In any event, the task has already been undertaken, if not with entire success. See Hugh Morris Gloster, *Negro Voices in American Fiction*, pp. 128-30; Bone, *The Negro Novel in America*, pp. 80-89; and the articles mentioned elsewhere. But the weakness found

the principal reason why some have decided to regard it as a novel.[37] But there is nothing of the novel in *Cane,* and while one may agree that here and there the influence of Sherwood Anderson[38] or of Joyce's *Portrait of the Artist* becomes manifest (perhaps especially the latter),[39] the manner nevertheless remains Toomer's own. The only literary genre to which one can assign the work is poetry, for ultimately the entirely personal meaning of Toomer's pilgrimage, and the poetic symbolism which gives it expression, are the elements that maintain the unity of this interlocking succession of poems, tales, sketches, and impressions that lead on to the book's final drama. But where does narrative end and poetry begin? How allot their proper shares to fiction and to autobiography? Where draw the boundary between novel and lyricism? All these questions beset the reader at every page of this astonishing book, many of whose threads have yet to be disentangled. Poetry always gains the upper hand.[40]

---

in all these studies is, on the one hand, their inadequate length and, above all, their inability or refusal to take into account the autobiographical elements in *Cane.* Yet nothing could be more obvious, especially in "Kabnis," the drama that makes up the third part of the work, and it is at bottom these elements that give unity to *Cane.* In "Kabnis," it is quite clear that Toomer depicted himself in the guise of Kabnis and Lewis, those two literally complementary characters, and that in so doing he symbolized his own inner cleavage. Paul Rosenfeld (*Men Seen,* p. 229) was only dimly aware that these elements were present, describing them merely as "semi-autobiographical" in the "earlier scenes" of "Kabnis." But Montgomery Gregory ("Cane," *The Crisis,* December, 1923, pp. 374-75) had a much more accurate insight into the meaning of "Kabnis" when he wrote: "Evidently the author's implication is that there must be a welding into one personality of Kabnis and Lewis." Though right on target, he failed to develop his idea, and in particular did not take the decisive step of proclaiming in no uncertain terms that we have to do here with Toomer himself. Thus an interesting detailed study has yet to be written, dealing with *Cane* as a "portrait of the artist as a young man."

[37] *Cane* was already classified as a novel in the brief biographical note on Toomer published in Locke, ed., *The New Negro,* p. 415. The same label is applied by Margaret J. Butcher, *The Negro in American Culture* (Mentor ed.), p. 147, unaccompanied by any justification. As for Bone (*The Negro Novel*), his decision to deal with *Cane* in the context of his book was purely arbitrary, and an avowal of his admiration for *Cane.* "Toomer was bootlegged into the book" — this was his reply, when we wrote to ask how he could defend the presence of Toomer in his dissertation. Thus, while the word "novel" has been used in connection with *Cane,* this has always been rather casually done, because no more precise categorization could readily be hit upon.

[38] The influence of Sherwood Anderson, already noted by Munson in his article in *Opportunity,* is more apparent, it seems to us, in the portraits of black women that form the first part of *Cane,* and in which the sensual note predominates. This is, too, the less personal part of *Cane.*

[39] See the concluding remark in note 36 above.

[40] See, for example, the description of the cabin where Kabnis is living, *Cane,* p. 157. To be noted in this passage is the symbolic value of the colors. In Toomer's eyes, the poetry of the South is the result of a natural harmony between blacks and the elements of nature. Thus the cracks between the planks, which are the

Cane can no more be summarized than can a painting by Pissarro or a composition by Debussy. Here the symbol reigns supreme, as if it alone could penetrate to the intangible depths of reality. Our task, then, must be to clarify the significance of *Cane* and to name the values it affirms. To this Toomer could doubtless have acquiesced, for he had written: "The true critic is a critic of meanings and of values."[41]

Cane is among the most significant first fruits of the Negro Renaissance, inasmuch as it was a return to the origins beyond the shame of slavery. One should not be afraid to state unequivocally that Toomer's Georgian sojourn, whose quintessence makes up the book, was at bottom the experience of purgation from the shame of slavery, an experience that he regarded as the unavoidable prerequisite for any liberation. "Essence-shame is man's lever on himself. Shame of a weakness implies the presence of a strength. He who feels ashamed of slavery can win freedom."[42]

The whitest of the Negro poets, Toomer saw himself as the living symbol of slavery's fundamental contradiction. He senses how master and slave confront each other in his bastard soul, and the poet in him projects this antinomy upon the Georgian landscape, which is all at once earth and sky, dusk and dawn, hideousness and beauty.[43] Finding his way back to the land of sugarcane and cotton, Toomer returns also to the origins of slavery, whose soul he sees rising to the sky like the smoke of the burning pine shavings in the evening air. It is slavery alone that has made of him a son of this earth, to which he addresses his "Song of the Son":

> Pour O pour that parting soul in song,
> O pour it in the sawdust glow of night,
> Into the velvet pine-smoke air to-night.
> And let the valley carry it along,
> And let the valley carry it along.

lips of the poet-winds, are black. Nevertheless Kabnis (which is to say Toomer himself, or one half of him) had not come seeking the beauty of the South. He must even ward it off by allying himself with the opposing elements that are symbolized by the opposite colors, the whiteness of the bed and that of the light, concerning which Toomer truthfully says that they do not afford enough protection. All that Kabnis wants to see in the South is the symbolic hideousness of slavery, as, for example, *Cane,* p. 161, last paragraph.

[41] *Essentials,* 62.

[42] *Ibid.,* 2.

[43] See (*Cane,* p. 218) Lewis's reproach to Kabnis (one half of Toomer reproaching the other half!): "Cant hold them, can you? Master; slave. Soil; and the overarching heavens. Dusk; dawn. They fight and bastardize you. The sun tint of your cheeks, flame of the great season's multicolored leaves, tarnished, burned. Split, shredded: easily burned."

O land and soil, red soil and sweet-gum tree,
So scant of grass, so profligate of pines,
Now just before an epoch's sun declines
Thy son, in time, I have returned to thee,
Thy son, I have in time returned to thee.

In time, for though the sun is setting on
A song-lit race of slaves, it has not set;
Though late, O soil, it is not too late yet
To catch thy plaintive soul, leaving, soon gone.

O Negro slaves, dark purple ripened plums,
Squeezed, and bursting in the pine-wood air,
Passing, before they stripped the old tree bare
One plum was saved for me, one seed becomes

An everlasting song, a singing tree,
Caroling softly souls of slavery,
What they were, and what they are to me,
Caroling softly souls of slavery.[44]

Into these "souls of slavery" — they included the poet's soul — the South
had impressed its own divisions, its sweetness along with its inhuman
cruelty. Toomer rediscovers this dualism as he looks at the body of a
woman, and in "Portrait in Georgia" he composes her hallucinatory portrait out of the elements of a lynching.[45]

Black women emerged from slavery physically diminished by their sufferings and humiliations. It is scarcely possible still to read in their faces
any trace of the African nobility of which they have been despoiled, and
which is symbolized by the primitive canoe whose silhouette the poet
imagines seeing between the wrinkles engraved in the forehead of the old
grey-haired woman in "Face":

Hair —
silver-gray,
like streams of stars,
Brows
recurved canoes
quivered by the ripples blown by pain,
Her eyes —
mist of tears
condensing on the flesh below
And her channeled muscles

[44] "Song of the Son," *ibid.*, p. 21.
[45] "Portrait in Georgia," *ibid.*, p. 50.

are cluster grapes of sorrow
purple in the evening sun
nearly ripe for worms.[46]

Slavery broke not only the Africans' bodies, but also their souls. It forced upon them a white god (the lower case has a meaning here!) and ceremonies without substance for them. Stealing their souls, it put in their place hollow phrases: that was their "Conversion."[47]

"Georgia Dusk" appears aimed at imbuing us with the feeling that, in the spiritual desert to which slavery has reduced the South, only the voice of African atavism remains to protect the rights of poetry and of the spirit. It alone still vibrates in harmony with nature, and thus it is recognized at least as a provisional value. As this voice rises in the evening air, the voices of the great pine trees and the choir of the cane fields respond. Together they send up to the stars an evening prayer which purifies the fallen bodies and gives them back a soul:

The sky, lazily disdaining to pursue
    The setting sun, too indolent to hold
    A lengthened tournament for flashing gold,
Passively darkens for night's barbecue,

A feast of moon and men and barking hounds,
    An orgy for some genius of the South,
    With blood-hot eyes and cane-lipped scented mouth,
Surprised in making folk-songs from soul sounds.

.   .   .

Smoke from the pyramidal sawdust pile
    Curls up, blue ghosts of trees, tarrying low
    Where only chips and stumps are left to show
The solid proof of former domicile.

Meanwhile, the men, with vestiges of pomp,
    Race memories of king and caravan,
    High-priests, an ostrich, and a juju-man,
Go singing through the footpaths of the swamp.

Their voices rise . . . the pine trees are guitars,
    Strumming, pine-needles fall like sheets of rain . . .
    Their voices rise . . . the chorus of the cane
Is caroling a vesper to the stars . . .

O singers, resinous and soft your songs
    Above the sacred whisper of the pines,

46 "Face," *ibid.*, p. 14.
47 "Conversion," *ibid.*, p. 49.

> Give virgin lips to cornfield concubines,
> Bring dreams of Christ to dusky cane-lipped throngs.[48]

At this point, however, Toomer diverges from the general tendencies of the Negro Renaissance. Just as he had no intention of castigating the South in *Cane*, he also had no intention of composing an apologia for his race and its African atavism. He had returned to the origins in order to rise above race, not to reestablish a bond with it. Thus, in the black hive, he feels like a drone which finds nourishment in the substance of the community, the better to take flight toward its own destiny ("Beehive").[49]

"Harvest Song,"[50] despite a certain obscurity, might well be seen as establishing the balance of profit and loss in Toomer's Georgian pilgrimage. Standing on the soil of his ancestors, the poet depicts himself as a harvester on the night harvesting is over. The whole harvest is right at hand, yet he is hungry, and the grain he crushes between his teeth is tasteless:

> I am a reaper . . . All my oats are cradled. But I am too
>   fatigued to bind them. And I hunger. I crack a grain.
>   It has no taste to it. My throat is dry . . .[51]

He would like to enter into communion with the other harvesters, his brothers, but something cuts him off from them, and he is afraid to hail them:

> My eyes are caked with dust of oatfields at harvest-time.
> I am a blind man who stares across the hills, seeking
>   stack'd fields of other harvesters.
>
> It would be good to see them . . . crook'd, split, and
>   iron-ring'd handles of the scythes. It would be good
>   to see them, dust-caked and blind. I hunger.[52]
>
> I fear to call . . .[53]
>
> My ears are caked with dust of oatfields at harvest-time.
> I am a deaf man who strains to hear the calls of other
>   harvesters whose throats are also dry.
>
> It would be good to hear their songs . . . reapers of
>   the sweet-stalk'd cane, cutters of the corn . . .

[48] "Georgia Dusk," *ibid.*, p. 22.
[49] "Beehive," *ibid.*, p. 89.
[50] "Harvest Song," *ibid.*, pp. 132-33.
[51] *Ibid.*, stanza 10.
[52] *Ibid.*, stanzas 3 and 4.
[53] *Ibid.*, stanza 6, line 1.

> even though their throats cracked and the strangeness
> of their voices deafened me.[54]

Hunger, blindness, and deafness are symbols of deficiency and frustration, while the harvest image, on the contrary, expresses riches, expansiveness, and contentment. The coexistence of these two series of antithetical images in the poem is significant, reflecting the inner division of a poet who is himself "a cracked grain like the oats."[55] It is this inner split that most obviously relates him to his racial brothers, the other harvesters, for are they not also "split" like the handles of their scythes? And must not this cleavage in their personalities be laid at the door of slavery since, again like the handles of their scythes, they are "iron-ring'd" as formerly the slaves' ankles had been?[56]

Thus it cannot be said that Toomer lacked identification with his people, since his own voluntary return to the people enabled him to discover that the elements at war within his own consciousness were also those dividing his people within theirs. But one cannot say that he made himself entirely one with the destiny of his people, for they had no choice but to assume the burden of slavery along with the burden of daily life, while Toomer had striven for an awareness of his inner division, not in order to accept it, but to transcend it.

Yet the conscious or subconscious content of these antithetical elements did not fully reveal itself to him; this may explain why he instinctively turned to the symbol as a means of reaching a synthesis. "Habentibus symbolum facilis est transitus."[57] Recent psychological studies have sought to show the value of the symbol as mediation:

> In this mediative property of the symbol, which allows it to function somewhat like a bridge, one may actually recognize one of the most ingenious and important provisions in the organization of the psyche. Indeed, given the dissociability characteristic of the psyche's nature, and given the presence of permanent threats to the structure of its unity, this mediative property of the symbol constitutes the only counterweight, the only real and natural balancing factor capable of ensuring health. . . .
>
> Inasmuch as it transcends the opposing elements and binds them into a

[54] *Ibid.*, stanzas 7 and 8.
[55] *Ibid.*, stanza 5, line 2.
[56] *Ibid.*, stanza 4.
[57] "For those who have a symbol the transition is easy." C. G. Jung was very much attached to this phrase, which he came upon in an old alchemical treatise. (Cited by Jolande Jacobi, "Archétype et symbole chez Jung," in *Polarité du Symbole*, Etudes Carmélitaines [n.p., 1960], p. 182.)

unified whole ... the symbol maintains the life of the psyche in a sort of permanent flux and channels it on to the outcome assigned by destiny.[58]

At all events, it is by means of the symbol that Toomer will seek to make himself whole, in that second stage of his poetic thought that is represented by "Blue Meridian."

3. BEYOND RACE: "BLUE MERIDIAN"

"Blue Meridian" is beyond a doubt the concluding step in a long process of meditation, for its central idea is already contained in embryo in an essay published seven years earlier and entitled "Race Problems and Modern Society."[59]

In this essay, Toomer begins by noting "the changes of forms and of modes"[60] that had occurred at a constantly accelerated pace during his own lifetime: "The principles of cohesion and crystallization are being rapidly withdrawn from the materials of old forms, with a consequent break up of these forms, a setting free of these materials, with the possibility that the principles of cohesion and crystallization will recombine the stuff of life and make new forms."[61] These cataclysms affect not only the material features of man's life but also the actual forms of relationships between men.[62]

Alongside this development there is, contrariwise, a strengthening of some other forms of modern society which, remaining exempt from the dissolution noted above, even tend to expand and establish themselves more firmly. In particular these are, according to Toomer, the Western world's economic, political, legal, and military concepts, which dig themselves in and work against the evolutionary forces.[63]

He proceeds by placing, within the context of these related yet hostile movements, the racial problems,[64] especially those of the United States, which cannot be considered apart from the other principal forms of the social order. Here the effect of the evolutionary factors is to bring about an ever closer resemblance between such Negro social types as the business-

---

[58] *Ibid.*, p. 185.

[59] In Baker Brownell, ed., *Problems of Civilization* (Princeton, N.J., 1929), pp. 67-114. On the other hand, there is no doubt that "Blue Meridian" continues the line of meditation to be found in *Essentials*, some lines of which reappear in the poem. We indicate them below as they occur.

[60] "Race Problems and Modern Society," in Brownell, ed., *Problems of Civilization*, p. 67.

[61] *Ibid.*, p. 68.

[62] *Ibid.*, p. 69.

[63] *Ibid.*, pp. 70-75.

[64] *Ibid.*, pp. 79ff.

man, politician, educator, student, writer, etc., and the corresponding white types. Yet, on the other hand, whites and blacks shut themselves up ever more tightly in their separatism with the consequence, for example, that interracial marriage becomes no less heinous in the eyes of blacks than of whites.[65]

Given this crystallization of the race question, Toomer is led to advocate, as a way out of the impasse, "a selective fusion of the racial and cultural factors of America, in order that the best possible stock and culture may be produced."[66]

Though the line of argument in this essay is buttressed by scientific considerations, Toomer's thinking is essentially that of a poet and humanist. We are, in any case, under no obligation to pass judgment on the feasibility of the plan, which concerns us only insofar as it may serve to throw light on the genesis of "Blue Meridian."

Race, in this poem, acquires a totally different dimension from what we encountered in *Cane*. As in the essay discussed above, it takes its place in the much vaster setting of the "Myth of America,"[67] to adopt Hart Crane's expression. For is not America indeed, as Walt Whitman declared it, "the race of races"[68] and also "the greatest poem"?[69] "Blue Meridian" quite certainly owes something to *The Bridge*,[70] but both alike are indebted to

[65] *Ibid.,* p. 99.

[66] *Ibid.,* p. 108.

[67] "What I am really handling, you see, is the Myth of America" (letter, dated September 12, 1927, to his patron Otto H. Kahn).

[68] Preface, 1855, to the first edition of *Leaves of Grass,* par. 5.

[69] *Ibid.,* par. 2.

[70] It would take too long, and would be irrelevant, here to make an exhaustive study of the relations between Jean Toomer and Hart Crane who, soon after the end of World War I, were both collaborators in the New Orleans *Double Dealer.* They also had a common interest in Ouspensky (see note 11 above). It may be that Crane was influenced by Toomer, rather than vice versa. For it would be necessary to examine whether the "black man in a cellar" in Crane's "Black Tambourine" (*White Buildings,* 1926) was not derived from the Father John of "Kabnis" (*Cane,* 1923). But, limiting ourselves to "Blue Meridian" and *The Bridge,* we note, among others, the following related elements: a certain formal resemblance in symbols and images (Crane's celebrated "curve," which appears to be akin to Toomer's "meridian"); such substantives as "disk," "discus," and adjectives like "radiant" (see the first draft of "Atlantis," which Crane sent to Wilbur Underwood in February, 1923, and which may be read in Frederic J. Hoffman, *The Twenties,* p. 227, n. 82); the symbolism of unity expressed by both poets not only in the image of the curve (Proem: "To Brooklyn Bridge," last stanza), but also in their resort to the Mississippi as a personage that blends past and present into one (compare "The River," and "Blue Meridian" lines 24-33, pp. 633-34; lines 682-92, p. 652); woman symbolizing unity for both poets (compare Pocahontas in "The Dance" and the unnamed but universally loved woman in "Blue Meridian," lines 544-61, p. 648); and others.

Whitman and, through him, to the American tradition born with the Pilgrim Fathers, according to which the New World must necessarily be new,[71] in the most literal sense of the word.

The fundamental thesis of "Blue Meridian" is the need for a regenerated America, to be achieved through the regeneration of each individual and each community composing it, of an America once more united around the spiritual dream of its founders.

> It is a new America,
> To be spiritualized by each new American.[72]

What must be found once more is the whole man in his primordial unity, whether this is brought about by the collective effort of millions of men or attained by an elite of apostles ("twelve men") among whom, as Toomer saw things, one would have to place the poets:

> Lift, lift thou waking forces!
> Let us feel the energy of animals,
> The energy of rumps and bull-bent heads
> Crashing the barrier to man.
> It must spiral on!
> A million men, or twelve men,
> Must crash the barrier to the next higher form.[73]

That Toomer's is truly a Whitman-like vision of the unity of mankind may be recognized in such passages of "Blue Meridian" as the following, where the nervy, muscular, elliptical style proceeds via a series of additions and emendations, jumping boldly from one image to the next but always maintaining a plenitude of vigor and conviction:

> We — priest, clown, scientist, technician,
> Artist, rascal, worker, lazybones,
> This is the whole —
> Individuals and people,
> This is the whole that stood with Adam
> And has come down to us,
> Never to be less,
> Whatever side is up, however viewed,
> Whatever the vicissitudes,
> The needs of evolution that bring
> Emphasis upon a part —

[71] See, in "Blue Meridian," the passage (lines 138-56, p. 637) beginning with "When the Spirit of mankind conceived / A New World in America...."
[72] *Ibid.*, lines 1-2, p. 633.
[73] *Ibid.*, lines 6-12, p. 633.

Man himself, his total body and soul,
This is the moving whole.

Men of the East, men of the West,
Men in life, men in death,
Americans and all countrymen —
Growth is by admixture from less to more,
Preserving the great granary intact,
Through cycles of death and life,
Each stage a pod,
Perpetuating and perfecting
An essence identical in all,
Obeying the same laws, unto the same goal,
That far-distant objective,
By ways both down and up,
Down years ago, now struggling up.[74]

When "the Myth of America" is approached on this level and from this viewpoint, one can see how relevant it is to the solution of the problem of unity as Toomer formulated it on the racial level. If the Negro's internal divisions were simply a variant of the divisions within America, then it would be possible to resolve them only through the regeneration and re-unification of *Homo americanus* himself. To begin with, it was necessary to discover why his original lofty dream had been corrupted.

In his search for the reasons that would explain this degradation, Toomer showed himself to be both more objective and more profound than most other Negro Renaissance poets. At the level on which his meditation moved, it could scarcely be otherwise. Every component making up America — whites from Europe, Negroes from Africa, the indigenous redskins — was severally and jointly responsible for the collapse of the American dream.

This is true, in the first place, because whites, blacks, and redskins alike, after distorting the image of their gods, thereupon abandoned them and left them to die. But in addition, after giving the best of themselves to America, they went on to give the worst:

The great European races sent wave after wave
That washed the forests, the earth's rich loam,
Grew towns with the seeds of giant cities,
Made roads, laid silver rails,
Sang of their swift achievement
And died, displaced by machines.
They say that near the end

---

[74] *Ibid.,* lines 34-59, p. 634.

> It was a world of crying men and hard women,
> A city of goddam and Jehovah
> Baptized in finance
> Without benefit of saints.[75]

The black race too must bear its share of blame for the decline of the American ideal. To the splendor of the common heritage it did indeed contribute the beauty and the fervor of its spirituals and secular songs, which epitomize universal human values. But it had not been able to exert on itself the effort required to redeem these values from the degrading slave matrix in which, through its own fault, it is still choking:

> The great African races sent a single wave
> And singing riplets to sorrow in red fields,
> Sing a swan song, to break rocks
> And immortalize a hiding water boy.

> I'm leaving the shining ground, brothers,
> I sing because I ache,
> I go because I must,
> Brothers, I am leaving the shining ground;

> Don't ask me where,
> I'll meet you there,
> I'm leaving the shining ground.

> But we must keep keep keep
>   the watermelon —
> He moaned, O Lord, Lord,
> This bale will break me —
> But we must keep keep
>   the watermelon.[76]

The symbolism of these three stanzas may call for some explanation. The fields of red earth are Georgia's, and it is the earth of which Toomer had already sung in *Cane*. Before they died of exhaustion, many blacks had not only worked on plantations as slaves but also as convicts in chain gangs. These were often used in building roads and, in the process, they had to demolish rock formations. The little water-carrier who hides away somewhere is one of the most pathetic and best-known characters in these anonymous black convict songs.[77] The second stanza successfully recovers

[75] *Ibid.*, lines 69-79, p. 635.
[76] *Ibid.*, lines 102-18, p. 636.
[77] "Water Boy." Text of this song in Victor Francis Calverton, ed., *Anthology of American Negro Literature*, pp. 231-32. There is a recording by Harry Belafonte on RCA 430-213, side 1.

the essence of the spirituals with their load of human suffering and their longing for another world which, more especially, would grant respite from all pain. With its use of the grotesque,[78] the third stanza stands in willed contrast to the lofty tone of the preceding stanzas. In it the watermelon symbolizes and sums up the stereotype — an absolute fiction concocted by the slave-holding mentality — of the inferior, subservient Negro. Toomer, however, makes use of this symbol to castigate the unawareness of Negroes also, since they had not merely failed to shake off this ghostly image imposed on them by others but had actually absorbed it into their own consciousness. In like fashion, the word "watermelon" is incorporated into the poem through the use of two lines actually taken from Negro work songs. If black men are divided within, it is because they have hitherto failed to purge the self of everything which, not being the self pure and unalloyed, degrades and denatures its primordial beauty.

The result of this perversion of the original dream, and of the fissure that has rent the individual's heart, is that every American, in a sense, has become a Negro:

> We're all niggers now — get me?
> Black niggers, white niggers, — take your choice.[79]

Like Hart Crane[80] and F. Scott Fitzgerald,[81] Toomer turns to the symbol of the airplane crash to depict this plunge into the abyss:

> An airplane, with a broken wing,
> In a tail-spin,
> Descends with terrifying speed —
> "Don't put me on the spot!" —
> From beings to no-things,
> From human beings to grotesques,
> From men and women to manikins,
> From forms to chaoses —
> *Crash!*[82]

If the original ideal has been transformed into a curse, man alone is responsible:

> It is because of thee, O Man,
> That the first prayer ends in the last curse.[83]

---

[78] Comparisons could also be drawn between Toomer, Crane, and Sherwood Anderson in their use of the grotesque.

[79] "Blue Meridian," lines 225-26, p. 639.

[80] "Cape Hatteras."

[81] *The Last Tycoon.*

[82] "Blue Meridian," lines 245-53, p. 640.

[83] *Ibid.,* lines 278-79, p. 641.

Man's greed for profit and the overall priority he has assigned to material civilization, the destroyer of primordial beauty, have not only disfigured the Creator's handiwork but even divided the creature against himself:

> On land are shadows not of trees or clouds,
> On materials marks not made by Nature,
> On men and women ravages no animal could make,
> On children brands,
> On life a blight not put by God —
> Gargoyle shadows,
> Finger marks,
> Ghosts like us,
> A blight in an image recognized,
> I having seen myself —
> O Man, that thy mask
> Streaks the space between the sun and earth,
> Streaks the air between thyself and thyself.[84]

Toomer, though surveying the whole of American civilization, does not let the race problem drop out of sight. He situates on the same plane the disfigurement of the human being by racial prejudice ("on children brands") and the fouling of nature by industrial proliferation.

If the source of corruption is man, man can also end it. A thousand ways are at his disposal, if he would vanquish and transcend himself:

> ... there is a great detour,
> Purgatories by many names.[85]

First one must break from the grip of fear, prejudice, and murderousness. Man must find the strength to detach himself from everything which, having been created by him, now possesses him and drags him to the abyss:

> That which you have held has got hold of you
> And would sink you as it goes down.[86]

A prime necessity, no matter what the context, is a great and generous act of emancipation, from which there will arise the fraternal love of man for man, in universal freedom. Rediscovering an élan that is truly Whitmanian, Jean Toomer summons up this liberating deed in a great litany, a full-throated heralding of the resurrection of regenerate man:

[84] *Ibid.*, lines 317-29, p. 642.
[85] *Ibid.*, lines 335-36, p. 642. See also *ibid.*, lines 391-419, p. 644, the passage: "Islanders, newly come upon the continents. . . ." In it, he summons "the islanders," among whom he certainly includes Negroes, to "disintegrate tribal integrators."
[86] *Ibid.*, lines 369-70, p. 643.

Mend and clean, and then —

Uncase the races,
Open this pod,
Free man from his shrinkage,
Not from the reality itself,
But from the unbecoming and enslaving behavior
Associated with our prejudices and preferences.
Eliminate these;
I am, we are, simply of the human race.

Uncase the nations,
Open this pod,
Keep the real but destroy the false;
We are of the human nation.

Uncase the regions —
Occidental, Oriental, North, South, —
We are of the Earth.

Free the sexes,
I am neither male nor female nor in-between;
I am of sex, with male differentiations.

Open the classes;
I am, we are, simply of the human class.

Expand the fields —
Those definitions which fix fractions
    and lose wholes —
I am of the field of being,
We are beings.

Uncase the religions;
I am religious.

Uncase, unpod whatever impedes . . .[87]

The second part of the poem[88] is devoted to the coming of the new man. In it there reappear themes and sequences already met with in the first part, but now they are transfigured.[89] Assuredly, the new America has yet

[87] *Ibid.*, lines 420-48, pp. 644-45. See also *Essentials*, 24.
[88] Beginning with line 483, p. 646.
[89] Here is a table of the principal recurrent lines to be noted in "Blue Meridian" (the numbers refer to the lines):
"It is a new America": 1-2, 183-87, 483-86, 562-71, 589-92; "Black Meridian": 3-5, 343-45, 717-23; "Lift, lift": 6-12, 60, 724-30; "Beyond plants": 13-17, 731-35; "O thou Radiant Incorporal": 18-23, 157-62, 736-41; "The Mississippi": 24-33, 682-92; "The old gods": 61-67, 593-600; "The old peoples": 68-82, 601-9; "Blood cannot mix": 83-93, 610-20; "The great African races": 102-18, 621-32; "The great red race": 119-36, 633-51; "It is because of thee": 95-96, 278-79.

to be inaugurated, but it has already been born within the poet's heart. Rising to the sphere toward which he dreams of leading all the men and women of his country, he at last savors the joys of inner unity regained, and in exaltation he would radiate this spiritual benefit to the whole of America.

Thus Toomer achieves the synthesis of the warring elements which, at the end of *Cane,* seemed irreconcilable. To bring this about, he had to break down every restrictive category ("uncase the races" — "free man from his shrinkage"). In short, he had to found a humanism which at the same time would be a spirituality.

For it cannot be doubted that unity is a God-given grace, a pure gift of the Spirit. That is why the poet repeatedly prays to the Radiant Incorporal:

> O thou, Radiant Incorporal,
> The I of our universe, hurl
> Down these seaboards, across these continents,
> The thousand-rayed discus of thy mind,
> And above our waking limbs unfurl
> Spirit-torsos of exquisite strength![90]

This also explains why unity, once achieved, remains something ineffable, which reason alone is powerless to grasp and which only the symbol is able to express without at the same time shattering it. Only the symbol can lead man to the zenith which the Creator, from all eternity, has allotted him in the heavenly azure. "A symbol is as useful to the spirit as a tool is to the hand."[91] Thus the Blue Meridian, the synthesis of the Black and White Meridians,[92] straightway soars aloft far higher than either of these separate forces could in isolation.

Azure, again, is the shade in which Toomer attires the new man, the spiritual synthesis of bygone antagonisms:

> A strong yes, a strong no,
> With these we move and make drama,
> Yet say nothing of the goal.
> Black is black, white is white,
> East is east, west is west,
> Is truth for the brain of contrasts;

---

[90] *Ibid.,* lines 736-41.

[91] *Essentials,* 5.

[92] This meaning remains implicit; it emerges from a comparison of the repetitive passages cited above, note 89, under "Black Meridian." It can also be read out of the meaning of the blue man (see the citation corresponding to note 93 below).

> Yet here the high way of the third,
> The blue man, the purple man
> Foretold by ancient minds who knew,
> Not the place, not the name,
> But the resultant of yes and no
> Struggling for birth through ages.[93]

With this, Toomer has welded all living men into a unity and even linked up into a living chain the whole of humanity past, present, and future.[94] Yet, as if this synthesis were still not sufficiently global, he returns once again to humanity's two streams and confers upon them the supreme unity in the redeeming symbol of the cross:

> Mankind is a cross,
> Joined as a cross irrevocably —
> The solid stream sourcing in the remote past,
> Ending in far off distant years,
> Is the perpendicular;
> The planetary wash of those now living
> Forms the transverse bar . . .[95]

Thus the ultimate driving force behind the whole body of Jean Toomer's work is his ardent longing for unity at the highest level of the spirit. Setting out from the immediate data of racial difference, he rapidly soars above them — too rapidly for the taste of those who, unable to imagine any universe not black and white, were not internally ready to join him in his pursuit of the Blue Meridian. They had expected him to be a poet of his race, but he resolved to be purely the poet of man. Did this provide sufficient reason for the accusation that he had repudiated his origins and abandoned his own people? One can scarcely believe that Jean Toomer, with a mind so tempered and with a soul so generous, could have toyed even fleetingly with the notion of treason. Quite to the contrary: it would seem that we must count him among the very great for having refused, for his own part and on behalf of his fellows, the shackles that are worn by men divided.

[93] "Blue Meridian," lines 652-63, p. 651.
[94] *Ibid.*, lines 664-74, pp. 651-52.
[95] *Ibid.*, lines 675-81, p. 652.

Chapter Eight: COUNTEE CULLEN

Together with Claude McKay, Countee Cullen was the black poet gifted with the most intense inner life, but he was also a most tormented personality. The particular circumstances surrounding his youthful years, an intellectual preparation acquired almost entirely outside his racial milieu, and, furthermore, particularly haunting personal problems — these were some of the influences that help to explain the strange note sounded by his lyric poetry. Its tone constituted a seemingly impassable barrier between the poet and the people of his own race.

Cullen, for them, soon became a great, misunderstood figure, and he found their lack of comprehension a burden hard to bear. But his direct experience of suffering was, for his inner life, a source of extraordinary enrichment.

His lyric gift was incontestable and, indeed, exceptional. But his poetry has none of McKay's fiery virility, and the treasures it encloses are, rather, those of a soul that at times indulged in an excess of sensibility and preferred to express itself in the half-tones and nuances of a high scrupulousness.

Now that so many years have elapsed since his death, it may not be too early to reassess the value of this work and to try, via the work, to reach and to understand the man.

1. CULLEN'S LIFE[1]

A Mysterious Childhood (1903-18)

A certain degree of mystery continues to hover over Countee Cullen's childhood and youth. The written and oral statements that we have been able to gather concerning the poet's earlier years frequently contradict each other. While apparently there can be little doubt that some accounts of his origins — most notably, those given by the poet himself — must be allotted the status of pious legends, the others do not on that account become entirely worthy of credence.

Cullen himself was very (taciturn) about his childhood, stating only that he was born on May 30, 1903, in New York and that he was raised "in the conservative atmosphere of a Methodist parsonage."[2] This has led to the assumption that he was actually the son of the Reverend Frederick Asbury Cullen, founder of the Salem Methodist Episcopal Church in Harlem, and of his wife Carolyn Belle Mitchell,[3] whereas he was really their adopted son,[4] the act of adoption, seemingly, never having been regularized.[5]

Another highly important source of information, since it is the only one to provide any details on these shadowy years, is a magazine article by an anonymous author who seems to have been particularly well informed.[6]

---

[1] This chapter was completely written before we became acquainted, in December, 1960, with the typescript of Beulah Reimherr's M.A. dissertation, "Countee Cullen: A Biographical and Critical Study" (University of Maryland, 1960), which clarifies certain details in the poet's life. But since our own conclusions are not affected by them in any way, we have not seen fit to reprint them in this biography. We corresponded with Mrs. Reimherr as she was engaged in research, and we are indebted to her for several pieces of bibliographical information, for which we take this occasion to thank her.

[2] *Caroling Dusk*, p. 179.

[3] For example, Stanley J. Kunitz and Howard Haycraft, "Cullen," *Twentieth Century Authors*.

[4] Arna Bontemps, "The Harlem Renaissance," *Saturday Review*, March 22, 1947, p. 12. In any event, the fact is today a matter of public knowledge. But, if this should still be necessary, the details provided by the Rev. F. A. Cullen in *From Barefoot Town to Jerusalem* would suffice to prove that it is factually out of the question that Countee Cullen could have been the son of the Rev. Cullen and of his wife — that is, if we accept the poet's birthdate as being correctly given. For the Rev. Cullen's wife died on October 5, 1932 (*From Barefoot,* p. 40) after twenty-five years of marriage (*ibid.,* p. 39), thus giving the date of 1907 for the marriage. Furthermore, the Rev. Cullen states that his marriage took place only a few months after he had met Carolyn Belle Mitchell for the first time (*ibid.,* p. 39). Thus the future spouses met for the first time no earlier than 1906, some three years after the poet's birth.

[5] This statement was made by Harold Jackman, a close friend of the poet's, in an interview he had the kindness to grant us in New York in October, 1958.

[6] "A Star Falls," *Headlines and Pictures* II, no. 8 (February, 1946), pp. 12-14.

The considerable number of precise facts mentioned, some of which it has been possible to verify elsewhere, indicate that it should be taken seriously. According to this article, Cullen was born in Baltimore and named Countee Leroy Porter; his father died while the poet was still quite small. Thereupon the mother left for New York with her only child. They lived in a depressing four-room apartment in a very dark building. We learn, still following this article, that the poet had a lonely childhood with no contacts whatever, except for his schoolmates. His mother's obesity left her practically immobile, and she received almost no visitors. Her financial resources were limited to what she succeeded in earning, highly irregularly, by taking as day pensioners the children sent her by the Children's Aid Society. The poor woman is said to have died on January 1, 1918, having had the time to recommend her son to a social service employee of the National Urban League, who saw to it that the boy was adopted by the Reverend Cullen and who also found him a job at ten dollars a week as valet to the actor John Drew, Jr.

According to the poet's widow,[7] however, Countee Cullen was born in Louisville, Kentucky,[8] and while still a baby was taken for adoption to the Reverend Cullen in New York. The poet's mother died in Louisville in September, 1940, and the poet attended the funeral.[9]

Yet another source declares that the woman referred to in the anonymous article was the poet's grandmother, not his mother. This emendation would make it possible to reconcile the two other versions.[10]

Finally, there is the enigmatic remark about Cullen's youth made by James Weldon Johnson: "There is not much to say about these earlier years of Cullen — unless he himself should say it."[11] This six-word afterthought is an invitation to reverie.

Whatever the truth of the matter, the belief imposes itself that the mystery surrounding Cullen's early years was desired, created, and carefully maintained by the poet himself, and respected by those close to him. He not only refrained from saying anything about his childhood; he also tried to throw people off the track by saying that he had been born in

---

[7] Ida M. Cullen, his second wife, today Ida M. Cullen-Cooper.

[8] Cullen's connections with Kentucky appear to be reliably established; see below our discussion of "The Ballad of the Brown Girl." Yet Beulah Reimherr tells us that nothing resulted from the investigations she undertook in the Vital Statistics Bureaus of both Louisville and Baltimore.

[9] In June, 1958, Ida Cullen-Cooper was kind enough to provide this information.

[10] Statement made by Harold Jackman (see note 5 above). There is every reason to accept it as accurate, since it appears confirmed by "Epitaph for My Grandmother," published in 1925 (*Color*, p. 46).

[11] James Weldon Johnson, *The Book of American Negro Poetry*, p. 219.

New York as the legitimate offspring of the Cullens. This is clearly not so. It is to be noted that, after signing himself Countee L. Porter,[12] and then Countee P. Cullen, at least until 1923,[13] he suddenly dropped the middle initial, as if it had become embarrassing, reminding him too insistently of the origins he was anxious to shake off. He took this step at the very time he was beginning to become well known and to be received in society.[14]

Cullen, then, appears to have aimed at the systematic repudiation of his childhood and through this, perhaps, of his mother also. As for the reasons that might have lain behind this attitude, it is unfortunately impossible to do more than conjecture.[15] Yet one thing is certain: on top of the feelings of inferiority he may have had, for racial reasons, he could not face the prospect of shouldering another form of inferiority, due to his social origins.

From the religious point of view, the Cullens were rigid fundamentalists, naïve and a trifle pedantic, as one realizes in perusing the Reverend F. A. Cullen's book, *From Barefoot Town to Jerusalem*. Their narrowly literal interpretation of the scriptures must have displeased that young intellectual, their adopted son, and it is likely that, more than once, filial devotion rather than conviction assured his compliance with the prescribed religious devotions.[16] The Reverend Cullen appears to have had a simplistic if not downright mechanical notion of the relations between man and God, which could scarcely satisfy so demanding a soul as the poet's.

Other factors also played a part in disturbing the conscience of the adolescent poet. There is some reason to believe that the marriage of the

[12] "Countee L(eroy) Porter" is, indeed, the signature attached to his first poem "To the Swimmer," *Modern School*, May, 1918, p. 142.

[13] In particular, the signature "Countee P. Cullen" is used with the sonnet "Christ Recrucified," *Kelley's Magazine*, October, 1922, p. 13, and can be noted a year later with his article "The League of Youth," *The Crisis*, August, 1923, p. 167.

[14] By the time of *Color* (1925), he has already become simply "Countee Cullen."

[15] If the poet was raised by his grandmother, his mother being the person who died in Louisville in September, 1940, the question arises why the mother did not bring up her child. Was he an illegitimate child, or did the circumstances of his mother's life make it impossible for her to have him around? We must be satisfied to voice these questions, without being able to provide answers. But Cullen's denial of his mother seems to have been a punitive action directed against her for having abandoned him, and at the same time an endeavor to carve out for himself a more respectable condition than was made available by his birth.

[16] Bontemps (for reference, see note 4 above) says, in particular: "A foster child, drawn into this shelter at an early age, he continued to cherish it gratefully. He paid his adopted parents a devotion, one is almost inclined to say a submission, only rarely rendered by natural sons."

adoptive parents was not altogether harmonious, and that the blame for this must be attributed to the Reverend Cullen's homosexual tendencies. Thus his adoption of the future poet may have been motivated by feelings that were more than paternal, and these may have been matched by certain inclinations on the adolescent's side.[17] Moreover, the favors the adoptive father heaped on the poet aroused the jealousy of other members of the family,[18] with the consequence that Countee Cullen, at the decisive age when he was about to become a man, found himself ripening in a rather muddied moral atmosphere.

The Productive Years (1918-35)

Cullen's first poetic efforts date from his high school years, which were spent at the De Witt Clinton High School in New York. "To the Swimmer," written when he was about fourteen, is a school assignment in free verse that was published by *Modern School* in May, 1918.[19] Of the same period is "Life's Rendezvous,"[20] whose title is a pastiche of that of Alan Seeger's poem, "I Have a Rendezvous with Death," and which was awarded first prize in a competition organized by the Federation of Women's Clubs.

Cullen entered New York University in 1922. There his poetic vocation was confirmed, with several of his major themes already becoming apparent. "Christ Recrucified" was published in *Kelley's Magazine* in October, 1922. He contributed to two of the most prominent Negro magazines, *The*

[17] These facts are widely known, though because of their nature they have never been put into writing. We mention them here because they both illuminate the poet's personality and serve to explain several of his poems that otherwise could not be understood (see, for example, "Fruit of the Flower," *Color*, p. 24; "Dad," *From Barefoot*, p. 10). As for the Rev. Cullen, whose marriage with Miss Mitchell remained without offspring, to judge by his own declarations he had a highly developed Oedipus complex: "I had resolved not to marry while my mother lived. I loved her so dearly and she loved me [so] dearly that I thought it would be impossible to share my love with a wife. Knowing or thinking that my mother would want to boss me and command me as she heretofore had done, also boss my wife, and that would bring about confusion, therefore, I didn't marry anybody while my dear mother lived. My mother was a wonderful woman ..." (*From Barefoot*, p. 10). This Oedipal attachment may usefully explain his feelings of special affection for the poet, his adopted son.

[18] See note 5 above.

[19] See note 12 above.

[20] The poem appeared in 1921 in *The Magpie*, the magazine of De Witt Clinton High School. It is not the same poem as that entitled "I Have a Rendezvous with Life," which was reprinted in *Caroling Dusk*, p. 180, after its prior publication in *Current Opinion*, May, 1924, p. 708. If the two texts are to be regarded as successive versions of the same poem, it was subjected to considerable revision, and Cullen's art had made astounding progress in the intervening period.

Crisis, then under the direction of W. E. B. Du Bois, and *Opportunity,* which the National Urban League had founded a short while before. *The Bookman,* the first magazine of wide circulation to print his poems, published "To a Brown Boy" in November, 1923. Soon all the major magazines opened their columns to him: *Harper's, The Century,* and *Poetry,* among others. In November, 1924, "The Shroud of Color" appeared in *American Mercury.*

The year 1925 turned out to be his *annus mirabilis.* "The Ballad of the Brown Girl," written in 1923, won him several awards, notably the Witter Bynner Undergraduate Prize, with the jury made up of Witter Bynner, Carl Sandburg, and Alice Corbin. New York University, before granting him his B.A. degree in June, elected him a member of Phi Beta Kappa. But, most especially, this is the year in which Harper published his first collection of verse, *Color,* which saw Cullen elevated to the summit of renown by his own people, and made him "the most widely acclaimed poet of all Negrodom."[21] In the fall he entered Harvard University; he received his M.A. the following summer.

Upon his return from a first trip to Europe and the Holy Land in November, 1926, he became assistant editor of *Opportunity* and for two years was in charge of "The Dark Tower," the section on literary criticism. He also compiled an anthology of American Negro poetry, *Caroling Dusk,* which stimulated a great deal of controversy when it appeared in 1927 because of the far from orthodox definition of Negro poetry advanced in the preface.

At least equally controversial, though for different reasons, was his second volume of poetry, *Copper Sun* (1927). Those who might be looked on as Negro nationalists were displeased at finding so many love poems, with only seven race poems among them. The numerical proportion of the two themes approximately reversed that found in *Color.* Also to be observed was a decided weakening of inspiration, a more artificial character, and, in general, a less vigorous, less dense, and less well-coined expressivity than in the earlier collection. After this interval of two years, the author of *Copper Sun* disappointed the expectations that had been aroused by *Color.*[22] The publication in brochure form of "The Ballad of the Brown Girl," which had been written several years before, did not attenuate the impression, circulating in 1927, that the poet's powers had declined.

[21] "A Star Falls." Two years after publication, more than six thousand copies of *Color* had been sold (Charlotte E. Taussig, "The New Negro as Revealed in His Poetry," *Opportunity,* April, 1927, p. 110).
[22] There may be a commonplace explanation for this sense that a weakening

This disappointing development was probably associated with the important decision that Cullen must have been envisaging at this time, and not without apprehension. While at New York University he had become acquainted with Yolande Du Bois, a graduate of Fisk University and daughter of W. E. B. Du Bois. She had visited Jerusalem with him in July, 1926. *Copper Sun* bore the dedication "To the Not Impossible Her," and there is every reason to believe that the unknown was indeed Yolande. In any event, one poem in the collection, "One Day We Played a Game," was unabashedly dedicated to her.[23] Had Cullen overcome his homosexual inclinations? Was he about to break with the past and prove it by getting married? Those who knew him well voiced their skepticism.[24] The unbelievable occurred, nevertheless, and on April 9, 1928, in the Reverend Cullen's own church, with great ceremony and in the presence of all the illustrious figures of America's black world, the poet married Yolande Du Bois.[25]

In the meantime, he had obtained a Guggenheim Fellowship in order

had occurred. Arna Bontemps has told us that, when *Color* appeared, Cullen still had enough unpublished poems on hand to constitute a second volume. Thus it may be assumed that the poems in *Color* and those in *Copper Sun* are practically identical in date, *Color* having been assembled from the better poems. *Copper Sun*, on the other hand, would thus be made up mainly of poems not deemed worthy of inclusion in the 1925 volume. But in the meantime they were certainly carefully reworked with a view to publication. For the extent of the revisions made by Cullen in his poems, see note 148 below.

23 Already "Brown Boy to Brown Girl," *Color*, p. 5, had the subtitle, "For Yolande."

24 After the break with Yolande, Cullen did not shrink from referring, in several poems, to the rumors that were circulating about him. There are veiled allusions in "Tongue-Tied," *The Black Christ*, p. 27. But most explicit, especially in the second part, is the poem "Two Poets," *ibid.*, pp. 34-35.

> "How could a woman love him; love, or wed?",
> And thinking only of his tuneless face
> And arms that held no hint of skill or grace,
> They shook a slow, commiserative head
> To see him amble by; but still they fed
> Their wilting hearts on his, were fired to race
> Once more, and panting at life's deadly pace,
> They drank as wine the blood-in-song he shed.

In another respect also this passage seems to be of central importance. To judge by the way he speaks here of his ethnic brothers, who condescendingly deplore his amorous setbacks, but who are still very much inclined to seek in his verses a stimulus for their faltering pride of race, it would not be surprising if about this time (when his marriage to Yolande Du Bois was a topic of general discussion) Cullen began, inwardly at first and then openly in his poems, to withdraw from his people. See also "A Thorn Forever in the Breast," which is cited and considered below.

25 On the ceremony, see "A Star Falls," and Langston Hughes, *The Big Sea*, pp. 274-75.

to continue studying in France. On June 30, 1928, in the company of his adoptive father and a friend, he left for Paris, where Yolande joined him in July. But she discovered only too rapidly, alas, that the marriage was "a tragic mistake."[26] After her return to the United States she sued for divorce; this was granted in the fall of 1929.

The bitterness following the collapse of his marriage left its mark on many of the poems included in *The Black Christ,* written in the main in Paris and published in 1929. The love theme, in particular, is dealt with in a disillusioned way — sometimes crassly so. On the other hand, his inner life gained in depth after his heart and his pride were thus afflicted, and in "The Black Christ," his longest poem, Cullen once again takes up and expands the dialogue with God already entered upon in "The Shroud of Color." In the new poem, he succeeds in orchestrating a spiritual synthesis which, despite its obvious formal blemishes, is not without grandeur.

But *The Black Christ* also writes a kind of *finis* to his work as a poet. As a result of his amorous setback there was an acceleration of his internal development, and his thinking, which had too early come to maturity, was marked by a kind of exhaustion. Apart from a few pieces that will appear in the same volume as his translation of Euripides' *Medea* (1935), his poetic achievement may be considered to have reached its conclusion with the 1929 collection. It will have proved to be but a sudden blaze, though astoundingly intense and rich, a few short years in duration. After that, this young old man of under thirty will arouse the distressing impression of having outlived himself.

For a moment, however, the hope could be entertained that he was about to renew himself in another literary form. In 1932 he published his novel, *One Way to Heaven,* which delves into the moral ambiguities of Harlem's religious life and satirizes the black intelligentsia. But this remained an isolated venture. Cullen had said all there was for him to say. His goal for the future was the silence which, in "A Wish"[27] and in "Self Criticism,"[28] he hoped he would have the strength to maintain.

---

[26] "A Star Falls."

[27] "A Wish," *The Black Christ*, p. 31:

> I hope when I have sung my rounds
> Of song, I shall have strength to slay
> The wish to chirp on any grounds,
> Content that silence hold her sway,
> My tongue not rolling futile sounds
> After my heart has had its say.

[28] "Self Criticism," *ibid.*, p. 38. Cullen was painfully conscious of the premature fading of his poetic gift. Shortly before the outbreak of World War II, he wrote to a friend: "My muse is either dead or taking a twenty-year sleep" (cited by Bontemps, "The Harlem Renaissance," *Saturday Review,* March 22, 1947, p. 13).

The Last Years (1935-46)

Cullen, who was passionately attached to France and its language,[29] continued his visits there every year until 1939.[30]

During the last twelve years of his life, he taught French in the Frederick Douglass Junior High School in New York, and it may be that his daily contact with young people gave him the idea of writing two books for children, *The Lost Zoo* (1940) and *My Lives and How I Lost Them* (1942).

In 1945 he worked on a play, "Saint Louis Woman," based on Arna Bontemps's novel, *God Sends Sunday,* and he prepared for publication an anthology of his own poems, *On These I Stand.* But he was to witness neither the performance of the one[31] nor the publication of the other.[32] The high blood pressure from which he had been suffering for several years suddenly grew worse, and he was admitted to Sydenham Hospital in New York, where he died on January 9, 1946.

The funeral ceremony, held in the Salem Methodist Episcopal Church, was attended by more than three thousand people.[33]

2. THE DICTATES OF THE PSYCHE

As we were making our way through the literary criticism written, between the two World Wars, on the poetical works with which we are dealing, we often thought that some critics of that time had a far too rigid notion of the standards to which, if grace was to be found in their eyes, all poetry written by Negroes must necessarily conform. Knowing the writer's color, they imagined that they knew *a priori* what he must say

In the poem "After a Visit" (*The Medea,* pp. 67-68) he is thoroughly ashamed of his silence. Yet "Interlude" (*ibid.,* p. 77) appeared to herald the renewal of his inspiration. It was only an illusion. Barely three months before his death, he again wrote: "I do not see myself publishing another book of verse for some time to come" (letter dated September 27, 1945, to Miss Amy Flashner, Countee Cullen file in the Negro Collection of Fisk University Library).

[29] Fisk University still has the certificate given the poet for the special courses (normal level, advanced class) he took at the Sorbonne from July 6 to August 14, 1931. His grades in the final examination were 18 out of 20 on the written, and 17 out of 20 on the oral.

[30] In September, 1940, Countee Cullen married for a second time, the bride being Ida Mae Robertson, whose acquaintance he had already made in 1930, and who was the sister of one of his very close friends.

[31] *Saint Louis Woman* had a New York run that began in March and ended in July, 1946.

[32] *On These I Stand* was published in 1947.

[33] See the obituary in the *New York Times,* January 13, 1946.

and how he must say it. This attitude has not disappeared completely, and in 1948 James D. Hart could still express the view that Cullen's poems "lack deep racial feeling in either idiom or rhythm."[34] Thus the writer would not merely be deprived of the free choice of his form; only through form would he be permitted the possibility of expressing "deep racial feeling."

Cullen incurred even more substantial disapproval because of the classical form of his verse and because his language contained many Victorianisms scorned by practitioners of the new poetry. Sometimes his lack of formal originality led to the hasty conclusion that he lacked sincerity of feeling: "He has borrowed the temperament of his poems. His interpretations and manner, his attitude of mind, are drawn, not from evidences of his personal and intimate life, but from a tradition entirely literary, and, by now, anemic."[35] When we set these judgments beside the title, "Race and a Poet," that Harry Alan Potamkin gave his article, the thought lies near at hand that basically he is reproaching Cullen for not having been more notably the spokesman of his entire race, as if the collective experience should necessarily absorb the individual's creative activity whenever the individual does not enjoy the privilege of being white. At the end of the article, there does appear to be confirmation that this was indeed the critic's line of argument: "The Negro folk has had its poet in Dunbar; will the Negro race produce a Synge?"[36]

Cullen, clearly, was the most unlikely of all the Negro poets to satisfy such standards, for the real substance of his lyric gift came from his individual experience at least as much as, if not more than, from the experience of the racial group to which he belonged and against whose encroachments he never ceased to defend himself with vigor. Even at

---

[34] James D. Hart, "Cullen," *Oxford Companion to American Literature.*

[35] Harry Alan Potamkin, "Race and a Poet," *New Republic,* October 12, 1927, p. 218. Ten years later Sterling Brown would express the view, concerning "The Black Christ," that this poem, like many others, "relies more upon literature than life" (*Negro Poetry and Drama,* p. 71). After the lapse of yet another ten years, Arna Bontemps spoke of his "tendency to get his inspiration, his rhythms and patterns as well as much of his substance from books" (*Saturday Review,* March 22, 1947, p. 12). A *New York Times* critic wrote what amounted to the same thing when he stated that Cullen was "just a little too much the product of our American colleges" (cited by Kunitz-Haycraft, "Cullen," *Twentieth Century Authors*). But Cullen found his most unjust critic in the person of J. Saunders Redding (*To Make a Poet Black,* pp. 108-12) who, together with many other unjustified reproaches, accuses him of having been "untouched by his times, by his conditions, by his environment" (*ibid.,* p. 108). While we cannot undertake here the detailed rebuttal of each of these declarations, at least we can hope that our study of Cullen's work will serve to clarify certain matters.

[36] Potamkin, "Race."

those moments when the poetic élan is most directly inspired by his color, his individual voice always dominates that of the group.

Thus it is hardly possible to treat him fairly unless one takes good care to allot its proper share to each of these two elements. The accusation is too easy that he never allowed his intimate personality to play a part in his poetry, when no attempt has been made to examine his work from this point of view. Yet any valid estimate of his work must, it seems to us, begin in this precise fashion.

We have already indicated what an excessive burden the shame of his origins was for him: the shame of his birth, which diminished him in his own eyes; the shame of the sin which, as he envisaged it, surrounded the circumstances of his adoption, and which exposed him to God's judgment; and especially the shame he felt at his color, which debased him in the eyes of other men and bent him beneath a weight he longed to shake off in death.

The Burden of Inferiority

We have spoken of the mystery in which he sought to plunge everything that concerned his real parents, and the place and circumstances of his birth and adoption. But the forgery to which he subjected his vital statistics could not by itself free him from his obsession with his origins. Sooner or later he had to find his way to the liberation that is reached only through avowal, and it was to his verse that he finally entrusted his conviction that a malevolent destiny had been imposed on him the day he was born. There had been a misdeal at the very outset, and this had falsified his whole existence.

Since his birth fell on a Saturday, May 30, 1903, he regarded Saturday as ill starred, for on that day, if we are to believe his account, a highly sinister band had presided over his arrival in the world. These phantom figures, Poverty, Pain, Death, and Sorrow, are evoked in the poem "Saturday's Child."[37] One also notes, for whatever the fact is worth, that he asserts he was born "on a night that was black as tar," and had "cut my teeth as the black raccoon,"[38] thus associating the color of his skin with the catastrophic atmosphere that surrounded his birth.

The notion that he was a "bad seed" sown in the world on an unlucky day is repeated in another poem, "Suicide Chant," in which Cullen's pes-

[37] *Color,* p. 18.
[38] "Raccoon" gives by aphaeresis "coon," which while designating the animal is also slang for "Negro." There can be no doubt that Cullen, in choosing this image, was aware of the ambiguity.

simism is transformed into forthright despair, which leads him to envisage suicide as the only way out of the dead end in which he had been placed by the circumstances of his birth:

> I am the seed
>   The Sower sowed;
> I am the deed
>   His hand bestowed
> Upon the world.
>
> .   .   .   .
>
> The seed of a weed
>   Cannot be flowered
>
> .   .   .   .
>
> Pull up the weed;
>   Bring plow and mower;
> Then fetch new seed
>   For the hand of the Sower.[39]

Here, to the dread constellation that had already met in "Saturday's Child," is added the name of the one ultimately responsible for letting the poet be born under an unlucky star, and whom he calls, as did the parable of the same name, the Sower. From his very beginnings, consequently, and with regard to those beginnings, Cullen sees himself involved in a struggle with God as his opponent. And, since the Sower sowed ill, all's to do again.

If, in his eyes, the adversary is God, it may be that he also feels himself guilty in God's sight. There would be no reason for surprise, if it should prove necessary to search for the origins of this feeling of guilt in the equivocal relationship that bound him to his adoptive father and to other persons of his own sex. It must not be overlooked that the adoptive father was also a man of God, and this may explain why, in "Fruit of the Flower," a poem replete with a sensuality he declares to have been inherited from his "father," he imagines he sees floating in his father's eyes the shadow of "some still sacred sin":

> There haunts them yet the languid ghost
>   Of some still sacred sin.[40]

This feeling of sinfulness depresses the poet and demeans him in his own eyes, for the consequence of his sin is that his heart, like his life, is a poorly written page:

[39] "Suicide Chant," stanza 1; stanza 4, lines 1-2; stanza 5, *Color,* pp. 87-88.
[40] "Fruit of the Flower," stanza 3, lines 3-4, *ibid.,* p. 24.

> . . . the ill-writ chart
> Small with virtue, big with sin.[41]

Nor can there be any doubt that his feeling of inferiority is also derived, by a more direct route, from his partial or total inability to lead a normal sexual life. Where he sees a sin committed before God, in the physical reality there is also a humiliating defeat before the love of woman. His marriage demonstrates this, and the poet is not oblivious of the fact. In a poem whose significant title is "Timid Lover," it would be difficult to overlook, expressed in terms scarcely veiled, the confessed impotence of a skittish lover[42] with masochistic[43] and fetishist[44] inclinations.

> I who employ a poet's tongue,
> Would tell you how
> You are a golden damson hung
> Upon a silver bough.
>
> I who adore exotic things
> Would shape a sound
> To be your name, a word that sings
> Until the head goes round.
>
> I who am proud with other folk
> Would grow complete
> In pride on bitter words you spoke,
> And kiss your petalled feet.
>
> But never past the frail intent
> My will may flow,
> Though gentle looks of yours are bent
> Upon me where I go.
>
> So must I, starved for love's delight,
> Affect the mute,
> When love's divinest acolyte
> Extends me holy fruit.[45]

If we have lingered a while over those aspects of Cullen's personality not immediately connected with his race, it is because of the importance, as it seemed to us, of stressing how fallacious any attempt would be that undertook to explain a man wholly by race. The sense of inferiority that overwhelmed him did not have a purely racial cause, and one must take

[41] "One Day I Told My Love," stanza 1, lines 3-4, *The Black Christ*, p. 54.
[42] *Ibid.*, stanza 4, lines 1-2; stanza 5.
[43] *Ibid.*, stanza 3, lines 1-3.
[44] *Ibid.*, stanza 3, line 4. Foot fetishism is a well-known phenomenon, and has often been described by psychopathologists.
[45] *Copper Sun*, p. 20.

fully into account the other emotional perturbations we have noted if one wishes to understand why Cullen, unlike the other poets of the Negro Renaissance, did not regard his race primarily as an object of pride. It is, indeed, difficult to conceive how emotionally he could dissociate as readily as is done in words, the concurrent facts of birth and color. Each unavoidably exerted an impact on the other, and he sensed how the fatal predestination he attributed to his birth also bore down upon his color:

> . . . being dark, forewilled to that despair
> My color shrouds me in . . .[46]

Each day undertook to demonstrate to him that the universe the white man had evolved for his own exclusive use had no more concern for the nonwhite than for the grain of dust trodden underfoot. It is his color that decides he will be barred from the most modest pleasures; color is the winding-sheet that shrouds him in despair, and the yoke that crushes him beneath its weight:

> . . . I am as dirt
> Beneath my brother's heel; there is a hurt
> In all the simple joys which to a child
> Are sweet; they are contaminate, defiled
> By truths of wrongs the childish vision fails
> To see; too great a cost this birth entails.
> I strangle in this yoke drawn tighter than
> The worth of bearing it, just to be a man.[47]

Indeed, how heavy the price that must be paid for the basic right of living like a human being! And, to be able to pay, he would have needed all the resources of a battler like McKay: his virility, his aggressiveness, and all his certitudes as well. But where could this man have found them, prey that he already was to the demons of guilt and doubt? Confronted by life's challenge, he was defenseless, prostrate, bloodless, and as though stricken with palsy:

> I am not brave enough to pay the price
> In full; I lack the strength to sacrifice.[48]

His lymphatic temperament caused him to overstate the dimensions of the sacrifice:

> . . . being dark, and living through the pain
> Of it, is courage more than angels have . . .[49]

[46] "The Shroud of Color," lines 3-4, *Color*, p. 26.
[47] *Ibid.*, lines 4-11.
[48] *Ibid.*, lines 12-13.
[49] *Ibid.*, lines 169-70, p. 34.

What else, then, can he hope for but death, which alone is able to deliver him from the burden once and for all?

Death the Liberator

In their analysis of the factors that give rise to "the need to liquidate totally the personality confronted by an ascendancy that has become intolerable,"[50] that is, the urge to suicide, psychiatrists have recorded that "delirious ideas of unworthiness, of guilt, of self-accusation, and mystical ideas may often lead certain subjects to a solution they regard as an inescapable or necessary obligation."[51]

This diagnosis admirably characterizes the psychic makeup of Cullen who, perhaps with the premonition of an untimely end, throughout his life rather resembled a dead man with a suspended sentence.[52] His writings are filled with the intense longing for a death that would set him free, when he does not go further and, in moments of despair, entertain the notion of suicide. It is also significant that he saw life as continuing only because death permitted it:

> . . . whatever lives is granted breath
> But by the grace and sufferance of Death.[53]

Barely twenty years old, he was already contemplating suicide. He revealed this to a number of friends,[54] and it was no doubt after some such avowal that Langston Hughes wrote for him, on the back of a letter that is preserved in the Fisk University library, "Song for a Suicide," with the dedication, "For Countee Cullen — November 18, 1925 — Washington":

> Oh, the sea is deep
> And a knife is sharp
> And a poison acid burns,
> But they all bring rest
> In a still, long sleep
> For which the tired soul yearns —
> They all bring rest in a nothingness
> From where no road returns.

This poem by Langston Hughes strangely echoes the poem which, in that

---

[50] Antoine Porot et al., "Suicide," *Manuel alphabétique de psychiâtrie*, p. 398, col. B.

[51] *Ibid.*, p. 399, col. A.

[52] See his poem "The Proud Heart," *The Black Christ*, p. 40, and in particular the last line: "The dead man lives, and none perceives him slain."

[53] "Sonnet Dialogue," *The Medea*, p. 86, lines 13-14.

[54] For this piece of information we are indebted to Arna Bontemps.

very same year (1925), Countee Cullen had designated as a *finis* redolent of despair and defeatism for his first volume of poems, *Color:*

REQUIESCAM

I am for sleeping and forgetting
All that has gone before;
I am for lying still and letting
Who will beat at my door;
I would my life's cold sun were setting
To rise for me no more.[55]

To forget all that has gone before, to discard a past not quite so easily obliterated as the record of one's vital statistics — that is the advantage he expects from death. "To liquidate totally the personality!"[56]

For Cullen, however, suicide remains at the speculation stage. It requires at least as much courage to carry out this ultimate act as to support the weight of existence, for one does not move without further ado from existence to oblivion. And again, a lesson that Langston Hughes drives home in his poem, one must have the dauntlessness to face the watery waste, the knife wound, or the scorching poison. Furthermore, actually to perform this deed with the aim of utterly annihilating the past would be another way of shouldering one's responsibilities, and that was the very thing from which Countee Cullen longed to be absolved.

At this stage on his despairing journey, when the depletion of his vital forces left him without even the possibility of self-procured ultimate forgetfulness, the same mystic tendencies that were in part at the base of his hankering after suicide brought him nearer to God. This can be truthfully called a conversion only in the etymological sense of the word, for, though he turned toward him whom he had never ceased to look on as his Creator, it was only to beg for an end to the existence he himself lacked the courage to terminate. The consequence of this turning to God was a strange dialogue, the subject of "The Shroud of Color."[57]

Here, as in "Suicide Chant," God is cast as the accused, for he had inflicted on the poet the malediction of his color. God defends this deed by revealing to his creature that the struggle for life is the supreme law of creation.[58] Even God is not exempt from this law, since only by struggle

---

[55] *Color*, p. 108.

[56] See note 50 above.

[57] Cullen was strongly influenced by Edna St. Vincent Millay. "The Shroud of Color," in particular, owes a great deal to "Renascence" (1912). Nor should one overlook the necessity of situating the theme of suicide, as handled by Cullen, within the much vaster context of the Lost Generation.

[58] "The Shroud of Color," lines 88-89, *Color*, p. 30, and *ibid.*, lines 111-12, p. 31.

could he assert his divinity against a rebellious Lucifer. However, the three visions God conjures up to convince the poet fail to do so, since the poet rejoins that strength for the struggle is found only in those who are not afflicted by the curse of color.

Realizing the force of this rebuttal, the Eternal at last hits upon the decisive argument that will refute the poet's despair and give him new strength with which to live. In a final ecstasy, there is displayed before the poet's eyes the long battle for liberty waged by the Africans, who have not been compelled by all the cruelties they suffered either in their homeland or in exile to abandon the hope of once again becoming free men.[59]

If Africa, despite the huge dimensions of its defeat, has never lost faith in its destiny, how can the poet, whose trials are as nothing compared with those of the mother country, still yield to despair?[60]

But the new inner equilibrium the poet has reached in this way continues to be precarious, for it rests on a quibble, and after one has finished reading "The Shroud of Color" it is impossible to say whether faith in God or Garvey's prophetic mantle saved the poet from his despair. His rejection of suicide is not outspokenly based on either of the two. But it is crucial that the Gordian knot of shame has not been severed. If the poet grudgingly accepts life it is because, when all is said and done, he is suspended between shame at his color and shame at the notion of betraying it:

> Lord, not for what I saw in flesh or bone
> Of fairer men; not raised on faith alone;
> Lord, I will live persuaded by mine own.
> I cannot play the recreant to these;
> My spirit has come home, that sailed the doubtful seas.[61]

The last line voices as a certitude what is in reality no more than a great illusion. The poet's soul has not been definitively purged of its hostility toward God, and both his oneness with his own people and his nay-saying to death as liberator will be called once again into question.[62]

Pride as Solace

Cullen's self-deception is linked, in fact, with the psychological value of the hypothesized act of self-slaughter. For suicide, in his mind, is not only a means of attaining forgetfulness; it is also a manifestation of his pride,

59 *Ibid.*, lines 149-67, pp. 33-34.
60 *Ibid.*, lines 176-80, p. 34.
61 *Ibid.*, lines 182-86.
62 See below the citation from "Mood" (1929).

a means of haughtily refusing communion with the people among whom
destiny has set him but whom he fundamentally despises.

> I think an impulse stronger than my mind
> May some day grasp a knife, unloose a vial,
> Or with a little leaden ball unbind
> The cords that tie me to the rank and file.[63]

If dreams of suicide may be attributed to pride, this clearly can only be the
pride of a powerless man who, confronting the actual spectacle of his
powerlessness and bafflement, attempts to lull himself and — at least in his
own imagination — the world in the supreme illusion that he has retained
the key to power:

> But when I will, World, I can go,
> Though triple bronze[64] should wall me round,
>
> .   .   .   .
>
> Within myself is lodged the key
> To that vast room of couches laid
> For those too proud to live and see
> Their dreams of light eclipsed in shade.[65]

But feelings are not in every instance what they appear to be, since transmutation into their own opposites can easily occur. La Rochefoucauld,
who had already noted this instability of the passions,[66] is less bold when
it comes to pride: "It seems that nature, which so wisely situated the
organs of our body to ensure our happiness, also endowed us with pride
so that we might be spared the distress of recognizing our imperfections."[67]
We would gladly go even further than this, affirming that pride and shame,
which are supposed to be antithetical, may simply constitute two aspects
of the same feeling. When Cullen imagines how death would separate him
from the common herd, he may be exhibiting pride, but he also confesses
his shame at being associated with it. And who could say, when he asserts

[63] "Mood," lines 1-4, *The Black Christ,* p. 17.
[64] "Bronze" has often been used as an equivalent for "black" or "Negro." Thus
the Associates in Negro Folk Education, Washington, D.C., published before World
War II a "Bronze Booklet" series, containing various informational pamphlets that
sought to spread a knowledge of Negro culture. In Cullen's lines, the prison constructed of triple bronze is, therefore, that in which he is enclosed by color.
[65] "Harsh World That Lashest Me," stanza 4, *Color,* p. 107.
[66] "The passions often give rise to others that are their own opposites. Avarice
sometimes produces prodigality, and prodigality avarice; one is often resolute out
of weakness and bold because of timidity." (François de La Rochefoucauld,
Maximes, suivies des réflexions diverses [Paris, 1935], p. 72; or see *Réflexions
morales,* XI.)
[67] *Ibid.,* XXXVI.

that he could not survive the collapse of what he calls his dream, whether the decisive factor is too much pride or an excess of shame?

For pride, in Cullen's case, is not a natural, spontaneous movement, the driving force of the whole personality, as it is with McKay. Rather, it is the equivalent of an attitude carefully formulated to disguise an instinctive self-contempt. Thus it becomes at the same time a mask and a kind of discipline. This phenomenon is submitted to a clear analysis in a sonnet written after the breakdown of the poet's marriage with Yolande:

> Be with me, Pride; now Love is gone, stay by;
> Let me nought hear but your metallic tone,
> With nothing gaze but your unflinching eye.
> Uplift me, Pride; compel the listless bone,
> The inert hand, the brain that still would think
> Upon its hurt, and most on that which gave
> The wound; be my clear fountain whence I drink
> Travail and toil from now until the grave.
> Cling to me, leeches pinned on either hand,
> As to a horse the reins he cannot shake,
> Which bid him go, and go he must; or stand,
> And though he strive there is no step to take.
> Be stronger than this heart . . .[68]

Whether seen as leeches attached to his hands in order to hinder their movements or as reins laid upon him as a constraint thwarting the spontaneity of his nature, pride, within Cullen's deepest being, is still a foreign element that has been deliberately imposed on his true personality. Thus, whenever we see him make a display of racial pride, we can never shake off a lingering doubt as to the validity and substantiality of such a pride which, in the last analysis, might be no more than a mask presented to the world outside.

3. RACE AND THE AFRICAN HOMELAND

As is true also for his personality, no aspect of Cullen's work can be considered entirely apart from the datum of color. Even when not directly arising from color, his emotional states are affected by its repercussions and, in their turn, they influence the potentialities of his racial consciousness. In his poetic thinking the very Divinity moves from black to white and back again in an utterly natural anthropomorphism, so revealing the close interdependence of racial consciousness and religious feeling. Conse-

[68] "Sonnet," *The Medea,* p. 89. See, too, his epitaph "For Myself," lines 3-4, *Color,* p. 72.

quently, in a totality each of whose elements is so inextricably interwoven with every other element, it is particularly difficult to satisfy the requirements of clarity in analysis by determining the main lines of articulation, without at the same time cutting into and distorting the living material.

In the preceding pages, we have already endeavored to disengage the psychic substratum from this totality. But the goal could be achieved only by allowing, despite ourselves, the spiritual and racial factors to have their say. It will prove equally impossible entirely to demarcate the racial and religious themes, or even to deal with them without referring once more to the dictates of the psyche. Thus, before setting out in the infinitely complex universe of the reverberations of color, we may more prudently examine first the relation of race to the other elements with which it necessarily coexists.

Race in Cullen's Poetic Universe

An examination of the tendencies manifested in the evolution of his poetic themes enables one to distinguish, in Cullen's work, two different periods marked off by the moment of reassessment represented in his life by the year 1927.

In his inner development, the primacy of race is scarcely noticeable after an early extroverted phase,[69] during which his behavior tended to seek an adjustment to the surrounding environment. This reaction to racial tensions is an instinctive phenomenon, on a par with the attitude of most of his racial brothers. There is no point in looking elsewhere for any deeper reason that would explain the success of *Color* (1925) from the moment of its publication. When he sang of the burden of color and of its nobility,

> ... I ... whose fount of pride,
> Dear distress, and joy allied,
> Is my somber flesh and skin,
> With the dark blood dammed within
> Like great pulsing tides ...[70]

and above all when he nostalgically evoked the memory of the African homeland, black America had no difficulty in recognizing its own states of soul in those of the poet. Through the voice of this young black bard of twenty-two, the whole black race was expressing itself. "A poet for the

---

[69] "The *extraverts* are attuned to objective realities, exteriorize their reactions and orient their behavior in the direction of adjustment to the environment, while the *introverts* practice interiorization and take refuge in autism" (Porot et al., "Extraversion," *Manuel*).

[70] "Heritage," lines 23-27, *Color*, p. 37.

Negro race!" exclaimed Eric Walrond, convinced that "dissecting the cosmos of the Negro spirit is Countee Cullen's ultimate concern."[71] But this was only a fraction of the truth, no doubt the most alluring, but for the poet not the most vital. It won over black opinion for the poet, whose themes were found entrancing but which, in terms of their real significance in Cullen's poetic universe, were misunderstood. For all his glorification of the African heritage, and despite the superiority he claimed for black over white — did this justify the extrapolation that made of him the spokesman of the black race? At least one attentive reader of *Color* replied in the negative. With greater acumen than Eric Walrond, doubtless because she was aided by her twin intuitions as a woman and as a poet, Babette Deutsch instinctively laid her finger on the true center of gravity of Cullen's poetic universe when, in a diagnosis as precocious as it was insightful, she ventured the opinion that "the color of his mind is more important than the color of his skin."[72] Cullen's subsequent career as a poet demonstrated in countless ways that she was right.

Despite surface appearances, his racial experience was indeed but one factor in what might be called his problem, and the basic urge behind his poetry must be sought in his scruples of conscience. This is what Arna Bontemps was saying when he declared, somewhat bluntly, that "Cullen was a worrier."[73] Even while Cullen was exploring the dimensions of his color, there occurred an imperceptible shift in its value. Its significance, which had been a collective one, now shrank until it corresponded to the limits of the poet's individual consciousness. As the demands of the spirit grew more insistent, color itself became spiritualized and amounted, in the end, to no more than an array of symbols that swirled around Cullen's reflections on his destiny.

This tenuous thread of symbolism, whose purely inner relevancy was not at first appreciated, enabled the racial community to maintain for some time longer the illusion that, through a shared loyalty to color, it was in communication with the poet. But they were no longer speaking a common language. The poet's eyes, raised above the contingency of race, were already turned toward the Creator who bore the ultimate responsibility and to whom he, the black poet-prophet, sought to lead his whole people. Unfortunately, his own followed him not on the rugged paths of the spirit. Little by little, a gulf widened between them and him, so that

[71] Eric Walrond, "A Poet for the Negro Race," *New Republic,* March 31, 1926, p. 179.

[72] Babette Deutsch, "Let It Be Allowed," *Nation,* December 30, 1925, p. 764.

[73] Bontemps, "The Harlem Renaissance," *Saturday Review,* March 22, 1947, p. 12.

the poet found himself a stranger in the midst of his own people. His lonely itinerary to the heights then became an actual Calvary on whose summit he, like another Christ, was crucified between the exigencies of his color and his loyalty to his individual ideal:

> A hungry cancer will not let him rest
> Whose heart is loyal to the least of dreams;
> There is a thorn forever in his breast
> Who cannot take this world for what it seems;
> Aloof and lonely must he ever walk,
> Plying a strange and unaccustomed tongue,
> An alien to the daily round of talk,
> Mute when the sordid songs of earth are sung.
>
> This is the certain end his dream achieves:
> He sweats his blood and prayers while others sleep,
> And shoulders his own coffin up a steep
> Immortal mountain, there to meet his doom
> Between two wretched dying men, of whom
> One doubts, and one for pity's sake believes.[74]

Thus the first period is followed by one characterized by introversion,[75] during which Cullen retreats ever further within himself. He has not severed all contacts with the external world, but this world is ever more often experienced as a cause of suffering for which he seeks a balm in his mystic dialogue with Christ.

It need scarcely be said that there is no absolute rupture between these two phases of his inner development. The last echoes of the African theme still resound faintly in the 1929 volume, and the colloquy with Christ had been inaugurated in *Color*. From one end of his work to the other, and more markedly than in the case of any other black poet, color and spirituality are inextricably intertwined. But as the former loses im-

[74] "A Thorn Forever in the Breast," *The Black Christ,* p. 39. The following note will also help to explain this sonnet.

[75] T. Kammerer describes introversion, or autism, in this interesting way, which may well throw a singular light on this period in Cullen's life: "Polarization of the subject's entire mental life around his inner world, with loss of contact with the exterior world. The patient lives with the intimate world of his desires, his anxieties, his sensibility, and his imagination — which, for him, are the only realities. The external world is but an appearance or, at least, a world that cannot possibly interact with his own world. Because of this attitude, the patient becomes utterly opaque and his behavior incomprehensible. In the less pronounced forms, contacts are still possible between the inner and outer worlds, but the patient is distressed by his inability to exteriorize his sensibility in appropriate expressions and, on the other hand, the external world constantly hurts him and forces him to shut himself up in his ivory tower" (in Porot et al., "Autisme," *Manuel*).

portance, his spiritual preoccupations take on ever clearer shape and soon outrank all else.

It is a change of course that happens rather early in the poet's career, and by the time *Copper Sun* was published in 1927 it may be considered an established fact. The critics were quite taken aback by that volume. Meeting with hardly any of the racial hyperboles they had noted in *Color,* they reached the conclusion, as we have seen, that the writer "has borrowed the temperament of his poems,"[76] and that his verse no longer had its source in his own inner experience. In a word, the blunt indictment was that his lines lacked sincerity.

In part in order to answer these critics — but also, assuredly, because he was trying to obtain a clearer view of his own inner self — Cullen in that same year repeatedly published rectifications concerning both his general conception of the part that should be played by the Negro poet and the actual hidden sources of his own inspiration. Such declarations, of which the essential is reprinted in his anthology *Caroling Dusk* (1927), unavoidably were treated in the black world as somewhat scandalous. They not only clashed head on with generally accepted opinions but also permitted the surmise that Cullen, as he tried to clarify attitudes hitherto left vague, was at the same time intent on establishing his distance from, and on making himself more or less independent of, the racial community to which he belonged.

Taking issue with the standpoint of James Weldon Johnson who, in 1922, had called his anthology *The Book of American Negro Poetry,* Cullen denied that one could speak of an American Negro poetry. He puts it this way, in his preface for *Caroling Dusk:*

> I have called this collection an anthology of verse by Negro poets rather than an anthology of Negro verse, since this latter designation would be more confusing than accurate. Negro poetry, it seems to me, in the sense that we speak of Russian, French, or Chinese poetry, must emanate from some country other than this in some language other than our own. Moreover, the attempt to corral the outbursts of the ebony muse into some definite mold to which all poetry by Negroes will conform seems altogether futile and aside from the facts. This country's Negro writers may here and there turn some singular facet toward the literary sun, but in the main, since theirs is also the heritage of the English language, their work will not present any serious aberration from the poetic tendencies of their times. The conservatives, the middlers, and the arch heretics will be found among them as among the white poets; and to say that the pulse beat of their verse shows generally such a fever, or the symptoms of such an ague, will

---

[76] See note 35 above.

prove on closer examination merely the moment's exaggeration of a physician anxious to establish a new literary ailment. As heretical as it may sound, there is the probability that Negro poets, dependent as they are on the English language, may have more to gain from the rich background of English and American poetry than from any nebulous atavistic yearnings toward an African inheritance.[77]

This line of argument is undeniably specious and, as Saunders Redding pertinently remarked, "The answer to all this seems to be: Chinese poetry translated into English remains Chinese poetry — Chinese in feeling, in ideas."[78] The essential weakness of Cullen's definition lies in its total (and doubtless deliberate) failure to recognize social realities. Also, if it was a vain decree that sought to constrain all poetry written by Negroes within a single mold, it was no less unrealistic to require the Negro poet to neglect utterly the racial context that conditioned every instant of his existence as a human being, and to suppose that he could derive sustenance exclusively from the Anglo-Saxon cultural past in which, both *de facto* and *de jure*, his share had always been a limited one. In keeping with the example of W. S. Braithwaite's poetry — it is noteworthy that *Caroling Dusk* is dedicated to him — the poetry that Cullen envisages could be written only within the confines of an ivory tower,[79] and by a poet disincarnate, lacking all sense of solidarity with his racial group, and who had deliberately cast off the contingency of his color. And this, indeed, is what Countee Cullen wanted to be and do.

At the time of the publication of *Copper Sun*, he made what amounted to the declaration that racial feeling was a close-to-spontaneous element in his poetry: "Most things I write, I do for the sheer love of the music in them. Somehow or other, however, I find my poetry of itself treating of the Negro, of his joys and his sorrows — mostly of the latter, and of the heights and depths of emotion which I feel as a Negro."[80] A little later that same year, however, he said to a journalist from the *New York World*: "I want to be known as a poet, not as a Negro poet."[81] He returns to the charge in *Caroling Dusk,* where he says, in direct reference to himself: "He has said perhaps with a reiteration sickening to some of his friends, that he wishes any merit that may be in his work to flow from it solely as the expression of a poet — with no racial consideration to bolster it up. He is still of the same thought."[82] This wealth of detail inevitably turns our

---

[77] *Caroling Dusk,* p. xi.
[78] Redding, *To Make a Poet Black,* p. 110.
[79] See note 75 above, end of quotation from Kammerer.
[80] Statement printed on the back inner flap of the dust jacket for *Copper Sun.*
[81] Cited in *The Light* (Chicago), September 24, 1927, p. 12.
[82] P. 180.

thoughts to Dunbar. He, as it happens, is the only black celebrity to whom Cullen ever devoted a poem,[83] and perhaps it is permissible to see in this the avowal of an affinity with a kindred personality. The two poets did not find themselves in even remotely similar situations. In origins and education Dunbar was of the people, to whom he allotted an important place in his poetry. But he would have wished this part of his achievement to be considered minor compared to the other part, from which the people and their language were both excluded.

Cullen is already a much more characteristic product of the black bourgeoisie, having been exposed to all its pressures as he grew up in the Harlem home of a Methodist minister. The whole course of his education took place in schools and universities with a majority of whites, and theirs were the standards and prejudices he unconsciously absorbed. He had scarcely any close associations with the people of his own race, and he had no sense of communion with them. The people, as a result, make no genuine contribution to his work in verse, and popular Negro themes and forms are entirely absent from it.[84]

It would even seem that Cullen always sensed the existence of some incompatibility between restrictions of any kind that might be imposed on the poet because of his color, and the universality that is the distinguishing mark of poetry. Perhaps, indeed, one should find much more than a mere quip in the final couplet of the sonnet, described by James Weldon Johnson as "the two most poignant lines in American literature":[85]

> I doubt not God is good, well-meaning, kind,
> And did He stoop to quibble could tell why
> The little buried mole continues blind,
> Why flesh that mirrors Him must some day die,
> Make plain the reason tortured Tantalus
> Is baited by the fickle fruit, declare
> If merely brute caprice dooms Sisyphus
> To struggle up a never-ending stair.
> Inscrutable His ways are, and immune
> To catechism by a mind too strewn
> With petty cares to slightly understand
> What awful brain compels His awful hand.
> Yet do I marvel at this curious thing:
> To make a poet black, and bid him sing![86]

[83] Epitaph "For Paul Laurence Dunbar," *Color*, p. 70.
[84] It does not seem possible, in fact, to treat "The Ballad of the Brown Girl" as a Negro ballad. See the discussion of this poem below.
[85] Johnson, *Book of American Negro Poetry*, p. 220.
[86] "Yet Do I Marvel," *Color*, p. 3.

In any event, up to the very end Cullen will maintain his determination to be independent of his racial group, even at the risk of being called a traitor by his own:

> Then call me traitor if you must,
> Shout treason and default!
>
> . . . .
>
> I'll bear your censure as your praise,
> For never shall the clan
> Confine my singing . . .
> How shall the shepherd heart then thrill
> To only the darker lamb?[87]

However, the distance that his haughty attitude and contempt for his color induced him to observe with respect to his people does not appear to have exerted on his muse the beneficial effects he had anticipated. The illusory independence thus won bears a much closer resemblance to isolation within which his inspiration, tragically cut off from the only sources that could provide fulfillment, was doomed to a premature sterility.

A Black among Whites

It was this isolation, as much as his unstable, tormented personality, that made him an ambiguous personage lingering on the immaterial frontier that separates the two races. He could not move to a forthright identification with one or the other, rather like the near-whites whose anguish he depicted in one quatrain:

> Ambiguous of race they stand,
> By one disowned, scorned of another,
> Not knowing where to stretch a hand,
> And cry, "My sister" or "My brother."[88]

If his color had permitted it,[89] who knows whether he too might not have been tempted by the experience of those who, relying on their almost white complexions, cross the racial frontier and go off to live as unsuspected immigrants amid the racial majority, where they find equality and forgetfulness of the past? The twin poems of "Two Who Crossed a Line" deal with this subject. "He Crosses"[90] presents the crossing of the racial frontier as a punitive expedition as well as a youthful escapade, since the

[87] "To Certain Critics," *The Black Christ*, p. 63.
[88] "Near White," *Color*, p. 11.
[89] Cullen was very dark-skinned.
[90] "Two Who Crossed a Line (He Crosses)," *Color*, p. 17.

young black in the poem, after sowing havoc far and near in the hearts of the white belles, and savoring alike the delights of vengeance and those of the forbidden fruit, prudently returns to his base, filled with contempt for his victims.

This poem's presentation of the problem of "passing" is curiously optimistic, however, and should perhaps be regarded as an act of wishful thinking or of braggadocio on Cullen's part. By relating imaginary erotic exploits he would, in this interpretation, have sought compensation for his inability to carry them out in the real world, even on less spectacular lines.

Altogether more tragic is the case of the heroine in "She Crosses,"[91] her psychological torments being subjected to a much more subtle and plausible examination. It is with a much heavier heart that she crosses the fatal line, and those close to her, as they watch her depart, are torn between condemnation and the desire to do likewise. She too comes back — but vanquished, not victorious, and with the fruit of an ephemeral liaison in her arms. Her face bears the traces of her disillusionment and shame at having served as a mere plaything and victim in the white world.

Quite remarkable in "She Crosses" is the discretion with which Cullen suggests rather than depicts the frustration that has beset this human creature. The white world, too, is barely present in this drama in which it is nevertheless a protagonist — and, whatever condemnation it may deserve, this remains implicit, the poet letting the reader formulate it as he chooses.

Only rarely does one observe Cullen in a frontal attack against white America. A rebellious stance would not have been in keeping with his temperament, and to the extent that some of his poems may be interpreted as protests, the method employed is usually an indirect one.[92] Because of the primacy he attributes to the spiritual, he more often chooses to address his plaints to the Creator, not to the creature. Besides, experience had taught him that nothing good can come of a dialogue with people whose passions and prejudices have blinded them, and that the simple demonstration that he was their equal would not prevent their continuing to look on him as an inferior.[93]

It follows from all this that the crass details of the incidents through which race prejudice was expressed did not occupy the central place in

---

91 "Two Who Crossed a Line (She Crosses)," *ibid.*, p. 16.
92 With the possible exception of "Scottsboro, Too, Is Worth a Song," *The Medea*, p. 96.
93 "To My Fairer Brethren," *Color*, p. 23.

his work, and that it was not his main concern to paint the portrait of racist America. This entity most often lurks in the shadows, and its presence is to be divined only by contemplating the sufferings it inflicts on the soul of the poet. He will convey to us nothing of those before he has first worked out the symbols that correspond to them. Cullen is sensitive to their reverberations above all — and this reaches beyond the superficial wounds caused by the evil of race prejudice — in the very roots of his being, which are the center from which his song most readily soars upward:

> If for a day joy masters me,
> Think not my wounds are healed;
> Far deeper than the scars you see,
> I keep the roots concealed.
>
> They shall bear blossoms with the fall;
> I have their word for this,
> Who tend my roots with rains of gall,
> And suns of prejudice.[94]

Yet there are several poems in which Cullen tackles more directly, and occasionally quite concretely, some features of the poisoned atmosphere that presides over relations between the races.

One of the earliest is "The Ballad of the Brown Girl,"[95] a narrative poem of more than two hundred lines, subtitled "An Old Ballad Retold." If the poem's prefatory remarks may be believed, the legend sprang up in Kentucky:

> Oh, this is the tale the grandams tell
> In the land where the grass is blue,
> And some there are who say 'tis false,
> And some that hold it true.[96]

However that may be, the setting is undoubtedly the South. Young Lord Thomas, who is loved by a white girl and a brown but reciprocates only the love of the former, nevertheless unwillingly agrees, under the influence of his mother, to marry the latter for her acres and her gold, despite the slur that besmirches the race of this girl without a name:

> She is the dark Brown Girl who knows
> No more-defining name,

[94] "Confession," *Copper Sun*, p. 8.
[95] This poem is available both as a separate pamphlet (1927) and in *On These I Stand*, pp. 175-82. Since the latter publication is more widely distributed, all references are to it. The poem had previously appeared in the *Pittsburgh Courier*, December 5, 1923, signed "Countee P. Cullen."
[96] Stanza 1, *On These I Stand*, p. 175.

> And bitter tongues have worn their tips
> In sneering at her shame.[97]

The white, by way of contrast, is the prototype of the Anglo-Saxon girl whose purity the laws of the South are designed to shield:

> ... lily maid,
> And pride of all the south.[98]

When she suddenly appears as an uninvited guest at the wedding feast, Lord Thomas greets her all the same and seats her beside him. However, instead of drinking to the health of bride and groom from the cup of wine he has offered her, she dashes it to the ground and censures Lord Thomas's choice:

> I came to see your bonny bride,
> I came to wish you well.
>
> .   .   .   .   .
>
> But, Thomas, Lord, is this your bride?
> I think she's mighty brown;
> Why didn't you marry a fair, bright girl
> As ever the sun shone on?
> For only the rose and the rose should mate,
> Oh, never the hare and the hound,[99]

This condemnation of interracial marriage is also a slight directed against the race and person of the young bride, and she demands reparation. When Lord Thomas hesitates to avenge her, she pulls out a dagger and stabs her rival to death, whereupon she herself is slaughtered by none other than Lord Thomas. The drama is concluded when he, stricken by insanity, takes his own life.

We have not taken the necessary steps to discover whether the origin of this tale indeed corresponds to the account given by Cullen, nor can we state that he has passed it on unchanged. But if the poem should be the reworking of a popular ballad, one feels almost authorized to declare that this must have been rather clumsily adapted by Cullen, who was barely twenty years old at the time of the poem's composition.

There are, actually, reasons to believe that the brown girl of the original ballad had brown hair only and that it was Cullen who burnished her skin, thus transforming a popular ballad into a poem with racial content.

The first argument in favor of this thesis is the implausibility of the in-

---

[97] Stanza 9, *ibid.*, p. 176.
[98] Stanza 4, *ibid.*, p. 175.
[99] Stanzas 25-27, *ibid.*, pp. 178-79.

gredients. One may overlook the title borne by the protagonist, since this
is not a historical impossibility and is, perhaps, called for by the archaic
nature of the ballad. There were, too, even prior to Emancipation, persons
of color who were free and in possession of considerable fortunes. But it
would be utterly deviant for the son of a prominent family to marry, in
a southern region and with all pomp and ceremony, a girl not of his own
race, and it is difficult to conceive how a popular ballad could crystallize
around such a forbidden theme. But Cullen's inadequate craftsmanship is
most clearly evidenced by his failure — once the element of race rivalry
has been introduced into the poem — to do anything with the situation
so created. For it is not the brown girl's race that constitutes the crux of
the matter but the fact that Lord Thomas, out of deference to his mother's
wishes and for purely material reasons, made a loveless marriage. This
blemish is particularly visible in the poem's moral, which could have remained unaltered if the heroines of the poem had both been white:

> O lovers, never barter love
> For gold or fertile lands,
> For love is meat and love is drink,
> And love heeds love's commands.[100]

Ultimately, one thing saves "The Ballad of the Brown Girl" and makes
it a rather successful poem. This is the art that Cullen displays in his
diction and in the rhythm and sonority of his lines, and also the skill with
which he captures the atmosphere so typical of the popular ballad of
other days.

But white America makes its presence felt more plausibly in such poems
as "Incident" and "Tableau," both of which deal with a black boy and a
white boy and lend concrete expression to the joint massiveness and flim-
siness of the wall which racial prejudice interposes between men of a different color. The first poem directs our attention to the ease with which
a child becomes imbued with the prejudices of his elders, while the second
stresses the forces of renewal that dwell within the freshness, purity, and
innocence of the child, against which the outmoded hatreds of adults will
one day find themselves powerless. "Incident," which is presented as the
poet's personal recollection, also insists upon the violent impact made upon
a child's consciousness by the hate-inspired insult, especially when this insult comes from the lips of another child and has been provoked by nothing
more than a smile, the universal gesture of brotherhood:

> Once riding in old Baltimore,
> Heart-filled, head-filled with glee,

[100] Stanza 42, *ibid.*, p. 181.

I saw a Baltimorean
Keep looking straight at me.

Now I was eight and very small,
And he was no whit bigger,
And so I smiled, but he poked out
His tongue, and called me, "Nigger."

I saw the whole of Baltimore
From May until December;
Of all the things that happened there
That's all that I remember.[101]

While these lines succinctly convey the past or present state of race relations, "Tableau" harbors the seed of a more brotherly future which will eliminate the fear that hides behind lowered shades and the racists' hypocritical expressions of indignation — of a future in which white and black will be as inseparably related as are lightning and thunder:

Locked arm in arm they cross the way,
The black boy and the white,
The golden splendor of the day,
The sable pride of night.

From lowered blinds the dark folk stare,
And here the fair folk talk,
Indignant that these two should dare
In unison to walk.

Oblivious to look and word
They pass, and see no wonder
That lightning brilliant as a sword
Should blaze the path of thunder.[102]

The same faith in a more equitable future finds expression in the sonnet "From the Dark Tower,"[103] where protest against the limits imposed on black destiny ends on a hopeful note: the day will come when blacks and whites will come to realize that they are destined not to oppose but to unite and complement each other, as the shades of night and the brilliance of the stars unite to form a whole.

Until that day, however, the superiority of white men is engraved like a national dogma across daily existence. When Uncle Jim, his philosophy deepened by long years of experience, declares that "white folks is white," only a giddy stripling could treat the remark as a tautology:

[101] "Incident," *Color*, p. 15.
[102] "Tableau," *ibid.*, p. 12.
[103] *Copper Sun*, p. 3.

314 Black Poets of the United States

> "White folks is white," says uncle Jim;
> "A platitude," I sneer;
> And then I tell him so is milk,
> And the froth upon his beer.
>
> His heart walled up with bitterness,
> He smokes his pungent pipe,
> And nods at me as if to say,
> "Young fool, you'll soon be ripe!"[104]

Racial inequality has consequences that can be seen implanted in the flesh of a black girl who ruined her hands working for white people:

> ... fevered blisters
> Made her dark hands run,
> While her favored, fairer sisters
> Neither wrought nor spun ...[105]

But it is not forbidden to laugh up one's sleeve at times at the vaunted superiority of the whites, and when Cullen writes, before the occasion has arrived, the epitaph of a white lady of his acquaintance, he takes a discreet pleasure in imagining the shock her naïve presumptions will meet with, the day she enters Paradise:

> She even thinks that up in heaven
> Her class lies late and snores,
> While poor black cherubs rise at seven
> To do celestial chores.[106]

But humor is only one safety valve for the hatred and frustration that well up within the heart, and the people evoked in the poem "Harlem Wine"[107] find in song, dance, and jazz an opiate that allows consoling dreams to arise, or a drunkenness that allows one to forget.

The only thought of Cullen himself was to escape the sufferings inflicted on him by a stepmotherly America, especially after he had discovered in France access to all that was denied him in his own land. In two sonnets, which are among the most beautiful he ever wrote, he expresses his gratitude to France for the delights of the freedom he could savor there. Here is the sextet of the first sonnet:

> As he whose eyes are gouged craves light to see,
> And he whose limbs are broken strength to run,
> So have I sought in you that alchemy

---

[104] "Uncle Jim," stanzas 1 and 2, *ibid.*, p. 9.
[105] "Threnody for a Brown Girl," stanza 6, *ibid.*, p. 5.
[106] Epitaph "For a Lady I Know," *Color*, p. 50.
[107] "Harlem Wine," *ibid.*, p. 13.

That knits my bones and turns me to the sun;
And found across a continent of foam
What was denied my hungry heart at home.[108]

The second finds terms perhaps even more poignant to express how precious a gift freedom is for a man long deprived of it:

I have a dream of where (when I grow old,
Having no further joy to take in lip
Or limb, a graybeard caching from the cold
The frail indignity of age) some ship
Might bear my creaking, unhinged bones
Trailing remembrance as a tattered cloak,
And beach me glad, though on their sharpest stones
Among a fair and kindly folk.

There might I only breathe my latest days,
With those rich accents falling on my ear
That most have made me feel that freedom's rays
Still have a shrine where they may leap and sear, —
Though I were palsied there, or halt, or blind,
So I were there, I think I should not mind.[109]

But even before he had discovered France and made it his second country, the urge to escape that was born of pain and frustration had already turned him, like millions of his racial brothers electrified by Garvey's preachments, toward the mirage of another substitute fatherland, Africa.

Garvey and the African Heritage

No one placed a literal interpretation on Garvey's crusading speeches that called for a return to the African homeland; few blacks understood his message as a summons to actual emigration. But his African mystique acted on all of them as an extraordinary stimulus to their racial pride. With his spectacular orchestration of this one fundamental idea, he convinced them of the greatness of the land of their ancestors, conjuring up a vision of the glorious past that had preceded slavery, whose shameful inner stain he exhorted them to expunge instantly.

Cullen was a psychically tormented young man during the period when Garvey ruled over Harlem, and he could not possibly have withstood the seductiveness of the black Moses.[110] No one sensed more acutely than he the need to vanquish his feelings of shame at his origins and his color.

---

[108] "To France," *The Medea*, p. 74.
[109] *Ibid.*, p. 91.
[110] *Black Moses* is the title of a book by E. David Cronon on Garvey (1955).

And, in truth, his poetry most strikingly echoes the less rational aspects of
Garvey's ideology, the proclamation of the natural nobility of Africa and
the Africans and of blacks' superiority over whites, and the Negrification
of the Divinity.[111]

Cullen, who because of his color felt himself to be dust beneath the
white man's heel, proceeded to create for himself and his scorned black
brethren a royal and even imperial African ancestry. In "The Ballad of
the Brown Girl," the brown-skinned girl comes to Lord Thomas on their
wedding day as might a queen, bedecked with jewels:

> The Brown girl came to him as might
> A queen to take her crown;
> With gems her fingers flamed and flared,
> Her robe was weighted down.[112]

When her defeated rival, the blond London, appears at the marriage feast
and insults her in the hearing of all the guests, she, queenlike, can hold in
check the anger that makes her blood boil.[113] But like a queen, too, she
demands satisfaction for the slur on her honor, and when Lord Thomas
hesitates to comply she herself avenges the insult, using an African dagger
she had been wearing in the guise of a diadem. Legend had it that in olden
times a black queen who had loved in vain had killed herself with it.[114]

Musing on Africa, Cullen was happy to find in his distant forebears a
nobility that gave the lie to the inferiority that was his in America:

> ... regal black
> Women from whose loins I sprang
> When the birds of Eden sang...[115]

For him who has eyes to see, this nobility still lives on in the haughty
carriage of members of the race, for instance, in that of a character in
"The Black Christ":

[111] Cullen certainly heard Garvey speak on one or more occasions, and Garvey
may even have been invited by the Rev. Cullen to speak in the Salem Methodist
Episcopal Church. In any case, Arna Bontemps has told us that he remembers
going one evening with Cullen to a lecture given in the church by another "black
prophet," George Wilson Becton, who, following on Garvey, fascinated the black
masses. It was the custom to listen to these preachings as though they were a performance, "a good show," as Bontemps puts it. Langston Hughes, who was also
present that evening, records his impressions in *The Big Sea*, pp. 275-78. See also
Claude McKay, *Harlem, Negro Metropolis*, pp. 83-85.
[112] Stanza 14, *On These I Stand*, p. 177.
[113] Stanza 29, *ibid*., p. 179.
[114] Stanzas 31 and 32, *ibid*., pp. 179-80.
[115] "Heritage," lines 4-6, *Color*, p. 36.

Jim's bearing spoke his imperial breed.[116]

Like a flash of lightning, it can be sensed traversing the body of a beautiful black girl with the gait of a queen:

> That brown girl's swagger gives a twitch
> To beauty like a queen.[117]

Even when white shopkeepers make fun of a fat, ugly black woman by poising on her head an unbecoming red hat, she still radiates her innate nobility:

> She went to buy a brand new hat,
> And she was ugly black and fat:
> "This red becomes you well," they said,
> And perched it high upon her head,
> And then they laughed behind her back
> To see it glow against the black.
> She paid for it with regal mien
> And walked out proud as any queen.[118]

This royal African blood, furthermore, had already given new black monarchs to the New World: Toussaint L'Ouverture was governor general, Dessalines was emperor, Christophe was king of Haiti. For his own benefit, but also for that of his whole race without even omitting black ragamuffins and hobos, Cullen sees in the glorious example of these "black majesties" a cause for pride and a hope for the future:

> "Lo, I am dark, but comely," Sheba sings.
> "And we were black," three shades reply, "but kings."[119]

The African heritage is not the preserve of a privileged few, for each and every one shares in it, in his humble way. The waiter in the Atlantic City hotel derives the grace and agility of his movements from the jungle,[120] as he does the pride that shines out beneath the mask of obsequious humility imposed by his occupation. But the women guests who linger for a moment to look at him may not realize, perhaps, that it is the blazing ardor of the African jungle that has taken on new life before their astonished gaze.

Atavistically African, too, is the gift of singing one's grief with all the

[116] "The Black Christ," line 274, *The Black Christ*, p. 80.
[117] "To a Brown Boy," *Color*, p. 8.
[118] "Colors (Red)," *Copper Sun*, p. 11.
[119] "Black Majesty," *The Black Christ*, p. 64.
[120] "Atlantic City Waiter," stanzas 1, 2, and 4, *Color*, p. 10.

moving profundity of the blues singer, to whom Cullen addresses these lines:

> You make your grief a melody
> And take it by the hand.
>
> Such songs the mellow-bosomed maids
> Of Africa intone
> For lovers dead in hidden glades.[121]

But black nationalism was not satisfied with the mere reminder that the black race also had its nobility. Fully to restore the balance after so many centuries of white hegemony, it was now essential to proclaim the superiority of black over white, and more especially the greater beauty of black women.

> They are much more beautiful, judging them by every physical measure that might be applied. They are better formed, of better carriage and fuller of life and female vanity. As a rule they are never ungracious. Negroes have not realized this fact, merely because they have had instilled into them for centuries the false doctrine that that only is beautiful which is white.[122]

To judge by two poems with almost identical titles, Cullen too had a spell of enthusiasm for the thesis that black women are the more beautiful. "A Song of Praise" is dedicated to "one who praised his lady's being fair." He no doubt was member of the black bourgeoisie, where there is a tendency to chose a spouse lighter than oneself,[123] and even in exceptional cases to marry a woman entirely white by ancestry. This is not necessarily the situation here, but the adjective "fair" that Cullen uses could apply to either white or near-white. The fact remains that, in his rejoinder to this praise of whiteness, he sets out not only to eulogize black beauty, in which he once again discovers the pride and grace of Africa, but widens the gulf by reproving white girls for their apathy, the insipidity of their fair hair, and the coldness of their blood.[124]

In the second poem, "Song of Praise" (there is no article),[125] the argument is developed in much the same way but the conclusion is much more

[121] "Colored Blues Singer," stanza 2, lines 3-4, and stanza 3, lines 1-3, *Copper Sun*, p. 10.

[122] From an article by J. Griffith which appeared in *The Crusader* (New York), September, 1919. Cited in *Radicalism and Sedition among the Negroes as Reflected in Their Publications*, 66th Cong., 1st Sess., *Senate Documents*, vol. 12, Document no. 153, p. 166.

[123] See, for example, Gunnar Myrdal, *An American Dilemma*, p. 698.

[124] "A Song of Praise (For One Who Praised His Lady's Being Fair)," stanzas 2-5, *Color*, p. 4.

[125] *The Black Christ*, p. 66.

openly controversial, since the poem comes close to asserting roundly that the man who has never loved a black girl does not know love. We note, incidentally, that in a poem whose aim it is to glorify blackness, it may be a strategic blunder to borrow from white people the expression "black as sin," and this barely a few months after the Negro cultural magazine *Opportunity* had editorially congratulated itself on the steadily decreasing frequency of such malicious associations of ideas. The work of a number of black poets was cited as proof of this, but Cullen was not among them.[126]

The two poems do not go very far in attributing an unfavorable meaning to whiteness, and it would probably be a mistake to see anything more in them than indications of a not very highly evolved racial pride. But Cullen does not leave it at that. In the wake of Garvey who, pushing to the limit his vision of the world through black spectacles, had negrified God and his angels, Cullen also created a black Christ and took him as the theme of one of his most deeply meaningful religious poems.[127] By making Christ black he won over to his cause the highest moral authority and the most venerated spiritual tradition of the inimical world in which blacks, because of their deportation from Africa, were forced to live. Black, in this fashion, was equated with goodness, right, and justice, with innocence wrongly victimized and beauty unjustifiably spurned. On the opposing side, white became a synonym for evil, violence, and brutality, and also for hypocrisy, ugliness, and perversity.[128] It was synonymous, too, with betrayal, as is made apparent in this couplet in which Simon of Cyrene, in accord with a fashion that the Negro Renaissance favored, is also made black and contrasted with Simon Peter, who thrice denied his Master:

> Yea, he who helped Christ up Golgotha's track,
> That Simon who did *not* deny, was black.[129]

The defective scansion of the first line, which does violence to the normal accentuation of the word "Golgotha," in no way diminishes the effectiveness of the insinuation voiced here.

Yet Garvey's influence alone is not sufficient to account for the breadth of significance that Cullen found in the antithesis between black and white. These, quite beyond their aesthetic or emotional impact, also formed the system of opposite poles between which the poet's conscience oscillated,

---

[126] "Blackness and Whiteness," *Opportunity*, April, 1928, p. 100.
[127] For these poems, see our Sec. 4 below.
[128] For the meaning attributed to these colors by the white mind see, for example, Myrdal, *An American Dilemma*, p. 100.
[129] "Colors (Black) — 2 —," *Copper Sun*, p. 11.

when he quested for a meaning he could give his destiny. Later on we will see how these colors, while functioning within the framework of racial conflict, nevertheless acquire their fundamental significance only by transcending it. It is this symbolism of color that leads to the very heart of the spiritual conflict in which the poet, as a person, is involved.

Africa as a Pagan Symbol

Concerning this conflict, in 1927 Cullen made this centrally important declaration: "Countee Cullen's chief problem has been that of reconciling a Christian upbringing with a pagan inclination. His life so far has not convinced him that the problem is insoluble."[180] This "pagan inclination," as he calls it, is actually a composite of remarkably heterogeneous elements which his poetic imagination chose to assemble around the symbol of Africa. In other words, every antagonism on every conceivable plane undergoes a transmutation that finally equates it with the basic antagonism, black versus white. So powerful, indeed, are the emotions enlisted by the racial conflict that its terminology imposes itself on every other conflict. Thus, to the hostile white God who was responsible for letting the poet be born under the evil star of color, the embattled poet opposes the pagan gods of the African homeland. We will not run ahead of ourselves here to make a detailed study of the conflict, and at this stage will simply consider what these symbols, the black gods of pagan Africa, really stand for.

For here we are concerned with symbols, and not with any African reality. If "Heritage" did not strike so excellently qualifed an observer as Sterling Brown as being altogether convincing,[131] and if Saunders Redding, taking over a number of terms from the poem, could write that "he cannot beat the tom-tom above a faint whisper nor know the primitive delights of black rain and scarlet sun,"[132] the reason is that neither had grasped the essentially symbolic nature, and the entirely inner and personal meaning, of Cullen's Africa.

Cullen's paganism, like Claude McKay's, is almost devoid of positive content, since it is above all a withdrawal from God. But whereas McKay's estrangement is motivated by a kind of rationalist skepticism concerning the Christian revelation, Cullen's has a predominantly emotional base, namely, his resentment at the Creator's having shown an inadequate degree of solicitude for him and his fellows. In Cullen's attitude there is an embryonic rebelliousness, directed against God rather than

---

[180] *Caroling Dusk*, p. 179.

[131] " 'Heritage,' for all its color and facility, does not quite convince" (Sterling A. Brown, *Negro Poetry and Drama*, p. 71).

[132] Redding, *To Make a Poet Black*, p. 111.

against white America, the one being the equivalent, in the poet's mind, of the other. In this atmosphere of revolt, everything traditionally opposed to Christian spirituality is posited as a value and given a black exponent. It need scarcely be pointed out that such a table of values is primarily subjective in nature and that it mirrors various allurements felt by the poet, with their source lying either in his imagination or in his flesh.

His poetic imagination appears to have given rise most directly to Cullen's inclination, exhibited in his first two volumes, to present the soul as a migrant that could be reincarnated after death. This notion is sufficiently close to the metempsychosis of the ancients to justify our taking over that term, though the poet's fantasy delights at times in adorning the theme with personal variations, in particular by linking to it the idea of the Negro's happier previous existence in the terrestrial paradise of Africa before it came under slavery's yoke.

In an obituary poem for a young brown girl, "Threnody for a Brown Girl," the poet advises the bereaved family not to place a slab of white marble on her grave:

> Lay upon her no white stone
> From a foreign quarry.[133]

Quite certainly, this is something other than the simple question of the color of a memorial stone. The poet is trying to prevent the commission of a sacrilege, the crushing of the dead girl beneath a weight whose white color would be doubly alien to her. White, here, is the symbol of a commitment, of a racial and spiritual allegiance,[134] and the use of white would mean doing violence, in the first place, to the deeper meaning of the dead girl's existence. It would also be a proclamation of faith, on the part of the survivors, in an eternal destiny as it is preached by the white enemies, and thus it would be a tacit adherence to their conception of man's place, and more especially the black man's place, in the ordering of the universe. Rather than a Christian eternity for the dead girl, the poet envisages her reincarnation into a plant or an animal, perhaps even into the body of another human being. This enables him simultaneously to proclaim, on the basis of metempsychosis, the requirement of love for one's neighbor as well as of kindness toward animals:

> Crush no bug nor nauseous worm
> Lest you tread upon her.

[133] "Threnody for a Brown Girl," stanza 9, lines 5-6, *Copper Sun,* p. 6.
[134] For white as symbol of a hostile God see, for example, "Gods," stanza 3, lines 1-2, *Color,* p. 101.

> Pluck no flower lest she scream;
> Bruise no slender reed,
> Lest it prove more than it seem.[135]

Cullen had already presented, at the beginning of his first volume, the notion of the transmigration of the soul within a meditation on his own demise, but only as a possibility. Strangely, this did not preclude a vague recognition of the existence of God, referred to by Cullen as the "Cryptic One" who refuses to give any clarification on this very question of metempsychosis:

> Who shall declare
>   My whereabouts;
> Say if in the air
>   My being shouts
> Along light ways,
>   Or if in the sea,
> Or deep earth stays
>   The germ of me?
>
> Ah, none knows, none,
>   Save (but too well)
> The Cryptic One
>   Who will not tell.[136]

Not only is there no direct recognition of God by the poet, who limits himself to accepting the reality of an omniscient being; he also reveals his will to paganism by using the biological term "germ" to designate the soul. It is noteworthy, furthermore, that for himself he looks forward to no so-called reincarnation, but only to the outflowing of his "germ" toward such elements as wind, sea, and earth. Should we see in this an idea borrowed from the pantheism of English Romantics like Shelley? That cannot be ruled out, but it should also be stressed that, for Cullen, the elements are symbols of primordial freedom in intimate unity with nature, the Negro's state in an ideal Africa that today is no more. In "The Shroud of Color," after the fourth vision through which God presents the African past to the poet, the poet actually finds himself living in this condition of primeval bliss and freedom by means of a blending into the elements:

> And I was wind and sky again, and sea,
> And all sweet things that flourish, being free.[137]

---

[135] "Threnody for a Brown Girl," stanzas 7 and 8, *Copper Sun,* p. 6.
[136] "To You Who Read My Book," stanza 5, and stanza 6, lines 1-4, *Color,* p. xiv.
[137] "The Shroud of Color," lines 156-57, *ibid.,* p. 33.

In a poem, "On Going," that is filled with a joyous serenity, the poet imagines that after his death he lives once more in the song of a bird or in the song of rain, so that he can return and speak to the woman who survives him. Yet he does not ignore the fact — for the body, too, has its destiny — that his decomposing substance will dissolve into the earth's great totality, giving nourishment to the plants which can then unfold their most beautiful flowers.[138]

The idea of metempsychosis is again utilized in the moving apostrophe to John Keats. In the leaves of trees, in buds and flowers can be heard the voice of the author of *Endymion*, since his survival in the midst of human-kind is a reality that must be postulated by anyone who has faith in poetry's immortality.[139]

Despite the remarkable frequency with which the theme of metempsychosis recurs in *Color* and in *Copper Sun*,[140] it is hardly likely that Cullen even fleetingly believed in the transmigration of souls as a reality. It was above all his poetic imagination that abandoned itself to the idea, in which the poet saw opportunities for thematic enrichment.

As for the sources of his notions concerning metempyschosis, it has seemed to us that such an inquiry would be insufficiently interesting to justify a prolonged examination. One might turn to Hindu and Egyptian traditional doctrines, and to such authors as Pythagoras, Plato, and Plotinus, and still reach no trustworthy conclusions. But Cullen may have sought inspiration in certain Negro folk beliefs, whose survival in the South is affirmed by several authors. Thus, in New Orleans, some old people assert even today that the two swans who can sometimes be seen on Lake Pontchartrain are the reincarnations of the voodoo priestess Marie Laveau and her daughter.[141] Even more noteworthy is the legend of the Flying Africans, which is told by Negroes living along the Georgia coast. This legend relates how some Ibos, who had been imported as slaves from the region of the Niger, chose, rather than to endure the humiliations of slavery, to walk singing into the sea and drown. Others, it is told, were changed into birds and flew back to their native Africa.[142]

Be that as it may, Cullen was not the only black celebrity to dream of metempsychosis in 1925, for Marcus Garvey, pondering the possibility of

[138] "On Going," *ibid.*, p. 105.

[139] "To John Keats, Poet, at Spring Time," *ibid.*, p. 103.

[140] See also, on the theme of metempsychosis, the poem "Words to My Love," *Copper Sun*, p. 22.

[141] Frederic Ramsey, Jr., *Been Here and Gone*, p. 136.

[142] Sterling Brown, "Negro Folk Expression," *Phylon*, fourth quarter, 1950, p. 324.

death as he entered the Atlanta penitentiary, offered this poetic thought to his adherents: "[If I should die in Atlanta,] look for me in the whirl-wind or the storm, look for me all around you, for, with God's grace, I shall come and bring with me the countless millions of black slaves who have died in America and the West Indies and the millions in Africa to aid you in the fight for liberty, freedom and life."[143]

These words were written too late to have had any influence on the poems that make up *Color*. But one toys with the notion of Cullen's having borrowed from Garvey both his longing for the lost African fatherland and his intuition of metempsychosis, and bringing them together in a poem. For Cullen actually wrote a poem to these specifications, and in "Brown Boy to Brown Girl" a young black in love, holding the hand of his beloved, tells her of his convictions:

> ... these alien skies
> Do not our whole life measure and confine.
> ... once in a land of scarlet suns
> And brooding winds, before the hurricane
> Bore down upon us, long before this pain,
> We found a place where quiet water runs;
> I held your hand this way upon a hill
> And felt my heart forebear, my pulse grow still.[144]

This is indeed the union of the Platonic "reminiscence," developed in the *Phaedo,* with the thesis of an earlier existence in the African paradise before this was ravaged by the hurricane that bore off into slavery the millions of Africans whose phantoms Garvey planned to resuscitate.

But the pagan elements grafted on to the theme of Africa did not all spring from Cullen's poetic imagination. One aspect at least lies much closer than did metempsychosis to the deeper urges of his being — and he, furthermore, was not alone in associating it with the black race. This association was also on the minds of the downtown New Yorkers who, in the 1920's, came up to Harlem in pursuit of special enjoyments of which they had been deprived in recent, comparatively austere years. In the murk of the cabarets and dance halls, bewitched by the beat of the jazz band's rhythm section, their eyes riveted on the lascivious undulations of the naked or almost naked black dancing girl, they had little trouble persuading themselves, with the powerful assistance of bootleg liquor, that the

[143] Marcus Garvey, "If I Die in Atlanta," *Negro World*, February 14, 1925. Cited by E. Franklin Frazier, *The Negro in the United States,* p. 530.
[144] "Brown Boy to Brown Girl," lines 7-14, *Color,* p. 5.

show constituted a genuine slice of African life, wild and primitive, and was an assertion and glorification of the hegemony of the senses and instincts.

However, just as with metempsychosis, Cullen does not always place this "pagan" element in a racial or religious context, and one comes across countless examples that simply ring the changes on the inexhaustible theme of *carpe diem*.[145]

Yet the true dimensions of the theme are realized only within the situation of black-white conflict. In "To a Brown Boy," the glorification of the body and the apology of instinct take on their meaning mainly because of what Cullen identifies them with, and that to which he opposes them:

> Lad, never dam your body's itch
> When loveliness is seen.
>
> For there is ample room for bliss
> In pride in clean, brown limbs,
> And lips know better how to kiss
> Than how to raise white hymns.[146]

Since the body is brown and thus symbolizes the superior physical qualities and beauty of the whole race, here it becomes a source of joy and pride, while instinct, whose voice can be heard in the tendencies of the flesh, is elevated to the rank of supreme guide, valid because spontaneous and in harmony with nature. In comparison the religion of the whites, symbolized by their hymns, is revealed as against nature and, consequently, hypocritical. There can be no doubt that their God must be viewed as just one instrument of slavery among others, that is, as a means of oppression expressly designed to maintain black inferiority. In the future one must free oneself of this God and resolutely trust in the voice of the race, sensed via the blood's hot tides. Thus Cullen does not merely set up instinct as an antithesis to Christian values; he integrates it at the same time in a great movement of racial emancipation, and for this the race's awareness of its own values is the essential foundation. "To a Brown Girl,"[147] which forms a unit with the preceding poem, implicitly follows the same line of reasoning.

[145] "To You Who Read My Book," stanza 9, *ibid.*, p. xv; "To the Three for Whom the Book," *The Black Christ*, p. 7; "To One Who Said Me Nay," last stanza, *Color*, p. 79; "Advice to Youth," *ibid.*, p. 80. *Carpe diem* and the glorification of the body are themes also favored by the Lost Generation, with which Cullen may be associated in many respects. See Malcolm Cowley, *Exile's Return*, p. 60. See also our note 57 above.
[146] "To a Brown Boy," stanza 1, lines 3-4, and stanza 2, *Color*, p. 8.
[147] "To a Brown Girl," stanzas 1 and 2, *ibid.*, p. 7.

It can hardly be conceived that this apotheosis of body and instinct could assume such magnitude or stir such distant reverberations, but for the presence of deep, obstinate roots within the poet's own nature. One need but recall the special difficulties that beset Cullen's sex life in order to realize what curious parallels his sensibility was able to establish between the glorification of the senses that was taking place in Harlem and the tyrannical sway that his own bodily inclinations exercised over his destiny. One must also bear in mind that the poet's nature was, at the same time, deeply and genuinely religious, in order to understand the battle which must have raged in his heart almost from the outset.

Indeed, a poem like "Heritage" has almost more merit as a mirror of the poet's inner struggle than as a paean of praise to an imprecise atavism of race, for, as Cullen explores the properties of the African heritage, what he discovers is above all himself. Thus in the long run his Africa takes on the guise of his own sensuality in somewhat altered form. While his reason proclaims that Africa means nothing to him, the voice of Africa unendingly comes to expression through his body's demands:

> What is Africa to me:
> Copper sun or scarlet sea,
> Jungle star or jungle track,
> Strong bronzed men, or regal black
> Women from whose loins I sprang
> When the birds of Eden sang?
> *One three centuries removed*
> *From the scenes his fathers loved,*
> *Spicy grove, cinnamon tree,*
> *What is Africa to me?*
>
> .   .   .   .
>
> So I lie, who find no peace
> Night or day, no slight release
> From the unremittant beat
> Made by cruel padded feet
> Walking through my body's street.
> Up and down they go, and back,
> Treading out a jungle track.
> So I lie, who never quite
> Safely sleep from rain at night —
> I can never rest at all
> When the rain begins to fall;
> Like a soul gone mad with pain
> I must match its weird refrain;
> Ever must I twist and squirm,

> Writhing like a baited worm,
> While its primal measures drip
> Through my body, crying, "Strip!
> Doff this new exuberance.
> Come and dance the Lover's Dance!"
> In an old remembered way
> Rain works on me night and day.[148]

"Heritage," at least throughout the first part, undeniably gives pride of place to the body. Incidentally, of course, the "new exuberance" of Western dress also stands for the alien civilization that must be discarded before one can rediscover oneself in the primordial state of the African earthly paradise. But the body is urged to strip more especially as a preparation for the celebration of the senses awaiting it in the love dance.[149] The poem pays some obeisance, no doubt, to local color. Thus the African forest, where "leprous flowers rear fierce corollas in the air," is traversed by huge bands of wild animals; bats and other barbaric flying things haunt its nights; in the shadows serpents lurk, and at the water's edge the big cats await their prey. Yet the primeval terror in which they plunge the immensity of Africa is ever softened by the sighs of the lovers and by the pledges of love they murmur in the grasslands:

> . . . tall defiant grass
> Where young forest lovers lie
> Plighting troth beneath the sky . . .[150]

The poet is haunted by the insistent rhythm of the drums which, across the jungle, call youths and girls to blend their bodies agleam with sweat in the frantic love dance:

> . . . I . . . always hear,
> Though I cram against my ear

[148] "Heritage," lines 1-10, 64-84, *ibid.*, pp. 36, 38-39. It is in connection with this passage that Locke speaks of the "paganism of blood" in Cullen (Alain Locke, "The Negro in American Culture," in Sylvestre C. Watkins, ed., *Anthology of American Negro Literature*, p. 170). In addition to this definitive version of "Heritage" appearing in *Color*, we have the earlier version of the poem, which occupied pp. 674-75 in the special number of the *Survey-Graphic* for March 1, 1925, edited by Alain Locke and entitled "Harlem, Mecca of the New Negro." While the definitive version has 128 lines, the earlier version has only 102, arranged very differently and with many variants. Locke took over this early version without any alteration in his volume *The New Negro*, pp. 250-53. This is an expanded form of the special number mentioned above. A comparison of the two versions reveals that Cullen made many corrections before passing the poem on for publication, that same year, in his first volume of verse.

[149] See also "The Dance of Love," *Color*, p. 19, which Cullen wrote after he had read *Batouala*, the novel by René Maran.

[150] "Heritage," lines 16-18, *Color*, p. 36.

> Both my thumbs and keep them there,
> Great drums throbbing through the air.[151]

> . . . . .

> . . . bodies sleek and wet,
> Dripping mingled rain and sweat,
> Tread the savage measures of
> Jungle boys and girls in love.[152]

A curious feature in each of these scenes is the special voluptuousness connected with African rain. For Cullen, it often has positively aphrodisiacal virtues and precipitates reactions that might almost be equated with a conditioned reflex. Yet to the best of our knowledge ethnologists have not recorded any cases in which such effects have been attributed to rain in Africa. Thus the inevitable conclusion is that this association of ideas is also Cullen's own, and that his having integrated it, by transposition, into the African heritage offers additional proof, if that should be necessary, of the basically subjective and symbolic character of his vision of Africa.

The special nature of the rain's reverberations on his sensibility is also quite meaningfully illumined by a stanza of "Fruit of the Flower," where it appears to symbolize a kind of communion of the senses that links the poet and his adoptive father:

> Why should he deem it pure mischance
> A son of his is fain
> To do a naked tribal dance
> Each time he hears the rain?[153]

Moreover, if the poet's widow is to be believed, rain did actually exercise a kind of voluptuous sway over Countee Cullen. As much as he was terrified of thunderstorms and thought he could effectively defend himself by shutting himself up in the house, to an equal degree he experienced rain as an invitation to open himself up to nature. As soon as rain began to fall, he stopped whatever he was doing and went outside to get soaked, sometimes for hours on end.[154] Considered in isolation this would be no great matter, but it is surely worth bearing in mind, to the extent that it

---

[151] *Ibid.*, lines 19-22, pp. 36-37.

[152] *Ibid.*, lines 48-51, p. 38.

[153] "Fruit of the Flower," stanza 5, *ibid.*, p. 24.

[154] We are indebted for this information to the kindness of Ida Cullen-Cooper. Arna Bontemps, for his part, has corroborated Cullen's addiction to walks in the rain, a taste they shared. As for Cullen's panic in stormy weather, this is confirmed by a letter the poet wrote his friend Harold Jackman and which bears the date October 22, 1944. The letter is preserved in the Negro Collection of the Atlanta University Library.

throws light, in Cullen's particular case, on the singularly obscure, irrational process of poetic creativity, and accentuates the prime importance of purely personal factors in his handling of themes involving race.

There can hardly be any doubt, then, that Cullen's pagan Africa must be viewed as the projection of half of himself — but no more than half, for just as the two parts of "Heritage" contrast the profane and the sacred and within each part depict the rational constituents of the Western World as locked in combat with the emotional forces of racial atavism, similarly the mystique of race and of its cradle in Africa is but the first stage in the poet's inner striving to effect a reconciliation between irreconcilables and so to attain the unity he longed for.

After emerging victorious from this first stage, he can speak of the pointlessness of "any nebulous atavistic yearnings toward an African inheritance."[155] For by then he had discovered that Africa was only a pretext for escape, an opportunity offered the individual to flee from the relevant reality around him into a cloudland of dream and illusion. When all was said and done, it was an invitation to flee from oneself. And so the dream of Africa becomes, in a way, transformed into the antithesis of any authentic inner life, for the individual is dispensed thereby from the struggle to transcend self, lulled to sleep on the path leading to spiritual values, and provided with an instantaneous gratification of the urges of a tormented psyche. Like jazz, Africa is both opiate and intoxicating whirl, not balm that heals once and for all, since nothing is gained beyond a provisional, illusive, emotional equilibrium.

Later Cullen encounters Christ and starts with him a dialogue whose vicissitudes we will now attempt to relate.

4. CHRIST AS SYMBOL AND REALITY

Among the religious themes of which Cullen's poetry has an unusual abundance, exceptional importance is given to Christ's figure, which haunted the poet throughout his life. As early as 1922 he published a sonnet entitled "Christ Recrucified." Every volume of his poetry, except perhaps *The Medea,* turns to the theme which, in his mind, was to have found its culmination in his longest poem, "The Black Christ," published three years after his visit to Jerusalem. Finally, the dying man left behind him an incomplete manuscript of three untitled sonnets, the subject being a dialogue between Christ and the poet.[156] Thus Cullen's religious sensibility

[155] See the text cited above, at the end of note 77.
[156] For the text of these unpublished poems, see our Appendix of such poems in the original French edition.

arrives at a certain unity within this theme, since around it he spontaneously grouped all the essential elements.

This unity, nevertheless, remains partly an illusion, for the figure of
Christ acquires widely different meanings from poem to poem. To begin
with, Cullen's very terminology fluctuates when he speaks of the deity,
which is either referred to as God, or the Lord, or the Cryptic One, or
sometimes as the Sower. The three persons of the Trinity are occasionally
distinguished, but only to the second are any distinctive attributes allotted.
Moreover, Christ is not always specifically treated as the second person of
the Trinity, at times being unqualifiedly God, and the poem would undergo no change in meaning if "Father" were substituted for "Son." All
in all, then, Cullen's practices are in conformity with popular usage, and
his terminology does not aim at theological rigor.

Christ as a Sign of Self-Contradiction[157]

What must concern us here reaches far beyond questions of terminology.
Some of the poems in which Christ appears present the white Christ who
symbolizes the race of oppressors and at times is their accomplice, an adversary of their joint victim, the black man. Other poems present the
crucified black Christ, the image and friend of the lynched Negro and
adversary of his executioner, the white man. In addition, though Christ
usually appears as an individual person, at times his image more or less
merges with the person of the poet.

It would be quite astonishing if such a contradiction within the symbol
were not the reflection of much deeper contradictions, of the kind already
noted in the tormented consciousness of blacks, who have been known to
be consumed with hatred for whites while at the same time making frantic
efforts to resemble them ever more closely. This contradiction that turned
some black men against themselves is not the least tragic aspect of the
"mark of oppression."[158] The slave system was riddled with contradictions,
beginning with the requirement that the master should be all at once oppressor and punisher and the protector who provided shelter, clothing, and
nourishment. But doubtless the primary contradiction is that which Cullen,
along with many others, instinctively traced back to the relationship between man and God. The white man shut himself up inside this contradiction on the day he decided he could at the same time abase his fellow
man to the level of an object and proclaim himself to be a Christian, affirming that his deed was the will of God and undertaking, into the bar-

[157] Luke 2:34.
[158] Title of the already mentioned work by Kardiner and Ovesey.

gain, to evangelize those he had enslaved. It was willed by the irony of fate that this basic contradiction, engendered in the white man's heart by his greed and hypocrisy, should be transmitted, as though it were a hereditary defect, to the black man[159] who depended on him for everything. Blacks did not remain unaware of the prodigious dilemma into which they had been forced in spite of themselves.

This contradiction within the Christ symbol enables us to penetrate more deeply, down to the level at which Cullen's racial consciousness and his conscience are closely intertwined. While meditating on the factors that oppose the two hostile races, he once more came upon the same irreconcilable elements that also divided the individual against himself and against God. In addition to their symbolic value in the conflict of races and cultures, the figures of the benevolent black Christ and the hostile white Christ are also the projection, onto another plane, of the poet's inner divisions. Behaviorist psychologists would tell us that what confronts us here is a conflict of roles complicated by a confusion of roles,[160] the latter finding its symbolic representation in an image of Christ who is made to contradict himself. It need not be emphasized that the contradiction lies not in Christ but in the poet, in whom it affects simultaneously a wide range of areas which, when brought into relationship, give rise to extraordinarily complex combinations. So it is advisable, before we enter upon a more detailed consideration, to remember the nature of the conflict in each area.

Quite clearly, at the bottom of it all is the racial conflict unchangingly identical with itself, and manifested in the black-white opposition we have so often met with. But upon this basic racial conflict there is grafted a cultural conflict in which Cullen, whose entire education intellectually tied him to the white Western world, found himself at odds with Negro folk standards. Too many obstacles cut him off from the popular conception of Christianity, too superficial, too narrow, and too closely akin to the Methodist fundamentalism that had irked him in his adoptive father's home, to win his adhesion.

At this level, the occasions for tension are at once multiplied, and problems grow even more acute because of the clashes and crossings between the racial, cultural, and spiritual areas.

What turns him away from the folk religion is also the credulity ex-

[159] Elkins's theories, the essentials of which have already been conveyed in our first chapter, may help in showing how this dualism was transmitted to the slave. See his *Slavery: A Problem in American Institutional and Intellectual Life,* Ch. 3.
[160] *Ibid.,* pp. 123ff.

hibited both toward the pastors in whom the people place their trust,[161] and toward God. How can anyone be so naïve as to believe and trust in Providence, when it blatantly favors only the undertakings of the white oppressors?

> Shall I never feel and meet the urge
> To bugle out beyond my sense
> That the fittest song of earth is a dirge,
> And only fools trust Providence?[162]

But what does Negro religious folklore have to say?

> Oh, give me Jesus,
> You may have all dis worl'![163]

Thus his very racial consciousness sets him in opposition to the naïve masses of his own people whom he despairs of ever saving despite themselves, but whose cause he will plead before a hostile God.

This, however, does not mean that he was not a Christian. Even at those moments when Christ appeared to him most hostile, Cullen thirsts for the Christian ideal of perfection and self-transcendence, and no one could have suffered more than he did from the sense of guilt that awareness of his sinfulness aroused in him. But since he found himself on hostile terms with Christ on the spiritual plane because of his sin, and on the racial plane also because Christ seemed to have abandoned the black race, it was tempting to unite the two terms on either side of the barrier — to promote the urges of the flesh to the rank of a positive value, indeed, of a black value that had been consecrated by the African gods who thus came to challenge the place held in his soul by the white Christ:

> Quaint, outlandish heathen gods
> Black men fashion out of rods,
> Clay, and brittle bits of stone,
> In a likeness like their own,
> My conversion came high-priced;
> I belong to Jesus Christ,

---

[161] In this connection, see also the portrait of religious life in his novel *One Way to Heaven.*

[162] "Self-Criticism," stanza 2, *The Black Christ,* p. 38.

[163] Chorus of the spiritual "Give Me Jesus." For the complete text, see James Weldon Johnson, *The Book of American Negro Spirituals,* I, 161. See, too, the passage in which Cullen mocks the people's faith in Providence ("The Black Christ," lines 352-55):

> "In His own time, He will unfold
> You milk and honey, streets of gold,
> High walls of jasper. . . ," phrases rolled
> Upon the tongues of idiots.

> Preacher of humility;
> Heathen gods are naught to me.
>
> Father, Son and Holy Ghost,
> So I make an idle boast;
> Jesus of the twice-turned cheek,
> Lamb of God, although I speak
> With my mouth thus, in my heart
> Do I play a double part.[164]

Those indeed are the terms of the antinomy, each with its retinue of overtones, reverberating and echoing through every level of consciousness. But how emerge from the antinomy, especially without sacrificing anything: either the black race, or white culture; the raptures of sin, or the friendship of Christ; Africa, or America? What a wager indeed!

He will try to rise to the occasion, nevertheless, by making Christ black and God a little less perfect:

> Ever at Thy glowing altar
> Must my heart grow sick and falter,
> Wishing He I served were black,
> Thinking then it would not lack
> Precedent of pain to guide it,
> Let who would or might deride it;
> Surely then this flesh would know
> Yours had borne a kindred woe.
> Lord, I fashion dark gods, too,
> Daring even to give you
> Dark despairing features where,
> Crowned with dark rebellious hair,
> Patience wavers just so much as
> Mortal grief compels, while touches
> Quick and hot, of anger, rise
> To smitten cheek and weary eyes.
> Lord, forgive me if my need
> Sometimes shapes a human creed.[165]

What we have here is a doubly anthropomorphic phenomenon or, one might say, an attempt to humanize Christ physically as well as morally. For, on the one hand, Cullen fashions a Christ in his own image, negrifying him and thus making him into a sort of idol, related to the African pagan gods that black men hew out of wood or stone, or model in a fistful of clay. By so doing, however, he deprives Christ of his divinity. His Christ

---

[164] "Heritage," lines 85-98, *Color,* p. 39.
[165] *Ibid.,* lines 99-116, p. 40.

has ceased to be Christ. The evidence for this becomes utterly incontrovertible as soon as one turns to the tentative sketch he has roughed out on the moral plane. Cullen, that creature of flesh and blood, is searching in Christ's human nature for some sign of a weakness which, if discovered, would make him seem more human, less perfect, and as a consequence nearer to the poet. He peruses his features for some indication of despair, for a touch of impatience, a heralded anger, or a spreading lassitude. But does he not realize that here too he is depriving Christ of his divinity by seeking to deny his perfection, which is his essential attribute? Yet the attempt is made again elsewhere. Not having abandoned a certain hankering after Lucifer, whose "sin-sweet voice" he had heard in "The Shroud of Color,"[166] Cullen would like to know of God whether he too, despite his perfection, had not retained in some recess of his memory at least the shade of a regret for Lucifer:

> God, Thou hast Christ, they say, at Thy right hand;
> Close by Thy left Michael is straight and leal;
> Around Thy throne the chanting elders stand,
> And on the earth Thy feudal millions kneel.
> Criest Thou never, Lord, above their song:
> "But Lucifer was tall, his wings were long"?[167]

Is there any need to stress the fact that countless dangers lay secreted in this approach to the unavoidable task of a synthesis that would vanquish his inner divisions and lead him to the goal of unity? As it turned out, and despite the admirable attempts he made in other ways to attain a truly Christian spiritual life, he never entirely succeeded in integrating his

---

[166] Line 131, *ibid.*, p. 32.

[167] "Dictum," lines 9-14, *The Black Christ*, p. 47. See also the poet's retort to his mother in "The Black Christ," lines 824-28:

> But Christ who conquered Death and Hell
> What has he done for you who spent
> A bleeding life for his content?
> Or is the white Christ, too, distraught
> By these dark sins His father wrought?

This is yet another attempt to stir up Divinity against itself. What we are confronted with here, on Cullen's part, appears to be the type of highly developed pathological anthropomorphism which Dr. Logre calls "automorphism": "Enclosed within its subjectivity, the ego projects into others its own feelings and desires. . . . The most frequently encountered type . . . of automorphism consists in attributing all our virtues (real or supposed) to those for whom we have a liking while, on the contrary, reserving our faults for our adversaries and the groups to which they belong. It follows, therefore, as Dr. Logre has noted, that 'the bill of particulars indicting our enemies is only a kind of involuntary examination of conscience which is repressed and transferred to the debit of someone else' " (Jean Maisonneuve, *Psychologie sociale*, p. 64).

racial self and his Christian self with the degree of perfection we have noted in McKay.

But we are anticipating the conclusions of this study. We must retrace a few steps and first try to circumscribe more closely the racial symbol represented by Christ.

One can understand how tempting it was to establish a parallel between the Calvary of the Son of God and the bitter hill that, for centuries, the sons of Ham had had to climb. In the Negro folk tradition that predated Cullen, blacks had become accustomed to recognizing themselves in the Hebrew people, the chosen of God, whereas white people, especially southern whites, were equated with the Egyptians and their Pharaoh, who held captive the people of Israel. The choice of the crucified Christ to symbolize the lynched Negro was a new idea, and it appears that its originator was indeed Cullen. We find it utilized for the first time in "Christ Recrucified," a sonnet published in *Kelley's Magazine* in October, 1922, and not subsequently reprinted in any collection of Cullen's poetry:

> The South is crucifying Christ again
> By all the laws of ancient rote and rule:
> The ribald cries of "Save yourself" and "Fool"
> Din in his ears, the thorns grope for his brain,
> And where they bite, swift springing rivers stain
> His gaudy, purple robe of ridicule
> With sullen red; and acid wine to cool
> His thirst is thrust at him, with lurking pain.
> Christ's awful wrong is that he's dark of hue,
> The sin for which no blamelessness atones;
> But lest the sameness of the cross should tire,
> They kill him now with famished tongues of fire,
> And while he burns, good men, and women, too,
> Shout, battling for his black and brittle bones.[168]

The sonnet is constructed with the greatest skill. It is presented as a religious poem, though the subject is entirely that of race. If the word "South" in the first line were omitted, no racial reference would appear in the two quatrains. But the full meaning is withheld from us until we reach the second tercet, for only then are the details of the lynching given: the flames of the bonfire and the struggle for the victim's charred bones, as each participant tries to carry away a piece to serve as a memento or a good-luck charm.

[168] "Christ Recrucified," *Kelley's Magazine*, October, 1922, p. 13. The sonnet is signed "Countee P. Cullen."

The poet, after making Christ black, shows his dexterity by treating his color as worse than a crime. It was a sin! The gain is threefold, in the first place because this answers like an echo a certain southern ideology which regarded the Negro's inferiority as part of the divine plan, since it atones for the sin committed by Ham.[169] It also maintains the unity of tone of the poem, which is religious. Finally, an even crasser light is thrown on the untenable attitude and the duplicity of the lynchers, who claim the right to judge Christ himself and to convict him of sin. Thus their crime turns, in the end, against themselves. Obviously Cullen is here trying to defeat the Southerners on their own ground by demonstrating that in one place they burn what elsewhere they worship. They are not only burning to death black servants they cannot do without; by lynching or simply mistreating them, they are treading underfoot the Christian principles on which they pride themselves and because of which they consider themselves, as the poet makes clear, to be "good men and women." They also negate their Christian principles by the zeal with which they carry away the bones of the lynched Negro, ready to display them proudly as though they were fragments of the true cross. This is a superstitious act on the part of people who accuse Negroes of being superstitious.

There is another poem on the topic of lynching which it would be pointless to cite, were it not that it reveals the mastery Cullen had acquired in the five-year interval that separates the two poems. One may regret the presence of several tedious passages in the nearly one thousand lines that make up "The Black Christ," but for the moment let us admire the concision — exhibited elsewhere, it made Cullen a master of the epigram — of this three-line tableau:

> The play is done, the crowds depart; and see
> That twisted tortured thing hung from a tree,
> Swart victim of a newer Calvary.[170]

But not only in the person of the lynched Negro is Christ's sacrifice undergone once more. His Calvary prefigures also that of the whole black people, crowned with thorns and crucified on a cross of the same color as the oppressors, for this people, after having foresworn the ancestors' African gods, had entrusted itself completely to Christ, for better and for worse:

> The thorny wreath may ridge our brow,
> The spear may mar our side
> And on white wood from a scented bough
> We may be crucified;

---

[169] Genesis 9:22.
[170] "Colors (Black) — 1 —," *Copper Sun,* p. 11.

> Yet no assault the old gods make
> Upon our agony
> Shall swerve our footsteps from the wake
> Of Thine toward Calvary.[171]

The sacrifice is all the more worthy to be associated with Christ's, since at bottom the black people harbor no resentment toward the oppressors. This prayer, placed by Cullen in the people's mouth, tends to demonstrate this:

> And if we hunger now and thirst,
> Grant our withholders may,
> When heaven's constellations burst
> Upon Thy crowning day,
> Be fed by us, and given to see
> Thy mercy in our eyes.[172]

All things considered, these poems built around the theme of the Passion are rather analogous to certain ambivalent spirituals, whose religious content is practically annulled by their racial significance.[173] It would appear to be primarily in the service of racial aims that Cullen is here utilizing the religious emotion he awakens in the reader, while the feelings expressed are of a collective rather than of a personal application. Does this amount to saying that he finds himself, via the Christ symbol, in perfect communion with his racial group? At no stage of his poetic career, indeed, would he seem so close to becoming the interpreter of the people's simple, confident, blind faith — and reciprocally, never again did they so trustingly view him as their poet. Yet at the very instant he is pleading the cause of the black people before a hostile God, he takes the greatest care to indicate his remoteness from their faith, so that in the end what he sends aloft to the Eternal is a "pagan prayer":

> Not for myself I make this prayer,
>   But for this race of mine
> That stretches forth from shadowed places
>   Dark hands for bread and wine.
>
> For me, my heart is pagan mad,
>   My feet are never still,
> But give them hearths to keep them warm
>   In homes high on a hill.

[171] "The Litany of the Dark People," stanza 2, *ibid.*, p. 13.
[172] *Ibid.*, stanza 3.
[173] One has in mind, especially, "Go Down, Moses," which Sterling Brown has described as being "the slaves' Marseillaise until the Civil War" ("Spirituals, Blues, and Jazz," in Ralph J. Gleason, ed., *Jam Session: An Anthology of Jazz*, p. 20). See also H. F. Krehbiel, *Afro-American Folksongs*, p. 21 and *passim*.

For me, my faith lies fallowing,
    I bow not till I see,
But these are humble and believe;
    Bless their credulity.

For me, I pay my debts in kind,
    And see no better way,
Bless those who turn the other cheek
    For love of you, and pray.

Our Father, God; our Brother, Christ —
    So are we taught to pray;
Their kinship seems a little thing
    Who sorrow all the day.

Our Father, God; our Brother, Christ,
    Or are we bastard kin,
That to our plaints your ears are closed,
    Your doors barred from within?

Our Father, God; our Brother, Christ,
    Retrieve my race again;
So shall you compass this black sheep,
    This pagan heart. Amen.[174]

Thus everything appears to be called into question, his friendship with God along with his union with his people. But a moment later, though still aware of the dimensions of his sin and how much it would cost him to give it up,[175] he once again starts to haggle with God, with the advance knowledge that the procedure will be of no avail:

I fast and pray and go to church,
    And put my penny in,

[174] "Pagan Prayer," *Color*, p. 20. See also, on Christ's abandonment of the black people, "Black Magdalens" (*ibid.*, p. 9), a poem about black prostitutes in which Cullen blends at least two distinct Gospel episodes, the one concerning Mary Magdalene (Luke 7:37-50) and the other on the woman taken in adultery (John 8:1-11). McKay already, in his "Harlem Shadows," had made a racial question out of the wretched state of these black prostitutes, but his formulation of the problem was a clumsy one. Cullen's poem is based on a more adroit insinuation which, as usual, is aimed against Christ and not against white folk: whereas Mary Magdalene had Christ to rehabilitate her, her black successors are in a "sorry plight" since Christ "forsook the cross to mount a throne." Whites are nowhere named, yet they are the target just as Christ is. All things considered, this poem of Cullen's is no more persuasive than is McKay's, for his "Magdalens" are black only in the title, and but for this indication of their color the text of the poem could apply equally readily to white prostitutes. Thus "Black Magdalens" must be placed among the poems in which the racial argument is an arbitrary addition.

[175] See also, on this topic, "Sonnet," *The Medea*, p. 82.

> But God's not fooled by such slight tricks,
>   And I'm not saved from sin.
>
> I cannot hide from Him the gods
>   That revel in my heart,
> Nor can I find an easy word
>   To tell them to depart;
>
> God's alabaster turrets gleam
>   Too high for me to win,
> Unless He turns His face and lets
>   Me bring my own gods in.[176]

Meanwhile he nevertheless continues to feel himself attracted to God as though toward a magnet, but it will become clear that, to see the true visage of Deity, Cullen must discover a way other than the deification of instinct.

Mysticism and Spiritual Experience

Several poems printed in *Color* already bring together the elements of an authentic Christian spirituality insightful enough to rise above the datum of color and substantial enough to serve as the foundations for the reconstruction of a shattered self. Admittedly, at this time the poet's faith is still engaged in a fearsome debate with mighty adversaries. The problem of evil remains a stumbling block that hampers Cullen in accepting without qualification a providential God, and the claims of instinct still make their voices heard. But certitudes already assert themselves, and these are all the more deeply rooted because they surge up unmediated out of intuition. Among them must be noted an unshakable belief in the immortality of the soul, resoundingly proclaimed from one collection of poems to the next and drowning out the tumultuous voice of the passions.[177]

But life must be breathed into these truths, if they are not to remain sterile. Before they could light up every instant of his existence, first all that was not of the spirit had to be brought to silence.[178] The poet had also to feel himself in the immediate presence of Christ in order to be set aflame by the fire of his ideal — his "dream," Cullen will say[179] — and

---

[176] "Gods," *Color*, p. 101.

[177] "Harsh World That Lashest Me," stanza 3, lines 5-8, *ibid.*, p. 107; "In Spite of Death," lines 5-14, *Copper Sun*, p. 55; "Counter Mood," lines 5-14, *The Black Christ*, p. 18.

[178] See "To Lovers of Earth: Fair Warning," *Copper Sun*, p. 51: "Give over to high things the fervent thought / You waste on earth. . . ."

[179] Speaking of Judas, Cullen says ("Judas Iscariot," stanza 4, lines 1-4, *Color*, p. 91):

in order, even more notably, to participate with him in a mystic union and thus further the work of redemption, as Simon of Cyrene had participated by carrying Christ's cross.

In "Simon the Cyrenian Speaks," beneath the features of Simon it is Cullen himself who communicates to us his mystic experience:

> He never spoke a word to me,
> And yet He called my name;
> He never gave a sign to me,
> And yet I knew and came.
>
> At first I said, "I will not bear
> His cross upon my back;
> He only seeks to place it there
> Because my skin is black."
>
> But He was dying for a dream,
> And He was very meek,
> And in His eyes there shone a gleam
> Men journey far to seek.
>
> It was Himself my pity bought;
> I did for Christ alone
> What all of Rome could not have wrought
> With bruise of lash or stone.[180]

What a distance we have come from the polemical poems referred to above! Now the dialogue has no need of words, and the race-motivated objections are instantly dissipated by the warmth that springs from the reciprocated gaze. The final stanza is perhaps not entirely without faults in structure, but there is no doubt as to its meaning: by accepting a mystical union with Christ, the sacrifice made by Simon of Cyrene, like the poet's own suffering, has advanced the task of Redemption.

Confronting the hostile world — not only the white world, but also that of the blacks who accuse him of having betrayed his race — Cullen likewise suffers, in a spiritual union with Christ, for the salvation of a people that is crucifying him:

> . . . one day he heard young Christ
> With far-off eyes agleam,
> Tell of a mystic, solemn tryst
> Between him and a dream.

See also the citation below. When Cullen establishes a parallel between himself and Christ, this "dream" is again present as a sign of the mystic union between Christ and the poet. As one example, see "A Thorn Forever in the Breast," which is quoted above in note 74.

[180] *Ibid.*, p. 14. See also the mystic experience recounted in "The Shroud of Color," which we have already discussed.

> I mount my cross . . .
> I drink the hemlock which you give
> For wine which you withhold . . .[181]

The parallel nowhere else finds clearer expression than in the sonnet "A Thorn Forever in the Breast,"[182] with, apparently, the consummation of the breach between the black people and the poet who, faithful to his "dream" as Christ had been, like him is abandoned by his own and is condemned to trudge up Calvary alone.

The poet, though suffering in unison with Christ, nevertheless avoids the presumption of equating his suffering with that of the Redeemer. At the very moment when he calls on him for help, he realizes how much lies between them, so that in itself the turning to Christ acts like a balm in assuaging his distress:

> Pity me, I said;
> But you cried, Pity you;
> And suddenly I saw
> Higher than my own grief grew.
> I saw a tree of woe so tall,
> So deeply boughed with grief,
> That matched with it my bitter plant
> Was dwarfed into a leaf.[183]

His mystic intimacy with Christ finds its culmination in "The Black Christ." This great poem is also his spiritual testament, where all the fundamental themes of his poetic achievement are taken up once more and placed in their ultimate perspective.

"The Black Christ": A Spiritual Testament

One may, of course, consider "The Black Christ" to be "a narrative poem about lynching."[184] Seen from this angle, its plot can be summarized in a few words. Jim is a young black driven by the misfortunes of his race to rebel against God, whereas his mother still clings blindly to her faith. One beautiful spring day Jim is walking along in the company of a white girl, when a white man sees them. The white insults the girl, whereupon the two men fight. Jim kills his opponent and then, as the law of the South requires, is himself lynched.

No one will fail to agree that it was Cullen's subsidiary aim to protest,

[181] "Harsh World That Lashest Me," stanza 2, lines 4-6, *ibid.*, p. 106.
[182] For this sonnet, see note 74 above.
[183] "Revelation," *The Black Christ*, p. 48.
[184] Brown, *Negro Poetry and Drama*, p. 71.

in this poem, against lynching, but it is also clear that this is a very minor aspect of the work.

The lynching of which it tells is, in any case, highly unusual. For, shortly after dying on the fatal tree, Jim is resuscitated — this demonstrates the persistence with which Cullen's imagination was struggling to round out the analogy already tentatively sketched in "Christ Recrucified," and to bring it to a conclusion. The theme, in the meantime, had grown considerably richer and more spiritual, and in the 1929 poem Jim's sacrifice derives all its meaning from its mystical union with Christ's. The drama of the lynching unfolds in keeping with that of the Passion, and at every instant the texture of Cullen's narrative allows the gospel texts to shine through.

Just as Christ had told his disciples of the coming Passion, Jim has an inkling that he will be lynched, and he speaks of it to his friends.[185] As they arrive to arrest their victim Jim's executioners, like those of Christ, were armed with clubs and carried torches,[186] and the shouts of "Lynch him!" echo the biblical "Crucify him!"[187] The episode with Pilate also has its counterpart in Cullen's poem:

> "So be it then; have then your way;
> But not by me shall blood be spilt;
> I wash my hands clean of this guilt."
> This was an echo of a phrase
> Uttered how many million days
> Gone by?[188]

Since Jim, like Christ, knows that his destiny must be fulfilled, he does not fear to anticipate the questions of the gang's leader and, unasked, to introduce himself:

> I am he whom you seek . . .[189]

After seizing him, one of the servants with the band strikes him in the face and draws blood;[190] but the lynchers lose their ardor when they see their victim at the point of death and, like the centurion and his men so many centuries ago, they are suddenly struck with terror.[191] At the last, as he is about to give up his spirit, Jim utters a final word to his mother

---

[185] "The Black Christ," lines 219-20; Matthew 26:2 and 46, etc.
[186] *Ibid.*, lines 634-35, 665; John 18:3, and Matthew 26:47.
[187] *Ibid.*, lines 645-46; Matthew 27:22 and 23.
[188] *Ibid.*, lines 652-57; Matthew 27:24.
[189] *Ibid.*, line 701; John 18:4-8.
[190] *Ibid.*, lines 735-39; John 28:22.
[191] *Ibid.*, lines 732-34; Matthew 27:54.

and brother.[192] The episode ends with an ecstatic outburst to celebrate the mystic nuptials[193] of Salvation's Tree with the victim who has been offered up as a holocaust on this new Calvary. Heaven becomes one with the earth, and transfigures the black victim:

> O Tree was ever worthier Groom
> Led to a bride of such rare bloom?
> Did ever fiercer hands enlace
> Love and Beloved in an embrace
> As heaven-smiled-upon as this?
> Was ever more celestial kiss?
>
> .   .   .   .
>
> Greet, Virgin Tree, your holy mate![194]

"The Black Christ" is not, however, summed up with the episode of Jim. Its real scope would be lost if one paid attention only to the narrative aspect, for with Cullen this is also, ultimately, a way of activating symbols so that they may confront one another. In this perspective, "The Black Christ" is a masterly reconstruction of the poet's inner drama. It retraces the long debate, already launched in "Heritage," whose protagonists are incredulity and faith, each of these parties to the confrontation being endowed with its entire accompaniment of racial and personal overtones, which in this poem are orchestrated into an imposing *da capo*.

In this internal confrontation, in which the poet functions not only as the narrator but also as the moderator whose role it is to synthesize the opposing elements, the mother stands for the people's unshakable Christian faith. She is one of the humble who believe without having seen and to whom, for this reason, the Lord has revealed mighty things he keeps hidden from the proud and the argumentative.[195]

The voice of the mother, as she speaks to her son in the humble setting of a southern cabin, at the same time is clearly that of faith speaking to the poet within his own heart. But the mother represents more than faith. She also symbolizes the people and, beyond them, the doubly ungrateful southern soil from which they draw their sustenance and in which, for hundreds of years, they have plunged deep roots.[196]

---

[192] *Ibid.*, lines 722-23; John 19:26.

[193] For a parallel between physical and mystical love, see Henri Sérouya, *Le Mysticisme*, pp. 35ff.

[194] "The Black Christ," lines 758-63, 774.

[195] *Ibid.*, lines 399-422.

[196] *Ibid.*, lines 92-97, 101-29. See also lines 170-76, in which his reliance on Providence is based on an explicit parallel between the black people and the people of Israel.

Thus Countee Cullen discovers, as had Claude McKay but along another path, the perennial strength of the trinity made up of earth, folk, and faith, all irrational values against which the young intellectual had rebelled in fiery protest in the days when he was winning his first triumphs as a poet.

Standing over against the values represented by the mother is the figure of Jim, who in many respects might well be looked on as the incarnation of the "New Negro." His whole being breathes pride of race and intolerance of any yoke. He also symbolizes the religious skepticism that sprang up in the heart of a whole race that had to witness unpunished injustice.[197]

The poet lends a voice to Jim's doubts in a passage in which, after mocking the passivity and silence of the Christian God, he sings the praises of antiquity's pagan gods and of their providential interventions:

> When Rome was a suckling, when Greece was young,
> Then there were gods fit to be sung,
> Who paid the loyal devotee
> For service rendered zealously,
> In coin a man might feel and spend,[198]

[197] *Ibid.,* lines 194-201.

[198] *Ibid.,* lines 373-77. This celebration of the pagan gods by a Christian poet belonging to an oppressed racial minority could be made the starting point for an interesting study in comparative literature. Let us call attention, in this connection, to the parallel aspects of the black poets we have been studying and the modern Jewish poets writing in Hebrew. In particular, it seems to us that an extremely instructive comparison could be drawn between the paganism of Countee Cullen and that of the Jewish poet Saul Tchernihovsky (1875-1943) who, having experienced the pogroms in his native Russia, reacted to God's inefficiency exactly as Cullen had done. His poem "Martyrs of Dortmund" is a forthright avowal of atheism, and this act of denial is directly based, like that outlined by Cullen, upon the continued silence of the Eternal, while the children of his chosen people are being massacred for their fidelity to his law. Turning away from God, Tchernihovsky then sings the praises of the pagan gods. See his poems "Before the Statue of Apollo" and "The Song of Astarte and Baal." Our ignorance of the Hebrew language has, regrettably, made it impossible for us to refer to the poet's work in the original. But we turned to the section devoted to him in the critical anthology by Menachem Ribalow, *The Flowering of Modern Hebrew Literature: A Volume of Literary Evaluation,* ed. and trans. by Judah Nadich (London, 1959), pp. 88-122. In order to convey some notion of the striking resemblance between Cullen and Tchernihovsky, we reproduce the following passages from the critical introduction that precedes the aforementioned poems of the Jewish poet: "He never had to break with the old hoary traditions; he was free of them from the start. . . . His generation sensed that he was *its* poet and crowned him poet laureate. But Tchernihovsky was different both in background and nature and so his early verse did not meet with the same response. It was simple, unsophisticated, and not particularly Jewish in either form or content" (p. 91). "Tchernihovsky is called the 'Greek' poet in modern Hebrew literature, the poet of paganism" (p. 92). "The contradictions peculiar to his poetry are to be found within his own soul. For

Beyond this, in the debate Jim also symbolizes a pagan value dear to Cullen's heart. That is sensual beauty, the love of which had spontaneously led him to Keats. One is reminded of Keats in reading the celebration of spring that is placed at the beginning of Jim's speech, as he is about to tell how the white man came upon him unawares.[199] From the narrative point of view, this forms too lengthy a parenthesis, but because of its symbolic value it rounds out the portrait of Jim. It cannot be doubted that in it Cullen sought to depict everything within himself that represented an obstacle on the path that ultimately led him to God.

The arguments advanced by the mother and by Jim do battle, throughout the poem, in the poet's own heart, and doubt appears to be on the point of winning when, after the lynching has been carried out and the mother and her surviving son abandon themselves to their grief inside their cabin, Jim suddenly manifests himself in the glory of his resurrection. Before this revelation of divine power and mercy, doubt finally is routed forever and the poet, another Doubting Thomas,[200] falls to his knees. He is overcome with remorse at the thought of all the blasphemies he had hurled at God, and which have been answered by the Divine mercy.

It is easy to understand why this long poem of 963 lines finally lost Cullen the sympathies of the black public. For the poem, with its mystical character, and despite the title and the theme of the narrative, is not essentially Negro in any way. Its very mysticism was condemned as child-

---

in addition to the struggle between Judaism and paganism in his poetry, there is the conflict between primitive civilization and the modern culture of which he is the exemplar. It is not easy for the poet of modernity to breathe the musty air of the ancients" (pp. 97-98). Concerning the divorce between Tchernihovsky and his people, the following lines from his poem "Man Is Nothing But..." offer us enlightenment:

> And my song is foreign, my song is
>   strange to the heart of my people,
> Barren it was when it appeared and barren
>   will it be when it departs,
> With no heart to absorb it and no echo to
>   reverberate.

One could with advantage compare, with this passage from Tchernihovsky, Cullen's sonnet "A Thorn Forever in the Breast." An available edition of Tchernihovsky is *Poems*, ed. L. V. Snowman (London, 1929). For a short but enlightening overall study of the problems that modern Jewish poets writing in Hebrew must confront, see André Néher, "Le Conflit du sacré et du profane dans la renaissance de l'hébreu," *Bulletin de la Faculté des Lettres de Strasbourg*, May-June, 1958, pp. 403-15.

199 "The Black Christ," lines 469ff.

200 *Ibid.*, lines 879-90, 903-4; John 20:24-29.

ish,[201] and one critic actually reproached the author for having dated the poem from Paris.[202]

There may be more meaning in this reproof than might be thought, for "The Black Christ" has affinities with a type of literature that could scarcely arouse any echoes in an American reading public. It is, as we see it, something like the transposition into another setting of a French medieval miracle play with, at the same time, the character of a votive offering, on the lines of a well-known Passion play which was expressly composed to give thanks to heaven for having spared a whole population the horrors of the plague.[203]

"The Black Christ" must be read as a poem of thanksgiving for the bestowal of the light of faith, as well as the translation into words of a contemplative experience. The religious exaltation that dictates the poem's entire structure bears the marks of the neophyte's sense of wonderment and his whole touching naïveté. With such characteristics, however, "The Black Christ" was inevitably inaccessible to all but a handful of readers.

It must be confessed that the poem has all the defects that correspond to its virtues. A mystical experience always retains a certain incommunicability, and in the present case the reader has to make a considerable effort of self-adaptation to remain attuned to the poet who, in his exaltation, sometimes leaves all trammels so far behind that he falls into incoherence and neglects the external form. The tetrameter, which he had always favored and which he uses throughout the poem, may be appropriate for the narrative passages, but the prolonged meditations, which occupy an important place, might have moved more freely in a less constricting meter. The presence of rhyme, too, disposed with impenetrable arbitrariness,[204] awakens a vague malaise and does injury to the sobriety

---

[201] "The childish mysticism of a bad dream," wrote Redding of "The Black Christ" (*To Make a Poet Black*, p. 112). Yet a critic writing in the *New York Times*, shortly after the poem had been published, expressed his admiration for "the force of the spiritual import" it carried (P. H., "Countee Cullen Has His Own Note," *New York Times*, December 1, 1929).

[202] Benjamin G. Brawley, *The Negro Genius*, p. 225.

[203] Oberammergau in Bavaria, 1634.

[204] It would be tedious to reproduce here the complete figures of our detailed counts on this point. Without providing references, we will limit ourselves to noting that some lines are left isolated, not rhyming with any other line; more than 50 percent of the lines are arranged in tercets rhyming *aaa*, and these are scattered throughout the poem; also, but only in the first quarter of the poem and in scattered fashion, one comes across four quatrains rhymed *aaaa* and one rhymed *abab;* the rest of the poem, or close to half, is in couplets. Many of the rhymes are weak, even very weak: love/of; aloft/waft; idiots/gluts; holocaust/blast; and also: me/me, swell/miracle, stoop/up. In the total picture, however, and given the length of the undertaking, these blemishes may be considered excusable. The disturbing

of the whole. In this connection one recalls Milton's view, and enthusiastically endorses it: "Rime [is] no necessary adjunct or true ornament of poem or good verse, *in longer works especially*. . . ."[205]

These reservations made, it must be avowed that this most sustained effort of Cullen's poetic inspiration finds, to the very end, accents of a deeply moving sincerity, and the undeniable beauty of a number of scenes within this great poetic fresco bespeaks the writer's quality of soul no less than his genius.

May we conclude by affirming that Cullen's reconciliation with God brought him exemption from all his conflicts? Beyond a doubt, the unmediated communion with Christ in the mystic experience, by strengthening his faith, simultaneously silenced the mutinies of reason and self-conceit. But it was in the wake of great suffering that he made his peace with God,[206] and this occurred all of a sudden, as though a ground swell had in an instant swept away all the obstacles that hitherto seemed unscalable. There is no indication of that slow progression in self-conquest we observed with Claude McKay; in the end, rather than raising himself up to God, Cullen lets himself be overwhelmed by him.

Consequently, it is hard to suppress the feeling that the precipitancy of this spiritual maturation left certain problems with no definitive solution. More particularly, while he appears to have discovered the permanent value embodied by the people, it is less likely that his sympathy went beyond the strictly spiritual. He had grown up apart from the people, and to the very end the people seem to have remained an abstraction for him.

All in all, and in spite of its extordinary density, his poetic achievement will stand less as a mirroring of the black soul than as a living testimony to the great spiritual adventure of a poet named Countee Cullen.

thing about the poem is not the haphazard distribution of the rhymes, but the fact that rhyme is used at all; see the following note.

205 John Milton, *Paradise Lost,* in a note entitled "The Verse" (italics added). The degree to which the English poetic sense rebels against rhyme, especially when the poem attains a certain length, can be seen from the spontaneity of the reaction exhibited by a critic writing in the *Scots Observer,* November 28, 1929, where he speaks of the "facility, inappropriateness, or even occasionally *the almost comic character of its rhyming*" in his discussion of "The Black Christ" (italics added). Against these observations one may set the opposing declaration made by Cullen himself, in Paris, to an American journalist: "I don't like free verse. . . . Verse comes out of me rhymed and metered. Free verse does not fit me" (*Chicago Daily Tribune,* Paris ed., March 5, 1930, in an article signed "Montparno" and entitled "Countee Cullen Declares Poetry a Matter of Personal Taste, Not One of Definition").

206 The break with Yolande Du Bois occurred during the summer of 1928; "The Black Christ" is dated Paris, January 31, 1929, but was not published until the following fall.

SECTION B: In Search of the People

Chapter Nine: JAMES WELDON JOHNSON

James Weldon Johnson was doubtless one of the most distinguished and influential personalities the black world has ever known. When he called him "the aristocrat of Negro Americans,"[1] Claude McKay correctly indicated the prestige he won in his career as educator, legal expert, diplomat, racial leader, journalist, and writer.

But the richly deserved reputation which he enjoyed often redounded a trifle overmuch to the credit of his poetic achievement. To be specific, one can scarcely justify praise as excessive as that voiced by Horace Gregory and Marya Zaturenska, who chose to present Johnson as "the only American Negro poet of the twentieth century who achieved poetic maturity."[2] No one would deny that American Negro poetry is greatly in his debt, but the services he rendered it by publishing its first anthology are at least as memorable as the body of his poetic writings.

These indeed suffer from a major blemish, their impersonal character. Johnson was a public figure, imbued with the reserve and moderation that official responsibilities call for, and he was excessively concerned with respectability and conformity. Only rarely did he show himself capable of the limitless abandon without which there can be no real poetic emotion. His verses reveal nothing or almost nothing of his own intimate depths, and may even seek to hide them from us. Johnson can hardly be classed as a lyric poet, since he is too often satisfied with a borrowed or purely

[1] Claude McKay, *Right Turn to Catholicism*, p. 24.
[2] Horace Gregory and Marya Zaturenska, *A History of American Poetry 1900-1940*, p. 392.

351

conventional lyricism. Compared with McKay's earliest American poems, those making up Johnson's first collection, which came out that same year, resemble less the work of a forerunner than of a man trailing behind his time.

His chief contribution to the poetic harvest of the Renaissance was *God's Trombones,* Negro sermons in verse in which, availing himself of the example of his contemporary John Millington Synge, he tried to carry over, into a more respectable idiom than the rough Negro dialect, the essentials of the naïve, clumsy religious lyricism of the oldtime Negro preacher.

In short, Johnson's writings in verse, with which we are here solely concerned, bear no relationship to the lofty position occupied in the movement of racial renewal by this man who had such a wide range of interests, and who throughout his life placed his intelligence at the service of his race.

1. BIOGRAPHY[3]

From Florida to Broadway (1871-1906)

James Weldon Johnson was born on June 17, 1871, in Jacksonville, Florida, where his parents had gone to live two years earlier. In the home circle he learned to avoid both excessive fear of the white man and the tendency to esteem him too highly. His father, James Johnson, had been born free in Virginia and had worked for a time in Nassau in the Bahamas, where blacks made up the majority and race relations were less disturbed than in the United States. His mother, Helen Louise Dillet, was from Nassau and numbered among her white ancestors one of Napoleon's army officers who had had to flee Haiti when that island became independent.

In the city of his birth the young James Weldon attended Stanton Central Grammar School, where the students were all black, and where his mother was a teacher. In 1887 he entered the preparatory division of Atlanta University and, later, the actual university, from which he graduated in 1894. He then took over the Stanton School, replacing the retiring principal. He remained as the head of this institution for eight years, patiently setting out to raise the level of teaching, and finally transforming the school into a secondary school.

[3] There is no biographical study of Johnson. For the bulk of our information we turned to the poet's autobiography, *Along This Way,* and to the pamphlet *James Weldon Johnson,* published by Fisk University on the occasion of the homage paid by the University to the poet's memory, April 21-23, 1939.

During this period he was beset by other ambitions, yet he did not know in what precise direction to turn. He founded a newspaper, *The Daily American,* in 1894, but despite initial success it disappeared after eight months of existence. He then began the study of law, combining his obligations as school principal with a position as trainee with a lawyer in his native city. In 1897 he was admitted to the Florida bar.

But his brother Rosamond's return to Jacksonville directed his energies elsewhere. Rosamond had completed his study of music in Boston and had just spent a year with an itinerant dramatic company, whose successes he described with great enthusiasm. His head was full of projects for songs and musical comedies, and he was very anxious to awaken his brother's interest. During the summer vacation of 1899 the two went to New York to find a producer for *Toloso,* the opera which they had written in collaboration. This bold venture died aborning, but their quest brought them in contact with all the leading figures in show business. Before leaving New York they wrote a song, "Louisiana Lize," for Bob Cole, and received fifty dollars in payment.

Back in Jacksonville, James Weldon wrote dialect poems in his spare time, modeling them on Dunbar's. Most of them, in his own view,[4] were very trite. Nevertheless, "Sence You Went Away" was accepted and published by *The Century* and, after Rosamond set it to music, it became a hit. For the anniversary of Lincoln's birth, February 12, 1900, they composed "Lift Every Voice and Sing," which Black America today regards as the Negro national anthem.[5]

From that time on, it became the Johnson brothers' regular practice to spend their summers in New York. Rosamond settled there permanently, waiting for James Weldon to do the same upon resigning from the Stanton School (1902). Show business was now their exclusive concern. They became Broadway personalities, signing contracts, entering into partner-

[4] *Along This Way,* p. 154.
[5] For the circumstances in which "Lift Every Voice" was written, see *ibid.,* pp. 154-56. The two Johnson brothers, who had intended this song to be sung for Lincoln's birthday at a recreational program of a Jacksonville school (February 12, 1900), were responsible neither for its widespread use nor for its adoption as the Negro national anthem. This appears to have been overlooked by Ernest Lyon, a Negro Methodist pastor in Baltimore, former U.S. Minister to Liberia and later Liberian consul in the United States, when he published his pamphlet *A Protest against the Title of James Weldon Johnson's Anomalous Poem as a "Negro National Anthem" as Subversive of Patriotism* (n.p., [1926]). In this pamphlet, whose contents had already appeared in *The Afro-American Journal,* Lyon asserts that the song divides Americans and that Negroes, who are American citizens like everyone else, recognize only one flag and one national anthem. Thus the utilization of the Johnson brothers' song must be discouraged, according to the writer, since to do otherwise would be to practice segregation.

ships, composing musical comedies, and writing hundreds of songs. These were sung in New York and were greeted with applause when the company headed by Rosamond and Bob Cole took them from coast to coast and even to Europe (1905).[6]

Yet these Broadway years were not devoid of intellectual profit for James Weldon Johnson. While continuing to write for the world of commercialized art, he did not abandon hope of raising the artistic level of the Negro song by freeing it from its greatest crudities and introducing into it a more authentic Negro character. "I now began," he wrote, "to grope toward a realization of the American Negro's cultural background and his creative folk-art, and to speculate on the superstructure of conscious art that might be reared upon them."[7] It was doubtless these preoccupations that induced him to take up his studies once again. He registered as a student at Columbia University and for three years (1903-6) he followed the courses of Brander Matthews. His life, in any case, was about to take on a new orientation that would allow him to realize his projects.

In the Service of Country and Race (1906-38)

During the 1904 campaign to reelect Theodore Roosevelt he had been asked to head a Negro Republican Club, set up for this very purpose with headquarters on 53rd Street. Two years after the Republican victory he was offered, as reward for his services, a post as consul in Latin America. In this role he served successively in Venezuela and in Nicaragua (1906-12). This sinecure enabled him to write his novel *The Autobiography of an Ex-Colored Man,*[8] which he brought out anonymously in 1912, and the bulk of his first collection of poems, *Fifty Years and Other Poems,* published in 1917.

However, since the State Department appeared little inclined to honor its promises of promotion, he resigned in 1913 and, the following year, joined the staff of the *New York Age,* where his editorials were published until 1924. In 1916 he was appointed secretary general of the N.A.A.C.P., and in its ranks he strove for fourteen years to defend the interests of his racial brothers. In 1920 he carried out an investigation of the extortions

[6] The company went to Europe in order to give a number of performances in London. But before that the Johnson brothers had a lively time in Paris and Brussels, spending the larger part of $13,000 they had received for one of their songs.

[7] *Along This Way,* p. 152.

[8] On Johnson as a novelist, see Robert A. Bone, *The Negro Novel in America,* pp. 45-49; and Hugh Morris Gloster, *Negro Voices in American Fiction,* pp. 79-82.

and abuses being committed in Haiti by the American forces of occupation, and in his own land he endeavored — unfortunately, without total success — to have Congress pass effective legislation dealing with lynching (defeat of the Dyer bill in the Senate, 1922).

But his most eminent services to his race were his labors to make known the cultural achievements of the Negro past. In this way he also had a decisive influence on the development of the Negro Renaissance. His first step in this new direction was his poem "The Creation," published by *The Freeman* in 1918, and which tried to provide a serious literary mold for the popular Negro sermon. Four years later, he gave America its first anthology of Negro poetry, *The Book of American Negro Poetry.* This was followed by the two volumes containing 120 *Negro Spirituals* (1925, 1926), with musical arrangements by his brother Rosamond and extensive prefaces that tried to throw light on the history and probable origins of these slave songs. Meanwhile he wrote other Negro sermons in verse, on the lines of "The Creation"; these, published in 1927 as *God's Trombones,* are often looked on today as his most impressive poetic achievement.[9] The same year also witnessed the publication of a second edition of *The Autobiography of an Ex-Colored Man,* but this time under his own name, and with an introduction by Carl Van Vechten.

In 1929, a Rosenwald grant allowed him to carry out his plan to write a history of the Negro in New York; this was *Black Manhattan* (1930).

He resigned as secretary general of the N.A.A.C.P. in 1931 to accept the chair of creative literature offered him by Fisk University. This gave him a major influence in the education of the rising black elite.

To remove the misapprehensions of those who had taken *The Autobiography of an Ex-Colored Man* to be the story of his life, he gathered his personal reminiscences and brought them out as *Along This Way* (1933). The following year, the lectures he had given at Fisk University on various aspects of the race question were published in book form as *Negro Americans, What Now?*

He had now become one of the outstanding personalities in Black America, and New York University invited him as a visiting lecturer in the fall semester of each academic year to give a course on the Negro's contribution to American culture (1934-37).

Finally, he published *Saint Peter Relates an Incident* (1935), a selection of the 1917 poems preceded by a new poem, written in 1930.

It proved to be his last book. He was killed in an accident in Wiscasset, Maine, on June 26, 1938, when a train crashed into his car at a railroad crossing.

[9] In particular, this is the opinion of Harriet Monroe (see note 122 below).

2. DUNBAR'S DISCIPLE

"I recognized his genius, and in a measure regarded myself as his disciple."[10] This avowal concerning Dunbar was made by Johnson in 1933 in his autobiography. But one could safely wager that those who read *Fifty Years and Other Poems* in 1917 had no need to await the author's admission before discovering the full dimensions of his debt to the younger man. There was, indeed, a striking resemblance between the two men, though Johnson rarely achieved the flights of genuine poetry so often incontestably attained by Dunbar in his best poems.

Johnson, like Dunbar, had the soul of an entertainer, at home in show business, eager to please, and always on the alert for a possible success. As a student at Atlanta University he already sang in a vocal quartet that toured New England to raise funds for the university. The repertoire consisted mainly of spirituals, but Johnson also appeared with the guitar and sometimes related a comic anecdote that, he relates, "proved to be a very popular one."[11] But it was above all from 1897 on, when his brother Rosamond returned to Jacksonville upon completing his musical education, that jointly with him James Weldon Johnson resolutely set out to provide songs and musical shows whose sole aim it was to conquer Broadway. For seven years his mind was centered upon show business, and a whole section of his first volume of poems is there to remind us that he spent longer as songwriter than as poet.

Poetry in Dialect

Under the collective title of "Jingles and Croons," the dialect poems make up one-third of the 1917 collection, some of them previously having been popular hits. Among these were "Sence You Went Away," "Ma Lady's Lips Am Like de Honey," and "Nobody's Lookin' but de Owl and de Moon." Though the first of these pieces had originally been published in *The Century,* they are all basically commercial pieces, put together with every necessary precaution to ensure monetary success. The following details given by Johnson on the origins of "The Maiden with the Dreamy Eyes" leave no doubt on that score:

> In those days the royalties of a writer depended largely upon the young fellow who would buy a copy of the song and take it along with him when he went to call on his girl.... In writing *The Maiden With The Dreamy Eyes* we gave particular consideration to these fundamentals. It needed

[10] *Along This Way,* p. 160.
[11] *Ibid.,* p. 103.

little analysis to see that a song written in exclusive praise of blue eyes was cut off at once from about three-fourths of the possible chances for universal success; that it could make but faint appeal to the heart or pocketbook of a young man going to call on a girl with brown eyes or black eyes or gray eyes. So we worked on the chorus of our song until, without making it a catalogue, it was inclusive enough to enable any girl who sang it or to whom it was sung to fancy herself the maiden with the dreamy eyes.[12]

In most of these poems Johnson rather unimaginatively follows Dunbar's themes and manner; he does not always even bother to change the title of the imitated poems or the names of the characters.[13] Here to be found once again are all the types of song that had been in circulation twenty-five years earlier: the naïve, sugary love song,[14] the cradle song with which the black mammy lulls her picaninny to sleep,[15] the story of the rival rural swains,[16] the fable that pays homage to Brer Rabbit,[17] and even, on occasion, a discreet hymning of the good old days[18] and of good oldtime Georgia.[19] Johnson's portrait of the Negro, in its main lines, still adheres to the minstrel tradition. He is carefree and optimistic,[20] plays the banjo,[21] eats watermelon[22] and 'possum,[23] and steals chickens and turkeys[24] — all traits necessary to arouse an easy sense of superiority in the white public.

Of all the poems in this section, only one can boast a certain originality. "Tunk," with the subtitle "A Lecture on Modern Education," is at the opposite pole from Daniel Webster Davis's "Stickin' to de Hoe," since it tends to demonstrate, in an amusing way, that the race's social progress must depend to a great extent on progress in its education. When he was writing this poem, Johnson must certainly have recalled his experiences

---

[12] *Ibid.*, pp. 179-80.

[13] See, for example, James Weldon Johnson, "The Rivals," *Fifty Years and Other Poems*, pp. 84-92, and Paul Laurence Dunbar, "The Rivals," *Complete Poems*, pp. 43-46. In both poems, Liza is the name of the girl the rivals quarrel over. With Dunbar, the incident took place "three an' thirty year ago" (line 1), while Johnson specifies that "dat's been forty yeahs ago" (line 3), etc.

[14] "Sence You Went Away," *Fifty Years*, p. 63; "Ma Lady's Lips Am Like de Honey," *ibid.*, pp. 64-65; "Nobody's Lookin' but de Owl and de Moon," p. 69; "Dat Gal o' Mine," p. 77.

[15] "You's Sweet to Yo Mammy Jes de Same," *ibid.*, pp. 70-71; "De Little Pickaninny's Gone to Sleep," p. 83.

[16] See note 13 above.

[17] "Brer Rabbit, You's de Cutes' of 'Em All," *ibid.*, pp. 81-82.

[18] "A Banjo Song," *ibid.*, p. 74, lines 1-3.

[19] "July in Georgy," *ibid.*, p. 73.

[20] "A Plantation Bacchanal," *ibid.*, pp. 71-72.

[21] See notes 18, 20 above.

[22] "July in Georgy," line 12; "The Seasons," *ibid.*, p. 78, stanzas 2 and 3.

[23] "The Seasons," stanzas 1 and 3; "'Possum Song," *ibid.*, pp. 79-80.

[24] "Answer to Prayer," *ibid.*, pp. 75-76; "An Explanation," p. 82.

as a onetime teacher in an out-of-the-way Georgia village,[25] where the Negro children attended school only during the summer months when Atlanta University students could earn a little pocket money by teaching school. Tunk was the name of one of the dunces in Johnson's class, and his entirely comprehensible ignorance was of the kind that condemned to wretched poverty and a primitive existence all the black rural folk left destitute on the fringes of the white majority's culture:

> W'en you sees a darkey goin' to de fiel' as soon as light,
> Followin' a mule across it f'om de mawnin' tel de night,
>
> Wukin' all his life fu' vittles, hoein' 'tween de cott'n rows,
> W'en he knocks off ole an' tiah'd, ownin' nut'n but his clo'es,
>
> You kin put it down to ignunce, aftah all what's done an' said,
> You kin bet dat dat same darkey ain't got nut'n in his head.
>
> Ain't you seed dem w'ite men set'n in der awfice? Don't you know
> Dey goes der 'bout nine each mawnin'? Bless yo' soul, dey's out by fo'.
>
> Dey jes does a little writin'; does dat by some easy means;
> Gals jes set an' play piannah on dem printin' press muchines.
>
> Chile, dem men knows how to figgah, how to use dat little pen,
> And dey knows dat blue-back spellah f'om beginnin' to de en'.
>
> Dat's de 'fect of education; dat's de t'ing what's gwine to rule;
> Git dem books, you lazy rascal! Git back to yo' place in school![26]

In the domain of dialect poetry, it was hard to do better than, or even as well as, Dunbar,[27] and in "Jingles and Croons" Johnson never attains the spontaneity of expression, the vivacious rhythm, or the melodiousness of his distinguished forerunner.

Moreover, Johnson would later repudiate, with as much vehemence as Dunbar had shown, this portion of his work[28] which had enabled him, in the century's opening years, to win a somewhat superficial popularity on Broadway. Yet some of his poems in standard English are scarcely less conformist than his dialect poems.

Religious and Patriotic Conformism

Since the avowal made in his autobiography five years before his death,

---

[25] See the account of this experience in *Along This Way*, pp. 107ff.

[26] "Tunk," *Fifty Years*, pp. 67-68, line 13 to end. The "blue-back spellah" is Noah Webster's famous dark blue spelling book, which was so extensively used in American grade schools that more than seventy million copies, it is estimated, were sold before 1900.

[27] This was Johnson's own opinion. See *Along This Way*, p. 159.

[28] On this topic, see "The Condemnation of Dialect" below.

we know that all Johnson's religious poetry came from the pen of an unbeliever.[29]

Under the influence of his maternal grandmother, who would have liked to see him become a minister, from the age of nine he had been forced into religious observances, inappropriate for a child, in the Methodist church which she attended. When she wanted him to be accepted as a full-fledged member, an argument broke out between her and her son-in-law; this aroused anxiety in the child. With it was blended his dislike for certain external religious practices common in the popular Negro churches:

> These combined factors at length produced reluctance, doubt, rebellion. I began to ask myself questions that frightened me. I groped within the narrow boundaries of my own knowledge and experience and between the covers of the Bible for answers, because I did not know to whom I could turn . . . I was alone with my questionings and doubts. . . . At fourteen I was skeptical. By the time I reached my Freshman year at Atlanta University I had avowed myself an agnostic.[30]

His openly proclaimed agnosticism led to some friction in Atlanta University, "a missionary-founded school, in which playing a game of cards and smoking a cigarette were grave offenses."[31] This experience, in which his frankness was poorly rewarded, may have given rise to the reserve with which he would henceforth surround his metaphysical convictions. Not only did he reveal nothing of his agnosticism in his poetry; quite the contrary, he strewed left and right declarations of trust in God the Creator and in Providence, as though he were speaking on his own account.

One sole feeble echo of his doubts regarding life after death can be heard in the last two lines of the sonnet "Sleep":

> Man, why should thought of death cause thee to weep,
> Since death be but an endless, dreamless sleep?[32]

But this is slight, compared to the numerous passages that could convince one of his religious orthodoxy.

Since he did not believe in God, why did he turn to him in prayer? Thus the envoi at the end of the 1917 collection begs the Almighty for inspiration and persuasive force:

[29] The definition of his agnostic attitude will be found in *Along This Way*, pp. 413-14. On his religious experience at home, see *ibid.*, pp. 21-31.
[30] *Ibid.*, p. 30.
[31] *Ibid.*
[32] *Fifty Years*, p. 50.
[33] *Ibid.*, p. 93. In the 1917 edition this poem does not bear the title "Envoy," which is to be found only in *Saint Peter Relates an Incident — Selected Poems by James Weldon Johnson* (1935), p. 103.

O God, give beauty and strength — truth to my words,[33]

and if that other personal request, "Prayer at Sunrise," does not expressly invoke the Deity, there can be no doubt that Johnson is thinking of him when he addresses the "greater Maker of this Thy great sun."[34] How could anyone guess he was an agnostic, hearing him proclaim:

... God's above, and God is love[35]

or again, when he offers this assurance to Horace Bumstead, president of Atlanta University:

... sure as God on His eternal throne
Sits, mindful of the sinful deeds of men,
— The awful Sword of Justice in His hand, —
You shall not, no, you shall not, fight alone.[36]

While maintaining that the universe had no purpose, in "Fifty Years" he nevertheless twice utters the conviction that the Negro's destiny is a part of God's great design:

A part of His unknown design,
We've lived within a mighty age;[37]

. . . .

Faith in your God-known destiny!
We are a part of some great plan.[38]

And in the celebrated poem "O Black and Unknown Bards," the principal merit he discerns in these bards who composed the spirituals is to have converted a race of idolators to Christ:

... the songs
That for your listeners' hungry hearts sufficed
Still live, — but more than this to you belongs:
You sang a race from wood and stone to Christ.[39]

Faced with such categorical declarations, one might feel tempted to conjecture that Johnson's agnosticism sometimes grew faint along the path, and that there were periods in his life when traditional religiosity

[34] "Prayer at Sunrise," *Fifty Years*, p. 51.
[35] "O Southland!" stanza 3, line 7, *ibid.*, p. 9. This passage may be compared with the last line of "Fragment," *ibid.*, p. 18: "God is not love, no, God is law."
[36] "To Horace Bumstead," *ibid.*, p. 10.
[37] "Fifty Years," stanza 5, lines 1-2, *ibid.*, p. 1.
[38] *Ibid.*, stanza 23, lines 3-4, p. 4.
[39] "O Black and Unknown Bards," *ibid.*, p. 8.

gained the upper hand. But nothing authorizes such a supposition,[40] and if we may trust his belated avowal in *Along This Way* (1933), his agnosticism remained unwavering to the very end.

> I have not felt the need of religion in the commonplace sense of the term. I have derived spiritual values in life from other sources than worship or prayer. . . .
>
> As far as I am able to peer into the inscrutable, I do not see that there is any evidence to refute those scientists and philosophers who hold that the universe is purposeless; that man, instead of being the special care of a Divine Providence, is a dependent upon fortuity and his own wits for survival in the midst of blind and insensate forces.[41]

Thus Johnson's religious poetry does not express his personal feelings; it merely conforms — in a way whose precise meaning is, in our view, most clearly apparent in certain commemorative poems that are semi-official in nature. The first of these, written in 1900, is "Lift Every Voice and Sing," which Black America spontaneously adopted as a Negro national anthem, and which ends with a fervent prayer to a providential God:

> God of our weary years,
> God of our silent tears,
> Thou who hast brought us thus far on the way;
> Thou who hast by Thy might
> Led us into the light,
> Keep us forever in the path, we pray,

[40] Except, perhaps, for this detail: during the summer of 1888, when there was an epidemic of yellow fever in Jacksonville, Johnson was in the employ of a local medical man, Dr. Summers. In the doctor's library he read *Some Mistakes of Moses* and *The Gods and Other Lectures,* but also *The Age of Reason* by Thomas Paine. This recollection, together with that of Ingersoll, may have helped to lend a slight tinge of deism to his agnosticism. But this influence, if indeed it ever existed, must have been minimal. See *Along This Way,* pp. 94ff.

[41] *Ibid.,* p. 413. To round out Johnson's confessions as contained in his autobiography, let us point out the existence of an essay on the foundations of morals, "The Origin of Sin," to the best of our knowledge never published, consisting of a six-sheet typescript preserved in the James Weldon Johnson file of the Negro Collection in Atlanta University. After making the arbitrary declaration that the origin of sin remains one of theology's mysteries, Johnson in this essay reaches the conclusion that the notion of sin was invented by man to enhance the natural pleasure he took in certain acts by adding that of the forbidden fruit. In the course of his argument he deplores the existence of a moral sense which, by bringing man into conflict with himself, is in large part responsible for making him unhappy. In a certain way, too, his moral sense makes man inferior to the animals. Johnson illustrates this point by citing Walt Whitman ("Song of Myself" 32, lines 1-5); but the way in which the problems are tackled awakens the impression that another influence was that of Mark Twain's *The Mysterious Stranger.*

> Lest our feet stray from the places, our God,
>   where we met Thee,
> Lest, our hearts drunk with the wine of the world,
>   we forget Thee;
> Shadowed beneath Thy hand,
> May we forever stand
> True to our God,
> True to our native land.[42]

The last two lines sum up the twin conformity of religion and patriotism that sounds the dominant note in *Fifty Years and Other Poems*. It is as though Johnson realized that, in a country where the inalienable rights of all men are officially derived from a gift made by their Creator,[43] the Negro could hardly expect to be heard until he had at least formally professed his faith in the existence of this Creator and his loyalty to his country.

God and country are no less closely associated in "Fifty Years," the commemorative poem written for the fiftieth anniversary of Emancipation and published by the *New York Times* on that very date: January 1, 1913. In it the liberation of the slaves is presented as God's handiwork, with Lincoln acting as the instrument of the Divine will:

> ... God, through Lincoln's ready hand,
> Struck off our bonds and made us men.[44]

On the soil of America, Negroes have undergone a multiple transformation;

> Far, far the way that we have trod,
> From heathen kraals and jungle dens,
> To freedmen, freemen, sons of God,
> Americans and Citizens.[45]

One may note, incidentally, the unflattering expressions used by Johnson in his references to Africa. Negroes had been living there in "heathen kraals" or even in dens like animals, from which God chose to remove them out of sheer mercy:

> Then let us here erect a stone,
> To mark the place, to mark the time;

[42] "Lift Every Voice and Sing," *Saint Peter Relates an Incident*, p. 102. Though this poem was written as early as 1900, it is not included in the 1917 collection.
[43] Declaration of Independence, par. 2.
[44] "Fifty Years," stanza 1, lines 2-3, *Fifty Years*, p. 1.
[45] *Ibid.,* stanza 4. In the 1935 edition, the second line has been changed to read: "From slave and pagan denizens." Stanzas 4 and 7 have also changed places.

> A witness to God's *mercies* shown,
> A pledge to hold this day sublime.[46]

The word "mercies" was bound to serve as an unpleasant reminder of that line of Phillis Wheatley's:

> 'Twas mercy brought me from my pagan land[47]

— as Johnson probably realized, for in the 1935 edition he put in its place the word "purpose," and also dropped from the poem the two following stanzas whose humility and submissiveness, both to God and to White America, was absolutely not the right thing, after the swath cut in its stormy passage by the nationalism of the Negro Renaissance:

> And let that stone an altar be,
> Whereon thanksgivings we may lay,
> Where we, in deep humility,
> For faith and strength renewed may pray.
>
> With open hearts ask from above
> New zeal, new courage and new pow'rs,
> That we may grow more worthy of
> This country and this land of ours.[48]

As was true of Dunbar, nothing in Johnson evokes rebellion or rebels. The heroes of whom he sings are all loyal, faithful national heroes, and not racial heroes. Most of them, too, are whites: the abolitionists Garrison, Phillips, and Lovejoy; John Brown, of course, and Lincoln the Emancipator.[49] He praises only two blacks: Crispus Attucks,[50] the first to fall in the struggle for the country's independence, and the humble standard-bearer who, though despised by all, loyally gave his life for his country at the battle of San Juan Hill:

> Black though his skin, yet his heart as true
> As the steel of his blood-stained saber.
>
> .   .   .   .
>
> Despised of men for his humble race,
> Yet true, in death, to his duty.[51]

His attitude toward the South is almost more submissive and senti-

[46] *Ibid.*, stanza 7 (italics added).
[47] See above, Ch. 1.
[48] "Fifty Years," stanzas 8 and 9, *Fifty Years*, p. 2.
[49] *Ibid.*, stanzas 24 and 25, p. 5.
[50] *Ibid.*, stanza 14, p. 3.
[51] "The Color Sergeant," *ibid.*, p. 11.

mental than Dunbar's. "O Southland!"[52] is the humble appeal of a weakling who asks for charity, and one would seek in vain for even the most muted protest against the abominations to which, as Johnson well knew, Negroes were being subjected in his own country.

Must we then brand Johnson a hypocrite?[53] His parade of religious orthodoxy is a paradoxical phenomenon, it must be confessed. Even Dunbar, though he seems to have been less grievously afflicted by doubt than Johnson, had bravely confided to his verses moving accounts of his problems with religious belief. But Johnson does not reveal himself, and speaks rather in the name of the racial or national community without allowing his own emotions to pour out. As for the avowal of his agnosticism, that will be judged opportune only in his declining years.

His behavior might appear to be dictated, in the first place, by a certain discretion, by the desire not to shock majority opinion and to respect its convictions. In any event, the following passage from his autobiography, in which he speaks of his lack of religion, would tend to convey that impression: "But I make no boast of it; understanding, as I do, how essential religion is to many, many people."[54]

Nevertheless, without making any display of his unbelief, he might have avoided affirming the antithesis of his real convictions and maintained a discreet neutrality. The miming of strong religious feeling was not called for.

Thus the thought arises that he conformed, to a very large degree, for reasons of diplomacy. Like humor in the dialect poems, the facade of religious orthodoxy fulfills the function of dissimulation and self-defense. In either case, the individual hides his real feelings behind ramparts constructed *ad hoc*, and the outer world, whose hostility must be appeased, is allowed to see only a mask which, in every respect, corresponds to the mythical portrait that prejudice has put together. Since, in the eyes of the majority, the Negro is deemed especially religious, it is better to acquiesce and to put on the externals of religion, if necessary, rather than offend the majority by showing oneself as one is. This is a kind of moral camouflage, or mimicry. As we have already stated, it is in order to strengthen the

[52] *Ibid.,* pp. 8-9.

[53] Johnson's own view was that the prayer meetings held at Atlanta University encouraged students in a hypocritical, conformist attitude: "I doubt not that there were students who enjoyed their prayer meetings and were spiritually benefited, but I believe the main effect was to put a premium on hypocrisy or, almost as bad, to substitute for religion a lazy and stupid conformity" (*Along This Way,* p. 81). For a similar remark on prayer, see *ibid.,* p. 44.

[54] *Ibid.,* p. 413.

Negro's claim to equal treatment that Johnson presents him as absolutely identical with the national ideal, which treats as indivisible belief in God and loyalty to one's country.

But Johnson's conformist behavior looks not only to the opinions of the white majority. In the tradition of his own race, too, the themes of religious orthodoxy have always been so closely intertwined with those of race that to separate them is almost unthinkable. Thus the religious themes survive and assert their authority, even after genuine religious feeling has practically evaporated. Involved here is a transfer of values, causing the religious theme to lose its sacral substance and to stand only for one racial theme among many others. The transfer seems to have occurred all the more easily because sacred and profane had been almost indistinguishable in the overall concept of Negro religion. This was true for both the ambivalent language of the spirituals and for the ambivalent figure of the Negro pastor, who was a racial as well as a spiritual leader.

Thus the poet, through the totality of signs constituted by the religious context of his poetry, no longer proclaims his adhesion to a metaphysical notion he had set aside long before. He announces his decision to remain one with a community that is at the same time national and racial.[55] How this finds expression is determined, ultimately, by social constraints no less powerful than those Dunbar had known. As a consequence, the bulk of Johnson's 1917 volume of poems, constructed around a conventional outlook, appears to us sadly lacking in that "spontaneous overflow of powerful feelings" which, according to Wordsworth,[56] is the distinctive mark of all good poetry.

3. JOHNSON AND THE NEW SPIRIT

If Johnson's lack of lyric upsurge and spontaneity leaves most of the poems in *Fifty Years and Other Poems* lagging behind Dunbar's work, an exception must nevertheless be made for a few poems which are characterized by a more mature racial consciousness, a less rudimentary critical sense, and a firmer tone with respect to White America. It is permissible, on the strength of these poems, to see in Johnson an immediate forerunner of the Renaissance.

---

[55] An analogous intention should probably be seen behind Johnson's gesture of agreeing, not long before he left for Fisk University, to become a deacon of Saint James Presbyterian Church in Harlem. On other occasions Johnson was a severe critic of the Black Church, which he charged with pretentiousness, corruption, inefficacy in practical matters, and a purely formal morality. On this, see *Negro Americans, What Now?* pp. 20-26.

[56] William Wordsworth, preface to *Lyrical Ballads* (1800 ed.).

Yet one must not follow John Hope Franklin[57] and base this assertion on "Fifty Years," in which the poet comes nowhere near the spirit that would imbue the New Negro. It contains fleeting references to Africa that are hardly laudatory, the estimate of the race's progress since reaching American shores seems excessively optimistic, and declarations of humility and loyalty far outweigh protest. This attitude was deliberate, for the poet thought it more appropriate to the celebration of Emancipation's fifty years than were the despairing stanzas that originally had concluded the manuscript poem, and which Johnson suppressed prior to publication.[58] Yet his dignity and moderation do not hinder his roundly denouncing injustice and servitude, with no attempt to minimize them, nor his restating forcefully the black race's right to an equitable share in the national heritage:

> For never let the thought arise
> That we are here on sufferance bare;
> Outcasts, asylumed 'neath these skies,
> And aliens without part or share.
>
> This land is ours by right of birth,
> This land is ours by right of toil;
> We helped to turn its virgin earth,
> Our sweat is in its fruitful soil.[59]

Johnson was not the man to throw down the gauntlet to America. He preferred to appeal to its reason and to persuade it that, since blacks and whites are irrevocably destined to live in association, the welfare of one group can only be maintained through assuring the welfare of the other. "To America" tries to convince America that it has the choice of making the black minority an element of strength for the nation or, on the contrary, a brake on its progress:

> How would you have us, as we are?
> Or sinking 'neath the load we bear?
>
> .   .   .   .
>
> Strong, willing sinews in your wings?
> Or tightening chains about your feet?[60]

But the question arises whether, in the poet's mind, the hour of this

[57] John Hope Franklin, *From Slavery to Freedom,* p. 493.
[58] On the writing of this poem, see *Along This Way,* pp. 289-91, where Johnson speaks of fifteen discarded stanzas. In *Fifty Years and Other Poems,* the poem has been cut down from 41 stanzas to 26 stanzas, and in the 1935 edition only 24 will remain.
[59] "Fifty Years," stanzas 10 and 11, *Fifty Years,* p. 2.
[60] "To America," *ibid.,* p. 5.

choice has not already passed. That, at least, is the conclusion one might derive from "Fragment," which offers a vision of the future hopelessly bogged down in past mistakes. While the country persisted in its prejudices and injustice, Johnson argues, its black population had unnoticeably been transformed for it into a divisive factor, a wedge inserted ever more deeply until the day came when, the split completed, the two halves of the nation rose against each other in bloody conflict:

> See! In your very midst there dwell
> Ten thousand thousand blacks, a wedge
> Forged in the furnaces of hell,
> And sharpened to a cruel edge
> By wrong and by injustice fell,
> And driven by hatred as a sledge.
>
> A wedge so slender at the start —
> Just twenty slaves in shackles bound —
> And yet, which split the land apart
> With shrieks of war and battle sound,
> Which pierced the nation's very heart,
> And still lies cankering in the wound.[61]

The wound in the nation's heart has not been cured thereby, the valor of the combatants has been expended in vain, and Johnson predicts that America's sin against its black minority will continue to weigh upon the future generations until it is at last expiated.

Yet he does not seem to have thought that the hostility dividing blacks and whites disproved the fact that they were destined to be brothers — quarreling brothers, perhaps, but brothers all the same. How else could he have given the title "Brothers" to a poem on lynching which, according to Sterling Brown, is "the most vigorous poem of protest from any Negro poet up to his time"?[62] How else could he have put these last words in the mouth of the Negro, as he dies at the hands of his lynchers:

> "Brothers in spirit, brothers in deed are we"?[63]

To behold the poet thus unflinchingly manifesting his faith in racial brotherhood leaves one divided between admiration for his idealism and awareness of a certain incoherence in the sequence of episodes that make up this "American drama."[64] The most authentic and gripping part of the

[61] "Fragment," stanzas 2 and 3, *ibid.*, pp. 17-18.
[62] Sterling A. Brown, *Negro Poetry and Drama*, pp. 50-51.
[63] "Brothers," last line, *Fifty Years*, p. 17.
[64] In the 1935 edition the poem is entitled "Brothers — American Drama" (*Saint Peter Relates an Incident*, p. 27).

poem is the forceful, realistic description of the lynching — which is the first of its kind in American poetry. With greater audacity than Dunbar in "The Haunted Oak," Johnson piles up the macabre details, depicts the flesh of the victim blistering in the flames and falling away in strips, and stresses the sadism of the killers who, when it threatens to end all too rapidly, throw water on the fire to slow it down, so that they may still revel in this ghastly spectacle. We may also admire the poet's notion of having the victim's last words arouse anguish in the minds of the lynchers. He does not, however, anticipate Cullen by suggesting to us that there is a parallel between this burning and the death of Christ on the cross, though he does eloquently suggest the victim's spiritual triumph and the moral defeat of triumphant brute force.

But how clumsily this powerful scene is introduced! It follows immediately, without the least psychological motivation, upon a no less implausible dialogue between the mob and the Negro they have seized. Doubtless it was Johnson's intention to demonstrate by concrete example that many lynchings had not a shadow of justification, and three lines before the end there is some mention of a "fiendish crime" the victim is said to have committed. But this does not eliminate the incoherence, which actually is double — for the lynching scene, to which is grafted the idea of brotherhood heralded by the title, has no organic connection with the first forty lines or so, which could have been utilized in a separate poem.

This earlier section appears to propound the thesis, later developed in Richard Wright's novels, that Negro criminality is due to the corruption whose victim he was, because of the treatment he suffered at the hands of the majority. Here are the actual terms in which the Negro of the poem defines himself, when the mob asks him who he is:

> ... I am that which lurks,
> Ready to spring whenever a bar is loosed;
>
> · · · ·
>
> The weight forever seeking to obey
> The law of downward pull — and I am more:
> The bitter fruit am I of planted seed;
> The resultant, the inevitable end
> Of evil forces and the power of wrong.[65]

Then comes an enumeration of all the trials, humiliations, and tragedies both physical and moral which have constituted the existence of the Negro in America, and which these lines sum up:

[65] "Brothers," lines 17-18, 21-25.

> ... I am
> No more than human dregs; degenerate;
> The monstrous offspring of the monster, Sin;[66]

So the Negro is no longer himself but has become, under the corrupting effect of oppression and injustice, an actual beast, having lost even the sense of belonging to any human race whatever:

> I claim no race, no race claims me ...[67]

It can be seen that, considered by itself, this first part of the poem lacks neither originality nor a certain grandeur. It might even have led logically to the lynching episode, but the connection would have required motivation — by showing us, for example, how the mob, suddenly made aware of its centuries-old crime against the black race, tried to cover this primordial crime by committing another. But nothing of this kind exists even in outline, and with the cry of "Enough!" the crowd silences the Negro and begins to lynch him.

The theme of brotherhood announced in the title also becomes obscured in the incoherence. Johnson presents it much more satisfactorily in another poem, "The Black Mammy." Frankly departing from the sentimentality the plantation tradition had attached to every mention of this figure, who often received a somewhat hypocritical veneration in the great families of the South, the poet is interested in and illuminates only the tragic aspect of the black nurse's situation. She must lavish the same generosity on her own child and on the other, who may one day crush him:

> Thou simple soul, as cuddling down that babe
> With thy sweet croon, so plaintive and so wild,
> Came ne'er the thought to thee, swift like a stab,
> That it some day might crush thine own black child?[68]

If Johnson rang so many changes on the theme of the hostile brothers, the reason is that this concept's internal contradiction, with its elements suggesting both fraternal love and the opposite, no doubt provided him with a fitting symbol for that other contradiction falsifying relations between blacks and whites who, though the children of the same fatherland and proclaiming the same ideal of liberty, nevertheless are divided by history and by descent.

Johnson hits upon the same contradiction once more, in different form, when he takes up the theme of interracial love in "The White Witch."

[66] *Ibid.*, lines 39-41.
[67] *Ibid.*, line 39.
[68] "The Black Mammy," lines 13-16, *Fifty Years*, p. 12.

This is probably the best poem in the volume, as it assuredly is the most "modern."

Yet, at first glance, the symbolism here may seem bewildering. Johnson himself has stated that many readers had found it obscure, but he adds that, for his part, he finds the meaning entirely clear.[69] In fact, however, the character who provides the poem's title has a complex meaning.

The white witch stands, in the first place, for the eternal feminine. As early as the second stanza the poet forthrightly declares that this is no old, toothless creature who terrifies little children; quite the contrary, she is adorned with all the charms of youth. Yet she is as old as the world.[70] Thus her bewitching nature is principally that of love.

This portrait is rendered more complex by the racial context into which it is introduced, for the white witch is also the incarnation of the Aryan racial type with blue eyes, fair hair, and lily-white skin.[71] At the same time she symbolizes the white purity which racist America is intent on defending against any admixture of black blood. Such, at all events, is the official doctrine, for in reality the attraction she possesses for the Negro is equaled only by the attraction she feels for him. Since she sees the Negro as closer to the state of nature than the white man, because he is still in close contact with the earth from which, like Antaeus, he derives his strength, the white woman rightly or wrongly attributes to him a greater sexual potency, and initially she expects him to reveal carnal delights hitherto unknown:

> Oh! she has seen your strong young limbs,
> And heard your laughter loud and gay,
> And in your voices she has caught
> The echo of a far-off day,
> When man was closer to the earth;
> And she has marked you for her prey.

> She feels the old Antaean strength
> In you, the great dynamic beat
> Of primal passions, and she sees
> In you the last besieged retreat
> Of love relentless, lusty, fierce,
> Love pain-ecstatic, cruel-sweet.[72]

Yet the witch of the poem is not only a passionate lover; she has also the undeniably maleficent character announced in the opening stanza:

[69] *Along This Way*, p. 306.
[70] "The White Witch," stanza 4, *Fifty Years*, p. 19.
[71] *Ibid.*, stanza 3.
[72] *Ibid.*, stanzas 8 and 9.

O brothers mine, take care! Take care!
The great white witch rides out tonight,
Trust not your prowess nor your strength;
Your only safety lies in flight;
For in her glance there is a snare,
And in her smile there is a blight.[73]

It would still be necessary to specify the danger against which Johnson warns his racial brothers. This is the very point at which the poem moves to the symbolic level. There is no question of the traditional punishment meted out to the Negro whose love for a white woman has become known. The danger is bound up, rather, with another feature in the portrait of the white witch. The poet, who tells us that he has already yielded to her charms,[74] has learned that beneath the fascinating exterior of the woman passionately in love she hides her vampire-like nature,[75] and that in the sexual embrace she seeks to rob of his substance the prey who lets himself be entrapped by her wiles. In particular, she is declared to be a "twin sister to the greedy earth,"[76] a possible allusion to the earth goddess Rhea, whose violent attachment to the god Attis ended in his emasculation.

Thus the poem's meaning reaches far beyond the theme of interracial love on which it is based, and in the last resort the white witch stands for the whole world of the white man. The reciprocal attraction between the two races is not only of the flesh; it is also felt throughout the many forms of civilization and culture, and in this lies, for the Negro, the chief risk of emasculation. By giving in to the powerful attraction the majority culture exerts on him, the Negro runs the risk of losing his own personality, together with his weapons of defense against the basic hostility of the white world. That is why Johnson advises him to seek safety only in flight.

Finally, it is possible to transpose into a historical context this vampirism, disguised beneath the outer signs of love, by seeing it as a characterization of the white man's striving for domination which, under the pretext of extending to Africans the blessings of civilization and the light of faith, reduced them to slavery and built an economic system on their continued exploitation.

At any level, consequently, at the heart of this poem — as was true also for the theme of the hostile brothers — is the association of those two opposites, love and enmity. Like James Edwin Campbell, who had obscurely sensed the profound meaning of the theme of interracial love in

73 *Ibid.*, stanza 1.
74 *Ibid.*, stanza 7.
75 *Ibid.*, stanza 5.
76 *Ibid.*, stanza 4, line 6.

"A Love Dream," Johnson does no more than state the terms of the antithesis. It will remain for others to raise the level of the debate and to
strive for a synthesis. But the fact remains that Johnson broke truly fresh
ground by endeavoring to elucidate, via this symbol, the extent of the basic
contradiction keeping the races apart. Especially if one bears in mind the
inadequacy of the few poems he published in 1935,[77] it is no exaggeration
to assert that his genuinely creative poetic effort is contained in its entirety
in the 1917 collection.

4. Folklore and Race: Their Rehabilitation

No less paradoxical than the religious feeling he displays in his poetry is
the strange attraction felt by Johnson the agnostic for the religious folklore of his race. One of the most remarkable poems in *Fifty Years* already
expressed his admiration for the unknown authors of the spirituals, and
his amazement that such noble songs could have sprung from the heart of
a race so obscure and so despised:

[77] In any event, with "The White Witch" Johnson reached a summit. This impression is confirmed by an examination of his 1935 volume, *Saint Peter Relates
an Incident,* consisting chiefly of poems that had already appeared in the 1917
collection, with only five new poems added. Of these, the only one with a racial
character is "Saint Peter Relates an Incident of the Resurrection Day" (pp. 13-
22). Originally published in 1930 in a limited edition, it was written to protest
against a particularly odious piece of racial discrimination committed by the
federal government, in connection with a pilgrimage of Gold Star Mothers to the
American military cemeteries in France. The black mothers were not allowed to
leave at the same time as the white mothers, who embarked on a luxury liner,
while the black mothers followed on an inferior vessel. In Johnson's poem, which
sets out to be humorous, Saint Peter tells the angels, long after time has ended,
how on Resurrection Day all the American patriotic groups came in a body to
witness the resurrection of the unknown soldier, and to escort him into paradise.
But when the tombstone was raised the unknown soldier, amid universal con-
sternation, turned out to be a Negro. For a moment the thought is entertained
of putting him back in the tomb, but then the whole throng disbands and forsakes
the unknown soldier, who makes his way into paradise alone, singing the spiritual
"Deep River." While this was an original idea, it was frittered away in this poorly
structured poem. There is a shocking imbalance between the central theme, which
extends over 56 lines of the fourth part, and the far too long introductory section
of 68 lines, often uninteresting and in dubious taste. The versification did not
profit from the speed with which the poem was written (see Johnson's remarks on
this, *Saint Peter Relates an Incident,* p. ix), and there are many rhythmic blemishes (in the first part alone, for instance, p. 13, stanza 3, line 4, and stanza 4,
lines 1 and 4, etc.). But the poem fails above all because Johnson is simply not a
humorist. This weakness was already noticeable in the poems of the 1917 collection
("Answer to Prayer," "An Explanation"), and in this new poem it is evident
beyond any gainsaying. Commonplace, vague notations (for example, in these
two lines of the second stanza: "The faces of the flaming seraphim / Were slightly
drawn, their eyes were slightly dim") too often are substituted for that incisive insight into reality that is one of the main sources of humor.

O black and unknown bards of long ago,
How came your lips to touch the sacred fire?
How, in your darkness, did you come to know
The power and beauty of the minstrel's lyre?
Who first from midst his bonds lifted his eyes?
Who first from out the still watch, lone and long,
Feeling the ancient faith of prophets rise
Within his dark-kept soul, burst into song?

· · · · ·

Not that great German master in his dream
Of harmonies that thundered amongst the stars
At the creation, ever heard a theme
Nobler than "Go down, Moses." Mark its bars,
How like a mighty trumpet-call they stir
The blood. Such are the notes that men have sung
Going to valorous deeds; such tones there were
That helped make history when Time was young.

There is a wide, wide wonder in it all,
That from degraded rest and servile toil
The fiery spirit of the seer should call
These simple children of the sun and soil.
O black slave singers, gone, forgot, unfamed,
You — you alone, of all the long, long line
Of those who've sung untaught, unknown, unnamed,
Have stretched out upward, seeking the divine.[78]

Of course, the poet did not share the faith whose expression he admires in the spirituals, and if with evident sincerity he praises their authors for having raised their souls to God, despite their debased condition, this merely proves that he was not narrowly sectarian. But, basically, the religious content of these songs did not interest Johnson except to the extent that it might move the nation's white majority. If he undertook to make the beauty of Negro folklore better known and appreciated, and with this purpose in mind brought out his two collections of spirituals, it was because he expected that the artistic and religious emotions thus awakened in the public would create a favorable climate likely to shake the foundations of the nation's prejudices. Significant in this connection is one passage in the preface to *The Second Book of Negro Spirituals* (1926) where Johnson, speaking of the spirituals, states:

For more than a half century they have touched and stirred the hearts
of people and effected a softening down of some of the hard edges of

[78] "O Black and Unknown Bards," stanzas 1, 4, 5, *Fifty Years,* pp. 6-7. The "great German master" of the text is probably Joseph Haydn.

prejudice against the Negro. Measured by lengths of years, they have wrought more in sociology than in art. Indeed, within the past decade and especially within the past two or three years they have been, perhaps, the main force in breaking down the immemorial stereotype that the Negro in America is nothing more than a beggar at the gate of the nation, waiting to be thrown the crumbs of civilization; that he is here only to receive; to be shaped into something new and unquestionably better.

This awakening to the truth that the Negro is an active and important force in American life; that he is a creator as well as a creature; that he has given as well as received . . . is, I think, due more to the present realization of the beauty and value of the Spirituals than to any other one cause.[79]

He had said the same thing about Negro poetry four years earlier, in the preface to his anthology *The Book of American Negro Poetry:*

The final measure of the greatness of all peoples is the amount and standard of the literature and art they have produced. The world does not know that a people is great until that people produces great literature and art. No people that has produced great literature and art has ever been looked upon by the world as distinctly inferior.

The status of the Negro in the United States is more a question of national mental attitude toward the race than of actual conditions. And nothing will do more to change that mental attitude and raise his status than a demonstration of intellectual parity by the Negro through the production of literature and art.[80]

These remarks hold true not only for the spirituals and for written poetry, but also for the sermons in *God's Trombones.*

Just as his two volumes of *Negro Spirituals* were intended primarily to make these songs better known, so it was the main object of *God's Trombones* to reveal the existence of the Negro folk sermon to the wider public. "A good deal has been written on the folk creations of the American Negro: his music, sacred and secular; his plantation tales, and his dances; but that there are folk sermons, as well, is a fact that has passed unnoticed."[81]

This is not the whole truth, however, for even before the earliest collections of slave songs, spirituals, and Negro sermons began to appear in the years following the Civil War, the general public had known of spirituals and Negro sermons, though in strange fashion, through the caricatures and parodies provided by the minstrels on the stage.[82] We have also seen the Negro sermon find its way into popular poetry with Irwin Russell,

[79] Pp. 18-19.
[80] P. 9 in the 1931 ed.
[81] *God's Trombones,* p. 1.
[82] *The Book of American Negro Spirituals,* pp. 13-14.

his example followed by Dunbar and some of his contemporaries. But, like the minstrels, all these poets treated the sermon as funny, with the ill-intentioned stock jokes further underlined by the use of a degraded form of speech baptized "Negro dialect" for the occasion. Thus the Negro sermons in verse of *God's Trombones* cannot properly be classified as a revelation, but rather as a rehabilitation — in the first place, of the Negro preacher, who here for the first time is no longer presented as a comic figure, and whose historic role in the service of the black people is thus emphasized:

> The old-time Negro preacher has not yet been given the niche in which he properly belongs. He has been portrayed only as a semi-comic figure. He had, it is true, his comic aspects, but on the whole he was an important figure, and at bottom a vital factor. It was through him that the people of diverse languages and customs who were brought here from diverse parts of Africa and thrown into slavery were given their first sense of unity and solidarity. He was the first shepherd of this bewildered flock.[83]

But from the rehabilitation of the Negro preacher it was Johnson's intention to proceed to that of the whole race. With that in mind, he at once forbade himself the use of Negro dialect, so that the reader would not be induced to adopt any of the unkind mental attitudes that dialect traditionally served to convey. For this reason it is possible, to some extent, to look on the sermons in *God's Trombones* as pieces of evidence in the indictment that Johnson, after 1917, took it into his head to pursue against Negro dialect. This consideration had such an influence on the composition of *God's Trombones* that we must linger over it for a moment before dealing with the work itself.

The Condemnation of Dialect

Shortly after Johnson had published *Fifty Years and Other Poems* (1917) — a third of which, let it not be forgotten, was made up of poems in Negro dialect similar to Dunbar's — he became this idiom's principal detractor.[84] His new stand seems to have been decided on by 1918, since "The Creation," which dates from this year and which he placed as the first sermon in *God's Trombones,* is not written in dialect. But not until 1922, in the preface to his anthology *The Book of American Negro Poetry,* did he first formulate his reasons for having come to condemn the dialect. He blamed it especially for being "an instrument with but two full stops,

[83] *God's Trombones,* p. 2.
[84] For Johnson's attitude to dialect, see *The Book of American Negro Poetry,* pp. 3-5, 40-42; *The Book of American Negro Spirituals,* pp. 42-46; *God's Trombones,* pp. 7-9; *Along This Way,* pp. 159, 336; *Saint Peter Relates an Incident,* pp. 69-70.

humor and pathos,"[85] and asserted "that there are phases of Negro life in the United States which cannot be treated in the dialect either adequately or artistically."[86] In these terms, the problem is obviously very poorly stated, and Johnson, as if aware of this, took it up again on the following page, specifying: "This is no indictment against the dialect as dialect, but against the mold of convention in which Negro dialect in the United States has been set."[87] But if the dialect was to be pronounced innocent the moment it had been accused, why was it brought into the case at all?

The real story behind this about-face may perhaps be found elsewhere. Much had changed since the days when Johnson reveled in his easily won successes on Tin Pan Alley, for now he was on the staff of a New York paper and was secretary general of the N.A.A.C.P, had an "in" with Congress and even the White House, and rubbed shoulders in New York and Washington, not with thespians any longer, but with people in society's loftiest circles. In a word he had become, as McKay put it, "the aristocrat of Negro Americans."[88] By repudiating dialect, Johnson at the same time turned his back on a whole segment of his own past and voiced his desire for a respectability whose usefulness, in his new situation, became more apparent every day.

Yet the dialect was too ready an alibi. If he had sought to be entirely sincere with himself, would he not have had to tell himself that he felt far less guilty for having written in dialect than for having presented his fellow blacks as idlers and thieves?[89] What, other than his own ambition, his eagerness to see his name displayed at the entrance of Broadway's music halls, had locked him into this "conventional mold"? If Dunbar had let himself be pulled in this direction, at least he had the excuse of financial need. But Johnson had never known hunger. He had a college degree, he had become a school principal and a lawyer at the Jacksonville bar, and he had abandoned all that for the vainglory and the royalties offered by the world of song and show business.

These are some personal aspects that must be borne in mind when evaluating Johnson's attitude toward dialect. He himself unintentionally revealed how inauthentic his attitude was, in the preface to the second edition of *The Book of American Negro Poetry*, in a passage that discusses the dialect poetry of Langston Hughes and Sterling Brown: "Several of the poets of the younger group, notably Langston Hughes and Sterling A.

[85] *The Book of American Negro Poetry*, p. 41.
[86] *Ibid.*
[87] *Ibid.*, p. 42.
[88] See note 1 above.
[89] See Sec. 2 above, "Dunbar's Disciple: Poetry in Dialect."

Brown, *do* use a dialect; but it is not the dialect of the comic minstrel tradition or of the sentimental plantation tradition; it is the common, racy, living, authentic speech of the Negro in certain phases of real life."[90] The distinction is valid, of course, but why not say outright that what has changed is not so much the dialect as the writers' basic outlook, and that in this lies the whole difference between the minstrel tradition of former days and the Negro poetry of the rising generation? The important thing is not any changes that Langston Hughes or Sterling Brown may have made in spelling the dialect, but the fact that they no longer portray other blacks as ignoramuses, lazybones, and thieves; they no longer present them exclusively as clowns who pass their lives laughing and strumming the banjo, but as human beings confronted by life's many problems — who laugh, of course, but who also weep, struggle, suffer, and die, crushed beneath the weight of injustice and their color. This is what makes good the sin of omission of which the minstrel and plantation traditions were guilty, and which such poets as Dunbar and Johnson, often too lightheartedly, chose to assume. The dialect itself was not evil; instead, it too often was but the innocent vehicle for evil.

Thus Johnson's thesis can scarely be defended. As it turned out, it won him no disciples, and a poet like Sterling Brown briefly but energetically expressed his refusal to participate in any condemnation of dialect.[91]

The Experiment of God's Trombones

The case thus adjudged, it remains nevertheless that Johnson's belated antipathy for dialect had noteworthy consequences in the free-verse sermons of *God's Trombones,* which he succeeded in making a typically Negro achievement while eschewing any use of dialect. Here is his own account of the origins of this experiment:

> What the colored poet in the United States needs to do is something like what Synge did for the Irish; he needs to find a form that will express the racial spirit by symbols from within rather than by symbols from without, such as the mere mutilation of English spelling and pronunciation. He needs a form that is freer and larger than dialect, but which will still hold the racial flavor; a form expressing the imagery, the idioms, the peculiar turns of thought, and the distinctive humor and pathos, too, of the Negro, but which will also be capable of voicing the deepest and highest emotions and aspirations, and allow of the widest range of subjects and the widest scope of treatment.[92]

[90] *The Book of American Negro Poetry*, p. 4.
[91] Brown, *Negro Poetry and Drama*, p. 77.
[92] *The Book of American Negro Poetry*, pp. 41-42.

We will not insist on the fact that the dialect itself could have met all these demands, since the work of Sterling Brown is there to prove it. Let us simply examine the means Johnson used to carry out the program he had set himself, and estimate the extent to which his experiment may be considered a success.

His intent in writing *God's Trombones* is succinctly expressed in these two sentences from the preface: "The old-time Negro preacher is rapidly passing. I have here tried sincerely to fix something of him."[93] The original idea was to begin the collection with a portrait of the preacher, "The Reverend Jasper Jones." Extant is a typewritten manuscript of this poem[94] of twenty-four rhymed couplets with the author's annotations, but it is so poor a piece that Johnson's final decision not to use it is easily understood. Thus, but for the references made in the preface, we have no direct portrait of the preacher, and to get an adequate view of him we must turn to the oratorical skills he displays in the opening prayer "Listen, Lord," and in the following seven sermons.[95]

The conventionality of these eight poems is already apparent from the fact that they are monologues, whereas in reality a part of the sermon, at least, would have consisted of a dialogue between preacher and congregation.[96] Here the presence of the latter is not even suggested, as it might have been by appropriate monologue technique — for example, by using the repeated question, as Irwin Russell and Page and Gordon had done. Nor is the monologue able to reproduce the oratorical gestures, always so important for the Negro preacher, who is equally actor and orator.

Thus Johnson, from the outset, imposed limits on his experiment. He had indicated what they were in the preface, and asked the reader to accept them.

In principle, the language of *God's Trombones* is normal English, not

[93] *God's Trombones*, p. 11.

[94] In the library of Atlanta University (James Weldon Johnson file in the Negro Collection).

[95] The titles of the seven sermons are "The Creation," "The Prodigal Son," "'Go Down, Death — A Funeral Sermon," "Noah Built the Ark," "The Crucifixion," "Let My People Go," and "The Judgment Day." Johnson himself recorded "Listen, Lord," "The Creation," "Go Down, Death," and "The Prodigal Son" on *Four Readings from "God's Trombones,"* Musicraft Album no. 21. For recordings made by others, see our discography in the Bibliographical Appendix. See, on the circumstances in which these sermons were written, *Along This Way,* pp. 335-37, 377-78.

[96] On the general problem of the Negro preacher, one may consult William Harrison Pipes, *Say Amen, Brother! — Old Time Negro Preaching — A Study in American Frustration.*

Negro dialect,[97] but here and there it is possible to note a few minor deviations from the norm. True, the dialect or familiar forms that creep in are for the most part American rather than specifically Negro. They include, for example, the intermittent usage of the double negation[98] and of the gerundive preceded by the preposition "a"[99] — except, however, in these two lines of "Noah Built the Ark," in which "a-going" is not just typically Negro but directly borrowed from the first line of a spiritual:

> God's a-going to rain down rain on rain.
> God's a-going to loosen up the bottom of the deep.[100]

Another Negro dialect form is the parasitical "a" often used by blacks to introduce a sort of syncopation into the English sentence:

> Lord — ride by this morning —
> Mount your milk-white horse,
> And ride-a this morning —[101]

or, again, in these lines:

> And the old ark-a she begun to ride;
> The old ark-a she begun to rock;[102]

Yet another Negro dialect form is the redundant recourse to the auxiliary "done," as in this example:

> And now, O Lord —
> When I've done drunk my last cup of sorrow —[103]

But such forms are exceptional;[104] no more than two or three dozen of them are to be noted in the more than 900 lines of *God's Trombones,* and their contribution to the effect Johnson was aiming at is but subsidiary.

Much more effective in giving these sermons their Negro character are

[97] *God's Trombones,* pp. 7ff.
[98] Of the type "they didn't make no sound," line 29 of "Go Down Death," *ibid.,* p. 28.
[99] Of the type "Jesus ... kept a-saying," *ibid.,* line 75, p. 30. Countless examples can be found throughout *God's Trombones.*
[100] Lines 115-16, *ibid.,* p. 35. See, for example, the title of the spiritual, "God's a-gwineter trouble de water."
[101] "Listen Lord," lines 16-18, *ibid.,* pp. 13-14.
[102] "Noah Built the Ark," lines 142-43, *ibid.,* p. 36. In these lines, the use of "begun" as a preterit is itself a dialect form.
[103] "Listen Lord," lines 40-41, *ibid.,* p. 14.
[104] To the examples cited above one should, however, add the instances when Johnson, incorporating into a poem a passage from a spiritual, leaves unchanged the dialect forms of the original. Such a case is the "gittin'" in the last line of "Listen Lord" (*ibid.,* p. 15): "To wait for that great gittin' up morning."

the countless, more or less extensive echoes of actual spirituals with which they are studded. Sometimes a mere word or expression that has long been familiar crops up in the sermon and by its own power suddenly evokes in the reader's mind the whole naïve imagery that makes up the religious context of the spirituals, to which the preacher untiringly returns to find subject matter for his sermon. There are the pearly gates and golden streets of the New Jerusalem, mentioned in Revelation;[105] the custom of calling Jesus "Mary's Baby,"[106] and the warning words to sinners and backsliders that they should repent before it is too late.[107] Elsewhere a line or two (or even an entire stanza) taken over bodily from a spiritual imperceptibly slips in at the end of a sermon.[108] This is the signal awaited by the congregation for their voices to join in with the preacher's; preaching then yields to song. And, finally, some sermons are constructed from beginning to end upon spirituals, borrowing their arguments and paraphrasing their lines. Thus "The Crucifixion" relies for its details on the spirituals "Look-a How Dey Done My Lord" and "Were You There When They Crucified My Lord."[109] "Let My People Go" is the account of Exodus, related on the lines of "Go Down, Moses," with its classical parallel between the people of Israel and the black people; whereas in "The Judgment Day," it is easy to pick out the very expressions used in the spirituals "In Dat Great Gittin' up Mornin'," "My Lord Says He's Gwineter Rain Down Fire," "My Lord, What a Mornin'," and "Too Late, Sinnah." These describe the Last Judgment, particularly the delicate mission of the Angel Gabriel who, with one foot on the mountaintop and the other in the middle of the sea, blows his trumpet gently at first and then "like seven peals of thunder" to awaken the dead and summon them before the Lord's throne.

Because of their somewhat immoderate resort to the texts of the spiri-

[105] *Pearly gates,* "Go Down Death," line 45, *ibid.,* p. 29; *golden streets,* line 27, p. 28; etc.
[106] "Listen Lord," line 44, *ibid.,* p. 14 (see the spiritual "Mary Had a Baby, Yes, Lord").
[107] See, for instance, "Too late, sinner! too late! / Good-bye, sinner, good-bye!" in "The Judgment Day," *ibid.,* p. 56, and the spiritual that begins with the words "Too late, too late, sinnah, hm, too late."
[108] At the end of "Listen Lord," *ibid.,* p. 15 ("In Dat Great Gittin' up Mornin'"); at the end of "The Prodigal Son," p. 25 ("When I Fall on My Knees"); at the end of "Noah Built the Ark," p. 37 ("My Lord Says He's Gwineter Rain Down Fire"); at the end of "The Crucifixion," p. 43 ("Were You There When They Crucified My Lord"); throughout "Let My People Go," pp. 45-52 ("Go Down Moses"); and at the end of "The Judgment Day," p. 56 ("My Lord Says He's Gwineter Rain Down Fire").
[109] Johnson, of course, does not let slip the opportunity to introduce the character of Simon of Cyrene who, in keeping with the tradition of the Black Church, is presented as a black (lines 58-61, *ibid.,* p. 41).

tuals, these last three sermons are the least original in the volume. Yet Johnson gives a correct idea of the preacher's technique, designed to move rather than convince his audience, alternately raising the congregation's hopes and filling them with terror, and arousing their pity by presenting scenes from Holy Writ as though these were taking place before their eyes. The preacher "sees" what he is describing, and his hearers "see" through his eyes:

> Up Golgotha's rugged road
> I see my Jesus go.
> I see him sink beneath the load,
> I see my drooping Jesus sink.[110]

When Eve yields to the serpent's wiles, the preacher is a witness to the scene.[111] Again, together with his parishioners, he relives the betrayal by Judas so vividly that one expects them at any moment to step in so as to change the course of events:

> Oh, look at black-hearted Judas —
> Sneaking through the dark of the Garden —
> Leading his crucifying mob.
> Oh, God!
> Strike him down!
> Why *don't* you strike him down,
> Before he plants his traitor's kiss
> Upon my Jesus' cheek?[112]

He is present, too, "on that great gettin' up morning": he "feels" the earth shudder, "sees" the graves burst open, and "hears" how the bones of those awakened from the dead click together.[113]

The most personal aspect of the preacher's art is what he creates out of his own fantasy with the aim of stirring the imaginations of his hearers. A ready fabulist, he constantly interpolates in order to supplement the bareness of the biblical narrative. Thus the creation of the world is unfolded before the eyes of the astounded congregation as though it were a fairy tale or a child's game:

> Then God reached out and took the light in his hands,
> And God rolled the light around in his hands
> Until he made the sun;
> And he set that sun a-blazing in the heavens.
> And the light that was left from making the sun

---

[110] "The Crucifixion," lines 54-57, *ibid.,* p. 41.
[111] "Noah Built the Ark," lines 35-36, *ibid.,* p. 32.
[112] "The Crucifixion," lines 26-33, *ibid.,* p. 40.
[113] "The Judgment Day," lines 32-41, *ibid.,* p. 54; see also lines 83-86, p. 56.

> God gathered it up in a shining ball
> And flung it against the darkness,
> Spangling the night with the moon and stars.
>
> .   .   .   .
>
> And the earth was under his feet.
> And God walked, and where he trod
> His footsteps hollowed the valleys out
> and bulged the mountains up.
>
> .   .   .   .
>
> ... God stepped over to the edge of the world
> And he spat out the seven seas —
> He batted his eyes, and the lightnings flashed —
> He clapped his hands, and the thunders rolled —[114]

His preaching ever relies on the concrete,[115] with an anthropomorphism that brings down to the human level the Eternal Father, who is addressed as one would speak to a friendly neighbor:

> O Lord — open up a window of heaven,
> And lean out far over the battlements of glory,
> And listen this morning.[116]

Particularly remarkable are the images the preacher uses to make himself understood by all. Witness the reproof administered to the Prodigal Son who has revolted against his Father:

> Young man —
> Young man —
> Your arm's too short to box with God.[117]

Naïve, homely, and extravagant in turn, but always direct and forceful, these images have no compunction about blending in with those of the Bible so unexpectedly at times as to be almost grotesque, as in this prayer uttered by the pastor for himself:

> And now, O Lord, this man of God,
> Who breaks the bread of life this morning —
> Shadow him in the hollow of thy hand,
> And keep him out of the gunshot of the devil.
> Take him, Lord — this morning —

[114] "The Creation," lines 14-21, 30-33, 36-39, *ibid.,* pp. 17-18.

[115] See, among other examples, the description of Babylon in "The Prodigal Son," line 38 to end, pp. 22-25, with its close similarities to many an American town, with its night clubs, dance halls, bars, and gambling houses.

[116] "Listen Lord," lines 10-12, *ibid.,* p. 13.

[117] "The Prodigal Son," lines 1-3, *ibid.,* p. 21.

> Wash him with hyssop inside and out,
> Hang him up and drain him dry of sin,
> Pin his ear to the wisdom-post,
> And make his words sledge hammers of truth —
> Beating on the iron heart of sin.
> Lord God, this morning —
> Put his eye to the telescope of eternity,
> And let him look upon the paper walls of time.
> Lord, turpentine his imagination,
> Put perpetual motion in his arms,
> Fill him full of the dynamite of thy power,
> Anoint him all over with the oil of thy salvation,
> And set his tongue on fire.[118]

If allowance is made for his borrowings from the Bible, from the spirituals, and from the Negro sermons he had heard, what then is the poet's share in *God's Trombones?* Johnson was certainly not the creator of these sermons but, as Synge remarked of his own indebtedness to the Irish people, every work of art results from a collaboration.[119] In *God's Trombones,* the artist is clearly present on every page, and he gives even while he receives. The simplicity and clarity, so striking in these poems, are the fruits of his efforts.[120] His musical sense is manifested in the choice of sonorities for the free-verse line which, in his hands, becomes docile and supple, and adjusts to the preacher's rhythm as well as to the rise and fall of his voice.[121] Taking what were, after all, the heterogeneous elements of his raw materials, the poet has marked them with the unity and the stamp of his own genius, so that these sermons, as they come from his hands, have undeniably become his own to some degree.

If he deserves any reproach, it might be for his excessive zeal in idealizing and refining — or, in other words, for having thought it necessary to impose too much respectability on essentially popular material whose crudity is one of its charms, as it is also a voucher for its authenticity. His sermons are still folklore, perhaps, but stylized folklore.[122]

---

[118] "Listen Lord," lines 22-39, *ibid.,* p. 14.

[119] John Millington Synge, *The Playboy of the Western World,* Preface (Everyman ed.), p. 107.

[120] Johnson, when speaking of the writing of "The Crucifixion," related how much trouble he had in achieving the effect of simplicity required by the poem (*Along This Way,* p. 377).

[121] It was in thinking of the preacher's vocal register that Johnson hit on his title: these Negro preachers are God's trombones. See, on this, the preface to *God's Trombones,* pp. 6-7.

[122] That is why it is hardly possible to compare Johnson and Joel Chandler Harris, as Harriet Monroe tried to do ("Negro Sermons," *Poetry,* August, 1927,

Johnson's experiment is not altogether comparable to Synge's, though this had been his source of inspiration. There was some desire in both cases, no doubt, to rehabilitate a racial community that had long been oppressed and mocked by a more powerful Anglo-Saxon people. Synge's work forms part of the Irish Renaissance, as Johnson's belongs to the Negro Renaissance. In each case the writer chose to produce a work that would be typically national or racial, while deliberately discarding the speech of the minority in favor of English. But even apart from the fact that, compared with Synge's lifework, *God's Trombones* is of modest dimensions, its themes were already set and its plots already mapped out, so that the role of inventiveness could only be negligible. Thus the poet's originality could hardly be exhibited except in his actual treatment of the material. While Synge did not overlook some opportunities for criticizing the Irish character, Johnson frankly aims at writing an apologia. Finally, even the linguistic experiment is not identical in the two writers. While Synge, utilizing the examples of folk speech which he had patiently collected, constructed for himself an extraordinary synthetic, artificial idiom, with intricate phrases and constructions that are his alone, Johnson relied much more widely on the English language's normal turn of phrase. Though making generous use, in his sermons, of fragments from the spirituals, he almost always provided them first with the respectable externals of standard English. What is Negro in *God's Trombones* is not the language as such, but the style and the outlook on life it reflects.

Successful as Johnson's experiment was, its success nevertheless remained limited and contingent, for it depended in large measure on forces lying outside the work itself and from which, in view of the nature of the theme, it profited. For any subject but this, it would have been hard to find so favorable a combination of circumstances.

This work, furthermore, was the offspring of an outdated mentality. Like its author, the work set out to have a Negro soul, but one garbed in the distinction and respectability of whiteness. Despite appearances, its tendency was at odds with that total coming to awareness marked by the Negro Renaissance, and no more is needed to explain why *God's Trombones* remained an isolated venture.

---

pp. 291-93). Her parallel is fundamentally erroneous — for, while Harris indeed "set down what he heard," this does not hold for Johnson with whom, quantitatively speaking, the elements borrowed from the Bible and the spirituals far exceed what he himself had collected. Johnson had not nearly the same intimate contact with the people as did Langston Hughes and Sterling Brown.

Chapter Ten: LANGSTON HUGHES

Langston Hughes's contribution to the Negro Renaissance is that of a highly original talent. Nourished from adolescence on the first fruits of the national poetic renewal then in full progress, he soon went on to discover the prophet and spiritual father of the movement, Walt Whitman. Among the others whom he would cherish at an early date was Paul Laurence Dunbar, whose modest birth and liking for the traditional poetic forms of the race established a kinship. But neither of these masters, to whom he gladly acknowledged his indebtedness,[1] could long maintain under his tutelage this youthful spirit that thirsted for independence and longed to follow the trail of its own genius. Before his twentieth birthday he had already displayed his own highly individual manner, and this was to become even more pronounced. Thus there is scarcely another poet for whom the endeavor to track down sources could prove less rewarding.

Instinctively in perfect harmony with the temperament of the black masses in the huge cities of our day, and abetted by a lively sensibility that rarely overlooked the imponderables affecting the psychology of his fellows, he was uniquely successful in capturing every subtlety in the atavistic rhythms that characterized his race and in marshaling them to express poetically some of the most significant moments of its life.

It did not take him long to emerge from a certain racial romanticism essentially oriented to the past in which, for a moment, the Negro Renais-

[1] See Stanley J. Kunitz and Howard Haycraft, "Hughes, Langston," *Twentieth Century Authors*, in which he states that the principal literary influences he had experienced were those of Dunbar, Sandburg, and Whitman.

385

sance appeared determined to remain fixed, and in jazz, that idiom of the masses of today, he soon discovered the instrument best fitted to express the rebelliousness of a whole people against the unworthy lot that some hoped to impose on them forever. The race would never, except for Claude McKay, produce a more fiery bard, and if the proximity of despair for a moment led him to seek beyond the nation's boundaries a solution for the misfortunes of his people, his name ever shone bright on the list of freedom's doughtiest defenders.

Langston Hughes was by far the most productive poet of the Negro Renaissance, and certain faults were the ransom that had to be paid. A sometimes excessive facility, an impulsiveness not always restrained by a judicious rein, a too frequent uncalled-for use of vulgarity for its own sake and, on occasion, the cultivation of originality at any price — those are the weaknesses most readily apparent. But they do not diminish the intrinsic worth of his achievement, which incontestably remains the freshest and most personal in the entire poetic production of the Negro Renaissance.

1. BIOGRAPHY[2]

The Restless Years (1902-24)

Born in Joplin, Missouri, on the first day of February, 1902, James Langston Hughes was not the "Negro, black as the night is black"[3] that one of his earliest poems speaks of. "You see," he declares in his autobiography, "unfortunately, I am not black."[4] He could count among his ancestors on his father's side a Jewish slave-dealer of Kentucky and a distiller of Scottish extraction. The maternal ancestry is no less variegated, with a white great-grandfather, Captain Ralph Quarles, himself a descendant of the English poet Francis Quarles, and a great-grandmother who sprang from the union of a Cherokee Indian woman from Carolina and a French merchant who came from the banks of the St. Lawrence. Let us add that his maternal grandmother, through her first marriage, became the wife of a Negro freeman who fell beside John Brown in the attack on Harpers Ferry. The poet's father, James Nathaniel Hughes, was a hard man set for

---

[2] There is no biography of Langston Hughes. Our information has come chiefly from his two autobiographical volumes, *The Big Sea* and *I Wonder as I Wander.* See also Kunitz and Haycraft, "Hughes," *Twentieth Century Authors;* "Hughes," *Who's Who in America* XVII (1932-33); and the short biographical notices in the main anthologies cited. For certain details, we are indebted to the poet himself.
[3] "Proem," *The Weary Blues,* p. 19.
[4] *The Big Sea,* p. 11.

gain. Shortly after the birth of his son, he decided to move to Mexico, where he would be immune from racial discrimination and where he hoped to make more rapid financial progress. But his wife, Carrie Mercer Langston, could not bear to settle in an unknown country, so distant from the familiar surroundings in which she had grown up. Thus husband and wife separated and the mother, on her own and often changing her place of residence as the next minor job offer required, could not continue to pay much attention to her son. When he was in the second grade in Topeka, she had to send him away to live with his grandmother in Lawrence, Kansas. When the grandmother died the boy, aged twelve, was taken in by friends of hers. Two years later his mother, who had remarried in the interval, had him join her in her new home in Lincoln, Illinois. But no sooner had he finished grade school in 1916 than the family moved to Cleveland, because of the high wages being paid by industry, which was besieged by orders coming from a war-torn Europe.

Langston Hughes had written his first poem for prize day at the Lincoln grade school and had been elected class poet. But it was in Cleveland's Central High School that he had the joy of seeing his first poems published in the school paper, *The Belfry Owl.* One of his teachers introduced him to the work of Amy Lowell, Vachel Lindsay, Edgar Lee Masters, and, most important, Carl Sandburg, who was to have a decisive influence on the future poet.[5]

The father, in the meantime, had expressed the desire to have his son with him for a while and to see to his future. So, at the age of eighteen and just out of Central High School, Langston Hughes went off to discover Mexico. As it turned out, however, incompatibility between father and son was almost total. The boy already had a poet's outlook on life and was eager to discover the earth and its inhabitants as fancy dictated, while the father talked of nothing but bookkeeping, college, and other forms of constraint — in a word, of a carefully mapped-out future, undertaken with all the application a businessman would require.

Though himself a Negro, he detested his racial brothers because they wasted their talents and let whites take advantage of them. The reason behind his divorce may have been that he despised his wife for humbling herself to take odd jobs from whites, though she had had a college education at the University of Kansas and had for a time held a teaching post in Oklahoma. But he, to escape such a comedown, had abandoned the United States for Mexico, and he hoped to achieve the same for his son.

Thus influenced by his father, who had promised to pay for his college

[5] "Carl Sandburg, my guiding star," he said (*ibid.,* p. 29).

education, Langston Hughes resigned himself to entering Columbia University in the fall of 1921, if for no other purpose than to put a few thousand miles between his father and himself. Besides, Harlem was only a step or two away, and this interested him far more than Columbia. "I didn't like Columbia," he confessed, "nor the students, nor anything I was studying!"[6] So he went to stage shows, read voraciously, missed an examination to attend the funeral of the actor Bert Williams, enthusiastically applauded Florence Mills, and set out to explore Chinatown.

With one year of study at Columbia behind him he decided not to return, but settled in Harlem and looked for work. He was soon to realize that, for a Negro, this was no easy matter. A Greek truck-gardener on Staten Island finally hired him. But, once the season had ended, he had to try his luck elsewhere. A florist took him on as delivery boy, but this was only to tide him over, for Hughes felt a too-long-denied yearning for adventure rising within him, and the desire to free himself from all the shackles of the past. The sea was calling him and, beyond it, the ancestral land of Africa. He signed up on a cargo vessel in June, 1923, and during the periods spent in port he was able to see something of the West African coast. But, before the hawsers were dropped, he insisted on proving to himself that one chapter of his existence had come to an end:

> I'd left a box of books in Harlem in the fall, and before we sailed I went after them. . . . But when I opened them up and looked at them that night off Sandy Hook, they seemed too much like everything I had known in the past. . . .[7] I leaned over the rail of the S.S. *Malone* and threw the books as far as I could out into the sea. . . .[8] It was like throwing a million bricks out of my heart — for it was not only the books that I wanted to throw away, but everything unpleasant and miserable out of my past: the memory of my father, the poverty and uncertainties of my mother's life, the stupidities of color-prejudice . . . the fear of not finding a job, the bewilderment of no one to talk to about things that trouble you, the feeling of always being controlled by others — by parents, by employers, by some outer necessity not your own. All those things I wanted to throw away. To be free of. To escape from. I wanted to be a man on my own, control my own life, and go my own way. I was twenty-one.[9]

Upon his return from Africa he signed up on a vessel bound for Holland, but when it put into port for the second time at Rotterdam in February, 1924, he decided to jump ship and make his way to Paris, this

[6] *Ibid.*, p. 85.
[7] *Ibid.*, p. 97.
[8] *Ibid.*, p. 3.
[9] *Ibid.*, p. 98.

being an old dream of his. His first job was as a doorman in a night club on the Rue Fontaine; then he was "second cook" at the Grand Duc on the Rue Pigalle. There, every morning at dawn when their work was over, American jazz musicians gathered for a jam session.

When the Grand Duc closed for the summer, Hughes seized the occasion to become acquainted with northern Italy, traveling with one of his fellow employees. On the journey he met with Alain Locke, whom he had gotten to know in Paris and who induced him to visit Venice. He also learned en route that Claude McKay, whom he greatly admired, was living in Toulon, and he decided to look him up. But the trip was brought to a halt in Genoa, for on the train he was robbed not only of all the money he was carrying but also of his passport. After some time of a hobo-like existence in the port of Genoa, he finally found a vessel heading for New York whose captain let him pay his way by doing minor jobs on board. After a number of calls in Naples, Sicily, and Spain, he once more found himself in Harlem on November 24, 1924, with two bits in his pocket.

Early Successes (1924-30)

He had scarcely arrived when he found out that his mother had been deserted by her second husband. He went to Washington to live with her, first working in a laundry, and then with Carter G. Woodson in the offices of the Association for the Study of Negro Life and History. Though the pay was adequate, he found this kind of work too restrictive, and finally he took a job as busboy in the Waldman Park Hotel. There, in 1925, he had the luck of a lifetime, on a day when Vachel Lindsay arrived to give a poetry reading. Here is Langston Hughes's own account of this memorable event:

> That afternoon I wrote out three of my poems, "Jazzonia," "Negro Dancers," and "The Weary Blues," on some pieces of paper and put them in the pocket of my white busboy's coat. In the evening when Mr. Lindsay came down to dinner, quickly I laid them beside his plate and went away, afraid to say anything to so famous a poet, except to tell him I liked his poems and that these were poems of mine. I looked back once and saw Mr. Lindsay reading the poems. . . .
>
> The next morning on the way to work, as usual I bought a paper — and there I read that Vachel Lindsay had discovered a Negro busboy poet! At the hotel the reporters were already waiting for me. They interviewed me. And they took my picture, holding a tray of dirty dishes in the middle of the dining room. The picture . . . appeared in lots of newspapers throughout the country. It was my first publicity break.[10]

[10] *Ibid.*, p. 212.

But at this instant, when Vachel Lindsay was directing the attention of white America to him, the black world was already familiar with his name, for several of his poems had been printed in *The Crisis,* in *Opportunity,* and in the special number of the *Survey Graphic* on the Negro, put together by Alain Locke. Into the bargain, *Opportunity* had just awarded him its first poetry prize, and Countee Cullen, to whom he had shown the poems he brought back from Europe, had introduced him to the leading figures, black and white, in the Negro Renaissance. This is the way in which he came into contact with Carl Van Vechten, who sponsored his first volume of poetry, *The Weary Blues,* which came out in January, 1926.

In this way, too, he got to know a New York woman, a patroness of the arts, who offered, as a Christmas present, to underwrite the cost of his college education. His European experiences had indeed awakened in him a fresh urge to understand better the world and its inhabitants. First he tried to get a scholarship at Howard University, but he found there a greater readiness to praise his poetry than to provide real help. So in the end he entered Lincoln University in Pennsylvania and emerged with a degree in 1929, having completed the studies he had begun at Columbia University.

But the three years spent at Lincoln were not devoted exclusively to study. On weekends and during vacations he took flight to Greenwich Village or Harlem, and in the summer of 1926, in collaboration with a group of Negro writers and intellectuals, he founded the short-lived magazine *Fire.* This aimed at being the artistic organ for the New Negro, and was so named because of the ambition to "burn" all the old, established ideas about Negroes.[11] The following year, Hughes had his first glimpse of the South, where he had been invited to read his poems. He pushed on as far as New Orleans, where he happened upon a vessel about to sail for Havana. He signed up on it for part of his vacation.

His poems and stories were now being printed in magazines of wide circulation, among them *Vanity Fair, Poetry, The New Republic,* and *The New Masses.* Knopf published a second volume of his poetry, *Fine Clothes to the Jew* (1927); it was imbued with a naturalism distasteful to the eminently respectable black bourgeoisie and was harshly treated by Negro critics. He also wrote a play, *Mulatto,*[12] which was not staged until 1935, and he began to work on a novel, *Not without Laughter.* The generosity

[11] For the *Fire* adventure, see *ibid.,* pp. 233ff.

[12] This play, written during the summer of 1928, while Hughes was working in the Hedgerow Theatre, Moylan Rose Valley, Pennsylvania, ran on Broadway for one year, and was then performed on tour for eight months.

of a wealthy Park Avenue patroness enabled him to finish this after he had left Lincoln University, and it appeared in 1930.[13]

A Literature of Commitment (1930-67)

However, public fascination with the Harlem revival had declined along with the stock prices on Wall Street. Economic disasters were bringing about profound changes in the country, and the first victim was the Negro. In the South he continued to be the victim of injustice as well. The Scottsboro case was stirring people's minds and, during a southern lecture tour undertaken after a trip to Haiti, Hughes went to the prison at Kilby, Alabama, and visited the eight young blacks who had been accused of raping two white girls on a freight train on March 25, 1931.

The poems written during these hard years are marked with pessimism and disillusionment (*Dear Lovely Death* [1931], and *A Negro Mother and Other Dramatic Recitations* [1931]). If any hope of a solution existed, he beheld it in the promises that the Soviet experiment appeared to offer to the disinherited of every race and clime. It was all the easier to sing its praises, since the reality of the Soviet Union was still scarcely known (*Scottsboro Limited* [1932]).[14] This tendency was strengthened after the poet's return from a voyage around the world, undertaken in 1932 and lasting a year. He first went to Russia, where he met Arthur Koestler and Boris Pasternak, and then visited China and Japan. His sympathy for left-wing circles was by now crystal clear. Early in 1934 he joined the editorial committee of *The New Masses,* and that same year he brought out his first volume of stories, *The Ways of White Folks.*

Then came the civil war in Spain, and he went there in 1937 as war correspondent for a group of Afro-American papers. He stopped in Paris on the way and, as delegate from the United States, attended the second

[13] See, on Hughes's novels, Hugh Morris Gloster, *Negro Voices in American Fiction,* pp. 184-87, 219-22; Robert A. Bone, *The Negro Novel in America,* pp. 75-77; and our short article, "Langston Hughes," *Informations et Documents,* January 15, 1961, pp. 30-35.

[14] The collection of poems *The Dream Keeper* (1932) was intended primarily for young people. It contains a selection of poems from the 1926 and 1927 volumes, and some twenty new poems, most of which have nothing racial about them. Other poems for youth were printed in Arna Bontemps, ed., *Golden Slippers: An Anthology of Negro Poetry for Young Readers.* See also *The Langston Hughes Reader,* pp. 143-56. Also for a youthful audience are *Popo and Fifina* (1932, in collaboration with Arna Bontemps); *The First Book of Negroes* (1952); *The First Book of Rhythms* (1954); *The First Book of Jazz* (1955); *The First Book of the West Indies* (1956); *The First Book of Africa* (1960); and biographies, including *Famous American Negroes* (1954); *Famous Negro Music Makers* (1955); *Famous American Negro Heroes* (1958).

International Writers' Congress in July, 1937. There he met, among other celebrities, Louis Aragon, André Malraux, Stephen Spender, W. H. Auden, Rosamund Lehmann, and Ilya Ehrenburg, and some of his poems were read in French translation by Jean-Louis Barrault. He also met once again Nicolas Guillén, who accompanied him to Spain. The experiences of these decisive years are mainly recorded in Hughes's autobiography, but they also leave their mark on the 1938 collection of poems, *A New Song*. It is noteworthy that the volume was published by the International Workers Order, with an introduction by Michael Gold and with a printing of 10,000 copies for trade-union comrades.

World War II inflicted no diminution on Langston Hughes's poetic productivity. In addition to the long poem, *Freedom's Plow* (1943), seven collections of poems, nearly all new, saw the light from 1942 on. They were *Shakespeare in Harlem* (1942), *Jim Crow's Last Stand* (1943), *Fields of Wonder* (1947), *One-Way Ticket* (1949), *Montage of a Dream Deferred* (1951), *Ask Your Mama* (1961), and *The Panther and the Lash* (1967), to which must be added some two dozen new poems contained in *Selected Poems* (1959). But the themes and the basic characteristics of this period are an extension of those found in the prewar work, and it cannot be maintained that the poet, over a span of twenty years, had really renewed himself.

In this intervening period a second collection of short stories, *Laughing to Keep from Crying* (1952), was published, and another novel, *Tambourines to Glory* (1958), which pokes fun at Harlem's social and religious life. In the two volumes of autobiography, *The Big Sea* (1940) and *I Wonder as I Wander* (1956), Hughes showed himself to be a close and intelligent observer of cultural, political, and social life, not only in his own country but also in the many foreign countries in which he had traveled. Furthermore, he continued to display a many-sided interest in the theater.[15] Several of his plays were performed on Broadway, and on two occasions (October, 1959, and February, 1960), collaborating with Robert Glenn, he tried the experiment of staging a portrait of Harlem that was put together from a number of his poems.

---

[15] After *Mulatto* (1935), his principal plays were *Little Ham* (1936), comedy in three acts; *Soul Gone Home* (1937), tragicomedy in one act; *Joy to My Soul* (1937), comedy in three acts; *Emperor of Haiti* (1938), tragedy in three acts; *Don't You Want to Be Free?* (1937), historic panorama in one act; *Front Porch* (1939), comic drama in three acts; *When the Jack Hollers* (1936), popular comedy in three acts (in collaboration with Arna Bontemps); *The Sun Do Move* (1942), musical drama in two acts; *Simply Heavenly* (1957), musical comedy in two acts. In more recent years he collaborated, as librettist or songwriter, with a number of composers, among whom were Kurt Weill, Joe Sherman, Jan Meyerowitz, and Granville English.

But the most original and most popular undertaking of these later years was the creation of the humorous personage Jess B. Simple ("just be simple") with whom, in *Simple Speaks His Mind* (1950), *Simple Takes a Wife* (1953), and *Simple Stakes a Claim* (1957), he conducts imaginary conversations that bring home to his readers the variegated aspects of Negro life and race relations in their own land.[16]

His sympathies for the far left resulted in his being summoned before Senator McCarthy's inquisitorial committee, but on March 26, 1953, he was absolved from censure.

Official recognition came to him at the fifty-first annual meeting of the N.A.A.C.P., held at the University of Minnesota in June, 1960, when he was awarded the Spingarn medal, instituted in 1914 by Professor Joel E. Spingarn and awarded every year to an outstanding Negro personality.[17]

2. From Racial Romanticism to Jazz

In an interview at which he spoke with the staff of *Phylon*, Hughes affirmed that the major aims of his work had always been "to interpret and comment upon Negro life, and its relations to the problems of Democracy."[18] Unquestionably, this definition corresponds by and large to the impression gained from a rapid perusal of the totality of his poetry — but might not the same be said with equal accuracy of other poets of the Negro Renaissance, of a Claude McKay or a Sterling Brown? Omitted from the formula is the distinctively personal character of the poet's vision of life and of his race's problems, for it tells us nothing of what specifically makes up Langston Hughes's manner.

Such poets as McKay, Toomer, and Cullen from the outset saw the external world in terms of their own consciousness and, even more precisely, of their conscience, which served them as a universal criterion. But Hughes's vision might almost be said to move in the opposite direction. He lives, basically, in terms of the external world and in unison with it, making himself one with the community and refusing to stand apart as an individual. His poetry, as a consequence, reflects collective states of mind as though they were *ipso facto* his own. Moreover, he only rarely launches into the painstaking self-analyses through which others sought to determine the exact boundaries of their individual persons.

This almost total merging of the poet's personality with his racial group

[16] These imaginary conversations were first printed in the *Chicago Defender,* where Hughes wrote regularly, beginning in 1945.

[17] See *The Crisis,* August-September, 1960, pp. 410-11, 422-23.

[18] "Some Practical Observations," by Langston Hughes and the editors, *Phylon,* fourth quarter, 1950, p. 307.

establishes Langston Hughes as, primarily, the poet of the masses. In him, Alain Locke declared, "the Negro masses have found a voice."[19] The masses, yes, rather than the folk — for this appears to constitute the difference that marks off Langston Hughes from Sterling Brown. The folk have roots, ties to the earth, while the masses whose joys and sorrows, both material and moral, are depicted by Hughes in the sometimes shocking hues of the naturalist palette, and with whom his own origins ensured obvious affinities, for the most part are flotsam, uprooted human beings as yet ill-fitted for the harsh, unfamiliar urban environment to which the barriers of segregation and the economic necessities of the epoch had driven them.

Nevertheless, this move in the direction of a naturalistic depiction of the black proletariat is not clearly discernible before the publication of *Fine Clothes to the Jew* (1927). There were premonitory signs, indeed, in *The Weary Blues,* published the previous year, but in many respects these poems were still highly romantic, with an African atavism lauded to the skies, the Negro presented as a stranger in Western civilization, and the color black idealized and glorified.

Racial Romanticism

Hughes's first poem, published in *The Crisis* in June, 1921, attracted the attention it did precisely because its author revealed the acute sensitivity to the racial past that Garvey, with his racial romanticism, was then trying to instill in the minds of all. "The Negro Speaks of Rivers" heralded the existence of a mystic union of Negroes in every country and every age. It pushed their history back to the creation of the world, and credited them with possessing a wisdom no less profound than that of the greatest rivers of civilization that humanity had ever known, from the Euphrates to the Nile and from the Congo to the Mississippi:

> I've known rivers:
> I've known rivers ancient as the world and older than the flow of human
> blood in human veins.
>
> My soul has grown deep like the rivers.
>
> I bathed in the Euphrates when dawns were young.
> I built my hut near the Congo and it lulled me to sleep.
> I looked upon the Nile and raised the pyramids above it.
> I heard the singing of the Mississippi when Abe Lincoln went down to New
> Orleans, and I've seen its muddy bosom turn all golden in the sunset.

[19] Review of *The Weary Blues, Palms* IV, no. 1 (1926), 25.

I've known rivers:
Ancient, dusky rivers.

My soul has grown deep like the rivers.[20]

The only definition of the Negro the poet was then willing to recognize as worthy was in terms of his African origins, his history, and his particular contribution to the civilizations in which he had been involved.

Yet unlike Countee Cullen, and perhaps because he was the only poet of the Negro Renaissance who had a direct, rather disappointing contact with Africa,[21] Hughes rarely indulges in a gratuitous idealization of the land of his ancestors.[22] If, in spite of everything, the exaltation of African atavism has a significant place in his poetry up to 1931, the reason is merely that he had not yet discovered a less romantic manner that would express his discomfort at not being treated in his own country as a citizen on a par with any other. If he celebrates Africa as his mother,[23] it is not only because all the black peoples originated there but also because America, which should be his real mother, had always behaved toward him in stepmotherly fashion.[24]

It is out of fear of its mighty, inhuman, cruel white civilization that he seeks reassurance by evoking and summoning to his aid the obscure powers of his African ancestors:

[20] *The Crisis,* June, 1921, p. 71. Reprinted in *The Weary Blues,* p. 51. The poem was dedicated to W. E. B. Du Bois. For a definition of the Negro from the same historical perspective, see "Proem," *The Weary Blues,* p. 19. The text of this poem was reprinted under the title "The Negro" in *The Dream Keeper,* p. 72; and with a variant in line 16 in *Selected Poems,* p. 8 ("Negro"). His acute historical sense is to be met with in a great many poems. See, for example, "Aunt Sue's Stories," *The Weary Blues,* p. 57; "The Black Clown," *The Negro Mother and Other Dramatic Recitations,* p. 8; "Prelude to Our Age," *Branch Library Book News* (New York Public Library), October, 1950, pp. 105-10. See also the poems examined below in connection with the theme of the American dream and, among the prose works, "The Glory of Negro History, a Pageant," *The Langston Hughes Reader,* pp. 465-80; as well as the article "The Need for Heroes," *The Crisis,* June, 1941, pp. 184-85, 206.

[21] "There was one thing that hurt me a lot when I talked with the people," declared Hughes, with reference to his trip to Africa. "The Africans looked at me and would not believe I was a Negro" (*The Big Sea,* p. 11).

[22] On one or two occasions, nevertheless, he also chose to imagine an Africa peopled by ebony kings and queens. Thus in the spectacle of a tiger taken captive by Hindu hunters he sees a fitting decorative motif for a screen that a prince might offer as a present to the black queen of some remote fairyland country: "...a prince's gift to some ebony queen / In a far-off land like a fairy scene" ("For an Indian Screen," *Opportunity,* March, 1927, p. 85). See also "When Sue Wears Red," stanza 2, *The Weary Blues,* p. 66.

[23] "My Africa, Motherland of the Negro peoples! And me a Negro! Africa!" *The Big Sea,* p. 10.

[24] "America never was America to me," he declares in the poem "Let America Be America Again," line 5, *A New Song,* p. 9.

> All the tom-toms of the jungle beat in my blood,
> And all the wild hot moons of the jungles shine in my soul.
> I am afraid of this civilization —
>> So hard,
>>> So strong,
>>>> So cold.[25]

The African forest and its trees, the jungle with its silvery moons — these are the romantic symbols of freedom of which the white man has deprived the colored peoples, so that he may enclose them in the cage of his civilization, as the tamer pens up wild beasts in his circus cages:

> I was a red man one time,
> But the white men came.
> I was a black man, too,
> But the white men came.
>
> They drove me out of the forest.
> They took me away from the jungles.
> I lost my trees.
> I lost my silver moons.
>
> Now they've caged me
> In the circus of civilization.
> Now I herd with the many —
> Caged in the circus of civilization.[26]

Another fine poem, "Black Seed," presents the Negroes of the diaspora as black seeds borne far away from their natural habitat by an alien wind to bloom in other people's gardens, where their flowers are cut by white-faced gardeners:

> World-wide dusk
> Of dear dark faces
> Driven before an alien wind,
> Scattered like seed
> From far-off places
> Growing in soil
> That's strange and thin,

[25] "Poem — For the Portrait of an African Boy after the Manner of Gauguin," *The Weary Blues,* p. 102. On the same subject, see also "Afraid," *ibid.,* p. 101. As for the beat of the African drum, it blends in like an accompaniment in numerous poems, even when the theme is not at all racial. It would require too much space to provide an exhaustive list here, but see, for instance, "Fantasy in Purple," *ibid.,* p. 46, and "Drum," *Dear Lovely Death* (first poem in this volume, whose pages are not numbered). This poem is also reprinted in *Selected Poems,* p. 87.
[26] "Lament for Dark Peoples," *The Weary Blues,* p. 100.

> Hybrid plants
> In another's garden,
> Flowers
> In a land
> That's not your own,
> Cut by the shears
> Of the white-faced gardeners —
> Tell them to leave you alone![27]

The real meaning of Hughes's African homesickness, it seems to us, is revealed in "Our Land," whose conclusion lets us divine that, when all is said and done, the Negro is not longing for the African sun, or trees, or parrots, but for the joy of loving and being loved:

> We should have a land of sun,
> Of gorgeous sun,
> And a land of fragrant water
> Where the twilight
> Is a soft bandanna handkerchief
> Of rose and gold,
> And not this land where life is cold.
>
> We should have a land of trees,
> Of tall thick trees
> Bowed down with chattering parrots
> Brilliant as the day,
> And not this land where birds are grey.
>
> Ah, we should have a land of joy,
> Of love and joy and wine and song,
> And not this land where joy is wrong.[28]

These romantic dreams of a lost Africa no doubt brought the poet of *The Weary Blues* much praise and sympathy, but dreams they remained. Later he will admit this, and will come to see that the resurrection of African greatness that Garvey had made seem so near at hand can be realized only in a remote and hazy future:

> Dream of yesterday
> And far-off long tomorrow:

---

[27] "Black Seed," *Opportunity*, December, 1930, p. 371.

[28] "Our Land," *The Weary Blues*, p. 99. See also, on the same subject, the poems "Fog," *Palms* IV, no. 1 (1926), 24, in which the poet, addressing the black boatmen who had come to reprovision the ship at Sekondi, on the Gold Coast, declares: "You do not know the fog / We strange so-civilized ones / Sail in always." See, too, "Disillusion," *The Weary Blues*, p. 104.

> Africa imprisoned
> In her bitter sorrow.[29]

Dreaming, in any case, formed no part of his real nature,[30] and one may wonder whether, even before the publication of *The Weary Blues,* and at the very moment he was writing some of the poems that would appear in it, he did not yield to the feeling that all this African romanticism was a whopping lie, an assemblage of words he used as "screens for thoughts," black garments he wove "to cover the naked body/Of the too white truth." This, basically, was the only kind of truth he could recognize in his civilized soul — or, in any event, that might well be the meaning of "Liars," published as early as the March, 1925, issue of the magazine *Opportunity:*

> It is we who are liars:
> The Pretenders-to-be who are not
> And the Pretenders-not-to-be who are.
> It is we who use words
> As screens for thoughts
> And weave dark garments
> To cover the naked body
> Of the too white Truth.
> It is we with the civilized souls
> Who are liars.[31]

He may have been lying also, when he so inopportunely praised the color black. This tendency to praise the color of his own skin was, indeed,

[29] "Motherland," *Jim Crow's Last Stand,* p. 15. Reprinted in *Fields of Wonder,* p. 97.

[30] "Poets who write mostly about love, roses and moonlight, sunsets and snow, must lead a very quiet life," wrote Hughes in "My Adventures as a Social Poet," *Phylon,* third quarter, 1947, p. 205. "Seldom, I imagine, does their poetry get them into difficulties. Beauty and lyricism are really related to another world, to ivory towers, to your head in the clouds, feet floating off the earth. Unfortunately, having been born poor — and also colored — in Missouri, I was stuck in the mud from the beginning."

[31] "Liars," *Opportunity,* March, 1925, p. 90. We may also note four other "African" poems by Langston Hughes: "Afro-American Fragment" (published in July, 1930, in *The Crisis,* and reprinted in the anthology edited by Langston Hughes and Arna Bontemps, *The Poetry of the Negro,* p. 102), already offers a much more realistic view of Africa than those to be found in *The Weary Blues.* "Call of Ethiopia" (*Opportunity,* September, 1935, p. 276) is an occasional poem concerning the invasion of Ethiopia by Mussolini's regiments. "Death in Africa" (*Opportunity,* August, 1941, p. 237), inspired by the battles of World War II that were fought in North Africa, indicates a renewal of his faith in the destiny of Africa. The poem, in which Hughes interrogates himself on the possible remedies for "death in Africa," ends with the following lines: "The drums and the witch doctors, helpless. / The missionaries, helpless. / Damballa, / Helpless, too?" Damballa is a voodoo god in Haiti and Dahomey. "Africa" (*Selected Poems,* p. 284) salutes the African awakening, "The new stride / In your thighs."

a persistent custom of the Negro Renaissance writer caught up in the
ardor of Garvey's black nationalism, but other writers had voiced their
praise with more nuances than Hughes employed. Countee Cullen let it
be known that his black skin brought him suffering as well as arousing his
pride, and the racial pride of Claude McKay was founded primarily on
his awareness of his dignity as a man. In Hughes's case, on the other hand,
the hymning of color is always accompanied by a certain gratuitousness, so
that is seems forced and artificial:

> The night is beautiful,
> So the faces of my people.
>
> The stars are beautiful,
> So the eyes of my people.
>
> Beautiful, also, is the sun.
> Beautiful, also, are the souls of my people.[32]

Hughes comes nearest to Countee Cullen's manner in "When Sue Wears
Red," where pride of color is based above all on the past greatness of the
race, translucent in the body of a black woman:

> When Susanna Jones wears red
> Her face is like an ancient cameo
> Turned brown by the ages.
>
> .   .   .   .
>
> When Susanna Jones wears red
> A queen from some time-dead Egyptian night
> Walks once again.[33]

"Songs to the Dark Virgin"[34] also pays homage to the beauty of the black
woman, in a way somewhat reminiscent of the oriental style of the Song
of Songs, but idealization of color goes over into paradox in "Poem to the
Black Beloved," when the poet sings of the beauty of a woman who is not
beautiful, and praises her virtue though she is not virtuous. Here is the
outstanding example of color venerated on its own account:

> Ah,
> My black one,
> Thou art not beautiful
> Yet thou hast

[32] "Poem," *The Weary Blues*, p. 58. Other parallel praises of blackness and the
night are to be found in "Dream Variation," *ibid.*, p. 43; "A Black Pierrot," p.
61; "Ardella," p. 64.
[33] "When Sue Wears Red," *ibid.*, p. 66.
[34] *Ibid.*, p. 63.

A loveliness
Surpassing beauty.

Oh,
My black one,
Thou are not good
Yet thou hast
A purity
Surpassing goodness.

Ah,
My black one,
Thou art not luminous
Yet an altar of jewels,
An altar of shimmering jewels,
Would pale in the light
Of thy darkness,
Pale in the light
Of thy nightness.[35]

Rebellion: Through a Glass Jazzily

Need one be astonished if, after they had been lulled by such dithyrambs in praise of their color and the land of their ancestors, some of Hughes's readers were almost nauseated when *Fine Clothes to the Jew* was published? The black critics, as it turned out, were almost uniformly negative in judging this second collection of poems. The *Pittsburgh Courier* used the headline, "Langston Hughes' Book of Poems Trash,"[36] and New York's *Amsterdam News* had "Langston Hughes — The Sewer Dweller."[37] The *Whip* of Chicago called him "The poet lowrate of Harlem."[38] In the eyes of Benjamin Brawley, professor at Howard University and "our most respectable critic,"[39] "it would have been just as well, perhaps better, if the book had never been published. No other ever issued reflects more

[35] "Poem to the Black Beloved," *ibid.*, p. 65. "Nightness," the last word in the poem, is evidently a coinage of the author's, who treats the substantive "night" as though it were an adjective. For other hymnings of the beauty of blackness, see "To the Dark Mercedes of 'El Palacio de Amor,' " p. 90; and "Epilogue," p. 109, lines 15-17. "Color" (*Jim Crow's Last Stand*, p. 7), which voices the pride of color, is certainly intended to be a rejoinder to Cullen who, in "The Shroud of Color," had compared his color to a shroud: "I would wear it / Like a banner for the proud — / Not like a shroud" (lines 1-3). On the evaluation of color, see also below, pp. 418ff.

[36] This citation, like those that follow, is taken from *The Big Sea*, pp. 266-67.

[37] Reference in note 36 above.

[38] A pun on the expression "Poet Laureate."

[39] *The Big Sea*, p. 266.

fully the abandon and the vulgarity of its age."[40] Eustace Gay, the literary critic of the Philadelphia *Tribune,* had this to say:

> It does not matter to me whether every poem in the book is true to life. Why should it be paraded before the American public by a Negro author as being typical or representative of the Negro? Bad enough to have white authors holding up our imperfections to public gaze. Our aim ought to be to present to the general public, already mis-informed both by well-meaning and malicious writers, our higher aims and aspirations, and our better selves.[41]

Allison Davis echoed all these criticisms when in August, 1928, he wrote in *The Crisis:* "For nearly ten years, our Negro writers have been 'confessing' the distinctive sordidness and triviality of Negro life, and making an exhibition of their own unhealthy imagination in the name of frankness and sincerity."[42] As he saw it, the whole movement awakened the impression that "Negroes are sincerely bestial,"[43] the responsibility for this lying with white writers like Carl Van Vechten, who had encouraged black writers, and Hughes in particular, to write in this fashion.

Hughes had already responded in advance to this hue and cry, at the end of an article published by *The Nation* on June 23, 1926. It amounted to a declaration of independence on the part of the younger generation of the Negro Renaissance:

> We younger Negro artists who create now intend to express our individual dark-skinned selves without fear or shame. If white people are pleased we are glad. If they are not, it doesn't matter. We know we are beautiful. And ugly too. The tom-tom cries and the tom-tom laughs. If colored people are pleased we are glad. If they are not, their displeasure doesn't matter either. We build our temples for tomorrow, strong as we know how, and we stand on top of the mountain, free within ourselves.[44]

This act of defiance undoubtedly had as its main addressee the black bourgeoisie,[45] which was subordinating everything to its concern that White America should be presented with a facade of unblemished respectability.

---

[40] *The Negro Genius,* p. 248.
[41] Cited in *The Big Sea,* p. 267.
[42] Allison Davis, "Our Negro 'Intellectuals,'" *The Crisis,* August, 1928, p. 268.
[43] *Ibid.,* p. 269. See, too, some remarks made by William Harrison about *Shakespeare in Harlem* in his review entitled "A Book of Light Verse," *Opportunity,* July, 1942, p. 219.
[44] "The Negro Artist and the Racial Mountain," *Nation,* June 23, 1926, p. 694.
[45] In the sentence preceding the passage cited above, members of "the smug Negro middle class" were invited "to turn from their white, respectable, ordinary books and papers to catch a glimmer of their own beauty."

Critics like Brawley were certainly aware of the fact that Negro life had its sordid aspects too, but they insisted that these should be kept under lock and key and away from public scrutiny, especially when the public was white. To Hughes's naturalism Brawley, the very incarnation of Comstockery and Victorian prudery, rejoined by citing Tennyson.[46] Taking his wishes for reality, he also made bold to affirm, in 1927, with a clairvoyance we can fully appreciate today: "Already, however, the day of jazz is over; charlatanry has defeated itself."[47]

Not only had the jazz age not come to an end; jazz had become the privileged channel for expressing the rebellion of modern man, especially the Negro, against the straitjacket of an inhuman industrial and commercial civilization that cut him off from the realization of his highest aspirations. "Jazz to me," said Langston Hughes, "is one of the inherent expressions of Negro life in America; the eternal tom-tom beating in the Negro soul — the tom-tom of revolt against weariness in a white world, a world of subway trains, and work, work, work; the tom-tom of joy and laughter, and pain swallowed in a smile."[48] Jazz, the favorite idiom of the black urban masses, would also become the habitual medium of the man who stood instantaneously revealed as their poet. Between them and him, jazz was the best and most natural means of communication,[49] for its rhythm was the actual rhythm of life:

> The rhythm of life
> Is a jazz rhythm.[50]

When, in Harlem, jazz is no longer heard, then life itself has departed:

> Life
> For him
> Must be
> The shivering of
> A great drum
> Beaten with swift sticks
> Then at the closing hour
> The lights go out
> And there is no music at all
> And death becomes

[46] Benjamin Griffith Brawley, "The Negro Literary Renaissance," *The Southern Workman*, April, 1927, p. 183.
[47] *Ibid.*, p. 184.
[48] "The Negro Artist and the Racial Mountain."
[49] See Hughes's "Jazz as Communication," *The Langston Hughes Reader*, pp. 492-94.
[50] "Lenox Avenue: Midnight," *The Weary Blues*, p. 39.

> An empty cabaret
> And eternity an unblown saxophone
> And yesterday
> A glass of gin
> Drunk long
> Ago.[51]

It is the accompaniment both of life here below and of life eternal:

> Play the *St. Louis Blues*
> For me when I die.
> I want some fine music
> Up there in the sky.[52]

The actual substance of jazz is Negro life, especially that of the great black metropolis. Between Harlem's heartbeats[53] and the beat of the rhythm section, between the frenzied swirl of Lenox Avenue and the gyrations of a record in the juke box, there are natural affinities, and thus possibilities of transmutation:

> I could take the Harlem night
> And wrap around you,
> Take the neon lights and make a crown,
> Take the Lenox Avenue busses,
> Taxis, subways,
> And for your love song tone their rumble down.
> Take Harlem's heartbeat,
> Make a drumbeat,
> Put it on a record, let it whirl,
> And while we listen to it play,
> Dance with you till day —
> Dance with you, my sweet brown Harlem girl.[54]

This is why Hughes calls Harlem "Jazzonia,"[55] the city of jazz.

[51] "Sport," *Fine Clothes to the Jew*, p. 40.
[52] "Request for Requiems," *One-Way Ticket*, p. 115. One may note that jazz does indeed still serve as a "Requiem" at the funeral of jazz players in the United States. The *Saint Louis Blues* was played at the funeral of its author, W. C. Handy, on April 2, 1958, in New York. Since then, a jazz funeral was celebrated in New Orleans for the clarinet player Alphonse Picou, and was followed by thousands of people who danced in the streets. For an illustrated account of the funeral, see "New Orleans Bids Goodbye to Alphonse Picou — Clarinetist Buried in Traditional Jazz Funeral," *Ebony*, May, 1961, pp. 55-65.
[53] "Jazz is a heartbeat — its heartbeat is yours," Langston Hughes also declared ("Jazz as Communication").
[54] "Juke Box Love Song," *Montage of a Dream Deferred*, p. 10.
[55] Title of a poem, *The Weary Blues*, p. 25. See also "Young Singer," *ibid.*, p. 28, and "Harlem Night Song," p. 62. On Harlem in Hughes's poetry, see the conclusion of this chapter.

In his fine poem "Trumpet Player: 52nd Street," Hughes analyzed with great subtlety and penetration the reasons that explain why jazz is so vitally important for the Negro:

> The Negro
> With the trumpet at his lips
> Has dark moons of weariness
> Beneath his eyes
> Where the smoldering memory
> Of slave ships
> Blazed to the crack of whips
> About his thighs.
>
> .   .   .
>
> The music
> From the trumpet at his lips
> Is honey
> Mixed with liquid fire.
> The ryhthm
> From the trumpet at his lips
> Is ecstasy
> Distilled from old desire —
> Desire
> That is longing for the moon
> Where the moonlight's but a spotlight
> In his eyes,
> Desire
> That is longing for the sea
> Where the sea's a bar-glass
> Sucker size.
>
> The Negro
> With the trumpet at his lips
> Whose jacket
> Has a *fine* one-button roll,
> Does not know
> Upon what riff the music slips
> Its hypodermic needle
> To his soul —
>
> But softly
> As the tune comes from his throat
> Trouble
> Mellows to a golden note.[56]

Thus in the first place jazz, like any other art form, is a means of escape,

[56] "Trumpet Player: 52nd Street," *Fields of Wonder,* p. 91.

another kind of addiction whose artificial paradises the poet equates with those obtained by the intravenous injection of a narcotic. For the popular masses in those immense ghettoes, the black districts of the great American cities, where human beings are chronically deprived of life's basic satisfactions, the temple of jazz, the nightclub, is also the sanctuary of an illusion, where floodlights replace moonlight and the sea's swaying immensity shrinks to the dimensions of a few sips of liquor from a shot glass. This transforming power of jazz is also forcibly expressed in "Harlem Dance Hall":

> It had no dignity before.
> But when the band began to play,
> Suddenly the earth was there,
> And flowers,
> Trees,
> And air,
> And like a wave the floor —
> That had no dignity before.[57]

Once the cabaret threshold is crossed, as though by magic every frustration and unhappiness disappears:

> Cabaret, cabaret!
> That's where ma man an' me go.
> Cabaret, cabaret!
> That's where we go —
> Leaves de snow outside
> An' our troubles at de door.[58]

It is no accident that jazz is nighttime music, for jazz and the night maintain a mysterious accord. In one poem, Hughes speaks of "the jazz-tuned night";[59] and in Harlem they conspire together to offer the Negro the longed-for forgetfulness:

> O, sweep of stars over Harlem streets,
> O, little breath of oblivion that is night.[60]

[57] "Harlem Dance Hall," *ibid.*, p. 94.
[58] "Minnie Sings Her Blues," *Fine Clothes to the Jew*, p. 64. For a highly significant poem on this same theme, see also "Flatted Fifths," *Montage of a Dream Deferred*, p. 29. Other observations on the atmosphere of liquor outlets have a graver tone ("Juice Joint: Northern City," *One-Way Ticket*, p. 67) or end in tragedy ("Death in Harlem," *Shakespeare in Harlem*, p. 57). "Lincoln Theatre" (*One-Way Ticket*, p. 46) establishes a parallel between the illusion offered by a show and jazz as a way of escape.
[59] "To a Black Dancer in the Little Savoy," *The Weary Blues*, p. 35.
[60] "Stars," *Fields of Wonder*, p. 101. See also, on the same theme, "Blues at Dawn," *Montage of a Dream Deferred*, p. 61.

All this, added up, makes of jazz the Negro's *carpe diem:*

> Tomorrow ... who knows?
> Dance today!
>
> . . .
>
> White ones, brown ones,
> What do you know
> About tomorrow
> Where all paths go?
>
> . . .
>
> Tomorrow ... is darkness.
> Joy today![61]

> Sun's going down this evening —
> Might never rise no mo'.
> The sun's going down this very night —
> Might never rise no mo' —
> So dance with swift feet, honey,
>   (The banjo's sobbing low)
> Dance with swift feet, honey —
>   Might never dance no mo'.[62]

As in the blues, of which this last poem is a variation, the pleasure of those who dance to the sound of jazz always has an admixture of despair:

> Stealing from the night
> A few
> Desperate hours
> Of pleasure
>
> Stealing from death
> A few
> Desperate days
> Of life.[63]

[61] "Harlem Night Club," *The Weary Blues,* p. 32.

[62] "Song for a Banjo Dance," *ibid.,* p. 36. Note also these lines from "Saturday Night" (*Fine Clothes to the Jew,* p. 41):

> Won't be nothin' left
> When de worms git through
> An' you's a long time
> Dead
> When you is
> Dead, too.
> So beat dat drum, boy!
> Shout dat song:
> Shake 'em up an' shake 'em up
> All night long.

[63] "Dancers," *Fields of Wonder,* p. 68.

Thus he who has the ear to hear can sense how the jazz band utters a sob, in the midst of the gaiety:

> Does a jazz-band ever sob?
> They say a jazz-band's gay.
> Yet as the vulgar dancers whirled
> And the wan night wore away,
> One said she heard the jazz-band sob
> When the little dawn was grey.[64]

With this we touch upon the fundamental reasons for the exceptional importance of jazz in Hughes's poetry. Unlike a Carl Sandburg, for example,[65] he finds in it much more than a mere literary theme. Hughes feels how, in genuine jazz, the whole soul of his race finds expression, with laughter often but a mask that hides tears. Let this phrase of the poet's, addressed to the "jazzmen" of a Paris nightclub:

> Play it,
> Jazz band!
> You know that tune
> That laughs and cries at the same time.[66]

stand beside this other poem in which he movingly depicts the black soul:

> Because my mouth
> Is wide with laughter
> And my throat
> Is deep with song,
> You do not think
> I suffer after
> I have held my pain
> So long?
>
> Because my mouth
> Is wide with laughter,
> You do not hear

64 "Cabaret," *The Weary Blues,* p. 29.

65 One may note, for example, the banality of such poems as "Jazz Fantasia," *Smoke and Steel* (*Complete Poems,* p. 179) or "Snatch of Sliphorn Jazz," *Good Morning, America* (ibid., p. 420) in order to appreciate fully all the novelty, and the lively personal contribution, that Hughes brought to jazz poetry.

66 "Jazz Band in a Parisian Cabaret," *Fine Clothes to the Jew,* p. 74. See also "The Big-Timer," *The Negro Mother and Other Dramatic Recitations,* pp. 12-15, in which Hughes offers us, in monologue form, the portrait of a local "big timer," who boasts of being on easy street. But the marginal "stage directions" with which the poem (in the manner of Vachel Lindsay) is provided enable the author to point out, concerning this character, the poignant contrast separating "the ironic gaiety of the music" — that is, of the jazz that accompanies the poem (p. 14, margin) — from "the tragic emptiness of his life" (p. 15, margin).

> My inner cry?
> Because my feet
> Are gay with dancing,
> You do not know
> I die?[67]

or, again, this avowal by a black buffoon:

> In one hand
> I hold tragedy
> And in the other
> Comedy, —
> Masks for the soul.
> Laugh with me.
> You would laugh!
> Weep with me.
> You would weep!
> Tears are my laughter.
> Laughter is my pain.
> Cry at my grinning mouth,
> If you will.[68]

Jazz, for Hughes, is thus but another form of the celebrated mask whose existence was revealed to us by Negro folklore,[69] and which Dunbar so poignantly evoked in his poem "We Wear the Mask."

On the other hand, the African rhythms of jazz make it a link with the land of his ancestors for the American Negro:

> My song
> From the dark lips
> Of Africa
> Deep
> As the rich earth
> Beautiful
> As the black night
> Strong
> As the first iron
> Black
> Out of Africa

[67] "Minstrel Man," *The Dream Keeper and Other Poems*, p. 38.
[68] "The Jester," *The Weary Blues*, p. 53. See also these two lines from "Homesick Blues" (*Fine Clothes to the Jew*, p. 24): "To keep from cryin' / I opens ma mouth an' laughs," and this definition of laughter in "Railroad Avenue" (*ibid.*, p. 27): "Laughter / Suddenly / Like a taut drum. / Laughter / Suddenly / Neither truth nor lie."
[69] See our Ch. 1, note 20.

Me and my
Song.[70]

This kinship has been authenticated many times by the analysts of jazz,[71] but with Hughes, especially in *The Weary Blues,* and also in the work of Cullen and Van Vechten, it functions within the romantic vision of a primitive, sensual Africa destined to please the patrons of the Harlem cabarets during the jazz era. In such poems as "To Midnight Nan at Leroy's,"[72] or "To a Black Dancer in the Little Savoy,"[73] the insidious rhythms of jazz are accompanied by the erotic convolutions of the naked black dancing girl with "breasts like the pillows of all sweet dreams,"[74] and the conjuring up of African love nights are in meaningful counterpoint with the Harlem nights spurred on by jazz:

> *Hear dat music . . .*
> *Jungle night.*
> *Hear dat music . . .*
> *And the moon was white.*
>
> Sing your Blues song,
> Pretty baby,
> You want lovin'
> And you don't mean maybe.
>
> *Jungle lover . . .*
> *Night black boy . . .*
> *Two against the moon*
> *And the moon was joy.*[75]

Thus the word "jazz" reacquires the entire erotic content it originally had in popular parlance.[76] More than that, this erotic content even projects

[70] "Me and My Songs," line 22 to end, *Jim Crow's Last Stand,* p. 26. The specifically racial, African quality of jazz is also stressed in "Negro Servant," *One-Way Ticket,* p. 70. In this poem, Harlem and the beneficent rhythms of Harlem jazz are presented as a haven of peace for the Negro who has spent a harassing day serving white men, and this sanctuary status allotted the world of jazz is the direct consequence of the similarity between its rhythms and those of the tribal dance in the African countryside, evoked by the poem in a delicate filigree. See also "Danse Africaine," *The Weary Blues,* p. 105.

[71] See, for instance, the first part ("The Pre-History of Jazz") of Marshall W. Stearns, *The Story of Jazz,* pp. 11ff.

[72] *The Weary Blues,* p. 30.

[73] *Ibid.,* p. 35.

[74] *Ibid.* See also "Nude Young Dancer," p. 33.

[75] "To Midnight Nan at Leroy's," stanzas 2-4, *ibid.,* p. 30.

[76] One may note H. L. Mencken's declaration: "To jazz has long had the meaning in American folk-speech of to engage in sexual intercourse" (*The American Language,* Suppl. II, p. 709). Nor should it be forgotten that jazz was born in Storyville, which was the New Orleans brothel quarter.

itself onto and tinges a number of nature poems. "Poème d'automne"[77] and "March Moon"[78] deal with striptease sessions transposed into a natural setting. In the first the poet compares the trees, in their autumnal dress of reddish leaves (scarlet is the traditional color of the prostitute and the adulteress) to young courtesans waiting for their lovers, the autumn winds, to disrobe them with a refined science before lavishing mordant kisses upon them:

> The autumn leaves
> Are too heavy with color.
> The slender trees
> On the Vulcan Road
> Are dressed in scarlet and gold
> Like young courtesans
> Waiting for their lovers.
> But soon
> The winter winds
> Will strip their bodies bare
> And then
> The sharp, sleet-stung
> Caresses of the cold
> Will be their only
> Love.[79]

In the second poem it is the moon that the wind amorously disrobes of its veils of cloud, and the poet seizes the opportunity to castigate the heavenly luminary as shameless, as he does the black girl with her midnight writhings in Leroy's cabaret.

These are the principal connections discovered, in a rapid survey, between Negro life and the jazz spirit in Hughes's work. This spirit may be looked on as a philosophy of life, a state of mind or point of view that at every moment affects the poet's vision of things. Though it does not always function as a theme in its own right, it nevertheless constitutes the geometrical locus of every theme and so, in a way, makes for the unity of the poet's work.

But it also influences the poem in its conception, form, and technique. In Dunbar's writings we had already noted several attempts to introduce into written poetry the rhythms and the spirit of Negro popular music. Hughes is almost alone in having taken up this trend anew, but it is not

[77] *The Weary Blues,* p. 45.
[78] *Ibid.,* p. 47.
[79] "Poème d'Automne."

altogether certain that his experiments on these lines have invariably produced especially admirable achievements.

The method contained the roots of its own weakness. Jazz depends to a great extent on the powers of improvisation possessed, at least in principle, by the individual instrumentalists. Moreover, and particularly in the jam session, jazz may become an entertainment basically devoid of any rule or rigorousness, an ill-defined arabesque around a given theme which in its vagueness can be taken up and interpreted as each player chooses. In these conditions it can readily be conceived that both the superb and the lamentable may emerge from the experiment, especially when it is carried out on the scale favored by Hughes. In his introduction for *The Weary Blues* Van Vechten remarked that the experimental poems in the volume "have a highly deceptive air of spontaneous improvisation."[80] Countee Cullen, who himself neither practiced nor cared for this sort of poem, rejoined, in his critique of the same volume: "I do not feel that the air is deceptive."[81] It is indeed difficult to look on as other than improvisations, in the plainest sense of the word, such pieces as "Negro Dancers," of which the first stanza runs:

> Me an' ma baby's
> Got two mo' ways,
> Two mo' ways to do de Charleston!
> > Da, da
> > Da, da, da!
> Two mo' ways to do de Charleston![82]

Yet here there is at least a minimum of rhythm. But what can be said of the following lines, which appeared twenty-five years later in *Montage of a Dream Deferred?*

> Daddy,
> don't let your dog
> curb you![83]

Under the title of "Warning," this "poem" is a mere witticism, inspired

[80] "Introducing Langston Hughes to the Reader," *The Weary Blues*, p. 13.
[81] "Poet on Poet," *Opportunity*, February, 1926, p. 73, col. A.
[82] *The Weary Blues*, p. 26. This utilization of the cry by Hughes is less typical than in "Blues Fantasy" (*ibid.*, p. 37). Its use will become general in the later collections of poems, reaching its full development in *Montage of a Dream Deferred*, and it will assist to some degree in accentuating, though superficially, the atmosphere of his jazz poetry. It is recognized that the Negro folk cry is one of the elements at the origin of jazz. On this topic, see the article by the musicologist Willis L. James, "The Romance of the Negro Folk Cry in America," *Phylon*, first quarter, 1955, pp. 15-30, in which the assertion is made: "Jazz is largely Negro cries sung or played or both" (p. 28).
[83] "Warning," *Montage of a Dream Deferred*, p. 11.

by the signs to be met with in every New York park: "Warning, Curb
your dog." In the name of jazz, we have been led well beyond the limits
that even the most broadminded and indulgent critic must place around
what it has been agreed to call poetry.

We hasten to add that the above examples are extreme cases, cited in
order to show the danger that lurks behind the decision to make a principle out of the jazz-style spirit of improvization and playfulness, especially
in the absence of taste, that ultimate rein applied to every freedom.

In any event, other attempts seem more readily acceptable, having at
least the validity of conscious experiments. Thus "Harlem Night Club,"
cited above several times, is both a poem highly evocative of the jazz
band's rhythms and crescendos and a splendid portrayal of the desperate
frenzy with which the dancers, before it is too late, try to squeeze the last
drop of pleasure out of life:

> Sleek black boys in a cabaret,
> Jazz-band, jazz-band, —
> Play, plAY, PLAY!
> Tomorrow . . . who knows?
> Dance today!
>
> .   .   .   .
>
> Jazz-boys, jazz-boys, —
> Play, plAY, PLAY!
> Tomorrow . . . is darkness.
> Joy today![84]

Interesting, too, is the experimental technique of "The Cat and the Saxophone." Like an orchestra score, the poem consists of two parts, bass and
tenor, which the typography enables one to distinguish immediately, and
which proceed together. The lines printed in capital letters are, furthermore, the text of a popular song; they constitute the sonorous setting of a
cabaret within which there takes place the conversation of two lovers,
which is printed in the normal way. On the value of this experiment,
Cullen wrote: "This creation is a *tour de force* of its kind, but is it a
poem?"[85]

[84] "Harlem Night Club," *The Weary Blues*, p. 32. The pulsing rhythm of jazz
is particularly well rendered in "Saturday Night" (*Fine Clothes to the Jew*, p.
41) and in "Ma Man" (*ibid.*, p. 88). In the latter poem, which is a blues, the
rhythmical structure of the first stanza is especially admirable, with the subtle
rhythms of Afro-American music very effectively recalled to life by the insertion,
between the main beats that distinguish the blues, of a certain number of secondary
beats, which leads to that fractioning of the rhythm so characteristic of genuine
jazz. On this topic, see also the remarks made in our Ch. 1.
[85] Countee Cullen, "Poet on Poet," *Opportunity*, February, 1926, pp. 73-74.

EVERYBODY
Half-pint, —
Gin?
No, make it
LOVES MY BABY
corn. You like
liquor,
don't you, honey?
BUT MY BABY
Sure. Kiss me,
DON'T LOVE NOBODY
daddy.
BUT ME.
Say!
EVERYBODY
Yes?
WANTS MY BABY
I'm your
BUT MY BABY
sweetie, ain't I?
DON'T WANT NOBODY
Sure.
BUT
Then let's
ME,
do it!
SWEET ME.
Charleston,
mamma![86]

This endeavor arises out of the frame of mind that can be found in many poets contemporary with Hughes and, all in all, it may be looked on as neither more nor less blameworthy than some of E. E. Cummings's and Guillaume Apollinaire's experiments, and with these it must no doubt be grouped.

But jazz technique not only affected the structure of the individual poem; it was also capable of influencing the ordering of a whole collection of poems. Timid gestures in this direction were already to be observed in *Fine Clothes to the Jew,* which opens with the first stanza of a blues and ends with the second stanza of the same blues,[87] so that the sequence of poems making up the collection is, in a sense, a string of variations on the

[86] "The Cat and the Saxophone (2 A.M.)," *The Weary Blues,* p. 27. For a similar experiment, see "Closing Time," *Fine Clothes to the Jew,* p. 32.
[87] *Fine Clothes to the Jew,* p. 17: "Hey!" and p. 89: "Hey! Hey!"

theme announced at the outset. Though no less restricted in scope, the poet's intention is even more clearly indicated in the volume entitled *Fields of Wonder,* whose first poem is called "Heaven."[88] But, when the identical poem is reprinted at the end of the volume, it is called "Reprise,"[89] just as in a jazz piece the opening theme is later echoed by certain instruments or by the ensemble.

The most ambitious experiment undertaken by Hughes in this domain is, however, *Montage of a Dream Deferred.* The author himself sketches the basic idea in these terms:

> In terms of current Afro-American popular music and the sources from which it has progressed — jazz, ragtime, swing, blues, boogie-woogie, and be-bop — this poem on contemporary Harlem, like be-bop, is marked by conflicting changes, sudden nuances, sharp and impudent interjections, broken rhythms, and passages sometimes in the manner of the jam session, sometimes the popular song, punctuated by the riffs, runs, breaks, and disctortions of the music of a community in transition.[90]

Thus the writer invites us to look on the ninety poems or so, varying greatly in length, that form this collection, as one large-scale composition that evolves on the same lines as a jam session. The unity of the whole comes from the fundamental theme of the "dream deferred" — that is, the frustration that is felt by the residents of Harlem, the black metropolis. As in a jam session, this underlying theme is first indicated ("Dream Boogie"[91]), then clearly stated, and then developed and picked up as each instrument in the band successively paraphrases it, weaves arabesques around it, and responds one to the other. Here, the instruments are represented by the voices or the awarenesses of different personages. These include, for instance, children ("Children's Rhymes"[92]), a friend ("Buddy"[93]), a dancer ("Dancer"[94]), a tenant ("Ballad of the Landlord"[95]), young veterans ("Flatted Fifths"[96]), a prostitute ("Evening Song"[97]), or a host of other characters ("Same in Blues"[98]) whose exact

[88] *Fields of Wonder,* p. 3.
[89] *Ibid.,* p. 115.
[90] *Montage of a Dream Deferred,* the unnumbered pages at the beginning of the volume.
[91] *Ibid.,* p. 3.
[92] *Ibid.,* pp. 5-6.
[93] *Ibid.,* p. 9.
[94] *Ibid.,* p. 21.
[95] *Ibid.,* p. 24. (This poem had already been printed in *Jim Crow's Last Stand,* p. 20.)
[96] *Ibid.,* p. 29.
[97] *Ibid.,* p. 64.
[98] *Ibid.,* p. 72.

identity is not made known to us. The poet, nevertheless, in each poem delineates for us the particular aspects that the basic theme of frustration assumes in their lives. Again, as in the jam session, this basic theme is sometimes interrupted by the digressive introduction of incidental or conflicting themes, or even by simple ornamental figures devoid of all meaning.[99] Finally, at times the *coda* of the musical phrase executed by one "instrument" is taken up and repeated by another "instrument," as though it were an echo.[100]

Though one may at first feel somewhat bewildered by the cavalier blending of the most elevated, serious themes with others that are utterly inept or banal, apparently with no other motivation than the temperamental quirks of the "instrumentalists," it still cannot be denied that the procedure experimented with in *Montage of a Dream Deferred* succeeds in conveying a pretty lively impression of the manifold forms and nuances of existence in the teeming city complex known as Harlem.

It should be stressed, too, that one factor in the relative success of the experiment, and by no means the least weighty, has nothing to do with jazz technique in any precise sense, for the vitality of the work largely depends on the idiom used. This is not some artificial dialect plastered together *ad hoc,* but a natural hybrid between the vital slang of the jazz fan and the equally picturesque idiom of the Harlem district, the "Harlem jive."[101]

These attempts to fuse jazz and poetry are interesting, praiseworthy technical experiments. Despite this fact, it is impossible not to deplore the way in which they sometimes, with an overdone frivolousness, step outside the bounds beyond which there can be no genuine hope of serving authentic jazz and, even less, of serving poetry. Hughes himself sensed, it would seem, that certain weaknesses were inherent in the manner adopted in *Montage of a Dream Deferred*. It will be seen below how, in a more recent experiment entitled *Ask Your Mama,* the jazz element is less in the actual poetry than in the marginal accompaniment. Consequently the poetry not only reacquires a certain autonomy; it also attains a balance that the poet, had he been less devil-may-care and of a surer taste, would never have let loose.

[99] "Figurine," *ibid.,* p. 9; "Figurette," p. 19.
[100] This device aims at stressing the antiphonal character or, in other words, the dialogue structure, of jazz. See, for example, p. 7, the poem "Sister" and the "Comment on Stoop" that answers it; p. 18, the poem "What? So Soon" and the "Comment against Lamp Post" that answers it; and p. 51, "World War II," which ends on an "Echo."
[101] On jive, see Dan Burley, *Original Handbook of Harlem Jive.*

3. THE POETRY OF THE MASSES

We have just seen how jazz constitutes an idiom, a state of mind, and a method. But is it only that, and might it not, without forming a theme in its own right, have its own thematic content nevertheless?

There is no gainsaying that Hughes, throughout his poetic career, made great efforts to widen the gamut of subjects that could be handled in the spirit and with the technique that distinguish jazz. His boldest experiments in this direction, as we have said, are found in *Montage of a Dream Deferred,* where the weightiest problems and most elevated topics, including social and political justice, are by these means closely associated with Negro existence at its most basic level.

But because of the folk origins of the elements that make it up, jazz prefers to seek its thematic material within a narrowly circumscribed range. For it has its very own social setting, that of the black proletariat, the direct replacement of the repressed slave class of a former day, and this latter has also passed on its social and economic circumstances, together with its moral blemishes. On the other hand — and this no doubt explains why it was predestined to become the language of revolt — jazz still recalled its roots sunk deep in folklore which, as we saw, sometimes had given vent to protest by lauding disorderly behavior and by systematically using obscenity.

It was chiefly through the blues that jazz took over both this social context and the urge to shock, and it is noteworthy that the same elements found their way into the work of Hughes also via the blues. Though his first volume, despite its title, contained only a small number of blues, more than one-third of the poems in *Fine Clothes to the Jew* were blues in form, and the others were every whit as much in their spirit.

At the same time we find ourselves transported into the social setting of the blues, whose particular viewpoint the poet makes his own. That means an end to all idealization of race or color and, in particular, an end to the quest for some artificial sustenance that would justify race pride. Henceforth the only voice is that of mass social reality, in all its unvarnished brutality.

In this way, and with the aid of the economic consequences of the 1929 crash, racial consciousness little by little turns into class consciousness. Like the leader W. E. B. Du Bois, Hughes discovers that "the mass of Negroes in the United States belong distinctly to the working proletariat."[102] In this fashion these masses, which the Negro Renaissance had hitherto known

[102] W. E. B. Du Bois, "Marxism and the Negro Problem," *The Crisis,* May, 1933, p. 104, col. A.

only through their folklore, acquire a new dimension, ceasing to be merely a racial minority with its own culture and traditions and becoming a social class defined, essentially, by its economic deprivation, which it shares with all the disinherited of the earth whatever their race or nationality.

Thus Hughes's poetry offers us two parallel portraits of the black masses: one in the naturalistic tradition of the blues, the other on the lines of the Marxist critique.

The Social Setting of the Blues

Like all lyric poetry, the blues is most frequently concerned with love. There is nothing particularly racial about it in this respect, which lies outside our field of concern. Yet it has a highly personal manner, disabused, cynical, and brutal, of describing the instability of the couple and the more sordid aspects of what, for want of a more appropriate term, must be called love. Hughes, in "Beale Street Love," claims to tell us what it means in the black districts of Memphis:

> Love
> Is a brown man's fist
> With hard knuckles
> Crushing the lips,
> Blackening the eyes, —
> Hit me again,
> Says Clorinda.[103]

In his blues, and in other poems reflecting the same frame of mind, he runs the gamut of amorous disillusionment and the plans for vengeance that spring from it. A plethora of ill-starred passions and ill-used partners are betrayed, deserted, or exploited with a cold-blooded vileness matched only by the blatant cynicism of the guilty, who themselves proclaim all the vicious deeds they have committed:

> I'm a bad, bad man
> Cause everybody tells me so.
> I'm a bad, bad man.
> Everbody tells me so.
> I takes ma meanness and ma licker
> Wherever I go.
> I beats ma wife an'
> I beats ma side gal too.
> Beats ma wife an'
> Beats ma side gal too.

[103] "Beale Street Love," *Fine Clothes to the Jew*, p. 57.

> Don't know why I do it but
> It keeps me from feelin' blue.[104]

In the first stanza of "Evil Woman," what at first appeared to be a promise to behave better finally turns out to be the decision to wreak an even more terrible vengeance:

> I ain't gonna mistreat ma
> Good gal any more.
> I'm just gonna kill her
> Next time she makes me sore.[105]

We will not linger over this theme, which is foreign to our purpose and which Hughes used and misused without attaining much freshness.[106] Thus he aroused the feeling that he was stagnating and justifies, here at least, the reproach made by Benjamin Brawley that the man who had claimed to destroy the old-time clichés was creating new ones that scarcely outpointed the old.[107] We should bear in mind, however, that the brutal vision conveyed by the blues was not restricted to amorous matters only; it affected other aspects of life as well and, more especially, the way in which color was treated.[108]

The glorification of blackness on the lines practiced by some poets of the Negro Renaissance and, more especially, in *The Weary Blues,* was largely the affair of intellectuals. The masses had scarcely been affected by it except through Garvey's campaign which, since its theories had no

[104] "Bad Man," *ibid.,* p. 21.

[105] "Evil Woman," *ibid.,* p. 62.

[106] Here are the most important poems in which this theme is to be found (the page numbers are given). In *Fine Clothes to the Jew:* "Misery," 19; "Suicide," 20; "Bad Man," 21; "Gypsy Man," 22; "Beale Street Love," 57; "Cora," 58; "Workin' Man," 59; "Bad Luck Card," 60; "Evil Woman," 62; "Dressed Up," 64; "Lament over Love," 81; "Gal's Cry for a Dying Lover," 82; "Young Girl's Blues," 83; "Midwinter Blues," 84; "Listen Here Blues," 85; "Hard Daddy," 86. In *The Dream Keeper and Other Poems:* "Wide River," 37. In *Shakespeare in Harlem:* "Twilight Reverie," 3; "Supper Time," 4; "Bed Time," 5; "Sunday," 7; "Pay Day," 8; "Letter," 10; "Evil," 15; "Hope," 16; "Declaration," 22; "Free Man," 31; "Brief Encounter," 42; "Morning After," 44; "In a Troubled Key," 49; "Only Woman Blues," 50; "Down and Out," 101; "Love Again Blues," 103; "Widow Woman," 107; "Fired," 112; "Early Evening Quarrel," 113; "Announcement," 115; "50-50," 117; "Evil Morning," 118; "Lover's Return," 119; "Reverie on the Harlem River," 123. In *One-Way Ticket:* "Mama and Daughter," 31; "S-sss-ss-sh!" 33; "Honey-Babe," 40; "Late Last Night," 95. In *Montage of a Dream Deferred:* "Sister," 7; "Preference," 8; "Question," 9; "Ultimatum," 10; "What? So Soon!" 18. In *Selected Poems:* "Miss Blues'es Child," 113; "Homecoming," 135; "Delinquent," 133.

[107] Brawley, *The Negro Genius.*

[108] On the value of color in the blues, see Paul Oliver, *Blues Fell This Morning,* pp. 78ff. and *passim.*

real base in American social reality, made only a transitory impact. Investigations such as that carried out by the sociologist Charles H. Parrish proved, furthermore, that even within the racial group there had always been deep-seated prejudices against individuals of extreme pigmentation, whether at the very light or the very dark end of the spectrum.[109] But to this day such prejudices are seldom openly admitted and, through a kind of unspoken agreement, they remain "a family matter." So it is not hard to imagine the anger aroused by *Fine Clothes to the Jew,* in which black is no longer assimilated to "beautiful like the night" but frankly linked with every kind of pejorative epithet.

"Evil Woman," for example, implicitly finds a cause-and-effect relationship between the woman's malevolence and her very dark skin color. Moreover, though black was officially admitted to be the thing, this poem gives us to understand that the "blue-gummed woman" — that is to say, one who was as black as could be imagined — was no longer popular and had gone out of fashion:

[109] Charles H. Parrish, "Color Names and Color Notions," *Journal of Negro Education,* Winter, 1946, pp. 13-20, has this to say: "Although few Negroes are willing to concede the validity of the assertion that color plays any significant role in the organization of Negro society, there is ample evidence that differences in skin color receive at least verbal recognition in the Negro community" (p. 13). From Parrish's article we borrow this table (p. 16), a partial summary of the results of the investigation he undertook of 400 pupils in a Negro secondary school, in order to discover what ideas they most frequently associated with a given skin color. The answers are given in percentages.

	Light	Medium Brown	Dark
Hard to get along with	23.2	9.9	52.5
Think they are better	74.7	9.4	2.9
Sweet and affectionate	15.5	57.7	7.9
Sensitive about color	16.8	4.6	68.4
Aggressive about rights	31.9	28.4	22.8
Physically stronger	6.5	12.1	59.4
Teacher's favorites	62.6	19.6	5.0
Excluded from sororities	0.23	8.7	75.0

It must be observed that this table expresses opinions, not objective facts. Furthermore, while the investigator has reduced to a mere three categories (light, medium brown, dark) the variations in skin pigmentation, in reality these run into the hundreds with an individual name for each. Thus, proceeding from lighter to darker, one meets with: half white, "yaller," high yellow, fair, bright, yellow, light, dirty yellow, high brown, olive, light brown, "teasing brown," creole brown, medium brown, brown, brownskin, tan, dark brown, chocolate brown, dark, black, rusty black, "ink spot," blue black, "tar baby" (p. 14), not to mention innumerable other terms less often used, such as: clinker, comeon-tan, blackout, jungle yellow, honest black, stove-pipe blonde, won't stop black, etc. (p. 13). In "Harlem Sweeties" (*Shakespeare in Harlem,* pp. 18-20), Hughes himself attempted to provide a list of skin colors for all the beauties in the moneyed district of Harlem, Sugar Hill.

> I can't have no woman's
> Got such low-down ways,
> Cause a blue-gummed woman
> Ain't de style now days.
>
> I brought her from de South
> An' she's goin' on back
> Else I'll use her head
> For a carpet tack.[110]

Black now becomes a synonym for ugliness,[111] and the black girl's natural destiny is to be poor[112] and wretched.[113] It is also her customary fate to be deceived or even deserted by her husband or lover, whose aesthetic ideal is the light-skinned woman and not the "black beloved" praised by the poet in *The Weary Blues* for her very blackness. That is the burden of the girl's lament in "Black Girl":

> ... it seems like always
> Men takes all they can from me
> Then they goes an' finds a yaller gal
> An' lets me be.
>
> .   .   .   .   .
>
> Can't help it cause I'm black.
> I hates them riney yaller gals
> An' I wants ma Albert back.[114]

The fallen girl in "A Ruined Gal" curses her mother for having born her:

> Damn ma black old mammy's soul
> For ever havin' a daughter.[115]

And if the bad character in "Death of Do Dirty" is treated by everyone as bad, his black color is to blame:

> They called him Do Dirty
> Cause he was black.[116]

[110] "Evil Woman," stanzas 3 and 4, *Fine Clothes to the Jew*, p. 62.
[111] "Black an' ugly" is how the girl in "Gal's Cry for a Dying Lover" (*ibid.*, p. 82) describes herself.
[112] "Po' an' black" ("Sinner," *ibid.*, p. 53).
[113] "Misery," *ibid.*, p. 19.
[114] "Black Gal," *ibid.*, p. 66. ("Riney" is the customary term applied to those with a coppery skin and hair color.)
[115] "A Ruined Gal," *ibid.*, p. 63.
[116] "Death of Do Dirty: A Rounder's Song," *ibid.*, p. 36. For other evaluations of color see, in *Shakespeare in Harlem*, "Daybreak," p. 6, and "Me and the Mule," p. 29; and, in *Montage of a Dream Deferred*, "Nightmare Boogie," p. 58, and "Argument," p. 62.

This new scale of values that the poet adopted from the time of *Fine Clothes to the Jew* clearly belongs to a particular social milieu. While other writers of the Negro Renaissance, above all such novelists as Jessie Faucet, had chosen to demonstrate that Negro society also had its respectable bourgeois elements, Hughes on the contrary seems determined to restrict this society to the most materially and morally wretched class, the one with which he was best acquainted from having lived its life for so many years.

The blues people are largely made up of a mobile mass of perennial misfits who are possessed, to use Sterling Brown's expression, by "a itch fo' travelin','"[117] and who are condemned to remain rootless wherever they go:

> Gimme six-bits' worth o' ticket
> On a train that runs somewhere.
> I say six-bits' worth o' ticket
> On a train that runs somewhere.
> I don't care where it's goin'
> Just so it goes away from here.[118]

In a different guise from jazz and the dream of Africa, traveling satisfies in the most literal sense the need for escape felt by the Negro, and it also offers him the same kind of relief:

> I got a railroad ticket,
> Pack my trunk and ride.
>
> . . . .
>
> Got a railroad ticket,
> Pack my trunk and ride.
> And when I get on the train
> I'll cast my blues aside.[119]

Many expect that strange scenes will deliver them from the antagonistic climate that weighs on them in the South:

> These Mississippi towns ain't
> Fit fer a hoppin' toad.[120]
>
> . . . in West Texas where de sun
> Shines like de evil one,
> There ain't no reason

117 "Long Gone," line 7; Sterling Brown, *Southern Road*, p. 8.
118 "Six-Bits Blues," stanza 1, *Shakespeare in Harlem*, p. 37.
119 "Blues Fantasy," *The Weary Blues*, p. 37.
120 "Bound No'th Blues," stanza 4, lines 5-6, *Fine Clothes to the Jew*, p. 87.

> For a man
> To stay![121]

They set off for anywhere, with no prospect of returning and a one-way ticket ("One-Way Ticket"), provided only that they can get away from the South:

> I pick up my life
> And take it with me
> And put it down in
> Chicago, Detroit,
> Buffalo, Scranton,
> Any place that is
> North and East —
> And not Dixie.[122]

But what they are really fleeing from is the absence of respect and affection:

> Once I was in Memphis,
> I mean Tennessee.
> Once I was in Memphis,
> Said Tennessee.
> But I had to leave cause
> Nobody there was good to me.[123]

Then, in the great cities of the North where they have come in search of a more human existence, their hopes are often blasted:

> When I was home de
> Sunshine seemed like gold.
> When I was home de
> Sunshine seemed like gold.
> Since I come up North de
> Whole damn world's turned cold.[124]
>
> Folks, I come up North
> Cause they told me de North was fine.
> I come up North
> Cause they told me de North was fine.
> Been up here six months —
> I'm about to lose my mind.[125]

The moment arrives when longing for the region of their birth gains the upper hand, when they are ready to set off on the return journey:

[121] "West Texas," last stanza, *Shakespeare in Harlem*, p. 79.
[122] "One-Way Ticket," *One-Way Ticket*, p. 61.
[123] "Gypsy Man," stanza 2, *Fine Clothes to the Jew*, p. 22.
[124] "Po' Boy Blues," stanza 1, *ibid.*, p. 23.
[125] "Evenin' Air Blues," stanza 1, *Shakespeare in Harlem*, p. 38.

I went down to de station.
Ma heart was in ma mouth.
Went down to de station.
Heart was in my mouth.
Lookin' for a box car
To roll me to de South.

Homesick blues, Lawd,
'S a terrible thing to have.
Homesick blues is
A terrible thing to have.
To keep from cryin'
I opens ma mouth an' laughs.[126]

Thus, in a way, the blues may be regarded as the lyric expression of the disillusion felt by the immense human tide that the Great Migration sent flooding over the northern cities, where these songs followed in its wake.

Disillusionment of this sort is at the antipodes from any racial pride. Hughes brings this home to us in a poem like "Prize Fighter." While the black boxer is traditionally looked up to as an idol by his people, the champion of this poem is, on the contrary, well aware of how stupid it is to continue on this road:

Only dumb guys fight.
If I wasn't dumb
I wouldn't be fightin'.
I could make six dollars a day
On the docks
And I'd save more than I do now.
Only dumb guys fight.[127]

No less disillusioned is the elevator boy ("Elevator Boy"[128]) about to walk off the job because he finds it too monotonous; the sleeping car porter ("Porter"[129]) who gags on repeating "Yes, Sir!" a thousand times a day to make a living; and the working man ("Workin' Man"[130]) who, getting back home after a hard day's work, finds his house topsyturvy and his wife departed.

---

126 "Homesick Blues," stanzas 2 and 3, *Fine Clothes to the Jew,* p. 24. For other poems dealing with migration see, for instance, "Migration," *Fields of Wonder,* p. 99, which also takes up the issue of the prejudice felt by northern Negroes against those who have just arrived from the South; "Stranger in Town," *One-Way Ticket,* p. 41; "Migrant," *ibid.,* p. 125; "Not a Movie," *Montage of a Dream Deferred,* p. 16; "Neighbor," *ibid.,* p. 63; "Good Morning," p. 71.
127 "Prize Fighter," *Fine Clothes to the Jew,* p. 33.
128 *Ibid.,* p. 38.
129 *Ibid.,* p. 39.
130 *Ibid.,* p. 59.

Few are those who, like the boy in "Brass Spittoons," can still derive
a naïve satisfaction from performing their humble task:

Clean the spittoons, boy.
  Detroit,
  Chicago,
  Atlantic City,
  Palm Beach.
Clean the spittoons.
The steam in hotel kitchens,
And the smoke in hotel lobbies,
And the slime in hotel spittoons:
Part of my life.
  Hey, boy!
  A nickel,
  A dime,
  A dollar,
Two dollars a day.
  Hey, boy!
  A nickel,
  A dime,
  A dollar,
  Two dollars
Buys shoes for the baby.
House rent to pay.
Gin on Saturday,
Church on Sunday.
  My God!
Babies and gin and church
and women and Sunday
all mixed up with dimes and
dollars and clean spittoons
and house rent to pay.
  Hey, boy!
A bright bowl of brass is beautiful to the Lord.
Bright polished brass like the cymbals
Of King David's dancers,
Like the wine cups of Solomon.
  Hey, boy!
A clean spittoon on the altar of the Lord.
A clean bright spittoon all newly polished, —
At least I can offer that.
  Com' mere, boy![131]

[131] "Brass Spittoons," *ibid.,* p. 28. Youthful memories probably are at the origin

Rare, too, are those with an occupation they can so readily own up to, for Hughes seems early to have established as his specialty the portrayal of a half-world peopled with unwed mothers and prostitutes,[132] pimps,[133] homosexuals,[134] and drug addicts,[135] together with drunks,[136] gamblers,[137] bad men, and killers.[138] In such volumes as *Fine Clothes to the Jew,* *Shakespeare in Harlem,* and *Montage of a Dream Deferred,* these social types practically represent the norm, so that a disorderly existence becomes the typical one. It may not be going too far to see, in this inversion of values, one of the remoter consequences of the revolutionary spirit incarnated in jazz — a music that Plato might have had specifically in mind when he wrote these sentences of *The Republic:*

> Beware of changing to a new kind of music, for the change always involves far-reaching danger. Any alteration in the modes of music is always followed by alteration in the most fundamental laws of the state. . . . The first beginnings of lawlessness in music are very hard to detect. . . . It is looked on as an amusement which can do no harm. All it does . . . is gradually to

of this poem. "When I was in the seventh grade, I got my first regular job, cleaning up the lobby and toilets of an old hotel near the school I attended. I kept the mirrors and spittoons shined and the halls scrubbed" (*The Big Sea,* p. 22).

[132] See, for example, in *The Weary Blues,* "To Midnight Nan at Leroy's," p. 30; "To a Little Lover-Lass, Dead," p. 31; "Young Prostitute," p. 34; "Port Town," p. 74; "Natcha," p. 79; "To the Dark Mercedes of 'El Palacio de Amor,' " p. 90; in *Fine Clothes to the Jew,* "Ruby Brown," p. 30; "A Ruined Gal," p. 63; in *Shakespeare in Harlem,* "Cabaret Girl Dies on Welfare Island," p. 66; "Ballad of the Girl Whose Name Is Mud," p. 91; "Midnight Chippie's Lament," p. 105; and in *Montage of a Dream Deferred,* "Evening Song," p. 64; etc. In Hughes's poems, it is not always easy to distinguish between the spouse, the mistress, and the professional prostitute, so closely alike are the portraits. See also note 106 above.

[133] See, for example, "Lincoln Theatre," line 14, *One-Way Ticket,* p. 46; "White Felts in Fall," *ibid.,* p. 109; "Sylvester's Dying Bed," *Shakespeare in Harlem,* p. 67. With this category one may associate that of kept men; the principal examples of this are given in note 106 above.

[134] "Café: 3 A.M.," *Montage of a Dream Deferred,* p. 32.

[135] "Gauge," *ibid.,* p. 31.

[136] "Ballad of Gin Mary," *Fine Clothes to the Jew,* p. 35, and countless poems whose chief theme is jazz and cabaret.

[137] See, for example, "Crap Game," *ibid.,* p. 34. In several other poems one can also find more or less extended references to playing the numbers: "Railroad Avenue," *ibid.,* p. 27; "Laughers," p. 77; "Madam and the Number Writer," *One-Way Ticket,* p. 11; "Numbers," *Montage of a Dream Deferred,* p. 18; "Hope," *ibid.,* p. 68; *Ask Your Mama,* pp. 62, 78. For a short explanation of how the numbers game works see, for instance, the article by Winthrop D. Lane, "Ambushed in the City — The Grim Side of Harlem," *Survey Graphic,* March, 1925, p. 692.

[138] See, for example, "Ballad of Do Dirty," *Fine Clothes to the Jew,* p. 36; "Ballad of the Killer Boy," *Shakespeare in Harlem,* p. 87; "Ballad of the Sinner," *ibid.,* p. 85. Many other examples will be found among the poems cited in note 106.

establish and quietly to insinuate itself into manners and customs. From these it issues in greater force and penetrates men's mutual dealings; from mutual dealings it advances, with the utmost insolence ... to laws and constitutions, till in the end it overturns all things public and private.[139]

"To laws and constitutions!" Langston Hughes was finally accused of having endangered the laws and the constitution of the United States with his subversive writings,[140] when the rebellious spirit inherent in jazz was joined in him with the revolutionary ideology that had sprung from Marxism.

Class Consciousness

It was Margaret Larkin, in her review of *Fine Clothes to the Jew,* who first characterized Langston Hughes as "Proletarian Poet." Speaking of poems like "Railroad Avenue," "Brass Spittoons," "Prize Fighter," "Elevator Boy," "Porter," and "Saturday Night," she observed that they "have their roots deep in the lives of workers. They give voice to the philosophy of men of the people, more rugged, more beautiful, better food for poetry, than the philosophy of the 'middle classes.' "[141] Yet the poet's social concerns are still remarkably limited in this collection. The proletariat is undoubtedly present, but it is as yet only the black proletariat. Besides, the vision of proletarian wretchedness was so strongly colored by the blues and jazz manner that it might not have been taken very seriously. Finally, to speak of the proletariat is to speak of class consciousness, and even of class struggle, but in *Fine Clothes to the Jew* one scarcely perceives any clear opposition between the folk types it evokes and another social class. If, indeed, they consider themselves as exploited, then the exploiters are whites,[142] or Jews,[143] so that the bond uniting them is, ultimately, their sense of forming a racial community, and not any sort of class consciousness.

Not that this awareness was lacking in Langston Hughes — from childhood on he had kept his eyes wide open to the hazardous conditions of the

---

[139] *Republic,* IV, 424 (trans. A. D. Lindsay, Everyman's Library ed., p. 109).

[140] See pp. 393, 436.

[141] Margaret Larkin, "A Poet for the People — A Review," *Opportunity,* March, 1927, p. 84.

[142] See, for example, "Ruby Brown" (*Fine Clothes to the Jew,* p. 30), which deals with a girl of this name who is paid better by whites now that they visit her in a brothel, compared with what she earned by working in their kitchens; and "Porter" (*ibid.,* p. 39), already considered above.

[143] See "Hard Luck" (*ibid.,* p. 18), on the Jewish old-clothes dealer who takes advantage of the Negro's financial distress to buy his best clothes from him for next to nothing. See also, on this theme, "Ballad of the Pawnbroker," *Shakespeare in Harlem,* p. 95.

social setting in which he had grown up. He had already written, at the age of fourteen, a poem that estimated, with a lucidity seldom found in a child, the weight of human suffering that was the concomitant of industrial production:

> The mills
> That grind and grind,
> That grind out steel
> And grind away the lives
> Of men —
> In the sunset their stacks
> Are great black silhouettes
> Against the sky.
> In the dawn
> They belch red fire.
> The mills —
> Grinding new steel,
> Old men.[144]

At the time of writing, however, the concept of a society split into rich and poor, into capitalists and their victims, was doubtless further away from the young author than was the example of Carl Sandburg (by whom, as Hughes himself has stated,[145] these lines were inspired). For him, as for most of his racial brothers, the most important dividing line his experience had revealed to him was that of color, and if one was hungry and thirsty, and poor and unhappy, the basic cause was one's blackness. This was the perspective common to the volumes published in 1926 and 1927 — and also, indeed, to a large part of Hughes's later work.

Before the black writer could come to see totally new dimensions in the structure of society, the specter of economic crisis had to stalk Harlem's teeming streets, and the wealthy art-lovers who had been underwriting the existence of a number of figures in the Negro Renaissance had to tighten their purse strings. Certainly the adage "Last hired, first fired" retained its validity, and the Negro was the first victim of the crisis. Yet he was not alone, and among those who rode out the ordeal blithely enough were some Negroes,[146] as well as whites. Color was not the sole criterion deter-

[144] This untitled poem is cited in *The Big Sea*, p. 29.
[145] *Ibid.*, p. 28. The *Chicago Poems* had just appeared (1916), and one of them, "Mill-Doors," which refers to factory doors "that call and wait and take you then for — how many cents a day? ... and you are old before you are young," seems to have directly inspired the poem by the young Hughes.
[146] Class rivalry within the Negro racial group moved Hughes to relatively few poems. The earliest is probably "To Certain Negro Leaders" (in Nancy Cunard, *Negro Anthology*, p. 427), which denounces the collusion between the leaders of the black race and whites who subsidize them to keep the black lower classes "in

mining affluence or poverty, and if hitherto it had been possible to regard the Negro as held down by race prejudice alone, now it became clear that, like many poor white people, he was being victimized by the greed of the big industrialists and landowners.

This newly acquired social conscience finds an outlet in "Sharecroppers," in which Hughes outlines the economic situation of the rural proletariat made up of the southern Negro tenant farmers:

> Just a herd of Negroes
> Driven to the field,
> Plowing, planting, hoeing,
> To make the cotton yield.
>
> When the cotton's picked
> And the work is done,
> Boss man takes the money
> And we get none.
>
> Leaves us hungry, ragged
> As we were before,
> Year by year goes by
> And we are nothing more
>
> Than a herd of Negroes
> Driven to the field —
> Plowing life away
> To make the cotton yield.[147]

The last stanza repeats the first, and so closes the circle. In this way the poem evokes the economic iron band that enables the landowners to keep their black sharecroppers in bondage, while the latter, perpetually robbed of the fruits of their labor, have no chance of breaking out.

The only means of escape would be for the Negro to become aware of

---

their place." "Seashore through Dark Glasses" (*One-Way Ticket*, p. 45) satirizes the black bourgeoisie, nauseated at the spectacle of lower-class people intoxicated by the frenzy of jazz. Finally, in *Montage of a Dream Deferred*, two parallel poems, "Low to High," p. 42, and "High to Low," p. 43, successively formulate the people's complaints against the bourgeoisie, and the reasons the latter believe they have for feeling ashamed of the common herd. In "Projection" (*ibid.*, p. 26), the poet imagines what would happen if, miraculously, these two extremes of black society should one day become reconciled. Rather different in nature are the dozen poems, unequal in quality, which form the first section of *One-Way Ticket*, pp. 1-27, under the title of "Madam to You — The Life and Times of Alberta K. Johnson," and in which Hughes satirizes the bourgeois aspirations of a woman of the people better endowed with ambitions than with intelligence or money. See also *Ask Your Mama*, sec. 6, "Horn of Plenty," and *passim*.

[147] "Sharecroppers," in Granville Hicks et al., eds., *Proletarian Literature in the United States: An Anthology*, p. 167. The poem was reprinted in *Shakespeare in Harlem*, p. 77.

his proletarian status and to make common cause with the rest of the proletariat:

> Not me alone —
> I know now —
> But all the whole oppressed
> Poor world,
> White and black
> Must put their hands with mine
> To shake the pillars of those temples
> Wherein the false gods dwell
> And worn-out altars stand
> Too well defended,
> And the rule of greed's upheld —
> That must be ended.[148]

This poem, in which Langston Hughes attains the noble male vigor of a Claude McKay, is significantly entitled "Union." The title, in addition to its central meaning, also points to perspectives of more or less universal trade-union solidarity.

This was the time when American proletarian writers, both white and black, began to look around for each other, publishing joint works of social protest in such so-called proletarian anthologies as *Unrest* (1929, 1930, 1931) and *Proletarian Literature in the United States* (1935). It was no longer the time for Negro anthologies, for the notions of caste and race now took second place to, or were even eliminated by, the idea of class.[149]

---

[148] "Union," *A New Song*, p. 31. For other poems expressing the unity of the proletariat see, in *A New Song*, "Chant for Tom Mooney," p. 13; "Kids Who Die," p. 18; "Sister Johnson Marches," p. 26; and "Chant for May Day," p. 14. This last is orchestrated in Vachel Lindsay's manner, and is intended to be spoken by the voice of a worker successively accompanied by groups including from ten to a hundred voices "multiplying like the roar of the sea" (the poet's directives). Other examples of "orchestrated poems" can be found in *The Negro Mother and Other Dramatic Recitations;* but, in particular, see *Ask Your Mama*.

[149] Significant for the transition from race consciousness to class consciousness are the two successive versions of the poem "Florida Road Workers." The first version (published in *Dear Lovely Death* [1931]; also in Cunard, *Negro Anthology*, p. 427) puts these words in the mouth of a Negro worker who is building a road which he himself will never have the means to utilize: "White folks ride —/And I get to see 'em ride" (lines 14-15). The second version (*One-Way Ticket*, p. 91) alters these lines to read: "Rich folks ride/And I get to see 'em ride." Note, also, this passage of imaginary conversation attributed to the accused youths in the Scottsboro case, in the play *Scottsboro Limited:*

7TH BOY: Well it's sho too bad
         How when you ain't got no job
         Things get sad.
5TH BOY: I ain't got no job.

One of the earliest poems written by Hughes in this new climate was his "Advertisement for the Waldorf-Astoria,"[150] with long prosaic lines and dense paragraphs which were also used by other proletarian poets like Kenneth Fearing, and once again revealed the already established influence of Sandburg. This poem, based on an advertisement that appeared in *Vanity Fair* to announce the opening — in the midst of the Depression — of the new Waldorf-Astoria Hotel, denounced as scandalous and a provocation of the people the scarifying luxury of this oasis for the wealthy implanted in the midst of New York's poverty. Repeating in an ironic mode the words of the advertisement, the poem invited the down-and-outs, the unemployed, and the bums, who were spending the night on a subway bench with a newspaper as their only covering, to come and take their ease in the Waldorf-Astoria:

Take a room at the new Waldorf, you down-and-outers —
sleepers in charity's flop-houses.

· · · ·

Have luncheon there this afternoon, all you jobless.
   Why not?
Dine with some of the men and women who got rich off of your labor,
   who clip coupons with clean white fingers because your hands dug coal,
   drilled stone, sewed garments, poured steel to let other people draw dividends and live easy.[151]

1st Boy: Neither is I, but I wish I had.
2nd Boy: Looks like white folks is taking all de work.
5th Boy: Is niggers got *exclusive* rights on work?
3rd Boy: Shut up, boy!
4th Boy: He ain't joking, Perk.
2nd Boy: All them little town jobs we used to do,
           Looks like white folks is doin' 'em now, too.
1st Boy: Just goes to prove there ain't no pure nigger work.
6th Boy: Look a-yonder you-all, at dem fields
           Burstin' wid de crops they yields.
           Who gets it all?
3rd Boy: White folks.
8th Boy: You means de rich white folks.
2nd Boy: Yes, 'cause de rich ones owns de land,
           And they don't care nothin' 'bout de po' white man.
3rd Boy: You's right. Crackers is just like me —
           Po' whites and niggers, ain't neither one free.

[150] For the text of this poem, with details on the circumstances of its composition, see *The Big Sea*, pp. 320-23.

[151] *Ibid.*, pp. 321-22. For other echoes of social misery from this time on, see "Ballad of Roosevelt," printed in *The New Republic* of November 14, 1934 (reprinted in *New Republic Anthology*, p. 478); "Broke," *The Negro Mother and Other Dramatic Recitations*, pp. 4-7 (however, this poem is still in the blues tradition; in any case, the person concerned ends up by escaping his poverty through

This invitation to rush in for the spoils is softened by the accompanying ironic smile, but in "Park Bench" the menace is already more clearly formulated, and the prospect of a "big night" is envisaged:

> I live on a park bench.
> You, Park Avenue.
> Hell of a distance
> Between us two.
>
> I beg a dime for dinner —
> You got a butler and maid.
> But I'm wakin' up!
> Say, ain't you afraid
>
> That I might, just maybe,
> In a year or two,
> Move on over
> To Park Avenue?[152]

The tone rises to an even higher pitch in "Pride," another poem whose splendid violence Claude McKay would not have repudiated, and which ends with the gesture of the clenched fist, the sign of proletarian unity throughout the world:

> Let all who will
> Eat quietly the bread of shame.
> I cannot,
> Without complaining loud and long,
> Tasting its bitterness in my throat,
> And feeling to my very soul
> Its wrong.
> For honest work
> You proffer me poor pay,
> For honest dreams
> Your spit is in my face,
> And so my fist is clenched —
> Today —
> To strike your face.[153]

marriage to an ugly girl he does not love, but who offers the attraction of having been able to keep her job, and who is also a good cook); "If-ing," *Shakespeare in Harlem*, p. 32; "Out of Work," *ibid.*, p. 40; "Ballad of the Man Who's Gone," p. 87; "Ennui," *Selected Poems*, p. 131.

[152] "Park Bench," in Hicks et al., eds., *Proletarian Literature in the United States*, p. 168. This poem was reprinted in *A New Song*, p. 12. Hughes was well acquainted with Park Avenue, where his rich patroness lived "in a large apartment, with attendants in livery at the door" (*The Big Sea*, p. 312).

[153] "Pride," *Opportunity*, December, 1930, p. 371. The poem was reprinted in *A New Song*, p. 16, with a few variants.

The bread of shame is probably what is earned by agreeing to work for less than trade-union wages, as Negroes were sometimes asked to do, so that they could be used as strike-breakers.[154] But the time for inner divisions is over, and the poet calls on all workers to unite and revolt:

> Revolt! Arise!
> The Black
> And White World
> Shall be one!
> The Worker's World![155]

In the name of the black worker, he even goes so far as to offer his hand to all white workers in the South, so that together they may seize control of the means of production:

> White workers of the South,
>> Miners,
>> Farmers,
>> Mechanics,
>> Mill hands,
>> Shop girls,
>> Railway men,
>> Servants,
>> Tobacco workers,
>> Sharecroppers,
>> GREETINGS!
>
> I am the black worker,
>> Listen:
>
> .   .   .   .
>
> Let us forget what Booker T. said,
> "Separate as the fingers."[156]
> Let us become instead, you and I,
> One single hand

[154] On the problems of employment during this period, the magazine *Opportunity* for the corresponding years is a highly valuable source. See, for a summary, E. Franklin Frazier, *The Negro in the United States*, Ch. 23.

[155] "A New Song," lines 49-53, *A New Song*, p. 25. The first version of this poem should also be read in *Opportunity*, January, 1933, p. 23, for it contains many highly important variants, and is accompanied by this editorial comment in a footnote: "This poem of Langston Hughes strikes a note of defiance hitherto unheard among Negro poets except in the bitter tones of Claude McKay." See also note 176 below.

[156] An allusion to the famous phrase uttered in Atlanta by Booker T. Washington in his address at the opening of the Cotton States Exposition, September 18, 1895: "In all things that are purely social we can be as separate as the fingers, yet one as the hand in all things essential to mutual progress."

That can united rise
To smash the old dead dogmas of the past —
To kill the lies of color
That keep the rich enthroned
And drive us to the time-clock and the plow
Helpless, stupid, scattered, and alone — as now —
Race against race,
Because one is black,
Another white of face.

.   .   .   .

We did not know that we were brothers.
Now we know!
Out of that brotherhood
Let power grow!

.   .   .   .

Let union be
The force that breaks the time-clock,
Smashes misery,
Takes land,
Takes factories,
Takes office towers,
Takes tools and banks and mines,
Railroads, ships and dams,
Until the forces of the world
Are ours!
White worker,
Here is my hand.[157]

These revolutionary ideas were, of course, mainly Communist-inspired. Thus Hughes came under the same influences as a considerable number of his fellow citizens, who turned toward the Soviet Union in the hope of finding the solution to their own problems.

The years 1933 and 1934 were a madly hopeful time when it seemed that great changes in the economic system were already under way. Russia in those days didn't impress us as a despotism or as the great antagonist in a struggle for world power; it was busy within its own boundaries trying to create what promised to be a happier future. "We are changing the world!" the Young Pioneers used to chant as they marched through the streets of Moscow. Here too it seemed that everybody was trying to change the world and create the future; it was the special pride and presumption of the period.[158]

[157] "Open Letter to the South," lines 1-13, 19-31, 47-50, 55-66. *A New Song*, pp. 27-28.
[158] Malcolm Cowley, *Exile's Return*, p. 11.

Though Langston Hughes denied, on several occassions, that he had ever belonged to the Party,[159] his sympathy for the Communist ideology was evident even before his stay in the Soviet Union.[160] It does not appear to have been affected by this experience and, at least between 1932 and 1944, traces of this sympathy are to be found in his work from time to time.

The first traces are noticeable in *Scottsboro Limited* (1932), a play in verse which provides an imaginary rendering of the arrest, sham trial, and incarceration of the eight Negro youths accused of rape in the celebrated Scottsboro case. As the accused are being led from the court to their separate cells, on several occasions there rises from among the spectators a "Murmur of Red Voices":

> We'll fight for you, boys. We'll fight for you.
> The Reds will fight for you.
>
> .   .   .   .
>
> And the red flag, too, will talk for you.[161]

Though the accused hesitate at first, for they have always been told that Communists are dangerous people better left severely alone, in the end they accept the help so generously offered, and together with the "red voices" they herald the new Negro who will emerge from this great act of proletarian brotherhood:

> *8th Boy:*   Now out of the darkness
> The new Red Negro will come:
> That's me!
>
> .   .   .   .
>
> The voice of the red world
> Is our voice, too.
>
> *Red voices:* The voice of the red world *is* you![162]

[159] This declaration was already contained in a press release of January 3, 1945, a typewritten copy of which we received from Langston Hughes. He repeated the statement when summoned before the Senate Committee on Permanent Investigations in March, 1953 (see the *Washington Post* for March 27, 1953). It is also to be read in *I Wonder as I Wander*, p. 122.

[160] According to a telegram from the American Communist Press Agency (now in the Schomburg Collection, Langston Hughes file), Hughes stated on June 18, 1932, on the eve of his departure for Russia via Germany, that Communism was the only force leading an active fight against the poverty and wretchedness of Negroes. Also see below our remarks on *Scottsboro Limited*, "Goodbye, Christ!" and "Always the Same," all published in 1932 before Hughes had visited the USSR.

[161] *Scottsboro Limited.*

[162] *Ibid.*

The conclusion is an apotheosis, with "a great red flag rising to the strains of the *Internationale*."[163]

The solidarity of the world proletariat beneath the liberating red flag is also the theme of a poem published by *The Liberator* of November 4, 1932. "Always the Same" aimed at showing that, throughout the world, the blood of the exploited workers was doomed to be converted "into Dollars Pounds Francs Pesetas Lire"

> Until the Red Armies of the International Proletariat,
> Their faces black, white, olive, yellow, brown,
> Unite to raise the blood-red flag that
> Never will come down.[164]

Almost at the same moment *The Negro Worker* printed "Goodbye, Christ!"[165] which stressed more particularly the atheistic aspect of international Communism.

The Spanish Civil War,[166] and then World War II,[167] gave Hughes the opportunity to present Communism as anti-fascist and to praise the Red Army as guarantor of world liberty.

The acme of this evolution was, no doubt, a poem published in 1944 and entitled "One More S in the U.S.A.," with the refrain:

> Put one more S in the U.S.A.
> To make it Soviet.

[163] *Ibid.*, stage directions.

[164] "Always the Same," lines 46-49. This poem was reprinted in Cunard, *Negro Anthology*, p. 427. On related themes see, for instance, "Ballad of Lenin," in Hicks et al., eds., *Proletarian Literature in the United States*, p. 166, reprinted in *A New Song*, p. 20; and, in a more conservative tone, "In Explanation of Our Times," *Selected Poems*, p. 281.

[165] *The Negro Worker*, November-December, 1932. (This magazine, published monthly at times and bimonthly at others, was the organ of the International Trade Union Committee of Negro Workers. It was founded in 1931 and appeared first in Hamburg, where it was published from Rothesoodstrasse 8, and later in Copenhagen. The editorial committee included, among others, George Padmore and Charles Woodson.) "Goodbye, Christ!" was reprinted, in two slightly different versions, in Cunard, *Negro Anthology*, p. 428, and in Benjamin Elijah Mays, *The Negro's God as Reflected in His Literature*, pp. 238-39.

[166] "Song of Spain," *A New Song*, p. 21. (This poem originally appeared in January, 1937, on unpaginated sheets bearing the title *Deux poèmes par Federico Garcia Lorca et Langston Hughes. Les Poètes du monde défendent le peuple espagnol* — numéro trois — composé à la main par Nancy Cunard et Pablo Neruda, n.p.) See also "Moonlight in Valencia: Civil War," in Thomas Yoseloff, ed., *Seven Poets in Search of an Answer* (New York, 1944), p. 51.

[167] See "Good Morning, Stalingrad!" in Yoseloff, *Seven Poets*, p. 44 (reprinted in *Jim Crow's Last Stand*, p. 27); "The Underground — To the Anti-Fascists of the Occupied Countries of Europe and Asia," *ibid.*, p. 51; "When the Armies Passed," *Fields of Wonder*, p. 109.

> One more S in the U.S.A.
>   Oh, we'll live to see it yet.
> When the land belongs to the farmers
>   And the factories belong to the working-men —
> The U.S.A. when we take control
>   Will be the U.S.S.A. then.[168]

The last two lines offer a multicolored fireworks display:

> Come together, fellow workers,
> Black and white can all be Red![169]

It is a trifle startling to think that the U.S. Senate should have called a committee of investigation into session to examine these works, whose naïveté and childishness far outweigh subversive import.[170] Setting aside the inept and sometimes even grotesque character of such lines, in all this Communist propaganda[171] one senses something irredeemably false. As Charles I. Glicksberg has pertinently remarked,[172] the Negro is deeply rooted in the American tradition, and he desires above all else to see the promises of democracy extended to include him.

Besides, what the Negro especially suffers from is White America, not capitalist America. This being so, if the latter is Sovietized, can he then

---

[168] "One More S in the U.S.A.," (New York) *Sunday Mirror*, October 8, 1944, p. 22. Reprinted as *corpus delicti* in the *Congressional Record* (Senate), April 1, 1948, p. 3910. This is followed (pp. 3910-11) by a list, one and a half columns long, of the organizations and committees of the far left to which Hughes is said to have belonged.

[169] "One More S in the U.S.A."

[170] One should probably see more than a quip in Hughes's rejoinder to a Russian Communist who asked him why he was not a member of the Communist party. The reason was, he replied, that jazz was "officially taboo in Russia." When the Russian tried to convince him that jazz was decadent bourgeois music, Hughes replied: "It's my music, and I wouldn't give up jazz for a world revolution" (*I Wonder as I Wander*, p. 122). The U.S. Senate was not alone in taking a dim view of Hughes's pro-Communist works. Though he was officially absolved after his last appearance before the Senate Committee on Permanent Investigations, the poet was still beset by deep-rooted animosities. Six years after, the *American Mercury* could still print a violent, ill-intentioned article which, in essence, demanded that the poet and his *opera omnia* be placed on the index. See Elizabeth Staples, "Langston Hughes: Malevolent Force," *American Mercury*, January, 1959, pp. 46-50.

[171] The poems just cited are probably not the only poems written by Hughes in this vein, and it should be possible to find others in various periodicals. But as it was our intention to throw light on one facet of the poet's work, not to take issue with the opinions held by the man, we did not believe that any useful purpose could have been served by continuing our researches in this direction.

[172] Charles I. Glicksberg, "Race and Revolution in Negro Literature," *Forum*, November, 1947, pp. 300-308. See also Wilson Record, "Extremist Movements among American Negroes," *Phylon*, first quarter, 1956, pp. 17-23.

hope for more humane treatment from the former? A man so closely familiar with these problems as was James Weldon Johnson entertained no illusions about that.[173]

Religion and the Masses

It is one thing to realize the utopian character of such speculations, and something else to grasp what it was, in the heart of the man, that had called them into being. The attraction of Communist ideology for Hughes went far beyond the vision of a social and economic revolution, whereupon proletarians black and white would jointly exercise the powers and take over the possessions of the former ruling classes. To opt for Communism was not only to reject a social hierarchy, an economic system, or a political regime — it was also to revolt against a moral order that was content to treat the black man as but half a man, and especially it meant to spurn the theology on which this moral order claimed to be based.

The revolt against God that explodes so brutally in "Goodbye, Christ!" can be clearly seen as the poet's desperate attempt to escape the clutches of this moral order by undermining its very foundations. For, if Christ were a mere myth and the Bible a book of pure imagination, the whole value system of the dominant society would collapse, leaving ground free on which to erect a new concept of man:

> Listen, Christ,
> You did alright in your day, I reckon —
> But that day's gone now.
> They ghosted you up a swell story, too,
> Called it Bible —
> But it's dead now.
>
> .   .   .   .
>
> Goodbye,
> Christ Jesus Lord God Jehova,
> Beat it on away from here now.
> Make way for a new guy with no religion at all —
> A real guy named
> Marx Communist Lenin Peasant Stalin Worker ME —[174]

[173] For Johnson's opinions on this matter, see *Negro Americans, What Now?* pp. 7-12; and *Along This Way*, p. 411.

[174] "Goodbye, Christ!" lines 1-6 and 17-22, in Cunard, *Negro Anthology*, p. 428. Critiques originating in this view of things are also to be found scattered through "Kids Who Die" (*A New Song*, p. 18), where the poet denounces the "money-loving preachers" (line 28), and in "Song of Spain" (*ibid.*, p. 23), where the Franco forces are accused of "dropping bombs from a Christian steeple / On the people" (lines 69-70).

Though Hughes, endeavoring to defend himself against those who accused him of atheism, later declared that he had never shared the views expressed in this poem, in which one should simply see a characterization of "the extreme right as seen by the extreme left,"[175] it is difficult not to believe that a personal religious crisis had preceded the writing of "Goodbye, Christ!"

This theory seems confirmed by another poem of the same period, since in several passages it efficaciously modifies the violence and blindness of "Goodbye, Christ!" Far from denying the existence of Christ or the historicity of the Scriptures, the first version of "A New Song" expresses regret that the Negro had never really shared in the Christian community.

The poet accuses the slave religion of an earlier day, as it may still be met with in the spirituals, of having served only as an opium for the sufferings of a people, being a device for hypnotizing the vicitims of oppression and for enabling them to forget that their life was but a slow form of death. As for the sacrifice of Christ himself, Hughes denies that it had taken place on behalf of black people who, excluded in effect from the fruits of the Redemption, can expect liberation only as the result of their own efforts:

> Bitter was the day
> When . . .
> . . . only in the sorrow songs
> Relief was found —
> Yet no relief,
> But merely humble life and silent death
> Eased by a Name
> That hypnotized the pain away —
> O, precious Name of Jesus in that day!
>
> That day is past.
>
> I know full well now
> Jesus could not die for me —
> That only my own hands,
> Dark as the earth,
> Can make my earth-dark body free.[176]

[175] "Concerning 'Goodbye, Christ!' " a press release of January 3, 1945, a typewritten copy of which was given us by the poet.

[176] "A New Song," lines 10-11, 21-33, *Opportunity*, January, 1933, p. 23. In the version printed in *A New Song*, p. 24, the most important of the lines cited above (lines 24-28, 30) were eliminated, so that this second version acquires an irreproachable religious orthodoxy. "Sorrow-songs" is the term used by W. E. B. Du Bois for the spirituals; in his *The Souls of Black Folk* (1903), the fourteenth chapter bears the title "Of the Sorrow Songs."

This religious crisis of 1932 was not the first the poet had experienced. When he was going on thirteen, a great revival was held in Lawrence and "Aunt Reed," with whom he had been living since the death of his grandmother, took him one evening to the service that had been specially organized "to bring the young lambs to the fold."[177] While he was sitting on the "mourners' bench," he remembered having been told that, on being saved, one could see, hear, and feel the coming of Jesus. One after another, the "young lambs" left the mourners' bench as they were "miraculously" converted, in the midst of general hysteria. Finally only Langston Hughes and another boy his own age remained untouched by grace. It was getting late, and the delirious crowd redoubled its shouts and prayers around the two young recalcitrants. Hughes's neighbor at last whispered to him: "God damn! I'm tired o' sitting here. Let's get up and be saved." As the other boy walked forward, Langston continued to hesitate, seated on the bench, for he had still not heard and seen Jesus. He was particularly astounded that the other boy, who had not seen Jesus either, had not been at once struck by a thunderbolt for having taken God's name in vain and for having lied in church. Reassured by this mark of impunity, he wound up the proceedings by going forward too. He thus played at being converted, but that night in his bed he wept bitterly.

> I buried my head under the quilts, but my aunt heard me. She woke up and told my uncle I was crying because the Holy Ghost had come into my life, and because I had seen Jesus. But I was really crying because I couldn't bear to tell her that I had lied, that I had deceived everybody in the church, that I hadn't seen Jesus, and that now I didn't believe there was a Jesus any more, since he didn't come to help me.[178]

This revolt of the thirteen-year-old and that of the mature man both vent the same feeling of spiritual frustration. They are also akin in seeking to reject, not so much God himself, as a nexus of outworn views on the divine-human relationship to which the poet, who longed to be straightforward toward himself and his fellows, would no longer assent. Here Hughes's attitude falls in with that of many intellectuals in the "talented tenth" who, resolutely determined on total emancipation, turned their backs both on the white man's Christianity, since they saw it as one of the last vestiges of enslavement that had survived the abolition of slavery, and the formalist religion of the traditional Negro churches, whose faded, simple-minded rituals did little to disguise the absence of a strong spirituality,

---

[177] *The Big Sea*, p. 18. See *ibid.*, pp. 18-21, for the account of this first religious crisis.
[178] *Ibid.*, p. 21.

and which were ill able to find an adequate response for the anguished questions that were tormenting the enlightened intellects of the younger generation.

But in Hughes's case these rebellious gestures proved quite transitory.[179] For they were gestures only, and not those crises of conscience[180] that seize upon certain delicate souls and shake them to their very depths. McKay, Toomer, and Cullen did not hesitate occasionally to estrange their fellows in order to follow the paths of the spirit. But Hughes was not of their dimension — and, again, his ties with the black people were so strong and enduring that he could not have repudiated them for long. Thus his religious poetry, with the exceptions we have noted, is essentially inspired by the folk traditions, and any criticism that he voices is fleeting and incidental.[181]

Langston Hughes as the poet of jazz was also well fitted to make himself the interpreter of the orgiastic religion of black people of the lower classes, where the spirit is less sure of a role than the heart and the senses. Between religious exaltation and that other exaltation of the human creature that finds an outlet in jazz there is, indeed, a basic identity of nature and func-

---

[179] "Goodbye, Christ!" was never reprinted in any volume. As for the passages in "A New Song" that reflected his religious revolt, they were carefully suppressed when the poem was reprinted in a volume. See our note 176 above.

[180] A poem like "Christ in Alabama," *Scottsboro Limited*, has, despite appearances, no religious content. Analogous in inspiration to Cullen's "Christ Recrucified," this poem, shocking rather than profound, is above all an indictment of the South, but Hughes himself does not ever seem to have felt personally involved in the contradiction whose presence at the center of white Christianity he denounced (for his own remarks on this poem, see *I Wonder as I Wander*, p. 46). He was fully justified, no doubt, in noting the all too blatant divergency between the doctrine and the practices of his adversaries. But if he had not remained at the surface of these problems, how could he persistently have avoided proceeding to the sounding of his own conscience? All things considered, religious problems are reduced to social problems in his eyes, while the richness and the complexities of the inner life seem to have been a closed book for him. See also, in the same vein, "Poem for Rich Churches" and "Not for Publication," which appear in our Appendix of hitherto unpublished poems in the original French edition.

[181] Since they lack both interest and originality, we neglect such childish productions as "Heaven," *Fields of Wonder*, p. 3 (see also *ibid.*, p. 83, "Personal"; p. 88, "There"; etc.) or the facile Christmas greeting card verse of "Four Christmas Poems," *The Crisis*, December, 1958, pp. 614-16. Let us point out, nevertheless, an isolated attempt in the genre of the Negro sermon, "Sunday Morning Prophecy," *One-Way Ticket*, pp. 35-37, doubtless inspired by the example of James Weldon Johnson. Yet, unlike Johnson's sermons, Hughes's poem barely rises above the humorous or satirical genre and, like some of the sermons written by Irwin Russell, it ends with the pastor's inevitable appeal for the congregation's financial support.

tion.[182] Whoever late in the evening has entered one of the countless store-front churches in the black districts of American cities[183] has inevitably associated the show offered by such a religious service with the other show, taking place at the same time and a mere two steps away, in a dance hall. In both establishments the shouts and rhythms are the same and, in both, human beings who all day have been tense, inhibited, blocked, and frustrated in their work with white people now find the identical powerful means of release and forgetfulness in the whirl and frenzy of the dance, whether profane or sacred. In both places they have come together with their own kind in a brotherly jostling that banishes all constraint, and their bodily exaltation is thoroughly capable of summing up the thousand emotions which have found no other outlet.

This identity between the profane and sacred modes of Negro lyric expressivity has been underlined in recent years by ethnology and by jazz criticism,[184] but it is already quite apparent by 1927 in such volumes as *Fine Clothes to the Jew,* which in the section entitled "Glory! Halleluiah!" contains what are undoubtedly the best poems written by Hughes in this manner.

"Moan" is in every respect the perfect religious equivalent of the blues. The structure of the poem heralds the fact, for its six stanzas are actually stanzas for the eye only. In reality, each is a long blues line that has been split for typographical reasons, with the second stanza repeating the first, and the fifth the fourth. Had the visual presentation been different, the poem would have appeared as a blues, with two stanzas of three lines each:

182 Richard Wright has very properly stressed the quotient of sexual excitement common to both these types of exaltation: "Protestant ministers have put to religious use the forces and capacities of sexual arousal inherent in the convulsionary songs; they have used the spirituals as aphrodisiac music. In Africa, the same sort of trance exists. When their faithful experience orgasm, the sorcerers cry out to them that the god is entering their bodies. One can thus understand why it is such a short way from the art of Ray Charles to that of the black preachers. The former says in plain language what the latter conceal behind more harmless words. . . . In the spirituals and in the songs of Ray Charles, I repeat, there is the same erotic exaltation. This aspect of black music has too often been passed over in silence. There is in the faith of the mystics and in the faith of most Negroes a sexual component which respectable people, because they are terrorized by it, dare not admit, but which must be emphasized" (Richard Wright, "Le Jazz et le désir," *Les Cahiers du Jazz,* no. 4 (June, 1961), pp. 53-54).
183 Of course, these observations hold good also for many churches in the rural South.
184 Note, for example, the remark of Frederic Ramsey, Jr., to the effect that many blues singers end their careers in churches, and that the blues and the spirituals are intimately related. *Jazzmen* (New York, 1939), pp. 115-16. See also the very thorough article by Mimi Clar, "Le Jazz moderne et la musique d'église," *Les Cahiers du Jazz,* no. 4 (June, 1961), pp. 16-39.

> I'm deep in trouble,
> Nobody to understand,
>   Lord, Lord!
>
> Deep in trouble,
> Nobody to understand,
>   O, Lord!
>
> Gonna pray to ma Jesus,
> Ask him to gimme His hand.
>   Ma Lord!
>
> I'm moanin', moanin',
> Nobody cares just why.
>   No, Lord!
>
> Moanin', moanin',
> Feels like I could die.
>   O, Lord!
>
> Sho, there must be peace,
>   Ma Jesus,
> Somewhere in yo' sky.
>   Yes, Lord![185]

But the poem is related to the blues above all on account of the emotions voiced, those of a person whose unhappiness arouses no sympathy among his fellows, and whose weariness would turn to despair but for the prospect of finding a haven of peace in Jesus.

In "Feet o' Jesus" the same weariness reappears in a being overwhelmed by life's difficulties, who throws himself at the feet of Jesus because suffering has swelled to oceanic proportions:

> At de feet o' Jesus,
> Sorrow like a sea.
> Lordy, let your mercy
> Come driftin' down on me.[186]

In such poems as "Fire" and "Angels' Wings," one comes on the same element of self-accusation already noted, especially in what is known as the "bad man blues":[187]

> Fire,
> Fire, Lord!
> Fire gonna burn ma soul!

[185] "Moan," *Fine Clothes to the Jew*, p. 51.
[186] "Feet o' Jesus," stanza 1, *ibid.*, p. 47.
[187] See, for example, the blues cited in the text corresponding to note 104 above.

> I ain't been good,
> I ain't been clean —
> I been stinkin', low-down, mean.
>
> . . . .
>
> I been stealin',
> Been tellin' lies,
> Had more women
> Than Pharaoh had wives.
>
> Fire,
> Fire, Lord!
> Fire gonna burn ma soul![188]
>
> De angels wings is white as snow,
>   But I drug ma wings
>   In de dirty mire.[189]

This self-contempt should not be confused with the pure act of Christian humility, nor even with the avowal made in the confession of one's sins, for the individual, instead of simply admitting his faults, derives a kind of morbid pleasure from deliberately badmouthing himself. The specifically racial character of this procedure, which delivers the individual from what oppresses him and perhaps redeems him in his own eyes, is clearly exposed when the enumeration of his sins and miseries is followed — as though this also were a sin for which he is responsible — by a reference to the contemptible color of his skin:

> Have mercy, Lord!
>
> Po' an' black
> An' humble an' lonesome
> An' a sinner in yo' sight.
>
> Have mercy, Lord![190]

But all that the most roughhewn individuals require to obtain solace and release is the primal cry which, as we have seen,[191] forms the embryo of all Negro lyric expression, both profane and sacred. To this simple cry the primitive soul entrusts the task of uttering everything it has been unable to understand and explain in detail, and it is determined that this cry, compensating all by itself for human weaknesses and shortcomings, shall in spite of all manifest the resolve of the creature to participate in

[188] "Fire," lines 1-6 and 17-23, *ibid.,* p. 50.
[189] "Angels' Wings," lines 6-8, *ibid.,* p. 52.
[190] "Sinner," *ibid.,* p. 53.
[191] See our Ch. 1, note 82; also note 82 of this chapter.

the communion of the saints. Such cries are uttered in "Shout,"[192] in "Spirituals,"[193] in "Mystery,"[194] or in "Sliver of Sermon,"[195] and Hughes has singled out their meaning with unerring precision in "Communion":

> I was trying to figure out
> What it was all about
> But I could not figure out
> What it was all about
> So I gave up and went
> To take the sacrament
> And when I took it
> It felt good to shout![196]

As well as demonstrating the close relationship between jazz rhythms and those of religious folk poetry, these poems perform the service of revealing the essentially emotional character of traditional Negro religion. Here and there a name does appear which might indicate a vague acceptance of some area of Christian doctrine but, as Jean Toomer put it in "Conversion," all we have in that is "weak palaver." There can be little doubt that this is a religion without any definite dogma whose goal is, above all, to stir up passions and inflame bodies. This indicates the enormous importance that here, as with jazz, falls on the rhythmic element, which Hughes once again shows he can interpret with extraordinary sensitivity and subtlety.

4. AMERICAN DEMOCRACY: PROMISES AND REALITIES

> I am the American heartbreak —
> Rock on which Freedom
> Stumps its toe —
> The great mistake
> That Jamestown
> Made long ago.[197]

[192] *Fine Clothes to the Jew*, p. 49.
[193] *Fields of Wonder*, p. 113.
[194] *Montage of a Dream Deferred*, p. 55.
[195] *Ibid.*, p. 56. See also "Testimonial," *ibid.*, p. 57. For other religious poems on popular lines see, in *Fine Clothes to the Jew*, "Judgment Day," p. 45; "Prayer Meeting," p. 46; "Prayer," p. 48; and, in *The Dream Keeper*, "Ma Lord," p. 55, whose first line ("Ma Lord ain't no stuck-up man...") already emphasizes the extent to which this sort of religious expressiveness characterizes the most deprived social levels.
[196] "Communion," *Fields of Wonder*, p. 98.
[197] "American Heartbreak," *Selected Poems*, p. 9.

One should not exaggerate the scope of Hughes's proposal to add another S to the U.S.A. in order to sovietize it. Even less should one hastily proceed, as some have done,[198] to take it as a badge of anti-Americanism. This gesture, much like the poet's cult of Africa, was evoked in particular by a highly understandable impatience, or perhaps even a momentary feeling of despair, at beholding how the promises of American democracy had never been fulfilled for his own race. There is every reason to believe that, to the very extent his faith in the American democratic ideal was deep and sincere, he finally came to find it intolerable that this ideal should remain a dead letter for a large number of his fellow citizens.

When he did rise up in protest, it was never against this ideal,[199] but against all those who, while paying it lip service, set out to ensure that they would be its exclusive beneficiaries. It was against these people, too, that in the hope of hastening the dawn of genuine freedom and equality he saw fit to conclude a pact with what he probably later realized had been the devil.[200] In any event, this step put him in excellent company, and he does not deserve to be branded an enemy of democracy any more than do men like Hemingway and Malraux, who stood beside him during the Spanish Civil War.

In fact, if there is one characteristic that only a great deal of bad faith could deny was his, it is his fundamental attachment to the ideal of democracy. His work, descended from Sandburg's and Whitman's, is to a great extent a sincere, ardent panegyric of the American dream, but the man who composed it retained enough lucidity to include in the story the tribu-

[198] See Staples, "Langston Hughes: Malevolent Force," and the article by Hughes, "My Adventures as a Social Poet," *Phylon,* third quarter, 1947, pp. 205-12.

[199] Unless one interprets in the opposite sense the last three lines (55-57) of "A New Song" (*A New Song,* p. 25). There Hughes, after summoning workers black and white to unity and revolt, ends thus: "A new dream flames / Against the / Sun!" In the author's mind, was this "new dream" really different from the "American dream" and destined to replace it? We do not think so, for a few lines above (36-44) was the declaration: "... now / In many mouths / Dark mouths where red tongues burn / And white teeth gleam — / New words are formed, / Bitter / With the past / But sweet / With *the* dream." The italicization of the definite article is ours, for it is the decisive word here. What is novel is the words that are formed — or, to put it differently, what now is spoken is the language of revolution, laden with the accumulated bitterness of the past. But these new words that are uttered are sweetened by the concrete hope of finally being able, by utilizing them, to achieve "the" dream, the unchanging dream that for so long has been carried in one's heart.

[200] See this assertion, made to a journalist and printed in the *Washington Post* of March 27, 1953: "He said he underwent 'a complete reorientation of my thinking ... about four or five years ago.'"

lations to which freedom was exposed. He recalled, too, that the passion for reform also counted among the most authentic traits of the national tradition.

The American Dream

His very earliest volumes evoke the traditional image of the dream in passionately hymning the primacy of the ideal, from which alone life derives its meaning and its value:

> Hold fast to dreams
> For if dreams die
> Life is a broken-winged bird
> That cannot fly.
>
> Hold fast to dreams
> For when dreams go
> Life is a barren field
> Frozen with snow.[201]

This ideal represents a universal value. It is the bond which enables the poet to feel his union with others: as he watches sailors about to set sail, he is glad to think that in their hearts they carry "dreams, like me."[202]

The poet is obliged to serve that value, and he calls himself "The Dream Keeper." In other words, as a poet he looks on himself as entrusted with the specific mission of keeping the flame of the ideal ever alive and shielding it from anything that could corrupt it or besmirch its purity:

> Bring me all of your dreams,
> You dreamers,
> Bring me all of your
> Heart melodies
> That I may wrap them
> In a blue cloud-cloth
> Away from the too rough fingers
> Of the world.[203]

But, more frequently than it incorporates this barely defined ideal, in Hughes's eyes the dream represents the democratic ideal of liberty and equality. The history of the dream is for him, in this sense, the actual history of the founding and building of America. This is the great epic re-

---

[201] "Dreams," *The Dream Keeper*, p. 7. See also "Dream Dust," *Fields of Wonder*, p. 79, and "Beale Street," *ibid.*, p. 18.

[202] "Water Front Streets," *The Weary Blues*, p. 71, lines 7-8.

[203] "The Dream Keeper," *ibid.*, p. 94.

counted in the two hundred lines of "Freedom's Plow,"[204] in many respects the most Whitman-like of all his poems. The dream was there from the beginning:

> First in the heart is the dream.[205]

America's earliest builders, starting out from nothing, had as their sole materials the faith, strength, and resolve to build that filled their hearts:

> With billowing sails the galleons came
> Bringing men and dreams, women and dreams.
>
>   .   .   .   .
>
> Some were free hands
> Seeking a greater freedom,
> Some were indentured hands
> Hoping to find their freedom.
> Some were slave hands
> Guarding in their hearts the seed of freedom.
> But the word was there always:
>   FREEDOM.[206]

From the pooling of all these individual dreams there then rose up the great communal dream called America:

> Thus the dream becomes not one man's dream alone,
> But a community dream,
> Not my dream alone, but *our* dream.[207]
>
>   .   .   .   .
>
> America is a dream.[208]
>
>   .   .   .   .
>
> America!
> Land created in common,
> Dream nourished in common.[209]

Like Whitman,[210] Hughes believes that it is in the hearts of the people that the original dream continues to survive most genuinely true to itself:

[204] This poem was first published in pamphlet form in 1943. Though twice reprinted (1944 and 1946), it is not easy to come by today. Thus all our references are to the reprinting that occupies pp. 291-97 of *Selected Poems*.
[205] *Ibid.*, line 9, p. 291.
[206] *Ibid.*, lines 33-34 and 40-47, p. 292.
[207] *Ibid.*, lines 21-23, p. 291.
[208] *Ibid.*, line 140, p. 295.
[209] *Ibid.*, lines 155-57, p. 296. See, on almost the same theme, "America," *Opportunity*, June, 1925, p. 175.
[210] See, for instance, this passage from the 1855 preface to *Leaves of Grass*, par. 3: "Other states indicate themselves in their deputies — but the genius of the

America is a dream.
The poet says it was promises.
The people say it *is* promises — that will come true.
The people do not always say things out loud,
Nor write them down on paper.
The people often hold
Great thoughts in their deepest hearts
And sometimes only blunderingly express them,
Haltingly and stumbling say them,
And faultily put them into practice.
The people do not always understand each other.
But there is, somewhere there,
Always the *trying* to understand,
And the *trying* to say,
"You are a man. Together we are building our land."[211]

Thus he is led to assert emphatically that the dream of black people has always been closely blended with the American dream. When the slaves sang, "Keep your hand on the plow! Hold on!"[212] or when Frederick Douglass cried out: "Better to die free than to live slaves!,"[213] were they in any way at odds with Jefferson proclaiming that "all men are created equal . . . endowed by their Creator with certain inalienable rights . . . among them life, liberty and the pursuit of happiness,"[214] or with Lincoln asserting that "No man is good enough to govern another man without that other's consent"?[215] If these words do not apply to everyone, then they have no meaning for anyone.

Their particular significance for the Negro, and the assurance of hope and confidence in the future that they have always brought him, were plainly stated by Hughes in "The Negro Mother,"[216] a figure incarnating the enduring qualities of the race:

United States is not best or most in its executives or legislators, nor in its ambassadors or authors, or colleges or churches or parlors, nor even in its newspapers or inventors — but always most in the common people. . . ."

[211] *Ibid.*, lines 140-54, pp. 295-96. In a note to his French translation of "Freedom's Plow," Renaud de Jouvenel (*Europe*, February-March, 1959, p. 149) expresses the view that the second line cited above may contain an allusion to *America Was Promises* by Archibald MacLeish.

[212] "Keep your hand on the plow! Hold on!" is a traditional Negro song, the first phrase of which occurs several times in "Freedom's Plow" (lines 124, 127, 158, 189, 198) and provides the title of the poem.

[213] This famous phrase of Douglass's occurs in lines 108-9 and 170-71.

[214] This passage from the Declaration of Independence is to be found in lines 89-93, and is used in part in line 166.

[215] *Ibid.*, lines 100-103 and 167-69.

[216] This poem, along with other monologues furnished with directions as to

God put a dream like steel in my soul.
Now, through my children, I'm reaching the goal.

. . . .

Sometimes, the valley was filled with tears

. . . .

But I had to keep on till my work was done:
I *had* to keep on! No stopping for me: —
I was the seed of the coming Free.
I nourished the dream that nothing could smother
Deep in my breast — The Negro Mother.
I had only hope then, but now through you,
Dark ones of today, my dreams must come true:

. . . .

Oh, my dark children, may my dreams and my prayers
Impel you forever up the great stairs —
For I will be with you till no white brother
Dares keep down the children of the Negro Mother.[217]

The day has not yet dawned, alas, that makes the American dream a
reality for all. True, the poet rejoices at even the least trace of movement
toward equality. Thus he warmly salutes the Negro captain of the *Booker
T. Washington* who, in the midst of world war, leaves port with a mixed
crew of blacks and whites, for Hughes is glad to see in this the promise
of more brotherly tomorrows:

More than ship then,
Captain Mulzac,
Is the BOOKER T.,
And more than captain
You who guide it on its way.
Your ship is mankind's deepest dream
Daring the sea —
Your ship is flagship
Of a newer day.[218]

Yet, up to this point, more frequent are the occasions for regretting the
debasement of the dream and for struggling against the shadows that

staging and musical accompaniment in the manner of Vachel Lindsay, was first
published in a brochure entitled *The Negro Mother and Other Dramatic Recitations*, pp. 16-18. Since the brochure is practically unobtainable, we refer to the
reprinting of the poem in *Selected Poems*, pp. 288-89.
    [217] *Ibid.*, lines 21-22, 27, 30-36, 51-54.
    [218] "To Captain Mulzac," lines 61-69, *Jim Crow's Last Stand*, p. 18. For an-
other poem written during World War II and dealing with the dream theme, see
"Oppression," *Fields of Wonder*, p. 112.

assail it from all directions. Like his first masters Whitman and Sandburg, like his fellow black Toomer, and like so many other American poets of the period, Langston Hughes never tires of proclaiming the absolute necessity for all to do what they can to save the democratic ideal.

> It was a long time ago.
> I have almost forgotten my dream.
> But it was there then,
> In front of me,
> Bright like a sun, —
> My dream.
>
> And then the wall rose,
> Rose slowly,
> Slowly,
> Between me and my dream.
> Rose slowly, slowly,
> Dimming,
> Hiding,
> The light of my dream,
> Rose until it touched the sky, —
> The wall.
>
> Shadow,
> I am black.
>
> I lie down in the shadow.
> No longer the light of my dream before me,
> Above me.
> Only the thick wall.
> Only the shadow.
>
> My hands!
> My dark hands!
> Break through the wall!
> Find my dream!
> Help me to shatter this darkness,
> To smash this night,
> To break this shadow
> Into a thousand lights of sun,
> Into a thousand whirling dreams
> Of sun![219]

[219] "As I Grew Older," *The Weary Blues*, pp. 55-56. "Song" (*The Dream Keeper*, p. 41) is another poem built around the theme of the wall that a man must beat down with his bare black fists. "Dusk" (*Fields of Wonder*, p. 108), which utilizes the same images, nevertheless ends on a hopeful note: walls have been seen to crumble, dusks to turn into dawns, and chains to fall.

But this is a gigantic task, for all America must be regenerated so that it may become once more the dream it used to be, and so that it may at last become, for the Negro, the true country that for him it had never been:

> Let America be America again.
> Let it be the dream it used to be.
> Let it be the pioneer on the plain
> Seeking a home where he himself is free.
>
> (America never was America to me.)
>
> Let America be the dream the dreamers dreamed —
> Let it be that great strong land of love
> Where never kings connive nor tyrants scheme
> That any man be crushed by one above.
>
> (It never was America to me.)
>
> O, let my land be a land where Liberty
> Is crowned with no false patriotic wreath,
> But opportunity is real, and life is free,
> Equality is in the air we breathe.
>
> (There's never been equality for me
> Nor freedom in this "homeland of the free.")
>
> .   .   .   .
>
> O, yes,
> I say it plain,
> America never was America to me,
> And yet I swear this oath — America will be![220]

This splendid confidence is scarcely to be met with again, except in the concluding lines of "A New Song,"[221] and here it is based on the union of all proletarians and on revolution. Elsewhere disillusionment and bitterness seldom fail to intrude in the evocation of the dream, whose long-awaited realization is every day postponed again.

"The Colored Soldier"[222] is one of the bitterest poems ever written to denounce the emptiness of the sacrifice made by Negro American soldiers killed during World War I. They set out to save democracy, but their sacrifice only strengthened the reign of injustice. All in all, it would have been better if they had never returned from overseas to see what had been

---

[220] "Let America Be America Again," *A New Song,* pp. 9-11. An earlier version of this poem had already appeared in *Esquire,* July, 1936. A third version will be found in Hughes and Bontemps, *The Poetry of the Negro,* pp. 106-8.

[221] Lines 43-44 and 55-57, *A New Song,* p. 25. See, however, our note 199 above.

[222] *The Negro Mother and Other Dramatic Recitations,* pp. 1-3.

made out of their dream! Lynchers had "strangled"[223] and "spit in the face of my dream";[224] the Ku Klux Klan had delighted "at making mincemeat of my dream,"[225] while the Negro, now as always, continues to be a "dreamer of dreams to be broken."[226]

This theme of a dream betrayed crests in a very special way in the volume which Hughes titled *Montage of a Dream Deferred* (1951). Jazz, which had strongly influenced the tone and structure of the poems in the volume, did something to soften the acrid disillusionment which they voice.[227] Without bathing the poet's vision in total serenity, at least jazz provides a certain detachment that sometimes almost attains the heights of stoicism.[228] With advancing age the poet did not maintain the same tone of militant or demanding ardor, and he more frequently showed himself to be deliberately solemn or wrapped in pensiveness. Then, too, the numerous digressions taking him far from the central theme situate this within a perspective of less urgency, and the sudden changes of tone interrupt[229] at every instant a train of thought so grievous that it is natural to seek some distraction.

This volume is a genuine whole. It is not easy to single out individual poems within the overall experiment, but the motif of the dream is both ubiquitous and incomprehensible. Like a flash of lightning it traverses the elements of this "montage," many of which amount to no more than a snatch of verse, and nowhere is it fully developed. Besides, it is not so much the dream itself as its reflection in the individual lives of countless Harlem dwellers that is offered us, so that it is glimpsed as the sum of these reflections and, consequently, as something no less composite than life itself.

There can be no doubt that this dream is no longer something to be exalted, but a vision degraded through trampling, shoving, and abuse.[230] As the title of the volume indicates, this degradation is primarily due to the dream's excessive postponement. One can but wonder, as does the

[223] "The Bitter River," line 16, *Jim Crow's Last Stand*, p. 11.
[224] *Ibid.*, line 60, p. 13.
[225] "Note to All Fascists, Nazis and Klansmen," *ibid.*, p. 8.
[226] "The Bitter River," line 65, *ibid.*, p. 13.
[227] There are too many examples, in this volume, of the blending of the themes of jazz and freedom for all of them to be cited. See, for example, "Dream Boogie," p. 3; and "Dream Boogie: Variation," p. 68. Reference can also be made to what has already been said on *Montage of a Dream Deferred*, above.
[228] Especially in "Harlem," *Montage of a Dream Deferred*, p. 71. See also "Likewise," *ibid.*, p. 66.
[229] See, for example, "Dream Boogie," *ibid.*, p. 3; "Children's Rhymes," p. 6; "Likewise," p. 66; etc.
[230] "Kicked around," says Hughes. See "Same in Blues" (last line), *ibid.*, p. 73; and "Comment on Curb," p. 74.

poet, whether it will succumb to some kind of rot or, on the contrary, explode like a time bomb:

> What happens to a dream deferred?
>
> Does it dry up
> like a raisin in the sun?
> Or fester like a sore —
> And then run?
> Does it stink like rotten meat?
> Or crust and sugar over —
> like a syrupy sweet?
> Maybe it just sags
> like a heavy load.
>
> *Or does it explode?*[231]

But another reason for degradation is that it is the dream of individuals whose lives are also degraded through having been deprived of the most modest satisfactions. There are the young people whose education has been repeatedly interrupted by poverty and displacement and who, at the age of twenty, still await the opportunity to finish their secondary schooling. And there are the elderly couples who, in the twilight of their days, still dream of the enameled stove they longed for when they got married, and which is still beyond their reach.[232]

Thus the final impression left by *Montage of a Dream Deferred* is that the Negro dream is a mitigated form of the American dream and that, forming a parallel to Harlem, that black islet in the midst of a white island, it is a tiny dream lost from sight within the great American dream:

> Dream within a dream,
> Our dream deferred.[233]

[231] "Harlem," *ibid.*, p. 71. It is in this poem that Lorraine Hansberry found the title for her play, *A Raisin in the Sun* (1959).

[232] "Deferred," *ibid.*, p. 48. See also "Same in Blues," p. 72.

[233] "Island," *ibid.*, p. 75. The theme of "tomorrow" in Hughes's work is analogous to that of the dream. Through another image the same hopes are expressed. Its evolution over the years follows the same declining curve, as confident optimism gives way to disillusionment. In "Epilogue," *The Weary Blues*, p. 109, later entitled "I, Too" (*The Dream Keeper*, p. 76, and *Selected Poems*, p. 275), one of Hughes's most often cited poems, he declared, in effect: I too am America. Today I am still forced to eat in the kitchen; but I am growing up, and tomorrow when there are guests, I too will be seated at the family table. "Poem," *The Weary Blues*, p. 108 (which we have cited above, p. 161), viewed tomorrow as adorned with a dazzling flame; and in "History" (*A New Song*, p. 19) much the same hope was uttered. See too "Dark Youth of the U.S.A.," *The Negro Mother and Other Dramatic Recitations*, p. 19 ("today's dark child, tomorrow's strong man"). But in a more recent utilization of the theme ("Tomorrow," *Montage of a Dream De-*

The Poet and Reality

Alongside the dream motif which is, for him, basically an occasion for reflection and meditation, Hughes more directly and concretely treated democracy's problems in what might be called a poetry of combat, often written under the pressure of events.

Yet this second manner, whose more or less immediate object is protest or a demand for redress, could not have arisen without a preliminary decision in the conflict of allegiances that divided him between his actual country and the land of his ancestors. He had first to convince himself that his dream of a return to Africa was unrealizable, and he had to admit openly that the destiny of his race was irrevocably tied to that of American democracy.

During the period which he required to reach a clear understanding of these truths, the longing for Africa was in itself almost enough by way of protest.[234] It was more than this, for its concomitant was the outright rejection of America[235] and the refusal of all discussion with it — with the consequence that no true protest could develop until the African theme had declined in importance.

As with the longing for Africa, there is something curiously romantic in the way Hughes took up the racial problem in his earliest poems. As though still subject to the influence of Dunbar, whose poetry had been a delight to him in his younger years,[236] he was less concerned with pleading for racial justice than with analyzing the often contradictory feelings aroused in him by the South which, at this time, he had never seen — and which, therefore, often represents a concept rather than a reality for him.

The South is the opponent envisaged more or less openly by Hughes in

_____

ferred, p. 30), "tomorrow's" date finds itself, just like the realization of the dream, postponed *sine die:* "Tomorrow may be / a thousand years off: / .... / Some dawns / wait." The study of this theme is very briefly outlined in John W. Parker's article, "Tomorrow in the Writings of Langston Hughes," *College English,* May, 1949, pp. 438-41.

[234] On this topic, see pp. 395-96 above.

[235] This includes the rejection of the city also. See "Disillusion" (*The Weary Blues,* p. 104), in which the poet bids Harlem what he believes is a final and irrevocable farewell. The simplicity mentioned in the poem is undoubtedly that of the land of his ancestors. Moreover, the poem is included in a group with several other "African" poems. But, underneath this theme of the return to Africa, one can sense the burgeoning, as one could in McKay's early poems, of something more, perhaps, than the disillusion of the title — of a certain disgust aroused in the newcomer by the city and its way of life, which he would prefer never to know again.

[236] See, in particular, *The Big Sea,* p. 28.

two of his earliest poems, "Cross"[237] and "Mulatto,"[238] both constructed
on the romantic theme of the tragic mulatto.[239] While the former poem
modestly limits itself to sketching the allegedly tragic case of the individual
born to a white father and a black mother, the latter more clearly voices
the rebellion of the mulatto against the white father who refuses to acknowledge him. Although "Mulatto" launches violent attacks against
southern racial etiquette, whose backers claim to be the protectors of
the purity of the white race while not denying themselves the pleasure of
engendering "little yellow bastard boys,"[240] it is nevertheless not certain
that these are purely combative poems. The theme is admittedly irrelevant,
given that American racial categories do not, as in the West Indies, allot
any special place to the mulatto, so that his lot is neither more nor less
tragic than that of any other individual classified as a Negro.[241] Hughes
knew all this. But if the theme of the mulatto continued to fascinate him
all the same,[242] it is probably because this theme allowed him scope for
expressing his own feelings concerning his father, who had not merely
abandoned the woman by whom he had had a son, but also had not
shrunk from revealing to the son the contempt he felt for his mother. Thus
the mulatto's hatred, and his rebellion against his father, may be also (if
not primarily) the hatred and rebelliousness felt by the poet himself.[243]

[237] *The Weary Blues*, p. 52.
[238] *Fine Clothes to the Jew*, pp. 71-72.
[239] On the utilization of the mulatto theme in American literature, see Sterling
A. Brown, "Negro Character as Seen by White Authors," *Journal of Negro Education*, April, 1933, pp. 179-203 (the section devoted more especially to the mulatto
occupies pp. 192ff.).
[240] "Mulatto," lines 24-25, *Fine Clothes to the Jew*, pp. 71-72. On the theme of
interracial love, Hughes generally remains rather discreet. But see "Red Silk Stock-
ings" (*ibid.*, p. 73), which is somewhat reminiscent of Fenton Johnson's "The
Scarlet Woman," since both poems tend toward the assertion that America reserves
prostitution as the only profession for the black girl. See also "Mellow" (*Montage
of a Dream Deferred*, p. 30), which treats with irony the fascination some white
women feel for black celebrities, the color difference contributing additional zest
to their sexual encounters.
[241] Hughes admits that "the problem of mixed blood in America is, to be sure,
a minor problem," yet he finds it "a very dramatic one" because one of the parents
remains "in the pale of the black ghetto," while the other is "able to take advantage of all the opportunities of American democracy" (*The Big Sea*, p. 263).
[242] In the addition to these two poems, see the play *Mulatto* (1949), and the
opera based on it, which bore the title *The Barrier* (music by Jan Meyerowitz);
also two short stories, "Father and Son," *The Ways of White Folks*, pp. 200-248,
and "African Morning," *Laughing to Keep from Crying*, pp. 15-20. The theme
of the mulatto in the totality of Hughes's writings has been well studied by Arthur
P. Davis, "The Tragic Mulatto Theme in Six Works of Langston Hughes," *Phylon*,
second quarter, 1955, pp. 195-204.
[243] On the relations between the poet and his father, see our biographical note,
and *The Big Sea*, pp. 39-49.

Why is "Mulatto" given a southern setting? Is it merely because the two races are mingled more intimately there than anywhere else in America? The problem the poem claims to examine is not restricted to the South, so it may be surmised that Hughes, influenced by the tales he had heard, may have come to regard the South as the symbol and incarnation of all evil. To treat the South alone as guilty — is this not a means of hurling far from himself, and attributing to someone he had not even met, both the origin of and the responsibility for this evil? The complaint voiced in "The White Ones" does indeed affect all whites, without distinction:

> ...why do you torture me
> O, white strong ones,
> Why do you torture me?[244]

But many other poems of protest are directed exclusively against the South. This holds in particular for "The South," a poem built entirely on antitheses. The southern region is depicted, as Edwin Campbell had done, as a mistress from whose charms the Negro regretfully takes his leave as he goes off to woo the more humane but colder North. The memory of James Weldon Johnson's white sorceress may also, perhaps, have inspired some of the antithetical elements composing the portrait of this mistress,

> Beast-strong,
> Idiot-brained.
>
> .   .   .   .
>
> Beautiful, like a woman,
> Seductive as a dark-eyed whore,
> Passionate, cruel,
> Honey-lipped, syphilitic —[245]

whom the poet situated, on Campbellian lines, amid the legendary, voluptuous sweetness of the South:

> Cotton and the moon,
> Warmth, earth, warmth,
> The sky, the sun, the stars,
> The magnolia-scented South.[246]

This poem, like that addressed to the South by Dunbar many years earlier,

---

[244] "The White Ones," *The Weary Blues*, p. 106.
[245] "The South," lines 5-6 and 13-16, *ibid.*, p. 54. Here one seems to hear also echoes of Toomer; see "Georgia Dusk," *Cane*, p. 22: "...some genius of the South/With blood-hot eyes and cane-lipped scented mouth."
[246] *Ibid.*, lines 9-12.

is almost the story of a rejected lover, but with this difference: the problem of lynching is raised without either ambiguity or indulgence.[247] The South is presented here as a mass of contradictions, as it is, too, in "Magnolia Flowers," where the poet paints the impressionistic portrait of a land gentle and cruel at the same time, half legend and half reality. He finds out its true face one evening as he goes off to look for undiscoverable magnolias (the gentle legends) and unexpectedly happens on a lynching party that is almost over (cruel realities) :

> The quiet fading out of life
> In a corner full of ugliness.
>
> I went lookin' for magnolia flowers
> But I didn't find 'em.
> I went lookin' for magnolia flowers in the dusk
> And there was only this corner
> Full of ugliness.
>
>   'Scuse me,
>   I didn't mean to stump ma toe on you, lady.[248]

Hughes never stopped returning, from time to time, to the theme of lynching. He sometimes deals with it via the lament of a young black girl for her vanished lover ("Song for a Dark Girl"[249]); sometimes it arises in advice given to a young black who has been falsely accused and who is fleeing his pursuers ("Flight"[250]); or, again, the story is put in the mouth of a black nurse ("Southern Mammy Sings"[251]) who sings about it to little children.

While most of these poems are designed to move the reader by stressing the cruelty and horror of these inhuman acts, at least two of them set out to demonstrate that the Negro is not the only (indeed, that he is not the

---

[247] *Ibid.*, lines 7-8.

[248] "Magnolia Flowers," *Fine Clothes to the Jew*, p. 70.

[249] *Ibid.*, p. 75.

[250] *Dear Lovely Death* (unpaginated brochure). The poem was reprinted in *One-Way Ticket*, p. 55.

[251] *Shakespeare in Harlem*, p. 75. For other poems dealing with lynching, in addition to those named below, see "Blue Bayou," *Jim Crow's Last Stand*, p. 10 (reprinted in *One-Way Ticket*, p. 53); "The Bitter River," *Jim Crow's Last Stand*, p. 11; "Freedom," *ibid.*, p. 7; "Silhouette," *One-Way Ticket*, p. 56; and more or less fleeting allusions in a great number of other works. Racial violence is also the theme of the entire volume entitled *Scottsboro Limited*. See also "Ballad of Ozie Powell," *A New Song*, p. 17 (Ozie Powell was one of the accused in the Scottsboro case); "Ku Klux," *Shakespeare in Harlem*, p. 81; "The Ballad of Margie Polite," *One-Way Ticket*, p. 75 (deals with a race riot in Harlem, perhaps the 1943 riot); "Roland Hayes Beaten," *ibid.*, p. 86; "Third Degree," p. 130; and "Who but the Lord?" p. 73.

actual) victim of lynching. In "Lynching Song," "the black boy spins" from the rope but "the white folks die."[252] The poem implies that such crimes endanger all our lives and, quite particularly, all our liberties. The same message is imparted by the fine poem "Georgia Dusk":

> Sometimes there's a wind in the Georgia dusk
> That cries and cries and cries
> Its lonely pity through the Georgia dusk
> Veiling what the darkness hides.
>
> Sometimes there's blood in the Georgia dusk,
> Left by a streak of sun,
> A crimson trickle in the Georgia dusk.
> Whose blood? . . . Everyone's.
>
> Sometimes a wind in the Georgia dusk
> Scatters hate like seed
> To sprout its bitter barriers
> Where the sunsets bleed.[253]

World War II had a decisive influence on the general characteristics of Negro literature in America, and a particularly strong effect on Hughes's poetry of combat. Unlike World War I, which had led to a hardening of racial oppression, the second war marked the setting-off point for considerable progress in the domain of civil rights.[254] In place of the sterile nationalism of the first postwar period, there now arose a frankly integrationist tendency, whose aim it was to obtain without further delay for the Negro the benefits of the "Four Freedoms" which President Roosevelt,

[252] "Lynching Song," *A New Song,* p. 30; reprinted in *One-Way Ticket,* p. 58.
[253] "Georgia Dusk," *Selected Poems,* p. 279.
[254] In the spring of 1941, the Negro trade-union leader A. Philip Randolph, by threatening a march on Washington, forced President Roosevelt to issue the famous Executive Order 8802 which set up the Fair Employment Practices Committee (June 25, 1941), aimed at abolishing all discrimination within firms involved in national defense. On this, see Gunnar Myrdal, *An American Dilemma,* pp. 414ff., 851-52. These laws were adopted after the war by various northern industrial states. As for elections, the white primaries were abolished (*Smith v. Allbright,* 1944). Segregation in trains crossing state lines was practically abolished as a consequence of certain judicial decisions (*Morgan v. Virginia,* 1946, and *Henderson v. U.S.,* 1950). On this topic, see "Lunch in a Jim Crow Car," *Selected Poems,* p. 280. A Supreme Court decision (*Shelley v. Kramer,* 1948) declared discrimination in housing to be illegal. This outlawed the practice of restrictive covenants, which Hughes dealt with in his poem of that name, *One-Way Ticket,* p. 64. ("Ballad of the Landlord," *Jim Crow's Last Stand,* p. 20, and "Madam and the Rent Man," *One-Way Ticket,* p. 9, take up the same problem.) Finally, segregation in schools, already shaken by judicial decisions handed down as early as 1950 (*Sweatt v. Painter,* Texas; and *McLaurin v. Oklahoma State*), was disposed of by the Supreme Court's history-making decision of 1954.

upon American entry into war, had promised to obtain for the other peoples of the world: [255]

> The President's Four Freedoms
> Appeal to me.
> I would like to see those Freedoms
> Come to be.
>
> If you believe
> In the Four Freedoms, too,
> Then share 'em with me —
> Don't keep 'em all for you.
>   .   .   .   .
> Freedom's not just
> To be won Over There.
> It means Freedom at home, too —
> Now — *right here*.[256]
>
> I tire so of hearing people say,
> *Let things take their course.*
> *Tomorrow is another day.*
> I do not need my freedom when I'm dead.
> I cannot live on tomorrow's bread.[257]

Occasional poetry now comes to occupy a more important place than ever in Hughes's work, and a volume like *Jim Crow's Last Stand* is almost entirely given over to it. Though often excellent as a weapon, it nevertheless clings too closely to the actual event to succeed in long retaining its interest. Already many of the writings of this period are of value only as historical documents. Examples are "Jim Crow's Last Stand,"[258] which expressed the hope that the bombs dropped on Pearl Harbor would deal a death blow to segregation; "Dear Mr. President,"[259] a protest against racial discrimination in the armed forces;[260] and even "Freedom Train,"[261] in which the poet comments ironically on the Freedom Train sent abroad

[255] Message to Congress, January 6, 1941.
[256] "How about It, Dixie," stanzas 1, 2, 6, *Jim Crow's Last Stand*, p. 9.
[257] "Democracy," lines 10-14, *ibid.*, p. 6.
[258] *Ibid.*, p. 29.
[259] For the text of this poem, see Yoseloff, ed., *Seven Poets*, pp. 46-47.
[260] This was at last abolished by President Truman in 1948.
[261] *The New Republic*, September 15, 1947, p. 27. The poem was reprinted in *Selected Poems*, p. 276, but with variants which effectuate a kind of "updating" of the poem, this made necessary by concrete developments taking place between 1947 and 1959. The necessity for this is sufficiently eloquent in itself: it clearly demonstrates the weakness of all this occasional literature. For other poems of the same kind, see especially "The Black Man Speaks," *Jim Crow's Last Stand*, p. 5; "Ballad of Sam Solomon," *ibid.*, p. 22; etc.

for propaganda purposes by the United States, whereas freedom still did not exist in southern trains.

Yet among all these poems of demand and protest there are some which, because of their picturesqueness and imaginative originality, have kept their pristine freshness. Until the day segregation has become no more than an evil memory, one will be captivated by an unpretentious piece such as "Merry-Go-Round," which exposes the absurd irrationality of the adult world with the implacable logic of childlike innocence:

> Where is the Jim Crow section
> On this merry-go-round,
> Mister, cause I want to ride?
> Down South where I come from
> White and colored
> Can't sit side by side.
> Down South on the train
> There's a Jim Crow car.
> On the bus we're put in the back —
> But there ain't no back
> To a merry-go-round!
> Where's the horse
> For a kid that's black?[262]

Some have deplored the fact that, in the midst of a world war, Langston Hughes chose to defend freedom by resorting to such trivial themes, and that he did not always make the trumpet sound in defending the greatness of democracy.[263] But of this one can be certain: whether sublime or humble, his verses always bear the stamp of unchallengeable sincerity, and no poet has ever found more moving tones to utter Freedom's beautiful name:

> There are words like *Freedom*
> Sweet and wonderful to say.
> On my heart-strings freedom sings
> All day everyday.
>
> There are words like *Liberty*
> That almost make me cry.
> If you had known what I knew
> You would know why.[264]

[262] "Merry-Go-Round," *Shakespeare in Harlem*, p. 80.
[263] Note in particular this observation made by William Harrison in his critique of *Shakespeare in Harlem* (*Opportunity*, July, 1942, p. 219): "At the present fateful hour when the very national independence of our country is threatened by the forces of Axis enslavement . . . a special task is imposed upon a Negro poet to be more than 'characteristic,' to rise above and expand beyond his usual self."
[264] "Refugee in America," *Fields of Wonder*, p. 105.

5. TOWARD A SYNTHESIS

A few months before his sixtieth birthday, Langston Hughes published, with *Ask Your Mama — Twelve Moods for Jazz* (1961), his first new collection of poems in ten years. Both in form and in thematic content the volume confirmed the tendencies already dominant in his earlier work, and in relation to which it acquired the importance of an attempted synthesis.

In terms of form, *Ask Your Mama* sums up forty years of experimentation. The physical appearance of the work shows that we confront an experiment. The book, shorter than it is wide, has the shape of an album; the inspiration for the brightly colored decorations, both outside and inside, comes from the shapes of abstract art. The paper sets itself apart through its brick color, and in turning the pages one discovers that the spread is printed alternately in sepia and in blue. Finally, just as E. E. Cummings and Kenneth Rexroth had chosen to use only lower case, here Langston Hughes prints everything in capitals.

The claim is that we still have to do with jazz poetry. Incidentally, the volume is dedicated to Louis Armstrong, "the greatest horn blower of them all."[265] But, compared with *The Weary Blues* or even *Montage of a Dream Deferred,* the definition of jazz poetry seems to have evolved considerably. True, we are once again asked to look on the eight hundred or so lines that form this work as a single long poem[266] divided into twelve movements, each of which represents a variation on a basic theme. The line endeavors (successfully, on a number of occasions) to awaken the impression that we are listening to the rhythm section of a jazz band, whether in an overture:

> IN THE
> IN THE QUARTER
> IN THE QUARTER OF THE NEGROES
> WHERE THE DOORS ARE DOORS OF PAPER . . .[267]
> SINGERS
> SINGERS LIKE O —
> SINGERS LIKE ODETTA — AND THAT STATUE . . .[268]

[265] *Ask Your Mama,* Dedication.

[266] *Ibid.,* facing the page cited in the preceding note: "The author wishes to thank the editors of *Poetry, The Village Voice, Voices, The Crisis* and *Jazz Today* for permission to reprint those sections of *this* [italics added] poem previously published in their pages." See also two pages further on: "The traditional folk melody of the *Hesitation Blues* is the leitmotif for *this* [italics added] poem."

[267] *Ibid.,* p. 3.

[268] *Ibid.,* p. 41.

DE —
DELIGHT —
DELIGHTED! INTRODUCE ME TO EARTHA . . .[269]

or in a finale with the picking up of cues:

IN THE QUARTER OF THE NEGROES
WHERE NEGROES SING SO WELL
NEGROES SING SO WELL
SING SO WELL
SO WELL.
WELL?[270]

or when the rhythm section suddenly rises in volume and the rumble of the drum underlines the anger rising in the Negro quarter:

FILIBUSTER VERSUS VETO
LIKE A SNAPPING TURTLE —
WON'T LET GO UNTIL IT THUNDERS
WON'T LET GO UNTIL IT THUNDERS
TEARS THE BODY FROM THE SHADOW
WON'T LET GO UNTIL IT THUNDERS
IN THE QUARTER OF THE NEGROES.[271]

In places, too, one has the impression that the repetition of words and phrases seeks to create an echo effect of the kind used for a number of years past by some singers of popular songs:

I WANT TO SEE MY MOTHER MOTHER
WHEN THE ROLL IS CALLED UP YONDER
IN THE QUARTER OF THE NEGROES.[272]

GRANDPA, DID YOU HEAR THE
HEAR THE OLD FOLKS SAY HOW
HOW TALL HOW TALL THE CANE GREW
SAY HOW WHITE THE COTTON COTTON
SPEAK OF RICE DOWN IN THE MARSHLAND . . .[273]

YES, SUBURBIA
WILL EVENTUALLY BE
ONLY IN THE SEA . . .
MEANWHILE
OF COURSE

[269] *Ibid.*, p. 69.
[270] *Ibid.*, p. 19.
[271] *Ibid.*, p. 7.
[272] *Ibid.*, p. 13. The first two lines are taken from the spiritual "When the Saints Go Marching In."
[273] *Ibid.*, p. 71.

> OF COURSE
> OF COURSE
> ON A MUDDY TRACK
> IN THE QUARTER OF THE NEGROES
> NEGROES
> NEGROES
> SOME HORSE MIGHT
> SLIP AND BREAK
> ITS BACK . . .[274]

Finally, as in *Montage of a Dream Deferred*, the development of the theme is underlined by riffs or interrupted by breaks, both features of jazz. These breaks utilize the phrase "Ask Your Mama," which is also the title of the volume and which we will refer to later.

But elsewhere the jazz technique is not so boldly employed as formerly and, all in all, *Ask Your Mama* represents a step backward compared with *Montage of a Dream Deferred*, since the jazz effects are no longer to be found exclusively in the poetry. Here the marginal directions so dear to that great troubadour of American poetry, Vachel Lindsay, appear once more. Hughes had experimented with them for the first time in 1931, in *The Negro Mother and Other Dramatic Recitations*, and had not resorted to them again.[275]

Yet in the interval, and especially after World War II, he had ceaselessly experimented in the area of the poetry recital with jazz accompaniment. In 1958, for instance, he had recorded *The Weary Blues* with Henry Red Allen's band.[276] After that, he performed from one end of the country to the other with a number of the best jazz groups in the land. This must be regarded as primarily a return to the best poetic traditions of the race and, in particular, to the global art form that Dunbar already conceived poetry to be. Hughes thus established himself as the most authentic wearer of Dunbar's mantle.

But this experiment was not racial alone; it was also American. For years jazz poetry was the rage in all the avant-garde circles of the United States, most notably among those of the "Beat Generation." One of the promoters of the movement and a veteran of experiment, Kenneth Rexroth, gave numerous poetry recitals to the accompaniment of jazz in the

---

[274] *Ibid.*, p. 57. There are countless examples of these echo effects in this volume. See, for instance, pp. 27 (manger, manger) and 71 (woman, woman), etc.

[275] In the reprinting of "The Negro Mother" in *Selected Poems*, p. 288, he had even left out the indications placed at the beginning of the poem as originally published.

[276] See the reference to this recording, and to a selection of other records of this kind, in our Bibliographical Appendix, "Discography."

cafés of San Francisco and elsewhere. We turn to him for a definition of this kind of poetry:

> What is jazz poetry? It isn't anything very complicated to understand. It is the reciting of suitable poetry with the music of a jazz band, usually small and very quiet. Most emphatically, it is not recitation with "background" music. The voice is integrally wedded to the music and, although it does not sing notes, is treated as another instrument, with its own solos and ensemble passages, and with solo and ensemble work by the band alone. ... It returns poetry to music and public entertainment as it was in the days of Homer and the troubadours. It forces poetry to deal with aspects of life it has tended to avoid in the recent past. It demands of poetry something of a public surface — meanings which can be grasped by ordinary people — just as the plays of Shakespeare had something for both the pit and the intellectuals in Elizabethan times, and still have today.[277]

This is the vein in which *Ask Your Mama* was conceived, and the poems in it no longer strive through their own means alone to reproduce the jazz orchestration. To underscore his themes, the poet openly relies on a musical accompaniment whose own evolution is meticulously ordered in the marginal directions on every page. Thus music and poetry reciprocally support each other, and their respective themes incessantly meet and intersect in a sort of dialogue, in which it is possible to see a modern equivalent of the antiphonal pattern so characteristic of the Negro lyric genius.

But *Ask Your Mama* satisfies Kenneth Rexroth's definition in yet another way. As a poet of the masses, Hughes had always maintained in the forefront of his mind the importance of not cutting himself off from the people. A consequence of his all too insistent efforts not to exceed their range was his occasional lapse into triviality. But this volume bears witness, on the contrary, to his strong desire to provide something for "the pit and the intellectuals" alike.

For the first time Hughes pays obeisance to the usage (established by T. S. Eliot half a century ago) of providing a poem with notes. These are but summary, however, and they differ vastly both in inspiration and manner from those given in *The Waste Land*. In fact, they are only a kind of

[277] Kenneth Rexroth, "Jazz Poetry," *Nation*, March 29, 1958, pp. 282-83. On jazz and literature, see also the same author's "Disengagement: The Art of the Beat Generation," in Gene Feldman and Max Gartenberg, eds., *The Beat Generation and the Angry Young Men* (New York, 1958), pp. 323-38. Let it also be noted that even before World War II Rexroth was in contact with circles of blacks. In any event, this supposition appears justified by the fact that his first poetic efforts appeared in 1937 in the WPA anthology, *American Stuff*, pp. 36-38 (excerpts from "The Apple Garths of Avalon"), side by side with those of Negro writers such as Richard Wright, Claude McKay, Sterling Brown, Robert Hayden, etc.

condensation of the "argument" of each of the twelve movements and do little to enlighten the "poetically unhep" for whom, in principle, they are intended.[278] Yet the mere fact of the poet's having sensed the need for this explanatory apparatus demonstrates his awareness that, for the first time, he was offering for our contemplation poetry that was often recondite.

The esoteric character of much of this work is derived from the complex and highly personal manner of the poet's thought. The influence of Carl Sandburg had by now receded into the past, and one is reminded rather of the obscurity of a Wallace Stevens by more than one passage in *Ask Your Mama*. The perceptible relationship between image and reality tends at times to shrink into total unintelligibility; as with Joyce, it can be sensed that the words summon one another and come together no longer at the bidding of a thought seeking vigorous expression, but on the basis of kindred sonority and structure:

> IN THE QUARTER OF THE NEGROES
> WHERE THE DOORS ARE DOORS OF PAPER
> DUST OF DINGY ATOMS
> BLOWS A SCRATCHY SOUND.
> AMORPHOUS JACK-O'-LANTERNS CAPER
> AND THE WIND WON'T WAIT FOR MIDNIGHT
> FOR FUN TO BLOW DOORS DOWN.
> BY THE RIVER AND THE RAILROAD
> WITH FLUID FAR-OFF GOING
> BOUNDARIES BIND UNBINDING
> A WHIRL OF WHISTLES BLOWING
> NO TRAINS OR STEAMBOATS GOING —
> YET LEONTYNE'S UNPACKING.[279]

If doors are said to be "of paper" in Negro quarters in the South, that asserts that the inhabitants are threatened by violence at any time. Danger prowls, day and night; this is symbolized here by the dirty atomic dust (there are clean atom bombs and others that are not clean) which the world has come to see as its greatest menace. But for southern Negroes that danger is less immediate than the other, incarnated by the members of the Ku Klux Klan who, torch in hand, prance about before midnight not far from the predestined victims of their punitive night raid. The Negro quarters are traditionally situated close to the river and the railroad which, with the boundless fluidity of their silvery ribbons, appear to facili-

---

[278] *Ask Your Mama*, p. 84: "Liner Notes — For the poetically unhep."
[279] *Ibid.*, pp. 3-4. To be noted are the associations dust/dingy, wind won't wait, for/fun, doors/down, river/railroad, fluid/far-off, boundaries/bind/unbinding, whirl/whistles.

tate departures for far-off horizons, but which actually are boundaries that segregation has made it almost impossible to traverse. Only the occasional return of a local woman who unpacks her things demonstrates that once in a while the frontier has been crossed.

Ask Your Mama has no shortage of passages that require equally careful elucidation, but at least in some instances a sufficient familiarity with the black world and its history opens the way to the innermost secret of this poetry. Then one can realize in what measure the art of Hughes here strives to achieve a powerful synthesis of the totality of his previous work:

> IN THE QUARTER OF THE NEGROES
> WHERE TO SNOW NOW ACCLIMATED
> SHADOWS SHOW UP SHARPER,
> THE ONE COIN IN THE METER
> KEEPS THE GAS ON WHILE THE TV
> FAILS TO GET PEARL BAILEY.
> SINCE IT'S SNOWING ON THE TV
> THIS LAST QUARTER OF CENTENNIAL
> 100-YEARS EMANCIPATION
> MECHANICS NEED REPAIRING
> FOR NIAGARA FALLS IS FROZEN
> AS IS CUSTOM BELOW ZERO.
> MAMA'S FRUITCAKE SENT FROM GEORGIA
> CRUMBLES AS IT'S NIBBLED
> TO A DISC BY DINAH
> IN THE RUM THAT WAFTS MARACAS
> FROM ANOTHER DISTANT QUARTER
> TO THIS QUARTER OF THE NEGROES
> WHERE THE SONG'S MAHALIA'S DAUGHTER
>
>   .   .   .   .
>
> WHEN NIAGARA FALLS IS FROZEN
> THERE'S A BAR WITH WINDOWS FROSTED
> FROM THE COLD THAT MAKES NIAGARA
> GHOSTLY MONUMENT OF WINTER
> TO A BAND THAT ONCE PASSED OVER
> WITH A WOMAN WITH TWO PISTOLS
> ON A TRAIN THAT LOST NO PASSENGERS
> ON THE LINE WHOSE ROUTE WAS FREEDOM
> THROUGH THE JUNGLE OF WHITE DANGER
> TO THE HAVEN OF WHITE QUAKERS
> WHOSE HAYMOW WAS A MANGER MANGER
> WHERE THE CHRIST CHILD ONCE HAD LAIN.[280]

[280] *Ibid.*, pp. 25-27. The image of Niagara may also contain an allusion to the

Admirable is the masterly virtuosity with which the symbol moves along, rebounds, and grows richer stage by stage, while revealing in its passage the highly diverse unity of the black world and the strength of the bonds that link it to its past. The "snow" of the second line symbolizes both the alien climate into which the Negro has been transplanted and the color of those who have forced their civilization on him. Against this white background the shadows, or Negroes, now stand out all the more sharply, but these shadows are at the same time those that still darken the picture of American democracy. For economic deprivation is still unconquered (the last coin goes into the gas meter and so barely permits the flame — that is to say, life — to burn on feebly), and integration is not yet achieved (the black artist Pearl Bailey could not be seen on television because of the racial discrimination still prevailing in show business). At this point, the snow symbolism takes another turn: it is said to be "snowing" on television when the picture is disturbed, and this signifies the whites who still prevent the gears of democracy from functioning freely. Still a brief while away from the celebration of the centenary of Emancipation, January 1, 1963, it is high time to repair the defective mechanism.

Immediately, the image of snow and cold leads to the image of a frozen Niagara, whose whole symbolic import will not be revealed to us until a little later. For the moment, memories of the South that has been left behind disintegrate, like the cake Mama has sent from Georgia that is nibbled at as the record of the black singer Dinah Washington turns on the phonograph. But the crumbs of the cake, as they fall into the rum that was manufactured by other Negroes on a distant island, accomplish the symbolic reconstitution of the unity of the black race, just as the Negro rhythms of the West Indies breathed out by the alcoholic spirits blend in with those of the black American singer Mahalia Jackson.

We soon come back to the image of the cold which, by depositing hoar frost on the window panes, erects an opaque screen between the Negro and the outside world. But the cold also freezes over Niagara, transforming it into a huge, fantastic monument to the memory of one of the most famous leaders of the Underground Railroad of slavery days, Harriet Tubman, who led runaway slaves along this route to freedom and was helped in her task by Quaker farmers. By putting up the runaways in their haymows, they echoed the charitable gesture that had, long ago, allowed Jesus to find shelter in a manger. Harriet Tubman, who was always armed when she went on her missions, was able to boast, when her career had ended, that she had never let her train derail and had never lost a single passenger.

Niagara Movement, which would later give rise to the N.A.C.P. On this, see p. 152 above.

From the thematic point of view, *Ask Your Mama* offers a striking summary of the American black world at this time, and even of the entire black world, for Hughes's technique enables us to sense their profound unity. Unlike *Montage of a Dream Deferred*, which was split into a great number of separate, relatively disconnected poems, the 807 lines of *Ask Your Mama* form a practically uninterrupted sequence, for the twelve movements making up this jazz symphony are not like so many watertight compartments. Quite the contrary — the themes copiously overlap from one section into another, spreading out, disappearing, and surging up anew at intervals, through the suggestion of a single word or phrase, as in a symphony a theme that has previously been developed by the whole orchestra is repeated in the midst of another passage by one instrument or by only one section of the orchestra.

Thus the unity of the whole is formed primarily by the strict cohesiveness of the themes. These all have as their center Negro life, as we are reminded by the periodic recurrence of the line

IN THE QUARTER OF THE NEGROES.[281]

This "Negro quarter" swells to the dimensions of the black world, including the blacks of the African fatherland as well as all those in the diaspora. The scene shifts from North to South, from the United States to the West Indies and Africa, and even to the Latin Quarter. Contemporary allusions and references to the increasingly important role played by the black man today are frequent, so that *Ask Your Mama* could be used to compile a veritable black *Who's Who* which would include, along with the black artists, writers, and leaders of America North and South, all the great political figures of the new African countries, and also certain other leaders at odds with the Western world, such as Castro and Nasser. Wherever there are nonwhites, the poet seems to be saying, they face the same problems. Thus his technique tends to make us aware of the unity of the Third World, as in the following line which melts three Negro writers, Alioune Diop, Aimé Césaire, and Léopold Sedar Senghor, into a single personage:

ALIOUNE AIME SEDAR SIPS HIS NEGRITUDE.[282]

[281] This expression, sometimes slightly modified, is the verbal *leitmotiv* of the poem just as the "Hesitation Blues" is its musical *leitmotiv*.

[282] *Ibid.*, p. 70. This merging of three persons into a single person is not an isolated phenomenon in this poem. See also the merging of the Voodoo divinities in the "Gospel Cha-Cha" section, *passim*, esp. p. 51; the merging of the street names in the Negro quarters of different American cities in the "Ask Your Mama" section, pp. 61ff.; and, in general, scattered widely throughout the poem, the merging of all the names, persons, and places whose unity or basic solidarity the poet wishes to stress. Again, this is but one of the devices that endow this work with

Humor is not necessarily barred from the presentation of these personages; especially to be relished is this reference to W. E. B. Du Bois's
advanced age:

> METHUSELAH SIGNS PAPERS W.E.B.
> ORIGINAL NIAGARA N.A.A.C.P.[283]

Confronting this monolithic portrayal of the black world, and associated
in a similar way, are to be seen the former colonial powers and the segre-
gationists of the southern United States — whose ghosts, even after their
departure from life, still let their shadows fall in silhouette on the "black
quarter."[284] Numerous tensions persist between these two worlds, and the
theme of the dream deferred obstinately returns in this volume in new
and endlessly varied forms. The musical *leitmotiv* of the poem is, furthermore, the "Hesitation Blues,"[285] which raises at intervals the haunting
questions of equality and freedom:

> TELL ME HOW LONG —
> MUST I WAIT?
> CAN I GET IT NOW?
> ÇA IRA! ÇA IRA!
> OR MUST I HESITATE?
> IRA! BOY, IRA![286]

It is but a step from the French revolutionary chant of "Ça ira!" to the
anger evoked by the Spanish word *ira* in the last line, and on more than
one occasion in this poem Hughes harks back to his old militant tone to
belabor the Southerners who are too ready to charge with subversion and
anti-American activities those Negroes who are only fighting for their
rights.[287] Gains have indeed been made, but too often they remain more
theoretical than real:

> IN THE QUARTER OF THE NEGROES
> WHERE THE PENDULUM IS SWINGING
> TO THE SHADOW OF THE BLUES,

its synthetic, "blended" style; one may also note the suppression of many articles,
the use of the present participle instead of a verb with a person as subject (see the
example cited in note 279, particularly the four lines before the end), and
the suppression, in relative clauses, of the relative pronoun and the verb "to be."
The sparse punctuation also contributes to this effect; and where it does occur, the
typographical rendering is such as to make it almost invisible.
   [283] *Ibid.*, p. 70. Here again is an allusion to the Niagara Movement. See our
remark on this in note 280, above.
   [284] See *ibid.*, p. 19.
   [285] *Ibid.*, marginal directions, pp. 7, 28, 29-30, 42, 45, 83.
   [286] *Ibid.*, p. 13.
   [287] *Ibid.*, pp. 14, 72-74.

> EVEN WHEN YOU'RE WINNING
> THERE'S NO WAY NOT TO LOSE.[288]

Then again, the economic situation of the Negro continues to be hazardous, for what is only a lull in business for whites is a real economic crisis for the Negro:

> WHITE FOLKS' RECESSION
> IS COLORED FOLKS' DEPRESSION.[289]

Yet from the entire poem there rises a vision of the future that is clearly more confident and optimistic than in *Montage of a Dream Deferred*. In spite of the odds against him, the Negro cherishes in his heart the hope that one day his dream will come true:

> THE REVEREND MARTIN LUTHER
> KING MOUNTS HIS UNICORN
> OBLIVIOUS TO BLOOD
> AND MOONLIGHT ON ITS HORN.[290]

Another new feature is the far from negligible place that humor now occupies in Hughes's poetry, whereas in his earlier works his talents as a humorist were hardly displayed outside his prose. Thus the first section of "Cultural Exchange" ends on the Swiftian dream of a South turned topsy-turvy — one of the passages in *Ask Your Mama* most likely to be cited time and again:

> DREAMS AND NIGHTMARES...
> NIGHTMARES...DREAMS! OH!
> DREAMING THAT THE NEGROES
> OF THE SOUTH HAVE TAKEN OVER —
> VOTED ALL THE DIXIECRATS
> RIGHT OUT OF POWER —
> COMES THE *COLORED HOUR:*
> MARTIN LUTHER KING IS GOVERNOR OF GEORGIA,
> Dr. RUFUS CLEMENT HIS CHIEF ADVISOR,
> ZELMA WATSON GEORGE THE HIGH GRAND WORTHY.
> IN WHITE PILLARED MANSIONS

[288] *Ibid.,* p. 31.

[289] *Ibid.,* p. 32. There are numerous references to the Negro's indigence; but at times, also, the poet ironically points out that those involved are themselves responsible for their chronic lack of cash. See in particular pp. 61-62.

[290] *Ibid.,* p. 70. On a number of occasions, the unicorn symbolizes the ideal. See also pp. 64-65. It is far from certain what gave rise to this symbol, apart from the creature's fabulous, unreal nature. Martin Luther King was a pastor in Montgomery, Alabama, when these lines were written. He continued on his course to achieve his goal and refused to be deterred by the threat of violence. (The reference to moonlight recalls the nocturnal violence so frequent in the South.)

SITTING ON THEIR WIDE VERANDAS,
WEALTHY NEGROES HAVE WHITE SERVANTS,
WHITE SHARECROPPERS WORK THE BLACK PLANTATIONS,
AND COLORED CHILDREN HAVE WHITE MAMMIES:
    MAMMY FAUBUS
    MAMMY EASTLAND
    MAMMY PATTERSON.
DEAR, *DEAR* DARLING OLD WHITE MAMMIES —
SOMETIMES EVEN BURIED WITH OUR FAMILY!
    DEAR OLD
    MAMMY FAUBUS!
CULTURE, THEY SAY, *IS A TWO-WAY STREET:*
HAND ME MY MINT JULEP, MAMMY,
    MAKE HASTE![291]

The margin has the indication that the band should impishly strike up "Dixie!" This is truly the plantation tradition stood upon its head.

It should also be noted that for the first time there appears, alongside the theme of the dream endlessly deferred, that of the dream come true. The whole section entitled "Horn of Plenty" is given over to it. After an overture that lists the outstanding financial successes of Negroes in show business, sports, and elsewhere, the poet introduces us to the recesses of the psychological universe of the Negro who has made it. At least one passage in this section might well have an autobiographical application:

GOT THERE! YES, I MADE IT!
NAME IN THE PAPERS EVERY DAY!
FAMOUS — THE HARD WAY —
FROM NOBODY AND NOTHING TO WHERE I AM.
THEY KNOW ME, TOO, DOWNTOWN,
ALL ACROSS THE COUNTRY, EUROPE —
ME WHO USED TO BE NOBODY,
NOTHING BUT ANOTHER SHADOW
IN THE QUARTER OF THE NEGROES,
NOW A NAME! MY NAME — A NAME![292]

Yet whites will only grudgingly admit that this is so. They look with a jaundiced eye on the Negro who has climbed the social ladder, and they continually try to make him feel this by asking malicious questions. These

[291] *Ibid.,* pp. 8-9. The personages satirized here were all living at the time. Rufus Clement was president of Atlanta University; Zelma Watson George, a black sociologist; Orval Faubus, governor of Arkansas; John Patterson, governor of Alabama; James Eastland, senator from Mississippi. The last three were all dyed-in-the-wool Southerners.

[292] *Ibid.,* p. 43.

questions are inserted into the body of the poem like breaks interrupting for an instant the progress of the jazz symphony, and the Negro snubs them with the impudent rejoinder: "Ask Your Mama!"

> AND THEY ASKED ME RIGHT AT CHRISTMAS
> IF MY BLACKNESS, WOULD IT RUB OFF?
> I SAID, ASK YOUR MAMA.[293]
>
> YET THEY ASKED ME OUT ON MY PATIO
> WHERE DID I GET MY MONEY!
> I SAID, FROM YOUR MAMA![294]
>
> THEY ASKED ME AT THANKSGIVING
> DID I VOTE FOR NIXON?
> I SAID, VOTED FOR YOUR MAMA.[295]

Thus, in sum, it seems that there are sound reasons for regarding *Ask Your Mama* as the poet's attempt to achieve a huge synthesis. This does not mean that all antitheses have been conquered and reconciled; some of them have hardened into a new opposition, and if we were able to declare above that this poem represents, in certain respects, a return to the past, this is especially true of the poet's religious attitude, which takes us back to the period when the first version of "A New Song" was published (1932-33).

If we are to believe the short note that the poet wrote for the section entitled "Gospel Cha-Cha," religion still is the opium of the people — the refuge, that is to say, of those who are still in need of escape because they have not yet succeeded financially: "Those who have no lawns to mow seek gods who come in various spiritual and physical guises and to whom one prays in various rhythms in various lands in various tongues."[296]

The white God never sets foot in the Negro quarter, for he knows that the moonlight would expose his whiteness:

> IN THE QUARTER OF THE NEGROES
> WHERE AN ANCIENT RIVER FLOWS
> PAST HUTS THAT HOUSE A MILLION BLACKS
> AND THE WHITE GOD NEVER GOES
> FOR THE MOON WOULD WHITE HIS WHITENESS

---

[293] *Ibid.,* p. 8.

[294] *Ibid.,* p. 43. The money mentioned here was used by a Negro who had "made it" to buy himself a house in a Long Island suburb.

[295] *Ibid.,* p. 70. For other examples of this break, see pp. 46, 58, 62. On page 32, the question receives no answer: "THEY ASKED ME RIGHT AT CHRISTMAS / WOULD I MARRY POCAHONTAS?" Perhaps the question must be interpreted as a reference to mixed marriage, to which the poet's reaction is that the best answer is no answer.

[296] *Ibid.,* p. 90.

AND THE NIGHT MIGHT BE ASTONISHED
AND SO LOSE ITS REPOSE.[297]

But elsewhere this white God finds himself in conflict with the black crucified Christ, whose image seems to come at the end of "Gospel Cha-Cha,"
which is filled with the frightful witches' sabbath conducted in the Negro's
soul by such Voodoo divinities as Damballa and Erzulie, by Negro American preachers represented by John Jasper and Daddy Grace, and finally
by Jesus and his Virgin Mother:

> I TRIED
> LORD KNOWS I TRIED
> DAMBALLA
> I PRAYED
> LORD KNOWS I PRAYED
> DADDY
> I CLIMBED
> UP THAT STEEP HILL
> THE VIRGIN
> WITH A CROSS
> LORD KNOWS I CLIMBED
> BUT WHEN I GOT
> JOHN JASPER JESUS
> WHEN I GOT TO CALVARY
> UP THERE ON THAT HILL
> ALREADY THERE WAS THREE —
> AND ONE, YES, ONE
> WAS BLACK AS ME.[298]

As was so frequently found in his earlier works, the expression of the
poet's religious feeling remained consistently wrapped in ambiguity, and
he tended to project outside the internal contradictions he had not yet
transcended. Thus, in his own personal case, the synthesis had not yet
been accomplished.

Conclusion: Langston Hughes and Harlem

No portrait of Langston Hughes would be complete without mention of
the countless bonds that grew between Harlem and the poet over the years.
The great black metropolis, first celebrated in poetry by Claude McKay,
was the center around which Langston Hughes organized his life and his

---

[297] *Ibid.*, p. 36. This river is probably the Jordan, very often alluded to by the
spirituals in a symbolic sense.
[298] *Ibid.*, pp. 51-52.

work. At twenty he had sought shelter there after dropping out of Columbia University, and when his *Wanderjahre* finished it was there that he settled down. Mecca of the New Negro, temple of jazz, refuge of the black masses fleeing the South, rallying point for Negroes from all over the world, focus of revolution, headquarters of countless sects, supreme living incarnation of the great dream of freedom and equality in which, despite and against every disappointment, neither the poet nor his racial brothers ever ceased to believe — Harlem sums up in itself the poet's every theme and all the aspects of his highly diverse personality. Thus no one would deny today that Hughes had become the outstanding poet of Harlem.[299]

Yet he is also much more than that, for in his work Harlem is symbol as much as reality. When late at night jazz at last falls silent, and one perceives in the nocturnal stillness the heartbeat of the great black city;[300] when, standing "on the edge of hell," "remembering the old lies, the old kicks in the back,"[301] a greatly provoked Harlem at last gives vent to its rage; when at last, at certain moments, those Harlemites who have fled from its "bitter dream"[302] and sought anonymity among the whites cannot think of it without a heart grip — then there can be no doubt that, beneath the poet's magic wand, Harlem miraculously overflows its boundaries and takes on the dimensions of all Black America.

But neither Harlem nor the race to which he belonged can claim to possess Langston Hughes entirely, for he voiced, beyond any frontier of color, the eternal aspirations of all men whose love is freedom.

---

[299] Arthur P. Davis has roughed out a portrait of Hughes as poet of Harlem in "The Harlem of Langston Hughes' Poetry," *Phylon,* fourth quarter, 1952, pp. 276-83.

[300] "Summer Night," *The Weary Blues,* p. 103.

[301] "Puzzled," *One-Way Ticket,* p. 71.

[302] "Passing," *Montage of a Dream Deferred,* p. 57.

Chapter Eleven: STERLING BROWN

The poetry of Sterling Brown was matured in hard times. When *Southern Road* appeared, in 1932, the first great upsurge of the Negro Renaissance had subsided, and the whole country was probing the reasons for its disarray ever since the fall of 1929, when poverty seemed to have acquired permanent squatter's rights.

The vogue of Harlem had encouraged the facile tricks that befitted a certain exhibitionistic trend, but now they were no longer appropriate. The heady frenzy had yielded to a sobering disillusion. Influenced by the pessimism that rose out of failure in the face of adversity, a critical outlook took the place of a fatuous optimism and immeasurable praise for the grandeur of the race. It was a critique more willing than ever to absorb the engaging explanation put forward by historical materialism.

Disillusionment with the present also affected the vision of the past, and so there sprang up a new sense of the unsevered tragic thread in the race's destiny. Between the lyrically voiced suffering of an enslaved people and the emotions kindled in the poet by contemporary hardships, unexpected relationships became apparent, and in this reciprocal immediacy the past and the present were stripped, coldly and lucidly, of one illusion after another. Religious faith, too, was swept away in this maelstrom of plummeting values.

If Sterling Brown succeeded in salvaging from despair what remained of man after the storm had subsided, it was essentially because he had drawn from past experience an unshakeable faith in the eternal potentials of his race. Pending the day when hopes would materialize, disillusionment was best concealed under the sometimes deceptive appearances of humor.

1. Folk Strength and Folk Frailties

The Negro Renaissance was not a total, unquestioning return to the tap-roots, and the movement's most prominent writers often showed themselves less eager to link up with the past than to break with it. The reason why so much energy had been devoted to defining the New Negro was, precisely, the desire to underline the many differences that marked him off from what formerly had been. In the eyes of a man like James Weldon Johnson, the cultural heritage of slavery undoubtedly retained a considerable measure of historic interest, but it is obvious that the anonymous authors of the songs and lyrics he strove to bring back to life could not serve him as masters in the art of thinking. The past that Langston Hughes celebrated lay, for the most part, in the centuries that had preceded slavery, and the citified Negro we meet with in his poetry has little in common with the black peasant of another day.

Sterling Brown's[1] work takes issue with that of his predecessors in the sense that it represents a living rebuttal of the notion that a great gulf separates the outlook of the New Negro from the spirit exhibited in slave poetry. He is not satisfied, as Hughes had been, to borrow only the forms of his verse from the storehouse of folk poetry. He imbues himself with its spirit, its practical philosophy, its humor, and its speech — which, for him,

---

[1] Sterling Allen Brown was born May 1, 1901, in Washington, D.C., where his father was a professor at Howard University. After schooling in that city, he went to Williams College in Massachusetts and was awarded his B.A. in 1922. The following year he earned his M.A. at Harvard. He taught successively at Virginia Seminary and College in Lynchburg, at Fisk University, Nashville, Tennessee, and at Lincoln University in Missouri. In 1929, he became professor of American Literature at Howard University. He also functioned as visiting professor at Atlanta University, New York University, the University of Minnesota, and Vassar College. Between 1936 and 1939 he was editor on Negro Affairs in the Federal Writers' Project of the WPA, was awarded a Guggenheim fellowship for 1937-38 and, from 1939 on, worked with the Gunnar Myrdal group on the huge research project on the American Negro, the conclusions of which were published as *An American Dilemma*. He has published articles in numerous periodicals, including *The Crisis, Opportunity, Phylon, New Challenge, The New Republic,* and various jazz magazines.

His poems were included in three annual anthologies edited by Benjamin Albert Botkin and published as *Folk-Say* (for precise references, see our bibliography) before they were gathered in Sterling Brown's own, and only, volume, *Southern Road* (1932). More recently a new group of poems was published in the anthology edited by George Kumler Anderson and Eda Lou Walton, *This Generation*.

Of all the recent black American poets, Sterling Brown is the most accomplished reader of his own works. The following recordings, consequently, will be found especially enjoyable: *Works of Sterling Brown and Langston Hughes,* Folkways FP 90, side one ("Break of Day," "Sharecroppers," "Slim in Hell," "Old Lem," "Old King Cotton," "Putting on Dog"); and *Anthology of Negro Poets,* Folkways FP 91, side one, tracks 3 and 4 ("Long Gone," "Ma Rainey").

have lost none of their validity, and have permitted him to handle present-day themes with undeniable originality. These themes, as a consequence, take on the depths and the characteristic profiles that mark his genius. In his poetry, past and present hail and respond to one another, and through this interplay each becomes endowed with fresh meaning and a new dimension. Thus Alain Locke was right in his assertion, made on the appearance of *Southern Road,* that Sterling Brown had found "a sort of common denominator between the old and the new Negro."[2]

This sense of continuity in the racial spirit was not won by the poet through some extraordinary gift of insight. Thanks to his parents, both of whom had studied at Fisk University, where more than elsewhere a taste for the beauty of the slave songs is cultivated, he had indeed inherited an unusually close affinity with the folk genius. But his poetic achievement is marked, above all, by a deep, direct acquaintance with the black soul's many facets such as can be acquired only by a patient, thorough study of the people, carried out with a sturdy independence of mind on a par with the sympathy he felt.

It remains necessary to indicate the limits within which he situates the people. Hostile to the rowdy atmosphere of the city, where popular traditions are commercialized and prostituted, Brown was instinctively drawn to the South, which he has traversed in every direction, listening to the songs of his ethnic brothers on the very soil of their destiny, remote from the Harlem cabarets where others grew drunk on din.[3] The antithesis of Langston Hughes, poet of the city, Sterling Brown is poet *par excellence* of the soil. This is where the blues and ballads came to birth, in the forms he loves to adopt for his own poetry; where one can encounter, in their full, living authenticity, the wisdom and the vision that had given sustenance to the anonymous poets of former days and into which he too plunges, so that he may pass these treasures on, in all their freshness, to us. There too one can still hear, in its richness and pristine purity, the meaty, image-loving speech that folk language has always been.

[2] Alain Locke, "Sterling Brown: The New Negro Folk Poet," in Nancy Cunard, *Negro Anthology,* p. 115.

[3] Sterling Brown is an isolated figure. He never had much contact with the other writers of the Harlem group, and he insisted that an exaggerated importance had been attributed to Harlem in the New Negro Movement: "The New Negro is not to me a group of writers centered in Harlem during the second half of the twenties. Most of the writers were not Harlemites; much of the best writing was not about Harlem, which was the show-window, the cashier's till, but no more Negro America than New York is America" ("The New Negro in Literature, 1925-1955," in Rayford Logan et al., eds., *The New Negro Thirty Years Afterward,* p. 57).

Strong in the certainties he acquired through exposure to these realities, Sterling Brown — not through ringing manifestoes or lengthy prefaces, but quite directly through his poetry itself — demolishes the allegations of those who held that the language of the people could no longer serve as an instrument for the poet. "The day of dialect as far as Negro poets are concerned is in the decline," Countee Cullen had declared;[4] and James Weldon Johnson had condemned dialect on the grounds that it was too restricted an instrument, having "only two stops — pathos and humor."[5] It was perhaps Sterling Brown's finest humorous touch, when he arranged to have the preface to *Southern Road* written by James Weldon Johnson himself, so that Johnson felt obliged to admit that Brown's poetry reopened the case that had resulted in the overly hasty condemnation of dialect. Johnson had made it his scapegoat, and now Brown demonstrated how wrong this was: he proved he could walk by walking.

By doing this, he also directed people's attention to the real nature of the problem. Of dialect one might say, as Aesop had said of language, that it was the best of things, and the worst. Evil lay not in dialect itself, but in the way it was used. Nothing that is natural for the people is reprehensible in itself. The poet still had the obligation, first to get to know the people, and then not to let them down, much less betray them. But dialect, as it had been used by the southern poets (by Russell, Page, and others of their school), was not the language of the people, but just one weapon of war among others that had been aimed at the Negro. Like the character traits they falsely attributed to their stock characters, the language they placed in the mouths of blacks was an argument designed to bolster their thesis. Their disciple Dunbar, and Dunbar's disciple Johnson, had been unable to break out of the infernal circle, in the first place because they had not observed the people closely enough, but in particular because both of them, writing for the world of popular song and show business, would have risked failure and might have forced themselves into silence, had they abandoned what the accepted convention looked on as Negro speech. Moreover, one cannot help but notice that, in taking over

[4] Countee Cullen, *Caroling Dusk*, p. xiv.

[5] James Weldon Johnson, *God's Trombones*, p. 7. The only time Brown reacted to this declaration of Johnson's was in *Negro Poetry and Drama*, p. 77, where he says of himself: "He is not afraid of using folk-speech, refusing to believe dialect to be 'an instrument of only two stops — pathos and humor.'" These diverging opinions concerning dialect did not, however, prevent Johnson and Brown from being excellent friends. Brown wrote the headnote for the selection of Johnson's poems included in Johnson's own anthology, *The Book of American Negro Poetry*, pp. 114-17; he also participated in the homage done Johnson after his death, in a ceremony held at Fisk University. See the brochure *James Weldon Johnson*, Department of Publicity, Fisk University (n.d.).

this conventional dialect, they also adopted, perhaps without any clear realization of the fact, other features in the portrait of the Negro that had been standardized in southern poetry. Thus dialect was worth precisely as much as the ideology it had been made to serve — and it was, in any event, inseparable from it.

Confronted by this state of affairs, Brown first brought to bear the weight of his independent outlook: he did not have to rely on his pen for his daily bread. More important, he was much better acquainted than his predecessors had been with the true visage of his people. His studies had been made on the scene, in the traditional habitat; he had studied the people in their literature; finally, his personal investigations led him to study also the way in which the people had been presented and, at times, misrepresented in the writings of his white compatriots.[6] He was thus excellently situated to defend whatever had an authentic folk origin, and to utilize it without incurring the blame directed against the dialect writers who had preceded him.

This also put him in a splendid position to denounce all the false portrayals of the people and of their art, and the poems that tackle these problems show him to be extraordinarily close to Claude McKay. In either writer, perhaps because they both had remained so deeply rooted in the soil, one discovers the same scrupulous respect for the racial heritage, and the same commitment to defend the purity of its memory against those whose behavior jeopardized it.

Though himself an ardent jazz fan, Brown was well aware of the abuses to which jazz had given rise, and of the impiety with which at times the most venerable treasures of folk poetry had been exploited and deformed by being uprooted from their natural context and delivered up to the appetites of the ignorant crowd.

"Cabaret"[7] is an experimental poem whose technique has precisely the aim of conveying the complex reasons why everything done by the Negro cabaret performers whom the poet presents to us sounds a false note. The meaning of the poem emerges from the confrontation of the three psychological levels on which it evolves, and which the typographical arrangement of the poem helps distinguish. From the outset, the value of this Negro art is falsified by the mentality of the cabaret guests, rich Jews and Anglo-Saxons searching for amusement in the company of women whose favors they expect to win by displaying their wealth and power. They also

---

[6] In our Bibliographical Appendix will be found a list of Sterling Brown's principal publications.

[7] *Southern Road*, pp. 115-18.

seek to demonstrate this power by shamelessly assuming the role of over-
lords vis-à-vis all the Negroes present. They, on their side, play the part
of circus animals, as they are expected to do. The employees fawn; the
fake "Creole Beauties from New Orleans" pretend to languish for a
birthplace which, in fact, they have never seen and whose proclaimed
happy life, celebrated by the orchestra, is in strange contrast with the
tragic existence that the black people really lead there. But the customers,
the performers, and the people are only three elements in the counterpoint, for the poem, by opposing myth to reality and superiors to inferiors,
also evokes the older polarity of masters and slaves. This is the historic
dimension that endows the poem with its full depth of meaning. In the
end, it is not the poet who condemns and effectively unmasks the whole
falsity of this alleged Negro art; it is instead the people, present on every
page of the poem and by whom, ultimately, the sham is laid bare.

"Children's Children,"[8] another poem in defense of Negro art, is laden
with bitter reproaches addressed to the younger Negro generation who
could no longer distinguish the cheap fakery of the commercial song from
the genuine beauty of the folk song which, in its simplicity and sparseness,
bears the weight of suffering from which it sprang. This disrespectful attitude of the young people of this period toward their racial heritage was
a sort of abdication of their Negro personality, and Brown saw it as analogous to the behavior of young Negro girls who, in order to resemble more
closely their white sisters, lightened their skin color and straightened their
hair.[9] Only ignorance of their own past could explain their willingness so
to depersonalize themselves:

> They have forgotten, they have never known,
> Long days beneath the torrid Dixie sun
> In miasma'd riceswamps;
> The chopping of dried grass, on the third go round
> In strangling cotton;
> Wintry nights in mud-daubed makeshift huts,
> With these songs, sole comfort.[10]

The same bitterness and disillusion seize the poet when, a pilgrim to the
area where Nat Turner's rebellion had raged,[11] he learns that the Negroes

[8] *Ibid.*, pp. 107-8.
[9] If Sterling Brown condemned this practice of women of his race, one reason
probably was that he wanted to show how out of touch with reality certain poets
of the Negro Renaissance were, when they claimed to take pride in their black skin
color.
[10] "Children's Children," *Southern Road*, p. 107.
[11] "Remembering Nat Turner," in Langston Hughes and Arna Bontemps, *The
Poetry of the Negro*, pp. 90-91. On Nat Turner's revolt of August, 1831, see

who live in this historic place today have forgotten the very name of the man who championed their freedom. Only one old white woman could tell anything of Nat, and she mixed up his deeds with those of John Brown. What a humiliation she inflicted on the poet by telling him that the post that had been erected in memory of the sacrifice made by Nat Turner and his companions had rotted away, and that local Negroes had divided up the wood to stoke their kitchen fires! Thus the poet, as he leaves the pilgrimage site, did not think of Nat Turner but of the post allowed to rot, just as the hero's memory had been allowed to die. The wood the Negroes had used as firewood becomes the symbol of the past's heritage on which they still live, even though they despise it. With an exaggerated optimism, many leaders of the race had presented the New Negro as a man with a memory, but Brown destroyed their illusions and directed their attention, on the contrary, to the saddening spectacle of a people forgetful of their past.

As for this past, which many of his predecessors had lauded to the skies, Brown found it to be less uniformly perfect, and alongside such heroes as Nat Turner he discovered other Negroes who were traitors to their race, spies, cowards, and renegades. "Memo: For the Race Orators"[12] emphatically called them to the attention of the race's spokesmen. There was no sense in burying these faithless brothers beneath a conspiracy of silence, for they had numerous progeny, and these must be awakened to their treason's effect on the destiny of the community. At a time when American society as a whole was shaken to its roots and sought those responsible for plunging it overnight from prosperity into indigence, Brown raised his voice to declare that, for the Negro also, the moment of truth had come. He demolished as he rebuilt, for he deemed it necessary that the people should become aware both of their strengths and of their frailties.

2. THE TRAGIC UNIVERSE OF STERLING BROWN

The dominant note in Brown's poetry is provided by his acute understanding of the tragic destiny that had been the black people's on American soil. No one previously had so meticulously orchestrated the dramatic atmosphere in which the characters were to play their parts; no one else had depicted the black man as so alone and powerless, confronting a universe all of whose elements are in league against him and with every avenue of

Roscoe E. Lewis, ed., *The Negro in Virginia,* pp. 178-81, and John Hope Franklin, *From Slavery to Freedom,* p. 211.

[12] For the text of this poem, see our Appendix of hitherto unpublished poems in the original French edition.

escape walled up in advance. Here the tragedy takes on truly global pro-portions, and the scene on which it is played out is no less hermetically sealed than was the closed world of slavery.

The Whites' Conspiracy

In Brown's poetry, the struggle of black against white appears not merely as an unequal battle — this is in full conformity with reality — but as a conspiracy carefully plotted long before and the execution of which pro-ceeds with all the inexorable precision of a piece of clockwork. This theme is worked out in particularly striking fashion in a poem like "Old Lem,"[13] which in its vigor has elements both of Carl Sandburg's somewhat brutal robustness and of the forceful realism of the protest songs of slavery days.[14] In a struggle that finds all the weapons in the hands of one side, neither courage nor even heroism are any use. The result is always foreordained, and the most fanatical resistance will be pulverized in the end. Whether the innocent Negro succumbs to the collective hysteria of a lynch mob set on him ("He Was a Man"[15]), or to the mindless panic of a rookie cop ("Southern Cop"[16]), his murderers will always find official justice on their side.

In a certain sense, Brown's anti-racist poetry may be said to have ceased to protest; it has gone far beyond. Protest takes place not only against, but also on behalf of, something. If Brown's forerunners could protest against the injustice that was victimizing their race, that was because they had faith in the democratic ideal the American nation so eagerly flaunted, and they invoked this ideal in demanding justice. Brown, on the other hand, has already lost all illusions concerning the practical efficacy of the "Amer-ican dream." He no longer believes in any ideal. As Richard Wright will do a little later in his novels, he is set on underlining, with the whole chill rigor of Marxist analysis, the political, social, and economic conditions that mathematically determine, so to speak, the destiny of the Negro within the American nation.

"Master and Man"[17] denounces the shameless exploitation of the black agricultural worker by his white employer, and bitterly traces the parallel

[13] "Old Lem," in Anderson and Walton, eds., *This Generation*, p. 645.
[14] "Old Lem" may be compared, more particularly, with the slave song cited by Brown in *Negro Caravan*, p. 446.
[15] "He Was a Man," in Robert Thomas Kerlin, ed., *Negro Poets and Their Poems*, pp. 259-60.
[16] For the text of this poem, see our Appendix of hitherto unpublished poems in the original French edition.
[17] See note 16.

between the prosperity enjoyed by the latter and the material and moral indigence of his employee.

In "Sam Smiley,"[18] a Negro veteran, who had been taught during World War I that patriotism consisted in killing as many as possible of the white men ahead of him, returned home to find his wife in prison for having killed the child she had had, during Sam's absence, by a rich white. When she died, Sam saw to it that her lover joined her beyond the grave, and he himself ended up dangling from the highest branch of an oak tree for having killed a white.[19]

Like the democratic ideal, the notion of trade-union solidarity seems unable to bring about, in the foreseeable future, a bond of brotherhood between the races. Either of these goals comes to resemble a trap that has been prepared to ensnare the black. It can lead to death; it does not enable him to live. Witness to this fact is the black hero of "Sharecroppers,"[20] shot down by his boss for refusing to reveal the names of the comrades, black and white, whom he had seen at the union meeting. As he gives up his life for his trade-union ideal, he does indeed declare his faith in inter-racial brotherhood — but this, it is quite clear, will not be achieved to-morrow. For the time being, as the specter of unemployment roams the land, white unionists do not hesitate to commit murder in order to get rid of a black locomotive engineer who refused to quit his job in their favor ("Break of Day"[21]). Thus the Negro worker has every reason to feel suspicious when a white union member offers him his hand and proposes an alliance against the bosses ("Colloquy"[22]).

The Black Man and His Fate

Southern Road depicts the Negro as the victim not of the white man alone, but of all that surrounds him. He is enslaved by the land he cultivates, victimized by the lawless natural elements whose predilection it is to fall on him, as he is victimized by his own fear and that of others, and by his own ignorance and credulity. In short he is exposed to a terrible fate whose whole pitiless cruelty is sung in the blues and whose effects the people had always sought to ward off by means of superstitious precepts passed from generation to generation.

[18] *Southern Road*, pp. 36-38.
[19] See also the bitter irony of "Let Us Suppose," the text of which is included in our Appendix of hitherto unpublished poems in the original French edition.
[20] See note 16.
[21] In Anderson and Walton, eds., *This Generation*, p. 648.
[22] *Ibid.*, p. 646.

The black peasant was practically chained to the earth by the cotton fields he cultivated. It was cotton that led to the importation of so many slaves into America, and cotton that for long years, until the recent introduction of labor-saving machinery to handle every aspect of growing and picking the crop, kept millions of Negroes prisoners in the South. It could not even be said that it enabled them to live — on the contrary, it let them go hungry, after good harvests as after bad:

> Ole King Cotton,
> Ole Man Cotton,
> Keeps us slavin'
> Till we'se dead an' rotten.
>
> Bosses us 'roun'
> In his ornery way,
> "Cotton needs pickin'!"[23]
> De Hell he say . . .
>
> Starves us wid bumper crops,
> Starves us wid po',
> Chains de lean wolf
> At our do'.
>
> .   .   .   .
>
> Cotton, cotton,
> All we know;
> Plant cotton, hoe it,
> Baig it to grow;
> What good it do to us
> Gawd only know![24]

The very farm dog is free to seek his fortune elsewhere, if he finds his rations doled out too sparsely. But the children of the black sharecroppers are chained to the farm by that tyrant cotton, just as their parents were:

> Cotton brought them
> And will keep them here.
>
> The spare-ribbed yard-dog
> Has gone away;
> The kids, just as hungry,
> Have to stay.[25]

[23] "Cotton Needs Pickin' " was the title of a song sung at Hampton Institute.
[24] "Old King Cotton," *Southern Road,* pp. 65-66. The author was moved to write this poem after reading Rupert B. Vance's book, *Human Factors in Cotton Culture* (Chapel Hill, 1929).
[25] "The Young Ones"; text of this poem in our Appendix of unpublished poems in the original French edition.

No less fearsome than subjection to "King Cotton" is the constant
menace exerted by the forces of nature upon the toiling black peasant, for
he is at their mercy. "Tornado Blues" provides a striking tableau of the
desolation strewn in its path by a tornado, to which Brown attributes the
traditional prejudices directed against racial minorities. Negroes and Jews
suffer most from the cataclysm, whose approach is depicted, in the style
of some blues songs, as a throbbing pack of giant airplanes:

> Black wind come a-speedin' down de river from de Kansas plains,
> Black wind come a-speedin' down de river from de Kansas plains,
> Black wind come a-roarin' like a flock of giant aeroplanes —
>
> Destruction was a-drivin' it and close behind was Fear,
> Destruction was a-drivin' it and hand in hand with Fear,
> Grinnin' Death and skinny Sorrow was a-bringin' up de rear.
>
> Dey got some ofays, but dey mostly got de Jews an' us,
> Got some ofays, but mostly got de Jews an' us,
> Many po' boys castle done settled to a heap o' dus'.
>
> .   .   .   .
>
> De Black wind evil, done done its dirty work an' gone,
> Black wind evil, done done its dirty work an' gone,
> Lawd help de folks what de wind ain't had no mercy on.[26]

If the tornado doesn't come, then the big river overflows its banks, depriving the Negro peasant of the patiently garnered modest fruits of his
daily labors. The Mississippi steals his arable land, his sticks of furniture,
and the few beasts in his stable; sometimes it even drags away his children
into death, and it does all this traitorously, unannounced, by night and
in secret:

> These know fear; for all their singing
>
> .   .   .   .
>
> These folk know grief.
> They have seen
> Black water gurgling, lapping, roaring,
> Take their lives' earnings, roll off their paltry
> Fixtures of home, things as dear as old hearthgods.
> These have known death
> Surprising, rapacious of cattle, of children,
> Creeping with the black water
> Secretly, unceasingly.

[26] "Tornado Blues," *Southern Road*, pp. 70-71. The poem forms part of a group
of three blues with the collective title "New Saint Louis Blues."

> *Death pick out new ways*
> *Now fo' to come to us,*
> *Black water creepin'*
> *While folks is sleepin',*
> *Death on de black water*
> *Ugly an' treacherous.*[27]

In the boundlessness of their despair, these unfortunate people are capable only of a single futile gesture. Powerlessly they turn to the implacable river and question it, as they would question a human being who had wantonly done them wrong:

> *What we done done to you*
> *Makes you do lak you do?*
> *How we done harmed you*
> *Black-hearted river?*[28]

All these scenes exhale a deep-seated sense of injustice suffered. Uncle Dan puts it all in the simple phrase he addresses to the Missouri, which has just borne off everything he owned:

> *Ain't got no right to act dat way at all!*[29]

Times of trial such as these enable the folk singer to exercise his function in society. For consolation in affliction, all gather to pool their griefs, to hear them sung and bewailed by the designated interpreter of the common despair, the woman blues singer. In a splendid poem dedicated to the great artist Ma Rainey, Brown reveals the close bond of feeling that unites the common people and the woman who, as she sings their distress, moves them to tears and so eases the burden weighing on their hearts:

> When Ma Rainey
> Comes to town,
> Folks from anyplace
> Miles aroun',
> From Cape Girardeau,
> Poplar Bluff,
> Flocks in to hear
> Ma do her stuff;
>
> .   .   .   .

---

[27] "Children of the Mississippi," *ibid.*, pp. 67-69. See, on the same theme, "Riverbank Blues," pp. 99-100; "Foreclosure," pp. 73-74; and "Strange Legacies," p. 96, which piles on top of the natural catastrophes already mentioned, drought, the boll weevil, and hog cholera.

[28] "Children of the Mississippi," *ibid.*, p. 69.

[29] "Foreclosure," *ibid.*, p. 74.

I talked to a fellow, an' the fellow say,
"She jes' catch hold of us, somekindaway.
She sang Backwater Blues one day,

. . . .

An' den de folks, dey natchally bowed dey heads an' cried,
Bowed dey heavy heads, shet dey moufs up tight an' cried,
An' Ma lef' de stage, an' followed some de folks outside."[30]

This harsh destiny, which condemned the folk to physical deprivation, also brought about its moral debasement. In either case, the forces affecting the individual resulted from a concatenation of events that is presented as inevitable, so that we are driven time and again to the implicit conclusion that man has no responsibility whatever for his destiny.

The prostitute in "Market Street Woman" is doubly derelict, in the sense that men no longer even stop to purchase her body; the reason she suffers this humiliation is because "life do her dirty in a hundred onery ways" and because bad luck haunts her irremediably:

Market Street woman is known fuh to have dark days,
Market Street woman noted fuh to have dark days,
Life do her dirty in a hundred onery ways.

. . . .

Put paint on her lips, purple powder on her choklit face,
Paint on her lips, purple powder on her choklit face,
Take mo' dan paint to change de luck of dis dam place.[31]

The central character of "Low Down," sunk in abject poverty and alone in the world since his wife left him and his son went to prison, is also convinced that bad luck dogs him and that, in the game of life he is in the process of losing, somebody has loaded the dice:

Some dirty joker done put a jinx on my po' soul.

Dice are loaded, an' de deck's all marked to hell,
Dice are loaded, de deck's all marked to hell,
Whoever runs dis gamble sholy runs it well.[32]

In "Dark of the Moon," a superstitious folk saying is used to explain the tragic destiny of a family of black farmers. Nothing must be undertaken, it is declared, on a moonless night because, strive as one will, failure is inevitable at such a time:

30 "Ma Rainey," *ibid.*, pp. 62-64.
31 "Market Street Woman," *ibid.*, p. 70. See, on a kindred theme, "Bessie," p. 41.
32 "Low Down," *ibid.*, p. 72.

> Plant a fence post
> On de dark uh de moon,
> Locust, oak, hickory,
> Any uh dose
> Yuh plant it fo' nothin',
> Yuh plant it fo' rottin',
> Is a ole head's sayin',
> An' a ole head knows.[33]

When the farmer's wife dies, the farmer places all his hopes in his son. Dan, who is a handsome youth, intelligent and highly promising, will take over the family farm in his turn. But one fine day, for no apparent reason, Dan falls into evil ways, spending his time in gambling and debauchery. He is dead drunk when his father is carried off to the grave, the victim of his chagrin. The farm is about to be sold, and the old people of the place, thinking of Dan, shake their heads and say:

> *"Must uh been bo'n*
> *On de dark uh de moon."*[34]

Johnny Thomas is a sort of tragic imbecile, his life an unbroken chain of catastrophes: he is kicked out of school and beaten by his father until the blood flows, whereupon he leaves home. He falls into the clutches of a trollop who extorts his last nickel from him and then pushes him into gambling and finally into murder. In the prison work camp where he has been sent to expiate his crime, he splits the skull of a warden who had been harassing him. He ends with a rope around his neck:

> Dropped him in de hole
> Threw the slack lime on,
> Oughta had mo' sense
> Dan to evah git born.[35]

Thus, as in many traditional blues, it is the woman who serves as instrument of fate. Her frivolousness brings misfortune to the man who, like Dan or Johnny Thomas,[36] lets himself be trapped by her wiles. But the outcome is equally fatal for the man who withstands feminine seductiveness. When we first hear of Georgie Grimes,[37] he is running away holding a suitcase as red as the crime he has just committed. He killed the woman

[33] "Dark of the Moon," *ibid.,* p. 19.
[34] *Ibid.,* p. 20. See also, on children who come to no good, "Maumee Ruth," p. 10.
[35] "Johnny Thomas," *ibid.,* p. 33.
[36] On the same theme, see "Pardners," *ibid.,* p. 81.
[37] "Georgie Grimes," *ibid.,* p. 22.

he blamed for his bad luck, but this does not change it, since here he is, pursued by a fear which, we well realize, will never leave him.

Love turns into an even more tragic misadventure when the lovers are not of the same race, as Brown seeks to demonstrate in his new version of the traditional ballad "Frankie and Johnny." Frankie might have come straight out of a novel by Erskine Caldwell. The daughter of a poor white, mentally retarded, cruel, and perverse, she never ceases to provoke Johnny, the black day-laborer, in the field where he is working. But after giving herself to him she tells her father, well knowing what her lover's fate will be:

> They swung up Johnny on a tree, and filled his swinging
>   hide with lead,
> And Frankie yowled hilariously when the thing was done.[38]

No poem more pathetically depicts the despair of the entire race than "Southern Road," a convict song in which the old lag relates in staccato fashion, in blues lines interrupted by his panting, his accursed destiny:

> Swing dat hammer — hunh —
> Steady, bo';
> Swing dat hammer — hunh —
> Steady, bo';
> Ain't no rush, bebby,
> Long ways to go.
>
> Burner tore his — hunh —
> Black heart away;
> Burner tore his — hunh —
> Black heart away;
> Got me life, bebby,
> An' a day.
>
> Gal's on Fifth Street — hunh —
> Son done gone;
> Gal's on Fifth Street — hunh —
> Son done gone;
> Wife's in de ward, bebby,
> Babe's not bo'n.
>
> My ole man died — hunh —
> Cussin' me;

[38] "Frankie and Johnny," *ibid.*, pp. 34-35. It is possible not to share the view of Louis Untermeyer when, in an otherwise highly favorable review of *Southern Road,* he speaks of "his unsuccessful variation of 'Frankie and Johnny,' a ballad which any genuine lover of folk-songs ought to let alone" ("New Light from an Old Mine," *Opportunity,* August, 1932, p. 250).

My ole man died — hunh —
Cussin' me;
Ole lady rocks, bebby,
Huh misery.

Doubleshackled — hunh —
Guard behin';
Doubleshackled — hunh —
Guard behin';
Ball an' chain, bebby,
On my min'.

White man tells me — hunh —
Damn yo' soul;
White man tells me — hunh —
Damn yo' soul;
Got no need, bebby,
To be tole.

Chain gang nevah — hunh —
Let me go;
Chain gang nevah — hunh —
Let me go;
Po' los' boy, bebby,
Evahmo' . . .[39]

The Negro Renaissance has furnished us with no other example of such virile despair. Here the entire spirit of revolt is already snuffed out and transcended, since it is seen as useless, and there is a stoic acceptance of destiny. Confronting a hostile universe, the black man knows that he is dolefully alone and has no surviving connection with an outside world that might offer him help or a gleam of hope.

As if to underline this isolation, the theme of Africa is utterly missing in Brown's work.[40] His black folk never utter the name of the land of their ancestors; they await from it neither sustenance nor consolation.

The Inanity of Faith

But their isolation is primarily metaphysical. No doubt at times they imagine God to be an ally, but this is mere illusion. For Brown, the facts made it their business a long time ago to demonstrate the opposite. Not only is God no friend of the Negro; he is not even his enemy. He remains totally indifferent to the black man's lot — that is, if he exists. From this

[39] "Southern Road," *Southern Road*, pp. 46-47. See, on a related theme, "Convict," *ibid.*, pp. 93-94.

[40] See, however, the opening lines of "Strong Men," *ibid.*, p. 51.

agnostic (or perhaps even atheistic) viewpoint, belief becomes futile and man is powerless to influence his own destiny, which increases the tragic character of his predicament.

The poet finds the true philosophy of existence on the lips of a fool who imagines he has received the command to carry the Word from village to village:

> *"You gotta walk that lonesome valley,*
> *You gotta walk it by yo'self,*
> *Nobody heah can a-walk it for you*
> *You gotta walk it by yo'self."*
>
> .   .   .
>
> *"Man wanta live,*
> *Man wanta find himself*
> *Man gotta learn*
> *How to go alone."*
>
> .   .   .
>
> "If man's life goes
> Beyond the bone
> Man must go lonely
> And alone,
> Unhelped, unhindered
> On his own . . ."[41]

Everyday reality cruelly belies the promises God made to his people in the Bible. Thus the victims of the Mississippi floods regard the story of Noah as a fable that has no relevance for them:

> *De Lord tole Norah*
> *Dat de flood was due,*
> *Norah listened to de Lord*
> *An' got his stock on board,*
> *Wish dat de Lord*
> *Had tole us too.*[42]

As a consequence, though they will not yet admit it, the people lend their ear to the whisperings of doubt.

> These, for all their vaunted faith, know doubt
> These know no Ararat;
> No arc of promise bedecking blue skies;
> No dove, betokening calm;[43]

[41] "Revelations," *ibid.*, p. 98.
[42] "Children of the Mississippi," *ibid.*, pp. 67-68.
[43] *Ibid.* See also this passage in "Cabaret," p. 117: "In Mississippi / The black folk huddle, mute, uncomprehending, / Wondering 'how come the good Lord /

God may be, as it is said, the ruler of the earth. If so, then he is an absentee master, no less rich than uncaring, who leaves the management of his estate to his steward the devil:

> God may be the owner,
> But he's rich and forgetful,
> And far away.[44]

When his promises do turn out to be true, sometimes it is in a back-handed way that involves tragic irony. "Chillen Get Shoes" is a bitterly cynical paraphrase of the spiritual "All God's Chillun Got Shoes," in which the people's faith pictured Providence as a huge hand-out of robes, shoes, and wings. In Brown's poem, on the contrary, if the little girl who envies Moll's shoes can be assured of one day having shoes just like them, that is because, like Moll, she has every likelihood of falling into prostitution:

> Hush little Lily,
>   Don't you cry;
> You'll get your silver slippers
>   Bye and bye.
>
> Moll wears silver slippers
>   With red heels,
> And men come to see her
>   In automobiles.
>
> Lily walks wretched,
>   Dragging her doll,
> Worshipping stealthily
>   Good-time Moll;
>
> Envying bitterly
>   Moll's fine clothes,
> And her plump legs clad
>   In openwork hose.
>
> Don't worry, Lily,
>   Don't you cry;
> You'll be like Moll, too,
>   Bye and bye.[45]

Could treat them this a way.' " See, furthermore, the poem "Crossing," the text of which is in our Appendix of hitherto unpublished poems in the original French edition.

[44] "Arkansas Chant"; text of this poem in our Appendix of unpublished poems in the original French edition.

[45] "Chillen Get Shoes," *Southern Road*, p. 110. The text of the spiritual "All God's Chillun Got Shoes" may be read in James Weldon Johnson, *Book of American Negro Spirituals*, I, 71.

The pointlessness of the hope the Negro had traditionally placed in God is underlined by the repetition of "bye and bye," the expression used in many spirituals to characterize the unspecified time when God would deliver his people:

> Bye and bye, I'm gonna lay down dis heavy load.[46]

"Rent Day Blues"[47] is a poem in the same key: when a couple no longer has enough money to pay the rent, the Lord in his mercy providentially makes available a handful of dollars; but the hint is clear that the daughter in the poem had obtained the money by prostituting herself, so that the devil is partly to be thanked that faith in Providence met with some measure of response.

The arraignment of faith as lacking material efficacy has always been a major theme in Negro poetry, but to it Brown adds his own greater bitterness and more chilling cynicism. One needs no great perspicacity to recognize in his manner the influence of the Marxist ideology that, under the impact of the years of economic crisis following the 1929 crash, came to have an ever greater appeal for Negro intellectuals — writers, economists, and sociologists alike.[48]

This hones to a sharper edge his satire of the Negro clergy. His pastors are no longer the harmless casuists of an Edwin Campbell or a J. Mord Allen, but exploiters from whom the people can expect no help.[49] When fun is poked at them, the humor is grim, and their behavior is usually not so much entertaining as revolting. The preacher in "Checkers"[50] is not satisfied merely to gamble; he mixes with gangsters and more than matches their foul language. The Negro bishop in "Slim Hears the Call"[51] is himself a onetime gangster who had discovered the ministry to be more rewarding. His ignorance did not prevent his growing outrageously rich at the cost of his credulous flock, thanks to "a pint of good sense, an' a bushel of bluff." He now has a wife who is "as purty as sin" and a secretary "twict as purty again," and he brazenly looks on the luxury with which

[46] Text of a spiritual cited by Brown in Langston Hughes and Arna Bontemps, eds., *The Book of Negro Folklore,* p. 287.

[47] This poem was published in Benjamin Albert Botkin, ed. *Folk-Say IV* (1932), section entitled "The Devil and the Black Man," pp. 246-56.

[48] In this connection, it is to be noted also that Brown, in his many discussions of the spirituals, always insisted upon the temporal meaning of the songs. See, for example, *Negro Poetry and Drama,* pp. 18ff.

[49] "Low Down," stanza 4, *Southern Road,* p. 72.

[50] *Ibid.,* p. 75.

[51] For this poem, see our Appendix of unpublished poems in the original French edition.

he has no trouble in surrounding himself as a concrete sign of heaven's approval and benediction of his ways.[52]

Who is to be blamed for this exploitation of the people? Whites, assuredly, who had taught Negroes "the religion they disgraced,"[53] but also the enduring, ineluctable concatenation of circumstances that keeps the people too ignorant to realize the uselessness of religious belief. The farmers in "The Young Ones," nailed to the earth by the cotton that lets them go hungry and extenuated by a plethora of children, are too stupid to accept the evidence that they are slaves. They persist in thanking the Lord for his alleged favors:

> Another mouth to feed,
> Another body to bed,
> Another to grow up
> Underfed.
>
> But their pappy's happy
> And they hear him say:
> "The good Lord giveth,
> And taketh away.
>
> "It's two more hands
> For to carry a row;
> Praise God from whom
> All blessings flow."[54]

Yet, while deploring the ignorance of the people, Brown has no blame to distribute because, in the first place, he knows that the people are not responsible for their own ignorance. Furthermore — and his attitude, in this, links up with that of James Weldon Johnson and Langston Hughes — he so greatly respects Negro folklore that he could not have wished to ban the especially abundant source of inspiration that, he realized, the people had always found in religious emotion. If this naïve faith had no other merit, at least it had developed the picturesque imagery in which the people sought to garb its overly simple notions of the beyond. Though it is replete with contradictions, beyond a doubt, the poet is moved to exhibit toward it an indulgence much like that felt by adults for the dreams of a child.[55]

[52] See also the poem "Slim in Hell," stanza 18, in Anderson and Walton, eds., *This Generation*, p. 648, in which Slim, whom the devil has invited to look around Hell, sees in one room a Baptist preacher with a girl on either knee.

[53] "Strong Men," *Southern Road*, p. 51. See also "Bitter Fruit of the Tree," in Anderson and Walton, eds., *This Generation*, p. 646, esp. lines 5-8.

[54] "The Young Ones"; text in our Appendix of unpublished poems in the original French edition.

[55] See, more particularly, in the poem "When de Saints Go Ma'ching Home"

Above all else, however, Brown shares the view that religion is the opium of the people, and what more soothing balm for suffering could he name? The people's illusions are better left intact, as with old Maumee Ruth who, lying on her death bed, knows nothing of the depraved existence that her son and daughter, degraded by drugs and drink, are living in the city:

> Preach her the lies about
> Jordan, and then

> Might as well drop her
> Deep in the ground,
> Might as well pray for her,
> That she sleep sound . . .[56]

Another consideration is that the people need to cherish the conviction of having, in religion and superstitious practices, an effective way to steer their own destiny. This illusion of power, though perhaps warding off despair, is nonetheless in tragic contrast with the reality of powerlessness.

Thus Scotty threatens, through the use of all sorts of magic powders made of pulverized black cat bones, to annihilate the whites who have been overworking his girl friend:

> Whuh folks, whuh folks; don' wuk muh brown too hahd!
> 'Cause Ise crazy 'bout muh woman,
> An' ef yuh treats huh mean,
> I gonna sprinkle goofy dus'
> In yo' soup tureen.

> •   •   •   •

> I got me a Blackcat's wishbone,
> Got some Blackcat's ankle dus',
> An' yuh crackers better watch out
> Ef I sees yo' carcass fus' —[57]

(*Southern Road,* pp. 12-18), a long description of the elect entering Paradise, as imagined by a wandering Negro piano player, who is dreaming as he plays the spiritual from which the poem borrows its title. His Paradise is essentially a turning of the tables by blacks against whites who, he dreams, will not be allowed to enter Paradise because of their wickedness. But then he remembers a white railroad man who once let him travel in a freight car, and he recalls another fine man who gave him food and shelter. And what will he do with the Yankee captain who lost his leg at Vicksburg? They must all find their place in Paradise: ". . . Mought be a place, he said, / Mought be another mansion fo' white saints, / A smaller one than his'n . . . not so gran'." As for the others, they can all go to Hell. See also, on a similar theme, "Sister Lou," *ibid.,* pp. 48-50, and "Virginia Portrait," pp. 27-28, last four lines.

[56] "Maumee Ruth," *ibid.,* pp. 10-11.

[57] "Scotty Has His Say," *ibid.,* pp. 23-24. Contrasting with this poem, which stresses the old-time superstitions, are "Old Man Buzzard" (pp. 29-30), in which

But these gestures are no less inefficacious than those the characters in "Memphis Blues" talked of making, in the event that Memphis should be wiped out by a tornado or swept away by the Mississippi:

> Watcha gonna do when Memphis on fire,
>   Memphis on fire, Mistah Preachin' Man?
> Gonna pray to Jesus and nebber tire,
>   Gonna pray to Jesus, loud as I can,
>   Gonna pray to my Jesus, oh, my Lawd!
>
> Watcha gonna do when de tall flames roar,
>   Tall flames roar, Mistah Lovin' Man?
> Gonna love my brownskin better'n before —
>   Gonna love my baby lak a do right man,
>   Gonna love my brown baby, oh, my Lawd!
>
> Watcha gonna do when Memphis falls down,
>   Memphis falls down, Mistah Music Man?
> Gonna plunk on dat box as long as it soun',
>   Gonna plunk dat box fo' to beat de ban',
>   Gonna tickle dem ivories, oh, my Lawd![58]

Then come, one after the other, the laborer who will push his wheelbarrow more vigorously than ever on that day; the drinker, cork in hand, who will empty his last bottle of whisky; the gambler who will roll his last seven. By placing on the same level the pastor's prayer and the actions of the five other characters, Brown seeks to show us that all of them are equally futile and powerless.

3. Means for Survival

Thus the Negro's destiny, as presented in Brown's work, is ultimately a depressing one. But his outlook strikes us as significantly more pessimistic than that of his predecessors because he practically excludes the spiritual forces from his universe. In some obscure way, a vital bond still subsisted between the black man and God in the writings of James Weldon Johnson and Langston Hughes. Sterling Brown, on the contrary, makes the situation

---

Fred, a Negro of the new generation, refuses to pay any attention to the dire predictions with which the buzzard tries to undermine his confidence in the future; "Conjured" (in Anderson and Walton, eds., *This Generation*, p. 645), which pokes innocuous fun at folk superstitions; and "Seeking Religion" (*Southern Road*, p. 21), a humorous paraphrase of the type of conversion customary in Negro folk churches. This poem was no doubt inspired by a short story by Dunbar, "Anner 'Lizer's Stumblin' Block," printed in Dunbar, *Folks from Dixie*, whose content is almost identical.

[58] "Memphis Blues," sec. 2, stanzas 1-3, *Southern Road,* pp. 59-61.

entirely clear: the black man suddenly finds himself isolated and must derive his whole strength from the people, who thus become the sole source of all true value.

Yet the people had never been more roughly criticized; all in all, the Negro could scarcely have survived the many antagonistic forces arrayed against him, had he not been able to call on a number of secret springs of resilience so that he could entertain at least the illusion of possessing a way out. Thus in Brown's poetry, as in that of the earlier poets, the possibility of escape continues to be an important means of survival for the black man.

When the big river overflows and threatens to destroy the black farmer and everything he owns, there is but one thing left for him to do, and that is to go away. The Negro of "Riverbank Blues," sitting on the bank of the Missouri, hears the river speak to him and urge him to stay. But he knows that the waters are treacherous, and something within him whispers that he had better depart:

> Dat is what it tole me as I watched it slowly rollin',
> But somp'n way inside me rared up an' say,
> *"Better be movin' ... better be travellin' ...*
> *Riverbank'll git you ef you stay ..."*[59]

The Negro of "Tin Roof Blues," disappointed by the inhuman city, expresses the antithetical desire to return to the land, where he may find once more a life setting with a scale that better befits a human being,

> ... de livin' what a man kin understand.[60]

"Long Gone" exemplifies the need to escape in its purest form. The speaker in the poem is a man

> With a itch fo' travelin'
> He cain't understan' ...[61]

He likes his home, where he is happy and loved, but his destiny repeatedly urges him on to other scenes and other people.

But there is no need to displace oneself geographically in order to escape. Thus Mose, saddened at having neither sweetheart, nor money,

59 "Riverbank Blues," *ibid.*, p. 100.
60 "Tin Roof Blues," *ibid.*, p. 105.
61 "Long Gone," *ibid.*, pp. 8-9. It may be noted that the recording of this poem by the author (reference in note 1 above) contains one stanza more than the text to be found in *Southern Road*. Long Gone is a traditional figure in Negro folklore, where he is sometimes known as Long Gone John. See also "Odyssey of Big Boy," *ibid.*, pp. 5-7.

nor fine clothes, turns to music to forget the dullness of his life as driver of a coal truck:

> . . . summer evenings
> Hard luck Mose
> Goes in for all
> The fun he knows.
>
> On the corner kerb
> With a sad quartette
> His tenor peals
> Like a clarinet.
>
> *O hit it Moses*
> *Sing att thing*
> But Mose's mind
> Goes wandering; —[62]

"Sporting Beasley"[63] finds compensation for his frustration in gaudy attire. Wearing a top hat, a Prince Albert coat, patent leather shoes, and white spats, and with a red carnation in his buttonhole, he flaunts it like a lord as he twirls his cane. He no longer inhabits the earth; he lives in an imagined world entirely of his own invention, in which he has endowed himself with a new identity. Scrappy ("Puttin' on Dog"[64]), a similar type, tries to dazzle those around him by wearing a silk shirt "pink as a sunset," skyblue suspenders, and red shoes.

All these personages, when their lives have become unlivable, find in escape a means of withstanding despair.

As for the poet himself, does he differ from them to any great extent? It would have been easy to understand, had the disillusioning portrait of the black man that he has painted for us ended in despair. The reason this does not occur is that he too has hit upon a way of escaping from an appalling reality. For it is an art of living that he has discovered in the humorous philosophy in which his race is steeped, and it may be more than a coincidence that Brown, the poet of the Negro Renaissance who most pitilessly excludes from his universe the whole range of religious forces, is at the same time the only truly humorous poet in the group.

Alongside its tragic depiction of the universe, *Southern Road* also offers us the light relief of its comic aspects. Yet in these two veins the themes

---

[62] "Mose," *ibid.*, p. 77. See, on alcohol as a way of escape, "Kentucky Blues," pp. 42-43.

[63] *Ibid.*, pp. 113-14.

[64] "Puttin' on Dog," in "The Devil and the Black Man" (reference in note 47 above).

are the same, as though stressing the fact that tragedy and comedy are linked and that, as the famous Negro folk song has it, laughter is a way of avoiding tears.[65] Thus humor marks the poet's resolve to break out of the fatal circle,[66] and to find in spite of all a way out on the hither side of despair.

Among all his humorous poems, in which he exercises his comic vein at the expense of whites no less than of blacks, the most remarkable are assuredly those which relate the adventures of Slim Greer. By creating this new hero of the tall tale, Brown provided Paul Bunyan and John Henry with a younger brother fully worthy of them. For Slim shows extraordinary skill in extracting himself from the most unbelievable situations. He brings to naught the vigilance of the most vigilant, and at the same time exposes the oddities of the people he brushes up against.

Thus he succeeds, in Arkansas, in passing as a white man, though his skin color is "no lighter than a dark midnight." The white woman he set up house with thinks he is a Spaniard or a Frenchman. He is found out at last, not because of his color, but through his way of playing the blues:

> An' he started a-tinklin'
> Some mo'nful blues,
> An' a-pattin' the time
> With No. Fourteen shoes.

> The cracker listened
> An' then he spat
> An' said, "No white man
> Could play like that ..."[67]

But he is more agile than the whites and makes his getaway, of course without suffering the least hurt.

"Slim Lands a Job" mocks the demands that southern white employers make of their black employees. Slim is going to be hired as a waiter in a restaurant whose owner is complaining about the slowness of the Negro he already employs, when the latter bursts into the room:

> A noise rung out
> In rush a man
> Wid a tray on his head
> An' one in each han'

[65] See Ch. 1, note 20.

[66] On humor, R. Escarpit has this to say: "It is the desire to break, and at the same time a means of breaking, the circle of automatisms which the deadly maternalism of life in society and, simply, life cause to crystallize around us, as a protection and as a shroud" (*L'Humour* [Paris, 1960], p. 127).

[67] "Slim Greer," *Southern Road,* p. 84.

> Wid de silver in his mouf
> An' de soup plates in his vest
> Pullin' a red wagon
> Wid all de rest . . .
>
> De man's said, "Dere's
> Dat slow coon now
> Dat wuthless lazy waiter!"
> An' Slim says, "How?"
>
> An' Slim threw his gears in
> Put it in high,
> An' kissed his hand to Arkansaw,
> Sweetheart . . . good-bye![68]

We meet Slim again in Atlanta, where the whites have passed laws "for to keep all de niggers from laughin' outdoors":

> Hope to Gawd I may die
> If I ain't speakin' truth
> Make de niggers do deir laughin'
> In a telefoam booth.[69]

When told about this rule on his arrival in Atlanta, he feels he is going to explode with laughter. He barely has time to skip past the queue waiting outside the phone booth and to dash inside — after dragging out the Negro who was there already. He laughs for hours on end, and the Negroes waiting in the lengthening queue groan in anguish as they wait their turn. In the end, Slim has to be taken away in an ambulance at the state's expense, so that things may return to normal in Atlanta.

Upon arriving in Paradise,[70] Slim is entrusted by Saint Peter with the job of inspecting Hell. In the description of his departure, and then of his visit to the various regions, Brown proves a master humorist. His gallery of portraits is reminiscent of a large fresco of Dubout's, in which each detail is a miracle of audacious suggestivity. Representatives of every vice pass before our eyes: gamblers, debauchees, the shameless, hypocritical preacher, the sellers of moonshine. By degrees, these tableaux begin to seem vaguely familiar, and Slim himself cannot refrain from commenting:

> . . . "Dis makes
> Me think of home —

[68] "Slim Lands a Job," *ibid.*, pp. 86-87. For another humorous poem on the relationship between white employers and black employees, see "Ruminations of Luke Johnson," pp. 25-26.

[69] "Slim in Atlanta," *ibid.*, p. 88.

[70] "Slim in Hell," reference in note 47 above. The poem is also printed in Anderson and Walton, eds., *This Generation*, pp. 647-48.

> Vicksburg, Little Rock, Jackson,
> Waco, and Rome"[71]

Immediately the devil laughs loudly and "turned into a cracker, wid a sheriff's star." Slim barely has time to escape and make his way back to Saint Peter, to whom he shamefacedly confesses that he has no report to make, since he had mixed up the South and Hell:

> Then Peter say, "You must
> Be crazy, I vow,
> Where'n hell dja think Hell *was*
> Anyhow?
>
> "Git on back to de yearth,
> Cause I got de fear,
> You'se a leetle too dumb,
> Fo' to stay up here . . ."[72]

But whites are not the only victims of the poet's mockery, and Brown's humor, where his own race is concerned, sometimes is so bitter that it borders on cynicism. This is true, for instance, of "Slim Hears the Call,"[73] which satirizes the black preachers who grow rich at the people's expense, and also of "Crispus Attucks McKoy,"[74] a mock-heroic poem which criticizes the excessive susceptibility and the misplaced patriotism of certain Negroes.

Sterling Brown's humor is never far removed from stoicism, and while the humorist wards off the blows inflicted by inequality in the immediate present, the stoic can glimpse the day when all the inequalities in the world will be reduced to nothing, once and for all, by that great equalizer Death.

In the parallel established between the rich white man and the poor black man in "Mister Samuel and Sam,"[75] the poet notes that in this world they are already equal in more than one respect. One of them drives a Cadillac and the other a little old Ford, but both cars break down; both of them make long speeches and say very little, one in the Chamber of Commerce and the other in his small Negro church; one goes into bank-

[71] *Ibid.*
[72] *Ibid.*
[73] For the text of this poem, see our Appendix of hitherto unpublished poems in the original French edition. See also pp. 493-94 above.
[74] This poem has not been published. For another humorous handling of the theme of lynching, see "A Bad, Bad Man," in "The Devil and the Black Man," reference in note 47 above.
[75] *Southern Road*, pp. 44-45.

ruptcy and the other hasn't a coin to bless himself with, but what difference does it make? When Mr. Samuel dies, everyone will know; Sam will die without any fuss. But the world will go on as before, and the two of them will be nothing but poor lost boys.

Stoicism and fatalism join hands in the beautiful "Memphis Blues":

> Nineveh, Tyre,
> Babylon,
> Not much lef'
> Of either one.
> All dese cities
> Ashes and rust,
> De win' sing sperrichals
> Through deir dus'...
> Was another Memphis
> Mongst de olden days,
> Done been destroyed
> In many ways...
> Dis here Memphis
> It may go;
> Floods may drown it;
> Tornado blow;
> Mississippi wash it
> Down to sea —
> Like de other Memphis in
> History.
>
> .   .   .   .
>
> Memphis go
> By Flood or Flame;
> Nigger won't worry
> All de same —
> Memphis go
> Memphis come back,
> Ain' no skin
> Off de nigger's back.
> All dese cities
> Ashes, rust...
> De win' sing sperrichals
> Through deir dus'.[76]

Like the gift of laughter to hide the tears, this male serenity in the face of adversity is one of the essential qualities of the race. If the black man has been able to resist a hostile universe and emerge victorious after more

---

[76] *Ibid.*, sec. 1 and 3, pp. 59-61. On this poem, see also p. 496 above.

than three hundred years, it is because he has had the courage to begin ever anew, even when all hope seemed lost:

> "Guess we'll give it one mo' try."[77]

Even beyond this, it is the actual fire of adversity that has forged the courage of strong men, whose irresistible advance not even all the humiliations and cruelties could bring to a halt:

> The strong men keep a-comin' on
> The strong men git stronger.[78]

What the black man was able to achieve yesterday, he can achieve again. Thus it is a profound faith in the continuity of the people and in their inexhaustible resources that finally leads the poet to hope, in spite of all:

> And yet we know relief will come some day
> For these seared breasts; and lads as brave again
> Will plant and find a fairer crop than ours.
> It must be due our hearts, our minds, our powers;
> These are the beacons to blaze out the way.[79]

[77] "Strange Legacies," *ibid.*, p. 96.

[78] "Strong Men," *ibid.*, pp. 51-53. This theme of the "strong men who keep a-comin' on" is found in several of Sandburg's poems, and Brown took it over from him. But it is also an inspirational idea for the Negro Renaissance. Because of his independence from the Harlem group (see, on this, note 3 above), and also because of his critical attitude toward the optimism of racial leaders, Brown made only a limited use of these themes. See, nevertheless, "To Sallie, Walking" (*ibid.*, pp. 39-40), which is a paean to the pride and attractiveness of the black woman. The same theme is at the base of the tall tale narrative poem "Glory, Glory" (Anderson and Walton, eds., *This Generation*, p. 649). On the need for a racial New Deal, see "Transfer" (*ibid.*, pp. 644-45). "Bitter Fruit of the Tree" (pp. 646-47) established the New Negro's refusal to accept white folks' traditional hocus-pocus, just as "Old Man Buzzard" (see note 57 above) recorded his rejection of the oldtime superstitions.

[79] "Salutamus," *Southern Road,* p. 123.

Chapter Twelve: CONCLUSION

Perhaps we may be allowed, by way of conclusion, to return briefly to our starting point and, at the close of our investigation, to examine the validity of our working hypothesis. The hypothesis of a reciprocal dependency, of greater or lesser immediacy, between racial and religious feeling was indeed the guiding idea behind our research. The plan of the book reflects it in some measure, and in the writing it was our constant concern never to let it disappear completely from sight.

That such a reciprocal relationship does indeed exist has been amply demonstrated by the analyses we have undertaken. In the case neither of folk poetry nor of written poetry is it enough to speak of a mere coexistence of the racial and religious themes. For always the moment arrives when the two themes become tied in a kind of vital knot, either because the racial problems force their way onto the metaphysical or moral level, or because the exigencies of religious faith bring about a change of direction or emphasis in the racial feeling.

Our introductory chapter dealt at sufficient length with the origins of this symbiosis. While noting its existence, we were obliged at the same time to stress its fragility, the responsibility for which rests directly on the contradictory terms that were employed in passing on to the slave the message of Christianity. We observed, more especially, that the spirituals did not always express religious feeling and that, in the secular songs, religious phraseology was sometimes utilized for the utterance of blasphemies and obscenities. Thus, prior to Emancipation, there had already taken place what must be called a secularization or, if the barbarous neologism is permissible, a racialization of religious feeling. Through a phenomenon of transference, God had come to be regarded as a member of the master race, which did not prevent Christianity from remaining, in the eyes of the oppressed, a vow that one day they would be set free. This resulted in the paradox of a God who was simultaneously friend and enemy, and thus we understand why, in the work of such twentieth-century black poets as Countee Cullen, Langston Hughes, and others, God was depicted sometimes as white and sometimes as black. In this fashion the religious problem was tightly enmeshed in the racial problem and to this day continues to be involved with it, even in writers such as James Weldon Johnson and Sterling Brown, who have shed their faith.

In the cases of Johnson and Dunbar we discovered, furthermore, that religious poetry fulfilled yet another function which may, perhaps, be traced back to slavery days. The master, as he listened to his slaves sing of the happiness awaiting them in the next world, may have told himself with a sigh of relief that they were not brooding on their wretched state here below and were not conspiring to find some way of escape. So the supposition is justified that, on occasion, a facsimile of religious emotion served to hide the slaves' true thoughts from their masters. In this sense a feigned religiosity may serve as a camouflage, much as humor does. In the absence of convincing counterarguments, this explanation may be considered valid for the orthodox religious poetry of Dunbar and Johnson. Not only did the religious conformism of these poets mask the antagonism they felt toward white people; it also testified to their deliberately sought identification with both the racial community and the national one.[1]

But really major choices were reserved for the following generation, the generation that entered upon the scene after the dislocation of the socio-religious order caused by Emancipation had exerted its full effect on people's minds. The religion of slavery, still current in the twentieth century in the folk churches, was now viewed as "the opium of the people" and as a brake on true emancipation. At the same time the folk, rehabilitated by the Negro Renaissance, advanced to the foreground, for in the folk lay the hope of tomorrow, which had to be defended against every enemy, including religious obscurantism. More than that, the folk became a value in its own right and was bound, by a seemingly natural development, to displace Christian values on the throne. Between God and the race, one felt constrained to choose.

----

[1] In this one can recognize another form of the psychic ambivalence whose terms are, on the one side, admiration for the white man, desire to resemble him, self-hatred, and, on the other side, hatred of the white man, self-pride.

Sterling Brown most forthrightly and most exclusively opted for race, while Langston Hughes, who took his stand only after lengthy deliberation, almost at once backtracked to a compromise position that left him close to the people but did not involve any definitive renunciation of Christian values. Neither for him nor for Brown was the choice accompanied by a real crisis of conscience, and this leads one to surmise that in the people they found an alternative value sufficient to meet their needs.

Why was this not equally true for McKay, Toomer, and Cullen? Were their spiritual demands perhaps less easily satisfied? There is no shortage of more specific explanations. They can all be summed up in the fact that these three men were much more thoroughly steeped in Western culture than were the others. McKay had been brought up like an Englishman. Even during what he referred to as his pagan period, he had come under the influence of the Church of England while, concurrently, his British mentor initiated him into Western rationalism. Cullen had received all his education in white schools and colleges, and the same holds true at least for Toomer's college experience. Finally, these three are unique in having studied abroad, and in France in particular.

If it does no more, the example of these three writers shows us that the spiritual conflict cannot be separated from the cultural conflict. One even reaches the conviction — and this might well be the gist of our conclusions — that this open or latent conflict between racial and religious feeling, which we have shown to exist in all the black poets we have studied, basically amounts to a cultural conflict. If the latter does not actually present itself as the opposition of Negro culture and Western culture, but appears masked as the irrational clash of the black race with the Christian religion, two reasons may be deemed responsible. On the one hand, Christianity was the first and, for a long time, the sole element in Western culture offered to the Negro. Thus it was inevitable that, in the Negro's eyes, the Christian God should have come to symbolize the slave master's twin face, both hostile and benevolent, and that of the white man and of his culture in general.[2] Besides, when the black poet took the oblique path of expressing in the form of hostility to God the pent-up aggressiveness which he did not choose to direct openly against the white man, he was only making a particular application of a spontaneous adaptive mechanism

[2] In any event Freud, in *The Future of an Illusion* (1928), had traced the idea of God back to the idealization of the father, wielder of authority and dispenser of everything necessary for the child's existence. These functions were also those of the master vis-à-vis the slave. And even in our day, in some instances, they have been those exercised by the white man with respect to the black. See Abram Kardiner and Lionel Ovesey, *The Mark of Oppression: A Psychosocial Study of the American Negro*, pp. 349ff.

well known to the psychologists, which allows the individual to survive in an inimical environment.

Let there be no misunderstanding, though. To state, as we have done, that the conflict between racial and religious feeling is basically a cultural conflict by no means justifies the inference that there is no such thing as a genuine spiritual conflict. In all our poets, with the possible exception of Toomer, this conflict is clearly apparent. Indeed, the spiritual conflict is the occasion and the rallying ground upon which the racial and cultural conflict tends to be centered — as, we believe, has emerged particularly clearly from our study of Countee Cullen. Yet it is still impossible to assert which of these conflicts precedes the other, for as the two cultures confront each other within a man's mind, the problem of evil is also there, imperiously demanding an answer.[3]

Again, the spiritual conflict leads the two groups of poets to very different conclusions. They all regard the traditional religion of the black masses as totally outworn, but while the folklorists reject the guardianship of a God conniving with the whites and claim to seek a more complete emancipation for their own people, on the other hand the spiritualists spurn the kind of Christianity that the black masses have debased and diminished by bringing God down to the level of their own mediocrity, almost totally evacuating its metaphysical content. Perhaps, too, they cannot accept God and the people as antagonistic values since, implicitly, the two of them would thus be established as equals and since, ultimately, this would amount to deifying the people, as some European totalitarian nationalisms have done.

Thus it is very largely over their evaluation of the people that the two groups of poets we have discerned find themselves at odds. For one group, the people are the source of all value, while for the other they are looked upon almost as a major obstacle to the spiritual emancipation of the individual and as a hindrance to his achieving integration in the vaster community of Western culture.

These spiritual considerations should not be overlooked in any assessment of the problems of literary expression to which we have repeatedly had occasion to refer. One is indeed led to believe that the discussions over

[3] Yet it is quite clear that, depending on the individual personality, one problem or another may take precedence. In this respect, it is worth mentioning that, in the poetry we have examined, the nostalgia for Africa takes shape only in those writers who have had no close contact with the soil. It is not manifested in McKay who, throughout his life, remained strongly attached to his Jamaican earth; nor in Toomer, who re-created for himself a bond with the soil of Georgia; nor in Brown, who is supremely the poet of the Southland. For them, the African mirage held not the least attraction. Thus the African theme is essentially a symptom of maladjustment.

such matters as the use of dialect and the borrowing of the traditional forms of folk art were no more than the surface reflection of dissensions lying much deeper, the most serious of these doubtless being metaphysical in nature.

The tragic example of Paul Laurence Dunbar was eloquent testimony to the fact that the selection of one or another style or language could be not merely a problem of literary aesthetics, but might imply a choice that involved the man in his entirety. One cannot hide from oneself the strange parallelism between Dunbar's contradictory attitudes toward poetry in dialect, which he kept on turning out while at the same time he condemned it, and the ambiguities of his religious verse in which, as we have seen, he alternately proclaimed his belief in God and his disbelief in a future life. The same ambiguities and the same parallels are to be found in the work of James Weldon Johnson, who was of the same generation. It is even more remarkable that, when these ambiguities come to be lifted, the metaphysical positions and the literary theories adopted split along the same line of cleavage. In so delicate a domain, which requires us to touch upon a man's most deeply held convictions, it would clearly be presumptuous to assert dogmatically what effects are due to what causes. Yet it is striking, to say the least, that James Weldon Johnson, Langston Hughes, and Sterling Brown, who were primarily responsible for the renewed use of Negro popular literary forms, should also have been the main critics of Christian belief and have found their way to varying degrees of unbelief, while Claude McKay, Jean Toomer, and Countee Cullen, whose poetry developed quite apart from any influence of the folk language and folk literary forms, were also the great Christian poets of the Negro Renaissance.

Each group also had its own distinctive conception of poetry, which in its turn was derived from a particular conception of the individual's situation and role in the community. For the folklorists, it is the community that generates the poetic function, providing the poet with his language, with the framework of the traditional forms, with the themes for his poetry, which are taken from everyday life, and even with his emotions. Thus the individual has no autonomous existence; he is taken over by the group and exists only for it and through it. At the same time, any inner life languishes or expires while, in its stead, particularisms are stressed and the specifically racial values are extolled. All this doubtless explains why these poets have been blamed for being insufficiently "rooted" in those humanist, Christian values on which Western civilization is based, and for offering only a "provincial view of life."[4]

[4] See Edward Bland, "Racial Bias and Negro Poetry," *Poetry*, March, 1944, pp. 328-33. This interesting article is nevertheless at fault by overgeneralizing. In keep-

Intolerant of any collective guardianship, the spiritualists stand out, by way of contrast, as the champions of individualism. Though they do not always herald the fact, in practice they reject dialect and the poetic forms they could have found in folk poetry, as though they feared that adoption of a form might also constrain them, unbeknownst to themselves, to adopt a way of thinking. Nor have they the least sympathy for the readily histrionic quality that is the mark of folk poetry, while for its favored comic approaches their own preoccupations are too solemn. Poetry, as they write it, is a preeminently individual art, a secret dialogue between the self and the self — or God, which is the same thing — in the course of which a personality patiently analyzes itself, explores its own boundaries, and defines the contacts it has freely chosen to maintain with the outside world. Though not oblivious to their own race, these poets penetrate so deeply into the black soul that they discover within it the basic aspirations shared by men of every race. As the poetic forms they use serve to demonstrate, they seek out the universal values that lie beyond all racial contingencies.

Thus it is from diverse angles that these several poets assay the prospects for the integration of the black man and his culture in the Western world. Like the slaves of yesteryear, whose condition in itself condemned them to abide within a passivity and a *de facto* irresponsibility, and who could expect nobody but their master to determine their fate, the folklorists seem to rely less on internal forces than on outside elements to bring about the miracle. For Sterling Brown, the more truly human future to which the black man is looking forward is simply his due, and it does not become especially clear how a personal effort on his part might be required, or even helpful, in forcing destiny's hand.[5] As for Langston Hughes, he leaves us with the feeling that a generous gesture by whites would be enough to make a reality of the promises of American democracy. And he would appear to believe, along with James Weldon Johnson, that the strong attraction which white men feel for some forms of Negro art, such as the spirituals and jazz, could in the long run soften hostile attitudes, without the Negro's having in any way to modify or abandon his particularism.

---

ing with outworn clichés, it valuates Negro poetry *en bloc*, as though it were a uniform, unchanging entity endowed with a life apart from the existences of its highly divergent creators. The statements made are valid, if they are limited to the poets we have called folklorists, and who were preoccupied with their quest for the people. But it is running against the obvious to maintain that the poets we have called spiritualists are less deeply rooted than other American or Occidental writers in humanist or Christian values. As this study has shown, such a declaration cannot survive a serious examination of the actual texts.

[5] Ch. 11, note 79.

This is not the view of the spiritualists, who scorn the notion that their fate might be decided apart from them and without their participation. They can see no value in any integration that has not first occurred in people's hearts where, as Cullen had declared, the key to every problem must be sought.[6] Assuredly they are not unmindful of the part the white man must play in bringing about racial reconciliation, but they think that reliance on others would prove illusory, that one must first raise oneself to a level where such a reconciliation becomes possible. This is what McKay was voicing when he declared that "segregation is not the whole sin" and that "the Negroes need salvation from within."[7] Like Toomer's "blue man," an understanding between the races can be achieved only after the contradictions within each man's heart have been overcome.

Thus, on the theme of the black man's integration within a civilization built by others, the work of each of these poets forms a treasury of feelings and reflections not only astonishingly varied, but also highly relevant to the present day. At a time when the consciousness of the nonwhite peoples everywhere has awakened to the determination to take over their own destinies, and when the white man, as a consequence, must redefine what his role shall be in a world on which he had formerly imposed his own criteria, the black poetry of the United States must be valued as a message that carries far beyond the national frontiers and deserves the attention of all men of good will.

[6] See Ch. 5, note 118.
[7] See Ch. 6, note 165. Also to be noted is this remark of Cullen's: "There is such a thing as working out one's own soul's salvation. And that is what the New Negro intends to do" ("The League of Youth," *The Crisis*, August, 1923, p. 167).

BIBLIOGRAPHICAL APPENDIX

It seems pointless to weigh down this bibliographical appendix by repeating some of the references already given, especially:

1. Works cited only incidentally and having no direct connection with our subject.

2. Bibliographical references for Negro poets prior to Dunbar and thus prior, also, to the period with which our study is concerned. We refer instead to the excellent bibliography in the work by Vernon Loggins, *The Negro Author: His Development in America,* which has lost none of its value.

3. Individual poems not reprinted in any volume. Our study, which is based on works published in volume form, does not claim to provide a complete bibliography of these isolated poems. Those that have actually been utilized have been mentioned only to the degree that they filled out certain aspects insufficiently documented by poems published between covers.

4. Individual articles in collective volumes. Only the latter have been included.

5. Certain works mentioned in the footnotes as supplementary documentation on one point or another, but not actually utilized in this study.

As for M.A. dissertations dealing with or touching on our subject, a certain number of which we were able to consult, we include all those that have been published. Of the others, we list only those that are more than mere compilations and can claim to be based on individual research.

Finally, it will be valuable to consult also complete files of the principal magazines containing the articles cited here, and more especially *The Crisis* (New York), *The Journal of Negro History* (Washington, D.C.), *The Journal of Negro Education* (Washington, D.C.), *Phylon* (Atlanta, Ga.), and *Présence Africaine* (Paris).

513

A. Bibliographies

In addition to the periodically published *Cumulative Book Index* and *Reader's Guide to Periodical Literature* which, unfortunately, fail to index many Negro publications, consult:

Leary, Lewis. *Articles on American Literature, 1900-1950.* Durham, N.C., 1954. xv + 437 pp.

Locke, Alain. *A Decade of Negro Self-Expression.* The Trustees of the John F. Slater Fund, Occasional Papers no. 26. Charlottesville, Va., 1928. 20 pp.

Merriam, Alan P. *A Bibliography of Jazz.* American Folklore Society, Bibliographical Series VI. Philadelphia, 1954. xiii + 145 pp.

Millett, Fred B. *Contemporary American Authors.* New York, 1940. xiii + 716 pp.

National Urban League. *Selected Bibliography on the Negro.* 4th ed., New York, 1951. 124 pp.

Porter, Dorothy Burnett. *North American Negro Poets: A Bibliographical Checklist of Their Writings, 1760-1944.* Hattiesburg, Miss., 1945. 90 pp.

Schomburg, Arthur Alfonso. *A Bibliographical Checklist of American Negro Poetry.* New York, 1916. 57 pp. (To all intents and purposes, this work has been superseded by the preceding entry.)

Spiller, Robert E., et al., eds. *Literary History of the United States: Bibliography.* 3rd printing, New York, 1953. xxii + 817 pp.

———, eds. *Literary History of the United States: Bibliography Supplement.* Ed. Richard M. Ludwig. New York, 1959. xix + 268 pp.

Woodress, James. *Dissertations in American Literature, 1891-1955, with Supplement, 1956-1961.* Durham, N.C., 1962. xii + 138 pp.

Work, Monroe. *Bibliography of the Negro in Africa and America.* New York, 1928. xii + 698 pp.

B. General Works

1. Psychology and Sociology

Jacobi, Jolande. "Archétype et symbole dans la psychologie de Jung." *Polarité du Symbole,* Etudes Carmélitaines, Desclée de Brouwer, 1960, pp. 167-206.

Maisonneuve, Jean. *Psychologie sociale.* Paris, 1950. 128 pp.

Memmi, Albert. *Portrait du colonisé, précédé du portrait du colonisateur.* Paris, 1957. 193 pp.

Mensching, G. *Sociologie religieuse.* Paris, 1951. 326 pp.

Porot, Antoine, et al. *Manuel alphabétique de psychiâtrie.* Paris, 1952. viii + 437 pp.

Sérouya, Henri. *Le Mysticisme.* Paris, 1956. 128 pp.

Wach, Joachim. *Sociologie de la religion.* Paris, 1955. 367 pp.

2. American Literature

Blankenship, Russell. *American Literature as an Expression of the National Mind.* New York, 1931. xviii + 731 pp.

Calverton, Victor Francis. *The Liberation of American Literature*. New York, 1932. xv + 500 pp.

Cowley, Malcolm. *Exile's Return: A Literary Odyssey of the 1920's*. Compass ed., New York, 1956. vi + 322 pp.

Gregory, Horace, and Zaturenska, Marya. *A History of American Poetry, 1900-1940*. New York, 1946. xi + 524 pp.

Hart, James D. *The Oxford Companion to American Literature*. New York, 1948. viii + 890 pp.

Hicks, Granville, et al., eds. *Proletarian Literature in the United States: An Anthology*. New York, 1935. 384 pp.

Hoffman, Frederic J. *The Twenties: American Writing in the Postwar Decade*. New York, 1955. xiv + 466 pp.

Kreymborg, Alfred. *An Anthology of American Poetry, Lyric America: 1630-1930*. Rev. ed., New York, 1935. xl + 654 pp.

———. *A History of American Poetry, Our Singing Strength*. New York, 1934. x + 643 pp.

Kunitz, Stanley J., and Haycraft, Howard. *Twentieth Century Authors: A Biographical Dictionary of Modern Literature*. New York, 1942. 1577 pp.

———. *Twentieth Century Authors: A Biographical Dictionary of Modern Literature, First Supplement*. New York, 1955. 1123 pp.

Lüdeke, Henry. *Geschichte der amerikanischen Literatur*. Bern, 1952. 656 pp.

Spiller, Robert E., et al., eds. *Literary History of the United States*. Rev. ed., New York, 1953. xxii + 1456 pp.

Trent, W. P., et al., eds. *The Cambridge History of American Literature*. 3 vols., 1917; 1 vol., New York, 1944. xvii + 380 pp., x + 430 pp., xiii + 678 pp.

Untermeyer, Louis. *American Poetry since 1900*. New York, 1923. xv + 405 pp.

3. American Music

Chase, Gilbert. *America's Music from the Pilgrims to the Present*. New York, 1955. xxiii + 733 pp.

Howard, John Tasker. *Our American Music, Three Hundred Years of It*. 3rd ed., New York, 1946. xxii + 841 pp.

Spaeth, Sigmund Gottfried. *A History of Popular Music in America*. New York, 1948. xv + 729 pp.

C. THE BLACK MAN IN THE UNITED STATES

1. Fundamental Problems

Aron, Birgit. "The Garvey Movement: Shadow and Substance." *Phylon*, fourth quarter, 1947, pp. 337-43.

Baker, Ray Stannard. *Following the Color Line: An Account of Negro Citizenship in the American Democracy*. New York, 1908. xii + 314 pp.

Baldwin, James. *Notes of a Native Son*. Boston, 1955. ix + 175 pp.

Bardolph, Richard. *The Negro Vanguard*. New York, 1959. 388 pp.

Bayton, James A. "The Psychology of Racial Morale." *Journal of Negro Education*, April, 1942, pp. 150-53.

Bennett, Lerone, Jr. "The Ghost of Marcus Garvey, Interviews with Crusader's Two Wives." *Ebony*, March, 1960, pp. 53-61.

"Blackness and Whiteness." *Opportunity*, April, 1928, p. 100.

Bontemps, Arna. *Story of the Negro*. 3rd ed., New York, 1960. xii + 243 pp.

Botkin, Benjamin Albert, ed. *Lay My Burden Down: A Folk History of Slavery*. Chicago, 1945; 4th printing, 1958. xxi + 298 pp.

Brawley, Benjamin Griffith. *Negro Builders and Heroes*. Chapel Hill, N.C., 1937. xi + 315 pp.

————. *A Short History of the American Negro*. 4th ed., New York, 1939. xv + 288 pp.

Carter, Elmer A. "Crossing Over." *Opportunity*, December, 1926, pp. 376-78.

Daykin, Walter L. "Nationalism as Expressed in Negro History." *Social Forces*, December, 1934, pp. 257-63.

Decraene, Philippe. *Le Panafricanisme*. Paris, 1959. 126 pp.

Du Bois, W. E. B. *The Souls of Black Folk*. Chicago, 1903. ix + 265 pp.

————. "Marxism and the Negro Problem." *The Crisis*, May, 1933, pp. 103-4, 118.

————. "On Being Ashamed of Oneself." *The Crisis*, September, 1933, pp. 199-200.

————. "Pan-Africa and New Racial Philosophy." *The Crisis*, November, 1933, pp. 247, 262.

————, and Washington, Booker T. *The Negro in the South: His Economic Progress in Relation to His Moral and Religious Development*. The William Levi Bull Lectures for 1907. Philadelphia, 1907. 222 pp.

Dunbar-Nelson, Alice. "The Negro Looks at an Outworn Tradition." *Southern Workman*, May, 1928, pp. 195-200.

Elkins, Stanley M. "The Question of 'Sambo': A Report of the Ninth Newberry Library Conference on American Studies." *The Newberry Library Bulletin*, December, 1958, pp. 14-40.

————. *Slavery: A Problem in American Institutional and Intellectual Life*. Chicago, 1959. viii + 248 pp.

Elmes, A. F. "Garvey and Garveyism: An Estimate." *Opportunity*, May, 1925, pp. 139-41.

Ferguson, Elizabeth A. "Race Consciousness among American Negroes." *Journal of Negro Education*, January, 1938, pp. 32-40.

Franklin, John Hope. *From Slavery to Freedom: A History of American Negroes*. 2nd ed., New York, 1956. xv + 639 + xlii pp.

Frazier, E. Franklin. "The Garvey Movement." *Opportunity*, November, 1926, pp. 346-48.

————. *The Negro in the United States*. Rev. ed., New York, 1957. xxxiii + 769 pp.

————. *Black Bourgeoisie*. Glencoe, Ill., 1957. 264 pp.

————, ed. *The Integration of the Negro into American Society*. Papers contributed to the Fourteenth Annual Conference of the Division of the Social

Sciences (Howard University, May, 1951). Washington, D.C., 1951. vii +
212 pp.

Glicksberg, Charles I. "Psychoanalysis and the Negro Problem." *Phylon,* first
quarter, 1956, pp. 41-51.

Hartt, Rollin Lynde. "The New Negro." *Independent,* January 15, 1921, pp.
59-60, 76.

Herskovits, Melville, J. "The Negro in the New World: The Statement of a
Problem." *American Anthropologist* XXXII (1930), 145-55.

———. "What Has Africa Given America?" *New Republic* LXXXIV (1935),
92-94.

———. *The Myth of the Negro Past.* New ed., Boston, 1958. xxix + 368 pp.

Himes, Joseph Sandy, Jr. "A Sociological Redefinition of the American Negro
Group." *Phylon,* second quarter, 1948, pp. 125-30.

"How the N.A.A.C.P. Began." *The Crisis,* February, 1959, pp. 71-78.

Hughes, Langston. "Our Wonderful Society: Washington." *Opportunity,* August, 1927, pp. 226-27.

———. "Democracy Begins at Home: What Shall We Do about the South?"
Common Ground, Winter, 1943, pp. 3-6.

Johnson, Charles S. "Public Opinion and the Negro." *Opportunity,* July, 1923,
pp. 201-6.

———. "After Garvey — What?" *Opportunity,* August, 1923, pp. 231-33.

———. "The Social Philosophy of Booker T. Washington." *Opportunity,* April,
1928, pp. 102-5, 115.

Johnson, James Weldon. *Black Manhattan.* New York, 1930. xvii + 284 + xvii
pp.

———. *Negro Americans — What Now?* New York, 1934. viii + 103 pp.

Kardiner, Abram, and Ovesey, Lionel. *The Mark of Oppression: A Psychosocial
Study of the American Negro.* New York, 1951. xvii + 396 pp.

Lewis, Roscoe E., ed. *The Negro in Virginia.* Compiled by workers of the
Writers' Program of the Work Projects Administration in the State of Virginia. New York, 1940. xii + 380 pp.

Locke, Alain. *Le Rôle du Nègre dans la culture des Amériques.* Port-au-Prince,
1943. 141 pp.

———, and Stern, Bernhard J., eds. *When Peoples Meet: A Study in Race and
Culture Contacts.* New York, 1942. xii + 756 pp.

Logan, Rayford. *The Negro in American Life and Thought, the Nadir: 1877-
1901.* New York, 1954. x + 380 pp.

———. *The Negro in the United States: A Brief History.* Princeton, N.J., 1957.
191 pp.

Lucas-Dubreton, Jean. "Le Moïse noir." *Les Œuvres Libres,* January, 1951,
pp. 81-116.

McCray, George F. "Race Pride." *The Crisis,* October, 1933, pp. 224-25.

McKay, Claude. "Soviet Russia and the Negro." *The Crisis,* December, 1923,
pp. 61-65; January, 1924, pp. 114-18.

———. *Harlem, Negro Metropolis.* New York, 1940. 262 pp.

McLean, Helen V. "Racial Prejudice." *Phylon,* second quarter, 1945, pp. 145-53.

Maquet, Jacques J. "Le Relativisme culturel." *Présence Africaine.* October-November, 1958, pp. 65-73; December, 1958-January, 1959, pp. 59-68.

Meier, August. "From 'Conservative' to 'Radical': The Ideological Development of W. E. B. Du Bois, 1885-1905." *The Crisis,* November, 1959, pp. 527-36.

Morse, George Chester. "The Fictitious Negro." *Outlook and Independent,* August 21, 1929, pp. 648-49, 678-79.

Morse, Josiah. "The Outlook for the Negro." *Sewanee Review,* April-June, 1920, pp. 152-59.

Murray, Florence, ed. *The Negro Handbook.* 4th ed., New York, 1949. 368 pp.

Myrdal, Gunnar. *An American Dilemma: The Negro Problem and Modern Democracy.* New York, 1944. lix + 1483 pp.

Ottley, Roi. *Black Odyssey: The Story of the Negro in America.* London, 1949. ix + 340 pp.

"Pan-African Congresses." *The Crisis,* October, 1927, pp. 263-64.

Park, Robert E. "The Conflict and Fusion of Cultures." *Journal of Negro History,* April, 1919, pp. 111-33.

———. "Die menschliche Natur und das Kollektiv-Verhalten." *Kölner Vierteljahrshefte für Soziologie,* 6th yr. (1926-27), pp. 12-20.

———. *Race and Culture.* Glencoe, Ill., 1950. xxii + 403 pp.

Parrish, Charles H. "Color Names and Color Notions." *Journal of Negro Education,* Winter, 1946, pp. 13-20.

Radicalism and Sedition among the Negroes as Reflected in Their Publications. Exhibit no. 10, pp. 161-87, in 66th Cong., 1st sess., *Senate Documents,* vol. 12, Document no. 153, "Investigation activities of the Dept. of Justice." Letter from the Attorney General transmitting in response to a Senate resolution of October 17, 1919, a report on the activities of the Bureau of Investigation of the Department of Justice against persons advising anarchy, sedition, and the forcible overthrow of the Government. Washington, D.C., Govt. Printing Office, 1919. Serial no. 7607. Letter of transmittal of A. Mitchell Palmer, Attorney General.

Record, Wilson. "Extremist Movements among American Negroes." *Phylon,* first quarter, 1956, pp. 17-23.

Reid, Ira de A. "Social Protest: Cue and Catharsis." *Phylon,* second quarter, 1955, pp. 141-47.

Rinder, Irwin D., and Campbell, Donald T. "Varieties of Inauthenticity." *Phylon,* fourth quarter, 1952, pp. 270-75.

Rose, Arnold Marshall. *The Negro's Morale, Group Identification and Protest.* Minneapolis, 1949. ix + 153 pp.

Schermerhorn, R. A. "The Northern Ideology and Negro Political Action." *Phylon,* fourth quarter, 1947, pp. 344-48.

Schoell, Franck Louis. *La Question des noirs aux Etats-Unis.* Paris, 1923. 284 pp.

———. *U.S.A.: Du Côté des blancs et du côté des noirs.* Paris, 1929. 242 pp.

————. *Histoire de la race noire aux Etats-Unis du XVII siècle à nos jours.* Paris, 1959. 248 pp.

Schuyler, George S. "Negroes Reject Communism." *American Mercury,* June, 1939, pp. 176-81.

Scott, Frank A. *An Inquiry into the Communist Program for the National Self-Determination of Negroes in the Black Belt.* M.A. dissertation, Howard University, 1951. v + 149 pp.

Simpson, George Eaton, and Yinger, J. Milton. *Racial and Cultural Minorities: An Analysis of Prejudice and Discrimination.* Rev. ed., New York, 1958. x + 773 pp.

Spencer, Samuel R., Jr. *Booker T. Washington and the Negro's Place in American Life.* Boston, 1955. ix + 212 pp.

Standing, T. G. "Nationalism in Negro Leadership." *American Journal of Sociology,* September, 1934, pp. 180-92.

Thurman, Wallace. "Negro Life in New York's Harlem: A Lively Picture of a Popular and Interesting Section." *The Light,* November 5, 1927, pp. ?; November 12, 1927, pp. 10-12, 46; November 19, 1927, pp. 7-9; November 26, 1927, pp. 8-10.

Washington, Booker T. *Up From Slavery.* New York, 1901; World's Classics ed., Oxford. xii + 244 pp.

————, et al. *The Negro Problem.* New York, 1903. 234 pp.

Weatherford, Willis D., and Johnson, Charles S. *Race Relations: Adjustment of Whites and Negroes in the United States.* New York, 1934. x + 590 pp.

Winston, Sanford. "Cultural Participation and the Negro." *American Journal of Sociology,* March, 1935, pp. 593-601.

Woodson, Carter G. *The Rural Negro.* Washington, D.C., 1930. xvi + 265 pp.

Wright, Richard. *White Man, Listen!* New York, 1957. 190 pp.

2. Religion

Billings, R. A. "The Negro and His Church: A Psychogenetic Study." *Psychoanalytic Review,* October, 1934, pp. 425-41.

Cullen, Countee. "The League of Youth." *The Crisis,* August, 1923, pp. 167-68.

Darrow, Clarence, and Jones, Robert Elijah. "The Religion of the American Negro." *The Crisis,* June, 1931, pp. 190-92.

Du Bois, W. E. B., ed. *The Negro Church.* Report of a Social Study made under the direction of Atlanta University; together with the Proceedings of the Eighth Conference for the Study of the Negro Problems, Atlanta University, May 26, 1903. Atlanta, 1903. viii + 212 pp.

Haynes, George E. "The Church and Negro Progress." *Annals of the American Academy of Political and Social Science,* November, 1928, pp. 264-71.

Herberg, Will. *Protestant, Catholic, Jew: An Essay in American Religious Sociology.* New York, 1956. 320 pp.

Holland, Jerome Heartwell. "The Role of the Negro Church as an Organ of Protest." *Journal of Negro Education,* April, 1942, pp. 165-69.

Johnson, Mordecai Wyatt. "The Faith of the American Negro." *The Crisis*, August, 1922, pp. 156-58.

Johnston, Ruby F. *The Development of Negro Religion*. New York, n.d. xxi + 202 pp.

McKay, Claude. "Mystic Happiness in Harlem." *American Mercury*, August, 1939, pp. 444-50.

Mays, Benjamin Elijah. *The Negro's God as Reflected in His Literature*. Boston, 1938. viii + 269 pp.

Mims, Edwin. *The Christ of the Poets*. New York, 1948. 256 pp.

Niebuhr, H. Richard. *The Social Sources of Denominationalism*. 1929; Meridian ed., New York, 1957. 304 pp.

Palmer, Edward Nelson. "The Religious Acculturation of the Negro." *Phylon*, third quarter, 1944, pp. 260-65.

Proctor, H. H. "The Theology of the Southern Slave." *Southern Workman*, November, 1907, pp. 584-92; December, 1907, pp. 652-56.

Puckett, Newbell Niles. "The Negro Church in the United States." *Social Forces*, March, 1926, pp. 581-87.

Sweet, William W. *The Story of Religion in America*. Rev. ed., New York, 1950. ix + 492 pp.

———. *Religion in Colonial America*. New York, 1953. xiii + 367 pp.

Wilson, Gold Refined. "The Religion of the American Negro Slave: His Attitude toward Life and Death." *Journal of Negro History*, January, 1923, pp. 41-71.

Woodson, Carter G. *The History of the Negro Church*. 2nd ed., Washington, D.C., 1945. xi + 322 pp.

Yinger, J. Milton. *Religion, Society and the Individual: An Introduction to the Sociology of Religion*. New York, 1957. 658 pp.

3. Negro Art

Barnes, Albert C. "Negro Art, Past and Present." *Opportunity*, May, 1926, pp. 148-49, 168-69.

———. "Primitive Negro Sculpture and Its Influence on Modern Civilization." *Opportunity*, May, 1928, pp. 139-40, 147.

Du Bois, W. E. B. "Criteria of Negro Art." *The Crisis*, October, 1926, pp. 290-97.

Guillaume, Paul. "The Triumph of Ancient Negro Art." *Opportunity*, May, 1926, pp. 146-47.

Munro, Thomas. "Primitive Negro Sculpture." *Opportunity*, May, 1926, pp. 150-52.

Paulme, Denise. *Les Sculptures de l'Afrique noire*. Paris, 1956. viii + 130 pp.

Schuyler, George S. "Negro-Art Hokum." *Nation*, June 16, 1926, pp. 662-63.

4. Folklore and Jazz

Ames, Russell. *The Story of American Folksong*. New York, 1955. xii + 276 pp.

Berdie, Ralph F. "Playing the Dozens." *Journal of Abnormal and Social Psychology*, January, 1947, pp. 120-21.

Brown, Sterling A. "The Blues as Folk Poetry." In Benjamin Albert Botkin, ed., *Folk Say*. Norman, Okla., 1930, pp. 324-39.

———. "Negro Folk Expression." *Phylon*, fourth quarter, 1950, pp. 318-27.

———. "The Blues." *Phylon*, fourth quarter, 1952, pp. 286-92.

———. "Negro Folk Expression: Spirituals, Seculars, Ballads and Songs." *Phylon*, first quarter, 1953, pp. 45-61.

Buermeyer, Lawrence. "The Negro Spirituals and American Art." *Opportunity*, May, 1926, pp. 158-59, 167.

Campbell, Elmer Simms. "Blues Are the Negroes' Lament." *Esquire*, December, 1939, pp. 100, 276-80.

Clar, Mimi. "Le Jazz moderne et la musique d'église." *Les Cahiers du Jazz*, no. 4 (1961), pp. 16-39.

Dollard, John. "The Dozens, Dialectic of Insult." *American Imago*, November, 1939, pp. 3-25.

Elton, William. "Playing the Dozens." *American Speech* XXV (1950), 148-49.

Finck, Henry T. "Jazz, Lowbrow and Highbrow." *Etude*, August, 1924, pp. 527-28.

Fisher, Miles Mark. *Negro Slave Songs in the United States*. Ithaca, N.Y., 1953. xv + 223 pp.

Gleason, Ralph J., ed. *Jam Session: An Anthology of Jazz*. New York, 1958. 319 pp.

Harris, Rex. *Jazz*. Rev. ed., Pelican Books, 1957. 272 pp.

Higginson, Thomas Wentworth. "Negro Spirituals." *Atlantic Monthly*, June, 1867, pp. 685-94.

Hodeir, André. *Hommes et problèmes du jazz*. Paris, 1954. 412 pp.

Hughes, Langston. "Songs Called the Blues." *Phylon*, second quarter, 1941, pp. 143-45.

Hughes, Langston, and Bontemps, Arna. *The Book of Negro Folklore*. New York, 1958. xxxi + 624 pp.

Jackson, George Pullen. *White and Negro Spirituals, Their Lifespan and Kinship*. New York, 1944. 349 pp.

James, Willis Laurence. "The Romance of the Negro Folk Cry in America." *Phylon*, first quarter, 1955, pp. 15-30.

"Jazz." *Opportunity*, May, 1925, pp. 132-33.

Johnson, Guy B. *John Henry, Tracking Down a Negro Legend*. Chapel Hill, N.C., 1929. x + 155 pp.

———. "The Negro Spiritual: A Problem in Anthropology." *American Anthropologist* XXXIII (1931), 157-71.

Johnson, James Weldon. *The Books of American Negro Spirituals*. 2 vols. in 1 (1925, 1926), New York, 1940. 187 pp., 189 pp.

Krehbiel, Henry Edward. *Afro-American Folksongs: A Study in Racial and National Music*. 4th ed., New York, 1914. xii + 176 pp.

Lomax, J. A. "Self-Pity in Negro Folk Song." *Nation*, August 9, 1917, pp. 141-45.

Metfessel, Milton, and Seashore, Carl E. *Phonophotography in Folk Music: American Negro Songs in New Notation.* Chapel Hill, N.C., 1928. x + 181 pp.

Odum, Howard W., and Johnson, Guy B. *The Negro and His Songs: A Study of Typical Negro Songs in the South.* Chapel Hill, N.C., 1925. ix + 306 pp.

Oliver, Paul. *Blues Fell This Morning: The Meaning of the Blues.* London, 1960. xx + 355 pp.

Pipes, William Harrison. *Say Amen, Brother! Old-Time Negro Preaching — A Study in American Frustration.* New York, 1951. i + 210 pp.

Puckett, Newbell Niles. *Folk Beliefs of the Southern Negro.* Chapel Hill, N.C., 1926. xiv + 644 pp.

———. "Race Pride and Folk Lore." *Opportunity,* March, 1926, pp. 82-84.

Ramsey, Frederic, Jr. *Been Here and Gone.* New Brunswick, N.J., 1960. xiii + 177 pp.

Stearns, Marshall. *The Story of Jazz.* Mentor ed., 1958. 272 pp.

Talley, Thomas W. "The Origins of Negro Traditions." *Phylon,* fourth quarter, 1942, pp. 371-76; first quarter, 1943, pp. 30-38.

Thurman, Howard. *Deep River: Reflections on the Religious Insight of Certain of the Negro Spirituals.* 1945; new ed., New York, 1955. 95 pp.

White, Newman Ivey. "Racial Traits in the Negro Song." *Sewanee Review,* July-September, 1920, pp. 396-404.

Whiteman, Paul. "What Is Jazz Doing to American Music?" *Etude,* August, 1924, pp. 523-24.

Work, John Wesley. *Folk Songs of the American Negro.* Nashville, 1915. 131 pp.

Work, John Wesley, Jr. *American Negro Songs.* New York, 1940. 259 pp.

Wright, Richard. "Le Jazz et le désir." *Les Cahiers du Jazz,* no. 4 (1961), pp. 53-54.

5. Minstrelsy

Brown, Sterling A. "A Literary Parallel." *Opportunity,* May, 1932, pp. 152-53.

Burtnett, J. G. "National Elements in Stephen Foster's Art." *South Atlantic Quarterly,* October, 1922, pp. 322-26.

Kahn, E. J., Jr. *The Merry Partners: The Age and Stage of Harrigan and Hart.* New York, 1955. 302 pp.

Matthews, Brander. "The Rise and Fall of Negro Minstrelsy." *Scribner's Magazine,* January-June, 1915, pp. 754-59.

Nevin, Robert P. "Stephen C. Foster and Negro Minstrelsy." *Atlantic Monthly,* November, 1867, pp. 608-16.

Rourke, Constance. *American Humor.* 1931; Anchor ed., New York, 1955. 253 pp.

Wittke, Carl. *Tambo and Bones: A History of the American Minstrel Stage.* Durham, N.C., 1930. ix + 269 pp.

6. The Plantation Tradition, etc.

Baskervill, William Malone. *Southern Writers.* Nashville, 1896-97. 404 pp. (This work was published in a number of installments.)

Birdoff, Harry. *The World's Greatest Hit, Uncle Tom's Cabin.* New York, 1947. xiv + 440 pp.

Brown, Sterling A. "Negro Character as Seen by White Authors." *Journal of Negro Education,* April, 1933, pp. 179-203.

———. *The Negro in American Fiction.* Washington, D.C., 1937. 209 pp.

———. "The American Race Problem as Reflected in American Literature." *Journal of Negro Education,* July, 1939, pp. 275-90.

Cash, Wilbur J. *The Mind of the South.* 1941; Anchor ed., New York, 1954. 444 pp.

Gaines, Francis Pendleton. *The Southern Plantation: A Study in the Development and the Accuracy of a Tradition.* New York, 1924. ix + 243 pp.

Gordon, Armistead C., and Page, Thomas Nelson. *Befo' de War: Echoes in Negro Dialect.* New York, 1895. vi + 131 pp.

Harris, Joel Chandler. *The Complete Tales of Uncle Remus.* Ed. Richard Chase. Boston, 1955. xxxiii + 875 pp.

Hubbell, Jay Broadus. *The South in American Literature 1607-1900.* Durham, N.C., 1954. xix + 987 pp.

Logan, Frenise A. "Old South Legend." *Phylon,* third quarter, 1950, pp. 234-39.

Macon, J. A. *Uncle Gabe Tucker; or, Reflection, Song and Sentiment in the Quarters.* Philadelphia, 1883. 181 pp.

Moody, Richard. "Uncle Tom, the Theater and Mrs. Stowe." *American Heritage,* October, 1955, pp. 28-33, 102-3.

Moore, Rayburn S. "Thomas Dunn English: A Forgotten Contributor to the Development of Negro Dialect Verse in the 1870's." *American Literature,* March, 1961, pp. 72-75.

Nelson, John Herbert. *The Negro Character in American Literature.* Lawrence, Kans. (University of Kansas Humanistic Studies IV, no. 1), 1926. 146 pp.

Nichols, Charles H., Jr. "Slave Narratives and the Plantation Legend." *Phylon,* third quarter, 1949, pp. 201-10.

Russell, Irwin. *Poems.* Introduction by Joel Chandler Harris. New York, 1888. xi + 112 pp.

———. *Christmas-Night in the Quarters and Other Poems.* Introduction by Joel Chandler Harris and historical sketch by Maurice Garland Fulton. New York, 1917. xxxviii + 182 pp.

Stanton, Frank Lebby. *Songs of the Soil.* Preface by Joel Chandler Harris. New York, 1894. xiv + 217 pp.

———. *Comes One with a Song.* Indianapolis, 1899. xv + 200 pp.

———. *Songs from Dixie Land.* Indianapolis, 1900. xiv + 239 pp.

———. *Up from Georgia.* New York, 1902. viii + 177 pp.

———. *Little Folks Down South.* New York, 1904. viii + 140 pp.

Weeden, Howard. *Shadow on the Wall.* Huntsville, Ala., 1899. 32 unnumbered pages.

———. *Bandanna Ballads.* Introduction by Joel Chandler Harris. New York, 1900. xiii + 92 pp.

————. *Songs of the Old South.* New York, 1901. xii + 96 pp.

————. *Old Voices.* New York, 1904. xii + 100 unnumbered pages.

Wolfe, Bernard. "Uncle Remus and the Malevolent Rabbit." *Commentary,* July, 1949, pp. 31-41.

D. BLACK POETRY

1. Black Literature

Allen, Samuel W. "La Négritude et ses rapports avec le noir américain." *Présence Africaine,* August-November, 1959, pp. 16-26.

Armond, Fred de. "A Note on the Sociology of Negro Literature." *Opportunity,* December, 1925, pp. 369-71.

Bone, Robert A. *The Negro Novel in America.* New Haven, 1958. x + 268 pp.

Boulware, Marcus Hanna. *Jive and Slang of Students in Negro Colleges.* Hampton, Va., 1947. 8 unnumbered pages.

Braithwaite, William Stanley. "The Negro in Literature." *The Crisis,* September, 1924, pp. 204-10.

————. "Alain Locke's Relationship to the Negro in American Literature." *Phylon,* second quarter, 1957, pp. 166-73.

Brawley, Benjamin Griffith. "The Negro in American Literature." *Bookman,* October, 1922, pp. 137-41.

————. "The Negro Literary Renaissance." *Southern Workman,* April, 1927, pp. 177-84.

————. *The Negro in Literature and Art in the United States.* New York, 1930. xii + 231 pp.

————. "The Promise of Negro Literature." *Journal of Negro History,* January, 1934, pp. 53-59.

————. *The Negro Genius.* New York, 1937. xiii + 366 pp.

Brown, Sterling A. "Our Literary Audience." *Opportunity,* February, 1930, pp. 42-46, 61.

————. "The Negro Author and His Publisher." *Quarterly Review of Higher Education among Negroes,* July, 1941, pp. 140-46.

————. "The New Negro in Literature, 1925-1955." In Rayford Logan et al., eds., *The New Negro Thirty Years Afterward.* Washington, D.C., 1956, pp. 57-72.

Burley, Dan. *Original Handbook of Harlem Jive.* New York, 1944. 159 pp.

Burma, John H. "Humor as a Technique in Race Conflict." *American Sociological Review,* December, 1946, pp. 710-15.

Butcher, Margaret Just. *The Negro in American Culture.* 1956; Mentor ed., New York, 1957. 240 pp.

————. *Les Noirs dans la civilisation américaine.* Paris, 1959. 323 pp.

Calverton, Victor Francis. "The Advance of Negro Literature." *Opportunity,* February, 1926, pp. 54-55.

————. "The New Negro." *Current History,* February, 1926, pp. 694-98.

———. "The Negro's New Belligerent Attitude." *Current History,* September, 1929, pp. 1081-88.

"A Challenge to the Negro." *Bookman,* November, 1926, pp. 258-59.

Chamberlain, John. "The Negro as Writer." *Bookman,* February, 1930, pp. 603-11.

Chesnutt, Charles W. "Post-Bellum — Pre-Harlem." *The Crisis,* June, 1931, pp. 193-94.

Davis, Allison. "Our Negro Intellectuals." *The Crisis,* August, 1928, pp. 268-69, 284-86.

Davis, John A., ed. *Africa Seen by American Negroes.* Paris, 1958. xii + 418 pp.

———, ed. *The American Negro Writer and His Roots.* Selected Papers from the First Conference of Negro Writers, March, 1959. New York, 1960. v + 72 pp.

"Debut of the Younger School of Negro Writers." *Opportunity,* May, 1924, pp. 143-44.

Du Bois, W. E. B. "The Negro in Literature and Art." *Annals of the American Academy of Political and Social Science,* September, 1913, pp. 233-37.

Fontaine, W. T. "The Mind and Thought of the Negro of the United States as Revealed in Imaginative Literature, 1876-1940." *Southern University Bulletin* (Scotlandville, La.), March, 1942, pp. 5-50.

———. "Vers une philosophie de la littérature noire américaine." *Présence Africaine,* February-May, 1959, pp. 153-65.

Frazier, E. Franklin. "A Folk Culture in the Making." *Southern Workman,* June, 1928, pp. 195-99.

Glicksberg, Charles I. "For Negro Literature: The Catharsis of Laughter." *Forum,* May, 1947, pp. 450-56.

———. "Race and Revolution in Negro Literature." *Forum,* November, 1947, pp. 300-308.

———. "Negro Americans and the African Dream." *Phylon,* fourth quarter, 1947, pp. 323-30.

———. "The Alienation of Negro Literature." *Phylon,* first quarter, 1950, pp. 49-58.

Gloster, Hugh Morris. "The Van Vechten Vogue." *Phylon,* fourth quarter, 1945, pp. 310-14.

———. *Negro Voices in American Fiction.* Chapel Hill, N.C., 1948. xiv + 295 pp.

Green, Elizabeth Atkinson Lay. *The Negro in Contemporary American Literature.* Chapel Hill, N.C., 1928. 94 pp.

Greever, G. "The Negro in Literature." *Dial* (Chicago), June 8, 1916, pp. 531-32.

Hercules, Frank. "An Aspect of the Negro Renaissance." *Opportunity,* October, 1942, pp. 305-6, 317-19.

Hughes, Langston. "The Negro Artist and the Racial Mountain." *Nation,* June 23, 1926, pp. 692-94.

————. "Harlem Literati of the Twenties." *Saturday Review of Literature*, June 22, 1940, pp. 13-14.

Ivy, James W. "Ecrits nègres aux Etats-Unis." *Présence Africaine*, June-July, 1959, pp. 66-76.

Jackson, Augusta V. "The Renascence of Negro Literature, 1922-1929." M.A. dissertation, Atlanta University, 1936. iv + 222 pp.

Jacobs, George W. "Negro Authors Must Eat." *Nation*, June 12, 1929, pp. 710-11.

Johnson, Charles S. "The Rise of the Negro Magazine." *Journal of Negro History*, January, 1928, pp. 7-21.

Johnson, James Weldon. "Race Prejudice and the Negro Artist." *Harper's Monthly Magazine*, November, 1928, pp. 769-76.

————. "The Dilemma of the Negro Author." *American Mercury*, December, 1928, pp. 477-81.

————. "Negro Authors and White Publishers." *The Crisis*, July, 1929, pp. 228-29.

Lash, John S. "On Negro Literature." *Phylon*, third quarter, 1945, pp. 240-47.

Lee, Ulysses. "Criticism at Mid-Century." *Phylon*, fourth quarter, 1950, pp. 328-37.

Locke, Alain. "American Literary Tradition and the Negro." *The Modern Quarterly*, May-July, 1926, pp. 215-22.

————. "Beauty Instead of Ashes." *Nation*, April 18, 1928, pp. 432-34.

————. "Art or Propaganda?" *Harlem: A Forum of Negro Life*. November, 1928, p. 12.

————. "The Negro's Contribution to American Art and Literature." *Annals of the American Academy of Political and Social Science*, November, 1928, pp. 234-47.

————. "1928: A Retrospective Review." *Opportunity*, January, 1929, pp. 8-11.

————. "This Year of Grace." *Opportunity*, February, 1931, pp. 48-51.

————. "We Turn to Prose: A Retrospective Review of the Literature of the Negro for 1931." *Opportunity*, February, 1932, pp. 40-44.

————. "Black Truth and Black Beauty." *Opportunity*, January, 1933, pp. 14-18.

————. "The Negro's Contribution to American Culture." *Journal of Negro Education*, July, 1939, pp. 521-29.

————. "A Critical Retrospect of the Literature of the Negro for 1947." *Phylon*, first quarter, 1948, pp. 3-12.

Loggins, Vernon. *The Negro Author: His Development in America.* New York, 1931. 480 pp.

Morpurgo, J. E. "The American Negro." *Forthnightly*, July, 1947, pp. 16-24.

"Negro Dialect." *Opportunity*, September, 1924, pp. 259-60.

"The Negro in Art — How Shall He Be Portrayed? — A Symposium." *The Crisis*, February, 1926, p. 165; March, 1926, pp. 219-20; April, 1926, pp. 278-80; May, 1926, pp. 35-36; June, 1926, pp. 71-73; August, 1926, pp. 193-94; September, 1926, pp. 238-39; November, 1926, pp. 28-29.

"A Note on the New Literary Movement." *Opportunity,* March, 1926, p. 80.

Park, Robert E. "Negro Race Consciousness as Reflected in Race Literature." *American Review,* September-October, 1923, pp. 505-16.

Redding, J. Saunders. *To Make a Poet Black.* Chapel Hill, N.C., 1939. xi + 142 pp.

———. "American Negro Literature." *The American Scholar* XVIII, no. 2 (Spring, 1949), 137-48.

———. "Contradiction de la littérature négro-américaine." *Présence Africaine,* August-November, 1959, pp. 11-15.

Schuyler, George S. "Carl Van Vechten." *Phylon,* fourth quarter, 1950, pp. 362-68.

Smith, William Gardner. "The Negro Writer: Pitfalls and Compensations." *Phylon,* fourth quarter, 1950, pp. 297-303.

Thornhill, Gertrude C. "The Negro Becomes a Literary Contributor." *Poet Lore* XXXIX (1928), 431-35.

Thurman, Wallace. "Nephews of Uncle Remus." *Independent,* September 24, 1927, pp. 296-98.

Van Doren, Carl. "The Younger Generation of Negro Writers." *Opportunity,* May, 1924, pp. 144-45.

———. "Negro Renaissance." *Century,* March, 1926, pp. 635-37.

Wagner, Jean. "Littérature nègre et littérature américaine." *Rives,* December, 1960, pp. 16-20.

"Why Negro Humor Is Dying Out." *Hue,* June, 1958, pp. 26-30.

2. Black Poetry

Bland, Edward. "Racial Bias and Negro Poetry." *Poetry,* March, 1944, pp. 328-33.

Bontemps, Arna. "The Harlem Renaissance." *Saturday Review of Literature,* March 22, 1947, pp. 12-13, 44.

Braithwaite, William Stanley. "Some Contemporary Poets of the Negro Race." *The Crisis,* April, 1919, pp. 275-80.

Brown, Sterling A. *Outline for the Study of the Poetry of American Negroes.* Prepared for use with *The Book of American Negro Poetry,* ed. James Weldon Johnson. New York, 1931. 52 pp.

———. *Negro Poetry and Drama.* Washington, D.C., 1937. 142 pp.

Ely, Effie Smith. "American Negro Poetry." *Christian Century,* March 22, 1923, pp. 366-67.

Glicksberg, Charles I. "Negro Poets and the American Tradition." *Antioch Review,* Summer, 1946, pp. 243-53.

Heath, Phoebe Ann. "Negro Poetry as an Historical Record." *Vassar Journal of Undergraduate Studies,* May, 1928, pp. 34-52.

Horne, Frank. "Black Verse." *Opportunity,* November, 1924, pp. 330-32.

Johnson, Charles S. "Jazz Poetry and Blues." *Carolina Magazine,* May, 1928, pp. 16-20.

Kerlin, Robert Thomas. "Present Day Negro Poets." *Southern Workman,* December, 1920, pp. 543-48.

———. *Contemporary Poetry of the Negro.* Hampton, Va., 1921. 23 pp.

———. "A Pair of Youthful Poets." *Southern Workman,* April, 1924, pp. 178-81 [Cullen and Hughes].

———. "Singers of New Songs." *Opportunity,* May, 1926, pp. 162-64.

———. "Conquest by Poetry." *Southern Workman,* June, 1927, pp. 282-84.

Kjersmeier, Karl. "Negere som Digtere." *Social Demokraten* (Copenhagen), January 17, 1925; trans. from the Danish as "Negroes as Poets" by E. Franklin Frazier, *The Crisis,* August, 1925, pp. 186-89.

Locke, Alain. "The Message of the Negro Poets." *Carolina Magazine,* May, 1928, pp. 5-15.

Morton, Lena Beatrice. *Negro Poetry in America.* Boston, 1925. 71 pp. (Actually, only pp. 1-36 deal with black poetry.)

"Negro Poets, Singers in the Dawn." *Negro History Bulletin,* November, 1938, pp. 9-10, 14-15.

Reddick, La Bertha. "The Element of Protest in the Poetry of the Negro." M.A. dissertation, Fisk University, 1940. 111 pp.

Rexroth, Kenneth. "Jazz Poetry." *Nation,* March 29, 1958, pp. 282-83.

Taussig, Charlotte E. "The New Negro as Revealed in His Poetry." *Opportunity,* April, 1927, pp. 108-11.

Thurman, Wallace. "Negro Poets and Their Poetry." *Bookman,* July, 1928, pp. 555-61.

White, Newman Ivey. "American Negro Poetry." *South Atlantic Quarterly,* October, 1921, pp. 304-22.

———. "Racial Feeling in Negro Poetry." *South Atlantic Quarterly,* January, 1922, pp. 14-29.

Wilk, Werner. "Negerdichtung?" In Kurt Ihlenfeld, ed., *Eckart Jahrbuch 1955-1956.* Witten and Berlin. 325 pp.

Work, Monroe N. "The Spirit of Negro Poetry." *Southern Workman,* February, 1908, pp. 73-77.

3. Specialized Anthologies

American Stuff: An Anthology of Prose and Verse by Members of the Federal Writers' Project. New York, 1937. xviii + 301 pp.

Bontemps, Arna. *Golden Slippers: An Anthology of Negro Poetry for Young Readers.* New York, 1941. xii + 220 pp.

Brawley, Benjamin Griffith. *Early Negro American Writers.* Chapel Hill, N.C., 1935. ix + 305 pp.

Brown, Sterling A.; Davis, Arthur P.; and Lee, Ulysses, eds. *The Negro Caravan.* New York, 1941. xviii + 1082 pp.

Calverton, Victor Francis, ed. *Anthology of American Negro Literature.* New York, 1929. xii + 535 pp.

Cromwell, Otelia; Turner, Lorenzo Dow; and Dykes, Eva B. *Readings from Negro Authors for Schools and Colleges.* New York, 1931. xii + 388 pp.

Cullen, Countee. *Caroling Dusk: An Anthology of Verse by Negro Poets*. New York, 1927. xxii + 237 pp.

Cunard, Nancy. *Negro Anthology*. London, 1934; reprinted, 1970. viii + 854 pp.

Dreer, Herman. *American Literature by Negro Authors*. New York, 1950. xvii + 334 pp.

Hughes, Langston, and Bontemps, Arna. *The Poetry of the Negro, 1746-1949*. New York, 1949. xviii + 249 pp.

Johnson, Charles S. *Ebony and Topaz: A Collectanea*. New York, 1927. 164 pp.

Johnson, James Weldon. *The Book of American Negro Poetry*. New York, 1922; new ed., 1931. xii + 300 pp.

Johnson, William Hallock. *Four Lincoln University Poets*. Lincoln University Herald, March, 1930. 16 pp.

Kerlin, Robert Thomas. *Negro Poets and Their Poems*. Washington, D.C., 1923; 4th ed., 1947. xxii + 354 pp.

Locke, Alain. "Harlem, Mecca of the New Negro." *Survey Graphic*, March, 1925, pp. 621-724.

———. *The New Negro*. New York, 1925. xviii + 452 pp.

———. *Four Negro Poets*. New York, 1927. 31 pp.

Magidov (alias Magidenko), R. *Negry Poĭut, Antologija Negritjanskoi Poezii*, Izdanie Soĭuza Russkikh Revoljutsionnykh Rabotnikov Iskusstva im. Maksima Gorkovo v S.A.S.Ch. New York, 1934. 80 pp.

Murphy, Beatrice M. *Negro Voices: An Anthoolgy of Contemporary Verse*. New York, 1938. 173 pp.

———. *Ebony Rhythm: An Anthology of Contemporary Negro Verse*. New York, 1948. 162 pp.

Watkins, Sylvestre C. *Anthology of American Negro Literature*. New York, 1944. xvii + 481 pp.

White, Newman Ivey, and Jackson, Walter Clinton. *An Anthology of Verse by American Negroes*. Durham, N.C., 1924. xi + 250 pp.

4. Poets Contemporary with Dunbar

Allen, J. Mord. *Rhymes, Tales and Rhymed Tales*. Topeka, Kans., 1906. 153 pp.

Campbell, James Edwin. *Driftings and Gleanings*. Charleston, W.Va., 1887. 96 pp.

———. *Echoes from the Cabin and Elsewhere*. Chicago, 1895. 86 pp.

Davis, Daniel Webster. *Idle Moments*. Baltimore, 1895. 81 pp.

———. *'Weh Down Souf and Other Poems*. Cleveland, 1897. 136 pp.

———. "Echoes from a Plantation Party." *Southern Workman*, February, 1899, pp. 54-59.

Woodson, Carter G. "James Edwin Campbell: A Forgotten Man of Letters." *Negro History Bulletin*, November, 1938, p. 11.

5. Paul Laurence Dunbar

Dunbar, Paul Laurence. *Oak and Ivy*. Dayton, Ohio, 1893. 62 pp. (This volume had already been published by December, 1892.)

————. *Majors and Minors.* Toledo, Ohio, 1895. 148 pp.

————. *Lyrics of Lowly Life.* Introduction by William Dean Howells. New York, 1896. 208 pp.

————. *Lyrics of the Hearthside.* New York, 1899. 227 pp.

————. *Lyrics of Love and Laughter.* New York, 1903. 180 pp.

————. *Lyrics of Sunshine and Shadow.* New York, 1905. 109 pp.

————. *Complete Poems.* New York, 1955. xxxix + 479 pp.

Achille, Louis T. "Paul Laurence Dunbar, poète nègre." *Revue Anglo-Américaine,* August, 1934, pp. 504-19.

Allen, Walker M. "Paul Laurence Dunbar: A Study in Genius." *Psychoanalytic Review* XXV, no. 1 (January, 1938), 53-82.

Arnold, Edward F. "Some Personal Reminiscences of P. L. Dunbar." *Journal of Negro History,* October, 1932, pp. 400-408.

Brawley, Benjamin Griffith. *Paul Laurence Dunbar, Poet of His People.* Chapel Hill, N.C., 1936. xi + 159 pp.

Burch, Charles Eaton. "The Plantation Negro in Dunbar's Poetry." *Southern Workman,* May, 1921, pp. 227-29.

————. "Dunbar's Poetry in Literary English." *Southern Workman,* October, 1921, pp. 469-73.

Cook, Will Marion. "Clorindy: The Origin of the Cakewalk." In Rosamond Gilder et al., eds., *Theatre Arts Anthology,* pp. 227-33. New York, 1950.

Cunningham, Virginia. *Paul Laurence Dunbar and His Song.* New York, 1947. ix + 283 pp.

Dunbar, Alice M.; Scarborough, W. S.; and Ransom, Reverdy C. *Paul Laurence Dunbar, Poet Laureate of the Negro Race.* Offprint of the October, 1914, issue of *The A.M.E. Church Review,* Philadelphia. 32 pp.

Gould, Jean. *That Dunbar Boy: The Story of America's Famous Negro Poet.* New York, 1958. viii + 245 pp. (For children.)

Howells, William Dean. "Life and Letters" (critique of *Majors and Minors*). *Harper's Weekly,* June 27, 1896, pp. 630-31.

Jenifer, George Davis. "The Services of Dunbar." *The Voice of the Negro,* June, 1906, pp. 408-9.

Johnson, Ralph Glasgow. "The Poetry of Dunbar and McKay: A Study." M.A. dissertation, University of Pittsburgh, 1950. v + 322 pp.

Lawson, Victor. *Dunbar Critically Examined.* Washington, D.C., 1941. xvi + 151 pp.

Terrell, Mary Church. "P. L. Dunbar." *The Voice of the Negro,* April, 1906, pp. 271-78.

Wiggins, Lida Keck. "Den of a Literary Lion." *The Voice of the Negro,* January, 1906, pp. 50-53.

————. *The Life and Works of P. L. Dunbar.* Naperville, Ill., 1907. 430 pp.

6. Minor Poets of the Negro Renaissance

Brown, Sterling A. "Two Negro Poets" (A. Bontemps, F. M. Davis). *Opportunity,* July, 1936, pp. 216, 220.

Davis, Frank Marshall. *Black Man's Verse.* Chicago, 1935. 83 pp.
————. *I Am the American Negro.* Chicago, 1937. 69 pp.
————. *Through Sepia Eyes.* Chicago, 1938. 10 pp.
————. *47th Street.* Prairie City, Ill., 1948. 105 pp.
Du Bois, W. E. B. *Darkwater: Voices from within the Veil.* New York, 1920.
  ix + 276 pp.
Johnson, Fenton. *A Little Dreaming.* Chicago, 1913. 80 pp.
————. *Visions of the Dusk.* New York, 1915. 71 pp.
————. *Songs of the Soil.* New York, 1916. 39 pp.

7. Claude McKay

McKay, Claude. *Songs of Jamaica.* Introduction by Walter Jekyll. Kingston,
  Jamaica, 1912. 140 pp.
————. *Constab Ballads.* London, 1912. 94 pp.
————. *Spring in New Hampshire.* Preface by I. A. Richards. London, 1920.
  40 pp.
————. *Harlem Shadows.* Introduction by Max Eastman. New York, 1922.
  95 pp.
————. *A Long Way from Home.* New York, 1937. 354 pp.
————. "On Becoming a Roman Catholic." *The Epistle* (New York), Spring,
  1945, pp. 43-45.
————. "Why I Became a Catholic." *Ebony,* March, 1946, p. 32.
————. *Selected Poems.* Introduction by John Dewey, biography by Max East-
  man. New York, 1953. 112 pp.
————. "Boyhood in Jamaica." *Phylon,* second quarter, 1953, pp. 134-46.
————. "Right Turn to Catholicism." MS., Schomburg Collection, New York.
  26 pp.
————. "My Green Hills of Jamaica." MS., Schomburg Collection, New York.
  82 pp.
Butcher, Philip. "Claude McKay — 'If We Must Die.'" *Opportunity,* Autumn,
  1948, p. 127.
Henriques, Fernando. *Jamaica, Land of Wood and Water.* London, 1957. 216 pp.
Hoehn, Matthew Anthony, ed. *Catholic Authors: Contemporary Biographical
  Sketches 1930-1947.* Newark, 1948. xvii + 812 pp. (McKay, pp. 467-68.)
Jackson, Blyden. "The Essential McKay" (critique of the 1953 edition). *Phylon,*
  second quarter, 1953, pp. 216-17.
Johnson, Ralph Glassgow. "The Poetry of Dunbar and McKay" (see above, Sec.
  5: Dunbar).
Smith, Robert A. "Claude McKay: An Essay in Criticism." *Phylon,* third quar-
  ter, 1948, pp. 270-73.
Tarry, Ellen. *The Third Door: The Autobiography of an American Negro
  Woman.* New York, 1955. ix + 304 pp.

8. Jean Toomer

Toomer, Jean. *Cane.* Preface by Waldo Frank. New York, 1923. xi + 239 pp.

———. "Race Problems and Modern Society," In Baker Brownell, ed., *Problems of Civilization*, pp. 67-114. Princeton, N.J., 1929.

———. *Essentials — Definitions and Aphorisms.* Chicago, 1931.

———. "Blue Meridian." In Alfred Kreymborg et al., eds., *The New Caravan*, pp. 633-53. New York, 1936.

———. *The Flavor of Man.* William Penn Lecture, 1949, delivered at Arch Street Meeting House, Philadelphia. 32 pp.

Du Bois, W. E. B., and Locke, Alain. "The Younger Literary Movement." *The Crisis*, February, 1924, pp. 161-63.

Gregory, Montgomery. "Cane." *Opportunity*, December, 1923, pp. 374-75.

Holmes, Eugene. "Jean Toomer, Apostle of Beauty." *Opportunity*, August, 1932, pp. 252-54, 260.

Munson, Gorham B. "The Significance of Jean Toomer." *Opportunity*, September, 1925, pp. 262-63.

———. *Destinations: A Canvass of American Literature since 1900.* New York, 1928. x + 218 pp.

Rosenfeld, Paul. *Men Seen: Twenty-four Modern Authors.* New York, 1925. x + 380 pp.

9. Countee Cullen

Cullen, Countee. "The League of Youth." *The Crisis*, August, 1923, p. 167.

———. *Color.* New York, 1925. xvii + 108 pp.

———. *Copper Sun.* New York, 1927. xi + 89 pp.

———. *The Ballad of the Brown Girl.* New York, 1927. 11 pp.

———. *The Black Christ and Other Poems.* New York, 1929. 110 pp.

———. *The Medea and Some Poems.* New York, 1935. vii + 97 pp.

———. *On These I Stand.* New York, 1947. x + 197 pp.

Benet, William Rose. "The Phoenix Nest." *Saturday Review of Literature*, February 23, 1946, p. 44.

Busey, Garreta. "The Legal Tender of Countee Cullen." *New York Herald Tribune Books*, August 21, 1927, p. 5.

Cullen, Frederick Asbury. *From Barefoot Town to Jerusalem.* New York, n.d. (1945?). 128 pp.

Davis, Arthur P. "The Alien and Exile Theme in Countee Cullen's Racial Poems." *Phylon*, fourth quarter, 1953, pp. 390-400.

Deutsch, Babette. "Let It Be Allowed." *Nation*, December 30, 1925, pp. 763-64.

Dillon, George. "Mr. Cullen's First Book." *Poetry*, April, 1926, pp. 50-53.

Eisenberg, Emmanuel. "A Not So Celestial Choir." *Bookman*, September, 1927, pp. 102-3.

Holley, Emile Trevelle. "And They Nailed Him to a Tree: A Study of the Poetry of Countee Cullen in His Book *The Black Christ*." *Carolina Magazine*, May 4, 1930, pp. 1, 7.

James, Bertha Ten Eyck. "On the Danger Line." *Poetry*, February, 1930, pp. 286-89.

McCormack, Margaret. "Countee Cullen." *Interracial Review,* May, 1939, p. 74.
North, Jessica N. "Mr. Cullen's Second Book." *Poetry,* February, 1928, pp. 284-86.
Potamkin, Harry Alan. "Race and a Poet." *New Republic,* October 12, 1927, p. 218.
Reimherr, Beulah Ottilda. "Countee Cullen: A Biographical and Critical Study." M.A. dissertation, University of Maryland, 1960. iv + 187 pp.
Robb, Izetta Winter. "From the Darker Side." *Opportunity,* December, 1926, pp. 381-82.
Root, E. Merrill. "Keats in Labrador." *Opportunity,* September, 1927, pp. 270-71.
Shillito, Edward. "The Poet and the Race Problem." *Christian Century,* July 17, 1929, pp. 915-16.
Smith, Robert A. "The Poetry of Countee Cullen." *Phylon,* third quarter, 1950, pp. 216-21.
Walrond, Eric. "A Poet for the Negro Race." *The New Republic,* March 31, 1926, p. 179.
Webster, Harvey C. "A Difficult Career." *Poetry,* July, 1947, pp. 222-25.
Woodruff, Bertram L. "The Poetic Philosophy of Countee Cullen." *Phylon,* third quarter, 1940, pp. 213-23.

10. *James Weldon Johnson*

Johnson, James Weldon. *Fifty Years and Other Poems.* Introduction by Brander Matthews. Boston, 1917. xiv + 93 pp.
———. *God's Trombones: Seven Negro Sermons in Verse.* New York, 1927. 56 pp.
———. *Along This Way: The Autobiography of James Weldon Johnson.* New York, 1933. 418 pp.
———. *Saint Peter Relates an Incident: Selected Poems.* New York, 1935. 105 pp.
———. *God's Trombones: Sermons noirs en vers.* Trans. Claude Julien. Paris, 1960. 109 pp.
———. "The Origin of Sin." MS., Negro Collection of the Library of Atlanta University. 6 pp.
Aery, William Anthony. "J. W. Johnson, American Negro of Distinction." *School and Society,* September 3, 1938, pp. 291-94.
Auslander, Joseph. "Sermon Sagas." *Opportunity,* September, 1927, pp. 274-75.
Collier, Eugenia W. "J. W. Johnson, Mirror of Change." *Phylon,* fourth quarter, 1960, pp. 351-59.
Cullen, Countee. "God's Trombones." *Bookman,* October, 1927, pp. 221-22.
Fisk University. *James Weldon Johnson.* Memorial brochure, Nashville, Tenn., n.d. (1939).
"J. W. Johnson, Negro American." *Christian Century,* July 13, 1938, pp. 860-61.
Loveman, Amy. "James Weldon Johnson." *Saturday Review of Literature,* July 9, 1938, p. 8.

Lyon, Ernest. *A Protest against the Title of James Weldon Johnson's Anomalous Poem as a "Negro National Anthem" as Subversive of Patriotism.* N.p., n.d. (1926). 15 pp.

Monroe, Harriet. "Negro Sermons." *Poetry,* August, 1927, pp. 291-93.

Potts, Eunice Bloodworth. "J. W. Johnson, His Legacy to Us." *Opportunity,* May, 1940, pp. 132-35.

Rosenberg, Harold. "Truth and the Academic Style." *Poetry,* October, 1936, pp. 49-51.

Villard, Oswald Garrison. "Issues and Men." *Nation,* July 9, 1938, p. 44.

11. Langston Hughes

Hughes, Langston. *The Weary Blues.* Introduction by Carl Van Vechten. New York, 1926. 109 pp.

————. "The Fascination of Cities." *The Crisis,* January, 1926, pp. 138-40.

————. *Fine Clothes to the Jew.* New York, 1927. 89 pp.

————. *Dear Lovely Death.* New York, 1931.

————. *The Negro Mother and Other Dramatic Recitations.* New York, 1931. 20 pp.

————. *Scottsboro Limited.* New York, 1932.

————. *The Dream Keeper and Other Poems.* New York, 1932. 77 pp.

————. *A New Song.* Introduction by Michael Gold. New York, 1938. 31 pp.

————. "Too Much of Race." Speech made by Langston Hughes at the Second International Writers' Congress, Paris, July, 1937. *The Crisis,* September, 1937, p. 272.

————. *Un Chant nouveau.* Trans. René Piquion. Port-au-Prince, 1940. 159 pp.

————. *The Big Sea: An Autobiography.* New York, 1940. 335 pp.

————. *Shakespeare in Harlem.* New York, 1942. xiv + 124 pp.

————. *Jim Crow's Last Stand.* New York, 1943. 30 pp.

————: *Freedom's Plow.* New York, 1943. 14 pp.

————. *Fields of Wonder.* New York, 1947. 115 pp.

————. "My Adventures as a Social Poet." *Phylon,* third quarter, 1947, pp. 205-12.

————. *One-Way Ticket.* New York, 1949. xvii + 136 pp.

————. *Montage of a Dream Deferred.* New York, 1951. 75 pp.

————. *Poèmes.* Trans. François Dodat. Paris, 1955. 89 pp.

————. *I Wonder as I Wander: An Autobiographical Journey.* New York, 1956. ix + 405 pp.

————. *The Langston Hughes Reader.* New York, 1958. x + 502 pp.

————: *Selected Poems.* New York, 1959. xii + 297 pp.

————. *Ask Your Mama: Twelve Moods for Jazz.* New York, 1961. 92 pp.

————, and the editors of *Phylon.* "Some Practical Observations: A Colloquy." *Phylon,* fourth quarter, 1950, pp. 307-11.

Arvey, Verna. "Langston Hughes Crusader." *Opportunity,* December, 1940, pp. 363-64.

Cullen, Countee. "Poet on Poet." *Opportunity,* February, 1926, pp. 73-74.

Davis, Arthur P. "The Harlem of Langston Hughes' Poetry." *Phylon,* fourth quarter, 1952, pp. 276-83.

————. "The Tragic Mulatto Theme in Six Works of Langston Hughes." *Phylon,* second quarter, 1955, pp. 195-204.

Dodson, Owen. "Shakespeare in Harlem." *Phylon,* third quarter, 1942, pp. 337-38.

Glenn, Robert. "Shakespeare in Harlem." *Criticism America,* March 19, 1960, p. 747.

Harrison, William. "Shakespeare in Harlem." *Opportunity,* July, 1942, p. 219.

Larkin, Margaret. "A Poet for the People — A Review." *Opportunity,* March, 1927, pp. 84-85.

Locke, Alain. "The Weary Blues." *Palms* IV, no. 1, 25-28.

MacLeod, Norman. "The Poetry and Argument of Langston Hughes." *The Crisis,* November, 1938, pp. 358-59.

Parker, John W. "*Tomorrow* in the Writings of Langston Hughes." *College English,* May, 1949, pp. 438-41.

Peterkin, Julia. "Negro Blue and Gold." *Poetry,* October, 1927, pp. 44-47.

Schoell, Franck Louis. "Un Poète nègre." *Revue Politique et Littéraire (Revue Bleue),* July 20, 1929, pp. 436-38.

Staples, Elizabeth. "Langston Hughes: Malevolent Force." *American Mercury,* January, 1959, pp. 46-50.

Wagner, Jean. "Langston Hughes." *Informations et Documents,* January 15, 1961, pp. 30-35.

12. Sterling Brown

Brown, Sterling A. *Southern Road.* Introduction by James Weldon Johnson. New York, 1932. xv + 135 pp.

Anderson, George Kumler, and Walton, Eda Lou, eds. *This Generation: A Selection of British and American Literature from 1914 to the Present with Historical and Critical Essays.* Chicago, 1939; rev. ed., 1949. xv + 1065 pp. (Sterling A. Brown, pp. 643-49.)

Benet, William Rose. "A New Negro Poet." *Saturday Review of Literature,* May 14, 1932, p. 732.

Botkin, Benjamin Albert, ed. *Folk Say.* Norman, Okla., 1930. 473 pp. (Sterling A. Brown, pp. 275-79.)

————. *Folk Say.* Norman, Okla., 1931. 354 pp. (Sterling A. Brown, pp. 113-23.)

————. *Folk Say.* Norman, Okla., 1932. 297 pp. (Sterling A. Brown, pp. 246-56.)

Locke, Alain. "Sterling Brown: The New Negro Folk Poet." In Nancy Cunard, *Negro Anthology,* pp. 111-15. London, 1934.

Untermeyer, Louis. "New Light from an Old Mine." *Opportunity,* August, 1932, pp. 250-51.

E. Discography

Anthology of Negro Poets. Ed. Arna Bontemps. Folkways FP 91. (Poems read by Langston Hughes, Sterling Brown, Claude McKay, Countee Cullen, etc.)

Anthology of Negro Poets in the U.S.A., 200 Years. Read by Arna Bontemps. Folkways FP 91-92. (Poems by Lucy Terry, Phillis Wheatley, Paul Laurence Dunbar, Jean Toomer, James Weldon Johnson, G. D. Johnson, Fenton Johnson, Frank Horne, Sterling Brown, Langston Hughes, Countee Cullen, Waring Cuney, Helene Johnson, Arna Bontemps, Claude McKay, etc.)

A Complete and Authentic Minstrel Show. Album P-1600. High Fidelity Somerset (Miller International Co., Media, Pa.).

Did You Ever Hear the Blues? Big Miller's choice of eleven deep blues by Langston Hughes. United Artists UAL 3047.

The Dream Keeper and Other Poems of Langston Hughes. Read by the author. Folkways FC 7104 (new no. FP 104).

Four Readings from "God's Trombones." By James Weldon Johnson. Musicraft Album no. 21.

The Glory of Negro History. Written and narrated by Langston Hughes. Folkways FC 17752 (new no. FP 752).

Jazz Canto. Vol. 1 — Poetry Jazz Album ("The Dream Keeper," "Night and Morn," "Daybreak in Alabama," by Langston Hughes). World Pacific PJ 1244.

Music from the South. 10 vols. Field recordings by Frederic Ramsey, Jr. Folkways FP 650-59.

Noël et Saint-Sylvestre à Harlem. Document Herbert Pepper. Ducrétet-Thomson 260 V. 069.

Poems by Langston Hughes. Langston Hughes reads from *The Weary Blues, The Dream Keeper,* and *Shakespeare in Harlem.* Asch Records 454.

Poetry of the Negro. Read by Sidney Poitier and Doris Belack. Glory GLP 1 (LP-G1-100). Poems by Paul Laurence Dunbar, James Weldon Johnson, Countee Cullen, Langston Hughes, etc.

The Rhythms of the World. Written and narrated by Langston Hughes. Folkways FC 7340 (new no. FP 740).

Singers in the Dusk. Poems with music as read by Charles Lampkin ("The Negro Speaks of Rivers," "Mother to Son," "Ballad of a Man Who's Gone," by Langston Hughes). Ficker Recording Service XTV 25689.

Spirituals et Folklore. Sung by Harry Belafonte. RCA 430-213.

The Story of Jazz. Written and narrated by Langston Hughes. Folkways FC 7312.

The Weary Blues. Poetry-jazz reading by Langston Hughes with Horace Parlan Quintet and Red Allen Quintet. MGM E-3697.

Works of Sterling Brown and Langston Hughes. Read by the authors. Folkways FP 90.

BIBLIOGRAPHICAL SUPPLEMENT
by Keneth Kinnamon

This supplement covers the decade between the compilation of Wagner's bibliography and the publication of this translation of his book. It is restricted (with one exception) to those sections most directly concerned with American Negro poetry from 1890 to 1940 — D2 through D12.

C4. Folklore and Jazz

Lovell, John, Jr. *Black Song: The Forge and the Flame.* New York, 1972.

D2. Black Poetry

Bone, Robert. "American Negro Poets: A French View." *Tri-Quarterly,* no. 4 (1965), pp. 185-95.

Bontemps, Arna. "The Black Renaissance of the Twenties." *Black World* XX (November, 1970), 5-9.

———. "A Memoir: Harlem, the 'Beautiful Years.'" *Negro Digest* XIV (January, 1965), 62-69.

———. "The Negro Contribution to American Letters." *The American Negro Reference Book.* Ed. John P. Davis. Englewood Cliffs, N.J., 1966. Pp. 850-78.

Bronz, Stephen H. *Roots of Negro Racial Consciousness: The 1920's: Three Harlem Renaissance Authors.* New York, 1964.

Cartey, Wilfred. "Four Shadows of Harlem." *Negro Digest* XVIII (August, 1969), 22-25, 83-92.

Chapman, Abraham. "Black Poetry Today." *Arts in Society* V (1968), 401-8.

———. "The Harlem Renaissance in Literary History." *CLA Journal* XI (1967), 38-58.

Collier, Eugenia W. "Heritage from Harlem." *Black World* XX (November, 1970), 52-59.

————. "I Do Not Marvel, Countee Cullen." *CLA Journal* XI (1967), 73-87.

Echeruo, M. J. C. "American Negro Poetry." *Phylon* XXIV (1963), 62-68.

Ellison, Martha. "Velvet Voices Feed on Bitter Fruit: A Study of American Negro Poetry." *Poet and Critic* IV (Winter, 1967-68), 39-49.

Emanuel, James A. "America before 1950: Black Writers' Views." *Negro Digest* XVIII (August, 1969), 26-34, 67-69.

————. "The Invisible Men of American Literature." *Books Abroad* XXXVII (1963), 391-94.

Ferguson, Blanche E. *Countee Cullen and the Harlem Renaissance*. New York, 1966.

Fullinwider, S. P. *The Mind and Mood of Black America: Twentieth Century Thought*. Homewood, Ill., 1969.

Furay, Michael. "Africa in Negro American Poetry to 1929." *African Literature Today* II (1969), 32-41.

Garrett, DeLois. "Dream Motif in Contemporary Negro Poetry." *English Journal* LIX (1970), 767-70.

Garrett, Naomi M. "Racial Motifs in Contemporary American and French Negro Poetry." *West Virginia University Philological Papers* XIV (1963), 80-101.

Gayle, Addison, Jr. "The Harlem Renaissance: Towards a Black Aesthetic." *Midcontinent American Studies Journal* XI (Fall, 1970), 78-87.

————, ed. *The Black Aesthetic*. Garden City, N.Y., 1971.

Haslam, Gerald W. "Two Traditions in Afro-American Literature." *Research Studies: A Quarterly Publication of Washington State University* XXXVII (September, 1969), 183-93.

Hill, Herbert. "The Negro Writer and the Creative Imagination." *Arts in Society* V (1968), 244-55.

Huggins, Nathan. *Harlem Renaissance*. New York, 1971.

Hughes, Langston. "The Twenties: Harlem and Its Negritude." *African Forum* I (1966), 11-20.

Jahn, Janheinz. *Neo-African Literature: A History of Black Writing*. New York, 1968.

Kent, George E. *Blackness and the Adventure of Western Culture*. Chicago, 1971.

Killens, John O. "Another Time When Black Was Beautiful." *Black World* XX (November, 1970), 20-36.

Kinneman, John A. "The Negro Renaissance." *Negro History Bulletin* XXV (1962), 200, 197-99.

Liebman, Arthur. "Patterns and Themes in Afro-American Literature." *English Record* XX (February, 1970), 2-12.

Littlejohn, David. *Black on White: A Critical Survey of Writing by American Negroes*. New York, 1966.

Margolies, Edward. *Native Sons: A Critical Study of Twentieth-Century Negro American Authors*. Philadelphia, 1968.

Moore, Gerald. "Poetry in the Harlem Renaissance." *The Black American Writer.* Ed. C. W. E. Bigsby. Deland, Fla., 1969. Vol. II, pp. 67-76.

"Negro Poetry." *Encyclopedia of Poetry and Poetics.* Ed. Alex Preminger, Frank J. Warnke, and O. B. Hardison. Princeton, N.J., 1965. Pp. 558-59.

Osofsky, Gilbert. "Symbols of the Jazz Age: The New Negro and Harlem Discovered." *American Quarterly* XVII (1965), 229-36.

Pool, Rosey. "The Discovery of American Negro Poetry." *Freedomways* III (1963), 46-51.

Redmond, Eugene B. "The Black American Epic: Its Roots, Its Writers." *The Black Scholar* II (January, 1971), 15-22.

Rollins, Charlemae. *Famous American Negro Poets.* New York, 1965.

Turner, Darwin T. *In a Minor Chord: Three Afro-American Writers and Their Search for Identity.* Carbondale, Ill., 1971.

Williams, Kenny J. *They Also Spoke: An Essay on Negro Literature in America, 1787-1930.* Nashville, 1970.

D3. Specialized Anthologies

Adams, William; Conn, Peter; and Slepian, Barry, eds. *Afro-American Literature: Poetry.* Boston, 1970.

Adoff, Arnold, ed. *Black Out Loud: An Anthology of Modern Poems by Black Americans.* New York, 1970.

————, ed. *I Am the Darker Brother: An Anthology of Modern Poems by Black Americans.* New York, 1968.

Baker, Houston A., Jr., ed. *Black Literature in America.* New York, 1971.

Barksdale, Richard K., and Kinnamon, Keneth, eds. *Black Writers of America: A Comprehensive Anthology.* New York, 1972.

Bell, Bernard W., ed. *Modern and Contemporary Afro-American Poetry.* Boston, 1972.

Bontemps, Arna, ed. *American Negro Poetry.* New York, 1963.

Chambers, Bradford, and Moon, Rebecca, eds. *Right On: Anthology of Black Literature.* New York, 1970.

Chapman, Abraham, ed. *Black Voices: An Anthology of Afro-American Literature.* New York, 1968.

Clarke, John Henrik, ed. *Harlem: Voices from the Soul of Black America.* New York, 1970.

Davis, Arthur P., and Redding, Saunders, eds. *Cavalcade: Negro American Writing from 1760 to the Present.* Boston, 1971.

Davis, Charles T., and Walden, Daniel, eds. *On Being Black: Writings by Afro-Americans from Frederick Douglass to the Present.* New York, 1970.

Emanuel, James A., and Gross, Theodore, eds. *Dark Symphony: Negro Literature in America.* New York, 1968.

Ford, Nick Aaron, ed. *Black Insights: Significant Literature by Afro-Americans — 1760 to the Present.* Waltham, Mass., 1971.

Hayden, Robert, ed. *Kaleidoscope: Poems by American Negro Poets.* New York, 1967.

———; Burrows, David; and Lapides, Frederick, eds. *Afro-American Literature.* New York, 1971.

Hughes, Langston, ed. *La Poésie négro-américaine.* Paris, 1966.

Jordan, June, ed. *Soulscript: Afro-American Poetry.* Garden City, N.Y., 1970.

Kendricks, Ralph, ed. *Afro-American Voices: 1770's-1970's.* New York, 1970.

Lomax, Alan, and Abdul, Raoul, eds. *3000 Years of Black Poetry.* New York, 1970.

Margolies, Edward, ed. *A Native Sons Reader.* Philadelphia, 1970.

Miller, Ruth, ed. *Black American Literature 1760–Present.* Beverly Hills, Calif., 1971.

Nicholas, Xavier, ed. *Poetry of Soul.* New York, 1971.

Patterson, Lindsay, ed. *An Introduction to Black Literature in America from 1746 to the Present.* Washington, D.C., 1969.

Randall, Dudley, ed. *Black Poetry: A Supplement to Anthologies Which Exclude Black Poets.* Detroit, 1969.

———. *The Black Poets.* New York, 1971.

Robinson, William H., ed. *Early Black American Poets.* Dubuque, Iowa, 1969.

Singh, Raman K., and Fellowes, Peter, eds. *Black Literature in America: A Casebook.* New York, 1970.

Stanford, Barbara Dodds, ed. *I, Too, Sing America: Black Voices in American Literature.* New York, 1971.

Turner, Darwin, T., ed. *Black American Literature: Poetry.* Columbus, Ohio, 1969.

D4. Poets Contemporary with Dunbar

Robinson, William H., ed. *Early Black American Poets.* Dubuque, Iowa, 1969.

D5. Paul Laurence Dunbar

Baker, Houston A., Jr. "Paul Laurence Dunbar: An Evaluation." *Black World* XXI (November, 1971), 30-37.

Butcher, Philip. "Mutual Appreciation: Dunbar and Cable." *CLA Journal* I (1958), 101-2.

Gayle, Addison, Jr. *Oak and Ivy: A Biography of Paul Laurence Dunbar.* Garden City, N.Y., 1971.

Turner, Darwin T. "Paul Laurence Dunbar: The Rejected Symbol." *Journal of Negro History* LII (1967), 1-13.

D6. Minor Poets of the Negro Renaissance

F[uller], H[oyt] W. "Arna Bontemps: Dedication and Bibliography." *Black World* XX (September, 1971), 78-79.

D7. Claude McKay

Bronz, Stephen H. *Roots of Negro Racial Consciousness: The 1920's: Three Harlem Renaissance Authors.* New York, 1964.

Cartey, Wilfred. "Four Shadows of Harlem." *Negro Digest* XVIII (August, 1969), 22-25, 83-92.

Collier, Eugenia. "The Four-Way Dilemma of Claude McKay." Atlanta, 1971.

Conroy, Mary. "Claude McKay: Negro Poet and Novelist." *Dissertation Abstracts* XXIX (1969), 3129A-3130A.

———. "The Vagabond Motif in the Writings of Claude McKay." *Negro American Literature Forum* V (1971), 15-23.

Cooper, Wayne. "Claude McKay and the New Negro." *Phylon* XXV (1964), 297-306.

———, and Reinders, Robert C. "A Black Briton Comes 'Home': Claude McKay in England, 1920." *Race* XI (1967), 67-83.

Drayton, Arthur. "McKay's Human Pity: A Note on His Protest Poetry." *Black Orpheus,* no. 17 (June, 1965), pp. 39-48.

Kent, George E. "The Soulful Way of Claude McKay." *Black World* XX (November, 1970), 37-51.

D8. Jean Toomer

Toomer, Jean. "Earth-Being." *The Black Scholar* II (January, 1971), 3-13.

Ackley, Donald G. "Theme and Vision in Jean Toomer's *Cane*." *Studies in Black Literature* I (Spring, 1970), 45-65.

Bell, Bernard. "A Key to the Poems in *Cane*." *CLA Journal* XIV (1971), 251-58.

Bontemps, Arna. "Introduction." *Cane*. By Jean Toomer. New York, 1969.

———. "The Negro Renaissance: Jean Toomer and the Harlem Writers of the 1920's." *Anger, and Beyond: The Negro Writer in the United States.* Ed. Herbert Hill. New York, 1966. Pp. 20-36.

Cancel, Rafael A. "Male and Female Interrelationship in Toomer's *Cane*." *Negro American Literature Forum* V (1971), 25-31.

Chase, Patricia. "The Women in *Cane*." *CLA Journal* XIV (1971), 259-73.

Dillard, Mabel M. "Jean Toomer: Herald of the Negro Renaissance." *Dissertation Abstracts* XXVIII (1968), 3178A-3179A.

Fullinwider, S. P. "Jean Toomer: Lost Generation, or Negro Renaissance?" *Phylon* XXVII (1966), 396-403.

———. *The Mind and Mood of Black America: Twentieth Century Thought.* Homewood, Ill., 1969.

Grant, Mary Kathryn. "Images of Celebration in *Cane*." *Negro American Literature Forum* V (1971), 32-34, 36.

Lieber, Todd. "Design and Movement in *Cane*." *CLA Journal* XIII (1969), 35-50.

McKeever, Benjamin F. "*Cane* as Blues." *Negro American Literature Forum* IV (1970), 61-63.

Mason, Clifford. "Jean Toomer's Black Authenticity." *Black World* XX (November, 1970), 70-76.

Reilly, John M. "The Search for Black Redemption: Jean Toomer's *Cane*." *Studies in the Novel* II (1970), 312-24.

Turner, Darwin T. " — And Another Passing." *Negro American Literature Forum* I (1967), 3-4.

———. *In a Minor Chord: Three Afro-American Writers and Their Search for Identity*. Carbondale, Ill., 1971.

———. "Jean Toomer (1894-1967)." *A Bibliographical Guide to the Study of Southern Literature*. Ed. Louis D. Rubin, Jr. Baton Rouge, La., 1969. Pp. 311-12.

———. "Jean Toomer's *Cane*." *Negro Digest* XVIII (January, 1969), 54-61.

D9. Countee Cullen

Bronz, Stephen H. *Roots of Negro Racial Consciousness: The 1920's: Three Harlem Renaissance Authors*. New York, 1964.

Collier, Eugenia W. "I Do Not Marvel, Countee Cullen." *CLA Journal* XI (1967), 73-87.

Daniel, Walter C. "Countee Cullen as Literary Critic." *CLA Journal* XIV (1971), 281-90.

Dorsey, David F., Jr. "Countee Cullen's Use of Greek Mythology." *CLA Journal* XIII (1969), 68-77.

Ferguson, Blanche E. *Countee Cullen and the Negro Renaissance*. New York, 1966.

Kilgore, James C. "Toward the Dark Tower." *Black World* XIX (June, 1970), 14-17.

Perry, Margaret. *A Bio-Bibliography of Countee P. Cullen, 1903-1946*. Westport, Conn., 1971.

Reimherr, Beulah. "Race Consciousness in Countee Cullen's Poetry." *Susquehanna University Studies* VII (1963), 65-82.

Turner, Darwin T. *In a Minor Chord: Three Afro-American Writers and Their Search for Identity*. Carbondale, Ill., 1971.

D10. James Weldon Johnson

Adelman, Lynn. "A Study of James Weldon Johnson." *Journal of Negro History* LII (1967), 128-45.

Bronz, Stephen H. *Roots of Negro Racial Consciousness: The 1920's: Three Harlem Renaissance Authors*. New York, 1964.

Copans, Sim J. "James Weldon Johnson et le patrimoine culturel des noirs africains." *Cahiers de la Compagnie Madeleine Renaud — Jean Louis Barrault* LXI (1967), 42-48.

Fullinwider, S. P. *The Mind and Mood of Black America: Twentieth Century Thought*. Homewood, Ill., 1969.

Jackson, Miles M., Jr. "James Weldon Johnson." *Black World* XIX (June, 1970), 32-34.

———. "Letters to a Friend: Correspondence from James Weldon Johnson to George A. Towns." *Phylon* XXIX (1968), 182-98.

Levy, Eugene. "Ragtime and Race Pride: The Career of James Weldon John-son." *Journal of Popular Culture* I (1968), 357-70.

Tarry, Ellen. *Young Jim: The Early Years of James Weldon Johnson.* New York, 1967.

Tate, Ernest C. "Sentiment and Horse Sense: James Weldon Johnson's Style." *Negro History Bulletin* XXV (April, 1962), 152-54.

———. "The Social Implications of the Writings and the Career of James Weldon Johnson." *Dissertation Abstracts* XX (1959), 1357.

D11. Langston Hughes

Hughes, Langston. *The Panther and the Lash: Poems of Our Times.* New York, 1967.

———. "Problems of the Negro Writer: The Bread and Butter Side." *The Saturday Review* XLVI (April 20, 1963), 19-20.

———. "My Early Days in Harlem." *Freedomways* III (1963), 312-14.

———. "I Remember the Blues." *Missouri Reader.* Ed. Frank Luther Mott. Columbia, Mo., 1964. Pp. 152-55.

———. "The Task of the Negro Writer as Artist." *Negro Digest* XIV (April, 1965), 65-75.

———. "The Twenties: Harlem and Its Negritude." *African Forum* I (Spring, 1966), 11-20.

———, ed. *Poems from Black Africa.* Bloomington, Ind., 1963.

———, ed. *New Negro Poets: U.S.A.* Bloomington, Ind., 1964.

———, ed. *La poésie négro-américaine.* Paris, 1966.

Bontemps, Arna. "Langston Hughes: He Spoke of Rivers." *Freedomways* VIII (1968), 140-43.

———. "Memories of Langston Hughes 1902-1967." *Negro American Literature Forum* I (1967), 12-13.

Cartey, Wilfred. "Four Shadows of Harlem." *Negro Digest* XVIII (August, 1969), 22-25, 83-92.

Combecher, Hans. "Zu einem Gedicht von Langston Hughes: 'Minstrel Man.'" *Die Neueren Sprachen* XV (1966), 284-87.

Davis, Arthur P. "Langston Hughes: Cool Poet." *CLA Journal* XI (1968), 280-96.

Diakhaté, Lamine. "Langston Hughes, conquérant de l'espoir." *Présence Africaine,* no. 64 (1967), pp. 47-50.

Dickinson, Donald C. *A Bio-Bibliography of Langston Hughes, 1902-1967.* Pref. Arna Bontemps. Hamden, Conn., 1967.

———. "Working with Langston Hughes." *Negro American Literature Forum* I (1967), 13, 15.

Dodat, François. *Langston Hughes.* Paris, 1964.

———. "Situation de Langston Hughes." *Présence Africaine,* no. 64 (1967), pp. 47-50.

Emanuel, James A. *Langston Hughes.* New York, 1967.

————. "The Literary Experiments of Langston Hughes." *CLA Journal* XI (1968), 335-44.

Finger, Hans. "Zwei Beispiele moderner amerikanischer Negerlyrik: Langston Hughes, 'Mother to Son' und Russell Atkins, 'Poem.'" *Literatur in Wissenschaft und Unterricht* II (1969), 38-46.

Fuller, Hoyt W., ed. "Langston Hughes Memorial." *Negro Digest* XVI (September, 1967), 31-48, 58-60.

Garber, Earlene D. "Form as a Complement to Content in Three of Langston Hughes' Poems." *Negro American Literature Forum* V (1971), 137-39.

Gayle, Addison, Jr. "Langston Hughes: A Simple Commentary." *Negro Digest* XVI (September, 1967), 53-57.

Gibson, Donald B. "The Good Black Poet and the Good Gray Poet: The Poetry of Hughes and Whitman." *Langston Hughes: Black Genius: A Critical Evaluation.* Ed. Therman B. O'Daniel. New York, 1971. Pp. 65-80.

Guillén, Nicolás. "Le Souvenir de Langston Hughes." *Présence Africaine,* no. 64 (1967), pp. 34-37.

Holmes, Eugene C. "Langston Hughes: Philosopher-Poet." *Freedomways* VIII (1968), 144-51.

Hudson, Theodore R. "Langston Hughes' Last Volume of Verse." *CLA Journal* XI (1968), 335-44.

Isaacs, Harold R. "Five Writers and Their African Ancestors." *Phylon* XXI (1960), 243-65, 317-36.

Jacobs, Leland. "Langston Hughes." *Instructor,* March, 1964, p. 28.

Jones, Eldred. "'Laughing to Keep from Crying': A Tribute to Langston Hughes." *Présence Africaine,* no. 64 (1967), pp. 51-55.

Jones, Harry L. "A Danish Tribute to Langston Hughes." *CLA Journal* XI (1968), 331-34.

Kaiser, Ernest. "Selected Bibliography of the Published Writings of Langston Hughes." *Freedomways* VIII (1968), 185-91.

Kearns, Francis E. "The Un-Angry Langston Hughes." *The Yale Review* LX (1970), 154-60.

Kent, George E. "Langston Hughes and Afro-American Folk and Cultural Tradition." *Langston Hughes: Black Genius: A Critical Evaluation.* Ed. Therman B. O'Daniel. New York, 1971. Pp. 183-210.

Kinnamon, Keneth. "The Man Who Created 'Simple.'" *The Nation* CCV (December 4, 1967), 599-601.

Kramer, Aaron. "Robert Burns and Langston Hughes." *Freedomways* VIII (1968), 159-66.

McGhee, Nancy B. "Langston Hughes: Poet in the Folk Manner." *Langston Hughes: Black Genius: A Critical Evaluation.* Ed. Therman B. O'Daniel. New York, 1971. Pp. 39-64.

Matheus, John F. "Langston Hughes as Translator." *CLA Journal* XI (1968), 319-30.

Meltzer, Milton. *Langston Hughes: A Biography.* New York, 1968.

Myers, Elisabeth P. *Langston Hughes: Poet of His People.* Champaign, Ill., 1970.

O'Daniel, Therman B., ed. *Langston Hughes: Black Genius: A Critical Evaluation.* New York, 1971.

———. "Langston Hughes: A Selected Classified Bibilography." *CLA Journal* XI (1968), 349-66.

———. "Lincoln's Man of Letters." *Lincoln University Bulletin* LXVII (July, 1964), 9-12.

Patterson, Lindsay. "Langston Hughes — An Inspirer of Young Writers." *Freedomways* VIII (1968), 179-81.

Patterson, Louise Thompson. "With Langston Hughes in the USSR." *Freedomways* VIII (1968), 152-58.

Presley, James. "The American Dream of Langston Hughes." *Southwest Review* XLVIII (1963), 380-86.

———. "Langston Hughes: A Personal Farewell." *Southwest Review* LIV (Winter, 1969), 79-84.

Prowle, Allen D. "Langston Hughes." *The Black American Writer.* Ed. C. W. E. Bigsby. Deland, Fla., 1969. Vol. II, pp. 77-87.

Quinot, Raymond. *Langston Hughes.* Brussels, 1964.

Rive, Richard. "Taos in Harlem: An Interview with Langston Hughes." *Contrast* XIV (1967), 33-39.

Rollins, Charlemae H. *Black Troubadour: Langston Hughes.* Chicago, 1970.

Waldron, Edward E. "The Blues Poetry of Langston Hughes." *Negro American Literature Forum* V (1971), 140-49.

Yestadt, Marie. "Two American Poets: Their Influence on the Contemporary Art Song." *Xavier University Studies* X (Fall, 1971), 33-43.

D12. Sterling Brown

Henderson, Stephen A. "A Strong Man Called Sterling Brown." *Black World* XIX (September, 1970), 5-12.

INDEX

Peterkin, Julia, 163
Peterson, Dorothy, 263
"Petrograd: May Day, 1923," 252
Phaedo, 324
Philadelphia Tribune, 401
The Philanthropist, 9
Phillips, Wendell, 363
Phylon, 393
Pinchback, Nina E. *See* Toomer, Nina E.
Pinchback, Pickney Benton Stewart, 260
Pise, Olivia, 45
Pissarro, Camille, 267
Pittsburgh Courier, 400
Plantations: and slavery, 6-8
"A Plantation Portrait," 118
Plantation tradition, 48; and Dunbar, 8-104; and Campbell, 134; and Davis, 138; and Hughes, 471
Plato, 323, 425
Plotinus, 323
"Poeme d'automne," 410
"Poem to the Black Beloved," 399
"The Poet," 109
Poetry: of the Negro Renaissance, 172-93; jazz defined, 464
Poetry, 180, 288, 390
The Poetry of the Negro, 263
Poets: black, theme after World War I, 177-93
Pope, Alexander, 19, 199
Porgy, 163
"Porter," 423, 426
"Portrait in Georgia," 268
Portrait of the Artist, 266
Potamkin, Harry Alan, 292
Pound, Ezra, 151
"The Power of Prayer," 51
Prairie, 261
Pravda, 202
"A Prayer," 124
"Prayer at Sunrise," 360
"The Prayers of God," 178
Preachers. *See* Pastors
Proletarian Literature in the United States, 429
"Promise," 121
Propaganda: and art, 170-72
Pride: and Cullen, 299-302
"Pride," 431

"Prize Fighter," 423, 426
Publishers: and black poets, 174
Pythagoras, 323

Quakers: and Toomer, 263
Quarles, Captain Ralph, 386
Quarles, Francis, 386
"Quashie to Buccra," 206-7

Race: and religion, xv, xxii, 505-11; and Dunbar, 95-104; and McKay, 223-25, 233; and Toomer, 272-81; and Cullen, 296, 301-29; and J. W. Johnson, 372-81; and Hughes, 393-415, 454; and Brown, 482-90
"Race and a Poet," 292
"Race Problems and Modern Society," 272
Radicalism: after World War I, 155-57
Radicalism and Sedition among the Negroes ... , 156
"Railroad Avenue," 426
Rain: and Cullen, 328
Rainey, Ma, 486
The Rape of Florida, 25
Readings from Negro Authors for Schools and Colleges, 176
Reconstruction, 39, 149
"A Recruit to the Corpy," 217
Redding, J. Saunders, xxii, 20, 306, 320
"Red Summer" of 1919, 155, 228
Reed, John, 201
Religion: and Dunbar, xvi, 123-25, 506; characteristics of Negro, 26-27; and Russell, 55-56; and Campbell, 135-36; and J. W. Johnson, 191, 358-62; and Brown, 192, 490-96; and Hughes, 192, 437-44, 472-73; and Cullen, 193, 304, 329-39, 507, 508; and McKay, 193, 247-57, 507; and Toomer, 193, 507; and race, 505-11
Renaissance: defined, 160
"Rent Day Blues," 493
"Reprise," 414
The Republic: quoted, 425-26
"Requiescam," 298
Rexroth, Kenneth, 461, 463-64
Rice, Thomas Dartmouth, 42-43
Richards, I. A., 202

A Note on the Author

Jean P. Wagner is professor of American Studies at the University of Grenoble III, where he has been teaching since 1962.

A native of Lorraine, he received his higher education in France, England, and the United States. He holds an Agrégation in English and a Doctorat d'Etat from the Sorbonne (1963), and has been the recipient of a Smith-Mundt research grant (1958) and a fellowship at the Centre National de la Recherche Scientifique, Paris (1959-62).

His other books include *Runyonese: The Mind and Craft of Damon Runyon*, and a French translation of Jean Toomer's *Cane*.

A Note on the Translator

Kenneth Douglas is a free-lance author and translator, residing in New York. He was formerly associate professor of French at Yale University, as well as editor of *Yale French Studies*. His most recent book, with Rosette Lamont, is *De Vive Voix: Lectures dramatiques* (1971).